# Thinking in Search of a Language

# Thinking in Search of a Language

## Essays on American Intellect and Intuition

*Herwig Friedl*

BLOOMSBURY ACADEMIC

NEW YORK • LONDON • OXFORD • NEW DELHI • SYDNEY

BLOOMSBURY ACADEMIC
Bloomsbury Publishing Inc
1385 Broadway, New York, NY 10018, USA
50 Bedford Square, London, WC1B 3DP, UK

BLOOMSBURY, BLOOMSBURY ACADEMIC and the Diana logo are trademarks
of Bloomsbury Publishing Plc

First published in the United States of America 2019

Bloomsbury Publishing Inc does not have any control over, or responsibility for,
any third-party websites referred to or in this book. All internet addresses given
in this book were correct at the time of going to press. The author and publisher
regret any inconvenience caused if addresses have changed or sites have ceased
to exist, but can accept no responsibility for any such changes.

A catalog record for this book is available from the Library of Congress.

ISBN:    HB:   978-1-5013-3271-5
         PB:   978-1-5013-3270-8
       ePDF:   978-1-5013-3273-9
      eBook:   978-1-5013-3272-2

Typeset by Integra Software Services Pvt. Ltd.

To find out more about our authors and books visit www.bloomsbury.com and
sign up for our newsletters.

*For Bettina*

# CONTENTS

# ACKNOWLEDGMENTS

When I think of the friends and colleagues who have inspired and supported my attempts to understand, interpret, and appreciate Emerson and the pragmatists, I cannot but think of myself as exceptionally fortunate. In a way, a seminar co-taught in the early 1980s with Dieter Schulz and David Robinson, then a guest professor at Heidelberg University, marks an important starting point; both, Dieter and David, have continued to be exemplary and encouraging through their important writings in the field. Christoph Schöneich, closest of friends, who passed away far too early, helped me gain confidence in myself; he generously and appreciatively read my earliest ventures in Transcendentalism. During a time of uncertainty and crisis in my early career, Hans Käsmann guided and successfully advised me with great care and sensitivity.

Since the 1990s and through today, at many a conference, Susanne Rohr, co-pragmatist and Germany's outstanding Peirce scholar, has always been a wonderful intellectual companion, energetic and philosophically challenging. Stimulating conversations and the continuing exchange of publications with Ulfried Reichardt have significantly deepened my understanding of pragmatist thinking.

During my tenure at Heinrich Heine University Düsseldorf, Christa Buschendorf became a friend and colleague who greatly expanded my awareness of the importance of classical and Renaissance literature and thinking for the Transcendentalists; Astrid Böger, Nicole Maruo-Schröder, and Georg Schiller opened new fields of inquiry and methodology and energetically supported pragmatist studies in my department. All four of them went on to pursue successful academic careers of their own.

It is one of the rewards of retirement in Berlin that a number of dear friends and colleagues, whose work has been truly inspirational over the decades (and continues to be so), are now close neighbors: I cannot think of my own efforts without the sophisticated and motivating examples of Winfried Fluck in cultural studies, of Ulla Haselstein on Gertrude Stein, of Heinz Ickstadt on the intellectual and aesthetic formation of American modernism, and of Joseph C. Schöpp's studies in Transcendentalism.

Among the students whom I had the privilege and pleasure to advise when they were writing their doctoral dissertations with me, Christa Grewe-Volpp, Thomas Krusche, Michaela Giesenkirchen, Jutta Rateike, Philipp Reisner,

Dennis Sölch, and Birgit Capelle have greatly expanded my understanding of Transcendentalism, pragmatism, and American modernism. It is wonderful that, among the outstanding younger scholars of today, my former doctoral student Jan Kucharzewski, Johannes Voelz, and Dustin Breitenwischer have become intellectual companions and friends whose innovative approaches I greatly admire.

America and its scholars have been personally and intellectually hospitable and encouraging: Robert O. Preyer has been the kindest and most generous of supporters ever since his year as guest professor at Heidelberg University in 1972–73; at Yale in the early 1970s Norman Holmes Pearson and R. W. B. Lewis graciously and importantly directed my research; and ever since the 1960s at Harvard, Daniel Aaron, in long and intense and intellectually exhilarating conversations, widened my horizon. To me, Harvard was a friendly place: Lawrence Buell, David Hall, and Werner Sollors were warmly welcoming not only during my several sojourns as Visiting Scholar; they and their work continue to be models and guidance through today.

Michael T. Gilmore was a close friend and a scholar of great intensity and sophistication; his sociocultural studies of Transcendentalism and nineteenth-century literature I continue to cherish. Roger F. Thompson's subtle studies of early New England history helped me understand and appreciate the background and antecedents of my chosen fields. Daniel and Helen Horowitz have importantly enriched my understanding of American cultural and social history and of the history of academic institutions.

This book would not exist, had it not been for the interest in my work, the loving care, energetic encouragement, and active support of Joan Richardson and Ross Posnock. Joan's work on pragmatism and Wallace Stevens, her deeply engaged discussions with me on philosophy and science and religion, and her friendship have created a sense of creative exhilaration that gives me great joy. Ross and his work on the Jameses, on dispositions and existential challenges of high modernist aesthetics, philosophy, painting, poetry, and prose have set new standards for me of what excellence and sophistication may mean. Ross helped me contact Bloomsbury Press, he inspired the title of the book, and, above all, his friendship and our shared interests made this project a pleasurable and exciting adventure of ideas for me.

At Bloomsbury Press, Haaris Naqvi was most kindly welcoming and supportive when I first submitted my proposal, and senior editorial assistant Katherine De Chant has been extraordinarily helpful and charmingly patient in advising me while preparing the manuscript. Without the editorial skill and academic expertise of Björn Bosserhoff, the manuscript would never have been prepared in the present form and in due time.

This book is dedicated to Bettina—a miniscule *thank you* for close to fifty wonderful years of being together.

# Introduction

*The poem of the mind in the act of finding*
*What will suffice.*

WALLACE STEVENS, "OF MODERN POETRY"[1]

The "tranquillized *Fifties*"—as Robert Lowell characterized the immediate post–Second World War era[2]—were, in one way, a leaden and uninspiring time of almost single-minded economic recovery efforts and of a widespread tendency to suppress the heavy moral burden of the recent past in my native Germany. In looking back, however, I am, more than ever before, surprised at how stimulating they were after all, as the time of preparation for an exciting personal intellectual journey that led me—fortunately and fortuitously, so it seems—from Heidelberg to Cambridge, Massachusetts, and from Gadamer and Heidegger to a lifelong fascination with and devotion to Ralph Waldo Emerson and William James, a fascination and devotion that helped motivate and inspire much of my teaching and, ultimately, encouraged me to publish this book. In the '50s, America as a culture only beckoned from afar when, for example, a young high school teacher, excited by the sudden and belated availability of modernist literature in post-fascist Germany, made us read Hemingway short stories in our first year of *Gymnasium* (high school) in 1954. More importantly, my reading during this decade opened a world that even today seems to me the most alluring, comprehensive, and inexhaustibly rewarding intellectual and spiritual realm possible, a realm of gentle transitions from literature to philosophy and religion (or spirituality), a realm without dogmatically imposed or rationalistically rigid demarcation

---

[1] *The Collected Poems of Wallace Stevens* (New York: Knopf, 1973), 239.
[2] "Memories of West Street and Lepke," in *Collected Poems*, ed. Frank Bidart and David Gewanter (New York: Farrar, Straus and Giroux, 2003), 187.

lines between fundamental intellectual and existential concerns, a realm of freedom where no single school of thinking and no exclusionary methodologies could claim hegemony.

Annual school prizes awarded by my provincial *Gymnasium* and selected by an admirably sophisticated teaching staff played a providential role in shaping predilections and forming horizons of great expectations. A translation of the *Dao De Jing* created a disquieting and, to this very day, challenging first insight into the, I believe, ultimately unfathomable relationship of language and thinking: "The name that can be named is not the eternal Name."[3] There is, possibly, I felt then, a thinking or knowing before and beyond naming; there is really no prison-house of language, or maybe, as Heidegger would maintain, we are spoken to by Being and then only do we respond and acquire language. Thinking—for example, thinking the *dao*—could be experienced as a never fully successful pursuit of final words, as a strenuous and disciplined search for an ultimately elusive language. Encounters with Dionysius Areopagita, Meister Eckhart, Jakob Boehme, and Angelus Silesius, readings recommended by my learned teachers of classical Greek, two elderly Benedictine monks, strengthened this sense that there is a thinking awareness *before* all saying. Hans-Georg Gadamer would later support this tentative intuition as he seriously entertains the idea of a pre-linguistic form of thinking awareness, of *Seinsdenken*, of thinking Being.[4]

Pierre Teilhard de Chardin's *The Phenomenon of Man*[5] and Katharina Kanthack's *Das Denken Martin Heideggers*[6] were farewell gifts by my school in the early '60s. Teilhard de Chardin gave me a sense of what I would later and in a variety of forms encounter and cherish as a philosophy of emergence and as an intriguing example of the possibility to envision a coalescence of natural science, philosophy, and religion. I did not know it, but I was being prepared for reading and appreciating Dewey and Whitehead. Katharina Kanthack's slender book on Heidegger came as a shock, as the sudden revelation of the possibility to think beyond the naïve dualism of subjectivity and objectivity. Dimly realized at the time, it would make me receptive for what Heidelberg University had to offer when I enrolled in 1963. Before that, however, the early 1960s had another formative experience in store: I persuaded my not excessively intellectual family to spend, I think, ten consecutive evenings listening to Karl Jaspers's

[3] *The Teachings of Lao-Tzu: The Tao Te Ching*, trans. Paul Carus (1913; New York: St. Martin's Press, 2000), 30.
[4] "Parmenides und die Meinung der Sterblichen," in *Der Anfang der Philosophie* (Stuttgart: Reclam, 1996), 143–4.
[5] I read the German edition: *Der Mensch im Kosmos* (Munich: Beck, 1959).
[6] [*The Thinking of Martin Heidegger*] (Berlin: De Gruyter, 1959).

radio lectures *Introduction to Philosophy*. The unpretentious clarity, the moral integrity, and the politically nonconformist courage of Jaspers, who had written and argued so vehemently against German rearmament and nuclear weapons in the 1950s, impressed me so deeply that the moralistic political excitement of the radical left in the late '60s seemed disingenuous by comparison. In addition, the enlightened and the existentialist as well as the political dimensions of Jaspers's philosophy harmoniously blended with his meditations on the transcendent dimension of existence, with what he called "the encompassing" (*das Umgreifende*). With the *Introduction* by Jaspers my literary, philosophical, and spiritual "pre-school days" had ended.

At college, even though my major subjects were American, English, and German literatures, philosophy turned out to be the formative discipline. Heidelberg University in the '60s was exciting and stimulating and demanding in philosophy. Gadamer's *Truth and Method* had just come out in 1960, Karl Löwith was still teaching, and the young Jürgen Habermas was spending several semesters as an adjunct professor in Heidelberg. Habermas's lectures and his writing on the public sphere did not really touch a chord, but his 1968 book *Erkenntnis und Interesse* did create a lasting impression. Here he presented a concept of interest as guiding knowledge that was closely, even if implicitly, modeled after the pragmatist interpretation of the term. Löwith, in his books and lectures, introduced me both to the Presocratics and their important role as catalysts for Nietzsche's radical modernism and to the epochal importance of Nietzsche's move away from the age of Goethe and Hegel. It was Gadamer, however, who was the guiding spirit at the center of my attempts to immerse myself in philosophy. I never warmed to Gadamer personally: he appeared too aloof, occasionally displaying a certain *hauteur*. And yet I attended his weekly three-hour lectures well into the 1980s when I moved on to Heinrich Heine University in Düsseldorf and the chair of American Literature and History of Ideas. These lectures proved formative. Breathtakingly elegant in their delivery, brilliantly improvised without the help of an extensive manuscript, Gadamer's lectures illuminated the transition from the Neo-Kantianism and epistemology of Cohen and Natorp to the difficult intensities of Heidegger's fundamental ontology. Gadamer's hermeneutics, the phenomenological elucidation of the situational dynamic of the processes of understanding and interpretation transcending objectivist constraints and subjective constructivism in an open-ended process, keeps guiding my attempts to read the historical unfolding of the American tradition of thinking to this very day.

It was 1965: Heidegger came to Heidelberg at the invitation of Gadamer. At first sight, what a disappointment! A short and stocky man with an impressive head, in a loden jacket that evoked an aura of the worst reactionary provincialism, he took the lectern in the grand Victorian lecture hall and then—he began to think. He did not instruct, he did not pontificate, there was no pretense. I was spell-bound by the meditative intensity, his full absorption in the subject, the careful search for words, the patient and sometimes painfully slow exegesis of the etymological backgrounds of German and Greek terms. The topics of the combined lecture and seminar sessions were Heraclitus and, later, Heidegger's own *Letter on Humanism*. Ever since, I simply cannot approach any thinker without asking the fundamental question as to their way of responding to or avoiding the indispensable core of all thinking, the problem of the ontological difference. Ever since, I cannot read any modern thinker without becoming aware of the way they—explicitly or implicitly—return to and revive the earliest, the primary thinking of, say, the Presocratics. Even though by now I have read a majority of the more than 100 volumes of the *Gesamtausgabe* (Complete Works), I do not consider myself a follower of Heidegger. The ontological difference as the key of keys in philosophy and the inescapable background of the dawn of thinking for an adequate appreciation of what it means to be modern, these two motifs and the indelible impression of what "doing thinking" could look and sound like, are what will stay with me as Heidegger's gift. As to his often appalling political opinions and anti-Semitic invectives, I would like to apply to Heidegger's *Seinsdenken* what Daniel Barenboim said when he was challenged by critics in Israel because he had dared to conduct Richard Wagner in Tel Aviv: the music is not anti-Semitic.

Slowly and with ever-growing fascination I spent much of the second half of the '60s in Heidelberg and at Cornell, reading everything by Henry James that was available in print. A Jacob Gould Shurman scholarship made it possible for me to prepare my doctoral dissertation on James at Cornell University's Olin Library in 1967–68, generously advised by M. H. Abrams and Arthur Mizener. I began to realize that, in encountering wide varieties of often radically different centers of consciousness in his novels and stories, I had entered a rich world of pluralist perspectivism without any substantialist dogmatic underpinning, without a single dominant belief, a world of open-ended experiential processes. The most intriguing feature of James's novelistic world and of his essayistic self-interpretation was the profusion of images that again and again overwhelmed any attempts by characters, narrators, or author to unequivocally conceptualize their widely differing forms of perceptual awareness. When the dissertation came out as a book in 1972, with the dry and ungainly title *Die Funktion der Bildlichkeit in den kritischen und theoretischen Schriften von Henry James: Ein Entwurf seiner Literaturtheorie*,[7] its third and final part presented James's implied literary theory as a pragmatist aesthetics.

---

[7][*The Function of Imagery in the Critical and Theoretical Writings of Henry James: An Outline of His Literary Theory*] (Heidelberg: Universitätsverlag Carl Winter, 1972).

In its essential features, Henry James's total vision, and especially his privileging of the perceptual, of imagery, over against conceptualization, implicitly but precisely paralleled William James's anti-intellectualist stance and, ultimately, his modernist pluralism and anti-foundationalism. I felt and I knew that I had found and begun to enter the philosophical, the existential, the cultural, and the moral space that I would assiduously and unceasingly study in order to be able to call it my own. Toward the end of *The Varieties of Religious Experience*, William James wrote: "The whole drift of my education goes to persuade me that the world of our present consciousness is only one of the many worlds of consciousness that exist."[8] To me, this is the true credo of a fundamentally liberal generosity, of an unaffected humility. Thinking Being as the unforeseeable proliferation of difference, as manifesting itself in a plurality of possible awarenesses, calls for a philosophical strategy or method that will shun all finality or closure: "The word 'and' trails along after every sentence. Something always escapes." "Ever not quite," James goes on to observe, "has to be said of the best attempts made anywhere in the universe at attaining all-inclusiveness."[9] Similarly, he thinks of reality as genuinely open and optional: "the word 'or' names a genuine reality."[10] This vision allows beings and their meaning to come into their own without any dogmatic conceptual prejudice. The worlds of our manifold consciousnesses keep opening into the yet-to-be-decided, the "or," the unforeseen, the truly new and essentially modern.

I spent Christmas of 1973, during my year of postdoctoral study at Yale, in Cambridge, Massachusetts, my future summer home, a few blocks from William James's house on Irving Street, and my wife presented me with the twelve-volume *Works of Ralph Waldo Emerson*, my cherished and to this very day indispensable 1888 Riverside Edition.[11] My first attempts to read Emerson were uncannily similar to Herman Grimm's experience in 1858. In an essay of 1865 Grimm, the first genuine German Emerson

---

[8] *The Varieties of Religious Experience: A Study in Human Nature*, vol. 13 of *The Works of William James* (1902; Cambridge, MA: Harvard University Press, 1985), 408. I will use the Harvard edition of James's *Works*, edited by Frederick H. Burkhardt, Fredson Bowers and Ignas K. Skrupskelis, throughout this book.

[9] *A Pluralistic Universe*, vol 4 of *The Works of William James* (1909; Cambridge, MA: Harvard University Press, 1977), 145.

[10] Ibid., 146.

[11] *The Works of Ralph Waldo Emerson* (Boston and New York: Houghton, Mifflin and Company, 1888). For me, this first comprehensive edition of Emerson's works represents and manifests the basis of all major interpretive efforts; it lays the ground for the historical emergence of what "Emerson" has come to mean. Redolent with the widest potential of readings actualized so far, it is indispensable in spite of the fact that later editions, especially the Harvard edition, have provided philologically more accurate texts. Thus, it will be used in all subsequent chapters. Abbreviation for references: W followed by Roman number of volume and page number.

enthusiast, remembers that reading Emerson was like encountering a new world, an authentic personality, a genuinely innovative language that at first puzzles and, at the same time, fascinates, a language that comes across as unprecedented with each successive reading.[12] Reading Emerson, for Grimm and for me as well, begins and continues in astonishment and wondering, in the *thaumazein* which according to Aristotle preceded and conditioned genuine philosophical thinking. In a sense, reading Emerson intensifies the Jamesian awareness of multiple worlds of consciousness. Each essay, and sometimes each single paragraph or even one aphorism after another, may open a new world, a different perspective, an unprecedented vista or vision. Again and again, alternative points of view are proposed and then abandoned, the Protean consciousness dons mask after mask. Thinking, as Emerson argues in "Circles," is essentially un-settling[13]; it does not allow one to find a reliable anchorage in the quicksand[14] of the ongoing and never completed search for an ultimately reliable language—all languages prove essentially fluxional, as he says in "The Poet."[15] There is no Emersonian philosophy, only thinking going on, a mode of thinking, as Stanley Cavell pointed out, which is on the way, a thinking that neither finds nor desires a real resting-place.[16] For Emerson, Being is radically "unsponsored, free" (in Wallace Stevens's phrase from "Sunday Morning"[17]). It demands, it calls for a thinking that returns again and again into the very beginning of a primary intuition without antecedents; it is a mode of thinking after the example of the "earliest inquirers" of ancient Greece.[18] William James's philosophical liberality that thinks plural worlds of consciousness emerging without the constraints and rigid determinations of antecedents helps me understand the central, the indispensable role of Emerson in founding anti-foundational American philosophy. Christmas 1973, the dissertation on Henry James and his pragmatist aesthetics published and twelve volumes of Emerson on the table, marks my very private sense of "graduation" without the trappings of that formal academic approval that came before and after.

What follows is best "told" by, is manifest in, the eighteen chapters of this book, some selected from roughly sixty scholarly essays published over the decades and some written exclusively for the present volume. The

---

[12]"Ralph Waldo Emerson," in *Neue Essays über Kunst und Literatur* (Berlin: Dümmler, 1865), 1–2.

[13]W II, 297.

[14]"Experience" W III, 58.

[15]W III, 37.

[16]"Thinking of Emerson," in *The Senses of Walden* (San Francisco: North Point Press, 1981), 136.

[17]*Collected Poems*, 70.

[18]*The Journals and Miscellaneous Notebooks of Ralph Waldo Emerson*, 16 vols. (Cambridge, MA: Belknap Press of Harvard University Press, 1960–82), vol. VII, 13. Abbreviation: *JMN*.

reader cannot but notice that these chapters have a tendency, especially in the second part on pragmatism, to return again and again to a limited number of key passages, to moments of what seem to me profound and indispensable insights by Parmenides, Heraclitus, Emerson, James, Dewey, Heidegger, Gadamer, and others. I am encouraged in this practice by a series of modernist interpretations of the relationship of identity and difference. In 1925, in *Experience and Nature*, John Dewey states: "recurrence makes novelty possible"[19]; in 1935, Gertrude Stein addresses "the important question of repetition" and concludes "I am inclined to believe there is no such thing as repetition," there are but differing forms of insistence or emphasis[20]; and in 1968 Gilles Deleuze calls upon our thinking to always elicit something new from repetition, to elicit difference.[21] This is what I try to do.

The two parts of this book, on Emerson and on American pragmatism, respectively, present consecutive as well as complementary modes of modernist, post-metaphysical strategies of thinking. The first part, *Philosophical Proteus: Varieties of Emerson's Thinking*, explores a variety of methods, a multiplicity of perspectives, an open-ended series of possible philosophical languages as the result of Emerson's basic intuition of the pre-verbal presencing of Being as a featureless openness or absence of a foundational *substantia*, as an abyss: "Under all this running sea of circumstance ... lies the aboriginal abyss of real Being."[22]

Chapter 1, "Emerson among the Presocratics," illustrates how Emerson eclectically returns to the earliest beginnings of Western thinking in Anaximander, Parmenides, Heraclitus, and Xenophanes. In recovering aspects of the ontology, the cosmology, and the rhetoric of supposedly unprecedented and thus primary thinking, he positions himself as the thinker of another, a second inception of philosophy that defines itself as modernist, as not constrained by the dogmatic demands of tradition. The ontological difference (in Heidegger's sense), the conception of the identity of Being and awareness, the rhetorical and ontological importance of paradox, and of sudden reversals (Gr. *metabole*) in Gadamer's interpretation,[23] the idea of compensation, the vision of an uncreated cosmos: these are major areas of congruence in which the elective affinity of the earliest thinking of the first

---

[19]*Experience and Nature*, vol. 1 of *The Collected Works of John Dewey: The Later Works, 1925–1953*, ed. Jo Ann Boydston (Carbondale, IL: Southern Illinois University Press, 1981) 47.

[20]"Portraits and Repetition," in *Stein: Writings 1932–1946*, ed. Catherine Stimpson and Harriet Chessman (New York: Library of America, 1998), 288.

[21]*Différence et répétition* (1968; Paris: Presses Universitaires de France, 1989), 103.

[22]"Compensation" W II, 116.

[23]"Heraklit-Studien," in *Der Anfang des Wissens* (Stuttgart: Reclam, 1999), 42–3.

axial age (Jaspers) and of the modernist reenactment of original philosophical intuition in Emerson (and, following him, in Nietzsche) become manifest. In the Presocratics, Emerson finds one of many possible languages to articulate "an original relation to the universe."[24]

A pervasive and foundational skepticism in Emerson concerns the possibility of ascertaining the essence, the true nature of all that exists, of the *Ding an sich*. Chapter 2, "Emerson; or, the Neopyrrhonist Skeptic," reads this ontological skepticism as a modern version of the Neopyrrhonist position most prominently represented by Sextus Empiricus. Suspension of judgment (*epoché*) is necessitated by the endless possibilities of contradictory points of view, which in their equipollence do not allow dogmatic positions. Like Sextus, Emerson does not dogmatically deny the possibility of ultimate knowledge; both encourage the proliferation of points of view, of endless seeking; both consider their versions of skepticism as preparing a religious disposition. Like the thinkers of the Platonic Academy, like Cicero, and like Hegel, Emerson reads Plato because of the very generosity of his multiple points of view as a Neopyrrhonist skeptic. Both skeptical Plato and Montaigne, as described in the essay on Montaigne in *Representative Men*, prepare the vision and language of Emerson's Neopyrrhonism, which is shown as pervasive and not limited to the radical questionings of "Experience."

Mysticism may be understood as both experiential identification of awareness and Being in the philosophical sense (Parmenides) and/or as religious *unio mystica* (Eckhart). For Emerson experience in both these senses is a radical and existential provocation of proper thinking that becomes manifest in the phenomenon of a "double consciousness." Chapter 3, "Mysticism and Thinking," is devoted to an Emerson challenged by the foundational mystical experience that will never result in a total transformation of that experience in language (Martin Buber) or fully realize the utopian promise of the initiating and overwhelming insight (Ernst Bloch). Thinking grounded in and provoked by a mystical intuition will always be a mode of thinking on the way (Stanley Cavell), a thinking whose authority is predominantly and exclusively valid for the person who underwent the mystical experience (William James). This tension or "doubleness" defines Emerson's thinking as one possible realization of the perennial philosophy always and again issuing forth from intuition without finding ultimate closure in systematic exposition.

The criticism of appropriations of Asian cultures as "orientalist" by Edward Said and his followers reveals an ideologically motivated hermeneutics of resentment. In contrast, Chapter 4, "Hosting Sa'di," attempts a careful consideration of Goethe's and Emerson's encounters with Persian poetry and prose, manifesting a hermeneutics of hospitality. The hermeneutic

---

[24]*Nature* W I, 9.

situation (Gadamer) of a hospitable encounter allows the Persian oeuvre of Sa'di in Emerson's reading to both remain the other, the alien, the past and, at the same time, to open itself to new possibilities of meaning in the welcoming atmosphere of the benevolent recipient. Emerson, the host in this hermeneutic encounter, is equally affirmed in his modern individuality as well as enriched and changed by the cultural potential of Sa'di's vision. A close reading of Emerson's prose commentaries on Persian literature and of his responses to Sa'di in his poems shows a far-reaching elective affinity in style, in religious and moral vision, and in existential disposition, while affirming an appropriate and respectful distance from the other.

Emerson develops a radical alternative to Hegel's philosophy of history and his history of philosophy. Like Marx and Kierkegaard he questions the validity and viability of a totalizing dialectic idealism. Chapter 5, "Resisting Hegel," reveals that the *History of Ancient Philosophy* by German historian of philosophy Heinrich Ritter (English translation 1838) and especially Ritter's interpretation of Heraclitus play a pivotal role, inspiring and supporting Emerson's resistance against Hegel's powerful model. In going back to Heraclitus's thinking as a dynamic vitalism in a world of eternal return and constant inchoation, Emerson prepares a post-metaphysical form of thinking Being and history. The terms *inchoation* and *transition* from Ritter's *History* make their way into Emerson's writing after 1838, signaling a vision of process as both iterative and continuous. Ritter's attacks on constructionist models of historical processes (Hegel) support Emerson's emphasis on the equal dignity of all individual philosophical intuitions and the concomitant denial of essential progress in thinking.

Poetry to Emerson is the true and future form of thinking, a necessary replacement of metaphysics whose conceptual categories are inadequate in and for a world of incessant dynamic changes. All formations of meaning in such a post-metaphysical world are masks of Proteus, temporary manifestations within processes of creation and de-creation, as Wallace Stevens would maintain. In Chapter 6, "Nature/Poetry," *self-reflexive poetry* in the poem "Art" is read as a mode of thinking about Being itself as a process of ceaseless re-valuation or troping of nature and reality. A *nature poem* like "The Snow-Storm" will support an interpretation as presenting a mode of thinking about reality as an endless series of un-grounded, non-foundational formations or masks of Being. Neither self-reflexive poetry nor nature poetry is a category designating stable and essential features; they are—like all linguistic and natural events—mere Protean masks of temporal realizations of the non-substantial Heraclitean flux of Being that all forms of poetry *think*.

Categories and clearly defined concepts, as demanded by Descartes, are absent in Emerson's post-metaphysical and anti-foundationalist thinking. The realm of culture and civility provides outstanding examples for his tendency to constantly transgress the stable definitions and essentialist fixations of phenomena like manners, conduct, behavior, character, fashion—terms merely pointing at fluid, transgressive events. Chapter 7, "Transgressive Manners," demonstrates that at the basis of Emerson's vision of social conduct, of manners, one may detect a philosophy of power as the guiding agency of constant self-overcoming modeled after the idea of the *hegemonikon* in Stoic philosophy as exemplified by Marcus Aurelius, an ethical and cultural ideal more recently revived and redefined for modernity by Martha Nussbaum. Historically Emerson, other than Norbert Elias, does not intuit a progressive melioration but rather contingent, unforeseeable shifts or tropings of the languages of manners—which include even Emerson's own tentative model of the Caesarian gentleman, which certainly found a strong echo in Nietzsche's ranking of forms of cultural power.

Emerson and Nietzsche realize a new dispensation of Being and thinking. Whitehead, Heidegger, and Susanne K. Langer all emphasize the fact that major philosophical paradigm shifts are not subjective human achievements but rather responses to new ways of Being manifesting itself. The modernist dispensation and the dramatic ontological change in Emerson, so thoroughly explored by Stanley Cavell in its foreshadowing of Nietzsche and Heidegger, are encapsulated in a momentous statement from "The American Scholar" where Emerson conceives of Being as power in the mode of an eternal return of the same.[25] Chapter 8, "Nietzsche's Emerson," focuses on Nietzsche's thinking about Being and becoming, on his ideas of fate and history and of becoming who one is, on the very reconciliation of fate and freedom, as these conceptions find themselves foreshadowed in major insights by Emerson into the ontological dimensions of fate, power, and history. Nietzsche's own way of becoming the thinker he is enacts the free acceptance of a fated past (Emerson) as the condition of the possibility of an authentic existence.

Chapter 9, "Emerson's and Dewey's America," deals with the differing, but intimately related, ways in Emerson and Dewey of thinking a particular dispensation of Being (Heidegger) called "America" as a contingent event. These differing, but related, ways reveal the radical turn away from philosophical, national, and cultural essentialism and from systematizing or teleological attempts to ground the histories of thinking and of social and political developments in Hegelian fashion. Both Emerson and Dewey practice what Cavell called "onward thinking,"[26] which maintains its unity and consistency in the processes of constant proliferation of difference. In this way the authority of all established entities (of antecedents in William James's sense), including conceptions of human nature, of national culture, even of race, is constantly imperiled and an experimental openness is experienced

---

[25] W I, 86–7.
[26] "Thinking of Emerson," 123–38.

and propagated, an existential gesture of letting be, an abandonment of all essentialist constraints. Both George Kateb's ontological idea of self-reliance and George Herbert Mead's vision of the ultimate guarantee of real democratic social cohesion in the privileged present owe themselves to Emerson's and Dewey's anti-essentialist intuitions of Being.

The nine ways of philosophical shape-shifting, of Protean transformations, discussed in the first part are a selection of possibilities of languages and fields of thinking in Emerson. Ultimately, no single position, interest, or language may claim exclusive or dominant or final authority. As Emerson says in "Plato: New Readings," "[t]he connection between our knowledge and the abyss of being is still real."[27] This connection becomes manifest in the inexhaustibility of possible realizations, of possible interests, of possible ways of thinking, of possible languages issuing from the powerfully absent presence, from the abyss of Being as it bodies forth ever new realizations and real newness.

In the second part of the book, *American Pragmatism: Thinking Modernism*, Emerson's modernist anti-essentialism and the profusion of his languages of thinking are complemented by the experimental and open-ended inquiries of William James and John Dewey. The modernist dimension of their thinking implies the possibility, above all, of escaping the constraints and rigid determinations of established fields of cultural formation. My emphasis on the modernist aspect of pragmatism, however, implies that the American historical antecedents and consequences of pragmatism recede somewhat into the background. Joan Richardson provides an absolutely necessary, an indispensable complement of my approach. *A Natural History of Pragmatism* offers an in-depth genealogy of pragmatism from Edwards to Stein and her refined interpretations in *Pragmatism and American Experience* subtly explore the transformations of the classical pragmatism of Peirce, James, and Dewey in thinkers like Cavell and Rorty.[28]

Both the primary philosophy of the Presocratics and modernist thinking, in its desire and attempt to recapture the moment of unprecedented initial meditation, may be said to arise from a realm outside the historically established fields of meaning in philosophy or poetry. Chapter 10, "American Thinking Out of Bounds," refutes the central vision and thesis of Pierre Bourdieu. Thinkers like Emerson, William James, and Charles Sanders Peirce, and poets like Wallace Stevens intuit an ontological and epistemological realm before any conceptualization and deterministic structuring in a cultural field. The free and experimental unfolding of the

---

[27]W IV, 84.
[28]*A Natural History of Pragmatism: The Fact of Feeling from Jonathan Edwards to Gertrude Stein* (Cambridge: Cambridge University Press, 2007); *Pragmatism and American Experience* (Cambridge: Cambridge University Press, 2014).

most ancient and of all radically innovative modern thinking positions itself
out of bounds in relation to established cultural, social, and philosophical
practices. In this way the emergence of the new, the modern, is assured.
Emerson's interpretation of intellect as unstructured awareness, James's idea
of pure experience, and Peirce's Firstness are the sites "out of bounds" that
permit a free and unconditioned, a genuine experimental newness.

An important modernist, post-metaphysical aspect of James's thinking
becomes manifest in his use of images as the essential way to convey his
approach to the question of Being. Chapter 11, "William James: Ontology
and Imagery," presents selected aspects of the interpretation of images in
Aristotle, in Rudolf Eucken, and in Hans Blumenberg that help argue that
images serve as bridges between mere presence and conceptualization,
as means of leading thinking back into the undifferentiated antecedent
totality of Being, and as placeholders of the inexhaustible reservoir of pre-
conceptual intuition. Images are the preferred rhetorical means to articulate
an indiscrete ontology (Hogrebe). James employs two major strategies to
make images do the work of ontological thinking: an open-ended series of
seemingly unrelated images such as "stuff," "mosaic," or "flux" may signal
the ultimate unavailability of Being for conceptual demarcation; variations
of one imagistic field like water allow thinking to transgress a world of
discrete entities in the direction of the pre-linguistic in-discreteness of Being
as event, as *Ereignis*.

The way in which William James keeps pursuing the question of Being
un-dogmatically and without expectation of a possible solution, the way he
privileges the phenomenal or the sensibly given over the conceptual, the way
he continues to juxtapose equipollent philosophical positions like monism
and pluralism (without dogmatic arbitration, even though with a clear
personal preference), the way he propagates the necessity to again and again
abandon inquiry in order to reach momentary resting-places that allow
for normal activity—all these, in Chapter 12, "William James: Ontological
Skepticism," can be shown as a modern version of the Neopyrrhonist
skepticism of Sextus Empiricus with its continuous, but never conclusive,
search of the skeptic (Gr. *zetetikos*) for essences, with its preference for the
testimony of the senses, with its desire for quietude (*ataraxia*) as a result of
the suspension of all ultimate judgment (*epoché*). Other than Cartesian and
post-Cartesian skepticism, James's modernist version of Neopyrrhonism
does not expect or desire a *fundamentum inconcussum*.

James's catalytic and often formative role in the propagation of global
modernist thinking is the wider context of Chapter 13, "Kitaro Nishida
and William James." The central importance of James's radical empiricism
and his concept of pure experience in the emergence of Kitaro Nishida's
philosophy and of the Kyoto School, however, must not obscure the fact
that Nishida himself did not always adequately appreciate the significant
convergence of Jamesian thinking and his own philosophy, partially based

as it is on Zen Buddhist thought. Nishida's wavering between a radical modernist Jamesian and an idealist European metaphysics was re-evaluated as expressing an essentially Japanese position in Keiji Nishitani's and Masao Abe's interpretations of Nishida. This is one result of the Japanese exceptionalism (*nihonjinron*) of the 1930s: a reductionist view of Western thinking as dualist and rationalist tending to obliterate the early cosmopolitan conversation between James and Nishida. Later Japanese scholars and American thinkers and critics like Thomas Merton and Andrew Feenberg have helped to redress the balance by their sophisticated interpretations of the idea of pure experience in James and Nishida.

Chapter 14, "The Necessity of the Lost Middle Voice," articulates a fundamental language problem that arises with the emergence of a modernist post-metaphysical disposition. The pragmatists, William James and John Dewey, on one side and Martin Heidegger on the other react differently to the problem of saying Being after the demise of traditional foundationalism. Instead of "inventing" a new terminology like Heidegger, James and Dewey draw attention to the difficulty of properly articulating Being as (flowing) event and/or as relational field. The problem posed by an indiscrete ontology demands that one acknowledge the insufficiency of language (of concepts) to say what *is*. James and Dewey develop different, but parallel, strategies to speak of Being (pure or primary experience) as an event preceding the formation of subject and object. Early (Indo-)European languages (Sanskrit and Greek) used the middle voice to express this event enacting itself without agent: this usage continues solely in Greek into the current Demotic. Most modern Indo-Germanic languages have lost the middle voice and thus cannot say Being directly: language has forgotten Being (*Seinsvergessenheit*). Varieties of metaphor in James and the pervasive co-presence of the active and passive voice in Dewey's sentences mark the absence of the middle voice. In this way they remember Being, which linguistically fell silent.

At first sight, Henri Bergson and William James seem to advance a parallel reconstruction of ontology. Their modernist approaches share one major methodological strategy: in their anti-intellectualism they both deny the possibility that concepts grasp or render Being itself. Chapter 15, "Polite Disagreements: James and Bergson," begins by looking at the correspondence of the two thinkers and the way it displays a slightly deceptive generosity in appreciating the vision and achievement of the other. At the same time, their very tact in reading the other conceals, or at least obscures, fundamental differences. While James advances a truly post-metaphysical indiscrete ontology that does justice to a pluralist vision, Bergson—despite his anti-intellectualist rhetoric—reaffirms a foundationalist entity, the *élan vital*, as the basis of an ontological dualism that inverts, but does not abandon, the Platonic vision of an ideal world of stability and a lesser world of becoming. Bergson's world of ideal becoming and ontologically deficient stability does not fully abandon metaphysical traditionalism, as does James when he discards all essentialist underpinnings of pluralistically emergent entities.

Chapter 16, "Congruences and Divergences: James, Bergson, Dewey," presents a discussion of modes of interdependence of stable facticity and flowing event as basic features in the description of Being and/as becoming in James, Bergson, and Dewey. The discussion leads to a deeper insight into the agreements and differences in their ontological presuppositions. This in turn makes it possible to evaluate the kind and degree of their respective forms of modernism in thinking. Aspects of emergent evolutionism, of indiscrete ontology, and of anti-intellectualist tendencies in all three thinkers seem to indicate a genuine family resemblance. James's pluralism and Dewey's refutation of all conceptual and ontological dualisms, however, reveal a major difference in their thinking in comparison with Bergson. James and Dewey abandon all metaphysical substantialization of both stable and dynamic aspects of Being; theirs is a radical turn away from metaphysics, whereas Bergson modernizes tradition, including Platonic and even Plotinian intuitions, without jeopardizing its metaphysical grounding. Bergson modernizes traditional metaphysics; James and Dewey are modern in abandoning it.

Two ultimately incompatible interpretations of the modern existential condition inform Charles Taylor's attempt to do justice to William James's philosophy of religion. In Chapter 17, "William James and Charles Taylor," the partially appreciative critique of James's philosophy of religion is shown to be almost exclusively focused on the centrality of individual experience in James. Taylor privileges the realm of the social imaginary and of communally available language whereas he accords a merely preparatory status to personal religious experience. In this way Taylor cannot properly appreciate James's vision of the mysticism of individual experience, which opens the realm of the numinous as an extension of human existence into the *More* of unbounded religious reality. Taylor revives the reductive social interpretation of religion by Émile Durkheim that Heidegger had implicitly refuted in 1921. Both Heidegger and James insist on the factuality of the religious as experiential event before all constraints by the social imaginary. Religious experience as existential reality can be articulated only in the form of testimony, be it that of the Bible, as in Heidegger's account of religiosity, or be it the cosmopolitan wealth of witnessing that James presents in *The Varieties of Religious Experience*.

Chapter 18, "The New," provides a summary highlighting the quintessential core of both the Emerson and the pragmatism sections. The new as the obvious central concern of modernist thinking and writing is intimately tied to a sophisticated ontological awareness of the importance of *nothingness* or "no-thing" in the American tradition. From Emerson and Thoreau through Dickinson to Stevens and Stein, moments of insight into the absence of circumscribed entities as factors in the emergence of the new play a major role. Their philosophical underpinning is provided by the liminal intuitions of Firstness in Peirce and of pure experience in James. Ernst Bloch has expanded and deepened these insights in his ontology of the not-yet, of a continuous move of the undefined no-thingness of mere existence toward the transitional fixations of essences, "real things," as the genuine event of newness. The American tradition of thinking novelty as the emergence from a no-thingness or sheer *thisness* culminates in John Cage whose (religious) awareness of a world arising from no-thing cheerfully contemplates its re-absorption in a Zen-like emptiness.

The eighteen chapters of this book are a part of my effort to critically appreciate and testify to the continuing, unceasing productive openness of Emerson's and of pragmatist thinking. In a sense, these chapters also attempt to realize the hermeneutic ideal that calls upon us not to hope for the impossible *telos* of an exegetic resting-place or closure, not to desire a final, an ultimate reading. For me, the plural worlds of Emerson and of James and Dewey speak out of the primordial, but always modern, experience of Being, of the non-substantial no-thing, of Emerson's abyss that allows beings, worlds, and their languages to emerge in inexhaustible proliferation. Existentially, this is both a daring and exhilarating, a risky and invigorating vision. For this existential condition Emerson found the image of "houses founded on the sea"[29] and William James intensified the intuition when he confessed that our "finite experience as such is homeless."[30] This, however, is not the homelessness of indigence and of despair; it is the homelessness of a thinking on the way that refuses to be settled. "People wish to be settled; only as far as they are unsettled is there any hope for them."[31]

---

[29]"Montaigne; or, the Skeptic" W IV, 154.
[30]*Pragmatism: A New Name for Some Old Ways of Thinking*, vol. 1 of *The Works of William James* (1907; Cambridge, MA: Harvard University Press, 1975), 125.
[31]"Circles" W II, 298.

# PART ONE

# Philosophical Proteus: Varieties of Emerson's Thinking

# 1

# Emerson among the Presocratics

The opening paragraph of Ralph Waldo Emerson's essay "Intellect" (1841) reads like an echo-chamber of Presocratic thinking, with sometimes clear and occasionally slightly blurred reverberations. The first two sentences rewrite the style and argumentative gestures of earliest Greek speculations on the relationships among material elements of the cosmos, even though neither the list of all the individual elements in Emerson's text nor their specific arrangement in an ascending scale could be called an exact or mirror image of actual Presocratic fragments or aphorisms. The fact that Emerson intersperses a few terms from contemporary chemistry and physics does not detract from the overall Presocratic aura of the passage:

> Every substance is negatively electric to that which stands above it in the elemental tables, positively to that which stands below it. Water dissolves wood and iron and salt; air dissolves water; electric fire dissolves air, but the intellect dissolves fire, gravity, laws, method, and the subtlest unnamed relations of nature in its resistless menstruum.[1]

In Diogenes Laertius's *Lives of Eminent Philosophers*, the interpretation of the interrelations among elements by Heraclitus offers a distant parallel of Emerson's text:

> Change is a path up and down, and the world is generated in accordance with it. For fire as it is condensed becomes moist, and as it coheres becomes water; water as it solidifies turns into earth—this is the path downwards. Then again earth dissolves, and water comes into being from it, and everything else from water (he refers pretty well everything to the exhalation given off by the sea)—this is the path upwards.

---

[1]"Intellect" W II, 303.

Exhalations are given off by the earth and by the sea, some of them bright and pure, others dark. Fire is increased by the bright exhalations, moisture by others.[2]

In the account of Anaximenes's cosmogony by the Christian theologian and critical chronicler of classical thinking Hippolytus (170–235 CE), a similar description is offered:

The heavenly bodies have come into being from earth, because mist rises from earth and is rarefied and produces fire, and the heavenly bodies are composed of this fire when it is aloft. There are also some earthy substances in the region of the heavenly bodies which orbit with them.[3]

Emerson's interpretation of the hierarchical relations among serially[4] emerging natural elements wears lightly the trappings of its scientific terminology ("negatively electric," "elemental tables," menstruum). Similarly, he uses rhetorical and argumentative features of archaic cosmological reasoning in a nonchalant way, re-enacting the style of ancient cosmology and cosmogony while he does not quite reproduce them in substance. First and foremost, however, the gestures and the tone of the passage from "Intellect" signal a beginning, a mode of inception, whether of ancient or of modern ways of thinking and reading *physis*, nature, in the Greek sense explicated by Heidegger, as that which arises of itself and comes into presence as an ordered world, a cosmos.[5] The passage (re-)enacts initial forms of interpreting nature philosophically and/or scientifically.

Emerson's imaginative cosmological hierarchy finds its culmination point and, at the same time, its all-encompassing and unifying container in the intellect. Intellect is the highest, the most pervasive, and the truly inclusive entity. In the Presocratic examples, the fire of Heraclitus may be said to function in a similar way. Intellect, like Heraclitus's fire, assumes the function of *arche*; it is both the principle, the first, in a logical sense, and it is the foundation, or ground of all that exists, in an ontological sense: "Intellect is the simple power anterior to all action or construction."[6] Intellect as *arche* is a major challenge for the thinker: "Gladly would I unfold in calm degrees a natural history of the intellect, but what man has yet been able to mark the

[2]Jonathan Barnes, *Early Greek Philosophy* (1987; London: Penguin, 2001), 55.
[3]Ibid., 24–5.
[4]The "interpretation of change in terms of a serial order" is seen as one of Anaximenes's important innovations in Milesian thinking; Philip Wheelwright, *Heraclitus* (1959; Oxford: Oxford University Press, 1999), 6.
[5]Martin Heidegger, *Heraklit*, ed. Manfred S. Frings, vol. 55 of *Gesamtausgabe* (1943–4; Frankfurt: Klostermann, 1994), 87–8.
[6]W II, 303.

steps and boundaries of that transparent essence?"[7] The "simple power" of the intellect is radically unstructured; there are no confining or defining lines that help the thinker in his effort to grasp, to conceive, to delimit, and thus to define it. Like the primordial water in Thales of Miletus, like the aboriginal air in Anaximenes, like the all-pervasive fire in Heraclitus, Emerson's intellect possesses no stable and lasting contours and thus escapes all conceptual circumscription. Anaximander found a wonderful term for this featureless quality, or rather: for the absence of all qualification, which seems to be a common factor in many of the elemental or foundational entities of the cosmos proposed by the early Greek *physiologoi*: Anaximander speaks of the *apeiron*, of that which displays no limitations or boundaries, inner or outer. It slips through all conceptual nets and, in displaying no qualities, qualifies as the origin of all qualitatively definable entities, as the Being of beings. In thinking this aboriginal simplicity,[8] Emerson becomes aware of a persistent challenge, of the necessity for all thinking to begin again and again when confronted with what came to be known as the question of Being. "The first questions are always to be asked."[9] Foundational or initial thinking is always a questioning,[10] and therefore, paradoxically, the inception of philosophy continues to be present.

Emerson, in thinking what he calls intellect, freely and eclectically moves about among the Presocratics. As he engages the persistent first questions and encounters the first tentative or experimental answers, he necessarily philosophizes as the correspondent of the always present, the eternally contemporaneous, primary thinkers:

> The history of opinions, any history of philosophy fortifies my faith in the treasuries of the soul by showing me that what dogmas I had supposed were the rare & late fruit of a cumulative culture, & only now possible to some recent Kant or Fichte, were the prompt improvisations of the earliest inquirers, of Parmenides, Heraclitus, & Xenophanes.[11]

Intellect as *arche* not only possesses no contours, but the traditional aspects, epistemological functions, and faculties commonly ascribed to intellect or mind do not structure "that transparent essence." Possible aspects or potential features of Emerson's vision of intellect show no specific or stable elements like ratiocination or knowledge or perception or ethical judgment

---

[7]Ibid.

[8]I have to remind myself that the simple, Lat. *simplex*, is that which is not folded; it has no outline, no fault-line, or break in its continuity, Gr. *apeiron*.

[9]W II, 303.

[10]On the importance of the question in philosophy and on the primacy of the question of Being in particular, see Martin Heidegger, *Einführung in die Metaphysik*, ed. Petra Jaeger, vol. 40 of *Gesamtausgabe* (1935/53; Frankfurt: Klostermann, 1983), 3–55, 80–99.

[11]*JMN* VII, 13.

or, quite generally, mental activity: "[e]ach becomes the other."[12] The negative qualifications of intellect prepare the starkly simple and powerfully oracular summary pronouncement: "Itself alone is."[13]

The term *intellect* is here fundamentally redefined by Emerson.[14] Intellect is the one and only *persistent* existent, it is a, or rather: it is *the* singularity, it is Being itself. If we look from Emerson's statement about Being in the direction of the future of American thinking, intellect as singularity without qualitative features and without exterior or interior relations may readily remind us of Charles Sanders Peirce's Firstness. In the context of the obvious Presocratic overtones and allusions in the opening paragraph of the essay "Intellect," however, one is also encouraged to look back and realize that Emerson's intellect—which alone *is* and which is one answer to the most central of the eternally recurring "first questions," the question of Being—is a version, an iteration, a recurrence of Parmenides's Being (*einai, on*). The first part of Parmenides's *Poem* argues that the only true way of thinking both leads to and emerges from the uncreated, indestructible, featureless, radically homogeneous, and everywhere self-identical Being, the "well-rounded ball" (*eukyklou sphaires*) that is "full of what is" (*pan d'empleon estin eontos*) and therefore "is all continuous; for what is approaches what is."[15] The plausibility of the convergence of the visions of Parmenides and Emerson is strengthened by Emerson's comment on the singular character of intellect as the *is*, as Being: "Its vision is not like the vision of the eye, but is union with the things known."[16] Parmenides had concluded: "Thinking and the object of thought are the same," and more succinctly: "Thought and being are the same" (*to gar auto noein estin te kai einai*).[17] Philip Wheelwright's interpretation of the central passage of the first part of Parmenides's poem is both subtle and simple: "The core of its meaning is put into a single word: *Esti*, 'Is.' Greek syntax permits, as English sometimes does not, the use of the verb without an expressed subject; our English linguistic habits make us want to say 'It is,' and then the purity of the utterance is spoiled, for the 'it' appears to raise a question."[18] Being is itself, it is a *one* (Gr. *hen*) without parts, it is

---

[12] W II, 303.

[13] Ibid.

[14] In other writings Emerson—due to his flexible terminology—uses intellect in a more traditional sense; see "Plato; or, the Philosopher" W IV, 62, where Being is defined as exceeding the limits of intellect.

[15] Barnes, *Early Greek Philosophy*, 84, 81 (Diels-Kranz B8: 43, 24–5).

[16] W II, 304.

[17] In the case of these two apodictic statements, I prefer the elegant and precise translation in Philip Wheelwright, *The Presocratics* (Upper Saddle River, NJ: Prentice Hall, 1966), 98 (Diels-Kranz B8: 34 and B3).

[18] Ibid., 92. Hermann Fränkel offers a similar interpretation in *Dichtung und Philosophie des frühen Griechentums* (1951; Munich: Beck, 1969), 403: "Die Aussage 'Ist', als Kernsatz der parmenideischen Lehre, hat kein Subjekt; sie ist ein sog. Impersonale wie '(es) regnet.'" ("The statement 'Is,' the core argument of Parmenidian teaching, possesses no subject; it is a so-called *impersonal* like '(it) rains'"; my translation.)

not a *substantia* of which existence may or must be additionally predicated; that would, absurdly, imply that Being as an entity is in need of Being as a quality. Emerson tries hard to appropriately express a similar intuition of the meaning of Being (intellect): "The intellect goes out of the individual, floats over its own personality, and regards it as a fact, and not as *I* and *mine.* He who is immersed in what concerns *person or place* cannot see the problem of *existence*. This the intellect always ponders."[19] Being transcends or precedes the person, subjectivity, the Cartesian *ego*, the *res cogitans*, and it transcends or precedes space, location, placement in the *res extensa* of the cosmos. In "Circles" Emerson had proposed a similar turn away from the Cartesian position on Being and knowing when he stated: "*so to be* is the sole inlet of *so to know*."[20] All that can be said of the "simple power" is that "Itself alone is" and that it ponders the problem of existence, that it is aware of Being. Being is at one with itself in this primary awareness; in *pondering* itself it *is* itself: "Thinking and the object of thought are the same."

Hans-Georg Gadamer has provided what I believe to be the most profound and subtle exegesis of this thought in his analysis of Parmenides's "*to gar auto noein estin te kai einai*" and—by implication—of Emerson's insight that existence/Being/intellect in pondering itself is itself. In the essay "Parmenides und die Meinungen der Sterblichen," Gadamer reminds us that we usually translate *noein* as *thinking*; however, one should not forget that the primary meaning of the word is not at all "meditative reflection in its interiority," but rather "a pure openness for everything that is." Speaking of the *nous* does not imply asking: *what* is it that we are aware of; rather, the word concerns the assertion that one is aware that something *is* (there). The etymology of the word, Gadamer explains, leads us back to the primary sense of the *presence* of something, as in animals scenting danger, a sensing of sheer Being or *existentia* that does not yet imply a precise knowledge of a *what* or of a concrete *essentia*. According to Gadamer, Parmenides seems to say, and for me Emerson echoes this thought, that it is Being itself which manifests itself and appears and thus *is* in and as sheer (as yet object-less) awareness (*noein*), a "sense of being which in calm hours rises,"[21] so that it may be present in an un-mediated way like the all-enveloping light of the day.[22]

Such a seemingly tautological interpretation of Parmenides—and by implication, of Emerson, as I read him—has puzzled and annoyed especially

---

[19] W II, 304 (my emphasis).
[20] Ibid., 299.
[21] Ibid., 64.
[22] I paraphrase Hans-Georg Gadamer, "Parmenides und die Meinung der Sterblichen," in *Der Anfang der Philosophie* (Stuttgart: Reclam, 1996), 143–4. Giorgio Agamben's reflection on the *aisthesis oti estin*, a sense of Being, in Aristotle presents a similar insight; see his "Friendship," trans. Joseph Falsone, *Contretemps: An Online Journal of Philosophy* 5 (2004): 5. See also my comments in Chapter 18, "The New."

English critics. Thus, in his philologically magnificently detailed and learned study of the Presocratics, Jonathan Barnes thinks that reading "Being exists" as Parmenides's central argument is untenable: "I am at a loss to understand that assertion; what in the world can be meant by 'Being exists'?"[23] Barnes's problem is due to his presupposition that Parmenides is a metaphysician in the Aristotelian sense who "attempts to discover, to elucidate, and to analyse the properties which must belong to every existent thing as such."[24] Barnes is obviously not interested in the ontological difference of beings ("existent thing[s]") and Being that arises with Parmenides's thinking. Being as the term *for* and as the thought and awareness *of* presence, Gr. *ousia* and G. *Anwesenheit*, is the central concern of German readers of Parmenides like Riezler and Gadamer and Heidegger.[25] Heidegger summarizes his exegesis of Parmenides thus: "Das Sein ist Gegenwart und Anwesenheit" ("Being is [the] present and presence").[26] When he says, "Itself alone is," Emerson thinks the temporal mode of Being as the uncreated and ceaseless presencing of a singularity in the way of Parmenides as interpreted by Gadamer. At the same time, Emerson foreshadows a reading like that of Heidegger because he is fully, even if only implicitly, aware of the ontological difference. Unlike Barnes, Emerson would not have been puzzled by statements like "Being is" or "Being exists" because, as we have seen, he does not simply equate Being/intellect with beings or things—be they subjects or spatially extended objects.

A second remarkable example of Emerson meditatively and speculatively perambulating among the thoughts and intuitions of the Presocratics can be found in the essay "Nominalist and Realist" (1844). Together with my interpretation of the opening passage from "Intellect" this will provide, I hope, sufficient micro-level correspondences to justify the thesis that Emerson is the first major modern thinker who, like Nietzsche and Heidegger after him, renews and reinvigorates philosophy by returning to and calling on and reviving and transforming the thoughts of philosophy's

---

[23]Jonathan Barnes, *The Presocratic Philosophers* (1979; Abingdon: Routledge, 2000), 162.
[24]Ibid., 176.
[25]In more recent English studies of the Presocratics, the German phenomenological approach and its central distinction of beings and Being again play no role whatsoever. For instance, Robin Waterfield argues: "Parmenides cannot mean, literally, that thinking and being are identical, but that they are co-extensive: thinking is the thinking of a thing [*sic*] as it is"; *The First Philosophers: The Presocratics and the Sophists* (Oxford: Oxford University Press, 2000), 51. It seems obvious to me, however, that Parmenides does not deal with *things* at all in part I of his poem, but rather and exclusively with Being, Gr. *on*, and thus not with *onta*, beings. Kurt Riezler argues that without the ontological difference the whole poem and its question of Being become empty, lifeless, and meaningless; *Parmenides: Übersetzung, Einführung und Interpretation* (1934; Frankfurt: Klostermann, 2001), 58.
[26]Heidegger, *Der Anfang der abendländischen Philosophie: Auslegung des Anaximander und Parmenides*, ed. Peter Trawny, vol. 35 of *Gesamtausgabe* (1932; Frankfurt: Klostermann, 2012), 174.

first and foundational thinkers. Nietzsche was to observe, following, as he did so often, the example set by Emerson: "Wir nähern uns heute allen jenen grundsätzlichen Formen der Weltauslegung wieder, welche der griechische Geist, in Anaximander, Heraklit, Parmenides, Empedokles, Demokrit und Anaxagoras, erfunden hat,—wir werden von Tag zu Tag *griechischer*."[27]

In "Nominalist and Realist," one may observe how Emerson becomes "more Greek" in Nietzsche's sense as he approaches, approximates, and appropriates the "Greek mind" of Anaximander, Heraclitus, and Parmenides. By no means an attempt to simply reproduce, let alone resolve, the medieval debate concerning the problem of universals, Emerson's essay is a balanced, a judicial presentation of the possibly equal claims of nominalist and realist, of monist and pluralist, of, as Emerson sometimes says, universalist and partialist positions. The final pages of the essay meditate on the tensions between different modes of particularizing and totalizing visions:

> If we were not kept among surfaces, everything would be large and universal; now the excluded attributes burst in on us with the more brightness that they have been excluded. "Your turn now, my turn next," is the rule of the game. The universality being hindered in its primary form, comes in the secondary form of *all sides*; the points come in succession.[28]

Things, individual beings, enter the bright light of phenomenality of presence, in sequential order; they appear in temporal succession and according to a law, to rules of a game. These rules determine that things, which co-exist only from a universalist point of view, keep replacing each other sequentially, in necessary and orderly fashion regulated by time. In this way Emerson evokes and meticulously rephrases the oldest preserved saying of Western philosophy by Anaximander, and he pays tribute to him by carefully attending to all of its important constitutive factors. I am quoting Anaximander in Philip Wheelwright's translation:

> The Unlimited [*apeiron*] is the first-principle of things that are. It is that from which the coming-to-be [of things and qualities] takes place, and it is that into which they return when they perish, by ... necessity, giving

---

[27]"Today we are approaching again all those forms of world interpretation, which the Greek mind invented in Anaximander, Heraclitus, Parmenides, Empedocles, Democritus, and Anaxagoras,—we are becoming more Greek by the day"; Friedrich Nietzsche, *Nachgelassene Fragmente 1884–1885*, vol. 11 of *Kritische Studienausgabe in 15 Bänden*, ed. Giorgio Colli and Mazzino Montinari (Munich: dtv, 1980), 679 (my translation). I will use this edition of Nietzsche's works throughout, abbreviated *KSA*.
[28]W III, 231.

satisfaction to one another and making reparation for their injustice, according to the order of time.[29]

Wheelwright explains:

> Each actually existing thing ... is a usurper; for during the time that it exists it "commits injustice" by preventing its opposite from existing; accordingly it must eventually pay the penalty by yielding up its overt existence and returning to its submerged place in the great qualitative reservoir [*apeiron*]. That, he [Anaximander] adds, is how time is ordered.[30]

If, following Heidegger, we do not read "injustice" and "penalty" as moral categories but as ontological conceptions, one understands that Anaximander speaks of processes of emergence and disappearance initiated and controlled by time as ontological "force."[31] Like Anaximander in Heidegger's interpretation, Emerson reads the coming-and-going of beings, their emergence and disappearance ("your turn, my turn"), as rule-bound events in a phenomenal world ("surfaces," "brightness") structured by time ("succession").

This particularized view of beings in a fundamentally temporal world is followed—in typical Emersonian fashion, that is, without any explicit argumentative transition—by the totalizing (or universalist) and *a*-temporal contemplation of Being as pure presence:

> It is the secret of the world that all things subsist and do not die, but only retire a little from sight and afterwards return again. Whatever does not concern us is concealed from us. As soon as a person is no longer related to our present well-being, he is concealed, or *dies*, as we say. Really, all things and persons are related to us, but according to our nature they act on us not at once but in succession, and we are made aware of their presence one at a time. *All persons, all things which we have known, are here present, and many more than we see; the world is full.* As the ancient said, the world is a *plenum* or solid; and if we saw all things that really surround us we should be imprisoned and unable to move.[32]

---

[29]Wheelwright, *Presocratics*, 54 (Diels-Kranz 12A9). I have omitted the adjective "moral" in Wheelwright's translation because, following Heidegger, I do not think that *dike* should be read as retributive justice in the sense of a moral world order; Heidegger, *Der Anfang der abendländischen Philosophie*, 12–13.

[30]Wheelwright, *Presocratics*, 53.

[31]Heidegger, *Der Anfang der abendländischen Philosophie*, 20–5. See also Fränkel, *Dichtung und Philosophie*, 304–5, who understands time in Anaximander's saying as the driving force (G. *Triebkraft*) which guarantees the continuity of the course of things.

[32]W III, 231 (my emphasis).

The vision of Anaximander of beings as they come and go in orderly fashion and in temporal succession is here complemented by the Parmenidian awareness of the stable presence of Being itself, "the unwavering heart of well-rounded truth," of Being as "ungenerated and indestructible, / whole, of one kind and unwavering, and complete. / Nor was it ever, nor will it be, since now it is, all together, / one, continuous."[33] Being in its totality is a singularity without past or future, an inescapable presence "since now it is." Thinking of the Being of beings instead of beings as such, Parmenides argues: "Look at things which, though absent, are yet present firmly to thought; / for you will not cut off what is from holding to what is"; and finally: Being is "all full of what is," *pan d'empleon estin eontos*[34]—or, in Emerson's words—"the world is full."

Gadamer explains that for Parmenides the *plenum* of Being, its unvarying presence, implies that it is *not* self-evident that the absent *is not* and that only present things exist; rather, the absent as such *is* (as) a presence.[35] Riezler had come to a similar conclusion in reading Parmenides: the *nous*, identical with Being itself, is persistently aware of absent things as co-present in their very absence.[36] Heidegger's analysis of the problem of Being and absence is closely related to Emerson's way of thinking and arguing: if there *is* something like the absent, it can only be absent within the circumference of presence; as far as the absent *is*, it is present in the *existential mode* of absence, even if it is not perceived.[37] Emerson correspondingly envisions all beings in their Being, all individual entities in so far as they *are*, as truly present in their—from a particularist point of view—seeming absence. The world in its Being, as *plenum*, for Emerson as for Parmenides, is immobile; it is a radical and inescapable presence: "if we saw all things that really surround us we should be imprisoned and unable to move."

In yet another of his abrupt shifts of perspective, Emerson then moves away from the totalizing Parmenidian contemplation of Being and considers the inner tensions within existence, the world of beings as it unfolds in time. The contrasts and conflicts between means and ends, agent and act, mind

---

[33]These are translations by Jonathan Barnes in *Early Greek Philosophy*, 79, 82.
[34]Ibid., 84, 83.
[35]Gadamer, "Parmenides und das Sein," in *Anfang der Philosophie*, 156.
[36]Riezler, *Parmenides*, 43.
[37]Heidegger, *Der Anfang der abendländischen Philosophie*, 176: "Gesetzt, es gäbe Abwesendes, und es gibt solches beziehungsweise, dann kann auch dieses Abwesende *nur abwesend sein in einem Umkreis von Anwesenheit*. Es ist *nur abwesend im Umkreis von Anwesenheit*, sofern es 'ist,' 'ist' es nur qua *anwesend*—es braucht aber nicht wahrgenommen zu sein." ("Suppose there were something absent, and something like this, so to speak, is, then this absent entity can only be *absent within a circumference of presence*. It is *absent only within a circumference of presence* insofar as it 'is,' 'is' only qua *present*—it does not have to be perceived"; my translation.)

and matter, right and wrong replace for a while the quiet plenitude of Being as the center of the essay's attention:

> We must reconcile the contradictions as we can, but their discord and their concord introduce wild absurdities into our thinking and speech. No sentence will hold the whole truth, and the only way in which we can be just, is by giving ourselves the lie; Speech is better than silence; silence is better than speech;—All things are in contact; every atom has a sphere of repulsion;—Things are, and are not, at the same time;—and the like. All the world over, there *is* but *one thing*, this old *Two*-Face ... of which any proposition may be affirmed or denied.[38]

By way of a series of abrupt reversals alternately replacing monist with pluralist ontological points of view and vice versa, Emerson's "Nominalist and Realist" has here reached a quintessentially paradoxical stand-point from which he intuits contradiction, dualisms, and plurality as the very manifestation of an inescapable unity of Being: "there *is* but *one thing*." Being is that which becomes phenomenally apparent in endless processes of emergent and disappearing beings which continue to exhibit mutually exclusive qualities that tend to replace each other abruptly and in this way call for a philosophical language of contradictions, a language of paradox. After engaging Anaximander and Parmenides, Emerson now finds himself, in vision and language, in the company of Heraclitus, probably the most prominent and congenial of his Presocratic interlocutors.

When he says, "Speech is better than silence; silence is better than speech;—All things are in contact; every atom has a sphere of repulsion," Emerson begins to present a series of radical contradictions, of paradoxes, as variations of a pattern established by Heraclitus, and he ends this series with an almost direct quotation of a saying by Heraclitus that he found in Heinrich Ritter's *The History of Ancient Philosophy* as: "all is and is not."[39] These stark contradictions imply ontological unity *by way of* or *as* fundamental tension in the ontic realm of beings, as "Two-Face." Karl Reinhardt's magnificent and highly influential interpretation of Heraclitus as complementing the ontological monism of Parmenides supports Emerson's Heraclitean insight. Reinhardt argues that in Heraclitus the power of contradiction is the essence of ontic reality, something which inherently belongs to and complements its ontological unity: truth is a paradox; everything in the world is antagonistic, but the contrasts and contradictions

---

[38] W III, 233 (my emphasis).
[39] Heinrich Ritter, *The History of Ancient Philosophy*, trans. Alexander J. W. Morrison (Oxford: Talboys, 1838), vol. I, 240. On the importance of Ritter's *History* for Emerson's understanding of both ancient philosophy and the history of thinking, see Chapter 5, "Resisting Hegel."

condition one another—opposition is the essence of all things and the world of antagonisms *is* the *one* and only true world.[40] Wheelwright has offered a similar reading of Heraclitus, which deserves to be quoted *in extenso* because it, almost uncannily, comes across as a tacit exegesis and justification of Emerson's judicial stance in "Nominalist and Realist," which presents ontological monism and ontic pluralism as equally justified and as both antagonistic and complementary philosophical positions. Wheelwright argues against a simplistic interpretation of Parmenides and Heraclitus as irreconcilable opposites:

> Granted that variety and change constitute a main theme, perhaps even *the* main theme for Heraclitus, there is nevertheless a second theme, running contrapuntally throughout the doctrine, which is equally indispensable— the theme expressed most plainly in Fr. 118 [i.e., Diels-Kranz B50], that "all things are one." It is misleading to call Heraclitus a pluralist without adding that he is somehow a monist as well, or to stress his doctrine of change, chance, and strife without adding that these characteristics, real and basic though they are, exist somehow counterbalanced by a tendency toward order, pattern, and harmony, which is equally inherent in what we must call (knowing that words fail us here) reality.[41]

Heraclitean fragments like the following make it plausible that the last paragraphs of "Nominalist and Realist" are deeply and pervasively imbued with the vision of a world of fundamental unity in Being that is paradoxically constituted by unceasing conflict and contrast among beings (Gr. *polemos*): "Opposition brings concord. Out of discord comes the fairest harmony"; "Into the same rivers we step and do not step"; "From out of all the many particulars comes oneness, and out of oneness come all the many particulars"; "Hesiod, whom so many accept as their wise teacher, did not even understand the nature of day and night; for they are one."[42] In Heraclitus all differences and all oppositions point toward ontological unity by the very fact of maintaining their tensions. Emerson, as we saw, responds by asserting that the One (Being) is a Two-Face and that the totality of Being conceived as nature (*physis*) "is *one thing and the other thing*, in the same moment."[43] The Emersonian thinker knows himself inescapably tied to this temporal world of successive and alternating as well as contradictory and conflicting and antagonistic phenomena. Like Heraclitus he finds his

---

[40]Karl Reinhardt, *Parmeniaes und die Geschichte der griechischen Philosophie* (1959; Frankfurt: Klostermann, 2012), 204, 208.
[41]Wheelwright, *Heraclitus*, 103.
[42]Ibid., 90–1. The traditional Diels-Kranz numbers are: B8, B49a, B10, B57.
[43]W II, 225.

integrity, his sincerity, his identity, his oneness, in admitting that the One as Being manifests itself as an endless contest, *polemos*, a war of perspectives within the One, "of which any proposition may be affirmed or denied." In proper paradoxical fashion, the thinker will then bear testimony to the true constitution and unity of Being and beings when he realizes "I am always insincere, as always knowing there are other moods."[44]

The sequence of Emersonian moves in the latter part of "Nominalist and Realist"—from a pluralistic contemplation of beings in their successive emergence and disappearance toward an evocation of the static fullness of ever-present Being, which culminates in a vision of the unity of Being paradoxically manifested in the inescapable and unceasing strife of a multiplicity of opposites—this sequence pays tribute to Anaximander, Parmenides, and Heraclitus, and to their individual philosophical intuitions. At the same time, Emerson implies the compatibility of the three thinkers and especially of Parmenides and Heraclitus, who are often and superficially understood as antagonists. They *are* antagonists, to be sure, but they are in opposition in the sense which testifies to unity: Parmenides complements his vision of Being with an analysis of the oppositional and changeable world of *doxa*, the unstable interpretations of reality by mortals, and Heraclitus intuits the One as it paradoxically comes to presence in the unceasing *polemos* or in the relentless flow of a co-eternal and irreducible, ever-changing multiplicity of beings. It would be impossible to be more Greek, *griechischer* in Nietzsche's sense, than Emerson enacting the return of Anaximander, Parmenides, and Heraclitus both in their irreducible individualities of vision and in their simultaneous, even though differing, celebrations of ontological unity in and as ontic multiplicity. In "Nominalist and Realist," the primary intuitions of the ontological difference at the core of early Greek thought return as the potential for that radical renewal of thinking which we have come to know as modernism.

As we have seen, Emerson's perambulations among the thinkers of the earliest beginnings sometimes result in the extended, condensed, and highly detailed appropriative and transformative responses exemplified by the passages from "Intellect" and "Nominalist and Realist." Such echoes on a textual micro-level are complemented by philosophical equivalences in Emerson and the Presocratics that pervade Emerson's thinking and writing more generally, on a macro-level that extends over more than just one essay; occasionally such features of more pervasive philosophical coalescence become manifest even without explicit references to specific Presocratic sayings. Emerson's awareness and understanding of his own position as a thinker makes him a natural ally of "the scholar of the first age"[45] who does

---

44Ibid., 235.
45"The American Scholar" W I, 89.

not rely on books or any other precedent, who existentially and intellectually entertains "an original relation to the universe"[46] and experiments "with no Past at [his] back."[47] This, for Emerson, is the characteristic disposition of primary thinkers, of the Presocratics. This is why he so intensely admires "the prompt improvisations of the earliest inquirers, of Parmenides, Heraclitus, & Xenophanes."[48] Their thinking is an immediate, a truly un-mediated and spontaneous ("prompt"), and thus ungrounded response ("improvisation") to Being itself; in Emerson's vocabulary such thinking experimentally articulates the challenge of aboriginal nature, of *physis* as unconditioned emergence.

Even though a considerable number of the critics and historians of Presocratic thinking insist on the importance of either shamanism, myth, the Seven Sages, the Orphic tradition, or Egyptian and Persian religious and philosophical thought as precursors and shaping influences on the Presocratics, Emerson's interpretation of their unconditioned and radically self-determined status as original thinkers[49] is not without important champions among historians, philologists, and philosophers. Fränkel, in his influential study of early Greek thinking and poetry, argues that, as far as we know, with the Presocratics a pure philosophy, separated from all foreign ties, appeared all of a sudden and without any discernible cause.[50] Gadamer insists that "Anfangen nichts Reflektiertes, sondern etwas Unmittelbares ist": beginning or inception is not something that is considered and enacted reflectively and intentionally; it is, rather, un-mediated.[51] From Gadamer's point of view any inception (G. *Anfang*), like that of Presocratic thinking, is a first and experimental step into a totally undetermined future,[52] or, in Emerson's words, a "prompt improvisation." Whereas for Heidegger the philosophical return to such beginnings or inceptions helps prepare or create the expectation of another, a restorative and redeeming, beginning in the future,[53] for Emerson the moment of the new dispensation of thinking is always now. Or as Whitman, inspired by Emerson, said: "There was never any more inception than there is now."[54]

---

[46]*Nature* W I, 9.

[47]"Circles" W II, 297.

[48]*JMN* VII, 13.

[49]As in so many other instances, Emerson is not necessarily consistent in his view of the unprecedented historical importance of the Presocratics. In "Plato; or, the Philosopher," he acknowledges predecessors of the Presocratics like the "Seven Wise Masters"; W IV, 48.

[50]Fränkel, *Dichtung und Philosophie*, 292: "Soweit wir wissen, erschien die reine, von allen fremden Bindungen gelöste, Philosophie plötzlich und ohne ersichtlichen Anlass."

[51]Gadamer, *Anfang der Philosophie*, 22.

[52]Ibid., 21.

[53]Heidegger, *Der Anfang der abendländischen Philosophie*, 97: "Das geschichtliche Wiederfragen der Seinsfrage als Wiederanfangen des anfänglichen Anfangs." ("Asking the question of Being again historically as a renewed inception of the initial inception"; my translation.)

[54]Walt Whitman, "Song of Myself," in *Leaves of Grass: Comprehensive Reader's Edition*, ed. Harold W. Blodgett and Sculley Bradley (New York: New York University Press, 1965), 30

The Presocratics not only provide a model for Emerson's view of himself as a primary thinker, a self-reliant thinker "of the first age," asking the perennial "first questions," but also present rhetorical patterns and strategies of reasoning that resurface in a majority of his essays and significantly structure the arguments. Heraclitus offers the most prominent parallels. An outstanding example is this aphorism: "It is one and the same thing to be living or dead, awake or asleep, young or old. The former aspect in each case becomes the latter, and the latter again the former, by sudden unexpected reversal."[55] We already encountered the thought of the co-presence of the living and the dead in a passage from "Nominalist and Realist." The important consideration now is the structure of the aphorism and of its argument that is concisely captured in the phrase "sudden unexpected reversal." Sudden reversals or turns or shifts in Emerson's essays are a most familiar and, for many, an irritating feature that has sometimes been misconstrued as the irresponsible evasion of conclusive philosophical commitments by the "man without a handle," as Henry James Sr. so charmingly satirized Emerson.[56] It is not just "Nominalist and Realist" where the title prepares the reader for a balanced and possibly unresolved presentation of mutually exclusive or, at best, complementary modes of thinking: examples of relentless reversals of thought, conviction, belief, or valuation proliferate in Emerson. The radical skepticism of "Experience" ends with a powerful and uplifting exhortation and the courageous assertion of a "will to believe." Like all portraits in *Representative Men*, "Plato; or, the Philosopher" is also pervaded by unmitigated contradictions: Plato is "the representative of philosophy" and the "balanced soul," his thinking offers "the pleasure of conversing with real being," and yet Plato's "theory of the world is a thing of shreds and patches" and "[i]n view of eternal nature Plato turns out to be philosophical exercitations."[57] The introductory chapter of *Representative Men*, "The Uses of Great Men," prepared the reader for the vacillations of Emerson's evaluation of greatness. The dogmatic assertion "we feed on genius" is implicitly undermined by the warning of the danger of becoming "underlings and intellectual suicides"[58] when we give in to this craving. Prominent examples of the thought pattern and the rhetorical strategy of systematic reversal in the *later* essays are the equally assertive pronouncements on the equipollence of fate and of freedom in "Fate" and the opposing claims advanced in the twin essays opening *The Conduct of Life*: "Fate" and "Power."

---

[55]Wheelwright, *Heraclitus*, 90–1 (Diels-Kranz B88).
[56]Qtd. in Ralph Barton Perry, *The Thought and Character of William James* (London: Milford, 1935), vol. I, 51.
[57]W IV, 44, 45, 64, 75, 76.
[58]Ibid., 30, 31.

Both Fränkel and Gadamer have interpreted the paradoxical structures of thinking and writing in Heraclitus in a way that helps to better understand the function and significance of the patterns of sudden reversals in Emerson's idiosyncratic appropriation or transformation of his Presocratic precursor. Fränkel argues that for Heraclitus Being in its totality is a relentlessly vibrating process of reversals and transformation that arises out of persevering tensions. Any process in Heraclitus should be interpreted as a continuous course of self-destruction and self-renewal.[59] Emerson had read in Ritter's *History of Ancient Philosophy*: "Before [the] force of perfect life nothing naturally can have persistence; it is the true, the ever-permanent; but, as the force of perfect vitality, it is without hinderance to its activity, so that nothing which it forms continues, but all is constantly in inchoation."[60] Emerson obviously understood the last phrase as a genuine aphorism by Heraclitus and confessed in his journals: "Ever & forever Heraclitus is justified who called the world an eternal inchoation."[61] The vision of a world of unremitting renewal, of ontological modernism, would necessitate a language that kept canceling or unsaying or at least questioning whatever had been stated before: reversals are of the essence of the vision of Heraclitean (and thus also of Emersonian) process philosophy, as Fränkel explains.

Gadamer adds an important aspect to our understanding of Emerson when he explains the prevalence and the importance of contradictions and reversals in Heraclitus. Gadamer differs from a number of other critics by insisting that the images of a flowing reality and the intuition of the unity of opposites support each other. The mysterious problem, Gadamer says, which becomes manifest behind all these contradictions, is this: the same shows without transition as the other, as an other. In all these examples, he continues, one finds the phenomenon the Greeks called *metabole* G. *Umschlag*, E. reversal), which is characterized by an abrupt suddenness. The experience of thinking at the basis of this vision is of the essential unreliability of all things that now show as this and then, all of a sudden, appear as fundamentally different.[62] Similarly, the equally unmediated reversals, which permeate so many of Emerson's essays, convey a world in which qualities and values change abruptly and most often without transition. The sudden turns of argument reveal a vision of ontic reality as essentially unreliable. As in Gadamer's interpretation of *metabole* in Heraclitus, the incessant shifts imply the absence of a reliable, or at least

[59]Fränkel, *Dichtung und Philosophie*, 432.
[60]Ritter, *History of Ancient Philosophy*, 236.
[61]*JMN* VII, 457.
[62]This is my paraphrase of Hans-Georg Gadamer, "Heraklit-Studien," in *Der Anfang des Wissens* (Stuttgart: Reclam, 1999), 42–3.

of a reliably recognizable, ground or foundation. Emerson has repeatedly articulated his sense of a fleeting and paradoxical world without firm underpinning. In "Compensation" he writes: "Under all this running sea of circumstance, whose waters ebb and flow with perfect balance, lies the aboriginal abyss of real Being."[63] The same philosophical sentiment is expressed in "Circles" where he intuits that "under every deep a lower deep opens."[64] The hope that one may find a solid and unquestionable basis as a safe haven for our existential condition is shattered in "Experience": "Gladly we would anchor but the anchorage is quicksand."[65] Being, which is not a *some-thing*, reveals itself in the ceaseless abrupt permutations of the world of beings, but it offers no stability. Heraclitus uses the images of the flowing ever-renewed and ever-changing river or of the all-consuming fire without fixed contours to indicate an ontological unity that refuses to be conceptually fixed; Emerson—correspondingly—knows only the "abyss of ... Being," a more than precarious anchorage, an absent presence of Being that paradoxically "sustains" the ceaseless ebb and flow of the conflicted and contradictory surface-world of mere beings.

The prefatory poem of the later essay "Illusions" (1860) is a powerful testimony and summary of the impact of the Heraclitean vision of a world of relentless change, of flowing transformations, of pervasive instability, and of ceaseless reversals. Emerson once again evokes an ontic totality without stable foundation: "Flow, flow the waves hated, / Accursed, adored, / The waves of mutation: / No anchorage is." All conflicting states of existence, as in so many of Heraclitus's sayings, reveal an identity only as they are engulfed by the endless processes of emergence and dissolution: "Sleep is not, death is not; / Who seem to die live. / ... They are all vanishing, / Fleeing to fables, / Cannot be moored." The world is an "endless imbroglio" of changes and (eternal) returns, which promises "power" and "endurance" for the individual being only as he is "Horsed on the Proteus," ready to accept existence as endless shape-shifting, as a process of never-ending turns and transformations.[66] The Protean character of the world calls for a rhetoric essentially structured by *metabole*. The sayings of Heraclitus and the essays and poems of Emerson again and again respond to this pro-vocation as they

---

[63] W II, 116.

[64] Ibid., 281.

[65] W III, 58.

[66] W VI, 292–3. Emerson's poem foreshadows Nietzsche's famous Heraclitean vision of the world as "ein Ungeheuer von Kraft, ohne Anfang, ohne Ende ... ein Meer in sich selber stürmender und fluthender Kräfte, ewig sich wandelnd, ewig zurücklaufend, mit ungeheuren Jahren der Wiederkehr"; *Der Wille zur Macht, KSA* 11, 610. (The world is "a powerful monster without beginning and end, a sea stormily raging within itself, forever changing and forever returning into itself through immensities of circular time"; my paraphrase.)

refuse to provide reliable resting-places in any single statement. As Emerson says: "I liked everything by turns and nothing long."[67]

In addition to Emerson positioning himself as a thinker of the first age and in addition to the important rhetorical strategies of paradox and argumentative reversal, the elective affinity with Presocratic philosophy manifests itself in a series of both major and minor motifs of Emerson's thinking. For the modern reader Heraclitus's fragment B 6 (Diels-Kranz) may be cryptic—which is not unusual for the dark thinker (Gr. *ho skoteinos*)— and also somewhat quaint: "The sun is new each day."[68] The saying, however, quite obviously and not at all mysteriously implies that what we see as natural processes characterized by continuity may alternatively be understood as a series that progresses by way of iteration. In "The American Scholar," Emerson evokes natural processes as the primary challenges for the thinker and he seems to echo Heraclitus when he says: "Every day, the sun; and, after sunset, Night and her stars."[69]

That this is not too fanciful a comparison is supported by a passage in "The Method of Nature": Emerson speaks of "[t]he wholeness we admire in the order of the world" and continues: "Its permanence is a perpetual inchoation. Every natural fact is an emanation, and that from which it emanates is an emanation also, and from every emanation is a new emanation."[70] The term "emanation" may seduce one to think of a Neoplatonic background for this passage; however, Emerson does not state or imply that there is an aboriginal One as the source of all emanations. Rather, the series of emanations is endless, without beginning or end. Natural processes of ceaseless renewal are iterative. The Heraclitean resonance is provided by the term "inchoation," the ever-new beginning as a permanent feature of the natural world according to Heinrich Ritter's interpretation of Heraclitus. I already noted that Emerson obviously considered the phenomenon of unceasing inchoation as an authentic Heraclitean conception and not just as a quite plausible interpretation by Ritter. Iteration or beginning again and again as a constitutive feature of natural phenomena in Emerson is obviously indebted to Heraclitus; iteration in the history of thinking is similarly an outcome of his encounter with Presocratic philosophy. Instead of a dialectically progressive unfolding of ideas as in Hegel, Emerson, encouraged by Ritter's study of early Greek thinking, preferred the idea of a succession of fully self-reliant, independent thinkers who realize that "[t] he first questions are always to be asked."[71] He cannot see an advance in

---

[67] W III, 236.
[68] Wheelwright, *The Presocratics*, 72.
[69] W I, 86.
[70] Ibid., 190–1.
[71] See Chapter 5, "Resisting Hegel," in this book.

depth or sophistication of thinking from Parmenides to Kant or Fichte.[72] Assuming a celestial perspective, Emerson amuses himself by envisioning the great thinkers of classical antiquity, from Heraclitus to Proclus, as forever youthful, as "babe-like Jupiters [who] sit in their clouds, and from age to age prattle to each other and to no contemporary."[73] The history of philosophy as iterative, as a series of inchoations, can be read both ways, as perennial and as unremittingly modern, as timeless but also as forever initial and primary.

Another important thematic convergence of Presocratic philosophy and Emerson's thinking is revealed in the way Heraclitus, Xenophanes, and Emerson envision the fundamental structure and the history of the cosmic order. Heraclitus says: "This universe, which is the same for all, has not been made by any god or man, but it has always been, is, and will be—an ever-living fire, kindling itself by regular measures and going out by regular measures."[74] The true Being of the world (fire) enacts itself in cyclical iterations of coming-to-be and self-destruction.[75] There is no original creation by an agent outside the energetic processes themselves. A similar view was advanced by Xenophanes in his fundamental critique of Greek polytheism and its anthropomorphic mythology. This critique, according to Eduard Zeller, provides the background for Xenophanes's theory that the totality of the world does not arise or pass away as do the beings in the world that we know.[76] Heinrich Ritter, whom Emerson had thoroughly studied, had argued: "the notion of incipiency appeared to Xenophanes so contradictory of the divine nature, that he rejected it altogether; and a singular argument has been attributed to him, maintaining that a beginning of being is, on the whole, inconceivable."[77]

Supported or encouraged by Heraclitus and Xenophanes, Emerson abandons biblical conceptions of creation and of a linear movement of the cosmos toward an apocalyptic finale. In this post-Christian view, he preserves and revives important aspects of the Presocratic cosmic imagination.[78] In "The American Scholar" Emerson expounds: "There is never a beginning,

---

[72]*JMN* VII, 13.

[73]*W* II, 322.

[74]Wheelwright, *Heraclitus*, 37 (Diels-Kranz B30). I prefer Wheelwright's translation over those by Jonathan Barnes and Robin Waterfield because he attempts to render the implications of the middle voice in the last clause more precisely: "Heraclitus does not think of the kindling and extinguishing as performed by an agency outside the fire itself"; ibid., 141.

[75]The question whether these cosmic cycles in Heraclitus imply a destruction by fire (Gr. *ekpyrosis*) after a cosmic time-span of 10,800 years and a consequent "fiery" rebirth is still a point of contention among critics.

[76]Eduard Zeller, *Die Philosophie der Griechen in ihrer geschichtlichen Entwicklung* (1919; Darmstadt: WBG, 2006), vol. I, 660–4.

[77]Ritter, *History of Ancient Philosophy*, 428–9.

[78]It is obvious that Nietzsche's idea of an eternal return of the same on a cosmic scale corresponds or is indebted to both Heraclitus and Emerson.

there is never an end, to the inexplicable continuity of this web of God, but always circular power returning into itself."[79] It is important to emphasize that God is not the name for a power outside the cosmos, the web. The text does not decide whether the divine web weaves itself or whether the cosmic web "creates" the divine. The continuity of the web, of the cosmos, is one of constant circular renewal of itself (iteration, inchoation) *by* and *through* itself. Emerson's philosophical return to the earliest cosmological and cosmogonic conceptions is—as in Nietzsche—both an overcoming and an abandonment of the Christian religious and metaphysical perspective and the initiation of the post-metaphysical dispensation with its emphasis on radical immanence. Remembering Heraclitus and Xenophanes, Emerson reclaims the innocence of becoming for a universe ontologically indebted only to itself.

The essay "Compensation" is not exactly a favorite among Emersonians. Even so it is worthwhile to look a little more closely at the implied Presocratic background of the idea, the pervasive theme, of compensation or polarity, as Emerson sometimes calls the fact of equalizing tendencies in natural and in moral history that tend to correct one-sidedness, excesses, or imbalances among beings. I will quote Anaximander's one preserved saying again: "The Unlimited [*apeiron*] is the first-principle of things that are. It is that from which the coming-to-be [of things and qualities] takes place, and it is that into which they return when they perish, by moral necessity, giving satisfaction to one another and making reparation for their injustice, according to the order of time."[80] Just or measured or appropriate retribution characterizes the sequential processes that take place in nature. In this way natural processes provide a model for the moral evaluation of actions among humans where one person usurps the place and the property that might empower someone else and is then justly "punished" by the retributive removal or loss of his seemingly unquestioned preeminence. Emerson's *poem* "Compensation," which serves as motto or preface for the essay, is printed on two consecutive pages:[81] the first page is devoted to compensatory balances among natural phenomena (black/white, tall/deep, tidal movements/balanced movements of planets); the second part, of equal length, describes necessary or fated compensations of deficiencies in human power or achievement. In this way the poem tends to mitigate, possibly even eliminate, the differences between compensations in the world of nature and in the moral universe. What Emerson does, in erasing the fundamental

---

[79] W I, 86–7.
[80] Wheelwright, *Presocratics*, 54. I do not omit the adjective "moral" in Wheelwright's translation here since Emerson in "Compensation" obviously allows for both natural and moral implications of compensatory events. Cf. footnote 29 above.
[81] W II, 89–90.

opposition of the natural and the moral order, was identified by Karl Löwith as a significant feature of the return of the early Greek philosophical vision, for instance, in Nietzsche. Löwith speaks of philosophy after Hegel as remembering the great Presocratic *physikoi* when it starts the important modern experiment of "re-translating" the human being into the nature of all things.[82]

Unity or the One as a theme, as an idea, as a motif of Emerson's thinking was significantly co-determined by Presocratic models. The unity or oneness of *the world* as an intuition or as a conception should be distinguished from the oneness of *Being* that I discussed at the beginning of this chapter. The texts inspired by or responding to the ontology of Parmenides deal with Being as the One, as uniform presence-ing, and distinguish it from beings. Being as the One is "determined" by the ontological difference. The Oneness or totality or unity of the world of beings, which I would like to address now, is an onto-theological conception with strong religious overtones in Emerson. This conception does not so much contradict as rather complement the interpretation of Being based on the ontological difference.

The world as the One is a relatively indistinct and ubiquitous notion in the histories of philosophical and of religious thought, with a great number of proponents. The important, even if not exclusive, role of Xenophanes in Emerson's meditations on cosmic unity is prepared by entries in the *Journals* as early as 1830–31, when Emerson was reading Joseph Marie de Gérando's *Histoire Comparée des Systèmes de Philosophie* (1822–23) and transcribed a great number of Presocratic fragments and comments on the Presocratics. Under the heading *Xenophanes* he noted: "In the last part of his life he said 'he could not be so happy as to know any thing certainly. Whichever side he looked all ran to unity—there was but one substance.'"[83] Emerson was obviously so taken by this comment that in 1831 he mistakenly attributed a similar saying to Heraclitus: "Heraclitus grown old complained that all resolved itself into identity."[84] In 1836 Emerson returned to the aphorism and, correctly, wrote in *Nature*, drawing again on the commentary by Timon of Phlius as reported by Theophrastus that he had found in de Gérando: "Xenophanes complained in his old age, that, look where he would, all things hastened back to Unity. He was weary of seeing the same entity in the tedious variety of forms. The fable of Proteus has a cordial truth."[85] The ever new world of shifting shapes is the dynamic realization of a powerful

---

[82]Löwith, *Nietzsches Philosophie der ewigen Wiederkehr des Gleichen* (1935; Hamburg: Meiner, 1978), 192. Löwith's term is *Rückübersetzung* (re-translation).
[83]*JMN* III, 368–9.
[84]Ibid., 266.
[85]W I, 48.

tendency that both creates and devours all beings. Emerson's poem "Pan"[86]
celebrates the splendor and the cruelty of this process in which we witness
"all things" as they "hasten back to Unity" and are thus annihilated after
their brief, their momentary and delusive self-sufficiency. In "Self-Reliance"
the melancholy connotations, the cruel and destructive aspects of the *way*
of the world have disappeared, and Emerson speaks—with religious awe
and echoing his notes on Xenophanes—of "the resolution of all into the
ever-blessed ONE. Self-existence is the attribute of the Supreme Cause, and
it constitutes the measure of good by the degree in which it enters into all
lower forms."[87] Later, the unifying dynamic of the cosmos re-appears as
eternally productive *natura naturans* in "Nature" (1844);[88] here Spinoza's
version of pantheism has supplanted or complemented Emerson's earlier
pantheistic ways of seeing the totality of the cosmos as suggested or inspired
by Xenophanes.[89]

The *tour d' horizon* of Emerson's philosophical encounters and
conversations with the Presocratics opens insight into an impressive variety
of textual echoes, of similarities in ontological, cosmological, as well as
methodological conceptions. The primary questions of the constitution
of the cosmos, of Being and of beings, of the challenges for a primary
and unprecedented mode of thinking, and of the paradoxes of conflicted
multiplicity as revealing unity, as well as a series of philosophical core themes
like the iterative character of physical and of historical events, the question
of the eternal subsistence of the world, the problem of compensation: all
these document a comprehensive elective affinity between Anaximander,
Xenophanes, Parmenides, and especially Heraclitus with Emerson's early
modern stance. Like Nietzsche, Emerson is able to abandon the constraints
of the metaphysical tradition in order to begin again with "no past at [his]
back." Paradoxically and plausibly at the same time, this project begins by
remembering what it means to be a primary thinker, to be "present at the
sowing of the seed of the world."[90] Modernist thinking as radical renewal
has to recover the very quintessence of first beginnings.

Emerson's responses to and transformations of Presocratic visions and
positions do not cohere. Not even the questions of the unity of Being or of the

---

[86] W IX, 309.
[87] W II, 70.
[88] W III, 172.
[89] Zeller reminds us that, according to Aristotle and Theophrastus, Xenophanes had seen
the world in its totality as the deity; *Philosophie der Griechen*, vol. I, 653. Contemporary
interpretations still support this nineteenth-century view of Xenophanes as pantheist:
"Xenophanes nannte dies All und Eine den Gott." ("Xenophanes called this One and All the
Deity"; my translation); Laura Gemelli Marciano, *Die Vorsokratiker: Auswahl der Fragmente
und Zeugnisse* (Düsseldorf: Artemis & Winkler, 2007), vol. I, 233.
[90] "Intellect" W II, 322.

underlying unity of the cosmos result in systematically unified conceptions. Inspired by the multiplicity of points of view in the Presocratic aphorisms and fragments themselves, Emerson offers experiments, he unsettles dogmatic convictions, he appreciates many perspectives, but—as we heard before—"nothing long." Thinking *after* the Presocratics, in a double sense, is a process for Emerson, a search for a philosophical language. The methods, the manifold *ways* of open-ended investigation—in the sense of continuous free experimentations—rather than system or dogma, become the hallmark of modern thinking, as Nietzsche once remarked.[91]

Focusing on the Presocratics is legitimate and productive. It allows us to see more clearly what Emerson considered to be central "first questions" that had to be entertained again and again, but it cannot do full and ultimate justice to Emerson's truly cosmopolitan outlook when he explores and revives and transforms earliest beginnings, true inceptions. The importance of Mencius, of the sayings of Zarathustra, of the *Upanishads* and of the *Bhagavad Gita* in Emerson's comprehensive recovery of a restorative origin[92] remind one that he is aware not only of the continuing challenge and inspiration of the Presocratics but also of what came to be called the axial age by Karl Jaspers.[93] As a thinker of the second axial age of the eighteenth and nineteenth centuries, Emerson accepted no cultural limits, he entered and restituted for us a philosophical *apeiron*, he revitalized un- or delimited and therefore always invigorating primal realms of both ancient and forever new ways of thinking of which the Presocratics are the outstanding and representative, but not the exclusive example.

---

[91]He said: "die werthvollsten Einsichten sind die Methoden"; *Der Antichrist, KSA* 6, 179 ("the most valuable insights are the methods"; my translation).

[92]Ross Posnock is one of the very few critics who has appreciated and subtly interpreted the importance of the ontological vision of Mencius for Emerson; see his *Renunciation: Acts of Abandonment by Writers, Philosophers, and Artists* (Cambridge, MA: Harvard University Press, 2016), 311. Indian and Persian religious thinking is comprehensively dealt with in Arthur Versluis, *American Transcendentalism and Asian Religions* (Oxford: Oxford University Press, 1993).

[93]Karl Jaspers, *Vom Ursprung und Ziel der Geschichte* (1949; Munich: Piper, 1949), 19–41.

# 2

# Emerson; or, the Neopyrrhonist Skeptic

Reading Emerson as a Platonic idealist is one of the long-standing, of the stubbornly recurring, and seemingly ineradicable prejudices of a considerable part of more conservative and traditionalist Emerson criticism and the hallmark especially of the common or popular perception of him as a thinker. More recent and highly sophisticated criticism, on the other hand, like the interpretations of such important and widely differing readers as, for example, Richard Poirier, David Robinson, Harold Bloom, Stanley Cavell, Lawrence Buell, Joan Richardson, Ross Posnock, or Branka Arsic, seems to consider Emerson's philosophical meditations on Plato and other thinkers of classical antiquity as far less central for a just appreciation of his foundational insights than his foreshadowing of great European and American moderns like Nietzsche, the pragmatists, or Wittgenstein. As a productive alternative and addition to these two well-established critical tendencies, it may appear rather daring and even Quixotic to draw attention to a thinker like Sextus Empiricus and to a mode of skeptical thinking that often goes by the name of Neopyrrhonism as avenues that promise to lead toward a different but maybe equally just appreciation of the core of Emerson's philosophy as a whole, as well as to a major re-evaluation of his interpretation of Plato and Platonism. The privileged role of Platonism for the development of European philosophy through Fichte, Hegel, and Schelling to Whitehead and Gadamer has obscured the importance of the often submerged alternative skeptical tradition. Its beginnings as a corrective in the Platonic Academy some seventy years after Plato have been constitutive and formative for a long philosophical lineage that—as we all know—counts Montaigne and, I will emphatically maintain, Emerson among its eminent descendants.

The factual basis that could help argue the case for the importance of the skeptics of classical antiquity and especially of its last and most prolific representative, Sextus Empiricus (late second to early third centuries CE), for Emerson is, at first sight, rather meager. Sextus is never named or quoted in any of Emerson's published writings and, as far as I could ascertain, the *Journals and Miscellaneous Notebooks* mention him just three times. When Emerson excerpted sayings of Pythagoras from Thomas Taylor's English translation of *Iamblichus' Life of Pythagoras*, he twice added "Sextus" to a quotation, indicating in this way that he realized that the aphorisms had been preserved in the writings of Sextus Empiricus.[1] More importantly, in 1830, when he read de Gérando's *Histoire Comparée des Systèmes de Philosophie*, Emerson copied sayings by Xenophanes together with comments by Sextus:

> Sextus Empiricus has preserved these words from [Xenophanes'] poem on nature which are as skeptical as one could desire[:] "No man knows any thing certain touching the Gods nor upon what I say upon the universal whole. None can. For if one should chance upon the truth—*he could not know he had obtained it*; but opinion spreads her veil over all things."[2]

Some thinkers of classical Greece saw Heraclitus, who played such a major formative role for Emerson, as a predecessor of the skeptics of the Platonic or Middle Academy (late fourth to second centuries BCE) and of later Neopyrrhonists like Sextus.[3] Emerson was aware of skeptical positions in Heraclitus as the *Journal* entries indicate which are devoted to aphorisms by Heraclitus transcribed from Heinrich Ritter's *The History of Ancient Philosophy*.[4] The commentary by Sextus on Xenophanes, however, is more significant: Sextus's words and the fragment from Xenophanes are "as skeptical as one could desire." As early as 1830 Emerson knew how to appreciate the profound skeptical view that, even though a person might accidentally have gained true insight, he would not be able to know that he had done so.

For a weightier factual underpinning of my attempt to argue the importance of Sextus's Neopyrrhonist position for Emerson, however, we have to look at Emerson's skeptical godfather, Montaigne. Visitors to Montaigne's study in his tower in Dordogne tend to be impressed by the fifty-seven Greek and Latin inscriptions Montaigne had incised on the rafters of the ceiling. As German novelist Uwe Timm recently wrote in a charming and insightful essay on his visit to Montaigne's tower, what impressed him most was the fact that as many as ten of these quotations

---

[1] *JMN* VI, 381.
[2] *JMN* III, 369.
[3] *Die Vorsokratiker*, vol. I, ed. Laura Gemelli Marciano (Düsseldorf: Artemis & Winkler, 2007), 452–3.
[4] *JMN* VI, 378–80.

are from Sextus Empiricus.[5] This indicates—not that it would surprise Montaigne scholars—how centrally important Sextus was for Montaigne's philosophical outlook. Montaigne read Sextus's *Outlines of Pyrrhonism* even and especially in times of political turmoil and civil war to instill in him and help him maintain an unperturbed inner balance and serenity (Gr. *ataraxia*).[6] Emerson, the early, avid, and devoted as well as lifelong reader of Montaigne, could in turn immerse himself in the central vision of Sextus Empiricus through the mediation and in the guise of Montaigne's thorough appropriation and transformation of Sextus.

Scholars usually roughly distinguish a common and colloquial use of the term *skepticism*, with its emphasis on doubt and especially on disbelief in religious matters, from the sophisticated skeptical traditions of classical antiquity on the one hand and the modern forms arising in the seventeenth century on the other.[7] Classical antiquity knows at least two major strands of skepticism: the skepticism of the Middle Academy, represented by Arcesilaus and Carneades in the third and second centuries BCE, and the Neopyrrhonist version beginning with Aenesidemus and Agrippa in the first century BCE which finds its culmination in Sextus Empiricus around 200 CE.[8] I would like to propose a different distinction. The skeptics of the Academy and the modern skeptics share one important fundamental strategy: their skeptical questionings end in a dogmatic assertion or with a solid and indubitable given and thus, in a sense, in abandoning or in the overcoming of a pervasive skepticism. The Greek Academics dogmatically and negatively assert that there is no way for humans to ascertain truth and in this way they end the skeptical search,[9] whereas the moderns positively find various realizations of a *fundamentum inconcussum* at the end of their skeptical quest:[10] be this Descartes' *cogito*, Hume's nature, Kant's unity of transcendental apperception, or Santayana's essences.[11] The other and

---

[5]Uwe Timm, *Montaignes Turm: Essays* (Cologne: Kiepenheuer & Witsch, 2015), 12.

[6]Herbert Lüthy, "Einleitung," in *Michel de Montaigne – Essais*, ed. and trans. Lüthy (Zürich: Manesse, 1953), 30–1.

[7]Markus Lammenranta, "The Pyrrhonian Problematic," in *The Oxford Handbook of Skepticism*, ed. John Greco (Oxford: Oxford University Press, 2008), 9.

[8]"Skepsis; Skeptizismus," in *Historisches Wörterbuch der Philosophie*, ed. Joachim Ritter et al. (Darmstadt: WBG, 1995), vol. IX, 938–74.

[9]John Greco, "Introduction," in *The Oxford Handbook of Skepticism*, 3–6; Lammenranta, "Pyrrhonian Problematic," 13; Jacques Brunschwig, "Skepticism," in *Greek Thought: A Guide to Classical Knowledge*, ed. Brunschwig and Geoffrey E. R. Lloyd, trans. Catherine Porter (Cambridge, MA: Harvard University Press, 2000), 937–56; "Skepsis; Skeptizismus," in *Historisches Wörterbuch* IX.

[10]José Luis Bermúdez, "Cartesian Skepticism: Arguments and Antecedents," in *The Oxford Handbook of Skepticism*, 53–79.

[11]George Santayana, *Skepticism and Animal Faith: Introduction to a System of Philosophy* (1923; New York: Dover, 1955), 70, 110, 126.

alternative tradition, from my point of view, could be said to thoroughly enjoy being skeptical. Their skeptical quest for truth never ends; they never abandon it. Sextus Empiricus, Montaigne, Emerson, and—among the pragmatists—James and Dewey, though not Peirce with his vision of an ultimate *telos* of all inquiries,[12] share this philosophical disposition. Their consistently tentative assertions of truths are transitional events during a never-ending journey toward an endlessly elusive goal.[13]

As the name indicates, these Neopyrrhonist skeptics believed or pretended to revive the philosophy of Pyrrho, who occupies a significant position in the history of thought, marking the transition from classical to Hellenistic thinking, from Plato to the Middle Academy and its form of skepticism that is characterized as negative metadogmatism since it dogmatically asserts the impossibility to achieve true insight.[14] Especially after the death of Aristotle, Pyrrho also stands for the skeptical turn against what was perceived as Aristotelian (positive) dogmatism. Pyrrho left no written testimonies. His disciple Timon of Phlius began by presenting Pyrrho "first and foremost as a master of happiness, as a moralist for whom the surest ways to achieve happiness are through insensitivity (*apatheia*) and imperturbability (*ataraxia*)." But Timon was also "the first person responsible for the shift in his master's thought toward a questioning of cognitive powers." This "alliance between the search for happiness and the critique of knowledge, which is found in Pyrrhon in a preparatory stage" is one essential feature of the later Neopyrrhonist vision.[15] Diogenes Laertius, in his *Lives of Eminent Philosophers*, summarizes Pyrrho's thinking: he "practiced a philosophy maintaining that things are inconceivable (*akatalepsia*) and demand suspension of judgment (*epoché*)"; and he adds specifically that Pyrrho is said to have denied "that things have essences which keep them separate from one another and self-identical: 'Nothing is in itself more this than that.'"[16] This decisive turn against Aristotle's law of the excluded middle and the implied denial of the possibility to really and distinctly know the essence of realities, of defined entities, of individual beings is a form of ontological skepticism that will be central to my reading of both Sextus Empiricus and Emerson's modernist version of Neopyrrhonism. Emerson himself mentions Pyrrhonism only twice. It is not possible to decide whether

---

[12]Charles Sanders Peirce, "The Fixation of Belief," in *Philosophical Writings of Peirce*, ed. Justus Buchler (New York: Dover, 1955), 10: "Doubt ... stimulates us to inquiry until it is destroyed."
[13]Brunschwig, "Skepticism," 939: "As for true Skeptics, they do not say that the truth is ungraspable, and they do not give up its pursuit; they profess 'to pursue the quest.'"
[14]The term was coined by Jonathan Barnes; see ibid.
[15]Ibid., 941–2.
[16]Quotations and paraphrases from Diogenes Laertius in Thomas McEvilley, *The Shape of Ancient Thought: Comparative Studies in Greek and Indian Philosophies* (New York: Allworth Press, 2002), 450–5.

he was speaking of Pyrrho's thinking, as far as it could be ascertained at all, or of Neopyrrhonism, or of skepticism in general in "Circles" and in "Spiritual Laws" where he attributes to "Pyrrhonism" first a moral and then an epistemological indifferentism or suspension of judgment (Gr. *epoche*).[17]

Sextus Empiricus's massive and carefully detailed, encyclopedic *Outlines of Pyrrhonism* provides the terms and ideas that can function as heuristic tools for a relatively precise presentation and analysis of basic assumptions and insights that characterize the classical and, as I would like to propose and make plausible, also the later and the modern versions of Neopyrrhonist skepticism in Montaigne or Emerson. I will limit myself to some of the central tenets. Sextus begins his book by distinguishing dogmatic, Academic, and skeptical thinking. Dogmatic thinkers, like Aristotle, argue that truth can be ascertained, Academic skeptics believe that it is inapprehensible, and "the Sceptics keep on searching."[18] This simple statement has far-reaching implications. In his major self-characterization as a thinker, Emerson calls himself "an endless seeker with no Past at my back."[19] The skeptics who ceaselessly search are called the seekers, Gr. *zetetikoi*, by Sextus. Both, the Neopyrrhonist *zetetikos* and Emerson's seeker, embark on an endless endeavor without closure and—as skeptics—with no certain, no dogmatically assured basis or *a priori* grounding to provide guidance, with no past at their backs; they are, as Emerson says, experimenters.[20] This is why Emerson's thinker urges himself to ceaselessly "look around" (*skopein*) and "Explore, and explore."[21] Sextus succinctly describes the skeptical method as a kind of experimentation: "The main basic principle of the Sceptic system is that of opposing to every proposition an equal proposition; for we believe that as a consequence of this we end by ceasing to dogmatize."[22] Emerson believes in a similar and ceaseless experimental search for "equipollent"[23] contrary assertions to every given judgment: "the mind goes antagonizing on"[24]; and he insists: "I accept the clangor and jangle of contrary tendencies."[25] The final pages of "Nominalist and Realist" also emphasize the skeptical method: "No sentence will hold the whole truth, and the only way in which

---

[17] W II, 296; ibid., 131.
[18] Sextus Empiricus, *Outlines of Pyrrhonism*, trans. R. G. Bury, Loeb Classical Library, vol. 273 (1933; Cambridge, MA: Harvard University Press, 2000), 3.
[19] W II, 297.
[20] Ibid.
[21] "Literary Ethics" W I, 179.
[22] Sextus Empiricus, *Outlines*, 9.
[23] Lammenranta, "Pyrrhonian Problematic," 14: "skepticism, as Sextus understands it, is not a thesis about the impossibility of knowledge or justified belief. It is an ability to find equipollent oppositions and the practice of using this ability to induce suspension of belief."
[24] "Experience" W III, 70.
[25] Ibid., 64.

we can be just, is by giving ourselves the lie."[26] As an example Emerson adds; "I assert that every man is a partialist ... and now I add that every man is a universalist also."[27] By this method dogmatic positions are continuously undermined and overcome: the result is a thorough suspension (Emerson occasionally says: "suspense") of judgment: Gr. *epoché*. *Epoché* precedes *ataraxia*, as Sextus explains, and *ataraxia*, imperturbability or quietude, is the ultimate existential, we might even say, the religious goal and result of the skeptical method of rigorous epistemological doubt:

> For the Sceptic, having set out to philosophize with the object of passing judgement on the sense-impressions and ascertaining which of them are true and which false, so as to attain quietude thereby, found himself involved in contradictions of equal weight, and being unable to decide between them suspended judgement; and as he was thus in suspense there followed, as it happened, the state of quietude in respect of matters of opinion.[28]

Quietude as a meditative relinquishment of anxiety concerning true reality has existential and religious implications in Sextus. It is an act or state of abandonment[29] that permits an unperturbed "assent to Being in general," as, preparing Emerson's stance, Jonathan Edwards had described the proper existential disposition of humans in *The Nature of True Virtue*. In "Montaigne; or, the Skeptic" Emerson condensed the transition from doubting toward quiet assent that Sextus had described so laboriously: "The ground occupied by the skeptic is the vestibule of the temple."[30]

Another central concern in Book I of Sextus's *Outlines of Pyrrhonism* is the insistence that sense impressions have to be taken for what they are and as they appear. He stresses the fact that "we shall, indeed, be able to state our impressions of the real object, but as to its essential nature we shall suspend judgment";[31] and he elaborates: "For while we are, no doubt, able to state what each of the underlying objects [of our perception] appears to be, relatively to each difference [in the physical condition of the perceiver], we are incapable of explaining what it is in reality."[32] The

---

[26]Ibid., 233.
[27]Ibid., 233–4.
[28]Sextus, *Outlines*, 19.
[29]This adds another shade of meaning to Branka Arsic's interpretation of the concept of "leaving" in Emerson; *On Leaving: A Reading in Emerson* (Cambridge, MA: Harvard University Press, 2010).
[30]W IV, 164.
[31]Sextus, *Outlines*, 37.
[32]Ibid., 53.

distinction between the certainty of perception and the incapability to assert real essence necessitates a linguistic correction: "But this point we must notice—that here as elsewhere we use the term 'are' for the term 'appear,' and what we virtually mean is 'all things appear relative.'"[33] With some passion Sextus returns to the problem of real being: "we are compelled to suspend judgment regarding the real nature of external objects."[34] The core of the skeptical vision is an ontological problem: the abiding uncertainty of the real nature of beings that keeps the skeptic as *zetetikos* searching and experimenting. If we simplify just a little, Sextus engages the problem of the *Ding an sich*, but he refuses Kant's negative metadogmatic position that legislates that it is forever, always, and necessarily inaccessible. Like the speaker in Robert Frost's wonderfully skeptical, almost Neopyrrhonist poem "For Once, Then, Something," the *zetetikos* keeps searching and hoping because he is "not simply someone who seeks or who has sought: he is someone who up to this point has done nothing but seek without finding, and who has the intention of continuing to seek, without giving up hope of finding."[35] In Emerson the necessary uncertainty of judgment of the skeptical mind looking for the ontological bedrock of all beings in one single *Ding an sich* or *substantia* finds expression in this perfect *epoché*: essence or nature "is *one thing and the other thing*, in the same moment."[36] The skeptic cannot decide on the *essentia* or *quidditas* of beings; in this situation, he sees himself forced to discard dogmatic Aristotelian logic and its law of the excluded middle; things may essentially just be "one thing and the other thing."

So far I have only sketchily adumbrated a few possible fundamental agreements in Neopyrrhonist and in Emerson's thinking. There is a dominant critical tendency to allow for a skeptical disposition in Emerson's writing in "Experience" (1844) at the earliest. Three major passages from earlier texts both question this view and help substantiate the claim for a pervasive skeptical Neopyrrhonist stance. In "Literary Ethics" (1838) we read:

> let us seek the shade, and find wisdom in neglect. Be content with a little light, so it be your own. Explore, and explore. Be neither chided nor flattered out of your position of perpetual inquiry. Neither dogmatize, nor accept another's dogmatism. Why should you renounce your right to traverse the star-lit deserts of truth, for the premature comforts of an acre, house, and barn?[37]

---

[33]Ibid., 79–81.
[34]Ibid., 93.
[35]Brunschwig, "Skepticism." 939.
[36]"Nominalist and Realist" W III, 225.
[37]W I, 179.

Wisdom arises out of and with the gesture of letting be, of abandoning the midday glare of a supposed absolute truth for the shade and twilight of uncertainty. The true seeker in his "perpetual inquiry," the *zetetikos*, resists the temptation to assert things dogmatically or be seduced by others to do so. He wanders in a desert place lit by the distant stars that give hope and motivate further seeking, even though they are or rather seem out of reach. As Emerson stated in "Circles," the endless seeker is he who prefers to be un-settled, a homeless thinker *on the way*,[38] thinking without closure.

In "Intellect" (1841) Emerson added to and deepened these echoes of the skeptical tradition from Sextus to Montaigne:

> He in whom the love of truth predominates will keep himself aloof from all moorings, and afloat. He will abstain from dogmatism, and recognize all the opposite negations, between which, as walls, his being is swung. He submits to the inconvenience of suspense and imperfect opinion ...[39]

One of the starkly incisive skeptical comments on the uncertain epistemological and existential human condition in "Experience": "Gladly we would anchor, but the anchorage is quicksand"[40] is obviously foreshadowed here in the image of the moorings that are not for the skeptical lover of truth to hold on to. Again, he is encouraged to abjure any dogmatism and instead to engage in the Pyrrhonian strategy of constantly looking for equipollent judgments that cancel each other's truth claims. In this way, the thinker exchanges the ease and the security of pretended fixed beliefs and accepts the difficult challenge of withholding judgment ("suspense" in the sense of suspension of judgment, *epoché*) and contenting himself with (mere) *doxai*, tentatively advanced, merely human opinions.

Reality itself, a passage in "Spiritual Laws" argues, is properly accessible or thinkable only as resisting all essentializing attempts to subject it to dogmatic and rigid conceptualizations in religious sects and philosophical schools:

> The wild fertility of nature is felt in comparing our rigid names and reputations with our fluid consciousness. We pass in the world for sects and schools, for erudition and piety, and we are all the time jejune babes. One sees very well how Pyrrhonism grew up. Every man sees that he is in the middle point whereof every thing may be affirmed and denied with equal reason. He is old, he is young, he is very wise, he is altogether ignorant.[41]

---

[38]Stanley Cavell, "Thinking of Emerson," in *The Senses of Walden* (San Francisco: North Point Press, 1981), 135–8.
[39]W II, 318.
[40]W III, 58.
[41]W II, 131.

The human being himself is truly and at all times essentially as undefined and undefinable, and lastly, as unknowable as is nature, reality, Being. The human being may *be* all things, may *have* all possible qualities, but, as far as we *know*, he is a "jejune babe." Equipollent contradictory assertions alone are adequate to describe him as well as the "wild fertility of nature." Faced with such evasions of certainty in the object world and in the human subject, *epoché* is the necessary outcome of our intuitions: "One sees very well how Pyrrhonism grew up."

The skeptical core intuition of Emerson is not springing up suddenly in "Experience"; basically nothing has changed in the remarkable consistency of his always daringly Protean oeuvre. Emerson has not matured after 1842, as some critics surmised; he has simply intensified his mature thinking by devoting an extensive essay to the exploration of features of our experience, of reality, and of our existential condition that necessitate skepticism. Such features were called *modes* or Gr. *tropoi* in Neopyrrhonism. Aenesidemus drew up a list of ten such *tropoi*; later skeptics like Agrippa added a group of five or just two.[42] One example may suffice: *tropos* number 1 in the list of ten considers the differences in the way things are experienced by humans and different animals. The discrepancies allow nothing but suspension of judgment concerning the essence, the *Wesen*, of reality, a reality continuing to elude our attempts to conceive, to grasp it. The Neopyrrhonist would not assert in negative metadogmatic fashion that reality can never be properly conceived; he goes on searching.

I propose that we consider the "lords of life" in Emerson's essay "Experience" as *tropoi*. Our moods, our temperament, the temporal succession and change, surfaces hiding unknowable or not existing depths, are conducive to, they demand an ontological skepticism. The evasiveness of the really real, "this evanescence and lubricity of all objects, which lets them slip through our fingers when we clutch hardest," the refusal of the essence, to be conceived (from L. *con-cipere*), to be G. *be-greifen* (grasped), is due to the fact that "[n]ature does not like to be observed."[43] Heraclitus, whom some ancients and some moderns read as a precursor of the skeptics, had said: *physis krypthestai philei*—nature loves to hide. Emerson conflates Heraclitus's intuition and the failure of concepts from the traditional skeptical point of view in order to clarify his position as ontological skeptic. For me, the most impressive of the many impressive assertions of necessary *epoché* in view of the always seductively elusive real reality is this: "Let us be poised and wise, and our own to-day. Let us treat the men and women well; treat them as if they were real; perhaps they are."[44] Wisdom implies poise, balance, and acceptance of this our condition;

---

[42]Cf. Sextus, *Outlines*, 25–93, 95–103.
[43]W III, 53.
[44]Ibid., 63.

it must accept and courageously bear the contradictions, the—once again—equipollent possibilities of, most radically, being and non-being. Out of the ultimate *epoché* concerning the reality of humanity itself, a skeptical ethos arises that dares accept the precarious ontological "as if" of all beings as the ungrounded condition of moral rectitude.

This ethical skepticism has its counterpart in the epistemological realm:

> We have learned that we do not see directly, but mediately, and that we have no means of correcting these colored and distorting lenses[45] which we are, or of computing the amount of their errors. Perhaps these subject-lenses have a creative power; perhaps there are no objects. ... Nature and literature are subjective phenomena; every evil and every good thing is a shadow which we cast.[46]

After this dramatically intense assertion of the achievements and ravages of modern subjectivism and its projective creation of a world of proliferating differentiations from individual points of view, the essay regains its balance and its productive skeptical indecision. It opposes the vision of the unity of living itself, of life, which, even though it may be imaged, is not reduced to a mere subjective representation but allows us to conceive it as inviolate unity: "Life will be imaged, but cannot be divided or doubled. Any invasion of its unity would be chaos."[47] The well-disposed reader may piously wish that Emerson privilege the latter position of the existential unity of life authentically lived as opposed to the subjectivist multiplicity of life individually represented and conceptualized. "Experience" as a whole and Emerson's oeuvre as whole, however, privilege nothing but the possible balance, the suspension of ultimate judgment that allows the wise and mature and imperturbable and fundamentally anti-dogmatic acceptance of all sides.

In "Circles" and in "Nominalist and Realist," Emerson celebrates the ceaseless search for judgments that replace and contradict established valuations and insights, and he maintains a continuous expectation of equipollent alternatives for all philosophical and ethical positions. The search and the expectation are manifest in the contingent shifts of the existential dispositions of humans, in their moods that "do not believe in each other"; they are obvious in the vicissitudes of scientific truth claims and literary values: "There is not a piece of science but its flank may be turned to-morrow, there is not any literary reputation, not the so-called eternal names

---

[45]The image of the colored lenses is another allusion to a saying of Heraclitus; it helps us see that for Emerson Heraclitus could indeed comfortably lend his authority to skeptical propositions.
[46]W III, 77.
[47]Ibid., 79.

of fame, that may not be revised and condemned."[48] Search and expectation help shake the stability of every person's seemingly essential beliefs and call for "the intrepid conviction that his laws, his relations to society, his Christianity, his world, may at any time be superseded and decease."[49] The ontological ground for this instability that cannot but induce a courageous skepticism is the fact that there "are no fixtures in nature"; that there "are no fixtures to men"; that all seemingly natural facts are "words of God, and as fugitive as other words."[50] In a world that allows no final, no absolute epistemological and ontological certainty, there is "[n]othing secure but life, transition, the energizing spirit. ... No truth so sublime but it may be trivial to-morrow in the light of new thoughts. People wish to be settled; only as far as they are unsettled is there any hope for them."[51] The very fact that there is no safety and no truth which can be dogmatically asserted, this fact makes for hope. The skepticism of a Neopyrrhonist *zetetikos*, an endless seeker with no past at his back, is hopeful because it is ready for life as "a series of surprises," because the possibilities of future moments of "total growths and universal movements of the soul" are never excluded, never certain, since these "masterpieces of God ... are incalculable."[52]

In "Nominalist and Realist" Emerson keeps a perfect balance[53] between two rival philosophical claims to offer the only adequate epistemological and ontological or cosmic interpretation of reality: nominalism is opposed by realism; pluralism is counterbalanced by monism. The essay carefully and plausibly juxtaposes each single dogmatic perspective and its opposing vision. The careful reader cannot but realize and accept a comprehensive *epoché*. In this skeptical stance, he is strongly encouraged and supported by the serene and charmingly anti-dogmatic and properly lighthearted, by the unperturbed self-confidence of the skeptic seeker's indefatigable openness: "Is it that every man believes every other to be an incurable partialist, and himself a universalist? I talked yesterday with a pair of philosophers; I endeavored to show my good men that I liked everything by turns and nothing long."[54]

---

[48]"Circles" W II, 286.

[49]Ibid., 288.

[50]Ibid., 282, 286, 293.

[51]Ibid., 298.

[52]Ibid.

[53]Russell B. Goodman has written a subtle and intriguing interpretation of "Nominalist and Realist": "Paths of Coherence through Emerson's Philosophy: The Case of 'Nominalist and Realist,'" in *The Other Emerson*, ed. Branka Arsic and Cary Wolfe (Minneapolis: University of Minnesota Press, 2010), 41–58. As so many other critics, however, Goodman cannot allow a radical and absolute and ultimate indecision or *epoché* in this essay or in Emerson's works in general. He tries very hard and, I believe, not quite successfully to find some aspects of a stable belief or, at least, a predilection for one side of the alternative posed by the text: "Emerson may be said to side with the nominalist"; ibid., 57.

[54]W III, 236.

In spite of all these strong skeptical statements by Emerson and my hopefully convincing interpretations, the case for Emerson as Neopyrrhonist skeptic remains weak and vulnerable and open to manifold objections as long as we do not critically deal with the lion in our path, with the traditional conception of Plato as Emerson's formative idealist ideal of a thinker. Before I do take a closer look at "Plato; or, the Philosopher," the first portrait in *Representative Men*, I would like to remind ourselves that reading Plato as skeptic is not as unheard of as one might commonly suppose. In ancient Greece, the *skeptikoi* "did not profess a system that we might call Skepticism, they practiced an activity known as *skepsis*," and the mentioning of an activity of *skepsis* does not always and necessarily mean that we deal with skepticism in the Pyrrhonian, Neopyrrhonist, or modern sense. *Skeptesthai*—"the frequentative form of the verb *skopein*"—means simply "examining with the eyes" and, by metaphorical extension, "examining with the mind, reflecting, studying"; thus, as Jacques Brunschwig reminds us: "[i]n one sense, all Greek philosophy is skeptical." It comes not as a surprise therefore that the New Academy, too, was "willing to consider the possibility that Plato may have practiced skepticism."[55] Once this possibility was accepted by applying the literal sense of the term and concept of *skepsis* to Plato's method, the careful consideration of his oeuvre as a whole began to convince ancients and moderns that the term *skepticism*, implying a comprehensive philosophical vision, might also characterize Plato. Thomas McEvilley argues that already "around the end of the fourth century B.C. [the Academy] ... began to emphasize the skeptical elements of Plato's oeuvre: the early aporetic dialogues, the Socratic profession of ignorance, the contradictions of the *Parmenides*, the denial of the written teachings in the *Seventh Letter*, and so on."[56] By the beginning of the first century CE, Plato was firmly established as a genuine skeptic. Cicero wrote in *Academica* I, 12, 46 on Plato: "cuius in libris nihil adfirmatur et in utramque partem multa disseruntur, de omnibus quaeritur, nihil certi dicitur."[57] Probably the most authoritative of all later and modern readings of Plato as skeptic is that of Hegel: in his *Logic* he calls Plato's dialogue *Parmenides* rather than Sextus the best "Dokument und System des ächten Skepticismus."[58] The *Parmenides* and the commentary by Proclus were of central importance for Emerson's appreciation of Plato's thinking. A critical review of defining statements in "Plato; or, the Philosopher" will help us see that Emerson's interpretation of Platonic thinking shares the emphasis on skepticism that we find in Cicero and Hegel.

---

[55]Brunschwig, "Skepticism," 937–8.
[56]McEvilley, *Shape of Ancient Thought*, 437.
[57]Qtd. in *Historisches Wörterbuch*, 942: "In his books nothing is affirmed, much is discussed in two [opposite] directions, everything is examined, nothing is maintained with certainty" (my translation).
[58]Ibid., 962: the best "document and system of genuine skepticism" (my translation).

"Out of Plato come all things that are still written and debated among men of thought":[59] like Whitehead, Emerson sees *all* future thinking as "footnotes to Plato." This implies, in terms of the list of indicators or defining features of skeptical thinking, the *tropoi* according to Sextus Empiricus, that a totality like Plato's philosophical cosmos must contain or exhibit or foreshadow the contradictions of all schools of thought: philosophy as a whole is full of irreconcilable visions, interests, points of view, and perspectives. It is a realm providing the basis for and, ultimately, necessitating skepticism and suspension of ultimate judgment (*epoché*). Emerson explains in detail:

> Plato absorbed the learning of his times,—Philolaus, Timaeus, Heraclitus, Parmenides, and what else; then his master, Socrates; and finding himself still capable of a larger synthesis,—beyond all example then or since,—he travelled into Italy, to gain what Pythagoras had for him; then into Egypt, and perhaps still farther East, to import the other element, which Europe wanted, into the European mind. This breadth entitles him to stand as the representative of philosophy.[60]

Such a plurality of radically differing positions and such hospitality in accommodating numerous varieties of thought, however, is apt to induce and imply indecision. Heraclitus and Parmenides and their respective visions of a dynamic and flowing universe as contrasted with static conceptions of essential Being provide an extreme example of equipollent alternative interpretations of reality. If both Heraclitus and Parmenides, and others, are absorbed in Plato, this would necessitate a pervasive skeptical *epoché* as the central feature of his "synthesis." The skeptical view, however, tends to prevail in Plato even when Emerson makes him consider the basic features of reality without recourse to previous thinkers and their contradictory perspectives: "Philosophy is the account which the human mind gives to itself of the constitution of the world. Two cardinal facts lie forever at the base; the one, and the two. ... Oneness and otherness. It is impossible to speak or think without embracing both."[61] The coexistence of monism and pluralism creates an *aporia* and, as in the case of the multiplicity of philosophical opinions and views, skepticism follows: it is impossible to present a final dogmatic solution to the problem of the constitution of the world as one or as a manifold, as Emerson goes on to explain: "These strictly-blended elements [the one and the many] it is the problem of thought to separate and reconcile. Their existence is mutually contradictory and exclusive; and each so fast slides into the other that we can never say what is one, and what it

---

[59] W IV, 41.
[60] Ibid., 44.
[61] Ibid., 49.

is not."[62] In Emerson's view Plato induces *epoché* and withholds a final and conclusive judgment: "we can never say." The conflict of the pluralist and monist visions is the central topic of the *Parmenides*; the problem is subtly and extensively entertained and argued, but it is not solved in this dialogue. As Emerson sees it, the philosophical problem of the one and the many tends to issue in *aphasia*: "we can never say what is one, and what ... is not." Like *epoché, aphasia*, or the suspension of speech, is one of the skeptic's possible reactions when he faces the ubiquitous conflicts of judgment in philosophical discourses. When Plato engages the highest and the most general philosophical entity or concept, Being itself, he faces and proposes a radical ontological skepticism: "[Being is] that of which every thing can be affirmed and denied: that 'which is entity and nonentity.' He called it super-essential. He even stood ready, as in the *Parmenides*, to demonstrate that it was so,—that this Being exceeded the limits of intellect. No man ever more fully acknowledged the Ineffable."[63] This is ontological skepticism as linguistic skepticism. *Epoché*, caused by the equipollence of affirmation and denial, culminates once again in *aphasia*: the acknowledgment of the Ineffable. Emerson read the Neoplatonic commentary by Proclus on Plato's *Parmenides* as a skeptical treatise: Proclus (412–85 CE) had annotated Plato on this matter, the fundamental ontological question of the Being of the One, as follows: since the highest, the One, cannot be qualified by either assertion or negation, "they [assertion and negation] fall short of the simplicity of the One. Indeed all truth is in it, but it is itself better than all truth. So how would it be possible to say anything true about it?"[64] While the mode of being of the cosmos, of the world, as both one and many results in indecision and *aphasia*, the question of the Being of the One itself issues not only in utter silence but in the abandonment of the idea of truth itself. The argument supported by Proclus when he reads Plato's *Parmenides* makes Emerson conclude:

> [Plato] has not a system. The dearest defenders and disciples are at fault. He attempted a theory of the universe, and his theory is not complete or self-evident. One man thinks he means this, and another that; he has said one thing in one place, and the reverse of it in another place. ... the *theory of the world* [i.e., Plato's philosophy] is a thing of shreds and patches.[65]

This passage, and I think that it is obvious, bears an uncanny resemblance to Cicero's characterization of Plato's thinking as thoroughgoing skepticism.

---

[62]Ibid., 50.
[63]Ibid., 61–2.
[64]*Proclus' Commentary on Plato's* Parmenides, trans. and ed. Glenn R. Morrow and John M. Dillon (Princeton, NJ: Princeton University Press, 1987), 601.
[65]W IV, 75.

Emerson concludes his evaluation of the Platonic philosophy: "In view of eternal nature, Plato turns out to be philosophical exercitations. He argues on this side and on that. The acutest German, the lovingest disciple, could never tell what Platonism was; indeed, admirable texts can be quoted on both sides of every great question from him."[66] Here again Emerson echoes Cicero, whether he knew his Plato critique in *Academica* or not: "He argues on this side and that. ... admirable texts can be quoted on both sides of every question from him." Cicero had said: "cuius in libris ... in utramque partem multa disseruntur." The Ciceronian position on Plato is applicable to Emerson himself: skeptical Plato and Emerson both show the evasion of ultimate, of dogmatic, of systematic judgments; they share the careful consideration of all sides; they avoid foundational ontological pronouncements. Emerson's Plato is not the idealist of the *Ideenlehre*, which, as an exclusive or dominant reading of Plato, is to a certain degree the invention or creation of especially German research in the history of philosophy. "Plato; or, the Philosopher" is remarkably reticent when it comes to the discussion of the realm of ideas. Emerson's Plato is the radical skeptic who presents, who allows, who appreciates all possible philosophical positions: the philosophies of Asia and Europe are equally cherished and accommodated in his thinking;[67] Heraclitus and Parmenides are both welcomed. Plato acknowledges the predominance of the one and that of the many at the same time, he quietly, without words and unperturbed, in *ataraxia*, contemplates the ultimate One, Being itself. The ontological skeptic is a philosophically and existentially "balanced soul";[68] he necessarily withholds final judgment, especially in ontology: *epoché* is his pervasive hallmark. In this sense we may say: Emerson's skeptical Plato is Emerson.

The indirect self-portrait of Emerson's ideal of a skeptical method and a proper style of skeptical thinking in the essay on Plato is complemented by his reading of Montaigne as the representative skeptic at the beginning of the modern era, the *Neuzeit*. Plato, Emerson's exemplary balanced soul, finds a proper equipollent alternative in equally balanced Montaigne whose chosen emblem was a "pair of scales."[69] The essay on Montaigne focuses not so much on the philosophical reasons for and the rhetorical realizations of a skeptical intuition or disposition; rather, it emphasizes the modes of *enacting* skeptical thinking and its existential implications: what does it feel like to think, *to be* radically skeptical in an ontological sense? Again, a series of brief quotations may illustrate the central points. The *conditio humana* is ontologically precarious: "You believe yourselves rooted and grounded

---

[66]Ibid., 76.
[67]Ibid., 53–4.
[68]Ibid., 54–5.
[69]"Montaigne; or, the Skeptic" *W* IV, 159.

on adamant; and yet, if we uncover the last facts of our knowledge, you are spinning like bubbles in a river, you know not whither and whence, and you are bottomed and capped and wrapped in delusions."[70] Early on in the essay on Montaigne, Emerson reads the world and the existential predicament humans find themselves in from a skeptical standpoint as lacking a solid and ascertainable grounding or foundation. The "last facts of our knowledge" reveal no solid ontological basis; the ultimate essence of human reality remains just as hidden as the true nature of all other beings, as Sextus had maintained. The world of the skeptic vision tends to offer no reliable orientation; the skeptic has no adequate sense of what reality really is; delusions prevail. We remember that in "Experience" Emerson had said succinctly: "Gladly would we anchor, but the anchorage is quicksand." If you want to render this uncertain and ultimately unknowable existential *conditio humana* in words and judgments, it demands the following method or strategy:

> If there are conflicting evidences, why not state them? If there is not ground for a candid thinker to make up his mind, yea or nay,—why not suspend the judgment? I weary of these dogmatizers. I tire of these hacks of routine, who deny the dogmas. I neither affirm nor deny. I stand here to try the case. I am here to consider, skopein, to consider how it is.[71]

The proper skeptical response to a world of fundamental uncertainty and unreliability is not what is called "negative metadogmatism"—the denial that anything can be known at all; *epoché*, the withholding of final judgment, of dogmatic assertion, implies a constant looking around, *skopein*, as to what the case may be without any attempt at closure, at concluding the inquiry. The ideal skeptic does not give up looking around: "Who shall forbid a wise skepticism, seeing that there is no practical question on which any thing more than an approximate solution can be had? ... There is much to say on both sides."[72] This aphoristic maxim is a reminder of what is commonly thought to have been the basic position of the founder of the skeptical school, of Pyrrhon. As I mentioned, he is said to have begun by observing that each single affirmative or dogmatic statement as to the essence of things could be undermined by an equally plausible opposing or counter-judgment whose final proof was as elusive as that of the initial statement. Thus it follows, Emerson argues:

> The philosophy we want is one of fluxions and mobility. The Spartan and Stoic schemes are too stark and stiff for our occasion ... We want a ship

---

[70]Ibid., 149.
[71]Ibid., 150.
[72]Ibid., 151.

in these billows we inhabit. An angular, dogmatic house would be rent to chips and splinters in this storm of many elements. ... [we need] a house founded on the sea."[73]

The flowing Heraclitean world, so often compared to the ocean, needs a flexible mode of thinking that easily and without "foolish consistency"[74] adapts to unforeseeably changing circumstances. For the skeptical schools of classical antiquity, the mode of thinking that opposed dogmatism, whose inflexible rigidity was inappropriate in a dynamic and contingent universe, was Stoicism. The proper habitation for human beings, the adequate philosophical shelter in all periods, is one that is responsive to and able to adapt to the storms of circumstance and the winds of doctrine. Our defining existential traits as humans who are exposed to this watery wilderness are necessarily contradictory, paradoxical, aporetic: "We are golden averages, volitant stabilities, compensated or periodic errors, houses founded on the sea."[75] Human existence in an ontologically unsettled and un-decidable world is coerced to accommodate and respond to the contingent and unforeseeable shifts and vagaries of what William James was to call the unpredictable cosmic weather of our phenomenal reality. But, even though ontological certainty and absolute existential safety are not available for the skeptic, there is a vista of transcendent hope and the possibility of religious acquiescence. For the Neopyrrhonist skeptics of classical antiquity this was manifest in the contemplative and quietist *ataraxia* issuing from the suspension of all judgments and their conflicts, whereas for Montaigne, for the modern skeptic, skepticism itself was the *way*: "The ground occupied by the skeptic is the vestibule of the temple."[76] Skepticism in Emerson's re-appropriation of the classical tradition and in his re-reading of Montaigne is the exact opposite of a religious skepticism in the sense of doubt or agnosticism: it is, I repeat, the always risky and troubled *way* toward contemplative existential and religious assurance, an attitude which allows that the numinous or holy come forth of itself for a human being who abandons all claims to decide what or who the ultimate reality, the divine truly is. The latter part of the essay on Montaigne asks: "Shall we say that Montaigne has spoken wisely, and given the right and permanent expression of the human mind, on the conduct of life?"[77] The first answer Emerson gives seems to question the legitimacy of a pervasive skeptical stance: "We are natural believers."[78] The text of the essay as a

---

[73]Ibid., 153–4.
[74]"Self-Reliance" W II, 58.
[75]W IV, 154.
[76]Ibid., 164.
[77]Ibid., 162.
[78]Ibid.

whole, however, is, in its pervasive inconsistency and because of its shifting points of view, more consistently skeptical and thus, again paradoxically, more religious or contemplative or believing than statements like "those superficial views we call skepticism"[79] would suggest. There is a difference between Montaigne's (and Emerson's own) skepticism and the vulgar or material skepticism that Emerson calls superficial: "This then is the right ground of the skeptic,—this of consideration, of self-containing; *not at all of unbelief*; not at all of universal denying, nor of universal doubting,— doubting even that he doubts; least of all of scoffing and profligate jeering at all that is stable and good."[80]

Sextus Empiricus himself already insisted that the true skeptic believes in the way the world shows phenomenally and that in his conduct the skeptic does not question social customs and cultural conventions—he does not propose "universal denying, [or] universal doubting." Radical doubt concerns the problem of real essence, of ontological grounding alone.[81] Emerson's skeptical meditations on doubt and belief—doing justice to Montaigne—culminate in this wonderful *epoché*: "The spiritualist finds himself driven to express his faith by a series of skepticisms."[82] The verbally, the conceptually unavailable realm of transcendent, of religious beliefs, undermines all single creedal judgments as merely dogmatic. The skeptic is called upon to save the faith; he will do so by preparing *aphasia* and contemplative *ataraxia* as his mind goes "antagonizing on." With this conviction, Emerson stands in a theological tradition that goes back to the earlier Renaissance readers of Sextus: in about 1630, François de La Mothe Le Vayer argued that skepticism supports true faith by destroying theologically rationalized beliefs: "la Sceptique se peut nommer une parfaite introduction au Christianisme."[83]

Neopyrrhonist skepticism, Montaigne's skepticism, Emerson's skepticism, and the skepticism of Emerson's Plato are guarantees of radical freedom. This freedom of philosophical thought, of religious faith, of existential conduct is generous; it is characterized by the gesture of letting concepts, of letting things, of letting thoughts be in the double sense of "letting be." The ability to respectfully entertain mutually exclusive thoughts and visions leads toward that unperturbed disposition of *ataraxia* that Nietzsche

---

[79]Ibid., 174.
[80]Ibid., 152–3 (my emphasis).
[81]Sextus, *Outlines*, 17: "The criterion, then, of the Sceptic School is, we say, the appearance, giving this name to what is virtually the sense-presentation. For since this lies in feeling and involuntary affection, it is not open to question. ... Adhering, then, to appearances we live in accordance with the normal rules of life, undogmatically, seeing that we cannot remain wholly inactive."
[82]W IV, 173.
[83]Qtd. in *Historisches Wörterbuch*, 935.

called Emerson's serenity. Both Nietzsche and Santayana have spoken of the exhilaration and strength of this kind of skepticism that is, I believe, indispensable for a just appreciation of Emerson. Nietzsche said: "Man lasse sich nicht irreführen: grosse Geister sind Skeptiker ... Die Stärke, die *Freiheit* aus der Kraft und Überkraft des Geistes *beweist* sich durch Skepsis. Menschen der Überzeugung kommen für alles Grundsätzliche von Werth und Unwerth gar nicht in Betracht. Überzeugungen sind Gefängnisse."[84] As so often, Nietzsche echoes Emerson here; skeptical Emerson asserted: "Every thought is also a prison; every heaven is also a prison."[85] In a similar vein Santayana celebrates the exhilarating and wild freedom of the skeptical mind: "Often the richest philosophies are the most sceptical; the mind is not then tethered in its home paddock, but ranges at will over the wilderness of being."[86]

---

[84]*Der Antichrist*, KSA 6, 236: "Don't be misled, great minds are skeptics. The strength, the *freedom* which arises from the power and over-power of the mind is proven by skepticism. People with convictions are of no account in all fundamental matters of worth and of worthlessness. Convictions are prisons" (my translation).
[85]"The Poet" W III, 36–7.
[86]Santayana, *Skepticism*, 67.

# 3

# Mysticism and Thinking

Several respected Emerson critics have doubted the authenticity and validity both of Emerson's mystically visionary moments as biographical facts and the relevance of mystical intuition in general for the evaluation of his thinking. In my attempt to reaffirm the mystical, the radically intuitive basis of Emerson's work as a whole, I would like to start by challenging two— as I think—typical, two representative voices in the camp of those critics who prefer to cast a sober and rationalist glance at the ecstatic passages in both his journals and essays. As early as 1942 Henry B. Parkes launched a thorough attack on the possibly heretical and antinomian implications of Emerson's thought. He denied any biographical and thus experiential basis for the central convictions of Emerson's mature work: "For the beliefs of Unitarianism he substituted a new set of beliefs. These beliefs were derived from books, and only the principles of their combination and certain deductions from them were in any way original."[1]

After the detailed biographical work of Ralph L. Rusk (1949) and of Gay Wilson Allen (1981), a position like that of Parkes seems difficult to maintain: both Emerson's epiphany in Charleston, South Carolina, on April 17, 1827,[2] and the experience that gave rise to the famous transparent-eyeball passage in *Nature* could easily have gained admission to the gallery of notable records of mystical experiences in William James's *The Varieties of Religious Experience*. The alleged lack of a mystical experience, though, is not the only reason for Parkes to call Emerson a pseudo-mystic.[3] After quoting Meister Eckhart on the unintelligibility of the "quiet Desert of the

This essay was previously published as "Mysticism and Thinking in Ralph Waldo Emerson" in *Amerikastudien/American Studies* 28, no. 1 (1983): 33–46. Reprinted by permission of Damien B. Schlarb, managing editor of *Amerikastudien/American Studies*.

[1]Henry B. Parkes, "Emerson," in *Emerson: A Collection of Critical Essays*, ed. Milton R. Konvitz and Stephen E. Whicher (Westport, CT: Greenwood Press, 1962), 124.
[2]Gay Wilson Allen, *Waldo Emerson: A Biography* (New York: Viking Press, 1981), 101.
[3]Parkes, "Emerson," 126.

Godhead," Parkes proceeds, dogmatically, to explain the difference between genuine and pseudo-mysticism.[4]

> It follows that there can be no relationship between the mystical experience and conduct …; when the mystic returns to the world he must obey the laws as before. Pseudo-mysticism, on the other hand, the mysticism of those who have not themselves had any genuine mystical experience, regards the divinity which man finds in himself as positive, giving positive commands—not as something so completely removed from sensible things that it can be described only in negatives.
>
> Not having had the true mystical experience, [Emerson] imagined that God in the soul was positive and gave positive commands.[5]

This passage quite obviously contains a number of highly problematic assertions. Meister Eckhart, on the basis of his mystical experiences and the consequent insight into the intellectual implications of mystical revelations, certainly did *not* obey the laws as before. The papal investigations conducted at the time of his death more than confirm that. The binding power of laws, both civil and ecclesiastical, and the obligations of social customs are frequently questioned in his sermons. Radical and often antinomian questioning of all traditional institutionalized order is one common denominator of a number of mystical texts both in the West and in Asia.[6] The critical, the revolutionary, the subversive potential of American Transcendentalist thought is one of the indicators of its family ties with the great mystical tradition. Parkes's animadversion against social upheaval in the wake of—sometimes—mystically inspired agitation, as in the case of many fourteenth-century spiritual revivals and even more prominently during the English Commonwealth (the Ranters), makes it sufficiently clear that he is more interested in supporting a conservative political ideology and theology than in doing justice to the mystical tradition. In *Atheismus im Christentum* Ernst Bloch has shown that the very cause and essence of great social reform movements can be interpreted as a mystically and thus intuitively gained affirmation of the inalienable and transcendent dignity

---

[4]The writings of Meister Eckhart contain no verifiable indications of a mystical experience that could serve to establish a biographical fact. All we have is the convincing religious intensity of the description and the intellectual rigor of the argument that follows.

[5]Parkes, "Emerson," 126, 131.

[6]Collections of genuine mystical texts include: William James, *The Varieties of Religious Experience: A Study in Human Nature*, vol. 13 of *The Works of William James* (1902; Cambridge, MA: Harvard University Press, 1985); Martin Buber, *Ekstatische Konfessionen* (Jena: Diederichs, 1909); Aldous Huxley, *The Perennial Philosophy* (New York: Harper, 1944); F. C. Happold, *Mysticism: A Study and an Anthology* (Harmondsworth: Penguin, 1963); and Hans Dieter Zimmermann, *Rationalität und Mystik* (Frankfurt: Insel, 1981).

of humanity.[7] It is certainly true that no genuine mystic claims an insight into detailed and specific moral tenets as an important and central aspect of her or his momentous experience. The relationship of the mystic to the socially established world is nevertheless, as Emerson said of himself in "Circles,"[8] basically *unsettling* even without the affirmation of a, for that matter, literally articulated positive or negative social or moral belief.

Parkes's statement that, in Emerson's view, the mystical experience results in positive commands is even easier to refute. The "wise silence"[9] as center of the mystical identification in "The Over-Soul" is always and without exception in Emerson's work conceived of as a speechless and untranslatable *that*, a pre-conceptual given, which underlies or precedes all articulate being-in-the-world; in that respect it is similar to William James's "pure experience." It is the basis of a great YEA-SAYING, but not an instruction manual guiding the details of our social, political, or religious behavior. In his essay on "Swedenborg; or, the Mystic" in *Representative Men*, Emerson made it one of his central critical points against Swedenborg that the literary presentations of his visions were too specific, his images too fixed, and his symbols too schematic: "I reply that the Spirit which is holy is reserved, taciturn, and deals in laws … The teachings of the high Spirit are abstemious, and, in regard to particulars, negative."[10] In terms of language and writing, all that can be said about a mystical experience is its occurrence, its *thatness*, but not its content, its *whatness*; or as William James argues: "It is a commonplace of metaphysics that God's knowledge cannot be discursive but must be intuitive, that is, must be constructed more after the pattern of what in ourselves is called immediate feeling, than after that of proposition and judgment."[11]

Thus "positive commands" in Parkes's sense of the word have no place in Emerson's mystical experience and in his attempts to deal with it in the medium of language. The importance of critical objections to a position like that of Parkes, the reprint of whose essay in Konvitz and Whicher's collection has given it a wider circulation, is shown by the fact that almost forty years later Gay Wilson Allen in his thorough, elegant, and balanced biography continues some of Parkes's problematic assertions. Even though he believes that he has some evidence for Emerson's mystical experiences, Allen still hesitates to call Emerson a mystic. He defines mysticism as the possibility of communication—not of identification—with the Infinite Mind and thereby cautiously brings Emerson back into the more orthodox

---

[7] Ernst Bloch in Zimmermann, *Rationalität und Mystik*, 357–8.
[8] W II, 297.
[9] "The Over-Soul" W II, 253.
[10] W IV, 134.
[11] *Varieties*, 322.

Christian fold.[12] Later in the book Allen obscures matters further by, on the one hand, doing justice to Emerson's Neoplatonic ancestry and the obvious connections with Indian thought, while, on the other hand, he calls all mysticism anti-social and ascetic. This is a highly problematic statement considering, for example, Bloch's claim for the majority of mystical writers in the medieval Christian tradition. A new and even more disturbing idea of mysticism is introduced in Allen's discussion of Emerson's lecture on "Demonology": "Anyone who regards his soul theories only as varieties of 'mysticism' might expect him to be more sympathetic with efforts to find 'truth' in dreams, omens, coincidences, luck, fortune-telling, magic, and so on."[13] This concept of mysticism, especially when used in vulgarized forms of Marxist ideology, was vehemently attacked by Bloch, who thinks of mysticism as "in Religion einbrechende Mystik, die als solche doch wohl nicht ganz, wie Vulgärmarxismus meint, mit Tischrücken oder Altweiberkohl zusammenfällt."[14]

In this way, two representative examples of earlier Emerson criticism, which are skeptical about the validity of his position as a member of the mystical tradition, reveal inadequate conceptions of mysticism as the basis of their judgments. Mysticism may be and has often been the origin of a radical questioning of established institutions and the authority of tradition, even though—and maybe because of the fact that—mystical experiences do not imply specific sociopolitical programs but, more fundamentally, encourage a profound existential re-orientation; mysticism tends to go—as does Emerson—beyond the theological tenets of established religion, as in the case of Meister Eckhart's non-Christian idea of a Godhead transcending the Trinity, and mysticism is, of course, not to be confused with magic and obscurantism. Mystical experience as an "event" forever beyond the possibilities of language to adequately render it, forever beyond the categories of time, space, subject, and object, is hard to verify as biographical fact. This holds for *all* mystical texts. The possibilities of the critic when faced with the assertion of a radically intuitive, that is, mystical, experience, such as gives rise to the transparent-eyeball passage in *Nature* (1836), are threefold: he may flatly disbelieve the possibility of all mystical insight, he may remain forever skeptical about its true basis without having anything to help him decide the question,[15] or he may follow the early example brilliantly set

---

[12]Allen, *Waldo Emerson*, X.

[13]Ibid., 334.

[14]Bloch in Zimmermann, *Rationalität und Mystik*, 381: "a mysticism invading religion which as such is certainly not—as vulgar Marxism surmises—fully identical with table rapping and old wives' tales" (my translation).

[15]Because of the trans-subjective nature of mystical insight, language can never be a reliable and exclusive indicator of the writer's sincerity. Erotic fervor, as in some Sufi texts or in Saint

by Stephen E. Whicher. Whicher discusses the change in Emerson after he became intuitively and thus intimately aware of the identity of self and SELF, of the ego and its divine ground: "The astonishing surge of pride and confidence that followed, however repugnant to Christians, is a genuine rebirth, and like all such unlooked-for spiritual unfoldings commands our respect and attention."[16]

When Martin Buber published his collection of mystical texts *Ekstatische Konfessionen* in 1909, he talked about the language problem in all mystically grounded works in his foreword "Ekstase und Bekenntnis" [Ecstasis and Confession]. He distinguishes two basic kinds of talking about IT:

> Sobald sie [the mystics] reden, sind sie schon der Sprache verfallen, die allem gewachsen ist, nur nicht dem Grund des Erlebens, der Einheit. Sobald sie sagen, sagen sie schon das *Andere*. Es gibt freilich eine allerstillstes Sprechen, das nur Dasein mitteilen, nicht beschreiben will.
>
> Von diesem Sprechen führen viele Stufen zu jenem Erzählen von Gott und seinen Gaben, das nicht erschrickt und umkehrt, sondern sagt und sagt. Es ist nicht weniger redlich, seine Sprache klingt nirgends gesprungen, wir wissen, dass es nicht lügt, sondern Gemeintes bekennt.[17]

In Buber's view, there is no single and absolutely reliable path in and through language that leads to a *final* assurance and an *absolute* certainty in these authentic confessions and in the philosophical works based on them. Following Whicher's early example I would like to pay my critical respects to Emerson guided by the attitude Buber takes when he tries to enter the spirit of one of Bernard of Clairvaux's sermons: "Ich glaube ihm sein Bekennen."[18]

\*

---

Teresa, has served the ends of mystics as well as the comic mode in Zen Buddhist writing; the disciplined rhetoric of Meister Eckhart seems quite as "adequate" as the complex symbolism of Boehme or Swedenborg.

[16]Stephen E. Whicher, *Freedom and Fate: An Inner Life of Ralph Waldo Emerson* (Philadelphia, PA: University of Pennsylvania Press, 1953), 21.

[17]Buber, "Ekstase und Bekenntnis," in Zimmermann, *Rationalität und Mystik*, 92–3: "... As soon as they [the mystics] speak, they are already caught up in a language which is equal to everything with the exception of the ground of their experience, the One. As soon as they speak, they say the *other*. But after all there is a speaking arising out of the deepest silence, which desires to simply say Being and does not wish to describe. 2. Many steps lead upward from that kind of speaking to that narrative of God and his gifts, which is not terrified and does not turn away, but keeps on saying. It is not less honest, its language does not sound flawed, we know that it does not lie but genuinely confesses what it intends" (my translation).

[18]Ibid., 92: "I do believe his confession" (my translation).

"Where do we find ourselves?" we may ask, using the opening question of Emerson's essay "Experience,"[19] after having tried to dispel some of the mists surrounding the core *and* starting point of Emerson's thinking: the mystically and thus experientially gained certainty concerning the basic identity of self and SELF, of soul and over-soul, of the human being and the divine, of individual being and Being.[20] The textual evidence for this belief, grounded, as I maintain, in experience, is to be found in the majority of Emerson's works, from the famous transparent-eyeball passage in *Nature* to the late "Natural History of Intellect"; it is prominent even in the so-called skeptical texts "Experience," "Fate," and the Montaigne essay in *Representative Men*.[21] But since we cannot satisfactorily talk about the essence of the mystical experience itself, cannot find a language fully appropriate for it, let alone prove it in rational discourse, where, then, do we find ourselves as critics?

We find ourselves drawn into a process of thinking based on the—for Emerson, the thinker and writer—axiomatic fact of an experience beyond the reach of conceptual justification and thus of rational thinking itself, a fact to which thinking nevertheless is intuitively and indisputably aware of owing itself.[22] The individualized consciousness that remembers the mystical event and then carries on conceptual thinking is characterized by a certain doubleness, a central feature of Emerson's "Man Thinking," the *persona* of his writings.[23] The task before us therefore contains three major points of interest: 1. a discussion of the authority of the mystically grounded consciousness from the point of view of subsequent being-in-the-world; 2. an analysis of the double consciousness; 3. the attempt to describe the essential features of thinking in Emerson.

---

[19]W III, 49.

[20]This series of intuitional identifications does not imply that they are conceptually identical; rather, the varieties of naming mystical unions implied by Emerson's variable terminology insinuate the possibility of a more basic a-verbal and pre-conceptual experience that is refracted either theologically or philosophically in varying contexts.

[21]I would not go so far as James M. Cox who says: "the intense intuitional moments of vision ... literally are the essays"; "R. W. Emerson: The Circles of the Eye," in *Emerson: Prophecy, Metamorphosis, and Influence*, ed. David Levin (New York: Columbia University Press, 1971), 71. The intuitional moment is rather a starting point recalled, remembered, and revived in writing; the process of thinking ever and ever again sets out from it in essay after essay.

[22]The most sophisticated analysis of the relationship between intuition and thinking, between, in Emersonian terms, intellect receptive and intellect constructive, is Branka Arsic, "Brain Walks: Emerson on Thinking," in *The Other Emerson*, ed. Branka Arsic and Cary Wolfe (Minneapolis: University of Minnesota Press, 2010), 59–97.

[23]Robert E. Spiller, "Four Faces of Emerson," in *Four Makers of the American Mind*, ed. T. E. Crawley (Durham, NC: Duke University Press, 1976), 22.

# The authority of mystical experience

Lawrence Buell has called the speaker of the early essays in particular "an experiencer of the holy" and he has paraphrased the hidden intention of the mystical passages especially in *Nature* as follows: "[R]eader, whatever we conclude from the formal analysis of nature that will follow, the original relation with the universe exists, for I have experienced it."[24] The important word here is *experienced*. In common parlance experience always implies a relationship between subject and object. It is the well-known hallmark of genuine mystical and intuitive experience, however, that it abolishes this distinction. The *unio mystica*, the ungrounded and therefore original relation with the world as totality, with nature, with the divine, with Being, encompasses and absorbs, it dissolves the experiencer as an independent entity; it is a genuine mystical event. In "The Over-Soul" we read:

> within man is the soul of the whole; the wise silence; the universal beauty, to which every part and particle is equally related; the eternal ONE. And this deep power in which we exist, and whose beatitude is all accessible to us, is not only self-sufficing and perfect in every hour, but the act of seeing and the thing seen, the seer and the spectacle, the subject and the object, are one
>
> The soul circumscribes all things. As I have said, it contradicts all [ordinary] experience. In like manner it abolishes time and space.[25]

Emerson repeats what has been said over and over again from the Daoists to the Neoplatonic school and Dionysius Areopagita, in Sufi texts and in the German tradition from Meister Eckhart to Jacob Boehme and Angelus Silesius, in the late medieval English mystics and in Emerson's own favorite Cambridge Platonists (lines from Henry More serve as a motto for "The Over-Soul"). Experience in terms of the sensualist interpretation of the concept is not applicable to mysticism (in mysticism "the subject and the object are one") and even Kantian terms are inappropriate; the *Anschauungsformen* of time and space are suspended. The single most significant statement in the passage above is: "we exist" in "this deep power." *Being* is ascertained, in the sense of: experienced in a non-dualist fashion, as the essential *a priori* before and beyond all conceptual knowledge or talk about it.

The essay "Intellect" elaborates on this. In this essay the word *intellect* in Emerson's flexible terminology is what he calls fluxional: it indicates both a pre-subjective and all-encompassing experiential awareness and

---

[24]Lawrence Buell, *Literary Transcendentalism: Style and Vision in the American Renaissance* (Ithaca, NY: Cornell University Press. 1973), 295, 287.
[25]W II, 253, 256.

what he calls constructive intellect, the rational and argumentative mode of conceptual judgments that is based on and always arises from intellect as pre-subjective, ontological awareness or intuition. In mystical awareness of Being it is true that "[l]ong prior to the age of reflection is the thinking of the mind" and "Intellect is the simple power anterior to all action and construction ... Itself alone is. Its vision is not like the vision of the eye, but is union with the things known."[26] This is an Emersonian echo and reconstruction of the foundational axiom of Western, of Presocratic ontology, namely of Parmenides's dictum: *to gar auto noein estin te kai einai*[27]—knowing awareness and Being are the same.[28] Some historians of philosophy have interpreted the vision of Being in Parmenides's poem as a mystical and pre-subjective experience of pure Being, as an ontologically, a philosophically momentous identificatory insight. Others have emphasized the predominantly religious character of the visionary experience, which the speaker of the poem is granted by the goddess.[29]

Structurally, Parmenides's poem and Emerson's work as a whole manifest a deep and pervasive, a primary fusion of religion and philosophy in allowing a strictly philosophical, that is, ontological, and, at the same time, a religious interpretation of the grounding mystical experience. Parmenides at the beginning of Western thinking and Emerson, as he initiates another beginning as philosophical modernism by returning to and recapturing one of the historically earliest moments of unprecedented intuition and intellection, Emerson and Parmenides both make it possible to accept philosophical and religious thought as intimately, as originally related, as different manifestations and results of an identical, of the initial mystical event.[30] The religious reading of the wordless experience will try to interpret it as divine; the philosophical exegesis will attempt to remember and explain

---

[26] W II, 305, 303–4.

[27] Parmenides, *Die Fragmente*, ed. Ernst Heitsch (Zurich: Artemis und Winkler, 1995), 16.

[28] In 1830 Emerson copied this saying from Marie Joseph De Gérando, *Histoire Comparée des Systèmes de Philosophie* (Paris: Eymery, 1822–23): "Thought & the object of thought are but one"; *JMN* III, 369.

[29] Among the by-now-classical interpretations of Parmenides Kurt Riezler's *Parmenides: Einführung und Interpretation* (1934; Frankfurt: Klostermann, 2001) may stand as an exemplary ontological reading, whereas Hermann Fränkel, *Dichtung und Philosophie des frühen Griechentums* (Munich: Beck, 1962) places Parmenides's poem in the context of religious thought and mysticism in early Greece, for example, Xenophanes (418). Gregory Vlastos also speaks of Parmenides's vision as a "strange blend of mysticism and logic" in "Parmenides' Theory of Knowledge," *Studies in Greek Philosophy*, vol. I, ed. Daniel W. Graham (Princeton, NJ: Princeton University Press, 1993), 162. Recently, Laura Gemelli Marciano has proposed a more balanced, both philosophical *and* religious, reading of Parmenides in her edition *Die Vorsokratiker*, vol. II (Düsseldorf: Artemis & Winkler, 2009), 6–95.

[30] Nietzsche maintained that not only religious but also central philosophical beliefs like the Greek *hen kai pan* have their origins in mystical intuitions. See "Die Philosophie im tragischen Zeitalter der Griechen," *KSA* 1, 813.

it as the revelation of the totality of nature, cosmos, law—of Being. As in Parmenides, what Emerson calls the mystically visionary intellection of Being precedes the constructive intellect, precedes and enables thinking as either philosophy or theology with their respective conceptual and rationalist apparatuses. Because he recaptures and re-enacts the very foundational moment of all thinking, as exemplified among others by Parmenides, in mystical intuition, Emerson allows for the paradoxical possibility of the eternal return of the unprecedented, he opens vistas of iterated originality. In experiencing, in manifesting, and in dealing with the mystical event, he performs the quintessential gesture of modernist thinking, a thinking that ceaselessly keeps emerging from the a-temporal *that*, a thinking "with no Past at [its] back."[31]

In his essay "Thinking of Emerson," Stanley Cavell has indicated the necessity to widen our concept of experience if we want to properly understand Emerson's modernist stature as a thinker and as a possible precursor of Heidegger. Cavell argues that in thinking of Emerson "what is wrong with empiricism is not the reliance on experience but its paltry idea of experience."[32] Even though Emerson in the passage quoted from "The Over-Soul" still adheres to the conventional use of the term "experience," it is obvious that the mystical moment and thus all intuition do have a definite and special experiential quality for him. A more generous and comprehensive interpretation of the term was introduced by William James in discussing the problem at hand—the authority of mystical experience:

Our own more "rational" beliefs are based on evidence exactly similar in nature to that which mystics quote for theirs. Our senses, namely, have assured us of certain states of fact; but mystical experiences are as direct perceptions of fact for those who have them as any sensations ever were for us. The records show that even though the five senses be in abeyance in them, they are absolutely sensational in their epistemological quality, if I may be pardoned the barbarous expression,—that is, they are face to face presentations of what seems immediately to exist.

The mystic is, in short, *invulnerable*, and must be left, whether we relish it or not, in undisturbed enjoyment of his creed.[33]

One may not be satisfied with expressions like "face to face presentations" that still imply the dualism of ordinary sensual experience, but on the whole James has widened our horizon beyond the confines of shallow empirical

---

[31]"Circles" W II, 297.
[32]Stanley Cavell, "Thinking of Emerson," in *The Senses of Walden* (San Francisco: North Point Press, 1981), 126.
[33]James, *Varieties*, 335–6.

rationalization. The important elements in his statement are the emphasis on the factual nature of mystical experience and the strict limitation of its authority as a guiding principle of thought and action within the world of the visionary himself. Emerson, the advocate of self-reliance, would certainly have agreed. The aversion to the forming of schools in Transcendentalist thinkers may well have one of its reasons in the insuperably individualized nature of their foundational insight.

The authority of mystical insight, then, resides above all in its facticity: this insight and experience are had and remembered as a given that grounds both thinking and acting:

> We learn that God *is*; that he is in me; and that all things are shadows of him. The idealism of Berkeley is only a crude statement of the idealism of Jesus, and that again is a crude statement of the fact [!] that all nature is the rapid efflux of goodness executing and organizing itself.[34]

The *fact* is accessible in its pure form not by way of religious teachings or philosophical systems and not by means of strictly referential language. It makes itself felt only in a direct confrontation, that is, by way of intuitional unification. Answering a critical letter by George Bush on the "Divinity School Address," Emerson talked about his conviction concerning the authority of his intuitions in religious matters:

> And why is not that conviction perfect? It is my habit to assume always as purely as I can, the attitude of an observer, & to record what I see. I am not responsible for the fact; for the truth of the record, I am ... what I see now,—the feeblest intellection, rightly considered,—implies all the vast attributes of the spirit, implies the uprising of the one divine soul into my particular creek or bay, & apprises me that the Ocean is behind.[35]

Using traditional (Neoplatonic) metaphors to grasp the One and the mysteries of emanation, Emerson posits the one fact he has to accept: the mystical intuition in its genuine, trans-subjective facticity waiting for language to—however inadequately or approximatively—say it.

A close look at some familiar passages in Emerson may help us appreciate the overpowering authority of this fact and its significance for his thinking. In "Self-Reliance" we find this passage on intuition, the mystical awareness of Unity, of the monistic constitution of Being:

> In that deep force, the last fact behind which analysis cannot go, all things find their common origin. For the sense of being, which in calm hours

---

[34]"Circles" W II, 289.
[35]*Letters* II, 156.

rises, we know not how, in the soul, is not diverse from things, from space, from light, from time, from man, but one with them and proceeds obviously from the same source whence their life and being also proceed. We first share the life by which things exist, and afterwards see them as appearances in nature, and forget that we have shared their cause. Here is the fountain of action and the fountain of thought.[36]

The realm beyond or, rather, before all original philosophical and religious (theological) speculation—be it ancient as in Parmenides or a modernist re-enactment of a historically primary intuition—is characterized not only by unity, it is *life* and is sensed or, rather, had as the very facticity of Being. Pure existence, before all differentiations into mind or matter, is the essence at the core of the mystical, of the intuitive moment. This, of course, is one of the reasons why the moment itself remains ineffable: "The soul answers never by words, but by the thing itself that is enquired after ... Do not ask a description of the countries toward which you sail. The description does not describe them to you; and to-morrow you arrive there, and know them by inhabiting them."[37]

The best term to adequately convey what is intuited and meant here and the only concept sufficiently indefinite to help us understand both the facticity and the authority of the central experience is *Being*.[38] In transcending all beings, it is known only by identification: "for *so to be* is the sole inlet of *so to know*."[39] In this radical inversion of the Cartesian *cogito ergo sum*, knowing is not, of course, a conceptual activity. Here knowing and/or thinking are a total awareness, the oneness of the moment of intuition and the pure presence of its "content." Emerson here once again implicitly evokes the earliest, the Parmenidian vision of the ontological ground as the identity of knowing awareness (Gr. *noein*) and Being (Gr. *einai*). In the texts collected as "Natural History of Intellect" in the early editions of his works, Emerson presents a kind of summary and he uses "Being" and "life" as terms in order to indicate the unquestionable given-ness of the transcending unity, which in his writings we know by so many names[40]—some with religious and some with more strictly philosophical connotations:

---

[36] W II, 64–5.

[37] "The Over-Soul" W II, 265–6.

[38] My decision to keep naming the "essence" of the universe of all beings Being is based on a passage in "Experience," where Emerson enumerates traditional philosophical and religious names for the ineffable and then summarizes: "In our more correct writing we give to this generalization the name of Being, and thereby confess that we have arrived as far as we can go"; W III, 75. Being in an Emersonian sense is not always fully compatible with Heidegger's use of the term since it may, in some passages, still possess onto-theological overtones.

[39] "Circles" W II, 299.

[40] The list of names for the all-encompassing unity in Emerson is long: Reason, Intuition God, Soul, Nature, the One, Beauty, Goodness, the Law, and, probably most adequate of all, Being or To Be, the least specific of all these terms.

To Be is the unsolved, unsolvable wonder. To Be, in its two connections of inward and outward, the mind and nature. The wonder subsists, and age, though of eternity, could not approach a solution. But the suggestion is always returning, that hidden source publishing at once our being and that it is the source of outward nature. Who are we and what is Nature have one answer in the life that rushes into us.[41]

The One, the process of Being without finality, the in-finite, the non-finite To Be without *telos* or closure is that which grounds all philosophical, all theological, that is, all conceptual thinking. It occasions wonder (Gr. *thaumazein*), the initial and initiating disposition of articulate thinking according to Aristotle. Ordinary human knowing and acting are always after the fact, the great and mysterious, the wonder-evoking fact, the event of Being or, rather, of To Be, which, in moments beyond our individual control, may manifest itself in its purity. Remembering this moment of mystical union, of transcendence, one may try and approach it by language, indirectly or "slant," as Emily Dickinson would have said, and one may even think about it without ever coming to *terms* with it. "We are wiser than we know";[42] maybe the emphasis should be: We *are* wiser than we *know*.

# The double consciousness

The mystical experience, properly speaking, does not pertain to the ordinary conduct of life; it cannot be fully integrated into the temporal sequence of events, petty cares, and the demands of an order we are used to call rational and historical. By its very nature the visionary moment resists complete transformation or integration into the world of practical affairs as much as it does withhold its essence from the grasp of language. But there it is, nevertheless, with its air of unassailable authenticity, its factual authority, a veritable *pièce de résistance* in the perpetual flow of existence. The recognition, description, and analysis of this state of internal affairs are one of the most important aspects of Emerson's oeuvre. The term Emerson occasionally uses to describe the existential dilemma of the human being, of the actual or at least potential mystical visionary, is "the double consciousness." Early on Emerson noted "an ambiguity in the term Subjective,"[43] which serves to designate both the individuality of a person and his ontological participation in or, rather, identity with a totality, that is, both his self and his

---

[41] W XII, 15.
[42] "The Over-Soul" W II, 263.
[43] JMN VII, 435.

SELF. For the later Emerson, in "Fate," "the propounding ... of the double consciousness"[44] was the solution for the ancient problem of the possible reconciliation of fate, of trans-individual determination, and of freedom as individualized human existence. Looking at Emerson's description of the perpetual wavering between ecstatic certainty of the individual's transcendent origin, dignity, and destiny, and the poverty and limitation of actual existence in time and space, one is able to discover that consciousness and subjectivity may, after all, not quite adequately cover all the aspects of the problem Emerson would like to convey: "There is a difference between one and another hour of life in their authority and subsequent effect. Our faith comes in moments; our vice is habitual."[45] In the journals we find the following remark: "I am *Defeated* all the time, yet to Victory I am born."[46] In "Circles" we read: "Our moods do not believe in each other ... Alas for this infirm faith, this will not strenuous, this vast ebb of a vast flow! I am God in nature; I am a weed by the wall."[47] The phenomenon of the double consciousness, of incompatible existential moods or dispositions far exceeds a mere epistemological problem. It seems to imply a fundamentally religious and, at the same time, a basically philosophical and, above all, an existential question. Stanley Cavell has importantly pointed out that moods for Emerson do possess existential, that is, ontological meaning. The two moods that Emerson describes as a fundamental binary pair constitute the basic possibilities of our existential relations with the universe, of our being in the sense of *Dasein*.[48] The alternations between ecstasy and despair, so frequent in Emerson, sometimes "leave the reader hard pressed to decide just where the weight of Emerson's argument lies."[49] It is rare that we find a statement that seems to imply the possibility of a permanent reconciliation or harmony between the remembered vision and the earthly, fallen state as in this sentence toward the ending of the exuberant "Over-Soul": "I, the imperfect, adore my own Perfect."[50] The religious attitude of adoration is hard to maintain and more often gives way to the despair that sets the tone for some parts of "Experience." In "Montaigne; or, the Skeptic" we read: "In every house, in the heart of each maiden and each boy, in the soul of the soaring saint, this chasm is found,—between the largest promise of ideal power, and the shabby experience."[51]

---

[44] W VI, 49.
[45] "The Over-Soul" W II, 251.
[46] *JMN* VIII, 228.
[47] W II, 286.
[48] Cavell, "Thinking of Emerson," 128.
[49] Joel Porte, *Representative Man: Ralph Waldo Emerson in His Time* (New York: Oxford University Press, 1979), 209.
[50] W II, 278.
[51] W IV, 176.

The double consciousness, the troubling coexistence of two basic existential moods in Emerson, the mystically gained assurance of identity with Being and the seeming aimlessness in a world of shifting values[52] call for a reconciliation, a fusion. This call is heard again and again in Emerson:

> To him who looks at his life from these moments of illumination, it will seem that he skulks and plays a mean, shiftless and subaltern part in the world. ... The worst feature of this double consciousness is, that the two lives, of the understanding and of the soul, which we lead, really show very little relation to each other; never meet and measure each other: one prevails now, all buzz and din; and the other prevails then, all infinitude and paradise; and, with the progress of life, the two discover no greater disposition to reconcile themselves. Yet, what is my faith? What am I? What but a thought of serenity and independence, an abode in the deep blue sky? Presently the clouds shut down again; yet we retain the belief that this petty web we weave will at last be overshot and reticulated with veins of the blue.[53]

Only when the SELF, the transcendent aspect of the ego, of the subject, is imagined to speak, does one get an inkling of the true nature of the relationship between the two manifestations of Being as human *Dasein*: "these hands, this body, this history of Waldo Emerson are profane and wearisome, but I, I descend not to mix myself with that or with any man. Above his life, above all creatures I flow down forever a sea of benefit into races of individuals."[54]

But this, of course, is a mere verbal projection. The essentially speechless, silent over-soul is given a voice in an ecstatic confession for one fleeting and transient moment. It is a hopeless endeavor for the thinker to try and harmonize the two fundamentally incongruent and yet radically interdependent existential dimensions of experiencing in one single and unified speech act: "the contrast between the transcendental Self and the actual insignificant individual adrift on the stream of time and circumstance"[55] is the necessary result of Emerson's, of all mystically grounded existence and articulation. Based on his comprehensive collection of mystical texts Martin Buber has generalized:

> In der Tat, ein Widerspruch ist aufgedeckt. Aber was kann er für die Beurteilung von Menschen bedeuten, die ihr Leben in der Pein eines

---

[52]See "Illusions," in *The Conduct of Life* W VI, 291–308.
[53]The "Transcendentalist" W I, 333.
[54]*JMN* VII, 435.
[55]Whicher, *Freedom and Fate*, 171.

ungeheuren Widerspruchs verbringen: des Widerspruchs zwischen dem Erlebnis und dem Getriebe, aus dem sie emporstiegen und in das sie hinabstürzen Mal für Mal? Das ist der Widerspruch zwischen der Ekstase, die nicht in das Gedächtnis eingeht, und dem Verlangen, sie für das Gedächtnis zu retten, im Bild, in der Rede, in der Konfession.[56]

Buber's interpretation of the predicament of the mystic is an indirect, but powerful, confirmation of my belief in Emerson's mysticism. The permanent contradiction between the mystical experience or intuition of Being and being-in-the-world is a quality of outstanding importance in all mystically grounded interpretations of human existence and one of the sources for their language of paradox. We can look at Buber's statement as a parallel version of the above quotation from "The Transcendentalist." Even the characterization of the world as *Getriebe* ("hustle and bustle") finds its counterpart in Emerson's "buzz and din." The so-called skeptical Emerson of "Experience" and of the Montaigne portrait is not a more mature writer who has outlived the transcendent enthusiasm of "The Over-Soul." Skepticism is a necessary concomitant of the ecstatic vision, skepticism is the adequate response of the self lost in the welter of ever-changing circumstance, but it is also, we have to remind ourselves, just one side of the double consciousness: "The ground occupied by the skeptic is the vestibule of the temple."[57]

When we look back at Emerson's earliest ancestor and his way of thinking on the basis of a mystical intuition of Being, when we look back at Parmenides, the fissure between the two dispositions, between intuiting the oneness of Being and the endless series of opinions (Gr. *doxa*) that dominate our thinking engagement with the world of the senses, this inescapable difference is manifest as the two seemingly irreconcilable parts of Parmenides's poem,[58] the founding text of the tradition that finds in Emerson its first modernist exponent. After this brief sketch of Emerson's interpretation of the existential predicament of the mystically grounded intuition of Being, the question arises: what then is the task, what are the defining features of thinking, of Man Thinking? It is, I may say, a formidable, a never-ending, an open-ended task. Emerson's representative philosopher Plato used the

---

[56]Buber, "Ekstase und Bekenntnis," 93–4: "Indeed, a contradiction has been uncovered. But what can it mean for the appraisal of human beings who spend their lives in the pain of such an immense contradiction: the contradiction between the momentous experience and the hustle and bustle, out of which they ascended and into which they will fall again and again? This is the contradiction between ecstasy, which will not enter memory, and the desire to save it in and for memory—in an image, in a discourse, in a confession" (my translation).

[57]"Montaigne; or, the Skeptic" W IV, 164.

[58]Part 1 of the fragmentary poem reports the speaker's journey to the abode of the goddess who opens and explains to him the intuition of pure Being, whereas Part 2 deals with the changeable, unreliable, and unstable opinions of humans.

doctrine of reminiscence to explain it. We may call that explanation fanciful, Emerson states, one possible metaphorical *attempt*, but even so the challenge remains: "the connection between our knowledge and the abyss of being is still real, and the explanation must be not less magnificent."[59]

# Thinking

In Emerson's eyes philosophy and theology are the permanent and never satisfactorily completed attempts to come to terms with the double consciousness, the basic existential feature of the human being. The moment of vision, of *unio mystica*, of one-ness with the "abyss of being," briefly opens a transient access to the a-temporal backdrop of our existence. At the same time, it initiates an exodus from this transcendent realm and sets in motion the never-ending process in which our awareness of our selves and our worlds tries to do justice to and verbally exhaust the magnificence of our transcendent origins, of the trans-conceptual given-ness of Being. The relationship between Being and thinking in Emerson is similar to the attitude taken by the great critic of enlightenment rationalism Johann Georg Hamann:

> "Nicht cogito, ergo sum, sondern umgekehrt, oder noch Hebräischer Est; ergo cogito," umschreibt [Hamann] seine fundamentale Einsicht in einem späten Brief an Jacobi. Nicht Denken ist das erste Prinzip, aus dem Wirklichkeit konstruiert wird, vielmehr ist Wirklichkeit ein Vorgegebenes, auf das Vernunft antwortet, Wirklichkeit ist Anrede an eine vernehmende Vernunft.[60]

Hamann's statement and the perceptive analysis by Reiner Wild point the way toward an adequate understanding of the status of thinking in Emerson:[61] thinking is the never fully completed attempt to respond to

---

[59]"Plato; or, the Philosopher" *W* IV, 84.

[60]Reiner Wild, "Einleitung," in *Johann Georg Hamann* (Darmstadt: WBG, 1978), 7: " 'Not cogito, ergo sum, but rather the other way round, or even more in Hebrew fashion Est; ergo cogito': this is the way [Hamann] paraphrases his fundamental insight in a late letter to Jacobi. The first principle, out of which reality is constructed, is not thinking; rather, reality is a primarily given to which reason responds; reality is a discourse addressed to a receptive reason" (my translation). Emerson's dictum in "Circles" characterizing the moments of vision, "the masterpieces of God," is an almost exact equivalent of Hamann's anti-Cartesian stance: "*so to be* is the sole inlet of *so to know*"; *W* II, 299.

[61]The difference between Hamann and Emerson consists in the fact that the *Est* is revealed to Hamann primarily in biblical texts and to Emerson exclusively in unmediated moments of mystical union.

the overwhelming experience of Being to which it, thinking, owes its very existence.

"Thinking as a partial act"[62] is an aspect of the total act of living, of existence as process, and this total act has at its core the tension between the unity of intuition and the partiality and temporality of thinking manifested in the double consciousness. Thinking as the articulate account of our temporality, our becoming, is thus necessarily open-ended and never totally resolved in a system. The essay "Circles" contains the most thorough analysis of the non-teleological character of Emerson's idea of thinking, a process without closure. Not even Plato, the philosophical master-mind in Emerson's gallery of representative men, has ever achieved a reconciliation or merger of thinking and the experiential realization of Being: "There [Plato] perishes: unconquered nature lives on and forgets him."[63] George Santayana's word ought therefore to be heeded: "He is never a philosopher, but always Emerson philosophizing."[64] On this basis Joel Porte has succinctly stated the task for the Emerson scholar: "We shall keep our eyes not so much on Emerson the finished thinker as on Emerson in the act of thinking, working his way indefatigably to that land's end which was always just disappearing over the horizon of his thought."[65]

Emphatically, then, there is no Emerson as a finished thinker, the very essence of thinking in Emerson is the formation of the next circle, the experimental process without systematic finality, the truly modernist gesture of ceaselessly making it new, or of beginning again and again, as Gertrude Stein saw it. Stanley Cavell has reminded us of the fact that Matthew Arnold's skepticism about Emerson's claim as a philosopher may be founded on an outmoded idea of philosophy: "We are by now too aware of the philosophical *attacks* on system or theory to place the emphasis in defining philosophy on a product of philosophy rather than on the process of philosophizing."[66] Looking at Emerson from this point of view one is well justified to rank him with the two other great destroyers of philosophical systems in the nineteenth century and thus with the kind of early modernist processual philosophy exemplified by Kierkegaard and Nietzsche.

Thinking in Emerson should be called the articulate aspect of the temporality of human existence, of the open-ended process of potentially persistent renewal. Satisfaction in thinking will never be in results, in final positions, or in conclusive judgments, not in systems, but only in the process of thinking itself with its continuous shifts and turns, its inner tensions and

---

[62]"The American Scholar" W I, 100.
[63]W IV, 76.
[64]George Santayana, "The Optimism of Ralph Waldo Emerson" (1886), qtd. in Porte. *Representative Man*, 21.
[65]Porte, *Representative Man*, xiii.
[66]Cavell, "Thinking of Emerson," 129.

contradictions; as the Emerson *persona* confesses, after encountering critical objections of "a pair of philosophers; I endeavored to show my good men that I liked everything by turns and nothing long."[67] The categorical imperative for proper thinking in Emerson as a function of living, which keeps arising from the unspeakable trans-temporal center of Being, is succinctly expressed in these last words from "Experience":

> in the solitude to which every man is always returning, he has a sanity and revelations which in his passage into new worlds he will carry with him. Never mind the ridicule, never mind the defeat; up again, old heart!—it seems to say,—there is victory yet for all justice; and the true romance which the world exists to realize will be the transformation of genius into practical power.[68]

This Transcendentalist *sursum corda* reinforces my principal argument. In the oscillation between solitary and intuitive identification with Being and a permanent going-forth or exodus[69] into the world of becoming, the "uses," the pragmatic dimensions of the mystical side of the double consciousness become apparent: it is the quiet center of an unceasing movement, a movement that may show itself in its total activity as life or in the partial acts of thinking, in endless attempts or experiments or essays by Man Thinking. Cavell has indirectly confirmed the mystical antecedents and implications of open-ended or onward thinking in modern philosophy by convincingly analyzing its beginnings in Emerson: "Onward thinking, on the way, knowing how to go on, are of course inflections or images of the religious idea of The Way, inflections which specifically deny that there is a place at which our ways end."[70] This is exactly the situation of thinking described in "Circles." Wherever thinking may start, it always sets out from the very center of Being that is everywhere and may always and contingently assert its presence in a moment of intuition. As a movement from the quiet center, though, whose circumference is nowhere, it is always on the way, pursuing "the flying Perfect, around which the hands of man can never meet."[71] Emerson, in speaking of center and circumference, thought he was using St. Augustine's definition of God,[72] or Being, when he tried

---

[67] "Nominalist and Realist" W III, 236.

[68] W III, 86.

[69] The most profound philosophical analysis of this going-forth and of its many forms of realization is Branka Arsic, *On Leaving: A Reading in Emerson* (Cambridge, MA: Harvard University Press, 2010).

[70] Cavell, "Thinking of Emerson," 136.

[71] W II, 281.

[72] Joseph Slater's notes for "Circles" in the Harvard edition of *The Collected Works of Ralph Waldo Emerson* (Cambridge, MA: Harvard University Press, 1979), vol. 2, 253–4, offer a variety of possible sources for this definition that Emerson might have used; the oldest

to articulate the terrible and exhilarating tension that always underlies thinking: it is the double consciousness in action.

Thinking that is certain of its mystical origin, of its beginning in the immediacy of intuition, this mode of thinking that knows itself as a never-ending task is radically revolutionary[73]: "Beware when the great God lets loose a thinker on this planet. Then all things are at risk. It is as when a conflagration has broken out in a great city, and no man knows what is safe, or where it will end."[74] Nietzsche was so impressed by this interpretation of the thinker as cosmically destructive force that he quoted the passage as a kind of summary at the end of his third *Untimely Meditation,* "Schopenhauer as Educator." The gesture here is Nietzschean and modernist but the threat to all humanly established order in Emerson is based on the intimate, the mystically achieved certainty and trust in the overabundance of the heart of the self that knows itself at one with the SELF, the arsenal of all power and potential. No finite thought and no finite order will ever fully contain and exhaust its possibilities. Its longing for adequate realization is endless and insatiable. "People wish to be settled: only as far as they are unsettled, is there any hope for them. Life is a series of surprises."[75]

The great Marxist philosopher Ernst Bloch, focusing his attention on the medieval Christian mystics, has described the origin of the persistent exodus of thinking, of such fundamentally moving *thinking on the way*: "Wer immer aber auszieht, kommt von einem Innen her."[76] This is not simply a plea to regain or at least remember a lost interiority. Bloch recognizes and articulates the powerful utopian element in all mystically based thinking, the true liberalization of thinking derived from the highest possible ideal of existing itself, an ideal that is not only posited but intimately intuited and authentically experienced:

So jedenfalls ist die kostbarste christliche Mystik, durch und durch ergreifend, *topisch-neu, utopisch-geladen mit dem Funken, der nicht untergeht.* Des Näheren, Nächsten aber: in diesem Subjektsein verbirgt sich hier der noch nicht herausgekommene Augenblick unserer selbst, das

---

textual evidence, however, not mentioned by Slater, is in the twelfth-century manuscript of the (possibly) fourth-century anonymous collection *Liber Viginti Quattuor Philosophorum* [Book of the 24 Philosophers]. See the Latin and French edition prepared by Françoise Hudry (Turnhout: Brepols, 1997), 7.

[73]An elegant exposition of Emerson's work as radical social criticism is Daniel Aaron, "Emerson and the Progressive Tradition," in Aaron, *Men of Good Hope: A Story of American Progressives* (1951; New York: Oxford University Press, 1969), 3–20.

[74]"Circles" W II, 288.

[75]Ibid., 298.

[76]Bloch in Zimmermann, *Rationalität und Mystik*, 351: "Whosoever departs and leaves home, emerges from an inner realm" (my translation).

ausstehend-präsente wirkliche Jetzt und Hier, ‚Nunc stans' (Augustin) des Wesens, zu dem wir Verwandlung sind.[77]

Bloch's brilliant phrase, "das ausstehend-präsente wirkliche Jetzt und Hier" ("the truly real Here and Now which is both present and yet always withholding its full emergence"), subtly interprets the existential predicament to which Emerson gave the name "the double consciousness." The ultimate perfection of the human being, her or his true being, is both present and *ausstehend*, that is, always waiting to come forth, to emerge, and be realized. The human being may be mystically certain of her or his identity with the true essence (*Wesen*), but she or he is nevertheless still on the way, permanently on the way as a thinking being in order to achieve the utopian realization of the innermost self. In Bloch, this always imminent, never fully achieved self-realization, of course, proceeds most significantly by work, in a broad sense including the work of the mind, that is, thinking. I have introduced Bloch in order to avoid the impression that my version of reading Emerson as a mystic has anything to do with fundamentalist primitivism or conservative emotionalism. Emerson may not always have been quite as radical as Bloch in his statements about so-called real political issues in his time. What I am concerned with here, however, is not *thoughts* of Emerson *about* social or political problems. I am interested in the *nature* of his thinking. Thinking in Emerson as an aspect of becoming or living is persistently non-teleological, open-ended, and in this way it is necessarily unsettling. It is based on the facticity of the double consciousness, the "'Nunc stans' ... des Wesens, zu dem wir Verwandlung sind" ("the 'nunc stans' ... of the true essence in the direction of which we tend to ceaselessly metamorphose"). This kind of thinking can only go on because it is certain of its origin or home, certain in moments of intuition and almost certain in the intermediate phases of belief in their reality. It is a courageous, a daring mode of being and thinking.

*

When Emerson wrote to Professor Max Müller in 1873, thanking him for the dedication of *Introduction to the Science of Religion*, he marveled at the surprising similarity of so many of the Indian texts from various epochs of religious history: "'Tis curious that in all these books are passages of

---

[77]Ibid., 359: "the most precious Christian mysticism is deeply moving, *topically-innovative, charged in a utopian fashion with the spark which never perishes.* Even closer or closest: in this mode of subjective existence that which has not yet fully emerged does hide, the truly real Here and Now which is both present and yet always withholding its full emergence, the 'nunc stans' (Augustinus) of the true essence in the direction of which we tend to ceaselessly metamorphose" (my translation).

grandeur, as if written by one majestic person."[78] Emerson did not believe in direct verbal inspiration, but he saw that the Hindu scriptures expressed a basic view of Being, a monistic philosophy and/or theology he had always regarded as closely related to his own experience and view of a transcendent onto-theological ground. In the late text "Natural History of Intellect" he confessed, "I am of the oldest religion."[79] The man who, at the beginning of his career as a thinker had called for an "original relation to the universe,"[80] who had seemingly despised all religious, philosophical, ethical, and political precedent, had to admit that he belonged to a tradition that, paradoxically, enabled him to be of the oldest religion and philosophy and, at the same time, made it possible for him to exist in a spiritually self-reliant and continuously innovative mode.[81] The tradition that goes back to the oldest religion and philosophy, to Parmenides or to Hindu scripture, may conveniently be known by the name of "the perennial philosophy." Speaking of Emerson, however, we should not use the term in its scholastic sense or in the way Leibniz applied it to denote the supposedly unassailable tenets of the philosophy of the ancients; even Karl Jaspers's understanding of perennial philosophy as the permanent conversation of the great texts of the history of philosophy is not wholly adequate. I would rather use it in the sense that gained some currency and even popularity because of Aldous Huxley's collection and study of important texts from the mystical tradition of the world published in 1944 as *The Perennial Philosophy*.

Huxley's historical and, even more so, his psychological investigations of the phenomenon are by now somewhat dated. The collection of passages from the great mystical philosophers is still useful, though. Looking at Emerson's lists of possible predecessors of Transcendentalism in "The Transcendentalist" or of the important successors of Plato in *Representative Men*, we detect a surprising similarity with compilations of textual mystical evidence like those of Huxley, of William James, or more recent ventures in this once again profitable field of publishing. Detailed analyses of Emerson's indebtedness to, say, Plotinus or Ralph Cudworth or Jakob Boehme are interesting and useful and shed more light on the methods of textual composition of Emerson, the inveterate eclectic syncretist, but I am concerned here only with the more general outlines of Emerson's spiritual and philosophical disposition: the mystical experience, the double consciousness, and the way of thinking as a result of both. "Idealism as it

---

[78]*Letters* VI, 246–7.
[79]W XII, 15.
[80]*Nature* W I, 9.
[81]The productive tension between self-reliant innovation and comprehensive reliance on tradition is magnificently and in-depth explored in Jan Stievermann, *Der Sündenfall der Nachahmung: Zum Problem der Mittelbarkeit im Werk Ralph Waldo Emersons* (Paderborn: Schöningh, 2007).

appears in 1842"[82] is one of numerous self-definitions by Emerson of his stance as a thinker. But the term "idealism" is not limited in its meanings to the German post-Kantians; idealism, as Emerson uses the term, is not a narrowly circumscribed philosophical position at all. Bishop Berkeley and Jesus are idealists in his view,[83] and Plato, the arch-idealist, is not the founder of a branch of Western philosophy, for Emerson he is above all the epitome, and his works are the *summa*, of the persistent questions of the perennial philosophy: "Mysticism finds in Plato all its texts."[84] The perennial philosophy offers no permanent solutions or final answers; it finds itself always called upon to explain and communicate again and again the silent center of self and SELF in the never-ending process called thinking: "No power of genius has ever yet had the smallest success in explaining existence."[85] Existence or Being or the Divine or Reason or Nature or Law: in Emerson's flexible terminology, the mystically given and revealed is the inescapable starting point of all genuine thinking the way he understands it. Each single individual within the tradition starts at that a-verbal and a-conceptual center that is everywhere and thus in him- or herself. In this manner a *community* of thinkers appears without depriving any of them of the privilege of "an original relation to the universe."[86] The way of their thinking is then to be seen as a unique version of the Way, of the "open road" that encompasses all specific and forever preliminary realizations.

We tend to believe in history; we almost superstitiously believe in the historicity and cultural determination of everything. We may, therefore, find it hard to accept, but we will probably not be able to approach and experience the disquieting, the revolutionizing center of Emerson's thinking unless we are ready to read him as a mystic and once again, as George Santayana did in 1900, place him in his proper philosophical and religious environment: "He belonged by nature to that mystical company of devout souls that recognize no particular home and are dispersed throughout history, although not without intercommunication."[87]

---

[82]"The Transcendentalist" *W* I, 311.
[83]"Circles" *W* II, 289.
[84]"Plato; or, the Philosopher" *W* IV, 42.
[85]Ibid., 77.
[86]*Nature W* I, 9.
[87]George Santayana, "Emerson" (1900), in Konvitz and Whicher, *Emerson*, 38.

# 4

# Hosting Sa'di

The guiding, the defining, the selective, and thus also the creative interest, which characterizes Ralph Waldo Emerson's approach to and his reading of medieval Persian poetry, is the core concern of this chapter. An elucidation and evaluation of Emerson's hermeneutics in this particular instance, however, quite clearly depends on my own understanding, my own reading of the essential features of the interpretive encounter, in its historical varieties, between Western readers and the so-called Orient. As I understand the evidence, the historically significant Western approaches to Islamic, Hindu, Buddhist, Daoist, and Confucian poetry, philosophy, and religion since the seventeenth and eighteenth centuries reveal three major hermeneutic strategies: *first*, we encounter the professedly dispassionate and ostensibly objectivist philological hermeneutics in the widest of senses, which issues primarily in the collecting, editing, translating, and annotating of major texts: Adam Olearius or Sir William Jones or Joseph Freiherr von Hammer-Purgstall or Max Müller or Paul Deussen may stand as admirable representatives of this mode of transcultural endeavor; *secondly*, one has to pay tribute to what I would like to call the hermeneutics of hospitality, which has long since attempted to allow Persian poetry, like any other Eastern or Asian or Oriental text, to unfold productively in a new cultural and historical moment and environment, be it by way of imaginative (re-)interpretation or creative appropriation and transformation: the achievements of Goethe, Thomas Moore, Emerson, Friedrich Rückert, or Edward FitzGerald may serve as prominent examples of an approach that welcomes the culturally as well as historically remote and seemingly alien text into a new setting and thus provides the conditions for the innovation, proliferation, and augmentation of meaning and literary as well as spiritual value; *thirdly*, and lastly, we have to acknowledge the hermeneutics of resentment that, for me, determines major postcolonial approaches to

This essay was previously published as "Emerson, Persian Poetry, and Sheikh Mosleho'd-Din Sa'di-ye Shirazi: The Hermeneutics of Hospitality" in *Orient and Orientalisms in US-American Poetry and Poetics*, ed. Sabine Sielke and Christian Kloeckner (Frankfurt: Lang, 2009), 33–57. Reprinted by permission of Peter Lang International Academic Publishers.

orientalism (rather than to the Orient). The third approach differs from the first two, since it has to be seen as a second-order hermeneutics: it does not primarily engage and read Persian or Indian or Chinese or Japanese texts and cultural achievements; rather, it reads the way "Oriental" cultures have been read in the West. The hermeneutics of resentment, poignantly represented above all by Edward Said's influential study *Orientalism*, subjects the possible failures and the undoubted successes of philological hermeneutics and of the hermeneutics of hospitality to a comprehensive and totalizing, often even totalitarian, politically motivated reductionist reinterpretation that invalidates, simplifies, and casts doubt on the legitimacy, the dignity, and often even the moral integrity of major testimonials in the productive, dialogic encounter between prominent individual representatives of world cultures.

One such productive encounter is that between Emerson and Sheikh Mosleho'd-Din Sa'di-ye Shirazi (1213/1219–92),[1] one of the seven greatest medieval Persian poets,[2] who is commonly identified by Western writers and scholars as either Saadi or Sa'di. Together with Samsu'd-Din Muhammad Hafiz, Sa'di represented the pinnacle of Persian poetic culture for Emerson. My remarks will be devoted to a descriptive definition and a tentative justification of the hermeneutics of hospitality as opposed to the orientalist implications of the hermeneutics of resentment. On this basis I will proceed and show the hermeneutics of hospitality at work in Emerson's general appreciation of Persian poetry and, in some detail, in the way it shapes his generous readings of Sa'di's work. Finally, I will try and interpret the poetic transformation of Emerson's vision of the Persian poet in his great poem "Saadi" in terms of the potential inherent in any true hermeneutics of hospitality.

In one of his many deeply appreciative comments on Emerson, Jorge Luis Borges called him "a classical writer and a gentleman," "a great intellectual poet, a skilled maker of aphorisms, a man who delighted in the varieties of being." This Emerson, the elegant literary, cultural, and philosophical pluralist, Borges adds, naturally also excelled as "a generous and sensitive reader of ... the Persians."[3] The generosity and sensitivity which Borges

---

[1] In my transcription of the name I follow the suggestion of the Iranian scholar Faramarz Behzad in his *Adam Olearius' "Persianischer Rosenthal": Untersuchungen zur Übersetzung von Saadis "Golestan" im 17. Jahrhundert* (Göttingen: Vandenhoeck & Ruprecht, 1970), 9. For the (relatively uncertain) dates I rely on Jan Rypka and his magisterial *Iranische Literaturgeschichte* (Leipzig: Harrassowitz, 1959), 242. Rypka gives Sa'di's full name as Saih Abu-'Abdi'llah Musariff(u'd-din) b. Muslih Sa'di.

[2] Goethe deals extensively with this "Siebengestirn" of (in his rendition of the names) Firdusi, Enweri, Nisami, Dschelaleddin Rumi, Saadi, Hafis, and Dschami who are said to best represent five hundred years of poetic excellence in Persia. See Johann Wolfgang Goethe, "Besserem Verständniß," in *West-östlicher Divan*, ed. Karl Richter et al., vol. 11.1.2 of *Sämtliche Werke nach Epochen seines Schaffens* (Munich: Hanser, 1998), 156–67.

[3] Jorge Luis Borges, "Thomas Carlyle, *On Heroes, Hero-worship and the Heroic in History*, and Ralph Waldo Emerson, *Representative Men*," in Borges, *Selected Non-Fictions*, ed. Eliot Weinberger, trans. Esther Allen, Suzanne Jill Levine, and Weinberger (New York: Penguin, 2000), 417.

recognizes in Emerson's reading of the Persian poets and which is, at the same time, manifest in Borges's own attitude toward the North American thinker, this generosity and this sensitivity of reading or, in other words, this hermeneutic hospitality is not prominent among the traits that postcolonial critics in the wake of Said's *Orientalism* tend to detect and value highly in their analyses of Emerson's or, for that matter, of any other Western writer's or thinker's responses to the literary, religious, and philosophical achievements of the so-called Orient. On the other hand, there is the long and impressive tradition of thorough, profound, carefully researched, and respectful criticism devoted to Emerson's encounter with and response to, above all and almost exclusively, Indian and Chinese literature, religion, and philosophy; this tradition, which manifests both the concerns of philological hermeneutics and the hermeneutics of hospitality, as I understand and as I will elucidate it, includes the major studies by Frederic Ives Carpenter, Arthur E. Christy, Carl T. Jackson, Arthur Versluis, and Alan D. Hodder.[4] John D. Yohannan's *Persian Poetry in England and America,* however, is the only truly comprehensive attempt to analyze Western responses to the great medieval Persian poets. His study includes a major, a meticulous and thorough, philological account and critique of Emerson's textual appropriations and English renditions of German translations of Persian poetic texts.[5] Emerson's response to Persian poetic culture has thus primarily or most importantly been evaluated in such a context of a philological hermeneutics. I find it desirable and mandatory to complement this approach by focusing on the hermeneutics of hospitality in Emerson's reading of Sa'di and by using Emerson's implied hermeneutic methodology as an adequate model for my own critical appreciation of Emerson reading Sa'di. The best way to introduce what I mean by a hermeneutics of hospitality should begin with a brief comment on my understanding of hermeneutics in general, followed by a tentative definition that will include an attempt to contrast the hermeneutics of hospitality with the hermeneutics of resentment.

One fundamental trait in Hans-Georg Gadamer's phenomenological interpretation of what he calls the hermeneutic situation, it will be remembered, is the fact that we are always and inescapably *in* it and *of* it, and that there is no way of objectifying it, of looking at it from the

---

[4]Frederic Ives Carpenter, *Emerson and Asia* (Cambridge, MA: Harvard University Press, 1930); Arthur E. Christy, *The Orient in American Transcendentalism: A Study of Emerson, Thoreau, and Alcott* (1932; New York: Octagon Books, 1968); Carl T. Jackson, *The Oriental Religions and American Thought. Nineteenth-Century Explorations* (Westport, CT: Greenwood Press, 1981); Arthur Versluis, *American Transcendentalism and Asian Religions* (Oxford: Oxford University Press, 1993); Alan D. Hodder, "'The Best of Brahmans': India Reading Emerson Reading India," *Nineteenth-Century Prose* 30 (2003): 1–32.
[5]John D. Yohannan, *Persian Poetry in England and America: A 200-Year History* (Delmar NY: Caravan Books, 1977), 113–34.

outside.[6] This situation is characterized by a dynamic historical horizon that always already includes the cultural tradition—though not as a fixed entity—and the persistently processual individual historical consciousness that engages that tradition in proliferating acts of interpretation.[7] These acts of interpretation are defined in their constantly progressing togetherness[8] by the situation itself[9] and not primarily by the dictates of a supposedly established (objective) past or by the (subjective) will to interpretive power of the present historical perspective. The continuous innovation of meaning as a result of this situational dynamics, by the way, reminds one strongly of the Emersonian interpretation of historical hermeneutic progression in his 1841 essay "Circles." If there is one aspect within the hermeneutic situation that Gadamer's phenomenological exegesis does not fully address or appreciate, it is the structuring agency of interest (in William James's and, later, Jürgen Habermas's use of the term, which, in *Erkenntnis und Interesse* (1968), was inspired by the precedent of James and Peirce). It is the kind of guiding interest active within the hermeneutic situation and the evaluation of the importance of that interest, which, in my view, account for the basic differences between a hermeneutics of resentment and a hermeneutics of hospitality. My own guiding interest in reading varieties of hermeneutic endeavor, be it confessed at the outset, is the rehabilitation of a hermeneutics of hospitality and a refutation of what I see as the reductionist and merely ideological implications of a politically motivated hermeneutics of resentment.

In spite of the various attempts by Edward W. Said, most recently in his "Preface to the Twenty-Fifth Anniversary Edition" of *Orientalism* (published in 2003, the year of his death), to mitigate the uncompromising harshness of its guiding culturally political interest, the hermeneutic situation in which he finds himself as a legitimately concerned public intellectual remains essentially structured by the desire to unmask "a style of thought and mode

---

[6]"Der Begriff der Situation ist ja dadurch charakterisiert, daß man sich nicht ihr gegenüber befindet und daher kein gegenständliches Wissen von ihr haben kann. Man steht in ihr, findet sich immer schon in einer Situation vor, deren Erhellung die nie ganz zu vollendende Aufgabe ist"; Hans-Georg Gadamer, *Wahrheit und Methode: Grundzüge einer philosophischen Hermeutik* (1960; Tübingen: Mohr, 1972), 285. Joel Weinsheimer and Donald G. Marshall translate this as follows: "The very idea of a situation means that we are not standing outside it and hence are unable to have any objective knowledge of it. We always find ourselves within a situation, and throwing light on it is a task that is never entirely finished"; Gadamer, *Truth and Method* (1975; London: Bloomsbury, 2013), 312.

[7]Gadamer, *Wahrheit und Methode*, 288.

[8]See ibid., 289, on "Horizontverschmelzung" ("fusion of horizons").

[9]The *situation* is thus revealed as language, as a "Mitte ... in der sich Ich und Welt zusammenschließen oder besser: in ihrer ursprünglichen Zusammengehörigkeit darstellen" (ibid., 449), that is, "a medium where I and world meet or, rather, manifest their original belonging together" (*Truth and Method*, 490).

of discourse perpetrated by Europeans upon various peoples and cultures of the non-Western world in the service, finally, of European colonial self-interests."[10] Said's reading of Western readings and "constructions" of the Orient is characterized by a fundamental distrust of even the seemingly most disinterested and benevolent of Western approaches to Eastern cultures; his program remains clear and distinct in spite of all prefatory disclaimers: "I myself believe that Orientalism is more particularly valuable as a sign of European-Atlantic power over the Orient than it is a veridic discourse about the Orient."[11] One does wonder what a veridic discourse might be and whether this would be limited to (supposedly unprejudiced?) readings by "Oriental" readers unimpeded by the asymmetrical power relations that have created, in *all* Western readings according to Said, *the* Orient as *we* know it.[12] This hermeneutics of reading Western interpretations of the Orient is structured by a pervasive, politically motivated suspicion and resentment. In spite of Said's impressive sophistication and wide-ranging cultural knowledge, the hermeneutics of resentment does not allow for or acknowledge the possibility of readings guided by interests other than those that reductively recognize again and again the same basic patterns of perceiving and construing and evaluating Oriental culture, skewed by the seemingly inescapable optics of domination and colonial motivation. Even the, at first glance, most well-meaning interpretations of Eastern literature ultimately reveal the ugly underbelly of the will to domination. Differences of individual achievement, of personal temperament, of political or religious belief, of historical or cultural situatedness among Western readers engaging Oriental cultures will thus ultimately be evened out; what remains and is exposed to our critical understanding is one vast monotonous desert of the eternally identical biased "constructedness" of all Western interpretations.

My not overly generous critique of Edward Said and the hermeneutics of resentment finds itself supported by what I see as the consequences of his methodological strategy in his followers. Malini Johar Schueller has analyzed "U.S. Orientalisms" in a book that is deeply indebted to Said and which finds additional theoretical support in Foucault's theories of power. Schueller wants to "pay particular attention ... to the deformative power of both particular writers and contexts."[13] And even though she acknowledges the possibility of individual writers resisting what she thinks of as the dominant imperialist discourse, her view of Emerson reading Oriental literature reveals all the structural properties of the hermeneutics

---

[10]Hodder, "'The Best of Brahmans,'" 3.
[11]Edward W. Said, *Orientalism* (1978; New York: Random House, 2003), 6.
[12]Ibid., 40.
[13]Malini Johar Schueller, *U.S. Orientalisms: Race, Nation, and Gender in Literature, 1790–1890* (Ann Arbor: University of Michigan Press, 1998), 8.

of resentment.[14] Reading Asia as predominantly "passive, spiritual, and incapable of action," Emerson is said to be not guided by an interest in the other but by a political motivation through which that other, the Orient, becomes subservient: "As my analysis of Emerson's Asian Oriental pieces demonstrates, Emerson's increasingly totalized visions of the Orient became much needed constructions through which he sought to maintain faith in what he saw as an increasingly fractured and rapacious New World."[15] The assumption of a "totalized vision" is possible only if one accounts for it in terms of a guiding political interest that predetermines the basic structure of the hermeneutic situation. In fact, a closer look at Emerson's characteristically varying and often contradictory readings of Indian, Chinese, or Persian poets shows a reader open to often unprecedented visions and revisions, not to mention the obvious fact that Mencius helps Emerson address totally different concerns than, say, the *Upanishads*, or Hafiz, or Sa'di. The implied and foundational resentment of Schueller's study of American readings of the Orient makes it necessary to ascribe to Emerson "binary distinctions between the West and the East, activity and passivity, dynamism and fate—distinctions that are often maintained to shore up a vision of the nation as a powerful imperial body."[16] Indeed, Emerson uses such binaries. However, true to his persistent strategy of troping or turning, of reversing each single statement and perspective, the opposite is also true. What is more, the binaries that Schueller observes are strongly contradicted by the evidence supplied by Emerson's reading of the *Bhagavad Gita*—a treatise, in part at least, on proper action and not at all on passivity—and by his appreciation of the Persian poets: the epic poetry of Firdausi, for instance, certainly does not invite any reader to visions of meek submissiveness. The politics that determine the guiding interest in the hermeneutics of resentment have a tendency to submerge and extinguish all distinguishing features that make up the fascinatingly varied landscapes of Western, of American, and of the manifold Emersonian readings of a great number of highly diverse Oriental cultures with their numerous unmistakably individual achievements. One thing is inadmissible in the practice of the hermeneutics of resentment: the possibility of a true, authentic, generous, friendly, altruistic, self-corrective, open-minded, productive, welcoming reading of the Oriental author or book, a reading that is not necessarily and primarily and always to be subjected to the corrosive of an obsessive, almost pathological suspicion and ingrained resentment. Emerson himself is a prominent, but certainly

---

[14]Ibid., 157–74. The chapter begins by dismissing Emerson's reading of Persian poets as subordinate to his interest in India; a closer look at some of his essays and especially the notebooks would contradict this statement, which reflects the dominant focus and interest of the majority of critical studies rather than Emerson's own preference.

[15]Ibid., 158–9.

[16]Ibid., 165.

not the only important, example of such a truly generous hermeneutics, a hermeneutics of hospitality.

It all comes down, then, to the kind of hermeneutic situation and its structuring interest in which the reader and her or his Oriental author or text find themselves. The examples of Goethe and, possibly inspired or at least encouraged by him, of Emerson will allow me to offer two related, though not quite identical, concrete instances of the hermeneutics of hospitality which I myself prefer to adopt and propagate and which, to begin with, I would somewhat abstractly characterize as follows: the basic and initial attitude of the reader in the situation of a hermeneutics of hospitality toward the distant and as-yet-unknown text or author is that of a host who is ready to extend a friendly welcome to his guest, to the, say, Oriental and medieval author or book. This situation of an open hospitality allows the guest to show himself at his best in the new cultural environment that he has entered; it allows the host both to be himself and yet, at the same time, to open himself up to and expose himself to the possibly unexpected and unforeseen challenges that the guest has to offer. The host is thus on the threshold leading toward a possibly new, a changed, and enriched identity. The guest is a guest only in the new environment, that is, he is necessarily different from what he is or rather was at home, in the culture and time of his origin. A proper guest would always conduct himself differently in his new environment from what he was or how he behaved at home; at the same time, the host will also be enacting a role different from that of his solitary self or that customarily assumed in his encounters with his contemporaries (or compatriots). Both host and guest become who they are in this very encounter. The encounter is the *situation* (Gadamer) out of which new meaning, new understanding, and a new significance arise in an unforeseen fashion that pays tribute to and yet changes, augments, and enriches who or what the host and guest were before the encounter. The earlier text or writer will most often have to be the guest: this entails the privilege and the responsibility for as well as the burden of interpretive decency on the later writer, that is, the host, the reader, the recipient. The situation, however, also allows the reader to consider himself the respectful guest of the foreign host culture that he approaches with consideration. Looked at it either way, the hermeneutics of hospitality is a warrant and a manifestation of the civility of the spirit.

In his comments on how to approach the Persian poets of the Middle Ages, his notes devoted to a better understanding of his *West-östlicher Divan* entitled succinctly "Besserem Verständniß," Goethe concretely adumbrated important features of a hospitable hermeneutics. He includes the translation of a letter written by the Persian ambassador at the court of St. Petersburg in 1816, which encapsulates the ethical mandate for a proper approach to a foreign culture and thus echoes Goethe's own position and practice: "Sey ein Freund der Fremden und Reisenden, denn sie sind als Mittel eines guten Rufs zu betrachten; sey gastfrey, schätze die Vorüberziehenden, hüte dich ungerecht gegen sie zu seyn. ... Ein wohldenkender Mann verbindet sich mit Fremden."[17] In these words of Mirza Aboul Hassan Khan, Goethe encounters the complement of his own injunctions concerning the reading of the other: he himself wishes to be considered a "Reisender ... dem es zum Lobe gereicht, wenn er sich der fremden Landesart mit Neigung bequemt, deren Sprachgebrauch sich anzueignen trachtet, Gesinnungen zu theilen, Sitten aufzunehmen versteht," even though he will always be recognizable as the guest by his "eignen Accent."[18] The accommodating gesture of the traveler as well as the welcoming disposition of the reader as host, that is, the historically later European reader, demands a polite openness approaching self-negation: "Wollen wir an diesen Productionen der herrlichsten Geister Theil nehmen, so müssen wir uns orientalisiren, der [mittelalterliche] Orient wird nicht zu uns herüber kommen."[19] The decorum of a proper hermeneutic host also mandates that he refrain from appropriation through misplaced comparisons of the other with his own culture: "Wir wissen die Dichtart der Orientalen zu schätzen, wir gestehen ihnen die größten Vorzüge zu, aber man vergleiche sie mit sich selbst, man ehre sie in ihrem eigenen Kreise, und vergesse doch dabey daß es Griechen und Römer gegeben."[20] Approached thus politely, the culturally remote and distant past will help renew the present of the host culture, the culture of the reader: "Wer den Dichter will verstehen / Muß in Dichters Lande gehen; / Er im Orient sich freue / Daß das Alte sey das Neue."[21] Goethe, we realize, can see himself in the situation of the hermeneutics of hospitality both as host and as guest, as traveler; in each case, however, his interpretive conduct is guided by an open-minded, an unprejudiced civility that allows the other author or text to reveal himself or itself freely and in those new and unforeseen dimensions encouraged by the hospitable environment of reception, so that "das Alte sey das Neue."

---

[17]Goethe, "Besserem Verständniß," 172–3. "Be a friend to strangers and travelers, for they are to be considered a means to acquire a good name. Be hospitable, respect those passing by, beware of being unjust to them. ... A well-meaning man obliges foreigners." Translation by Martin Bidney, http://www.katharinamommsen.org.

[18]Ibid., 130. "a traveler who will be worth hearing if he eagerly assimilates the ways of life of a strange country, tries to appropriate its forms of speech, and learns how to share views and comprehend customs"; "he still continues to be identifiable as a foreigner because of a distinctive accent" (trans. Bidney).

[19]Ibid., 187. "If we want to acquire an insight into all these works of splendid spirits, then we will have to Orientalize ourselves; the Orient will not come to meet us" (trans. Bidney).

[20]Ibid., 189. "We are able to appreciate the poetic art of the Orientals; we see in them the highest merits. But they should be compared with each other. We must honor them in their own right by forgetting that there once were Greeks and Romans" (trans. Bidney).

[21]Ibid., 250. "If the poet you would know, / To the poet's country go. / In the Orient it's true / What is old is what is new" (trans. Bidney).

Emerson reveals his own vision of a hermeneutics of hospitality not only in the implied strategies of his many concrete readings of major works of European and Asian cultures; he articulates the underlying philosophical assumptions in the introductory treatise "The Uses of Great Men" in his 1850 volume *Representative Men*, and he offers a comprehensive proto-phenomenological analysis of hermeneutics in the 1841 essay "Friendship," which, even though ostensibly devoted to an interpretation of human intimacy at its highest and most refined, does indeed provide us with a profound exploration of the structural and strategic properties of encounters with the other, be that so-called other a human being or a work of art. Like Goethe, Emerson investigates the dynamics of welcoming and being welcomed by the other—the seemingly remote, the alien, the historically earlier person or text—and the manifold ways in which the situation of encounter changes the participants in and through their mutually hospitable accommodation.

In "The Uses of Great Men," Emerson early on offers a prime example of his characteristic strategy of thinking through a problem by way of juxtaposing seemingly mutually exclusive statements in a rapid and ungrounded reversal in order to avoid any inadequate dogmatization that would be inappropriate for his world of Heraclitean flow and openness. The interest that should guide our readings and interpretations, our hermeneutic practice, is described in two ways. We read and study the unfamiliar because "[o]ther men are lenses through which we read our own minds." At the same time "[e]ach man seeks those of different quality from his own, and such as are good of their kind; that is, he seeks other men, and the *otherest*."[22] The encounter with the other person, author, and work opens a new perspective on the reading self and at the same time manifests the desire to find and appreciate the radically different; Emerson's proper reader is both self-centered and altruistic with equal intensity. The hermeneutic encounter allows two to be intimate in their difference. In "Friendship" in particular, Emerson provides what one could call an existential rationale for the hermeneutics of hospitality and/or intimacy. The essay deals with the other as both person and, implicitly, as text. The encounter is supposed to begin with a positive prejudicial attitude (*Erwartungshorizont*): "Of a commended stranger ... only the good and new is heard by us. He stands to us for humanity."[23] The hospitable mindset of the reader allows the guest, the "commended stranger," to open the unforeseen, the new, as that which is always and truly and universally positive. The welcome friend, the other worldview, the foreign work or text, change, strengthen, and exhilarate the self by becoming both an intimate while yet remaining himself or itself: "The

---

[22] W IV, 11.
[23] W II, 184.

only joy I have in his being mine, is that the *not mine* is *mine.*"[24] The result of the hermeneutic encounter, arising out of a hospitable predisposition, is an agreement, a reading, an interpretation, one new meaningful text that yet attests the presence and dignity of its constituents in their difference: "There must be very two, before there can be very one."[25] Like Gadamer, Emerson sees the encounter with the other, the remote, the distant, the tradition essentially as a *Gespräch*, as a dialogue. In this dialogue the hospitable disposition issues in a possible peace in which each partner, host and guest, maintains his existential centrality by the very act of sharing it with the other who both transcends and remains himself: "There can never be deep peace between two spirits, never mutual respect, until in their dialogue each stands for the whole world."[26] The hermeneutic encounter opens a new dimension of the reader's, that is, the host's, self while welcoming, encouraging, and preserving the otherness of "*the otherest.*" The mutual agreement in a successful reading or interpretation, the peaceful consonance based on a dialogue as a hospitable encounter, paradoxically allows two worlds to coexist as one, or one whole world to show as two. Emerson thinks the basic hermeneutic situation of the encounter of two persons in a friendly dialogue, or of reader and text in the act of interpretation, as a play of identity and difference, just as Goethe, more concretely, illustrates the encounter with a seemingly remote poetic culture as both the experience of a fair-minded traveler welcomed in a foreign land and the experience of a generous host allowing the stranger to unfold his identity on his own conditions in a new historical and cultural environment. Both Goethe and Emerson explore the dynamics of the hermeneutics of hospitality as a process in which host and guest are enriched by acknowledging and appreciating a difference; this process issues in a deepening of insight into the previously unsuspected, seemingly alien reaches of their respective selves. The situation of the hermeneutics of hospitality creates the possibility of knowing oneself in the other in unprecedented ways, and it creates the possibility of allowing the other, the older, the Oriental text to co-create a new world of meaning without abandoning its previous identity and selfhood.

I would now like to address the central concern of this essay, a demonstration of the hermeneutics of hospitality at work in Emerson's encounter with, firstly, Persian poetry in general, and then, secondly, with the, for him, exemplary personality[27] and literary achievement of Sa'di. The essay "Persian Poetry" is Emerson's most comprehensive attempt to

---

[24]Ibid., 199.
[25]Ibid.
[26]Ibid., 202.
[27]It has been pointed out that, originally, Emerson had planned to include Sa'di instead of Shakespeare as the model poet in his portraits of *Representative Men*; see Robert D. Richardson, Jr., *Emerson: The Mind on Fire* (Berkeley: University of California Press, 1995), 414.

welcome the great poets of the Persian Middle Ages as guests within the
horizon of the modern vision and to respectfully enter their world. In the
beginning, Emerson pays tribute to the achievement of Joseph Freiherr von
Hammer-Purgstall as a mediator whose translations and commentaries in
German had provided him with ample material for his own English versions
of Persian poetry just as they had inspired Goethe before him.[28] The opening
characterization of the cultural differences between the West and the Orient
seems to establish a stark contrast between a world of "secular stability"[29]
and one of existential violence and intensity. True to his pervasive strategy
of constantly troping and insistently subverting any seemingly dogmatic
standpoint, Emerson then proceeds to differentiate, refine, and ultimately
transcend the simple dualistic scheme of his opening proposition. In this way
the foreign guests are progressively made to feel at home in the hermeneutic
situation of the modern age. The cultural excellence of the "Eastern nations"
is valued because of their "highly intellectual organization" and the fact that
they "are exquisitely sensible to the pleasures of poetry."[30] In the context
of Emerson's table of values, the Persian poets and their culture have thus
been accorded the highest possible rank. In focusing on defining features of
Persian poetry as they reveal themselves to the generous and open-minded
reader, Emerson allows these traits to manifest themselves as salient:

> The Persians have epics and tales, but, for the most part, they affect
> short poems and epigrams. Gnomic verses, rules of life conveyed in a
> lively image addressed to the eye and contained in a single stanza, were
> always current in the East; and if the poem is long, it is only a string
> of unconnected verses. They use an inconsecutiveness quite alarming to
> Western logic.[31]

It is not too difficult to realize that in the Persians Emerson recognizes a
complement of his own stylistic preference for aphoristic and seemingly
unconnected textual units that deal with existential issues and the conduct
of life by using an intense and condensed imagistic technique. The host
identifies, or feels at home, with the guest rather than his own conventional
cultural environment when he realizes that the Persian poets, too, despise
a "foolish consistency."[32] As in the case of Emerson's retrieval of the
argumentative techniques of writing and the pre-metaphysical vision of the
Presocratics, the Persian poets in his generous reading provide a potential

---

[28] W VIII, 225.
[29] Ibid., 226.
[30] Ibid., 227.
[31] Ibid., 230–1.
[32] "Self-Reliance" W II, 58.

of renewal, of troping the established and petrified forms of seeing, writing, and thinking.

The by-far-longest part of "Persian Poetry" is devoted to Samsu'd-Din Muhammad Hafiz, "the prince of Persian poets."[33] Hafiz, for Emerson, recalls Pindar, Anacreon, Horace, and Burns and yet transcends them through "the insight of a mystic, that sometimes affords a deeper glance at Nature than belongs to either of these bards." At the same time he "accosts all topics with an easy audacity."[34] Here also, we see major concerns of the Emersonian vision emerge in the hermeneutic encounter with medieval Persia: the mystical intuition, the deep insight into nature, and a comprehensive concern with all aspects of reality. The ample quotations from Hafiz, which fill the remaining pages of the essay, are not simply illustrations or specimens; the guest within the hermeneutic situation speaks in his own voice. The sparse and interspersed comments of his host, however, continue to indicate that in the meeting of two different minds and poetic styles, the later poet or thinker is encouraged by traits that manifest his own potential and his visionary innovative desire foreshadowed in the other: Emerson uses his favorite, Heraclitean images of flux in order to characterize Hafiz, speaking of his "fluent mind," of his "large utterance" as "a river that makes its own shores" and detecting a vital "generosity of ebb and flow." Constant and ceaseless innovation is one of Hafiz's hallmarks, just as it is Emerson's basic gesture in "Circles," because Hafiz shows "a constitution to which every morrow is a new day"; as in Emerson the poetic speech of Hafiz is a metamorphosis through which the existential urges constantly pass "over into new form, at once relief and creation." Surprisingly, Emerson's Hafiz shows a critical "intellectual liberty, which is a certificate of profound thought" and which allows him to see "that the whole web of convention is the imbecility of those whom it entangles." Emerson goes so far as to welcome in Hafiz a religious truthfulness that may provoke "the accusation of irreligion"; in a triumphant summary appreciation, the predecessor poet reveals the highest goal of his reader and host and successor: "[h]is complete emancipation he communicates to the reader. ... Nothing is too high, nothing too low for his occasion. He fears nothing, he stops for nothing."[35] Emerson's Hafiz envisions a world of flux and constant innovation within which poetry provides the insight into, and creates, the constant metamorphosis.[36] He is a radical critic of the established order even in religious matters, a fearless egalitarian emancipator, a liberator, a *liberating god*—in the words of the essay "The Poet."[37] The hermeneutic

---

[33] W VIII, 231.
[34] Ibid., 232.
[35] Ibid., 235–6.
[36] Cf. W III, 34
[37] Ibid., 33, 35.

situation out of which Emerson's reading of Persian poetry in general and
of Hafiz in particular emerges both as an appreciation of "*the other-est*"
and, at the same time, as a looking at his own mind through the lens of
the other, this hermeneutic situation, structured by hospitable generosity,
makes for a dialogue, in which "each stands for the whole world."[38]

Emerson's second important and more extensive interpretation of Persian
poetry is part of the essay "The Superlative." The essay seems to imply one
of those obnoxious binary characterizations and evaluations of Western
and Eastern culture that have provided the munition for the relentless
attacks on Western orientalism by the adherents of the hermeneutics of
resentment. Sobriety and discipline seem to be the hallmark of the West,
Emerson insinuates, while an exuberant proliferation of images marks the
typical mode of expression in Oriental cultures.[39] Emerson's initial praise
of simplicity, of a plain style favored by the common people, and the
condemnation of the inflated and hyperbolic style and affectation among
the seemingly sophisticated classes and professions soon give way, however,
in his typical move of argumentative reversal, to a more balanced and
corrective vision: "The superlative is as good as the positive, if it be alive."[40]
The emphasis on vitality, or, using related favorite terms of Emerson's,
the insistence on energy and power as measure of proper and adequate
expression, prepares the reader for an appreciation of the superlative
expression in Persian poetry:

> Whilst in Western nations the superlative in conversation is tedious and
> weak, and in character is a capital defect, nature delights in showing us
> that in the East it is animated, it is pertinent, pleasing, poetic. Whilst she
> appoints us to keep within the sharp boundaries of form as the condition
> of our strength, she creates in the East the uncontrollable yearning to
> escape from limitation into the vast and boundless; to use a freedom of
> fancy which plays with all the works of nature, great or minute, galaxy
> or grain of dust, as toys and words of the mind; inculcates the tenet of a
> beatitude to be found in escape from all organization and all personality,
> and makes ecstasy and institution.[41]

---

[38] W II, 202.

[39] The abundance of daring imagery in Persian poetry is discussed thoroughly by Goethe in
"Besserem Verständniß" 184–92; hyperbole and profusion of similes and metaphors are, however,
also seen in Jean Paul's "oriental" style and yet, Goethe insists, there is "Übereinstimmung und
Differenz" (192), which make European and Persian superlatives similar in expression and
different in function. The most important (Western) academic study of Persian poetic imagery
is Annemarie Schimmel, *A Two-Colored Brocade: The Imagery of Persian Poetry* (Chapel Hill:
University of North Carolina Press, 1992).

[40] W X, 167.

[41] Ibid., 171–2.

At first sight, such a descriptive evaluation could easily support the idea of a simplistic, dichotomous, binary, and reductive opposition of Eastern and Western poetic styles in Emerson's view.[42] If we are true to the idea of a hermeneutics of hospitality, however, we easily detect that the ostensibly exclusive and essentialist characterization of Persian stylistics and mentality adumbrates features, which the host, Emerson, cherishes as his very own possibilities to transgress seemingly inescapable Western conventions, the site of his cultural conditioning. The desire "to escape from limitation" echoes the basic ethical and aesthetic mandate of Emerson's thinking so powerfully articulated in "Circles": "The only sin is limitation."[43] Similarly, the celebration of an "escape from all organization" through— paradoxically—institutionalized ecstasy recalls for us one of the concluding aphorisms of the earlier essay: "Nothing great was ever achieved without enthusiasm."[44] The gesture of the free play "with all the works of nature ... as *toys* ... of the mind" (my emphasis) quite obviously recalls the vision of rejuvenated man in the opening paragraph of the "Divinity School Address," rejuvenated man who experiences "his huge globe a toy."[45] As in "Persian Poetry" "*the otherest*" opens, reveals, affirms, and supports the creative and productive potential of the generous and open-minded hermeneutic host. Finally, Emerson's reading of the seemingly antagonistic stylistic ideals of the West and of Persia allows for the innovative symbiosis of both realms, so that the encounter with Persian poetry becomes the moment of a visionary innovation and liberation; the encounter with the seeming antagonist in matters of taste prepares the possibility to make it new:

> Meantime Nature, who loves crosses and mixtures, makes these two tendencies necessary to each other, and delights to re-enforce each peculiarity by imparting the other. The Northern genius finds itself singularly refreshed and stimulated by the breadth and the luxuriance of Eastern imagery and modes of thinking, which go to check the pedantry of our inventions and the excess of our detail. There is no writing which has more electric power to unbind and animate the torpid intellect than the bold Eastern muse.[46]

---

[42]Lawrence Buell prefers not to go beyond such a "first sight" when he argues that "Emerson does indeed repeatedly succumb to these dichotomies"; therefore, he thinks it "hard to conceive the allure of Persian poetry for Emerson except in terms of what Edward Said calls Orientalism"; Buell, *Emerson* (Cambridge, MA: Harvard University Press, 2003), 154, 153.

[43]W II, 287.

[44]Ibid., 300.

[45]W I, 119.

[46]W X, 173–4.

Like Nietzsche, who was obviously inspired by him in this as in so many other momentous particulars, Emerson thinks of transitional cultures, of hybrid phenomena, of "crosses and mixtures" as the truly productive, innovative, and therefore "unbinding," that is, emancipatory forces. The hospitable gesture in reading the foreign poetic style reveals its initially only hidden but, once it is openly recognized, truly powerful potential as an indispensable ally in the always ongoing renewal of human insight and its expression.

Of all medieval Persian poets Emerson extended the most intense, the most intimate, and the most sustained as well as the most liberally open-minded hermeneutic welcome to Sheikh Mosleho'd-Din Sa'di-ye Shirazi whose writings and character engaged his attention almost uninterruptedly for close to three decades from the early 1840s through the 1860s. Sa'di was born in Shiraz sometime between 1213 and 1219 as the son of a prominent and highly educated family. He left Shiraz possibly because of the Mongol invasion and continued his education at the Nizamiyya in Baghdad. Traditionally Sa'di's life has been divided into three periods of approximately twenty-five years each. After the first period of study, he seems to have traveled extensively. He is said to have been to Mecca at least fifteen times and to have been enslaved by the Crusaders and condemned to hard labor in Syria before he was ransomed and continued his explorations of Mesopotamia, Yemen, and parts of North Africa; finally, he turned farther East and is rumored to have reached the Punjab and Gujarat in India. The biographical reports agree that he returned to Shiraz in 1256. This is the beginning of the third and last period when his best-known works—the *Bustan* and the *Gulistan*—were completed in 1257 and 1258, respectively. The *Gulistan,* or *Rose Garden*, is a series of loosely organized exemplary narratives, essayistic meditations, and lyrical poems arranged in eight parts with headings such as "The Morals of Dervishes" (II) or "On Rules for Conduct in Life" (VIII). Ever since the first translations into Latin, French, and German in the seventeenth century, the *Gulistan* was highly regarded by prominent Western intellectuals like Herder or Franklin.[47] Emerson joins that tradition. The *Gulistan* was dedicated to Prince Sa'd b. Abi-Bakr b. Sa'd of Shiraz, whose name the poet assumed as his *takhallus*, or honorific pen-name.[48] The last, roughly thirty years of his life the venerable elder teacher (Sheikh) Sa'di spent in a monastery near Shiraz, highly respected as an intellectual, moral, and religious authority. He died in 1292 and was buried near his monastery, where his tomb is still extant.[49]

---

[47]On the early European translations, cf. Behzad, *Adam Olearius' "Persianischer Rosenthal,"* 9–17.

[48]The custom of choosing a *takhallus* is explained in Rypka, *Iranische Literaturgeschichte,* 101.

[49]My biographical sketch is indebted to Edward G. Browne, *A Literary History of Persia From Firdawsí to Sa'dí* (London: Fisher Unwin, 1906), 525–39; Henri Massé, *Essai sur le Poète Saadi* (Paris: Geuthner, 1919), 3–102; and Rypka, *Iranische Literaturgeschichte*, 241–5.

When Emerson began to read, study, and critically appreciate Sa'di, his horizon of expectations had been formed by the translations and the critical as well as biographical comments of Joseph Freiherr von Hammer-Purgstall (1818), James Ross (1823), and Karl Heinrich Graf (1846). Their summary evaluations of Sa'di's stature as a poet and intellectual may help one to understand Emerson's initial fascination with the Persian poet, and they will provide a point of departure to mark the new directions toward which his generous intellectual acceptance guided his readings as well as his critical and poetic dialogue with Sa'di. Von Hammer-Purgstall's *Geschichte der schönen Redekünste Persiens mit einer Blüthenlese aus zweyhundert persischen Dichtern* (1818) had already provided Goethe with deeper insight into Persian poetry, especially Hafiz, when he was working on the *West-östlicher Divan*. Sa'di is characterized in the introduction to the chapter "Dritter Zeitraum. Mystisches und moralisches Zeitalter. Dschelaleddin Rumi und Saadi."[50] The emphasis on the moral dimension of Sa'di's work, as distinguished from the emphasis on the mystical interiority of Rumi, is intensified by von Hammer-Purgstall's insistence that Sa'di is representative of the thirteenth century because of his "klare Besonnenheit und kältere Einbildungskraft."[51] Enlightened prudence, a sober imagination, and a moral concern with the conduct of life (cf. the eighth part of the *Gulistan*, "On Rule for Conduct in Life")—as distinguished from the intensity of true Sufi religious fervor in Rumi[52]—this, for Emerson, may have indicated that Sa'di could possibly be read as a Persian *representative man* on the model of Montaigne, as an enlightened and cosmopolitan skeptic. The Scottish translator James Ross (1759–1831) prefaced his version of the *Gulistan* with a longish introduction on "Shaikh Sadi" in 1823.[53] Emerson was thoroughly familiar with this translation and the essay, especially so since the essay was reprinted in the version of the *Gulistan* translated by Francis Gladwin for which Emerson wrote an important preface. Ross celebrates Sa'di as an "excellent moralist," "a Sufi of profound learning, or master in every branch of science, and accomplished in the polite arts" and stresses his "habitual love of seclusion" again and again compromised by the demands of "the busy world" around him; as far as his conduct is concerned Ross likes to believe

---

[50]Joseph Freiherr Von Hammer-Purgstall, *Geschichte der schönen Redekünste Persiens mit einer Blüthenlese aus zweyhundert persischen Dichtern* (Wien: Heubner und Volke, 1818), 137–220. Emerson's copy of von Hammer-Purgstall is in the Houghton Library of Harvard University.
[51]Ibid., 140.
[52]This indicates that a simple and unquestioning qualification of Sa'di as a Sufi poet does not really do him justice; cf. Buell, *Emerson*, 141. J. T. P De Bruijn in *Persian Sufi Poetry* (Richmond: Curzon Press, 1997) is therefore careful to distinguish between, on the one hand, thematic and formal elements of court poetry and the secular epic in Sa'di and, on the other, "the ethics of [a] moderate kind of mysticism Sa'di adhered to" (113–14).
[53]Sa'di, *Gulistan or Flower-Garden*, trans. James Ross (1823; London: Walter Scott Publishing, 1840), 1–58.

that, other than some Persian poets of the same age, Sa'di "was habitually temperate, sober, and chaste." Finally, and importantly, he is seen as a model of literary self-reliance: "he is a mannerist *sui generis*; not as implying servile imitation of any preceding admired model in Persian, but as constantly recurring to a manner of deliverance peculiarly his own."[54] The defining moral sense, the comprehensive learning, the oscillation between society and solitude, the sobriety (all of which Emerson had celebrated in "The Poet") and, above all, the radical refusal of imitation or indebtedness to precedent, these traits of Sa'di in Ross's interpretation certainly helped to shape a positive predisposition in Emerson. Karl Heinrich Graf, in the "Vorrede" to his 1846 German translation of the *Gulistan*, adds an interesting facet to the general appreciations of Sa'di that Emerson encountered. Graf shows that Sa'di's religious disposition makes him critical of all "Werkheiligkeit," which he severely condemns in order to emphasize the true piety that rests on faith and hope alone.[55] Graf supports this comment by quotations which leave no doubt that Sa'di advances a position which the Christian Protestant tradition could not but welcome. Sa'di's version of the emphasis on *sola fides* as the only true means of approaching the possible dispensation of divine grace must have appealed to the latter-day Protestant in Emerson.

It is interesting to note how these early general characterizations of Sa'di the person and his oeuvre have continued to inform major Western criticism with only a few variations here and there. A brief look at selected responses to Sa'di in the twentieth century helps one understand how Emerson's own hermeneutic encounter was prepared by preconceptions still, to a degree, valid today, and it makes one see how Emerson subtly differentiated and often went far beyond these preconceptions by means of his hospitable and critical openness to the appeal both of the overly familiar and of the sometimes only seemingly remote and alien in Sa'di. Edward G. Browne, in volume 2 of his influential literary history of Persia (1906), notes "the astute, half-pious, half worldly side" in Sa'di and comments that the pious sentiments are ultimately "eminently practical" and "devoid of … visionary quality." This image of the prudent and pragmatic moralist is not far from von Hammer-Purgstall's earlier judgment. In stressing that Sa'di's popularity "lies not in his consistency but in his catholicity,"[56] Browne adds an observation that hints at that stylistic similarity to Emerson with his preference for the aphoristic and gnomic expression that has already been noted above. Henri Massé in his comprehensive study emphasizes, as does Ross, the existential, social, and aesthetic values of independence, self-reliance, and liberty that would have necessarily intrigued Emerson: "La liberté, c'est ce qui, semble-t-il, sert de base à la morale sociale de Saadi:

---

[54]Ibid., 2, 6, 11, 25, 39.
[55]*Moslicheddin Sadi's Rosengarten*, trans. Graf (Leipzig: Brockhaus, 1846), XX.
[56]Browne, *Literary History of Persia*, 526, 532.

il faut, pour vivre heureux, travailler sans cesse à se rendre indépendant, non seulement de soi-même, mais des autres." Finally, in a sweeping generalization, Massé affirms the Western critical consensus concerning the pragmatic dimension of Sa'di's total philosophical and religious outlook: "Sa morale religieuse, de même que sa morale sociale, reste en somme essentiellement pratique."[57] Rypka, in his *Iranische Literaturgeschichte* (1955/59), accentuates the commonsense morality and a trace of skepticism, and thus joins the chorus of the voices who celebrate the practical wisdom of the Persian poet.[58] When, in his 1965 introduction to Edward Rehatsek's translation of the *Gulistan*, G. M. Wickens insists that "no Persian writer is more humanistic and humane than Shaikh Sa'di,"[59] this familiar vision with its early antecedents in von Hammer-Purgstall, Ross, and Graf marks what for Emerson as reader had from the very beginning defined the Montaigne-like fascination of his guest from thirteenth-century Shiraz.

Emerson's responses to Sa'di in his journals and published works are wide-ranging, persistent, varied, and they reveal a readiness to allow the Persian poet to show a multifaceted potential of inspiring his reader with new possibilities in thinking and writing. In 1843 Emerson excerpted a series of lengthy quotations from Ross's 1823 translation of the *Gulistan*, which, he gleefully notes, show "many traits which comport with the portrait I drew."[60] The portrait is, of course, the great poem "Saadi," which I will discuss toward the end of my considerations. *Notebook Orientalist* contains numerous translations of Sa'di's poetry from the German of von Hammer-Purgstall,[61] and *The Poetry Notebooks of Ralph Waldo Emerson* list no fewer than fifteen entries of frequently great length that prepare the poems devoted to the *persona* of Sa'di, that is, "Saadi" and "Fragments on the Poet and the Poetic Gift."[62] A major series of significant responses to Sa'di are found in the Notebook for 1863 when Emerson was preparing his "Preface" for the new edition of the *Gulistan*.[63] The sheer number of quotations and comments, translations, and transformations of Sa'di's writings in Emerson's notebooks indicates that the poet became for him one of "the scholar[s] of the first age,"[64] a representative of persistently innovative and innovating

---

[57]Massé, *Saadi*, 139, 194.
[58]Rypka, *Iranische Literaturgeschichte*, 243, 245.
[59]G. M. Wickens, "Introduction," *The Gulistan or Rose Garden of Sa'di*, ed. W. G. Archer, trans. Edward Rehatsek (New York: Putnam, 1965), 38.
[60]*JMN* IX, 37.
[61]*The Topical Notebooks of Ralph Waldo Emerson*, ed. Ralph H. Orth et al. (Columbia: University of Missouri Press, 1993), vol. II, 37–141. A biographical sketch of Sa'di is on p. 123.
[62]*The Poetry Notebooks of Ralph Waldo Emerson*, ed. Ralph H. Orth et al. (Columbia: University of Missouri Press, 1986), *passim*.
[63]*JMN* XV, 383–5, 396–7.
[64]"The American Scholar" *W* I, 89.

and invigorating wisdom. In 1843 he noted: "Like Homer and Dante & Chaucer, Saadi possessed a great advantage over poets of cultivated times in being the representative of learning & thought to his countrymen."[65] Emerson later used this comment on Sa'di in his portrait of Shakespeare in *Representative Men*. Sa'di is thus generously interpreted in two ways: as a global cultural presence of universal significance, like Shakespeare as a poet's poet, and at the same time as the teacher of his countrymen. Sa'di's poetry, in Emerson's hospitable reading, is always available as inspiration in and for the present; nevertheless, it also remains historically situated and honored and respected in the context of his proper culture. Interestingly, Emerson's view is partially echoed by Henry David Thoreau in a long and subtle meditation on identity and difference of reader and text in a journal entry for August 8, 1850. Thoreau, other than Emerson, however, discards the historically and culturally specific dimension of Sa'di. He appropriates, whereas Emerson allows for both contemporaneity and historical distance: "I know, for instance, that Sadi entertained once identically the same thought that I do, and thereafter I can find no essential difference between Sadi and myself. He is not Persian, he is not ancient, he is not strange to me."[66]

Emerson's published works display a multitude of allusions to Sa'di. A brief and slightly selective *tour d'horizon* of these often epigrammatic, aphoristic, and sometimes merely illustrative comments indicates clearly that Emerson does not subsume Sa'di under one single preconceived notion. In this respect, his hospitable hermeneutic method transcends the horizon of expectations and possible readings which von Hammer-Purgstall, Ross, and Graf had provided for him and which, as we saw, to a certain degree continues to shape major twentieth-century interpretive responses to Sa'di. The breadth of readings that Emerson's responses allow is manifested impressively when Sa'di, on the one hand, in "Swedenborg; or the Mystic" is shown as the rapt mystic "who, in his vision, designed to fill his lap with the celestial flowers, as presents for his friends" and then lost himself in the divine fragrance, and, on the other hand, is celebrated as true bard of "firm and cheerful temper," as a veritable worldly representative of the *gaya scienza* in "Shakspeare; or, the Poet."[67] Quite differently, the essay on "Beauty" finds in Sa'di a master of caricature and satire who excels in graphic descriptions of human deformity.[68] In the essay "Books" Sa'di is appreciated as an elegant literary conversationalist and *causeur* in the company of Boswell, Hazlitt, or Eckermann's conversations with Goethe.[69] In "Poetry and Imagination,"

---

[65] *JMN* IX, 38.
[66] *The Journal of Henry David Thoreau*, ed. Bradford Torrey and Francis H. Allen (Boston: Houghton, Mifflin, 1906), vol. IV, 290.
[67] W IV, 137, 206.
[68] W VI, 283.
[69] W VII, 199.

Sa'di is seen as one of the bards "who shall sing all our old ideas out of our heads, and new ones in" because he is the master of verse "which the angels testified 'met the approbation of Allah in Heaven.'"[70] And, ultimately, of course, Sa'di is also the wise moral counsel for Emerson, the teacher of proper social conduct, a Persian Montaigne, as when he quotes him in his "Lecture on the Fugitive Slave Law": "The Persian Saadi said: 'Beware of hurting the orphan. When the orphan sets a-crying, the throne of the Almighty is rocked from side to side.'"[71] The scope of Emerson's hermeneutic hospitality transcends the critically established frame; Emerson allows the potential of Sa'di's achievement a free play of possibilities of expression that range from visionary and mystical rapture to the joyful science of poetic celebration to the sobriety and enlightened sincerity of socially responsible criticism. Sa'di's work is thus not subordinated to any single and overriding "agenda" or concern of Emerson, the reader. The hermeneutic host respects and welcomes, encourages, and takes pride in the seemingly unlimited creative potential that continues to fascinate in his poetic guest.

Emerson's most intimate and significant encounter with and engagement of Sa'di's achievement is found, however, in his preface to the 1865 translation of the *Gulistan* by Gladwin[72] and in the poems in which the *persona* of Sa'di is invited to enact and unfold its potential of suggestion and inspiration for the modern mind. Emerson's preface[73] begins with a critical look at the common prejudices among Western readers that make a proper appreciation of Oriental poetry difficult or, for some, even impossible: "At first sight, the Oriental rhetoric does not please our Western taste." He elaborates: "I do not know but, at the first encounter, many readers take also an impression of tawdry rhetoric, an exaggeration, and a taste for scarlet, running to the borders of the negrofine,—or, if not, yet a pushing of the luxury of ear and eye where it does not belong."[74] But then, in one of his characteristic argumentative moves, Emerson undermines these initial and superficial evaluations: "These blemishes disappear or diminish on better acquaintance. Where there is real merit, we are soon reconciled to differences of taste. The charge of monotony lies more against the numerous Western imitations than against the Persians themselves"; and he adds pointedly: "The monotonies which we accuse, accuse our own."[75] The portrait of Sa'di

---

[70] W VIII, 65.

[71] W XI, 222.

[72] "Preface," *The Gulistan or Rose Garden. By Musle-Huddeen Sheik Saadi, of Shiraz,* trans. Francis Gladwin (Boston: Ticknor and Fields, 1865), III–XV.

[73] Lawrence Buell's important study of Emerson unfortunately insinuates that the essay "Persian Poetry" and the 1865 preface to the *Gulistan* are identical; see Buell, *Emerson,* 151.

[74] "Preface," IV–V.

[75] Ibid., V, VII.

at the center of the essay begins with a celebration of his versatility and profundity:

> Saadi exhibits perpetual variety of situation and incident, and an equal depth of experience with Cardinal de Retz in Paris, or Doctor Johnson in London. He finds room on his narrow canvas for the extremes of lot the play of motives, the rule of destiny, the lesson of morals, and the portraits of great men.[76]

The Persian poet displays a multiplicity of concerns under Emerson's benevolently interested gaze that recall not only features prominent in the appreciations of von Hammer-Purgstall or Ross, like a soberly enlightened empirical cultural criticism, but in the *Gulistan* Emerson also discovers themes that foreshadow or correspond to his own far-flung literary and philosophical interests: the study of social difference, the problem of fate, the foundational concern with the moral sentiment, or the study of great, or representative men. In a second step, Emerson adds Sa'di's vision of the pervasive and defining existential mood to the general description of his thematic interests:

> Saadi, though he has not the lyric flights of Hafiz, has wit, practical sense, and just moral sentiments. He has the instinct to teach, and from every occurrence must draw the moral, like Franklin. He is the poet of friendship, love, self-devotion, and serenity. There is a uniform force in his page, and, conspicuously, a tone of cheerfulness, which has almost made his name a synonyme [*sic*] for this grace. The word *Saadi* means *fortunate*. In him the trait is no result of levity, much less of convivial habit, but first of a happy nature, to which victory is habitual, easily shedding mishaps, with sensibility to pleasure, and with resources against pain. But it also results from the habitual perception of the beneficent laws that control the world. He inspires in the reader a good hope. What a contrast between the cynical tone of Byron and the benevolent wisdom of Saadi![77]

Again Emerson begins with the frame of expectations he shares with his contemporaries who emphasize the didactic and moralistic aspect of so many of Sa'di's sketches in the *Gulistan*. But then he asserts his own more generous vision, which allows traits in Sa'di to come forth which are rarely addressed by the translators and the critics: the benevolent ease and serenity, which Emerson stresses so strongly, are dimensions of his own existential

---

[76]Ibid., V.
[77]Ibid., VII–VIII.

disposition; Nietzsche, for example, was acutely aware of and deeply impressed by this feature in Emerson's mental constitution.[78] An elective affinity between Emerson and Sa'di manifests itself, which tempts me to say that Emerson found in Sa'di another practitioner of the *gay science*.

Sa'di, however, is appreciated by Emerson not only because of the variety of his literary and social interests and because of the serene mood that permeates his vision; he also excels—for his time and culture—as "the chief authority on religion."[79] Even though Sa'di often shows deference to the religious establishment and, like Hafiz, appears to accept the fatalistic implications of the Quran, he nevertheless seems not to be bound and hampered by the dogmatic implications of Islamic orthodoxy: "the Sheikh's mantle sits loosely on Saadi's shoulders, and I find in him a pure theism. He asserts the universality of moral laws, and the perpetual retributions. He celebrates the omnipotence of the virtuous soul."[80] The critical distance from the strict interpretation and practice of Islam, which characterizes so many of Sa'di's sketches of inadequate dervishes or other believers, allows Emerson to find in his Persian counterpart a non-orthodox theism, an awareness of compensation and of the presence of a pervasive moral law that is able to deify the "virtuous soul."[81] Here, once again, Sa'di becomes the intimate other of Emerson himself.

A final major point in Emerson's thorough analysis is devoted to Sa'di's style:

> Wonderful is the inconsecutiveness of the Persian poets. European criticism finds that the unity of a beautiful whole is everywhere wanting. Not only the story is short, but no two sentences are joined. ... 'Tis sand without lime,—as if the neighboring desert had *saharized* the mind. ... No topic is too remote for their rapid succession. The Ghaselle or Kassida is a chapter of proverbs, or proverbs unchaptered, unthreaded beads of all colors, sizes, and values.[82]

Emerson here repeats and deepens an observation he had already made in his essay "Persian Poetry." The prominence of very short stories, the epigrammatic concision, the loosely aphoristic brilliance, the rich profusion of disjointed comments, observations, and insights, all these do indeed wonderfully evoke the rhetorical style of Sa'di, especially in the *Gulistan*, and one may without effort apply the very same descriptive analysis to

---

[78]*Götzen-Dämmerung, KSA* 6, 120: "Emerson hat jene gütige und geistreiche Heiterkeit, welche allen Ernst entmuthigt ..." For "Nietzsche's Emerson," see Chapter 8 in this book.
[79]"Preface," IX.
[80]Ibid., X.
[81]Ibid.
[82]Ibid., XI.

Emerson's own style in his essays and, as we will see, also in some of his poems. Sa'di parallels and re-enforces, he supports and justifies tendencies and preferences in Emerson's own innovative approach to writing.

Sa'di becomes for Emerson a primary model and inspiration that emerges from the past and the distant East: "It is provincial to ignore [him]."[83] Sa'di belongs to world literature in Goethe's sense of the term. But for Emerson's hospitable cosmopolitanism, a mere respectful relegation of the poet into the archives of the so-called cultural memory would be dolefully insufficient. Reading Sa'di, "[w]e pass into a new landscape, new costume, new religion, new manners and customs, under which humanity nestles very comfortably at Shiraz and Mecca, with good appetite, and with moral and intellectual results that correspond, point for point, with ours at New York and London."[84] Reading Sa'di with a cosmopolitan open-mindedness, then, reveals a world that is as inspiringly new as the so-called New World: "Through his Persian dialect he speaks to all nations, and, like Homer, Shakespeare, Cervantes, and Montaigne, is perpetually modern."[85] The characteristic modernist gesture of retrieving the earliest beginnings of globally significant cultures as an arsenal with the potential of future innovation, this gesture assures, in Emerson's reading, the dignity of contemporaneity for Sa'di, and the promise of future enriching hermeneutic encounters with the Persian poet.

Two longer poems by Emerson are devoted to Sa'di as representative poet: "Saadi" and "Fragments of the Poet and the Poetic Gift." In these major creative responses, Emerson's guest from medieval Persia is celebrated as the emissary of one of the world's great literary cultures and, at the same time, as a herald of future, of modern creativity in the Emersonian sense. I would like to consider these poems as the culminating achievement of Emerson's hermeneutics of hospitality. Again, as in the case of the essays on Sa'di and Persia, my main focus will be on Emerson's reading rather than on Sa'di's texts.

The poet in his later years, the derwish Sa'di in his seclusion, the revered sage who resides in his monastery outside Shiraz, impresses Emerson as the incarnation of the quintessential poet in "Saadi." Society and solitude, the intimate relation and tension of these terms, which provided the title for volume VII of the *Works*, inform Emerson's awareness of the continuing, the model significance of the last phase of Sa'di's life. The first stanzas evoke the world of herds of animals, of groups of trees, of human collectives, of sociable communal life—and, in a kind of refrain, they insist: "But the poet dwells alone," "Wise Saadi dwells alone," "Good Saadi dwells

---

[83]Ibid., VI.
[84]Ibid., VII.
[85]Ibid., VIII.

alone."[86] Paradoxically, however, it is this very seclusion that ensures the social, the communal function of the poet and his poetry: "Yet Saadi loved the race of men,– / No churl, immured in cave or den; / In bower and hall / He wants them all, / Nor can dispense / With Persia for his audience"[87] True to the biographical reports and Sa'di's portraits of himself in the *Gulistan*, the poet is not an ascetic, and Emerson's friendly recreation contrasts the benevolent sage with the life-denying "[s]ad-eyed Fakirs":

> For Saadi sat in the sun,
> And thanks was his contrition;
> For haircloth and for bloody whips,
> Had active hands and smiling lips;
> And yet his rune he rightly read,
> And to his folk his message sped.
> Sunshine in his heart transferred
> Lighted each transparent word,
> And well could honoring Persia learn
> What Saadi wished to say ...[88]

Sa'di is appreciated and welcomed as the type of the wise and influential public intellectual, as *praeceptor Persiae* ("honoring Persia"); and while Emerson in this passage echoes the image of the poet created by himself and affirmed by successors like Jami in the fifteenth century, the poetic transformation also projects a poet of the future as a "professor of gay science," or, in Nietzsche's terms, echoing the Emersonian interpretation, a Zarathustra-like prophet of the "schenkende Tugend" ("bestowing virtue"). Sa'di, the poet of the past with an inexhaustible future opened in the hospitable reading of Emerson, this Sa'di goes playfully beyond all limitations of philosophical and theological systems ("Let theist, atheist, pantheist, / Define and wrangle how they list"); the post- or a-metaphysical thinker as poet is a veritable deconstructionist ("Fierce conserver, fierce destroyer"), an exuberant practitioner of *die fröhliche Wissenschaft*: "joy-giver and enjoyer."[89] In Sa'di's affirmative catholicity, of which Browne speaks in his *Literary History of Persia*,[90] Emerson finds the promise of a poetry that liberates because still "Man in man is imprisoned."[91] The poet as liberator reveals the presence of the divine in common and even in down-trodden humanity: "the Pariah hind / Admits thee to the perfect mind."[92] And

---

[86]Ibid., 114, 114, 115.
[87]Ibid., 114.
[88]Ibid., 116.
[89]Ibid., 117.
[90]Browne, *Literary History of Persia*, 532.
[91]W IX, 117.
[92]Ibid., 119.

lastly, the poet with his unlimited sympathy for the natural world, which so profusely endowed Sa'di with images and metaphors, this poet of nature is the present and future sole center of the meaning of the cosmos in its totality: "Suns rise and set in Saadi's speech!"[93] The poem benevolently recreates major features of the historical personality and the oeuvre of Sa'di and then allows these traits to show as productive, as creative, as prophetic of modern or future poetry as Emerson saw it. The power of the poet resides both in his historical achievement and in the unlimited potential of his future transformations in generous readings. Like Goethe's traveler in the Orient, however, Emerson has a double role in this poem. He is the appreciative voice of the present welcoming the guest from afar in his re-creation, but he might also be said to assume the garb of the predecessor poet in his remote culture. In this way, Emerson moves into the margins, away from his own culture, like the aged Sa'di, and in so doing, in transgressing the boundaries of his own social environment and cultural tradition, he becomes central as an innovator and *praeceptor Americae*.

"Fragments on the Poet and the Poetic Gift" at first sight seems just that: a loose collection of random observations on basic, on universal, on modern, on necessary features of poet and poetry. The fact that Emerson here combines very early and some later poems, collected under the sober and unappealing heading of "Appendix" in volume IX of the *Works*, may have contributed to the relative neglect of the "Fragments." A closer look, however, as always in Emerson, is highly rewarding. The "Fragments" begin with five numbered poems, all of which are devoted to an evocation of Sa'di; the following thirty-five poems or verse fragments are unnumbered. The poem that immediately follows number V of the Sa'di poems proper could easily be read as another poem dealing with the Persian poet or as the first of the verses that address an unidentified poet or are articulated by an unnamed poetic voice.[94] The Sa'di poems elegantly and impressively recapitulate the themes and motifs of "Saadi": the solitary existence of the poet, his marginal status and his national reputation, the anti-orthodox religious disposition, the egalitarian gestures, the cosmic reach of the poet's vision, and the joyful rendition of deep wisdom. Occasionally Emerson allows his guest to almost speak for himself, as in poem III when he transcribes Sa'di's celebrated appreciation of Hassan the camel-driver, who, in his devotion to his humble profession, impressed him more than all of Timur's military fame.[95] The first poem that follows the Sa'di poems continues to elaborate the motif of the poet as the only authentic witness of the natural world. From here on the seemingly fragmentary lyrical meditations on poetry

[93]Ibid., 118.
[94]W IX, 268.
[95]Ibid., 265–6.

and the poet can no longer be attributed to an identifiable historical or contemporary individual. What happens, then, in the course of "Fragments" is this: the boundaries of the *persona* of Sa'di slowly dissolve and merge with an (as-yet) anonymous poetic voice or presence that continues the open-ended work of creating and transforming meaning, the work of the endless metamorphosis of reality through human speech. "Fragments" very carefully documents what I have tried to work out as the fundamental strategy of Emerson's hermeneutics of hospitality: the guest is allowed to show himself at his best in the light of benevolent modern attention; in this light the inexhaustible potential of poetic meaning opens and adumbrates a future dimly emerging in outlines of potential significance. "Fragments" also pays tribute to Sa'di's stylistic strategy, especially in the *Gulistan*, namely that characteristic mode of thinking and writing which Emerson celebrated as the wonderful "inconsecutiveness of the Persian poets" in his "Preface." This "inconsecutiveness" is, of course, also Emerson's; it is the very quintessence of the essayistic and aphoristic mode.

"Fragments on the Poet and the Poetic Gift" is a masterful verse essay: it looks toward Sa'di as continuing inspiration and it manifests Emerson's present practice, while it generously acknowledges the inspiration of his Persian guest as a herald of the future. This poem substantiates what the essay "Friendship" had to say about the intimate encounter in the existentially and culturally significant situation of a hermeneutics of hospitality: "A friend is Janus-faced; he looks to the past and the future. He is the child of all my foregoing hours, the prophet of those to come, and the harbinger of a greater friend."[96] Sa'di the poet, Sa'di's work, is such a friend for Emerson; and in "Fragments" it becomes manifest what should be true for all our generous readings of the other person, the other work: "There must be very two, before there can be very one."[97]

---

[96] W II, 204.
[97] Ibid., 199.

# 5

# Resisting Hegel

Few genuine alternatives existed for a thinker of the first half of the nineteenth century who was faced by the totalizing historical and ontological system of Hegel's philosophy and who felt the necessity to escape that system's deterministic constraints imposed by its evolutionary and relentlessly dialectical unfolding of the absolute on its way toward an inevitable and full realization of its self-awareness in philosophical conceptualization. Like Marx, he could question the ontological premise of the system and put it back on its feet in the concretely experienced and enacted material reality of social conflict and resolutions, or he could, like Kierkegaard, invert the very concept of the *idea* as the unity of the finite and the infinite and insist that it is not the absolute, the *Weltgeist*, but rather radically individualized existence where that unity finds its ultimate realization.

I would like to discuss a—as I see it—momentous third possibility in the history of thinking, namely, the emergence of a post-metaphysical and anti-Hegelian mode of thought in Ralph Waldo Emerson, who provided the basis and the point of departure for the well-known later, truly modern and comprehensive, challenges to traditional Western metaphysics advanced by Nietzsche. Nietzsche's central philosophical intuitions like the overman, the will to power, and the eternal return of the same are most adequately understood as re-readings of originally Emersonian thought.[1] The emergence of a post-metaphysical mode of thought in Emerson may best be described in terms of a return, the return *to* the—or *of* the—(almost) lost beginnings of pre-European thinking in the fragments of the Presocratics, especially of Heraclitus.[2] In Emerson's return to the earliest documents of Western thinking the relatively pervasive German presence in American thought of

---

[1] See Chapter 8, "Nietzsche's Emerson," in this book, as well as my essay "Emerson and Nietzsche: 1862–1874," in *Religion and Philosophy in the United States of America*, vol I, ed. Peter Freese (Essen: Die Blaue Eule, 1987), 267–87.
[2] See Chapter 1, "Emerson among the Presocratics," in this book.

the Transcendentalist era makes itself, once again, felt in a way that has so far been almost completely overlooked—because, so it seems, the dedication to the art of painstaking philological attention to significant detail has more and more, sadly, receded into the background of our professional efforts at textual explication. This is my thesis: Emerson's own, his original, initial, and foundational non-metaphysical, and therefore anti-Hegelian, intuition was greatly supported, re-enforced, and refined by his encounter *with*, his thorough reading *of The History of Ancient Philosophy* by Heinrich Ritter.[3] Ritter's interpretation of Heraclitus and of the Presocratic unfolding of the history of Greek thinking served as a catalyst for Emerson in his project of finding a mode of both thinking and writing that would escape the intellectually totalizing coercions of the Hegelian system as the culmination point of Western metaphysical thought.

I would like to pause here ever so briefly and answer two subsidiary questions: firstly, how do I know this? And secondly, who was Heinrich Ritter, the German catalyst in Emerson's momentous and revolutionary re-interpretation of the historical progression of thinking? The important and catalytic connection between Ritter, Emerson, and Heraclitus is factually well documented. In their painstakingly detailed notes, the editors of the Harvard edition of *The Collected Works of Ralph Waldo Emerson*, of *The Journals and Miscellaneous Notebooks*, and of *The Topical Notebooks* have exhaustively identified the relatively numerous references to and quotations from Ritter's *History*. So far, however, no critic has discussed the importance and the impact of Ritter's work for Emerson's reading of the Presocratics and for his views of the beginning and the pattern of the unfolding of the history of thinking. While the impact of Emerson's thorough early reading of Joseph Marie de Gérando's *Histoire Comparée des Systèmes de Philosophie* (1822–23) and his access to early Greek thinking on the basis of his extensive study of Plutarch have received proper and deserved attention,[4] Ritter's role in the formation of Emerson's thinking has been overlooked. When one examines the references to and quotations from Ritter, both more general and very specific signs or symptoms of the effect of his work on Emerson become visible.

When Emerson begins his in-depth reading of Ritter's *History of Ancient Philosophy* in the English translation in four volumes that came out in 1838 (there are indications that he may have known the German version of 1829),

---

[3]Heinrich Ritter, *The History of Ancient Philosophy*, trans. Alexander J. W. Morrison, 4 vols. (1829–34; Oxford: Talboys, 1838–46).

[4]On de Gérando and Emerson, see Robert D. Richardson, *Emerson: The Mind on Fire* (Berkeley: University of California Press, 1995), 102–5; Edmund G. Berry, *Emerson's Plutarch* (Cambridge, MA: Harvard University Press, 1961).

his argumentative style changes radically: the semblance of a systematically reasoned unfolding of an argument that so deceptively characterizes *Nature* in 1836, and to a lesser degree also "The American Scholar" (1837) and the "Divinity School Address" (1838), this argumentative surface structure disappears and the characteristically disjointed, aphoristic style, the Heraclitean gestures of his mature work with its often irritating and abrupt changes of emphasis and point of view begin to prevail; we see this, for example, in "Literary Ethics," in "The Method of Nature," and above all in his 1841 *Essays*. In 1838 and 1839, Emerson extensively copies what he thinks of as sayings of Heraclitus from chapter VI in volume I of Ritter's *The History of Ancient Philosophy*. In the course of this note-taking, two of Ritter's key concepts find their way into the *Journals and Miscellaneous Notebooks* and the published works, concepts not used before: one is *inchoation* (in the sense of: beginning, inception or G. Beginn, Anfang, Anhub) and the other is *transition*. These concepts Emerson (wrongly but not without plausibility) believes to be genuine Heraclitean terms—they will become central for the articulation of his own most fundamental vision and philosophical belief. Last, and most certainly not least, Emerson's view and understanding of the history of philosophy itself begins to be articulated in ways that are indebted both to Ritter's thirty-seven-page "Introduction" to his *History* and to Ritter's interpretation of Heraclitus to which Emerson paid such close attention.

Who was Heinrich Ritter? Born in 1791 in Zerbst in the province of Anhalt, Ritter was a disciple of Schleiermacher's. After his doctorate from Halle and his Habilitation in Berlin in 1817, he began to publish his *magnum opus*, the massive twelve-volume *Geschichte der Philosophie*, in 1829, a highly regarded standard work of the nineteenth century completed in 1853, which was superseded only by Eduard Zeller's philologically more meticulous *Die Philosophie der Griechen in ihrer geschichtlichen Entwicklung* (1856–68). The first four volumes of Ritter's *History* were dedicated to the *Geschichte alter Zeit*; this is the work that Emerson studied in depth. Beginning in 1824, Ritter was *ausserordentlicher Professor* in Berlin during Hegel's tenure there, but he failed in his application for Hegel's chair after the latter's death in 1831. When one considers Ritter's decidedly un- or even anti-Hegelian view of the dynamics of the history of philosophy, this comes as no surprise. Ritter went on to professorships in Kiel (1833) and finally Göttingen (1837). He died in 1869.

Let me return to the momentous matter of resisting Hegel and his views of history, of Being, and of thinking, and thus abandoning almost 2,300 years of European metaphysics. I already indicated that Ritter introduced two terms that became central vehicles in Emerson's revolutionary thinking: *inchoation* and *transition*. With only slight variations Emerson used the following aphorism three times in his *Journals* and in the *Notebooks*: "Ever

& forever Heraclitus is justified who called the world an eternal inchoation."[5] Actually Heraclitus never wrote or said anything of the kind. Emerson keeps referring to a comment by Ritter on the idea of a "perfect force of life" in Heraclitus, a force that tends to overpower all individual entities:

> Before this force of perfect life nothing naturally can have persistence; it is the true, the ever-permanent; but, as the force of perfect vitality, it is without hinderance [sic] to its activity, so that nothing which it forms continues, but all is constantly in inchoation. Therefore it was, that to the mind of Heraclitus the eternal life of fire absorbs all persistence of individual phenomena, and of each individual thing; that with him, according to ancient testimony, "all is and is not; for though it does in truth come into being, yet it forthwith ceases to be;" and according to him, "all is in motion;" and he denied all rest and quietude.[6]

Emerson obviously appreciated the vitalistic dynamism that Ritter ascribed to Heraclitus and the idea that all beings, all entities tend to constantly overcome themselves in an endless process. In his essay "Circles," Emerson would elaborate this idea of an unceasing proliferation of destructive and reconstructive transformations of beings and meanings, an idea that clearly and distinctly foreshadows Nietzsche's interpretation of all processes as acts or events of (self-)overpowering. Emerson plausibly read "all is constantly in inchoation" not just as a comment by Ritter but as an authentic extension of Heraclitus's "all is and is not."

In his published work, Emerson used the term only once, but he used it for a central, for a truly axiomatic statement on the nature of nature, on the Being of natural beings in his 1841 lecture "The Method of Nature": "Its permanence," Emerson says of *natura naturans*, "is a perpetual inchoation."[7] The temporal dimension and extension of Being, of the world, of nature, does not primarily show as a meliorative and ascending tendency; rather, Being as time is both continuous and iterative. With the introduction of the term and vision of a perpetual inchoation, the post-Socratic edifice of metaphysics collapses: if all Being begins again and again, if all things exist iteratively and not in a dialectically evolutionary fashion, if the world *has* no beginning, but essentially *is* a beginning or a multitude

---

[5] *JMN* VII, 457. In *JMN* VI, 379, a variant of this saying is placed among a series of aphorisms by Heraclitus excerpted from Ritter: "All is, and is not. [...] (i.e. All is constantly in inchoation.)"; in *The Topical Notebooks of Ralph Waldo Emerson*, vol. 2, ed. Ronald A. Bosco (Columbia: University of Missouri Press, 1993), 353, we read: "*Heraclitus* called the world an eternal inchoation."
[6] Ritter, *History* I, 236.
[7] *W* I, 190.

of beginnings, if everything comes forth again and again contingently and not on the basis of a dialectical or any other rationalistic pattern, then there is no way of finding one single word or identifying concept for the highest or for a substantially underlying Being, no term like the Absolute, no single thing or entity that remains self-identical, no first beginning and no ultimate *telos* of either nature or history or thinking as in Hegel. In "The American Scholar," Emerson had already succinctly stated: "There is never a beginning, there is never an end, to the inexplicable continuity of this web of God, but always circular power returning into itself."[8] In "Circles," identifying true thinking with the power of fire, the symbol of the inner destructive as well as constructive dynamics of all becoming in Heraclitus, in "Circles" Emerson said dramatically: "Beware when the great God lets loose a thinker on this planet. Then all things are at risk. It is as when a conflagration has broken out in a great city, and no man knows what is safe, or where it will end."[9] This passage—which so deeply impressed Nietzsche that he quoted it in the concluding paragraph of his third *Untimely Meditation*, "Schopenhauer as Educator"—echoes the central cosmological intuition of Heraclitus as interpreted by Ritter: the world, or better: worlds exist and are experienced and *thought* as endless series of destructions by fire (*ekpyrosis* is the Greek term) followed by ever new fiery, that is, energetic and dynamic re-creations.

With the philosophical intuition of a world and of worlds and of all single beings in perpetual inchoation, Emerson had to abandon and did abandon, as we know, the search for a single, an exclusive and highest, name for an unchanging or underlying substance; he discarded the belief in enduring self-identical entities and in a first beginning and in a consummatory *telos* of history, whether in a Christian or Hegelian sense. With the help of Ritter's term *inchoation* Emerson reads the world as a relentlessly modernist event, a "beginning again and again"—as Gertrude Stein, remembering Emerson, was to define modernism. All beings, the world as a whole, and the human being are re-translated, as Karl Löwith put it in his interpretation of Nietzsche,[10] into the *nature* of all things as ceaseless change and innovation. The iterative and circular processes of Being (and of thinking Being) replace the one-directional thrust of the absolute as both *causa efficiens* and *causa finalis* of all Being. Thus, and at the same time, Emerson's vision, in the very act of becoming modern, returns to the oldest, the pre-European Heraclitean ontology of insistent and playful, of both constructive and de-structive renewal: the history of thinking in Emerson's

[8]Ibid., 86–7.
[9]W II, 288.
[10]Karl Löwith, *Nietzsches Philosophie der ewigen Wiederkehr des Gleichen* (1935; Hamburg: Meiner, 1978), 192.

reading is witness to a return of the beginning, or as Emerson once said of Anaximander: "how close is the first & the last step of philosophy."[11] Put differently, the incremental and evolutionary view of ontological and philosophical progression in the Hegelian mode, of history as a process of unceasingly adding insight onto itself in dialectic fashion, is replaced by an iterative pattern within which we may witness the possibly eternal return of the same, or, as Emerson said: "Hegel pre-exists in Proclus, and long before, in Heraclitus and Parmenides."[12] Emerson does not say, "Hegel is foreshadowed by Heraclitus," as Hegel himself maintained; rather, Emerson emphasizes that he pre-*exists*, is already and fully there as one option of thinking in Heraclitus, so that the history of philosophy does not so much progress as re-enact itself in each new and significant thinker, in constant inchoation.

The second term that testifies to the catalytic effect of Ritter in helping Emerson articulate his basic philosophical intuition more precisely is *transition*. In 1999 Jonathan Levin, in a thorough and important study of a pervasive pattern in American thinking, has given careful attention to Emerson's central "transitional dynamic."[13] Levin, however, does not mention the seminal role of Ritter for Emerson's appreciation of the concept of transition as an important heuristic tool for thinking a post-Hegelian world. In Ritter's Heraclitus interpretation, Emerson encountered the concept of transition continuously, like a leitmotif characterizing a core element and aspect of the ontological and cosmological insights of Heraclitus. Emerson read that Heraclitus "under the most opposite figures ... describes the transition from one form to another," that for Heraclitus "the phenomenal was ... conceivable as a transition-moment in the universal development," that "all the mundane phenomena" were "a something merely transitory," that "the grades of being" reveal "nothing but a transitory process," and that even *ekpyrosis*, the rhythmically recurring total conflagration or *Weltbrand* with a consequent renewal, was considered by Heraclitus as a mere "transition-point to a new formation of the world."[14] After 1838, after reading *The History of Ancient Philosophy* in the English translation, the term *transition* begins to abound in Emerson as he uses it in both a modernist revisionist and in a Heraclitean sense obviously inspired by Ritter: "Self-Reliance" states "Life only avails, not the having lived. Power ceases in the instant of repose; it resides in the moment of transition from a past to a new

---

[11]*JMN* III, 364.
[12]*W* VIII, 172.
[13]Jonathan Levin, *The Poetics of Transition: Emerson, Pragmatism, and American Literary Modernism* (Durham: Duke University Press, 1999), *passim.*
[14]Ritter, *History* I, 240, 263, 246, 247, 247.

state";[15] in "Circles" we find this aphoristic condensation: "Nothing is secure but life, transition, the energizing spirit";[16] the essay "Nature" (1844) has this to add: "If we look at her [i.e., nature's] work, we seem to catch a glance of a system in transition,"[17] that is, a system that negates itself, a system that exists by again and again abandoning its systematic character: this is a poignant distancing of all philosophical modes that would find their ultimate model in Hegel as the epitome of all systematic philosophizing. The late essay "Power" evaluates: "Everything good in nature and the world is in [the] moment of transition";[18] in "Poetry and Imagination" we read "the creation is on wheels, in transit, always passing into something else";[19] and finally, there are these wonderfully Heraclitean passages from the 1870 version of "Natural History of Intellect," which I would like to quote at some length:

> No wonder the children love masks and costumes ... The children have only the instinct of the universe, in which becoming somewhat else is the perpetual game of nature, and death the penalty of standing still ... The universe exists only in transit, or we behold it shooting the gulf from the past to the future. ... Transition is the attitude of power. ... The habit of saliency, of not pausing but proceeding, is a sort of importation and domestication of the divine effort into a man ... // Man was made for conflict, not for rest. In action is his power; not in his goals but in his transitions man is great. Instantly he is dwarfed by self-indulgence. The truest state of mind rested in becomes false.[20]

Three times Emerson uses transition (or transit) in this brief passage; he creates the vision of a world that cannot be held, cannot be arrested, and thus cannot be properly conceived, a world in Heraclitean flux that is therefore logically beyond conceptualization. Conceptualization, however, is the central, the most prominent and dignified of all metaphysical tools, the Hegelian magic wand *par excellence*.

Emerson thus repeatedly uses Ritter's second major heuristic term in this passage, which is in itself one of the most artfully condensed among his many evocations of Heraclitus: the playful children at the beginning of the quotation remind us that for Heraclitus the world itself is a child playing a board game; the fact that nothing stands still so obviously recalls the famous flux of all things; the insight that man was made for conflict rephrases the

---

[15] W II, 69.
[16] Ibid., 289.
[17] W III, 174.
[18] W VI, 71.
[19] W VIII, 10.
[20] W XII, 54–5.

centrality of *polemos* (i.e., conflict or war) for Heraclitus's interpretation of reality as contested. Maybe most importantly, the constant change of masks and costumes with which the passage begins strongly evokes that most powerful of Heraclitean descriptive interpretations of reality: namely, that reality and nature basically love to hide (Gr. *physis kryptesthai philei*), and when they show, reality and nature manifest themselves in a persistent *metabole*, that is, in a relentless and contingent, a willful and often unforeseeable *Umschlagen* or turning of one thing or quality or appearance, of one mask or costume, into another. *Metabole* or sudden *Umschlagen* or turning or reversal, Hans-Georg Gadamer explains in his "Heraklit-Studien" of 1990, is an indication of a "zugrundeliegende Denkerfahrung ... der essentiellen Unzuverlässigkeit alles dessen, was sich bald so und bald anders zeigt."[21] *Metabole* as philosophical intuition or stylistic strategy of sudden reversal is an indicator of a foundational, basic unreliability and ungroundedness of the phenomenal world that shows as this in one moment and quite differently in the next.[22] All of Emerson's writings after 1838 show these sudden breaks and shifts of direction or changes in argument. A prominent example is the essay "Nominalist and Realist," which argues the nominalist and the realist position with equal conviction and defends both a pluralist and a monist universe by shifting back and forth between the two visions. Toward the end of the essay, Emerson uses a series of Ritter's Heraclitus fragments and interpretations verbatim to defend his own "metabolic" strategy: "Speech is better than silence; silence is better than speech; ... Things are, and are not, at the same time ... All the universe over, there is but one thing ... of which any proposition may be affirmed or denied."[23] In the very last paragraph, confronted by two philosophers, who argue the nominalist and the realist position, respectively, the Emerson *persona*—in the kind of serene abandonment of all systematic seriousness, a serenity that Nietzsche so liked in Emerson—is made to say: "I love everything by turns and nothing long."[24]

One realizes: the catalytic function of Ritter's reading of Heraclitus and his interpretive terminology enable, they empower Emerson to allow the return of the Presocratic vision as an innovative, a modern critique of the totalizing systematics of Hegelian metaphysics, a philosophy in which—according to William James's scathing criticism of Hegel—the dignity of

---

[21]Hans-Georg Gadamer, "Heraklit-Studien," in *Der Anfang des Wissens* (Stuttgart: Reclam, 1999), 43.
[22]In Rod Coltman's translation the sentence in question reads: "The fundamental experience of thinking ... seems to be the essential unreliability of everything that shows itself sometimes in this way and sometimes in another"; Gadamer, *The Beginning of Knowledge* (New York: Continuum, 2002), 39.
[23]W III, 233.
[24]Ibid., 236.

all individual entities in their merely transitional existence and all single moments of unceasing and spontaneous, of contingent inchoation are ruthlessly subsumed under and subjected to a relentlessly "foredone reality."[25] With Ritter as terminological and heuristic support in reading Heraclitus for the purpose of philosophical resurrection, Emerson could more easily and elegantly move beyond Hegel: into the free realms of a truly modern and once again un-coerced vision of a world of ever new and unforeseeable, truly contingent possibilities (*inchoation*) and a restlessly flexible dynamic (*transition*).

However, the catalytic effect of Ritter's *History of Ancient Philosophy* was, as I already indicated, not limited to the liberating infusion of Heraclitean or quasi-Heraclitean terms into Emerson's thinking and writing. Beyond and maybe above the transformative effect of the terms *inchoation* and *transition* in Emerson's philosophical household, Ritter's conception of the way the history of thinking unfolds became a welcome support and affirmation in Emerson's own quietly insistent distancing from Hegel. In the 1820s, Emerson had read and quoted generously from the systematically organized histories of philosophy by de Gérando, Victor Cousin, and Wilhelm Gottlieb Tennemann, and he had occasionally paid his respects in his *Notebooks* to Hegel and his magisterial interpretation of the ways the *Weltgeist* manifests itself in the incremental, dialectical progression of thinking.[26] Emerson's early lectures and writings of the 1830s still show half-hearted attempts to organize the elements of both natural and cultural history in terms of evolution, progression, and, sometimes, melioration. To me it seems no coincidence that such traces of a vision of history as orderly and progressive process begin to disappear after 1838 when Emerson works on *Essays: First Series* and, at the same time, reads Ritter in English. "Society never advances,"[27] we read in "Self-Reliance"; and, even more pertinently, in "Literary Ethics" Emerson states: "Any history of philosophy fortifies my faith, by showing me that what high dogmas I had supposed were the rare and late fruit of a cumulative culture, and only now available to some recent Kant or Fichte,—were the prompt improvisations of the earliest inquirers; of Parmenides, Heraclitus, and Xenophanes."[28] This clearly indicates that, for Emerson, there is no real historical and incremental growth *of* or *in* the histories of thinking, of ideas, and of culture and society. But it is not quite true that "*any* history of philosophy" fortified his faith in the constant iteration and return of the most profound and significant philosophical

---

[25] William James, "On Some Hegelisms," in *The Will to Believe and Other Essays in Popular Philosophy*, vol. 6 of *The Works of William James* (1896; Cambridge, MA: Harvard University Press, 1979), 201.
[26] See "Index" for several entries on Hegel in *Topical Notebooks*, vol. 2.
[27] W II, 82.
[28] W I, 156.

insights. In the "Translator's Preface" to the English version of Ritter's *History* by Alexander J. W. Morrison, Fellow of Trinity College, Cambridge, Emerson could read that—other than the histories of philosophy by de Gérando, Cousin, and Tennemann—Ritter's *History of Ancient Philosophy* excelled because it was "[s]uperior to the low spirit of system, and equally indifferent [meaning: equally just and fair] to all [thinkers]" and so could "present every theory ... from the particular point of view it intentionally took up and labored to enlarge."[29] It is this pluralistic insistence on the unique validity of each individual point of view at any given time that accords Ritter's history of Greek philosophy an importance for Emerson beyond anything found in de Gérando or Hegel.

As Gadamer has reminded us, "Schleiermacher hatte im Unterschied zu Hegel ein besonderes Gefühl für die Individualität der Phänomene."[30] Ritter as Schleiermacher's disciple obviously continued to emphasize the priority of the single, individual instance rather than the authority of an overarching systematic totality. It is a similar insistence on the genuine validity of each individual philosophical point of view as unique that resurfaces in Emerson's "History" as the desire to do justice to the fact that each individual, each live being, writes or creates her or his history and world interpretation and philosophy as an authentic act whose value and dignity are not determined by any pre-ordained developmental, say dialectical, scheme—be it that of Tennemann, de Gérando, Cousin, or Hegel himself.[31] This is why "[a]ll history becomes subjective; in other words there is properly no history, only biography."[32] Similarly, the thinkers of antiquity from Heraclitus and Empedocles through Synesius and Proclus do not represent stages in a historical development or the systematic unfolding of dialectically consecutive insights or arguments for Emerson; they are each of them equal and coeval in their dignity: "these babe-like Jupiters sit in their clouds, and from age to age prattle to each other and to no contemporary."[33]

In the lengthy introduction to his history, Ritter himself relentlessly attacks what he calls the constructionist approach in writing the history of thinking. He never mentions anyone by name, but it is more than obvious that the central target is Hegel. In Hegel's dialectical constructionism, Ritter criticizes the loss of the *independent* individual worth and achievement of each thinker; he criticizes an insufficiently inductive approach to research and the arrogant pretension of a humanly possible, all-encompassing, final,

---

[29]"Translator's Preface" in Ritter, *History*, n.p. [3].
[30]Gadamer, *Anfang der Philosophie*, 13: "Unlike Hegel, Schleiermacher possessed a special sensibility for the individuality of phenomena" (my translation).
[31]In a footnote in the "Translator's Preface," Morrison mocks Hegel, the "German master" of Victor Cousin, because of his pretense "to be in full possession of all truth"; n.p. [3].
[32]W II, 15.
[33]Ibid., 322.

and absolute point of view that obliterates essential personal and cultural difference and jeopardizes the possibility of the unforeseen, of chance and contingency in the in fact always undecided future of thinking. When one looks at Ritter's interpretation of a proper history of philosophy and at his at times obsessed and unfair anti-Hegelian tirades in some more detail, one cannot but notice how many of his views were apt to reinforce Emerson's disposition as a thinker. Ritter criticizes the exclusive valuation of "systematic form and arrangement" in writing philosophy and its history: "it must not be overlooked, that there are also other modes of philosophical exposition equally valid and admissible … The instances of an Augustin, a Jacobi, and a Plato … will sufficiently illustrate our meaning."[34] Emerson would have appreciated the critique of exclusively systematic exposition and enjoyed the company of Augustine, Jacobi, and Plato.

At the center of Ritter's criticism of the Hegelian approach to the history of philosophy, we find a fundamental disagreement about method:

> we cannot sufficiently express our surprise that the constructive method should have been recommended for an historical work, be it of what kind it may. This procedure implies a perfect misconception of the historical method; for in every species of history, induction, *i.e.* the discovery of the general from the particulars, is the only legitimate mode of proceeding. We set out from certain individual facts already ascertained, and evolve therefrom a knowledge of the general principle; so in the department of physics; so, too, in the department of pure intellect. What schoolboy is ignorant of this?[35]

A purely deductive method, based on the comprehension of the *essence* and the final destination and fulfilment, the *telos*, of the history of thinking, is usually "but little troubled about the multiplicity of transmitted details."[36] Constructionists also overlook that history's "series of developments is … occasionally broken by external and contingent influences,"[37] and the writings of constructionists are deficient because they show "the absence of all estimate of the intrinsic value of individual efforts."[38] Emerson could see himself encouraged in his experimental, his essayistic engagement of the multiplicity of the real, the contingent, and the inescapably individual importance of humans and of events. The implication of the Hegelian system that the final destination and essence of the development of philosophical speculation could be known was a central target of Ritter's animadversion: "In order that this perfect

---

[34]Ritter, *History*, 14–15.
[35]Ibid., 34.
[36]Ibid., 17.
[37]Ibid., 23–4.
[38]Ibid., 24.

knowledge of the destination should be present and possible at a particular period, it would be necessary that the destination be actually attained at that particular time."[39] Ritter concludes: "Whoever, therefore, would not put an end to further inquiry must willingly admit that he does not possess this entire consciousness of the destination of his species."[40] Emerson's vision of the unending propagation and proliferation of thinking, its unending and always tentative, experimental advance into "Chaos and the Dark"[41] found itself supported and encouraged by Ritter's denial of a possible speculative closure of the historical progression of thinking.

In the "Conclusion" to the first volume of *The History of Ancient Philosophy*, Ritter wrote about Heraclitus and his position in the history of thinking: at the very beginning of philosophy, he had achieved "the highest flight that it was possible for a philosopher to reach, who, in his system of nature, was exclusively devoted to the dynamic view."[42] Emerson not only shared Ritter's high regard for Heraclitus as a possible model of a contemporary, a modern "dynamic view" as I tried to show in my discussion of *inchoation* and *transition*. Emerson could also read Ritter's anti-Hegelianism as a support for his own emerging *philosophiegeschichtliche* intuition that the true future modes of thinking would or could rewrite, recapture, revitalize what had been authentically said before in a history whose structure, if it had any, was iterative and not systematically progressive, a true beginning again and again, which allowed for the fullness of beings and events, for contingency and breaks in development, and abandoned all thought of speculative completion. The history of thinking would then, for Emerson and for the modern imagination, be, in its tendency, an endless series of nows or moments of deep insight. No single philosophical position could be accorded more dignity than any other just because it was thought or supposed to be closer to an imagined founding origin or, as in Hegel, closer to a culminating *telos* or *finale*.

Emerson once, in the *Topical Notebooks*, found this way of presenting his vision, supported by Ritter and exemplified, as so often, also by Heraclitus: "I think that Philosophy is still rude & elementary. It will one day be taught by poets. The instinct that led Heraclitus & Parmenides & Lucretius to write in verse, was just."[43] In Emerson and Ritter, as later in Nietzsche and Heidegger, and other than in Hegel, the thinkers of the future do have the possibility to *productively* (in the sense of *poiesis*) recapture and refashion the powerful potential of earliest beginnings as the free and as the unending, the persistently modern promise of the unprecedented in Being and in thinking.

---

[39]Ibid., 27.
[40]Ibid., 28.
[41]W II, 49.
[42]Ritter, *History*, 592.
[43]Emerson, *Topical Notebooks* 2, 349.

# 6

# Nature/Poetry

As a thinker Emerson envisioned poetry as the highest and as the ultimate form of human knowledge and wisdom. Poetry, for Emerson, not only resides in the neighborhood of thinking as in Heidegger,[1] it is seen as the form and mode of thought, as the "methodos" or way of thinking,[2] that will replace philosophy as metaphysics.[3] In the late "Natural History of Intellect," the lectures delivered at the invitation of President Charles William Eliot as "University Courses" on philosophy at Harvard in 1870 and 1871,[4] Emerson states:

> The analytic process is cold and bereaving and, shall I say it? somewhat mean, as spying. There is something surgical in metaphysics as we treat it.

This essay was previously published as "The Masks of Proteus: Emerson on the Nature of Poetry and the Poetry of Nature" in *Poetics in the Poem: Critical Essays on American Self-Reflexive Poetry*, ed. Dorothy Z. Baker (New York: Lang, 1997), 104–16. Reprinted by permission of Peter Lang International Academic Publishers.

[1]Heidegger described the relationship between thinking and poetry quite frequently in these terms; more extended analyses of thinking and poetry may be found in his *Hölderlins Hymnen Germanien und "Der Rhein,"* ed. Susanne Ziegler, vol. 39 of *Gesamtausgabe* (1934–5; Frankfurt: Klostermann, 1980), 3–8, and in *Hölderlins Hymne "Andenken,"* ed. Curd Ochwadt, vol. 52 of *Gesamtausgabe* (1941–2; Frankfurt: Klostermann, 1982), 5–17.

[2]See Stanley Cavell, "Thinking of Emerson," in *Ralph Waldo Emerson: A Collection of Critical Essays*, ed. Lawrence Buell (Englewood Cliffs, NJ: Prentice-Hall, 1993), 198. Cavell places Emerson deliberately at the beginning of the essential modernist movement in thinking leading from him through Nietzsche to Heidegger. In this context Cavell suggests a connexion between Emerson's "onward thinking" and Heidegger's way or "Weg."

[3]This idea that poetry will replace metaphysics in the future is an early version of Heidegger's view that metaphysics will find its completion in the sciences and be replaced by both thinking and poetry as the possible future versions of what is now called philosophy.

[4]On the invitation as a gesture of reconciliation and compensation by the Harvard establishment after more than thirty years of ignoring Emerson following the scandal occasioned by the "Divinity School Address" in 1838, cf. John McAleer, *Ralph Waldo Emerson: Days of Encounter* (Boston: Little, Brown, 1984), 588 ff.

Were not an ode a better form? The poet sees wholes and avoids analysis; the metaphysician, dealing as it were with the mathematics of the mind, puts himself out of the way of inspiration; loses that which is the miracle and creates the worship.

I think that philosophy is still rude and elementary. It will one day be taught by poets. The poet is in the natural attitude; he is believing; the philosopher, after some struggle, having only reasons for believing.[5]

In a familiar Romantic vein, traditional philosophy as metaphysics is accused of "murdering to dissect" the living totality of Being or the world. It loses "the miracle" that induces wondering awe (gr. *thaumazein*) as the foundation of all original and genuine thought and, instead, dogmatically creates the basis, the principles, and reasons for the veneration or worship of so-called eternal verities. The possibility of the existential act of believing and thus creating a world[6] is replaced, in metaphysics, by the reasons enforcing dependence on a pre-established order, a world that is already given. The poetic mode of thinking is active; it is self-reliant, whereas the metaphysical mode is authoritarian like a traditional theology.[7]

The most significant statement, however, in this brief passage is: "The poet is in the natural attitude." The poet agrees with Being as nature, he is of the world and in tune with it, he is attuned to its potential. In this innocent phrase, Emerson late in his career once again states one of the fundamental positions of his thinking: the necessity to see and understand the human being in accordance with nature, that is to say in agreement with Being "as it arises out of itself and thus becomes present."[8] The task of the poet as post-metaphysical thinker, we may somewhat prematurely conclude, is the existential act and the articulation of the belief in Being as nature.[9] This is why Emerson categorically demands: "Metaphysics must be perpetually reinforced by life ... must be biography."[10] And in the same context he redefines the uses of traditional metaphysical thinking: "I want

---

[5] W XII, 13.

[6] This is one of the aspects of Emerson's thought that clearly prepares the way for William James and his concept of the "will to believe."

[7] These ethical and political implications of the shift from metaphysics to a new mode of thinking are most clearly expounded in John Dewey's *The Reconstruction of Philosophy* (1920).

[8] This is an attempt to translate Heidegger's series of translations of the Greek word "physis," understood as the earliest words for Being: "Was von sich her aufgeht und anwest"; Heidegger, *Heraklit*, ed. Manfred S. Frings, vol. 55 of *Gesamtausgabe* (1943–4; Frankfurt: Klostermann, 1994), 141–8.

[9] In this, as in so many other ways, Emerson here prepares the ground for his successor Friedrich Nietzsche. Karl Löwith has described this shift in thinking from the metaphysical idealism of, for example, Hegel to Nietzsche as the process of re-naturalization (re-translating the human being back into the nature of things); *Nietzsches Philosophie der ewigen Wiederkehr des Gleichen* (1935; Hamburg: Meiner, 1978), 192.

[10] W XII, 12.

not the logic but the power."[11] Such intimations of "Lebensphilosophie" and the will to power not only foreshadow the core of Nietzsche's writings, they indicate that Emerson conceives of thinking as part of the vital design that emerges in the powerful realization of an individual nature, a significant biography. This kind of thinking is "in the natural attitude," and it will be the task of the poet to articulate it and voice the very being of nature for post-metaphysical times by replacing the philosopher as metaphysician.

In a journal entry dated October 25, 1840, Emerson adds a crucial new dimension to this vision of the poet as heir and successor of the metaphysician:

> I value the poet. I think all the argument & all the learning is not in the Encyclopedia, or the Treatise on Metaphysics, or the Body of Divinity, but in the sonnet & the tragedy. In my daily work, I retrace my old steps and do not believe in remedial force, in the power of change & reform; but some Petrarch or Beaumont & Fletcher filled with the new wine of their imagination write me a tale or a dialogue in which are the sallies & recoveries of the soul: they smite & arouse me with the sharp fife. & I open my eye on my own possibilities. They clap wings to the side of all the solid old lumber of the world & I see the old Proteus is not dead.[12]

Again the poets are named as adequate and necessary replacements of the thinkers within what came to be called, in our century, the onto-theological tradition of metaphysics. It is their essential function and service to make one perceive a world of real possibilities and real newness. The solidities of conceptual specification, the stability of repositories of systematic knowledge, the encyclopedias, are shown as but one possible appearance of an essentially fluid, a winged world of radical change and constant becoming. The presiding deity of this truly and forever new world, of "this new yet unapproachable America,"[13] is Proteus.

If it is the primary task of the thinker to articulate, to say and interpret Being or nature, and if the essential and indispensable thinker of the present and the future is the poet, because of his natural attitude, then the poet will face the constant challenge to render a world that shows as, or maybe is, a series of perpetual (dis)guises or masks in endless succession, a protean nature. This protean or ever-changing quality characterizes and invigorates not only the world, which metaphysics has hardened into the "old lumber"

---

[11]Ibid.

[12]*JMN* VII, 523–4. The passage quoted was used by Emerson in his essay "Circles" *W* II, 291–2; in the essay, however, the last sentence was reworked and the reference to Proteus was dropped.

[13]The phrase is from "Experience" *W* III, 73. See also Stanley Cavell, *This New Yet Unapproachable America: Lectures after Emerson after Wittgenstein* (Albuquerque: Living Batch Press, 1989).

of conceptual schemes; the passage from the journals shows that the protean aspect is as much an essential characteristic, an indispensable existential desire of the human being.

These preliminary meditations have yielded some provisional and preparatory results that may be useful in an attempt to approach the peculiar qualities that emerge and the problems that are raised once we turn our attention to Emerson's self-reflexive poetry, to his poetry "mirroring and examining itself."[14] The results may be tentatively stated as follows:

a.  If the poet succeeds or replaces the metaphysician, then poetry becomes the true form of thinking. Poetry "mirroring or examining itself" would then, essentially, think thinking or thought itself.

b.  The poet as "Man Thinking" liberates persons and things; he liberates the world, Being, or nature as a whole from the ossification of metaphysical interpretations[15] and thus envisions Being or nature as an endless and endlessly creative temporal succession of ever-changing masks.

c.  In Emerson, then, so we are led to expect, self-reflexive poetry would be poetry that is thinking thought, and this thought, the post-metaphysical or poetic thought, would think a protean world or, in other words, a radically temporal masked nature.

The outlines of a dilemma are beginning to emerge: within the presuppositions of Emerson's own thinking, self-reflexive poetry may be seen in poems trying to image or probe the essence, the nature of poetry as thinking; at the same time, because of the world, because of the Being, because of the nature this thinking thinks, poems dealing with nature as shifting and protean metamorphosis will shed light on thinking as poetry. The lines of division between self-reflexive poems dealing with the nature of poetry and poems rendering the poetry of nature, depicting the creativity underlying the constant play of masks or appearances, begin to blur. The shifting ground, the quicksand of Emerson's thinking and of Emerson's language,[16] threatens to engulf categories like self-reflexive poetry and nature poetry as neatly defined, clearly circumscribed, and properly delimited conceptual entities.

---

[14]Dorothy Z. Baker, *Mythic Masks in Self-Reflexive Poetry: A Study of Pan and Orpheus* (Chapel Hill: University of North Carolina Press, 1986), 3. This general definition is based on the by-now-classical German definition by Alfred Weber in his essay "'Kann die Harfe durch ihre Propeller schiessen?' Poetologische Lyrik in Amerika," in *Amerikanische Literatur im 20. Jahrhundert*, ed. Weber and Dietmar Haack (Göttingen: Vandenhoeck und Ruprecht, 1971), 181.

[15]"The Poet" W III, 33, 35.

[16]"Experience" W III, 58.

This is what we may suppose. We will understand the dilemma or problem more deeply and more appropriately if we let the poems themselves speak of and about their proper matter—if there is something as essentialist and substantial as a "proper matter" in Emerson. I have selected two poems as possible representatives of their respective tentative and preliminary categories, as specimens of self-reflexive poetry and nature poetry. The titles of the two poems seem to assure one of the comfortably stable validity of such traditional designations of subgenres: "Art" and "The Snow-Storm." In reading and thinking about these poems, however, the critic should keep in mind what Emerson says of the effects of true, of authentic thinking in "Circles":

> Beware when the great God lets loose a thinker on this planet. Then all things are at risk. It is as when a conflagration has broken out in a great city, and no man knows what is safe, or where it will end. There is not a piece of science but its flank may be turned to-morrow; there is not any literary reputation, not the so-called eternal names of fame, that may not be revised and condemned.[17]

Minding Emerson, the thinker, as characterized in this passage and in the opening remarks of this chapter, we are now ready for a—joyfully[18] destructive—critical analysis, which will be satisfied only when no or few conceptual stones will remain in place simply to remind us of our maybe necessary, but solely initial trust in the explanatory power of categories.

"Art" is the prefatory poem introducing the essay of the same title in *Essays: First Series*. Since art and poetry tend to be used in an identical fashion and in a generic sense in Emerson's work,[19] the poem "Art" may be read as a summary statement by the poet/artist as thinker on the subject of art or poetry as the proper mode or way of thinking. This possibility of reading the poem is not immediately apparent. The first lines are often quite legitimately seen as an Emersonian endorsement of a program for a democratic aesthetics:

---

[17] *W* II, 288.

[18] Emerson usually prefers rather cheerful self-characterizations of his activity as thinker. The militant or military tone of the passage in "Circles" should not make one forget that he essentially conceives of himself as a "professor of the Joyous Science"; *JMN* VIII, 8. In this capacity, he provided the model for the voice in Nietzsche's *Die fröhliche Wissenschaft*.

[19] In the following argument I, too, will use the terms "poetry" and "art" or "poet" and "artist" interchangeably. This usage is justified by the generous and generic sense in which Emerson himself applies the term "poetry" in the essay "The Poet" and elsewhere; the same may be said of the way he uses the word and the concept "art." "Poetry" and "art," then, tend to signify the creation, the making of meaningful configurations of signs or things.

Give to barrows trays and pans
Grace and glimmer of romance,
Bring the moonlight into noon
Hid in gleaming piles of stone;
On the city's paved street
Plant gardens lined with lilac sweet,
Let spouting fountains cool the air,
Singing in the sun-baked square.[20]

This is the Emerson who describes himself in "The American Scholar" thus: "I ask not for the great, the remote, the romantic ... I embrace the common, I explore and sit at the feet of the familiar, the low."[21] It is also the voice of a substantial citizen of Jacksonian America calling for improvements; his program sounds a little like another version of William Cullen Bryant's active promotion of the creation of Central Park in New York City. In short, the poet seems to introduce himself as egalitarian ecologist. However, if we not only consider what these lines demand, describe, and show in simple historical terms, if we *think* the world projected here, we may realize that Emerson calls for an act of re-valuation (the Nietzschean term is deliberately chosen). Values (high and low), symbolic temporal units (moonlight, noon), representative places (city, country/garden), and qualities (hot and cold) are not simply shown here as dialectical opposites. The "other" may always be transformed, metamorphosed; it may be brought into the vicinity of its supposed antagonist: we are introduced into a world of possible changes in valuation, of gradual transitions and tentative reconciliations of seemingly incommensurable parts or aspects. Such a world is no longer a place in which concepts or substances or categories or values are stable and forever well defined: the commanding voice of the poem changes a system of static oppositions into a living cosmos of temporal gradations in which aspects and values and qualities intermingle and change, and in which time itself always remembers and foreshadows or "contains" its prior or future possibilities ("Bring the moonlight into noon"). Aspects, appearances, faces, that is, *masks* of the world, are mere moments in a series of mutations that are promoted and kept alive for us by the powerfully commanding voice ("Give ... / Bring ... / Plant ... ") of the poet in this poem, the maker of meaning who reveals himself at the same time as one who un-makes traditional categories, values, oppositions, and divisions. It is obvious that this interpretation of the poem is guided by the conviction that Emerson initiates what we call modernism in a double sense: 1. his poet-figure is a precursor of the poet in Wallace Stevens's sense who de-creates a world as found in order to enable

---

[20] W II, 325; the poem is reprinted in W IX, 235.
[21] W I, 110.

us to project a reality according to our powers as makers (of sense) in a
post-metaphysical and post-religious time;[22] and 2. this poet, this voice in
the poem, re-values old value-systems, doing what, at least since Nietzsche,
is considered to be the first and foremost duty of the thinker. Returning to
the poem we hope for further support of this thesis from the text:

> Let statue, picture, park and hall,
> Ballad, flag and festival,
> The past restore, the day adorn
> And make each morrow a new morn.
> So shall the drudge in dusty frock
> Spy behind the city clock
> Retinues of airy kings,
> Skirts of angels, starry wings,
> His fathers shining in bright fables,
> His children fed at heavenly tables.

Traditional art forms ("statue, picture, park and hall") have a function
that goes beyond traditional interpretations of the offices of art and
poetry. Neither the "dulce" nor the "utile" is addressed here. Art or poetry,
sense-making as re-valuation through thinking, has to do with time. The
three dimensions, or "ecstases" of time in Heidegger's terminology—
past, present, and future—are transformed in a celebration of Being that
guarantees the creative presence of a dignified "it was" in a festive now
("the day adorn"), which, in turn, is the precondition for a perpetually
present existential, almost religious possibility of renewal ("new morn").[23]
Art or poetry thus functions in the context of a new existential "Entwurf"
based on a new sense of time. The single person realizes the grandeur of
his personal mythological past ("behind the city clock," "fathers shining in
bright fables") and the promise of a persistent future salvation ("children
fed at heavenly tables").

The poem has introduced the poet/artist as thinker. His task is not
analysis; it is the re-valuation of the conditions of existence. This re-valuation
is enacted because of his command (it is a "Setzung" or "Entwurf"); it
reconciles conceptually divided opposites and redefines time in a way that
makes the celebration of Being as time possible. The last part of the poem

---

[22]Wallace Stevens, "The Relations between Poetry and Painting," in *The Necessary Angel:
Essays on Reality and Imagination* (1951; London: Faber and Faber, 1960), 174 ff.
[23]Emerson thus articulates the program of modernism as it was announced, for instance, by
Ezra Pound in the famous phrase "Make it new." The intimate connection between modernism
proper and Transcendentalism is also established by Henry David Thoreau's use of the phrase
as a program of existential renewal and by his reference to its source in ancient Chinese culture
in chapter 2 of *Walden*, "Where I Lived, and What I Lived For."

is rather more essayistic than "poetic" in a conventional sense; the speaker openly avows the existential function of art/poetry:

> 'Tis the privilege of Art
> Thus to play its cheerful part,
> Man in Earth to acclimate
> And bend the exile to his fate,
> And, moulded of one element
> With the days and firmament,
> Teach him on these stairs to climb
> And live on even terms with Time;
> Whilst upper life the slender rill
> Of human sense doth overfill.

Art in Emerson has the existentially significant task of making the human being not only feel but be at home on this earth, in an existence that is understood as radically immanent. Emerson—like Nietzsche after him—reclaims the "Erdenreich"[24] for mankind. This is the cheerfulness of thinking as "joyous" or "gay science." It is surprising, though not puzzling, when we consider the affinities existing between certain thoughts in Emerson and Heidegger, that we should find a similar philosophical interpretation of poetry and Being in Heidegger's favorite poet-as-thinker Hölderlin. In a line Heidegger liked to quote again and again, Hölderlin says: "Voll Verdienst, doch dichterisch, wohnet / der Mensch auf dieser Erde."[25]

Emerson's poem, then, thinks Being (in the sense of Dasein and her/his dwelling) and time together; art/poetry teaches to "live on even terms with Time." As a radically temporal being, the human person is an exile; she or he never arrives to stay. Art as thinking reconciles with this fate and makes the human being feel at home in exile itself. The "upper life," finally, which "overfills" human sense, is not a promise of transcendent inspiration and guidance; rather, it assures the person of that excess of power (or life force) described in "Nature," which makes it possible to exceed each singular state of Being and "draw a new circle,"[26] that is, makes it possible to go on being human and temporal.

"Art," so we may conclude, ostensibly talks about or shows art/poetry at work. Taken at face value, it is a self-reflexive poem proper. The speaker powerfully commands and re-shapes reality in an act of re-valuation. In doing this, however, the poet/artist/speaker assumes the role of post-metaphysical thinker. The world he thinks and/or shapes is a world of gradations and

---

[24]Nietzsche, *Also sprach Zarathustra*, KSA 4, 393: "*so wollen wir das Erdenreich.*"
[25]Friedrich Hölderlin, "In lieblicher Bläue ...," in *Sämtliche Werke*, ed. Friedrich Beissner (Stuttgart: Kohlhammer, 1953), vol. II, 372.
[26]W II, 177, 300.

transitions and thus no longer a world of clear-cut dialectical oppositions—
one could say that in "Art," as in all of Emerson, we are moving from Hegel
toward Nietzsche. This world in which opposites merge or exist contiguously
or, as William James liked to say, "durcheinander," this world is thought as
radically, that is, basically temporal. Appearances and temporal phases hide
or reveal forever new possibilities: a masked protean universe is hinted at.
The poet/thinker, the maker of sense, has to integrate Dasein, the human
being, into this world; it is his task to justify existence or Being as time.

In our reading the genre or subgenre of the poem "Art" begins to show as
a mere mask: the title confidently announces a self-reflexive poem. Art and/
or poetry, though, undergo a radical change in the poem: they are revealed
as agents of a constant re-valuation; they assume the role traditionally
accorded to philosophy as metaphysics. Poetry or art in this poem about art
are strictly speaking about something else: they are about Being and time.
Art or poetry, so it seems, are a mask for an endeavor to think the world
as time, that is, as an endless succession of changes or masked appearances,
as the realm of Proteus. In such a world, concepts like self-reflexive poetry
may be useful only if we think of them as always hiding (and showing)
something else. If this is true, then the reverse must also be valid: a subgenre
like nature poetry may or must show as a mask always hiding something
else—maybe, among other possibilities, shifting and elusive aspects of self-
reflexive poetry.

"The Snow-Storm" envisions the dynamism and the shaping energies of
nature:

Announced by all the trumpets of the sky,
Arrives the snow, and, driving o'er the fields,
Seems nowhere to alight: the whited air
Hides hills and woods, the river, and the heaven,
And veils the farm-house at the garden's end.
The sled and traveler stopped, the courier's feet
Delayed, all friends shut out, the housemates sit
Around the radiant fireplace, enclosed
In a tumultuous privacy of storm.[27]

The opening line of the poem speaks of an apocalyptic event, of the
naturalized version of a transcendent and religious revelation. Nature
has replaced transcendence as the origin of power and signification. The
most noteworthy effect of the violence of natural forces unleashed by the
snow-storm is the disruption of all social organization and public life, but
other than Whittier, who used the first nine lines of "The Snow-Storm" as
a motto in "Snow-Bound: A Winter Idyl," Emerson is not interested in the

---

[27] W VIII, 42.

exploration of domestic charm, happiness, and sentiment.[28] The reader is rather invited to think about the characteristics of natural power manifested in the storm. The snow-storm hides and veils familiar things; it masks the world as we have come to know it and makes it unfamiliar; we dare say that the snow-storm de-creates a reality we have come to rely on. The poem will go on to show that this de-creation, the obliteration of familiar distinctions in the world of things, is the precondition for a new, even if only temporary, creation. The first nine lines show a force at work in nature that defamiliarizes by creating a disguise. The force itself is mysterious: it is undoubtedly and aggressively present, yet "[s]eems nowhere to alight." Strictly speaking it is an absent presence. This could be used as an abstract, but quite appropriate, definition of the character of Proteus, the ancient Greek water god who was later identified as a son of Poseidon and who was notorious for his evasiveness and shifting of shapes.[29]

The second and longer part of the poem makes us familiar with the effects of this powerful absent presence, the snow-storm, effects that depend on its masking and de-creative activity:

Come see the north wind's masonry.
Out of an unseen quarry evermore
Furnished with tile, the fierce artificer
Curves his white bastions with projected roof
Round every windward stake, or tree, or door.
Speeding, the myriad-handed, his wild work
So fanciful, so savage, nought cares he
For number or proportion. Mockingly,
On coop or kennel he hangs his Parian wreaths;
A swan-like form invests the hidden thorn;
Fills up the farmer's lane from wall to wall,
Maugre the farmer's sighs; and at the gate
A tapering turret overtops the work.
And when his hours are numbered, and the world
Is all his own, retiring, as he were not,
Leaves, when the sun appears, astonished Art
To mimic in slow structures, stone by stone,
Built in an age, the mad wind's night-work,
The frolic architecture of the snow.[30]

---

[28]On the difference between "fireside poets" like Whittier and Transcendentalist poetics, cf. Bettina Friedl and Herwig Friedl, "Dichtung als Institution: Die 'Fireside Poets' Bryant, Whittier, Longfellow, Holmes und Lowell," in *Amerikanische Lyrik: Perspektiven und Interpretationen*, ed. Rudolf Haas (Berlin: Schmidt, 1987), 38–62.
[29]"Proteus," in *Der kleine Pauly: Lexikon der Antike*, ed. Konrat Ziegler and Walther Sontheimer (Munich: Druckenmüller, 1972), vol. IV, 1196–7.
[30]W VIII, 42–3.

Natural force is seen and understood in terms of artistic creativity, here in terms of architecture; power within nature is characterized as fierce, savage, and mad, as excessive in energy ("overtops the work"). Like Emerson's ideal poet, the wind cares less for "number and proportion" than for "a metre-making argument,"[31] that is, for the expressive energy itself. One would not even need the "Parian wreaths" in the poem to sense that this creative force might deserve the name of Dionysus. Like Nietzsche Emerson envisions original creativity as a purely natural, as a barbarous event that creates the temporary condition of the possibility of culture as measured imitation, as careful, Apollinian representation. Creative nature, however, is an essentially unpredictable, pre-logical temporal event, a "Geschick," as Heidegger would say. The creative force arrives, we see not whence; it is present without settling, since it "[s]eems nowhere to alight," and it finally withdraws "as [if] he were not." This basic creative drive or power or force is not a substance in the way traditional metaphysics understood the term. It is a mysterious "Ereignis"—a temporary and unstable presence that we know by its masking of familiar reality. This masked reality, the precarious and fugitive creations of the snow, in turn makes another version or mask or appearance of reality possible, a mask we call art. What we are witnessing is a—potentially endless—series of shifting shapes, a sequence of metamorphoses, a constant turning of one aspect into another, a "troping" of reality.[32] Art or poetry as we know them, then, are merely phases or kinds of masks within universal processes of shape-shifting, aspects of an "essentially" Protean reality.

Emerson, as one of the indispensable founding figures of post-metaphysical thinking, like Nietzsche and like Heidegger, returns to the very beginnings of Western thought and retrieves forgotten and buried origins that in his works assume the character of starting points for new interpretations in the effort to overcome the spent metaphysical tradition. Emerson returns again and again, through direct and indirect quotation, as do Nietzsche and Heidegger, to the philosophical visions and fragmented sayings of Heraclitus. As we have seen in our reading of "The Snow-Storm," nature itself is shown as

---

[31]"The Poet" W III, 15.
[32]Richard Poirier has used this term in his two important analyses of Emerson's linguistic technique and practice: it seems, however, as if "troping" were not just a trait characterizing "logos," as Poirier sees it, but also, and in a privileged sense, "physis"; see *The Renewal of Literature: Emersonian Reflections* (New York: Random House, 1987) and *Poetry and Pragmatism* (Cambridge, MA: Harvard University Press, 1992). Brian Harding has carefully analyzed the relationship of the architectural and the musical metaphors in "The Snow-Storm" and other poems by Emerson as means to convey his vision of an essentially metamorphic nature and existence. His essay refrains, however, from relating these insights to Emerson's major concerns as a thinker; see "'Frolic Architecture': Music and Metamorphosis in Emerson's Poetry," in *Nineteenth-Century American Poetry*, ed. A. Robert Lee (New York: Vision/Barnes & Noble, 1985), 100–17.

creative force, as a maker. We know nature only, however, in a basically unpredictable sequence of appearances or masks, that is, in a progression of images, things, works, concepts making temporary sense. In a radically flowing, Heraclitean world of ceaseless construction and destruction, nature herself remains absent, she "[s]eems nowhere to alight." These insights are, most probably, indebted to Heraclitus's saying—fragment B 123[33]— that "nature likes to hide" ("physis krypthestai philei"). In the German translation "physis" is usually rendered as "das Wesen der Dinge," as "the essence of things or reality."

We may therefore conclude: a text like Emerson's "The Snow-Storm" is a nature poem in which the essence of nature remains hidden. Instead we witness, we are shown, we may read a succession of temporary appearances, of masks that hide something that is actually absent. Nature or the creative force, as Emerson so accurately and yet enigmatically stated in "Nature" (1844), "is still elsewhere."[34] This post-metaphysical power of/as nature has a definitive artistic or poetic potential. Like Wallace Stevens in "The Relations between Poetry and Painting," Emerson perceives the existence of "a universal poetry that is reflected in everything or ... a fundamental aesthetic of which poetry and painting are ... manifestations"[35] For Emerson, the essayist, there is forever "Art," the productive process of the world or Being as a whole, and there is "art" or poetry as human participations in the endless masquerade of sense-making.[36] A poem on nature by Emerson in the role of the poet as post-metaphysical thinker will thus always reveal things, or Being, or nature, as artistic or poetic creations by an absent presence. Such a poem will necessarily say something or show qualities of making sense for which the poem itself stands; the nature poem will most likely be a mask of a self-reflexive poem trying to think Being as time and therefore as the world of Proteus.

The concept of self-reflexive poetry, like all concepts in Emerson, may be seen as both endangered and vindicated. It is endangered because there seems to be no separate and definitive and essential entity "about which" a poem might be. On the other hand, anything might—temporarily and tentatively— be poetic, that is, show as sense made or emerging in a thoroughly dynamic and unstable world of forever shifting shapes. Like all words or terms in Emerson's thinking, "self-reflexive poetry" does not designate an entity or fix an essence; like all words and symbols it is "fluxional; all language is vehicular and transitive, and is good, as ferries and horses are, for

[33]*Heraklit: Fragmente*, ed. Bruno Snell (1926; Munich: Artemis, 1986), 36–7.
[34]W III, 184.
[35]Stevens, "Poetry and Painting," 160.
[36]Such a distinction between "Art" and "art" is insinuated by the essay "Art": W II, 325–43.

conveyance, not as farms and houses are, for homestead."[37] In the context of Emerson's post-metaphysical thought, the term and the subgenre ' self-reflexive poetry" acquires a fluid and a flexible meaning. The term is a good and comfortable conveyance on a *tour d'horizon* through Emerson's poetic achievement as long as we do not make the mistake and settle down on the homestead of a simple and single-minded meaning and application.

[37]"The Poet" *W* III, 37.

# 7

# Transgressive Manners

When one looks at manners as a well-defined, as a clear and distinct category of possible social, cultural, and literary analysis, it does become rather difficult to properly work out and appreciate the intricacies of Ralph Waldo Emerson's vision of, and his thinking about, manners and social conduct. The reason for this difficulty is relatively simple and almost obvious: Emerson's post-metaphysical mode of thinking does not permit, or make room for, *the concept of the category* any longer; the Emersonian vision radically questions the possibility to clearly delimit and to essentially define realms or categories of being, for example, of cultural reality, like manners or civility. The very concepts and terms are—and, ultimately, all language is—in Emerson's words from the essay "The Poet," "vehicular and transitive" and only good, he adds, "as ferries and horses are, for conveyance, not as farms and houses are, for homestead."[1] Emersonian terminology does not allow us to settle on the *terra firma* of conventionally or philosophically fixed meanings; such settling down or such linguistic homesteading would always conceal that any ground so covered by symbols or signs or verbal categories is after all but treacherous "quicksand."[2] Categories and concepts—seen from Emerson's anti-foundationalist and anti-substantialist position—are mere "conveyances"; they work and function in a pragmatic sense only when they lead us back, again and again, into the uncharted terrain of forever new experience, as, among other post-Emersonians, William James was to explain with great subtlety in *Some Problems of Philosophy*. Categories have the limited use of leading us back into ongoing, open-ended, and hopefully more and more enriched encounters with reality as forever transitional

---

This essay was previously published as "Emerson on Manners" in *Civilizing America: Manners and Civility in American Literature and Culture*, ed. Dietmar Schloss (Heidelberg: Winter, 2009), 173–84. Reprinted by permission of Universitätsverlag Winter GmbH.

[1] W III, 37.
[2] "Experience" W III, 58.

processes of experience.[3] The Cartesian ideal of clear and distinct concepts, of categories, which guarantee access to a stable reality, is undermined by Emerson; in his thinking the semantic content of words, of concepts, of signs tends to *transgress* precise and circumscribed boundaries and is always ready to fuse with neighboring fields of meaning.

Emerson actually—and for some, maybe, surprisingly—devoted considerable attention and in-depth meditations to the phenomena only tentatively circumscribed by the words "manners" and "civility." In addition to such lectures as the 1848–49 series with the title *Mind and Manners of the Nineteenth Century*, which concentrates on what we might call culture, his most remarkable contributions toward a "phenomenology" of aspects and forms of individual and collective or social human practice may be found in the two complementary essays "Character" and "Manners" in the collection *Essays: Second Series* (1844) and in the essay "Behavior" in *The Conduct of Life* (1860). These three essays will be at the center of my interpretation and my evaluation. Here Emerson employs—and these are only the most prominent and the most frequently used instances—the words "character," "conduct," "manners," "behavior," and "fashion" in order to articulate, typically from unpredictably shifting points of view, his philosophical interpretations of a field of fluid and transitional as well as transgressive phenomena, each of which seems always ready and about to merge into any of the fleeting manifestations designated by those other terms also available. Such Emersonian readings of manners and conduct are shared and continued and deepened, I would like to suggest, without my intending to demonstrate this in full detail here, by his literary descendants Thoreau, Whitman, and Dickinson as major representatives of the proto-modern American Renaissance, by the great pragmatist thinkers William James and John Dewey, by their literary counterparts Wallace Stevens, William Carlos Williams, and Gertrude Stein, as well as by such outstanding European Emersonians and modernist revolutionaries as Friedrich Nietzsche. Emerson initiates and facilitates a sweeping post-metaphysical modernist critique and re-valuation of the essentialist and categorial conceptions of established modes of social and cultural practice like manners.

I would like to begin and find my way toward an elucidation of Emerson's interpretations of manners (or conduct or behavior or character or fashion) by way of a brief discussion of what Emerson means by power (or force or energy or vitality)—another field of terminological profusion and, from the point of view of critical reception, of considerable *con*fusion.[4] Emerson's

---

[3]Jonathan Levin, *The Poetics of Transition: Emerson, Pragmatism and American Literary Modernism* (Durham, NC: Duke University Press, 1999), 17–44; Mark Bauerlein, *The Pragmatic Mind: Explorations in the Psychology of Belief* (Durham, NC: Duke University Press, 1997), 7–35.
[4]Michael Lopez, *Emerson and Power: Creative Antagonism in the Nineteenth Century* (DeKalb: Northern Illinois University Press, 1996), *passim*.

philosophy of manners—may it be confessed at the outset—is a philosophy of power.

"Power" is one of the many words in Emerson's flexible lexicon that—besides or in addition to "soul," "reason," "force," "energy," or "nature"—may designate Being, *das Sein*. "Life is a search after power," he writes, "and this is an element with which the world is so saturated,—there is no chink or crevice in which it is not lodged."[5] Productive and dynamic reality, life, is thus read as the ubiquitous and manifold tendencies in live entities toward self-realization by way of powerful self-overcomings, or, as Mark Bauerlein explains: "The most powerful Power applies itself to its own annihilation, cancels its dominion by breeding the Power that supersedes it."[6] Here the groundwork for Nietzsche's radical modernist philosophy of the will to power as a non-substantialist plurality of dispositional potentials is fully prepared.[7] In Emerson power is invoked again and again in order to elucidate, to interpret, to appreciate, to evaluate and rank character, conduct, behavior, manners, and fashion. Power is thus quite obviously not primarily understood as the precondition for the domination or subjection of others; rather, Emerson uses it in order to indicate potential, the possibility to do and to achieve, to constantly overcome any given state of existence, and thus to truly be in the state-less state of transition: "Life only avails, not the having lived. Power ceases in the instant of repose; it resides in the moment of transition from a past to a new state, in the shooting of the gulf, in the darting to an aim."[8] Life as performative self-realization is a manifestation of power not as a stable and essential, but as a dynamic and transitional reality: "Transition is the attitude of power."[9] If one reads life in such an ontological context, manners or conduct will necessarily have to lose any substantialist or categorial character; they tend to become dependent on a pluralist dynamics that ultimately can only undermine any unquestioned or authoritative viability buttressed by deceptively stable, by traditional social conventions. One of the often used and important alternative designations for what Emerson has in mind whenever he speaks of power is virtue in the root sense of Lat. *virtus*. The meaning of ethically proper and socially acceptable behavior, of good manners, is thus implicitly foreshadowed as dependent on the existential potential or *potestas*, on the power that may help ground any vital and significant human self-realization.

---

[5]"Power" *W* VI, 55.
[6]Bauerlein, *The Pragmatic Mind*, 19.
[7]Herwig Friedl, "Fate, Power, and History in Emerson and Nietzsche," in *Emerson/Nietzsche*, ed. Michael Lopez, spec. issue of *ESQ* 43 (1997): 267–93, *passim*. See also Chapter 8 in this book.
[8]"Self-Reliance" *W* II, 69.
[9]"Natural History of Intellect" *W* XII, 54.

"Character" may function as an intermediary term connecting power and conduct, or manners, or behavior. Character is predicated on the basis of a latent power; it shows as "a reserved force which acts directly by presence, and without means. It is conceived of as a certain undemonstrable force ... by whose impulses the man is guided but whose counsels he cannot impart."[10] Character may thus be understood as a mere given, as a "natural power" due to which "[a]ll individual natures stand in a scale, according to the purity of this element in them. The will of the pure runs down from them into other natures, as water runs down from a higher into a lower vessel. This natural force is no more to be withstood than any other natural force."[11] Power or force as realized in and as character, as the potential of agency, determines the individual's position on "a scale"; this, of course, may be read as another of the many foreshadowings of Nietzschean thinking as it posits classes or castes, a ranking of humans, determined by their natural, by their existentially defining powers of agency or *virtutes*. The reach and value of human agency and the kind, the dignity and importance, the manners and modes, of the interaction of a person with the world depend on such power and rank: "All things exist in the man tinged with the *manners* of his soul. With what quality is in him he infuses all nature that he can reach."[12] The power and rank of character allow a whole world to emerge, "all nature that he can reach," a world distinguished by the "manners of [the] soul," by the potential of who one authentically *is*. Such powerful manners also in-form, in the sense of "shape," the social realm: "Manners impress as they indicate real power."[13]

This then is Emerson's vision of the transition from "manners of the soul" to social manners: "*[M]en of character* are the conscience of the society to which they belong. The natural measure of this *power* is the resistance of circumstances."[14] The intensity and mode of being, the manners of a powerful personality, antagonize the established decorum; they resist and antagonize and thus transform, and in transforming essentially create a new desirable usage of a society, its manners as well as its *ethos*. Ethos should here be understood as the measure, the intensity, the authority of its *virtus*: "The openness that Emerson advocates undermines authority ruthlessly but only to institute new authority, an 'amelioration.'"[15] As we would expect, Emerson opposes character as a productive center to (mere) social arrangements as "frivolity": "Character is centrality, the impossibility of being displaced or overset. A man should give us a sense of mass. Society is frivolous, and shreds its day into scraps, its conversation into ceremonies and escapes."[16] And so we read: "the uncivil,

---

[10]"Character" W III, 90.
[11]Ibid., 94–5.
[12]Ibid., 95 (my emphasis).
[13]"Behavior" W VI, 181.
[14]"Character" W III, 96 (my emphasis).
[15]Bauerlein, *The Pragmatic Mind*, 23.
[16]W III, 98.

unavailable man, who is a problem and threat to society, whom it cannot let pass in silence but must either worship or hate,—and to whom all parties feel related, both the leaders of opinion and the obscure and eccentric,—he helps"; and Emerson adds by way of explanation: "Acquiescence in the establishment and appeal to the public, indicate infirm faith" if compared to "the instant presence of supreme power."[17] The civil order, societal manners are always in need of the supreme power of character—as corrosive, as corrective, as that which allows the manners of the soul, the great or grand style, as he was to say—to overcome the conventionalized arrangements, the mere mannerisms or fashions or frivolity of the established order. The revolutionary manners of the soul are not a private, a merely personal affair: "We shall one day see that the most private is the most public energy [or power]."[18]

For Emerson this insight is verified by the existence of a universal class of human beings, a class that is neither limited by region or culture nor constrained by historical circumstance: the—in one sense—classless class of the gentleman. The conduct, the manners, the civility of this cosmopolitan and timeless elite, this "select society, running through all the countries of intelligent men, [this] self-constituted aristocracy, or fraternity of the best"[19] of the "most *forcible* persons of every country" is the "result of the *character* and faculties universally found in men. It seems a certain permanent average ... [it is] that class who have most *vigor*"; in other words, from the same essay, "Manners": "Power first, or no leading class. ... the name [gentleman] will be found to point at original energy."[20] Significantly, "original energy" is the term which Whitman later found appropriate to characterize the communally representative voice of the poet as lawgiver and touchstone of existentially authentic manners in "Song of Myself."

Emerson goes on to define "the energetic class" as "[t]he rulers of society," as "men of the right Caesarian pattern." "My gentleman," he concludes, "gives the law where he is."[21] Ontologically and ethically speaking, Emerson's gentleman is the ruler of any social reality, of any set of manners and civility in which he may chance to find himself. Men of the "Caesarian pattern" manifest a behavior; they show individualized expressions of the "manners of the soul," which deserve the name "conduct." Emerson illustrates such conduct thus: "The famous gentlemen of Europe and Asia have been of this strong type ... They sat very carelessly in their chairs, and were too excellent themselves, to value any condition [i.e., an established class or conventional social status] at a high rate."[22] Here we are reminded of the provocatively

---

[17]Ibid., 99.
[18]Ibid., 111.
[19]"Manners" W III, 118.
[20]Ibid., 119, 121 (my emphasis).
[21]Ibid.
[22]Ibid., 123 (my emphasis).

self-assured and nonchalant gesture of Whitman's poet as "loafer," as self-reliant American *flaneur*: "I wear my hat as I please, indoors and out."[23]

Doubtlessly, the Caesarian pattern of such conduct that disregards pre-established social categories like class or regional culture is modeled on Emerson's vision of the Stoic emperor Marcus Aurelius. The not-always-properly-appreciated, important Stoic dimension[24] of Emerson's reading of individual conduct and social manners helps us to unveil the core of his basic intuition in a way that is related and similar to the elucidations that emerged from my discussion of questions of power. A brief excursion into Marcus Aurelius's *Eis heauton* (commonly and somewhat inadequately known under the title *Meditations*) may be of help here. The central category of individual and social conduct in Marcus Aurelius, whose specific meanings he inherited from Zeno of Citium and Chrysippus, is *to hegemonikon* (literally: "that which guides"). *To hegemonikon* is often translated as guiding reason, or will, or heart, or—significant in the context of my reading of Emerson—as character. If Emerson heard the connotations "will" and "character" in Marcus Aurelius's Greek text, he quite obviously also became aware of a further and implied double meaning of *to hegemonikon*: it is "*the authoritative part of the soul* (reason)," as it was used in the Stoic philosophy of Zeno, but also "*the governing part* of the universe, of the ether or sun," a usage found especially in Chrysippus.[25] From Emerson's perspective, human conduct— that is, powerful, proper conduct of a vigorous character after the Caesarian pattern—would thus be determined by the fundamentally related, even identical dynamic and productive forces of the world itself, of Being, and, at the same time, by the potential of the powerfully productive individual self who is nothing but a humanized version of that totality of generative energies or wills to power commonly named nature by Emerson.[26]

---

[23]Walt Whitman, *Leaves of Grass: Comprehensive Reader's Edition*, ed. Harold W. Blodgett and Sculley Bradley (New York: New York University Press, 1965), 77.

[24]Wesley T. Mott, "'The Age of the First Person Singular': Emerson and Individualism," in *A Historical Guide to Ralph Waldo Emerson*, ed. Joel Myerson (New York: Oxford University Press, 2000), 72.

[25]*A Greek-English Lexicon*, ed. Henry George Liddell and Robert Scott (1842; Oxford: Clarendon Press, 1968), 763.

[26]Cf. Bauerlein, *The Pragmatic Mind*, 24, 32. Robert D. Richardson, in *Emerson: The Mind on Fire* (Berkeley: University of California Press, 1995), 232–3, has provided us with one of the most succinct and enlightening analyses of the way *Nature* (1836) "marks the beginning of Emerson's rethinking of classical Stoicism," which even makes him describe *Nature* as "a modern Stoic handbook, Marcus Aurelius in New England." Richardson also provides one of the many possible quotations from Marcus Aurelius's *Eis heauton* that indicates Stoic thinking as not only one of Emerson's sources of his vision of self-reliance but also as a testimony to the conception of an identity of the guiding spirit in nature and man, the pervasive *hegemonikon*: "A man contains all that is needful to his government within himself. He is made [by nature] a law unto himself"; 152.

The opening statement, already partly quoted above, of Emerson's essay "Character" says that character is "a reserved force, which acts directly by presence and without means. It is conceived of as a certain undemonstrable force ... by whose impulses the man is *guided* but whose counsels he cannot impart."[27] Character is thus conceived and defined as the anthropomorphous agency of nature itself, the human presence of power as guiding energy: the *hegemonikon*. The opening paragraph of the essay "Behavior" in *The Conduct of Life* (1860) states that human manners as a visible language of the individual are "resulting from his organization and his will combined."[28] Organization in *The Conduct of Life* is the totality of the naturally given, also called "fate," whereas "will" is the individualized and free agency within that totality: conduct, thus, is the articulation of the world *and*, or of the world *as*, the individual. This is exactly what the Stoic technical term *to hegemonikon* in its double meaning of "authoritative part of the soul" and "governing part of the universe" conveys. The very phrase "the conduct of life" as well leaves it undecided who or what the "conductor," the *hegemonikon* is: is it life (or nature or fate or power or the world) that conducts or guides, or is it the person who conducts *a* or *her* or *his* life? Conduct, then, is indeed at the same time a very individual and a very public, even cosmic, affair, it is both the way of the world and Caesar's way, that is, the powerful, self-reliant, vigorous, and virtuous person's way. The ambiguous guiding force or power called character, *to hegemonikon*, Emerson adds, "is company for [the Caesarian individual], so that such men are often solitary, or if they chance to be social, do not need society but can entertain themselves very well alone."[29]

In the second chapter of her book *Cultivating Humanity*, Martha Nussbaum reminds us of Stoic culture as a viable model for a true cosmopolitanism. The education for the proper conduct of life in a future mature cosmopolitan culture demands that individuals be weaned from the sheltering constraints, "the warm nestling feeling," as Nussbaum phrases it, of their immediate and inherited cultural or social environment; they must be removed from the herd, as Nietzsche would have said. Nussbaum stresses the importance and the exemplary character of a cosmopolitan conduct of life for the Stoic model, writing that "[b]ecoming a citizen of the world is often a lonely business. It is, in effect, a kind of exile"[30]—just as Emerson had expressed this in "Character." Emerson and Thoreau carry on these particular important aspects of the Stoic cosmopolitan heritage

---

[27]W III, 90 (my emphasis).

[28]W VI, 163.

[29]W III, 90.

[30]Martha C. Nussbaum, *Cultivating Humanity: A Classical Defense of Reform in Liberal Education* (Cambridge, MA: Harvard University Press, 1997), 83.

into modernity; this is the way Nussbaum sees the connection. Being existentially solitary, an ontological exile, and, at the same time and because of that, a person after the Caesarian pattern: this, I believe, is the legacy of Marcus Aurelius in particular and of the *hegemonikon* in Emerson's reading of conduct that he designed for a continuously to-be-renewed, a modern version of Stoic cosmopolitan manners.

So far it may seem as if there was no truly or distinctly recognizable historical dimension in Emerson's account of manners or conduct or behavior or fashion, as if there were only timeless and universal patterns of powerfully natural self-actualization that help to question and overcome established, traditional regimes of social manners and decorum. In the essay "Manners," however, Emerson takes great care to develop his vision and interpretation of the historical emergence and unfolding of conduct. The argument begins in this energetically apodictic fashion: "There exists a strict relation between the *class of power* and the exclusive and polished circles. The last are always filled or filling from the first."[31] Behavior patterns and social practice, which become exemplary and create models of civility for all, are interpreted as the result, as the creation of the powerful, the Caesarian class of self-determined and thus, according to the originally Stoic vision, at the same time world-determined individuals. These creations, however, do not, cannot, and should not continue unchanged. Manners that become the dominant feature of a whole society have the inevitable tendency to mutate into what Emerson calls fashion; vital manners of self-determined and truly creative individuals become transpersonal and institutionalized; they ossify or become petrified, as Emerson liked to describe the process.

> Fashion, though in a strange way, represents all manly *virtue*. It is *virtue* gone to seed: it is a kind of posthumous honor. It does not often caress the great, but the children of the great: it is a hall of the Past. It usually sets its face against the great of this hour. Great men are not commonly in its halls; they are absent in the field: they are working, not triumphing. Fashion is made up of their children; of those who through the value and virtue [again in the sense of *virtus*] of somebody, have acquired lustre to their name, marks of distinction, means of cultivation and generosity, and, in their physical organization, a certain health and excellence, which secures to them, if not the highest power to work, yet high power to enjoy.[32]

Mark Bauerlein has provided a comprehensive and sophisticated summary of the implied historical, the grounding intuition of Emerson that pervades all of his comments on temporal processes:

---

[31] W III, 125 (my emphasis).
[32] Ibid. (my emphasis).

As soon as the first announcement [of any thought or rule of social practice and behavior] expands into law, into a repeatable, anonymous principle, the "truth" petrifies. This is the inevitable declension of vision: from original conception to habitual perception. First gratifyingly received as a colossal reshaping of an outworn world, on its common acceptance, vision passes into disposition, into a benign lethargy of works and days. ...

The second instance already marks a submissive present, a superior past. Regarding such repetitions as a conspiracy against genius, mind must move on, must be a continuum of fixations and dissolutions.[33]

Like all histories in Emerson, the history of civility and manners is thus a history of decadence—and Nietzsche certainly approved of and supported that reading—it moves as a continuum from self-creation, from individual world-making, to proper conduct in the Stoic sense to manners to mere fashion. The last stage of this developmental cycle is a necessary, a violent revolution that issues in new modes of exemplary living and doing that are imposed on the body politic and the social compact by new, powerful, that is, virtuous individuals or groups of individuals. Other than Norbert Elias, Emerson does not at all believe in a "ganz bestimmte Richtung," which is teleologically implicit in the process of civilization; other than Elias, Emerson does not assume a "festes Gerüst von Prozessen" within which the only seemingly contingent and volatile and the only seemingly tentative and experimental regional developments of the process of civilization may ultimately organize themselves and then finally result in a total vision of a cultural history, as proposed and beautifully illustrated in *Über den Prozess der Zivilisation*.[34] Like Nietzsche in *Der Antichrist*, Emerson thinks history not as meliorative but rather as an iterative process of invention and decline, marked again and again by revolutionary breaks and radical new beginnings, which is somewhat reminiscent of Jefferson's idea of necessarily recurring violent, rejuvenating upheavals. Emerson thinks of historical sequences as the unfolding of certain sets of manners and social conduct, of series of creation and decadence, of a "beginning again and again," as Gertrude Stein phrased her fundamental modernist intuition of historical developments of culture and civility in "Composition as Explanation"[35]—a lecture-essay heavily indebted, like so many of her insights, to Emerson. Nietzsche's vision

---

[33]Bauerlein, *The Pragmatic Mind*, 20.

[34]Norbert Elias, *Über den Prozess der Zivilisation: Soziogenetische und psychogenetische Untersuchungen* (Frankfurt: Suhrkamp, 1976), vol. 2, 444–5. The two quoted phrases could be translated as "in a well-defined direction" and "a solid scaffolding of processes."

[35]*Gertrude Stein: Selections*, ed. Joan Retallack (Berkeley: University of California Press, 2008), 218 ff.

in *Der Antichrist* impressively and succinctly captures and condenses the Emersonian argument proposed in "Manners" of a process of civilization and civility that does not at all correspond to a Hegelian progressive or cumulative and teleological pattern:

> Die Menschheit stellt *nicht* eine Entwicklung zum Besseren oder Stärkeren oder Höheren dar, in der Weise wie dies heute geglaubt wird. Der "Fortschritt" ist bloss eine moderne Idee, das heisst eine falsche Idee. Der Europäer von heute bleibt in seinem Werte tief unter dem Europäer der Renaissance; Fortentwicklung ist schlechterdings *nicht* mit irgendwelcher Notwendigkeit Erhöhung, Steigerung, Verstärkung.
>
> In einem anderen Sinne gibt es ein fortwährendes Gelingen einzelner Fälle an den verschiedensten Stellen der Erde und aus den verschiedensten Kulturen heraus, mit denen in der Tat ein *höherer* Typus sich darstellt: etwas, das im Verhältnis zur Gesamt-Menschheit eine Art Übermensch ist. Solche Glücksfälle des grossen Gelingens waren immer möglich und werden vielleicht immer möglich sein. Und selbst ganze Geschlechter, Stämme, Völker können unter Umständen einen solchen *Treffer* darstellen.[36]

Even more subtly than in "Manners" of 1844, these iterative and contingent modes of historical change in culture, in manners, in behavior, in conduct, or fashion are imaged and discussed in the late essay "Behavior." This is the opening paragraph:

> The soul which animates Nature [one could speak of power here] is not less significantly published in the figure, movement and gesture of animated bodies, than in its last vehicle of articulate speech. This silent and subtile language is Manners; not *what*, but *how*. Life expresses. A statue has no tongue, and needs none. Good tableaux do not need declamation. Nature tells every secret once. Yes, but in man she tells it all the time, by form, attitude, gesture, mien, face and parts of the face, and by the whole action of the machine. The visible carriage [behavior] or

---

[36]*Der Antichrist*, KSA 6, 171: "Mankind does *not* represent an evolution in the direction of the better or the stronger or the higher, in the way this is believed in today. 'Progress' is merely a modern idea, and this means it is a false idea. In his value the European of today stays far below the European of the Renaissance; development is simply *not* necessarily heightening, increase, strengthening. / In a different sense there exists a ceaseless success of individual cases, in utterly different places of the earth arising out of utterly different cultures, through which a *higher* type manifests itself: something which in its relation to mankind as a whole is a kind of overman. Such lucky instances of great success were always possible and will perhaps always be possible. Whole generations, tribes, and peoples even may, under certain circumstances, show as such a *hit*" (my translation).

action [conduct] of the individual, as resulting from his organization and his will combined [another name for *to hegemonikon*], we call manners. What are they but thought entering the hands and feet, controlling the movements of the body, the speech and behavior?[37]

Several pages later Emerson performs one of his famous, or, if you wish, notorious, reversals in argument that does not allow that one dogmatically rest on any single instance of his own analyses of any phenomenon whatsoever. This strategy of pervasive argumentative *metabole*, so obviously inherited from Heraclitus, leads to the following re-valuation of the initially celebrated silent and subtle language of manners:

But through this lustrous varnish the reality is ever shining. 'Tis hard to keep the *what* from breaking through the pretty painting of the *how*. The core will come to the surface. Strong will and keen perception *overpower* old manners and create new; and the thought of the present moment has a greater value than all the past. In persons of *character* we do not remark manners, because of their instantaneousness. We are surprised by the thing done ... Yet nothing is more charming than to recognize *the great style* [this will become a major term in Nietzsche] which runs through the actions of such.[38]

Language in Emerson, and I would like to come back to the opening observations of my essay, is a flexible tool, not a container of essentials; neither is the language of manners a safe haven of stable meaning. If employed properly, that is, in an existentially meaningful way, language in Emerson is the tool of meaning-making, of *poiesis*. Such language undergoes a continuous metamorphosis at the hands and instigation of the underlying contingent power-play of character, of nature, that is, through the actions of the *hegemonikon* as guiding principle in both self and world. These transformations and transmutations of language in Emerson were analyzed and interpreted with great intensity and deep insight by Richard Poirier under the heading of "troping."[39] The language of manners, we come to realize, is equally subject to tropings, to unforeseeable turns and relentless renewals at the hands of powerful realizations of that which simply is and ultimately refuses to be named, that which sometimes shows as nature, and sometimes manifests as a Caesarian self. Such tropings, however, indicate that the historical changes, the new beginnings in the iterative patterns of

---

[37]*W* VI, 163.
[38]Ibid., 180 (my emphasis).
[39]Richard Poirier, *The Renewal of Literature: Emersonian Reflections* (New York: Random House, 1987), *passim*.

the creation of manners and of decay into mere fashion, are acts not of conformity, of continuity, of tradition, and of obedience; they are, rather— and as we already heard—"resistance of circumstances," signs of character. Emerson's deep awareness of the power and dignity of human agency— before any social determination and uncontaminated by any antecedent collective imprint: things in which the deeply conservative passion of so much of contemporary cultural criticism may want us to believe—this deep awareness in Emerson of the un-mediated human potential makes him define true conduct and proper manners primarily as negations of the established, as violations of the current civility, as provocations of the prevailing social contract and its concomitant decorum. "Manners impress [only] as they indicate real power"[40]—and real power is un-mediated potentiality. This is also why Emerson repeats within a few pages his insistence on the grounding of all languages of civility on self-reliance and on the implied identity of self-reliance with powerful agency: "The basis of good manners is self-reliance"; and again: "Self-reliance is the basis of behavior, as it is the guaranty that the powers are not squandered in too much demonstration."[41] An existentially well-mannered existence implies and manifests an economy of power.

With his celebration of European and Asian Caesarian gentlemen who lounge so provocatively in their chairs, with these creators of an exemplary conduct of life and a great and original and self-reliant style in manners, with these models Emerson's text had, however, created its own fixed image of what conduct could or should be, an image in danger of establishing a precedent with the pretense to an authoritative sway over all succeeding generations who might thus be possibly bereft of an "original relation to the universe."[42] Emerson, however, is too careful and sophisticated a thinker and writer to become a victim of the very petrifications and ossifications he denounces: "The Emersonian conversion of intellect into action ... resists formal stasis, even the stasis of constant conversion."[43] In order to undermine the authority of his own narrative of manners-in-the-making and in order to dis-appoint the Victorian frames of reference that he has implicitly established and fixed by his celebration of the conduct of representative *men*, the later honorary vice-president of the New England Woman's Suffrage Association in a typical turning or troping of his own guiding beliefs invents two fictitious women, Gertrude and Blanche, who take us into a realm of conduct and manners as yet (in 1860) only insufficiently explored and not yet safely established, a realm of civility that is about to mark another, an imminent upheaval in the endless story or history of the tropings of the

---

[40]Ibid., 181.
[41]Ibid., 178, 182.
[42]*Nature* W I, 9.
[43]Bauerlein, *The Pragmatic Mind*, 21.

languages of human behavior: "Nothing can be more excellent in kind than the Corinthian grace of Gertrude's manners, and yet Blanche, who has no manners, has better manners than she; for the movements of Blanche are the sallies of a spirit which is sufficient for the moment, and she can afford to express every thought by instant action."[44] Blanche, the as-yet-to-be-defined whiteness of human conduct and manners, a whiteness so ambiguously dear to the imagination of the American Renaissance, Blanche as a new woman in an existential sense is, in Emerson's text, the truly unprecedented and therefore the authentic agent and powerful instigator of a future practice of more genuine manners. Emerson occasionally saw this possibility of a new departure in manners and conduct as imminent, and he exults in saying: "at this moment I esteem it a chief felicity of this country, that it excels in women."[45]

Ultimately, then, for Emerson, there are no such precisely circumscribed entities or categories or conceptions as social conduct, as manners and civility, as behavior and fashion. "Emersonian thinking hesitates" before such substantiations[46] because "[t]he only sin is limitation";[47] instead, he uses his flexible, his fluid terms in order to celebrate the unforeseen, the powerfully contingent possibility that humans and the forms of their social relations may yet again be different. This is why, for him, the genuinely civilized and well-mannered person is she or he who resists circumstances, resists that which has literally been built around us and, in the words of the essay "Circles," "hem[s] in the life."[48] In a modest way I have tried to imitate this Emersonian strategy in dealing with his vision of manners and civility. In discussing Emerson on manners and conduct, I thought it best to heed his advice and allow the mind to go "antagonizing on"[49] and encourage the concepts and the words to transgress their conventionally well-defined circumferences.

---

[44]W VI, 178.
[45]"Manners" W III, 145.
[46]Bauerlein, *The Pragmatic Mind*, 11.
[47]"Circles" W II, 287.
[48]Ibid., 284.
[49]"Experience" W III, 70.

# 8

# Nietzsche's Emerson

Radical changes or innovations in the history of thinking that characterize a whole new epoch are usually not sufficiently accounted for when we limit our attention solely to changing concepts, tenets, propositions, or systems of belief. In the context of his analysis of seventeenth-century rationalism and scientism, Alfred North Whitehead once briefly characterized the conditions of the possibility of new modes of thinking in a given historical era:

> There will be some fundamental assumptions which adherents of all the variant systems within the epoch unconsciously presuppose. Such assumptions appear so obvious that people do not know what they are assuming because no other way of putting things has ever occurred to them. With these assumptions a certain limited number of types of philosophic systems are possible, and this group of systems constitutes the philosophy of the epoch.[1]

In drawing attention to the formative potential of unconsciously and unwittingly held beliefs or apparently unquestioned fundamental assumptions, Whitehead merely adumbrates the problem. We might still want to know whether he believes in an individual or collective subject who or which, however unconsciously, assumes these fundamental assumptions or whether they do indeed—and this is the way I read Whitehead—simply and contingently occur and thus happen *to* subjects. Other twentieth-century

This essay was previously published as "Fate, Power, and History in Emerson and Nietzsche" in *Emerson/Nietzsche*, ed Michael Lopez, spec. issue of *ESQ: A Journal of the American Renaissance* 43 (1997): 267–93. Reprinted by permission of Johanna Heloise Abtahi, managing editor of *ESQ*.

[1]Alfred North Whitehead, *Science and the Modern World* (1926; New York: Free Press, 1967). 48.

thinkers have argued the case more decisively. Moving beyond the subject as foundation of historical change or belief, Heidegger has opened the possibility of our appreciating historical modes of thinking as dispensations of Being, as un-grounded challenges to which not only individual thinkers but whole eras feel constrained to respond. According to Whitehead and Heidegger, then, we would be obliged to characterize a radical change in thinking either as an unmediated and contingent occurrence of new fundamental assumptions or as the emergence of a new dispensation of Being. In both cases, the new era would be something that happened and not something humanly made or authored.

Following Whitehead, Susanne K. Langer has tried to find an appropriate terminology for major historical shifts in thinking. In the first chapter of *Philosophy in a New Key*, she speaks of "basic assumptions," of a "framework of thinking," or even of "common-sense notions about things in general." She draws our attention to the fact that it is the questions we ask rather than specified answers in a given philosophical system that determine the prevalent mode of thinking; she speaks of the "horizon" within which new possibilities of thought, or a new key, for that matter, may arise or be detected. For her, there are "tacit, fundamental way[s] of seeing things." A new mode of thinking owes itself to a new and basic idea. Such basic or fundamental ideas, she concludes, "are not theories; they are the terms in which theories are conceived; they give rise to specific questions, and are articulated only in the form of these questions. Therefore one may call them *generative ideas* in the history of thought."[2] The very profusion of Langer's terminology tends to obscure the fact that she cannot really account for what the sciences or the humanities might describe as a paradigm change. Again, as in the case of Whitehead, the question remains: who thinks these generative ideas, or how and why are they generated? At first sight Langer's implicit subjectivism seems to exclude the possibility that changes in thinking occur or emerge as challenges or dispensations of Being, as contingent ways the world may show itself in a manner unforeseen by a previous mode of thinking; her very concepts (idea, theory, conceive) insinuate a rationalist and metaphysical basis for all kinds of thinking. And yet, in a minor key, Langer's remarkable endeavor also indicates the possibility of a mode of speaking about radical change that goes beyond "rational assumptions" and "generative ideas." She is ever so implicitly aware of the fact that there have to be "tacit [!] ... ways of seeing things" and as-yet-unnamed modes for things to appear before they are conceptualized as ideas. The half-buried terminology of appearing and seeing acknowledges the always possible and unpredictable new manner in which things may make themselves known

---

[2]Susanne K. Langer, *Philosophy in a New Key: A Study in the Symbolism of Reason, Rite, and Art* (1942; Cambridge, MA: Harvard University Press, 1979), 3–6, 8.

by showing. Thus Whitehead's example, Heidegger's interpretation of the history of thinking as a history of the dispensation of Being, and Langer's very hesitation within the precincts of metaphysical conceptualization all point in the same direction: changes in thinking that may constitute the beginning of an epoch occur because of the way the *world* or *things* reveal themselves and because of the way they are then seen before they are being questioned or answered. This kind of ontological change, which is always accountable for a new departure, is realized by thinkers as a new and basic *intuition* or *vision* provoked by Being rather than as fundamental assumptions or ideas simply and unaccountably generated and then held by subjects.

Emerson and Nietzsche stand for the beginning of one of the most dramatic changes in the history of thinking. It was Stanley Cavell who first thoroughly comprehended the significant role of Emerson in helping to bring about the *way* or *methodos* of thinking that we have come to understand as the slow erosion and gradual overturning of (the possibilities of) metaphysical systems. In linking Emerson, Nietzsche, and Heidegger, Cavell has also set the agenda for a new understanding of the relationship between Emerson and Nietzsche.[3] Harold Bloom, Richard Poirier, and George Kateb have followed Cavell's lead in variously reading Emerson from the—sometimes implicit—perspective of the major philosophical changes commonly acknowledged in Nietzsche.[4] This approach has complemented the more traditional intensive and extensive research devoted to tracing Emerson's influence on Nietzsche in terms of thematic and sometimes only localized inspirations of single, even if singularly significant insights in the later thinker. The majority of attempts to deal with the relationship between Emerson and Nietzsche have thus been devoted to a study of terms, concepts, images, ideas, problems, and opinions shared by the two thinkers.[5]

---

[3]Stanley Cavell, "Thinking of Emerson," in *The Senses of Walden: An Expanded Edition* (1972; San Francisco: North Point Press, 1981), 121–38.

[4]Harold Bloom, "Emerson: Power at the Crossing," in *Ralph Waldo Emerson: A Collection of Critical Essays*, ed. Lawrence Buell (Englewood Cliffs, NJ: Prentice Hall, 1993), 148–58; Richard Poirier, *Poetry and Pragmatism* (Cambridge, MA: Harvard University Press, 1992); George Kateb, *Emerson and Self-Reliance* (Thousand Oaks, CA: Sage, 1995).

[5]George J. Stack's comprehensive *Nietzsche and Emerson: An Elective Affinity* (Athens: Ohio University Press, 1992) is certainly the first systematic presentation in English of the "many elements" (x) that Nietzsche may have adapted from Emerson. Contrary to Professor Stack's claim in his preface, however, there has been an in-depth research into the field since at least 1902 that has unearthed practically all the evidence that he so generously reassembles for the American reader. Major sources are: Georg Biedenkapp, "Der amerikanische Nietzsche," *Ernstes Wollen* 4 (1902/03): 246–9; Régis Michaud, "Emerson et Nietzsche," *La Revue germanique* 6 (1910): 414–21; Charles Andler, *Nietzsche: Sa vie et sa pensée* (Paris: Bossard, 1920–31); Julius Simon, *Ralph Waldo Emerson in Deutschland* (Berlin: Junker und Dünnhaupt, 1937); Rudolf Schottlaender, "Two Dionysians: Emerson and Nietzsche," *South Atlantic Quarterly* 39 (1940): 330–43; Fred B. Wahr, "Emerson and the Germans," *Monatshefte für Deutschen Unterricht* 33 (1941): 49–63; Hermann Hummel, "Emerson and Nietzsche," *New*

If, however, a momentous change in thinking like the beginning of the erosion of metaphysics is due to the way Being addresses thinkers, if a fundamental redirection of thought is due to the way a new and basic vision happens to them, then we may legitimately ask whether there is a common ontological core, a post-metaphysical response to a new dispensation of Being, a primary intuition shared by Emerson and Nietzsche that is not sufficiently recognized if we exclusively focus on common concepts, images, and themes in their thinking. What was it, we may ask, that kept Nietzsche's interest in Emerson alive beyond the fascination with the occasional aphorism or single existential or ethical interpretation of the *conditio humana*?

The ontological revelation and/or vision shared by Emerson and Nietzsche may be tentatively circumscribed by the Emersonian terms "fate," "power," and "history," provided we do not use these words as concepts in a metaphysical sense.[6] Emerson himself has insisted that language is a system of fluxional symbols, "vehicular and transitive, … good, as ferries and horses are, for conveyance, not as farms and houses are, for homestead"[7]— an idea that anticipates or projects Nietzsche's description of language as "bewegliches Heer von Metaphern" (a mobile army of metaphors).[8] Philosophical terms and terminologies are lost in the "quicksand"[9] of

---

*England Quarterly* 19 (1946): 63–84; Ernst Robert Curtius, "Emerson," in *Kritische Essays zur europäischen Literatur* (Bern: Francke, 1950), 189–203; Eduard Baumgarten, "Emerson – Nietzsche," *Internationale Zeitschrift für Erziehung* 8 (1939): 1–16; Eduard Baumgarten, "Mitteilungen und Bemerkungen über den Einfluß Emersons auf Nietzsche," *Jahrbuch für Amerikastudien* 1 (1956): 93–152; Stanley Hubbard, *Nietzsche und Emerson* (Basel: Verlag für Recht und Gesellschaft, 1958); Ingo Seidler, "'Den Blick fernhin auf Nordamerika richten': Zur Amerikaperspektive Nietzsches," in *Amerika in der deutschen Literatur*, ed. Sigrid Bauschinger et al. (Stuttgart: Kohlhammer, 1975), 218–28; Michael Lopez, "Transcendental Failure: 'The Palace of Spiritual Power,'" in *Emerson: Prospect and Retrospect*, ed. Joel Porte (Cambridge, MA: Harvard University Press, 1982), 121–53; Vivetta Vivarelli, "Nietzsche und Emerson: Über einige Pfade in Zarathustras metaphorischer Landschaft," *Nietzsche-Studien* 16 (1987): 227–63; Herwig Friedl, "Emerson and Nietzsche: 1862–1874," in *Religion and Philosophy in America*, ed. Peter Freese (Essen: Die Blaue Eule, 1987), vol. 1, 267–87; Michael Payne, "Emerson, Nietzsche, and the Politics of Interpretation," *CEA Forum* 18 (1988): 16–18; Irena S. M. Makarushka, *Religious Imagination and Language in Emerson and Nietzsche* (New York: St. Martin's Press, 1994). If these texts were properly consulted, one would hesitate to speak of "rumors about the affiliation between the writings" of Emerson and Nietzsche and of a field that "has not been explored"; Stack, *Nietzsche and Emerson*, vii.

[6]Michel Haar, "Nietzsche and Metaphysical Language," in *The New Nietzsche*, ed. David B. Allison (Cambridge, MA: MIT Press, 1987), 4–36, offers an excellent analysis of the changes in the function and reach of philosophical terms effected by Nietzsche's post-metaphysical vision.

[7]W III, 37.

[8]"Über Wahrheit und Lüge im aussermoralischen Sinne," in *Die Geburt der Tragödie, KSA* 1, 880. As before, I use the abbreviation *KSA* to refer to the *Kritische Studienausgabe* of Nietzsche's works, ed. Giorgio Colli and Mazzino Montinari (Munich: dtv, 1980).

[9]W III, 58.

illusory references that complicate linguistic orientation in Emerson and, at the same time, widen and invigorate[10] the possibilities of meaning-making, of *poiesis*, in a newly opened ontological realm. The three concepts of fate, power, and history may be said to create a field or to map a territory within which the Emersonian primary intuition of a new dispensation of Being may be articulated or imaged. Nietzsche's "conceptions" of "the eternal return of the same," of "the will to power," and—again—of "history" possibly serve a corresponding function for him without being exact equivalences of words that have no fixed significance in Emerson to begin with.

"The American Scholar" contains one of the most profound early pronouncements by Emerson on the way nature shows herself to the thinker, the scholar:

> There is never a beginning, there is never an end, to the inexplicable continuity of this web of God, but always circular power returning into itself. Therein it resembles his own spirit, whose beginning, whose ending, he never can find,—so entire, so boundless. Far too as her splendors shine, system on system shooting like rays, upward, downward, without center, without circumference,—in the mass and in the particle, Nature hastens to render account of herself to the mind.[11]

Nature speaks and the thinker responds; Being reveals itself as both nature and mind, as and through a world of possible correspondences without origin or *telos*, without center or delimitation. The highest, the supreme being, God himself, is an ambiguous entity, a doubtful agent: does he weave the web, is he identical with the web, or does the web—similar to the emerging deity of process philosophy—weave God? All beings in this world of natural and mental continuities without destination seem open to possibly endless readings or classifications, as Emerson goes on to explain. Emerson's new awareness foreshadows Nietzsche's famous vision of the world as "ein Ungeheuer von Kraft, ohne Anfang, ohne Ende ... ein Meer in sich selber stürmender und fluthender Kräfte, ewig sich wandelnd, ewig zurücklaufend, mit ungeheuren Jahren der Wiederkehr."[12] Nietzsche's powerful monster without beginning and end, stormily raging within itself, forever changing and returning into itself through immensities of circular time, is nothing but a hyperbolic version of Emerson's earlier interpretation. The core of the primary vision, the fundamental assumption literally provoked by a new dispensation of Being, however, is neither Emerson's web of

---

[10]Compare the concept of "troping" used by Richard Poirier in *The Renewal of Literature: Emersonian Reflections* (New York: Random House, 1987) and in *Poetry and Pragmatism* (Cambridge, MA: Harvard University Press, 1992).

[11]*W* I, 87.

[12]*KSA* 11, 610.

God nor Nietzsche's raging sea; the core of this world of nature and mind shows itself in the most original and innovative way as "circular power returning into itself." It is in this phrase, I would like to maintain, that we witness the new dispensation of Being: the very beginning of momentous implications explored by both Emerson and—responding to the same challenge or following Emerson's vision—by Nietzsche. The phrase "circular power returning into itself" poses a severe threat to any metaphysical and substantialist ontology—more severe, ultimately, than the denial of beginning and end, of Alpha and Omega, in the same quotation. The words "circular power returning into itself" are a new and unprecedented way of naming Being.

The first chapter of the second volume of Martin Heidegger's *Nietzsche* is entitled "Die Ewige Wiederkehr des Gleichen und der Wille zur Macht"; his critical interpretation of Nietzsche's concepts of the eternal return and the will to power is meant to show that Nietzsche's way of thinking the Being of beings is the ultimate and disastrous culmination of metaphysics. Even if one tends to disagree with Heidegger's historical analysis, the basic ontological insight in this chapter is important for an in-depth appreciation of Emerson's and Nietzsche's new departure in thinking Being. The thoughts of the will to power and the eternal return of the same think the identical ontological factuality according to Heidegger.[13] In this way the traditional difference between *essentia* and *existentia* is overcome: Heidegger sees this as a deficiency and speaks not so much of overcoming as of a forgetting of the difference.[14] However, if the will to power names the *essentia* or *quidditas*, that is, *what* something is, and if the eternal return of the same thinks this *essentia* in its *existentia*, or the fact *that* it is, then, Heidegger concludes, both terms speak of the "steadying" (Beständigung) of becoming in the mode of a continuous—and again "steady"—(self-)overpowering.[15]

It is not at all difficult to see that Emerson thinks the same thought when he speaks of "circular power returning into itself" as the basic feature of the way the world as nature shows in its Being. First, Emerson establishes the continuity, the temporal "steadiness" of becoming through the very circularity of the *essentia* of all beings, namely power. Secondly, if power is that which or what things are, then their that-ness or *existentia* is a constant circular return into their own what-ness or *quidditas* or *essentia*, that is, power. Power, the Being of beings, we may conclude, is a persistent,

---

[13]Heidegger, *Nietzsche II*, ed. Brigitte Schillbach, vol. 6.2 of *Gesamtausgabe* (1961; Frankfurt: Klostermann, 1997), 7.

[14]Ibid., 9.

[15]Ibid., 14. "Die ewige Wiederkehr des Gleichen trägt gleichsam ihr Wesen als ständigste Beständigung des Werdens des Ständigen vor sich her." ("The eternal return of the same propagates—so to speak—its essence as the steadiest steadying of the becoming of steadiness"; my translation.)

a continuous, a steady self-grounding of beings. The becoming of beings—their Being—is a self-conditioning. By their power, by their assertion of the possibility to become and thus to transcend any of their given states, they paradoxically also return into themselves and ground themselves again and again, incessantly, as radically temporal and yet as steady and continuous in their very becoming, weaving the web of God. Emerson's response to a new dispensation of Being, his generative idea, his primary vision differs in only one respect from that of Nietzsche. Emerson does not even articulate the duality of the eternal return and the will to power: the idea of circular power thinks the unity of *essentia* and *existentia* more radically and originally than Nietzsche's tortuous attempt to join and fuse two traditional metaphysical ontological categories like *essentia* (will to power) and *existentia* (the eternal return of the same). The earlier thinker—as Heidegger so often maintained in speaking of the Presocratics—opens the most radical and far-reaching implications of the new response to the new dispensation of Being.

If we look at Emerson's seminal post-metaphysical phrase of "circular power returning into itself" from this ontological perspective, we become aware of the expanse of the field that has been opened for thinking: 1. beings ground themselves in becoming what they are; they condition themselves, they owe themselves to themselves in their Being as becoming—maybe we could say, they are their own "fate"; 2. in the foundational, the creative act of continuously returning to themselves as they become what they are, they show as the very potential of becoming or "power"; 3. the constant and circular play of a powerful self-conditioning provides for continuity and thus for a self-generated and always individualized "history." The ontological turn beyond metaphysics in Emerson shows ontically, that is, in the way he reads so-called real events and things and (human) beings, in his interpretations of fate, power, and history. The essays entitled "Fate," "Power," and "History" were among those which Nietzsche studied again and again.[16] In reading the central ontological implications of these texts, we may deepen our understanding, our visionary awareness of the common, the identical ground of Emerson's and Nietzsche's fundamental or foundational "idea."

"Fate" is, in a way, Emerson's ontological *summa philosophiae*. The essay is as much about power and history as it is about fate itself. An essay like "Power" is more like a coda to "Fate," and "History" appears as the

---

[16]The best and most systematic and thorough as well as comprehensive information on the phases of Nietzsche's reading of Emerson is found in Baumgarten, "Mitteilungen und Bemerkungen" and in Hubbard, *Nietzsche und Emerson*. The early phase is systematically analyzed in Friedl, "Emerson and Nietzsche: 1862–1874." Stack provides useful English versions of the texts and of the detailed and in-depth German research in *Nietzsche and Emerson* as well as "Nietzsche's Earliest Essays: Translation and Commentary on 'Fate and History' and 'Freedom of Will and Fate,'" *Philosophy Today* 37 (1993), 153–68.

prelude of the mature considerations in *The Conduct of Life*, once we adopt the ontological perspective. Nietzsche at age 18 showed an extraordinary perception of Emerson's most revolutionary concerns when he wrote two early essays under the immediate impression of his reading the German translation of *The Conduct of Life* in 1862 and called these two sketches "Fatum und Geschichte" and "Willensfreiheit und Fatum." Focusing on the terms "freedom of the will," "fate," and "history," he responded to Emerson's primary vision of a radically changed dispensation of Being—a vision he continued to share and was never to abandon throughout his career.[17] As usual, Emerson carefully avoids a strict terminology in "Fate" so as not to create the impression that fate or its seeming opposite, power, stand as metaphysically solidified entities. Fate is often spoken of as necessity, determination, nature, or natural history—and power tends to assume the verbal guises or alternatives of freedom, spirit, and thought. Emerson stresses the fact that power and fate, freedom and necessity, are not even, strictly speaking, pairs in a binary opposition but rather possibilities of naming the way things are in a realm of gradual transitions without metaphysical fixation:

> to see how fate slides into freedom and freedom into fate, observe how far the roots of every creature run, or find if you can a point where there is no thread of connection. Our life is consentaneous and far-related. This knot of nature is so well tied that nobody was ever cunning enough to find the two ends.[18]

Every existent being, and thus also our human life, is determined by consent and relation, by will (the will to yea-saying, we might add in a Nietzschean vein) and by fate. Like the metaphysical opposites of the one and the many,[19] or the classical positions of metaphysics discussed in "Nominalist and Realist," freedom and fate, or power and determination, or spirit and nature, are aspects of Being and not (substantial) essences in themselves. The transgression of the ontological boundaries of *essentia* and *existentia* is echoed in the ontic realm as the literal delimitation, the un-defining of that which conditions and the act of conditioning itself. Being as becoming owes itself to itself:

---

[17]In "Emerson and Nietzsche," I have systematically explored all major motifs of Nietzsche's mature thought already to be found in these early exercises in Emersonian thinking. Stack, in "Nietzsche's Earliest Essays," emphasizes a selection of these.

[18]W VI, 40.

[19]Emerson erodes the binary opposition of the one and the many in his essay on Plato in *Representative Men* by using the very word "sliding" in order to indicate the continuity of these two—one might say, tentative—conceptions rather than their separate essentialist integrity: "each so fast slides into the other that we can never say what is one, and what is not"; W IV, 50.

The planet makes itself. The animal cell makes itself;—then what it wants. Every creature, wren or dragon, shall make its own lair. As soon as there is life, there is self-direction and absorbing and using of material. Life is freedom,—life in the direct ratio of its amount.[20]

The circular structure of Being asserts itself in the way beings are conceived in their individual becoming. The intensity of this becoming depends on the amount of life or power, on the *quanta* of power, as Nietzsche was going to say. One of the central concerns of "Fate," however, is specifically with the human being and her or his newly envisioned possibilities of becoming who one is.

The investigation of this crucial existential concern, of this *fundamentalontologische* problem concerning the Being of *Dasein*, which is so prominent in Emerson's "Self-Reliance" and in Nietzsche's late *Ecce homo: Wie man wird, was man ist*,[21] may best be guided by two momentous aphoristic propositions in "Fate." The first statement is introduced as a version of the Hindu idea of *karma*, a conception also advanced by Schelling: "in the history of the individual is always an account of his condition, and he knows himself to be a party to his present estate."[22] The temporal dimension of the Being of *Dasein*, her or his history, literally presents one with the conditioning factors of that which she or he has become. At the same time, fate or the conditions of becoming who one is must be seen as results of (free and powerful) acts of will, and consequently each one is "a party to his present estate." Necessity and freedom, fate and the power of self-fashioning, are varieties of reading the self. The past of the self, the conditions, may be read as fate, or they may be read as acts, as a series of active participations. This implies, at the same time, that the self may be said to incorporate an alien other, an "it" that she or he may accept as a yet to be acknowledged phase of self-hood. Returning into "it"-self the human being may appropriate the alienated or forgotten other that usually shows as the natural history of the species. In a powerful act of interpretive will, however,[23] the self may transgress its metaphysical idea of her- or himself as self-contained, as a self contained, and re-appropriate the past that only seems to be mere "condition," or fate, or determination, or the natural history of the species: "We must respect Fate as natural history, but there is more than natural history."[24] It is power, Emerson asserts, that enables the

---

[20] W VI, 41–2.

[21] *KSA* 6, 255–374.

[22] W VI, 18.

[23] The most thorough and the philosophically most sophisticated essay on the concepts of the will to power and on interpretation as an assertion of power is Wolfgang Müller-Lauter "Nietzsches Lehre vom Willen zur Macht," in *Nietzsche*, ed. Jörg Salaquarda (Darmstadt: WBG, 1980), 234–87.

[24] W VI, 26.

self to go beyond its dependency on previous conditions. The true self is the one that is not limited by her or his presence or present estate as a seemingly subjective and enclosed entity. The true self may say yes to its forgotten other, it returns in a circular motion into its own past and thus grounds the present self in the it-self while becoming who she or he is. This, however, as we saw in reading the passage on circular power in "The American Scholar," is the temporal gesture that characterizes (true) Being. In accepting the alienated past as her or his own, the self becomes who she or he is; the self achieves the fullness of Being, it becomes a *Dasein*.[25]

The second proposition that helps to deepen the understanding of the new ontological situation within which Emerson and Nietzsche find themselves obliged to redescribe the Being of the human being or *Dasein* reads:

> Just as much intellect as you add, so much organic power. He who sees through the design, presides over it, and must will that which must be. We sit and rule, and, though we sleep, our dream will come to pass. Our thought, though it were only an hour old, affirms an oldest necessity, not to be separated from thought, and not to be separated from will. They must always have coexisted.[26]

Awareness, knowing, intellect are agents of ontic, of real, of organic power. To know is to rule and dominate. Knowing Being, knowing the design of the intimate relationship of and the transitionality between fate and power enables the human being to fulfill her or his existential desire; "our dream will come to pass." The parallelism of "must will" and "must be" asserts that there is only one mode of Being and that true willing, the fully unfolded will to power which is aware of itself, the genuine existential desire, is the same as, is identical with the necessity of Being. Willing does not oppose fate, it does not battle the past, willing as the power of the human being may return into its conditioning, into what "must be," and may knowingly will its own becoming in the by now familiar, circular ontological structure. In willing fate and in revealing fate as the ossification of past willing,[27] our thought, the human being's existential awareness "affirms an oldest necessity." This affirmation of the oldest necessity is the precursor or equivalent of Nietzsche's yea-saying to the eternal return and to the steadiness of becoming, it is the foreshadowing of his un-conditioned ontological assent to what must be— *amor fati*.

---

[25]Heidegger's familiar term, characterizing the human being from the perspective of a fundamental ontology, literally denotes the place or "there" (Da), where Being (Sein) occurs. Both Emerson and Nietzsche obviously think human beings in a similar fashion as localized events of circular (self-)grounding.

[26]W VI, 31.

[27]Compare this passage in "Fate": "Every spirit makes its house; but afterwards the house confines the spirit"; W VI, 14.

One of the most intriguing philosophical problems in Nietzsche's *Also sprach Zarathustra* is his meditation on and his re-valuation of the meaning of time and thus of history in the ontological sense of the indispensable dimension of becoming.[28] In the chapter "Von der Erlösung" ("On Salvation"), Zarathustra meditates on the now and the "has been." He calls their relationship "*mein* Unerträglichstes,"[29] his most unbearable thought or burden. The problem for Zarathustra is the fact that the will, the will to power as "der Befreier und Freudebringer" (the liberator and bringer of glad tidings, the new evangelist), seems unable to overcome that which chains it and limits its freedom: the "it was," the past as an unmovable fate. The fact that beings owe themselves to an "other," that they are indebted in their very existence to something that seems alien to them, this is the ontological condition of guilt and bad conscience, this is the melancholy of existing,[30] which ultimately results in "Widerwille," in resentment. The chapter culminates in this prophetic pronouncement:

Alles "Es war" ist ein Bruchstück, ein Räthsel, ein grauser Zufall – bis der schaffende Wille dazu sagt: "aber so wollte ich es!"

Bis der schaffende Wille dazu sagt: "Aber so will ich es! So werde ich's wollen!"

Aber sprach er schon so? Und wann geschieht diess? Ist der Wille schon abgeschirrt von seiner eignen Thorheit?

Wurde der Wille sich schon selber Erlöser und Freudebringer? Verlernte er den Geist der Rache und alles Zähneknirschen?

Und wer lehrte ihn Versöhnung mit der Zeit, und Höheres als alle Versöhnung ist?

Höheres als alle Versöhnung muss der Wille wollen, welcher der Wille zur Macht ist –: doch wie geschieht ihm das? Wer lehrte ihn auch noch das Zurückwollen?[31]

---

[28]There are few really thorough investigations of the question of time in Nietzsche. I have been encouraged in my own attempts to think through the problem by these two outstanding and quite different interpretations: Joan Stambaugh, *The Problem of Time in Nietzsche*, trans. John F. Humphrey (Lewisburg, PA: Bucknell University Press, 1987) and David Wood, "Nietzsche's Transvaluation of Time," in *Exceedingly Nietzsche: Aspects of Contemporary Nietzsche-Interpretation*, ed. David Farrell Krell and David Wood (London: Routledge, 1988), 31–62.

[29]*KSA* 4, 179.

[30]Ibid., 180.

[31]Ibid., 181. This is my attempt at translation: "All 'it was' is a fragment and a riddle, a cruel chance—till the creative will says to it: 'but this is how I willed it!' / Till the creative will says to it: 'But this is how I will it! This is the way I will will it!' / But has it already spoken in this way? And when will this happen? Has the will already been released from the harness of its own stupidity? / Has the will already become its own savior and evangelist? Has it un-learned the spirit of revenge and all grating of teeth? / And who taught it reconciliation with time, and something that is higher than all reconciliation? / The will which is the will to power has to will something higher than all reconciliation—: but how does this happen to it? Who taught it to also will backwards?"

The past, Zarathustra explains, is a mere and contingent given unless the will (to power) accepts it and identifies with it as something willed. Then the past is grounded and, we might inelegantly add, it becomes relevant. The will, or power as event, if we use Emerson's rhetoric, has to encompass all dimensions of time: past, present, and future. A true and full existence beyond resentment would have to accept and will its own past otherness and its as-yet-unachieved future possibility. Only in this way, the will, Being as power, would become reconciled with time: it might even become something higher, namely time itself. Understood as identical with time and its three dimensions, the will to power as the Being of the human being would achieve salvation, it could gladly say yes to its own conditioning and to its as yet and forever open future. This new gospel is the ontological promise that the human being may one day accept her- or himself as Being and time. Being able to "will backwards," the human being *is* "circular power returning into itself." Nietzsche-Zarathustra's prophecy of salvation is one with Emerson's ontological vision. True Being as becoming grounds itself in returning into its own (alienated) past in order to guarantee the freedom of its future; this is the ultimate realization of self-reliance. Once the human being "must will that which must be," as Emerson says in "Fate," it is indeed true that "freedom is necessary."[32]

Nietzsche did not gradually *develop* this vision, this response to a new dispensation of Being as time, to the identity of will to power and eternal return, to the unity of freedom and fate in their circular interdependence. Rather, Nietzsche seems to have been immediately struck by this challenge and by Emerson's response in 1862; he returned to reading Emerson with great intensity in 1881 when he began to compose *Also sprach Zarathustra* and uttered the prophecy of the will's power to "will backwards,"[33] and he reaffirmed this generative idea when he added his favorite phrase "how to become who you are" as a subtitle to his last "autobiography" *Ecce homo* in 1888.

In his first essay inspired by Emerson and written during the Easter vacation of 1862, "Fatum und Geschichte," Nietzsche responds to Emerson's "History" and "Fate," the two opening texts of *Essays: First Series* and *The Conduct of Life*, respectively.[34] Nietzsche says:

Was ist es, was die Seele so vieler Menschen mit Macht zu dem Gewöhnlichen niederzieht und einen höhern Ideenaufflug so erschwert?

---

[32] W VI, 27.
[33] See Baumgarten, "Mitteilungen und Bemerkungen," 107 ff.
[34] See Herwig Friedl, "Emerson and Nietzsche" and Stack, "Nietzsche's Earliest Essays." Graham Parkes has greatly deepened our understanding of the psychological and biographical significance of this early encounter of Nietzsche and Emerson; see his *Composing the Soul: Reaches of Nietzsche's Psychology* (Chicago: University of Chicago Press, 1994), 35–42.

Ein fatalistischer Schädel- und Rückgratsbau, der Stand und die Natur ihrer Eltern, das Alltägliche ihrer Verhältnisse, das Gemeine ihrer Umgebung, selbst das Eintönige ihrer Heimat. Wir sind beeinflußt worden, ohne die Kraft einer Gegenwirkung in uns zu tragen, ohne selbst zu erkennen, daß wir beeinflußt sind.[35]

It is not difficult to see how this passage echoes Emerson in "Fate":

The menagerie, or forms and power of the spine, is a book of fate: the bill of the bird, the skull of the snake, determines tyrannically its limits. So is the scale of races, of temperaments; so is sex; so is climate; so is the reaction of talents imprisoning the vital power in certain directions.[36]

Nietzsche at age 18 had accepted Emerson's bleak view of the determining factors of natural history. The last sentence quoted from Nietzsche's early attempt, however, indicates where the solution will be found. If we do not know that we have been influenced or determined by the past, by the "it was," it follows that the possibility of a powerful insight may change the depressing, melancholy state of affairs, which he still remembers in the passage on salvation from *Zarathustra*. His solution will be and has to be Emerson's: "He who sees through the design, presides over it, and must will that which must be." A late fragment from the so-called *Dionysian Dithyrambs*, written in the summer of 1888, once again states the problem and the solution, Emerson's and Nietzsche's solution in "Fate" and in *Also sprach Zarathustra*, to the problem posed by the seemingly inflexible and majestically alien past and its antagonism to the free play of Being as the will to power in its now-ness; the solution is indeed none other than that of "circular power returning into itself," now expressed in terms of willing and determination:

so ist's jetzt mein Wille:
und seit das mein Wille ist,
geht Alles mir auch nach Wunsche—
Dies war meine letzte Klugheit:

---

[35] "Fatum und Geschichte," in *Frühe Schriften*, ed. Hans Joachim Mette (1934; Munich: Beck, 1994), vol. 2, 58. My translation does not attempt to gloss over Nietzsche's stylistic awkwardness: "What is it that so powerfully debases the soul of so many people and makes a higher flight of ideas impossible? A fatalistic structure of the skull and the spine, the social status and the nature of their parents, the everyday routine of their condition, the vulgarity of their surroundings, the monotony even of their home. We have been influenced, without bearing within us the power of reaction, without even knowing that we have been influenced and determined."
[36] W VI, 14.

ich wollte das, was ich muß:
damit zwang ich mir jedes "Muß" ...
seitdem giebt es für mich kein "Muß".[37]

Emerson had affirmed the progressive and retroactive self-constituting circularity of both nature and mind in "The American Scholar." Nietzsche deepened Emerson's insight by prophetically joining true or authentic (human) Being and time. The ultimate acceptance of the identity of fate and freedom, of power and eternal return, of *essentia* and *existentia*, was seen by both Emerson and Nietzsche as a promise rather than an existential fact. Emerson's thoughts on the fallen state of mankind, on the fragmentation of the human being in "The American Scholar," on his deficiencies when compared with nature in "The Method of Nature," and his so-called skepticism in "Experience" are well matched by Zarathustra's meditations on the deformed and despicable "last" or ultimate man. Both Emerson and Nietzsche-Zarathustra have to repeatedly remind themselves that they need courage to continue on the arduous road toward the overman or the *"plus* man," as Emerson said in "Power."[38] Nietzsche's recurring "Wohlan! Wohlauf! Altes Herz!" in *Also sprach Zarathustra* is a direct response to and equivalent of Emerson's "up again, old heart!" at the end of "Experience."[39] This kind of post-Christian *sursum corda* affirms that the overman and Emerson's *"plus* man" are possibilities and that the presently existing human being is, as Nietzsche says, a rope tied between animal and overman, a rope spanning an abyss[40]—or, in Emerson's phrase, the present human being shows her or his promise and power "in the moment of transition from a past to a new state, in the shooting of the gulf, in the darting to an aim."[41]

The true fulfillment would indeed be self-sufficient circularity. Nietzsche has envisioned this state and thus the true figuration of the overman as the Being of the child: "Unschuld ist das Kind und Vergessen, ein Neubeginnen, ein Spiel, ein aus sich rollendes Rad, eine erste Bewegung, ein heiliges Ja-Sagen."[42] This truly self-moved mover, this self-contained ecstasy and play,

---

[37]*KSA* 13, 53. "thus it is now my will: / and ever since this is my will, / Everything obeys my wishes and desires— / This was my ultimate and last prudence: / I willed that which I must [do or be] / in this way I forced any 'Must'... / ever since there is no 'Must' for me."

[38]*W* VI, 59. Nietzsche used the term "plus ..." frequently. He found the word used several times in the German translation of *The Conduct of Life*. See Emerson, *Führung des Lebens: Gedanken und Studien*, trans. E. S. von Mühlberg (Leipzig: Steinacker, 1862), 40, 42, 47, 49.

[39]*KSA* 4, 184; *W* III, 86.

[40]*KSA* 4, 16.

[41]"Self-Reliance" *W* II, 69.

[42]*KSA* 4, 31. I would suggest the following paraphrase for this passage: "The child is innocence and forgetting, a (constant) new beginning, a play, a self-moved wheel, a first (initial and initiating) movement, a holy yea-saying."

is a constant beginning, and as such it testifies to the will to power as the potentiality of becoming. At the same time she or he constantly grounds her- or himself in a past that is forgotten and overcome *as* past by this act of circular re-appropriation: this person is the innocent wheel of the eternal return or, in Emerson's phrase, circular power that does not owe itself to anything. Since the primary ontological intuition shared by Emerson and Nietzsche is not limited to the human or any other particular being, one must remind oneself, though, that all beings, that nature herself shares in this identity of Being as becoming and time. In "The Method of Nature" Emerson found this phrase for the Being of nature: "a work of *ecstasy*, to be represented by a circular movement."[43] Ecstasy is often used by Emerson to indicate the tendency of all beings to overpower themselves; it is his word to hint at the way the will to power shows. This literal "going beyond" is, however, also a going back in the sense of a grounding of becoming through reclaiming the past state of the ecstatic being. The wheel, the play of the innocence of becoming, characterizes all beings.

This ontological homology between nature and human being or *Dasein* is an important aspect of Emerson's "Power":

> Life is a search after power; and this is an element with which the world is so saturated,—there is no chink or crevice where it is not lodged,— that no honest seeking goes unrewarded ... All power is of one kind, a sharing of the nature of the world. The mind that is parallel with the laws of nature will be in the current of events, and strong with their strength. One man is made of the same stuff of which events are made; is in sympathy with the course of things; can predict it.[44]

Life as becoming is a search after, a desire for, a will to power. Power is obviously seen as the Being of all beings, as that which saturates and permeates every single being. Heraclitus, who is so often quoted by Emerson and Nietzsche, said that nature likes to hide (her essential Being).[45] In Emerson, however, this tendency of the Being of beings to withdraw is no match for the desire of beings to participate, to fully and powerfully be their Being. Since power is a participation in the nature or Being of the world, the human being or *Dasein* is seen as ontologically identical with nature as process, as ecstatic unfolding of the will to power. Event and entity, event and human being are one. In "Fate" Emerson had written: "The secret of the world is the tie between person and event. Person makes event, and event

---

[43] W I, 192.
[44] W VI, 55, 58.
[45] Heraklit, *Fragmente: Griechisch und Deutsch*, ed. Bruno Snell (Munich: Artemis, 1986), B 123: "Das Wesen der Dinge versteckt sich gern." ("The essence of things likes to hide"; my translation.)

person."[46] Being as powerful becoming dissolves the boundaries between entity and eventuality, between "subject" and history. This succinctly describes, analyzes, and thinks what Nietzsche called the "Rückübersetzung," the literal re-translation of the human being into nature.[47] Karl Löwith has explained this motif in Nietzsche's thinking as his central cosmological— and I would add, ontological—concern:

> Ein "Vorspiel der Philosophie der Zukunft" sind Nietzsches Schriften nicht dadurch, daß er an einen künftigen Wandel im Wesen des Menschen dachte, den man vorbereiten oder gar wollen könnte, und zu dessen Herbeiführung er sich den Übermenschen erdachte, sondern dadurch, daß er – in Erinnerung der vorsokratischen *physikoi* – den großen Versuch unternahm, den Menschen in die *Natur* aller Dinge "zurückzuübersetzen."[48]

In reading Emerson's thoughts on the relationship of person and event, Nietzsche could not only perceive the continuity of nature and *Dasein* and the reintegration of the human being into the world as process, his basic intuition of the structure of Being as time was re-enforced: "Person makes event, and event person." If the human being and events are made of the same "stuff," as Emerson says in "Power," then the circular interdependence of process and human agent is guaranteed ontologically. The vision reveals that, ultimately, there is only power. Fate now appears merely as a word indicating the insufficiently understood and not yet appropriated past, a past into which the human being has to be re-translated in order to make it her or his own. In this act of re-translation, the circular and transitional relationship and ultimate identity of event and person, of fate and power, become apparent. It is obvious that in such passages of Emerson's writings and in their ontological implications Nietzsche would find a sufficient basis for his critique of the subject as separate entity and, as a consequence, a starting point for his demolition of the idea of determination as a necessitarian interaction of distinct causes and effects.[49] Instead, Emerson's

---

[46] W VI, 42.

[47] *Jenseits von Gut und Böse: Vorspiel einer Philosophie der Zukunft* [*Beyond Good and Evil: Prelude to a Philosophy of the Future*], KSA 5, 169.

[48] Karl Löwith, *Nietzsches Philosophie der ewigen Wiederkehr des Gleichen* (1935; Hamburg: Meiner, 1978), 192. I suggest this translation: "Nietzsche's writings are a 'Prelude of a Philosophy of the Future' not because he thought of a future change in the essence of man, which one could possibly prepare or even will, and for the realization of which he conceived of the overman, but rather because—remembering the Presocratic *physikoi*—he started the great experiment of 're-translating' the human being into the nature of all things."

[49] Müller-Lauter has thoroughly analyzed these critiques in "Nietzsches Lehre vom Willen zur Macht," 261.

ontological interpretation of a world of power transcending the separation of person and event could result in the repeatedly stated insight, in *Jenseits von Gut und Böse*[50] and in Nietzsche's late notes toward a theory of the will to power, that power does nothing but enact its own ultimate consequences in every moment.

If person and event are not only interdependent but names for aspects of a continuum, then "person" has to be thought of as one important name for process or for history. In "Fate" Emerson said: "History is the action and reaction of these two, Nature and Thought; two boys pushing each other on the curbstone of the pavement. Everything is pusher and pushed; and matter and mind are in perpetual tilt and balance, so."[51] "Nature," we have understood, may be the term designating the realm of fate, whereas "thought" or "spirit" may indicate the possibilities of the free play of power antagonizing fate. Basically, however, both power and fate, nature and thought, are of the same kind; they are aspects of the Being of the world: the image of the two boys asserts the identity and the difference of these players in a precarious field (the curbstone). Their contingent play is called history: a continuity of persons or events in which the roles assumed (pusher and pushed, action and reaction, fate and power) are "slid[ing] into the other" as Emerson had already stated of power and fate in order to avoid the attribution of metaphysical essentials and the fixation of a binary opposition when speaking of the continuities of Being.

Nietzsche was obviously fascinated by Emerson's conception of history; the 1862 essay "Fatum und Geschichte" testifies to that fact. "History" is the essay that has supplied the greatest number of direct references to Emerson throughout Nietzsche's career: the image and the idea of the sphinx as reading her own riddle, the motto selected for the first edition of *Die fröhliche Wissenschaft*, the concept of nomadic thinking[52]—these and many other passages indicate that Nietzsche did read Emerson's vision of history as a central aspect of his thinking, of his new ontological perspective. A famous statement like "All history becomes subjective; in other words, there is properly no history, only biography"[53] may have encouraged Nietzsche to write so very often in the autobiographical mode in order to ascertain the historical significance of his own thinking.[54]

The most important ontological insights, however, seem to be contained in two succinct phrases of the essay. Firstly, Emerson states: "We must in ourselves see the necessary reason of every fact, see how it could be and must

---

[50]*KSA* 5, 37.

[51]W VI, 46.

[52]This is presented in painstaking detail by Baumgarten in "Mitteilungen und Bemerkungen," 101–2.

[53]W II, 15.

[54]Parkes has most convincingly explored this connection in *Composing the Soul*, 35 ff.

be."[55] The self is here seen as the place, as the *there* in the sense of *Da*sein, where necessity and possibility, fate and power as freedom are grounded. The self, however, is also an event, as we saw in reading "Power." The Being of *Dasein*, of the human self, as time is the realm of the interplay of power and fate. This temporally progressive *there*, however, is always focused in the present; the present as a constantly evanescent event is the domain of true Being—as this second major ontological statement in "History" asserts: "All inquiry into antiquity ... is the desire to do away with this wild, savage, and preposterous There and Then, and introduce in its place the Here and the Now."[56] Nietzsche included this passage in the selection of paraphrases from Emerson that he entered into separate notebooks late in 1881 and early in 1882 while conceiving the central ontological ideas of *Also sprach Zarathustra* and while writing the first two parts of the book.[57] Nietzsche's paraphrase intensifies Emerson's statement and reads: "Dieses planlose rohe widersinnige Dort und Jetzt soll verschwinden und an seine Stelle das Jetzt und Hier treten."[58] The gesture is familiar from Nietzsche's second *Unzeitgemässe Betrachtung,* "Vom Nutzen und Nachtheil der Historie für das Leben." The *Untimely Meditation* on the uses and disadvantages of history for life asserts the existential prerogative of the present over against the past as a possible repository of models, values, and meaning. The appropriation of the past from the perspective of a powerfully asserted present point of view, however, is also the concern of the fully developed ontological interpretations which Emerson offers in "Fate" and which Nietzsche proposes in *Also sprach Zarathustra*. Here reading and making history become one with true temporal Being. When Emerson says in "Fate," "He who sees through the design ... must will that which must be,"[59] he deepens the vision from "History" and the interpretation of the human being as the origin and place of "could be" and "must be." And when Nietzsche prophesies the possibility of powerfully overcoming the "it was" and of making the will to power "will backwards," he also expands the Emersonian injunction from "History" to transform the "There and Then" into the "Here and Now," going beyond the "mere" cultural critique of the second *Untimely Meditation,* while he unfolds the ontological underpinning of his earlier work inherited from Emerson.

The map of Being sketched by Emerson uses the flexible terms "fate," "power," and "history" in order to facilitate the experience of thinking a new dispensation of Being, a revolutionizing generative idea. Nietzsche, in

---

[55] W II, 16.

[56] Ibid.

[57] *KSA* 9, 618–22, 666–72.

[58] Ibid., 666. "This chaotic and brute and absurd There and Then must disappear and the Here and Now must take its place" (my translation).

[59] W VI, 31.

reading Emerson throughout his career, returned to his predecessor and met
again and again, the challenge to appropriate the ontological thought of
the other as his own authentic achievement. Emerson's vision of the will
to power and the eternal return of the same, his version of *amor fati* and
the endeavor to become who one is, was both to be acknowledged and
overcome. Nietzsche's recognition of Emerson's significance was at the same
time generous and secretive.[60] In the privacy of his notebooks, he called
Emerson *the thinker* of the nineteenth century whose wealth of thinking was
unsurpassed, even though sometimes darkened by the verbal ground glass
of German idealism.[51] The thinker who stylized himself as the homeless
wanderer on icy Alpine heights of thought showed himself overcome by
emotion in confessing that Emerson provided a real home for him, that
he was too close to him for words of appropriate praise.[62] In *Ecce homo*,
Nietzsche said that Plato used Socrates as a semiotics for Plato, that he
read his own thought into the older *alter ego*.[63] Emerson had stated, in
*Representative Men*, that "[o]ther men are lenses through which we read our
own minds."[64] The intimate relationship between Emerson and Nietzsche
shows in the very words they use in order to characterize relationships.
On a level that goes beyond mere appreciation and biographical factuality,
however, we realize that the encounter of Emerson and Nietzsche proved
a testing ground for the very ontological revolution that they experienced
and shared. In the creative intensity of 1888, Nietzsche characterized the
existential disposition of Emerson and of himself in a way that goes beyond
mere psychology. Aphorism 13 of *Götzen-Dämmerung* says about Emerson:
"Emerson hat jene gütige und geistreiche Heiterkeit, welche allen Ernst
entmuthigt; er weiss es schlechterdings noch nicht, wie alt er schon ist und
wie jung er noch sein wird, – er könnte mit einem Worte Lope de Vega's
sagen: 'yo me sucedo a mi mismo.'"[65]

Nietzsche not only celebrates an almost Mediterranean serenity in
Emerson's thinking, he above all attributes to his Being a temporal dimension
that reaches far back into the past and extends into an unforeseeable future.
This is not about Emerson's fame or the future of his reputation as the

---

[60]See Baumgarten, "Mitteilungen und Bemerkungen," 152.
[61]I have paraphrased this note dated "Fall 1881": "der gedankenreichste Autor dieses
Jahrh[underts] ist bisher ein Amerikaner gewesen (leider durch deutsche Philosophie
verdunkelt—Milchglas)"; *KSA* 9, 602.
[62]"Emerson—Ich habe mich nie in einem Buch so zu Hause und in meinem Hause gefühlt als—
ich darf es nicht loben, es steht mir zu nahe"; ibid., 588.
[63]"Dergestalt hat sich Plato des Sokrates bedient, als einer Semiotik für Plato"; *KSA* 6, 320.
[64]*W* IV, 11.
[65]*KSA* 6, 120. "Emerson possesses that benevolent and spirited serenity which discourages all
heavy seriousness; he simply doesn't know how old he is already and how young he will yet
be—he could possibly say of himself quoting Lope de Vega: 'yo me sucedo a mi mismo'" (my
translation).

quotation from Lope de Vega seems to prove: Emerson as thinker *is* his own immemorial past, his fate, and—at the same time—the potential, the power of his unlimited future; as thinker he is the very *exemplum* of his own existential vision. In his self-portrait as both a *décadent* and as a new beginning in *Ecce homo*, Nietzsche says of himself: "Das Glück meines Daseins, seine Einzigkeit vielleicht, liegt in seinem Verhängniss: ich bin, um es in Räthselform auszudrücken, als mein Vater bereits gestorben, als meine Mutter lebe ich noch und werde alt."[66] This passage thinks Nietzsche's own Being, the temporal mode of his existence, in a way that parallels his interpretation of Emerson. Nietzsche envisions himself as reaching back into a seemingly unavailable, a dead past (the father); at the same time, this very past (the mother) is the guarantee of an extended future. Emerson and Nietzsche are seen as both fated and free, as determined by the burden of the past and as empowered to overcome this affliction: this circular structure, once again, is the very condition of the possibility of their (common) history.

At the end of his wonderfully painstaking study of Nietzsche and Emerson, Stanley Hubbard modestly summarized his insights and concluded that, after all, Emerson was not Nietzsche.[67] If one considers not so much their biographies and their psychological profiles, but rather dwells on the essential challenge to and of their thinking, one will have to both agree and disagree with Hubbard. Emerson is not Nietzsche. However, Nietzsche as a thinker responding to a new dispensation of Being could only become who he was by appropriating the fated antecedent other, called Emerson, enacting that significant circular move of a powerful return into a seemingly obstinate past that alone guarantees the possibility of a new history of thinking.

---

[66]Ibid., 264. "The good fortune of my existence, maybe its uniqueness, resides in its fatedness—I will express it in the form of a riddle: as my father I have already died, as my mother I am still alive and will grow to be old" (my translation).
[67]Hubbard, *Nietzsche und Emerson*, 178.

# 9

# Emerson's and Dewey's America

Thinking America is radically and fundamentally different from advancing opinions, offering critical evaluations, and proposing historical explanations of the culture and the political system of the United States based on research and theory within the fields of political science, of cultural, or of social history. Thinking America precedes any scholarly or scientific approach in a logical, in an onto-logical, rather than a temporal, sense. Scholarly disciplines and the sciences, as Heidegger once remarked, do not think.[1] Thinking articulates the realm and reach of Being within which the development of historical events and their scholarly explanations are possible as well as accessible in an essentially unforeseeable, yet specific, way. This does not at all invalidate the importance of historical scholarship and of the social sciences. Thinking, however, elucidates the way Being has always already been dispensed at a certain time: as that localized opening of potentiality within which a phase of history and its scholarly explorations may then unfold. Thinking proper responds to these dispensations of Being, as Heidegger explained in *Was heisst Denken?*

I use *dispensation* as a translation of Heidegger's term *Geschick*. *Geschick*—in the literal sense of the word preferred by Heidegger in so many instances—means the totality of all significance that is given or sent or dispensed at a certain time. Heidegger does not imply an author or agent who or which dispenses the way things are and signify. The late work "Zeit und Sein" offers the phrase "Es gibt Sein" in order to indicate

This essay was previously published as "Thinking America: Emerson and Dewey" in *Negotiations of America's Cultural Identity*, ed. Roland Hagenbüchle and Josef Raab (Tübingen: Stauffenburg, 1999), vol. 2, 131–56. Reprinted by permission of Stauffenburg Verlag GmbH.

[1] *Was heißt Denken?* ed. Paola-Ludovika Coriando, vol. 8 of *Gesamtausgabe* (1951–2; Frankfurt: Klostermann, 2002), 9.

that Being itself is radically contingent.[2] The "it" (Es) that "offers Being as a gift" or, rather, "dispenses Being" (gibt Sein) is a present absence. In this way the *Geschick*, the dispensation of Being, retains its numinous character without specifying a theological or metaphysical presence as a source or origin. The *OED* explains the traditional religious connotations by defining *dispensation* as a "special dealing of Providence with a community, family, or person" and adding a theological definition: "A religious order or system, conceived as divinely instituted, or as a stage in a progressive revelation, expressly adapted to the needs of a particular nation or period of time."[3] By abandoning any specific divine or metaphysical origin of the dispensations of Being, Heidegger enables us to think the ungrounded emergence of historical periods and regional or national cultures as realities that do not arise from our metaphysically guaranteed and religiously guided individual or collective human efforts, possibilities, and capabilities. Historical eras and nations may thus be understood without resorting to a transcendent authority or a mythic origin as the initiators of human events and their significance.

Such a view of the contingent background of the dispensations of Being also implies that it is neither the explicit or implicit metaphysical system nor the abundance of possibly critical political or cultural opinions in the work of a philosopher that account for the ultimate significance of his thinking. Rather, it is the often silent, but always regulative and formative, presence of his sense or primary intuition of Being that explains his status and importance as a thinker. The specific dispensation and the unique sense of Being by which he feels addressed are not historical phenomena in a traditional way since they are without grounding in antecedent events. Therefore they are challenges of *Seinsdenken*, of thinking Being, of onto-logy in a genuine sense. A thinker who properly responds to this challenge will then be a modern, a post-metaphysical thinker. His effort to articulate Being provides the frame for all scholarly understanding of historical, regional, or national cultural specifics.

It is my thesis that the cultural and political world which we call America can be philosophically interpreted as owing itself to a specific mode of the dispensation of Being. This mode found its major early modern ontological expression in Emerson's works. Emerson's response to the *call* or address of Being in and as America may be seen as the first post-metaphysical approach to thinking ever to occur. Two hundred years after its inception, two hundred years after the emergence of America in 1620 or thereabouts, Emerson finds one of the profoundest ways of giving a voice to the unique mode of Being revealing itself as a *new* world in an ontological sense. In the twentieth century, John Dewey's thinking continues the Emersonian project in the

---

[2]Martin Heidegger "Zeit und Sein," in *Zur Sache des Denkens*, ed. Friedrich-Wilhelm von Herrmann, vol. 14 of *Gesamtausgabe* (1969; Frankfurt: Klostermann, 2007), 9.
[3]*Oxford English Dictionary* (Oxford: Clarendon Press, 1933), vol. 3, 481.

most comprehensive fashion. This does not imply that other thinkers from Roger Williams and Jonathan Edwards through William James and Stanley Cavell have neglected or remained deaf to this challenge.[4] Emerson and Dewey, however, seem to have provided the most expansive and penetrating response to the specific call of Being in America.

This thesis, then, also insinuates that Heidegger's idea of a contingent *temporal* sequence of the dispensations of Being may be too limited and that the underlying ontological "structure" of all human history should be expanded to accommodate significant *regional* or *spatial* differences in addition to the temporal dimension. Heidegger's Eurocentric view does not allow for any other sequence of contingent dispensations of Being than the one we know as extending from the Greeks through modern European history, with its corresponding ontological thinking. The meditations of the late Heidegger on Japanese thought in *Unterwegs zur Sprache*[5] seem to attest an awareness of possible multicentered occurrences of Being; given his inflexible anti-Americanism, however, the New World was never a serious candidate for inclusion in Heidegger's tentative moves beyond his European provincialism in thinking the history of Being.[6]

The works of Emerson and Dewey quite obviously contain an abundance of *opinions* on matters political and cultural in America. This is not only true of texts that respond to specific historical moments—as does Emerson's "Progress of Culture" (1867), for instance, which addresses the problems, the promises, and achievements of the post–Civil War era, or Dewey's *Freedom and Culture* (1939) with its spirited defense of a reconstructed idea of American democracy against the joint threats of fascism and Stalinism.[7] Emerson's "Circles" is a profoundly philosophical text first and foremost, and yet we do find a considerable number of metaphors

---

[4]A similar awareness of Emerson's significance informs Cavell's *This New Yet Unapproachable America: Lectures after Emerson after Wittgenstein* (Albuquerque: Living Batch Press, 1989).

[5]*Unterwegs zur Sprache*, ed. Friedrich-Wilhelm von Herrmann, vol. 12 of *Gesamtausgabe* (1959; Frankfurt: Klostermann, 1985).

[6]Heidegger's anti-Americanism shows in his early essays collected later in *Holzwege* it is prominent in his indictment of the gigantic as an essential trait of modern technology in *Beiträge zur Philosophie (Vom Ereignis)*, in *Einführung in die Metaphysik*, and, at least implicitly, throughout his late works. This merely shows that neither American culture nor American thinking was ever really seriously considered by the provincial in Heidegger—and, for that matter, by most European thinkers and academics to this very day. At the same time, Heidegger's anti-Americanism reveals the obvious, namely, that his opinions are infinitely less interesting than his thinking. See especially *Holzwege, Einführung in die Metaphysik*, and *Beiträge zur Philosophie (Vom Ereignis,* = volumes 5, 40, and 65 of *Gesamtausgabe* (Frankfurt: Klostermann).

[7]W VIII, 195–222. All quotations from Dewey refer to the *Collected Works of John Dewey*, ed. Jo Ann Boydston (Carbondale, IL: Southern Illinois University Press, 1977–2008). *The Middle Works*, comprising the years 1899–1924, are abbreviated *MW; The Later Works* (1925–53), *LW*. For *Freedom and Culture*, see *LW* 13, 63–188.

and symbolic attitudes along the way that reflect Emerson's political opinions, even though the work as a whole goes far beyond mere *doxa*. When Emerson states that "People wish to be settled; only as far as they are unsettled is there any hope for them,"[8] the concepts of a persistent removal and the refusal to acknowledge "settling" as an ultimate goal of human existence clearly bespeak a receptivity for and sensitivity to the spirit of the expansionist 1840s, even if Emerson remained critical of military adventures like the Mexican-American War that he condemned in his famous "Ode. Inscribed to W. H. Channing." Similarly, while Dewey's *summa philosophiae, Art as Experience* (1934), may be the most significant work on art as the quintessential mode of human experience or human existence written by a twentieth-century thinker, it does articulate beliefs and opinions that qualify as sociopolitical in the narrow sense of the word. Dewey's insistence on making art accessible to the common man is not only an important facet of his thinking, it is also the proclamation of a political, an ideological belief not so far from the prevailing cultural concepts of the New Deal. Critical appreciations that narrowly focus on Emerson's and Dewey's *opinions* concerning the national identity, or the essential Being, of America tend to place the two thinkers at opposite ends of a possible political and cultural spectrum. Emerson is commonly seen as an advocate both of individuality and of individualism, with a growing tendency toward a laissez-faire ideology, whereas there is hardly one significant interpretation of Dewey that does not stress the communitarian aspects of his idea of a democratic society in America. That Sacvan Bercovitch's somewhat one-sided and, one regrets to say, Eurocentric reading of Emerson's meditations on individuality may be successfully challenged, this has been convincingly shown by the political theorist George Kateb in his recent book *Emerson and Self-Reliance*.[9] Kateb has demonstrated that Emerson's existential and argumentative strategies provide the proper philosophical basis for a liberal and individualistic but, at the same time, for a truly tolerant communitarian democracy. Even so, however, significant disparities in the *opinions* of the two thinkers concerning the social and political order in America remain.

It is therefore surprising and, at first sight, seemingly inconsistent that Dewey, in his centennial essay on Emerson (1903),[10] describes his predecessor as the quintessential philosopher of democracy and, by implication, as the model of all thinking about America, including his own. It is at this point that one is faced with the obligation to distinguish between the necessarily different historical responses and opinions of Emerson and

---

[8] W II, 298.
[9] Sacvan Bercovitch, *The Rites of Assent: Transformations in the Symbolic Construction of America* (New York: Routledge, 1993), 307–52; George Kateb, *Emerson and Self-Reliance* (Thousand Oaks, CA: Sage, 1995).
[10] "Emerson – The Philosopher of Democracy" *MW* 3, 184–92.

Dewey concerning America and its democratic culture *and* the way both thinkers think the dispensation of Being within which American institutions, culture, and politics may show for what they are in a process of historical development and continuous differentiation.[11] A meditation on the meaning of Being in American thinking implies the possibility that the "onward thinking," which Cavell's essay "Thinking of Emerson" finds so significant[12] because it moved away from the fixed ground of traditional metaphysics and thus toward the philosophical modernism of Nietzsche and Heidegger, that this onward thinking also opens the way, the *methodos*, of thinking Being in America, which issues in Dewey's works. "Onward thinking," in my view, would imply the possibility that, in thinking the ungrounded dispensation of Being called America, Emerson and Dewey were faced with and responded to a totality of givens whose central trait consists in the mode of remaining the same through a constant proliferation of differences.[13] An unceasing production of refusals to "settle," to use Emerson's term in "Circles," may prove to be the prominent feature of the way Being occurs and things are in and as America. The persistence of such "unsettling" thinking as a response to the American dispensation of Being could then also account for the identity in difference in Emerson and Dewey when thinking America. In a first step I would therefore like to establish the continuity in difference between Emerson and Dewey as a basis for a discussion of their response to and interpretation of the call of Being in and as America.

When Dewey had overcome his early allegiance to Hegel by means of a rigorous critique, he began to slowly position himself within the American tradition of thinking. His 1903 essay "Emerson – The Philosopher of Democracy" is, ever so indirectly, a landmark in his attempt to claim the possibility of a new mode of thinking in and for a new world. "The Development of American Pragmatism" (1925) and the, for Dewey, exceptional autobiographical essay "From Absolutism to Experimentalism" (1930), which briefly details his philosophical development, also belong with the very small group of writings on his own place within the world of American thought.[14] It is therefore fitting and appropriate to study Dewey's

---

[11]Dewey has thoroughly analyzed the differences of the meaning of democratic America during the Revolution and at the beginning of the twentieth century in chapters 3 and 7 of *Freedom and Culture*.

[12]Stanley Cavell, "Thinking of Emerson," in *The Senses of Walden: An Expanded Edition* (1972; San Francisco: North Point Press, 1981), 123–38.

[13]If this and some of the following remarks sound as if my readings of the American dispensation of Being in Emerson and Dewey were attributing postmodernity to these thinkers, one might do well to remember that the postmodern condition may indeed be a contemporary French idea but that it has always been an American existential and ontological experience. The interest of a writer like Baudrillard in America may have a deeper reason than the perspective of the cultural critic is able to account for.

[14]*LW* II, 3–22; *LW* V, 147–60.

brief tribute to Emerson with care since it promises insight into the basic and common philosophical concern of American thinking at the very moment when it becomes aware of its own unfolding.

In "Emerson – The Philosopher of Democracy," Dewey celebrates Emerson's poetical thinking as a radically new beginning that is comparable to and will one day serve as the replacement of the long and dignified metaphysical tradition of thought inaugurated by Plato. In the opening paragraph, Dewey appreciates the way Emerson goes beyond the traditional forms of philosophical writing and discovers "a logic that is finely wrought," a silent method, in Emerson's own words, which underlies his "brilliant insights and abrupt aphorisms."[15] This silent, this pre-linguistic intuition opens the dispensation of Being in a way that, as we will presently see, allows the persistent and undetermined free unfolding of all beings and thus facilitates the very possibility of a democracy[16] of all entities. The poetic aspect of Emerson's thought, in the original sense of the Greek *poiesis*, is of philosophical significance for Dewey. In stating that Emerson is "a maker rather than a reflector,"[17] Dewey quite appropriately claims Emerson as the ancestor of the pragmatic turn from antecedents to consequences, as the initiator of a shift from a conception of truth as representation to an idea of truths as strategies of possible conduct. If, as Dewey goes on to say, "perception was more potent than reasoning"[18] for Emerson, he clearly aligns his thought with William James's repeated re-valuations of the relative truth-claims of perceiving and conceptualizing that he discussed in *The Principles of Psychology* (1890) and continued to explore through the late *A Pluralistic Universe* (1908) and the posthumous *Some Problems of Philosophy* (1911). The privileges of perception, understood pragmatically, guarantee an openness that keeps overcoming the tendency of all essentializing conceptions to achieve closure, to establish precedent, and thus to predetermine the order of things. The silence intuited by Emerson as the core of Being opens a world of unconditioned and unobstructed becoming. This is why Dewey goes on to characterize Emerson's thinking as an exploration of "the ways of things," as an investigation of "the paths by which truth is sought."[19] The pervasive metaphor of the open road in his tribute to Emerson indicates that Dewey conceives of Emerson's thought as providing the foundation for or at least as participating in the American

---

[15]*MW* 3, 184.

[16]Ontologically speaking, democracy means the authority of all singularities or beings in their actual presence (or presence-ing), whether these beings are understood as things or ideas or humans. Unless otherwise specified, my use of the word "democracy" implies this specialized meaning.

[17]*MW* 3, 185.

[18]Ibid.

[19]Ibid., 186.

national mythology of exploratory motion; at the same time, he claims him for the pragmatist mode of experimental and onward thinking. It is not the state of affairs among human beings or things of nature but rather the enactment, the process, of their production that ontologically count for Emerson. It is not the *essentia* of things but rather their dynamic way of being, their *existentia*, which is significant. For Dewey, Emerson has already overcome what James liked to call the "block-universe" of both metaphysical rationalism and of an unreconstructed sensationalist empiricism that has not yet been transformed into a pragmatist *radical* empiricism. Because "Emerson knew something deeper than our conventional definitions"— that is, conceptualizations—he moved toward a poetic mode of thinking that could also be found in "Euripides and Plato, Dante and Bruno, Bacon and Milton, Spinoza and Goethe."[20] It is obvious that Dewey sees his own thinking as philosophically complementing Emerson's "poetic" vision so that "Emerson and Dewey" would form another significant pair exploring the reaches of poetic thinking. More than thirty years would pass, however, before Dewey was ready to present his own ultimate intuition of the plural worlds of experience freely fulfilling themselves as processes of art in *Art as Experience* (1934). The future of thinking, Dewey insinuates in 1903, will be determined by a new way of conceiving the relationship of literature and philosophy—in this way Dewey thinks like Heidegger, with whom he shares so many important philosophical concerns in spite of their vast differences in matters of ideology and opinion.[21] Dewey, inspired by the example of Emerson, propagates an open field, a Western expanse of free ontological inquiry: "Looked at in the open, our fences between literature and metaphysics appear petty—signs of an attempt to affix the legalities and formularies of property to the things of the spirit."[22]

Dewey's pervasive critique of unwarranted appropriation makes him think the things of the spirit, the matter of thinking—that is, Being itself— as a realm within which radical freedom prevails. There is not one single privileged kind of access called philosophy in the Emersonian mode of approaching and responding to the call of Being. The ways of thinking are pluralistic, they show as art, as literature, as philosophy; they are democratized and may be understood as achieving the identical goal (of thinking Being) in their very difference. A *proprium*, something proper or persistently essential, may be ascribed neither to Being nor to thinking Being; Being is the property of no one and of no single way of thinking it. Dewey detects the creative significance of free thinking also in Emerson's

---

[20]Ibid.

[21]See Herwig Friedl, "John Dewey und Martin Heidegger über die Kunst: Prolegomena zu einem kritischen Vergleich," in *Literaturimport transatlantisch*, ed. Uwe Baumann (Tübingen: Narr, 1997), 167–92.

[22]*MW* 3, 187.

meditations on the human being. The human being possesses no solid or antecedent substance or unchanging essence or *proprium*. Like Being itself and any other single entity—a nation, for example—"the individual man is only a method, a plan of arrangement."[23] This is why Dewey appreciates "Emerson's whole work as a hymn to intelligence, a paean to the all-creating, all-disturbing power of thought."[24] In 1903 Dewey sees in Emerson the proto-pragmatist, the precursor of his own instrumentalist works to come, especially of *Art as Experience*, and he recognizes in him the herald of the thinker who encourages the possibility to conceive of the world as a plurality of creative intelligences.

In spite of the significance of art and poetry as paradigms of post-metaphysical thinking for both Emerson and Dewey, the American mode in Emerson's thought emerges most prominently in the fact that, for Dewey, Emerson is the thinker of democracy. The thinker of democracy is always and at the same time the thinker of the present moment, of self-reliance, and of common experience. Dewey makes it clear that these philosophical motifs in Emerson pertain to the center of his thinking, his way of envisioning Being. All thinking past and present is to be subjected "to the test of trial by the service rendered the present and immediate experience."[25] This is not merely a political program or a psychological encouragement. Dewey is not concerned with Emerson's opinions but with his thinking. The pragmatic test of all thinking in the present implies that the fullness of Being, the authority of existing, is always now and in its plural and common manifestations. This means that, for Emerson and Dewey, Being is always in the fleeting present and therefore, paradoxically, never fully present, never ultimately established, never irremediably authoritative. Being is always itself in the now. This is to say, it and all the beings under its dispensation are always identical and always on the way to be different. This is one way of understanding what both thinkers intuit when they think Being, when they think America. The connection between Being, the present, and America as democracy becomes even clearer in this passage:

> [Emerson] finds truth in the highway ... His ideas are not fixed upon any Reality that is beyond or behind or in any way apart, and hence they do not have to be bent. They are versions of the Here and the Now, and flow freely. The reputed transcendental worth of an overweening Beyond and Away, Emerson, jealous for spiritual democracy, finds to be the possession of the unquestionable Present.[26]

---

[23]Ibid.
[24]Ibid.
[25]Ibid., 189.
[26]Ibid., 189–90.

Emerson thinks spiritual democracy. Spiritual democracy, however, as Dewey explains, is not a metaphysical, a transcendent or transcendental entity grounded in "an overweening Beyond and Away." It is accessible to a mode of thinking that keeps responding to a realm of absolute immanence in Heraclitean flux. Being is radically temporal. It arises out of the "unquestionable Present." The present is the one and only authority; this is why it cannot be questioned. The present is the moment of Being. The authority of Being is constantly renewed or turned, or troped, as Richard Poirier might say. Every response to Being, every human, every natural, every political or institutional, every national entity or identity called America is merely a "version," in the literal sense of a "turning," of "the Here and the Now." The ontological aspect of democracy, as the way in which America is thought by Emerson, is its refusal to be "settled," or fixed, or defined, or conceptualized with a claim to continuing validity. Dewey makes Emerson prepare the momentous shift in thinking which he himself has described as the move from antecedents to consequences in his *Reconstruction in Philosophy* of 1920 and which he explored in depth in *The Quest for Certainty* of 1929. This shift is not merely important because it provides the basis for the pragmatic theory of truth, or because it ideologically supports the emancipation from all pre-established authorities. At the core of this radical turn, we find the American thought of Being as time in the way Emerson envisioned it, in the way it was shaped and re-shaped by James and Dewey till it found one of its major comprehensive articulations in George Herbert Mead's magnum opus *The Philosophy of the Present* (1932). Mead unfolded the democratic and anti-authoritarian lineaments of Being as presence-ing that were prepared by his predecessors. Now-ness erodes all authority and all domination: it is ontologically communitarian for Mead and as such it is democratic.[27]

Having engendered this line of American thinking, Emerson may be said to have thought the "national identity" by questioning its essentialist stability and to have responded to and articulated the dispensation of Being in America in an exemplary and historically productive fashion:

> thinking of Emerson as the one citizen of the New World fit to have his name uttered in the same breath with that of Plato, one may without presumption believe that even if Emerson has no system, none the less he is the prophet and herald of any system which democracy may henceforth construct and hold by, and that when democracy has articulated itself it will have no difficulty in finding itself already proposed in Emerson.[28]

---

[27]George Herbert Mead, *The Philosophy of the Present*, ed. Arthur E. Murphy (Chicago: Open Court, 1932).
[28]*MW* 3, 191.

Emerson's thought is seen as poetic and non-systematic like Plato's, and therefore Dewey finds this thinking fit to provide the condition of the possibility of a major historical sequence of systematic unfoldings of the meaning of his basic intuition. Just as Plato inaugurated the series of systematic expositions of his fundamental vision that we call the history of Western metaphysics, so Emerson will be seen as the equally non-systematic *fons et origo* of all historically possible democratic systems of thought. The non-systematic is the space of the true, of the foundational thinker, and of the contingent dispensation of Being to which he responds, a space within which subsequent historical specifications are possible and necessary. This also implies that anything that unfolds within this space is not predetermined and therefore free. There is no conceptual framework in Emerson that binds the succeeding thinkers and constrains their vision of possible versions of democratic existence. Being itself, as intuited and interpreted by Emerson, has opened and guaranteed their freedom.

This makes it abundantly clear that in Emerson's thinking "democracy" as a central ingredient of the "national identity," of Being in America, is in itself not a political system but an ontological precondition of egalitarian culture(s). Democracy, in the way Dewey reads Emerson, is the mode or way or dispensation of Being that makes proliferating versions of democratic realization possible in their essentially unforeseeable variety and plenitude.[29] It is necessary that within the sway of such an experience of Being any fixation of a circumscribed solidity like a national identity will always find itself challenged and troped and ultimately defeated by the very Being within which it tried to unfold. The American way of Being, as thought, as answered, and as read by Emerson and Dewey, keeps subverting any stable identities that endanger the letting-be of new beings and of innovative modes of existence: this is why Emerson thinks a spiritual democracy, according to Dewey. Democracy, in this specific sense, is—once again—not a political, a social, or a cultural state of affairs, even though it may prevail in any of these specific modes of existence; rather, it designates a version of the order of things in progress and as process among humans, a version commonly called America.

At the very end of his portrait of Emerson as the thinker of Being in America, at the end of the implicit portrait of his future self as a thinker in the mirror of his precursor, Dewey dwells on the true form of human existence. The true thinker, the visionary soul, is characterized in Emerson's own words: "It lies in the sun and broods on the world."[30] Emerson foreshadows what

---

[29]In case this be thought a naïve and overly idealistic view of what America "really" is, the reader should consider that my ontological interpretation merely outlines what Being means in America. Racial tensions, economic problems, crime also *are*, they are specific beings in the field of Being which thinking opens for our appreciation.

[30]*MW* 3, 191.

Nietzsche described in an image of Mediterranean serenity as the great noon of human existence, as an existential mood that Heidegger in turn called *Gelassenheit*, a term often translated as "releasement." Emerson, Nietzsche, and Heidegger think the fullness of human existence as a letting-go and a letting-be: a letting-go of all claims to appropriation and to domination by the (antecedent) other and a letting-be of the true Being of the self that Emerson named self-reliance. Dewey interprets this Emersonian existential gesture as the fulfillment of a democratic form of life beyond control and mastery. Thus he concludes his profound meditation on Emerson by equating Being and the human being, by locating Being in human existence as the place or "there" of true Being. In this way Emerson and Dewey, and (the early) Heidegger, join in identifying human existence as *Dasein*. Dewey gives his "assent to the final word of Emerson's philosophy, the identity of Being, unqualified and immutable, with Character."[31]

Emerson's response to Being as America is appreciated by Dewey as a *foundational* act of thinking. And yet, paradoxically, this foundational intuition of Being as America, as spiritual democracy, as the union of Being and character, functions by letting each singular moment, each singular existence, and each singular subsequent act of thinking be what it is. In this denial of an original, a grounding, a totalizing authority, the American dispensation of thinking allows Dewey to be who he is by continuing through difference what was begun by Emerson. In a second and a third step, I would now like to dwell ever so briefly on the specific forms of thinking Being as and in America in the way they show in Emerson's and in Dewey's writings, whose very differences allow us to speak of a true continuity in American ontology.

As the indispensable thinker of his time and place, Emerson conveys his sense of America most often through his meditations on Being even if the nation and the country are not directly addressed. The American dispensation shows directly in the way Emerson thinks what *is*. And, according to the presuppositions of this paper, thinking what is, in Emerson, necessarily means thinking America as an ontological event. In "Self-Reliance," Emerson speaks of the absent, the unknowable ground of our existence:

> the sense of being which in calm hours rises, we know not how, in the soul, is not diverse from things, from space, from light, from time, from man, but one with them, and proceeds obviously from the same source whence their life and being also proceed. [32]

The awareness of Being is an unforeseeable, a contingent gift that lets everything in nature and in the human being be. The awareness of Being

---

[31]Ibid., 192.
[32]W II, 64.

establishes a world in which things are both together and in which they exist as their separate selves. The awareness of Being allows for unity and for multiplicity, for the one and the many, for identity and difference.

The meaning of Being is thoroughly explored in "Circles" where Emerson succinctly states: "There are no fixtures in nature" and "There are no fixtures to men."[33] These parallel sentences articulate Emerson's insight that Being as a whole, here named nature, is not a "state" of affairs. This is why it defies conceptualization, it cannot be fixed in a term, it cannot be held within the limits of a definition. The same is true of the human being. The person is the place of Being and as such it possesses no delimitation, no solidity, no specificity like any other being or thing. What metaphysics calls subject and object, subject and world, are held together by that nameless silent principle that Dewey found at the center of Emerson's thinking. The realm of Being, which challenges thought and which defies concepts in "Circles," is characterized by constant ecstatic self-overcoming and by the ultimate and radical evanescence of all singular beings, whether they are parts of nature or human beings. The image of the expanding and proliferating circles helps to visualize this ontological event. Being as the power or virtue of becoming, or self-overcoming, or constant differentiation, shows in a "moment of transition" as Emerson states in "Self-Reliance."[34] It calls for a proper response in thought: "The mind now thinks; now acts."[35] This simple phrase from "The American Scholar" reminds us that for Emerson the fleeting moment, the now, is the true temporal space of Being and its thought. Thinking is always present, but never at home; it is "unsettled" or "nomadic." The concept of nomadic thinking in Emerson's "History" inspired Nietzsche to use the term—Gilles Deleuze, in his work on Nietzsche, made "nomadic thought" a catchword of the postmodern sensibility;[36] he forgot its American origin, though. Thinking Being in Emerson, then, is on the way, it is literally a method, it is onward thinking. The transitional moment, which Harold Bloom has studied in detail in his "Emerson: Power at the Crossing,"[37] keeps eroding all established and possibly authoritative significations of this kind of thinking. At the same time it provides the possibility of permanent tropings of meaning within the space-time of such a dispensation of Being. Poirier has shown in *Poetry and Pragmatism*[38] how the mode of troping meanings establishes a unique American cultural

---

[33]Ibid., 282, 286.
[34]Ibid., 69.
[35]Ibid., 99.
[36]See, e.g., Gilles Deleuze, "Nomad Thought," in *New Nietzsche: Contemporary Styles of Interpretation*, ed. David B. Allison (Cambridge, MA: MIT Press, 1977), 142–9.
[37]Harold Bloom, "Emerson: Power at the Crossing," in *Ralph Waldo Emerson: A Collection of Critical Essays*, ed. Lawrence Buell (Englewood Cliffs: Prentice-Hall, 1993), 148–58.
[38]Richard Poirier, *Poetry and Pragmatism* (Cambridge, MA: Harvard University Press, 1992).

tradition from Emerson through the pragmatists and the authors of literary modernism. It is Emerson's significant insight that the tendency of all singular beings to maintain themselves is negated or undermined by Being itself; the temporality of Being enables and commands Emerson to think each single being as "unsponsored, free"—as Wallace Stevens said in the last stanza of "Sunday Morning."

The moment, the now, the present thus becomes for Emerson's intuition of Being the temporal "location" of an eternal return, of what he calls "circular power returning into itself" in "The American Scholar."[39] This momentous phrase provided Nietzsche with the problem of thinking the will to power and the eternal return together, as possible "features" of Being. Emerson's American vision thinks power as the *virtus* or potential of all becoming. In making each single being become what it is (to use another Nietzschean phrase), Being as power goes forward. At the same time it may paradoxically be said to "return" because, in sending a being on its way toward becoming its self, it lays the foundation of this single being as an entity always differing from itself. Being in this way makes all things and persons be; at the same time, it denies them any foundational authority since Being as power makes them be themselves only as they are on the way toward themselves in a persistently unsettling motion.

In "Nature" Emerson found a different way of speaking of the elusive, non-essentialist ways of Being. He describes in some detail how the contemplation of nature never allows a sense of full presence. We may understand nature as one of the many terms Emerson used in order to speak of Being without fixing it in one inadequate conceptualization. His summary of the felt evanescence of Being as nature is another impressive attempt, or *essay*, to say Being and, at the same time, to un-say it: "It is the same among the men and women, as among the silent trees; always a referred existence, an absence, never a presence and satisfaction."[40] The Being of what was in traditional metaphysics called objects and subjects is equally evasive. No single existent being in Emerson's world is able to maintain and establish itself so as to exert authority, because of its ontological precedence or persistent presence. This is why it may be said that all people and things share a democratically constituted universe, a universe in which, ontologically speaking, each individual and each "generation" may and must claim the possibility of a new and unhampered appropriation of their respective worlds. Emerson thinks a kind of ontological Jeffersonianism. A universe or a world that is thought in such a fashion will demand or even necessitate a particular attitude toward each single existent being. This attitude George Kateb defines as mental self-reliance: "Mental or philosophical self-reliance

---

[39] W I, 87.
[40] W III, 185.

means, precisely, the readiness to treat with sympathetic understanding ideas and values that have no sympathy for each other."[41]

Kateb's work on the philosophical and ontological foundations of the political phenomenon of a democratically organized society provides a fascinating view of the way Emerson's basic assumptions as a thinker, of how his ontology presents a mode of appreciating the ontic realm of concrete democratic practice. Kateb does not limit the concept of self-reliance to an individualistic existential experience or resolve—this would be the usual and, in its way, quite appropriate reading of Emerson. He defines self-reliance also as a philosophical attitude toward a conflictual social reality. In the war, the *polemos*, of ideas, values, and desires, Kateb detects the ontic reality whose underlying ontological principle is a radical pluralism or persistent inner differentiation of Being. The appropriate attitude of a thinker toward such a dispensation of Being is the "sympathetic understanding" of conflicting positions. This sympathetic understanding, however, is not a mere liberal indifference. It is an active assent to real diversity as the expression of an inevitable and persistent divisibility of whatever comes into existence. This is why Kateb also calls this attitude one of "sympathetic withholding."[42] In his programmatic outline of the basic ideas of his book, Kateb shows the way philosophical self-reliance[43] issues in a comprehensive democratic and non-essentialist idea of America:

> Self-reliance as a method of thinking with its own intrinsic value means more than any substantive commitment to a particular value, principle or idea, or to any practice or institution that embodies or derives from them ...
>
> One relies on oneself rather than seeking support in external commitments. One stays within oneself in order to enter imaginatively into all the commitments that social life displays, and must display. One increases the amount of value in the world by keeping oneself from embracing favorite ideas and works exclusively.
>
> Emerson is persuaded of two things: every position is held for at least plausible reasons and perhaps for necessary ones; and every position is inevitably accompanied by or engenders an opposition that is also (though not always equally) plausible or necessary and also narrow ...

---

[41]Kateb, *Emerson and Self-Reliance*, 4.

[42]Ibid.

[43]It should be noted that Kateb thinks of Emerson as a thinker who privileges mind over matter (56), an idealist and latter-day Platonist. He does implicitly acknowledge Emerson's pre-modern potential by allying him with his successor Nietzsche throughout, but he does not attribute a radical turn toward a new sense of Being to him. Nevertheless—and this is important for my argument—the (political and social) world surveyed by the Emersonian philosophical mind is, for Kateb, in its very Being an irreducible plurality possessed of an almost Jamesian aversion to closure.

That antagonists need each other for the sake of their own sanity is shown, Emerson thinks, in the political sphere where parties goad, check, and define each other. But antagonism—not just in politics—is the health of the whole world: its value is perpetual and to be preferred over synthesis or diluted compromise. ...

In the work he does, [Emerson] displays and inspires what we may call the democracy of intellect; he gives an example of the spirit of democracy at its best. That is self-reliance.[44]

Like Dewey, Kateb believes in Emerson's foundational role in thinking spiritual democracy, that is, in thinking the dispensation of Being in America. Thoreau said in "Walking" that "[i]n Wildness is the preservation of the World,"[45] that the as-yet-unappropriated is the true resource of all creative becoming. When Kateb says that Emerson believes that "antagonism ... is the health of the whole world," he voices a similar ontological idea. The forever undecided character of the world as a Heraclitean conflict, as a *polemos*, makes it impossible for any position or being to assume precedence and authority and stable and unchallenged identity forever. The struggles and debates in public life are the ontic aspects of the way Being is dispensed in the American realm. Kateb's argument culminates in the idea that true thinking that responds to this state of affairs will have to be a "sympathetic withholding," an attitude actively impartial, judicial, and caring at the same time. This attitude, so I would claim, is the existential dimension of true thinking which Dewey describes in his tribute to Emerson and which, in the high modernist thought of William James, might bear the name of the "gospel of relaxation"; it might also, in Heidegger's terminology, qualify as the true ethos of letting-be or *Gelassenheit*. It is this very attitude that assures the ability to truly enter, as Kateb says, "the commitments that social life displays."[46] The transition from the individualist point of departure in Emerson to Dewey's communitarian preference in thinking Being and defining democracy in America thus shows as that specific identity in difference that may well be the central trait of the American dispensation of Being.

Taking my clue from Kateb's methodology, I would like to end these brief remarks on Emerson thinking Being as America by looking at the way

---

[44]Ibid., 6–7.

[45]Henry David Thoreau, "Walking," in *The Writings of Henry David Thoreau* (Boston: Houghton, Mifflin, 1897), vol. 9, 275.

[46]Emerson is not yet given sufficient credit for the important communitarian aspects of his oeuvre, for his celebration of the "free and helpful [!] man" of whom he speaks in "Man the Reformer"; W I, 218. David Robinson has thoroughly explored this aspect, especially in the later works, in *Emerson and the Conduct of Life* (Cambridge: Cambridge University Press, 1993).

he makes transitions felt from the ontological to the ontic, from thinking Being to opinions on beings, including aspects of democratic and national culture. In "Progress of Culture," an 1867 essay that, like so many of his later writings, has not been sufficiently appreciated, Emerson uses the term *culture* to express the process through which the person becomes who she or he is; he makes the concept describe the evolution of true Being:

> I find the single mind equipollent to a multitude of minds, say to a nation of minds, as a drop of water balances the sea; and under this view the problem of culture assumes wonderful interest. Culture implies all which gives the mind possession of its own powers; as language to the critic, telescope to the astronomer. Culture alters the political status of an individual. It raises a rival royalty in a monarchy. 'Tis king against king.[47]

The way toward a human being's true existence is seen as providing a powerful alternative to everything that is. In the political realm, this means the abolition of hierarchy and the replacement of dominance by difference. The "rival royalty" inaugurated by the fully emancipated person allows for a balance of powers, for the tug of war between the "equipollent" forces of Being in a realm of differing individual centers. But it is not only the stability of traditional hierarchies that is challenged here. Through culture, as the process of becoming a true self, a mode of Being spreads that defies the claims of totalizing collectives like nations. A true human existence as Emerson thinks it, an individual *Dasein* under the American dispensation cannot but actively differ from the totalities of "block-universes"—be they vertically structured, like monarchies, or horizontally, like ethnically defined nation-states. From the perspective of Emerson's American experience of Being, this implies that "all history is a record of the power of minorities, and of minorities of one."[48] The single person as the fullness of Being in the "each-form," which William James so profoundly analyzed in *A Pluralistic Universe*, the single (human) Being is a threat to and a challenge of all historical ossifications. The single person keeps the dispensation of Being happening as the proliferation of difference, which is the central topic of essays like "Circles." On the ontic level of social reality, this means that a community, or a nation, or any collective of persons or ideas or things, will be truly communitarian only if it allows the single existence to be. In other words, communities only exist as provisional entities whose task it is to let all beings be or become who they are; the community and the collective is the transient mediator, the non-essential catalyst of true Being as temporally proliferating difference.

---

[47] W VIII, 206.
[48] Ibid., 208.

In "New England Reformers," Emerson said: "The union is only perfect, when all the uniters are isolated."[49] The single and singular person is the guarantee of a subversion of collective and persistent entities which is called for by the specific dispensation of Being called America which Emerson thinks. A totality like a society or a nation and its identity can only be thought on the basis of an evasion. Bercovitch, therefore, speaks quite appropriately of Emerson's "subversive infusion of individuality into the very concept of nationhood."[50] Emerson argues his case most impressively in "Courage":

> People wrap themselves up in disguises, and the sincere man is hard to reach. A man is concealed in his nation, concealed in his party, concealed in his fortune, and estate, concealed in his office, in his profession, concealed in his body at last, and it is hard to find out his pure nature and will.[51]

This is a statement on Being and (in-)authenticity; Emerson's words, in his customary flexible vocabulary, are sincerity, disguise, concealment, pure nature, and pure will. Any established social mode of existence, any fixed and identifiable form, like the body even, precludes that the authentic volatility, the "pure nature and will," of the single being or person unfold. Anything that absorbs true Being and its singularity and constant temporal differentiation, anything that replaces relentless becoming by means of a pretense of stability, lasting consistency, collective identity, or abstract universality betrays true Being and makes it inauthentic, offers a mere semblance of presence.

Thinking democracy and thinking America as a dispensation of Being in the Emersonian way disavows the possibility of a national identity in the sense of a stable and solidified totality of beings, because this state of affairs, this static version of temporal Being, would make being a person inauthentic and therefore un-democratic: "A man is concealed in his nation." A national identity called America would not really let beings be. It comes as no surprise, therefore, that Emerson does not believe in the concept of "race" as denoting an essentialist entity, either. Race, in its prominent nineteenth-century double meaning of *Volk* and ethnic group, is always a deceptive

---

[49] W III, 253.
[50] Bercovitch, *The Rites of Assent*, 345. It does remain a puzzle, though, at least for this reader, why Bercovitch believes that the very subversion of the concept of nationhood brings Emerson "to the verge of a sweeping repudiation not only of his society, but of his culture"; ibid., 320. I cannot but read Emerson as radically affirmative of American culture: this is why he has to be the relentless critic of its constant tendency to lose itself in essentialized interpretations and practices of its own fundamental beliefs.
[51] W VII, 245.

and mythological unity that veils the real conflicting multiplicity of warring factors in every "racial" or national entity. The opening paragraph of chapter IV, "Race," in *English Traits* states the case succinctly:

> An ingenious anatomist has written a book to prove that races are imperishable, but nations are pliant political constructions, easily changed or destroyed. But this writer did not found his assumed races on any necessary law, disclosing their ideal or metaphysical necessity; nor did he, on the other hand, count with precision the existing races, and settle the true bounds; a point of nicety, and the popular test of the theory. The individuals at the extremes of divergence in one race of men are as unlike as the wolf to the lapdog. Yet each variety shades down imperceptibly into the next, and you cannot draw the line where a race begins or ends.[52]

If one had assumed that Emerson's denial of the essentialist presence of the nation might yet leave the concept of race intact as a kind of substantial substratum, this passage clearly indicates that he maintains that there is no unchangeable and stable entity called race. There is no metaphysical necessity for it; this kind of being called race has no essential Being, it does not even possess the necessary limits or limitations to facilitate a definition. This is why Emerson, in opening the next chapter "Ability," treats the distinction of the Norman and the Saxon race within England as mythical, as an ideological invention.[53]

If there is no communitarian essence in the way the American dispensation of Being is thought by Emerson, if there is no nation and no substantial biological or cultural identity of a collective called race, in scrutinizing the ontic realm called America one might at least hope for the belief in stable political structures. The belief in democratic institutions, which could guarantee the very diversity at the heart of the American thought of Being, this belief would provide one resting place, one solid support in the quicksands of Emerson's ontological imagination. There is, however, no more radical vision of the insubstantiality, the non-essential way of Being, of the sheer phenomenality of institutions than in this wonderful passage from "Politics":

> Hence, the less government we have, the better,—the fewer laws, and the less confided power. The antidote to this abuse of formal Government, is, the influence of private character, the growth of the Individual; the appearance of the principal to supersede the proxy; the appearance of the wise man, of whom the existing government is, it must be owned, but

---

[52] W V, 47.
[53] Ibid., 75.

a shabby imitation. That which all things tend to educe, which freedom, cultivation, intercourse, revolutions, go to form and deliver, is character; that is the end of nature, to reach unto this coronation of her king. To educate the wise man, the State exists; and with the appearance of the wise man, the State expires. The appearance of character makes the State unnecessary. The wise man is the State. He needs no army, fort, or navy,— he loves men too well; no bribe, or feast, or palace, to draw friends to him; no vantage ground, no favorable circumstance. He needs no library, for he has not done thinking; no church, for he is a prophet; no statute book, for he has the lawgiver; no money, for he is value; no road, for he is at home where he is; no experience, for the life of the creator shoots through him, and looks from his eyes.[54]

The ecstatic vision of the true individual as the authentic form of Being indicates, once again, that Being, for Emerson exists only in the each-form, in difference. The institutions, rules, laws, and regulations of established society are so many denials of true Being; they are constantly to be overcome. The forms of political, religious, and economic institutionalization hide Being from itself—their mode of existence is inauthentic. The "dogma of no-government and non-resistance," as he explains in the "Stonehenge" chapter of *English Traits*,[55] is the true American idea: it is the idea of letting the human being fully be. One should, however, not overlook that Emerson's vision of the utopian achievement of true Being as human *Dasein* is not a "state" of affairs. In their true existence, we read in "Circles," there are "no fixtures to men." In summarizing these observations on the ontic realm and its ontological underpinnings, in re-considering what Emerson might call authentic, we find that there is not only no nation, no race, no state in Emerson thinking America, there is also no human nature.

The third and last part of my attempt to describe the continuities and differences in the way Emerson and Dewey think Being as America is devoted both to a summary analysis of Dewey's version of a fundamental ontology and to a direct comparison of his position with Emerson's thinking. Their shared sense of Being in America implies a basically identical view of human nature in Emerson and Dewey. Human nature may be seen as one of the privileged places, in an ontological sense, where Being occurs. For Emerson, as we saw, the human being is not really himself but rather a channel or method or way through which the soul, reason, power, an aboriginal self or, one may suggest, Being itself—as another word for the ultimately nameless event—issues into a constantly renewable and often self-contradictory becoming as a process of both defining and un-defining,

---

[54] W III, 206–7.
[55] W V, 272.

of de-constructing, individual identity. This is why Emerson celebrates inconsistency in "Self-Reliance." The true self is always on the way to being its own other and in the process of denying any momentarily acquired solid and substantial identity. In *Freedom and Culture* (1939), Dewey has argued that human nature is not an essential antecedent endowment of a person but rather a momentary result of the multiple interactive processes taking place between what we tend to call culture and what we have learned to describe as the person.[56] For both Emerson and Dewey, human nature is not natural or *a priori*, human nature is an event that is always just about to occur. This leads Dewey to argue against all attempts to define a culture or a society or a nation on the basis of "human nature." In his own specific way, he continues the argument begun by Emerson in *English Traits*. Dewey's thorough refutations of Hobbes, Rousseau, Hegel, and Mill in chapter 5 of *Freedom and Culture*, "Democracy and Human Nature,"[57] make us aware of the fact that the democratic quality of the as yet to be achieved and constantly to be reconstructed American democracy is not an essential trait grounded in (human) nature but a process of experimental innovation without antecedents.

Dewey's mode of thinking the human being in *Freedom and Culture* facilitates the approach to his interpretation of Being as such. When he observes that the Marxist equation of conservative and radical attitudes and beliefs with certain social classes is easily falsified, he takes this as

> sufficient disproof of the notion that the problem can be stated as one of the relation of *the* individual and *the* social, as if these names stood for any actual existences. It indicates that *ways of interaction* between human nature and cultural conditions are the first and the fundamental thing to be examined, and that the problem is to ascertain the effects of interactions between different components of different human beings and different customs, rules, traditions, institutions—the things called "social."[58]

There are no essential beings called individuals and social conditions. What truly *is*, "the first and the fundamental thing[s]," the principal modes of Being, the *arche*, should be called "*ways of interaction*," processes, events that temporarily result in the nominalized, and easily and mistakenly essentialized, beings called individual or society, human nature or cultural condition. Being itself is an event of producing differences: "All that we can safely say is that human nature, like other forms of life, tends to

---

[56]See chapter 2, "Culture and Human Nature" *LW* XIII, 80–98.
[57]Ibid., 136–55.
[58]Ibid., 86.

differentiation."[59] In order to show that thinking of human nature as a true essence is an ontological error, Dewey demonstrates that Hobbes's negative evaluation of the desire for gain may show as the positive feature of the capability for free and creative competition in John Stuart Mill. He concludes:

> Neither competition nor cooperation can be judged as traits of human nature. They are names for certain relations among the actions of individuals as the relations actually obtain in a community.
>
> This would be true even if there were tendencies in human nature so definitely marked off from one another as to merit the names given them and even if human nature were as fixed as it is sometimes said to be ...
>
> But the alleged unchangeableness of human nature cannot be admitted.[60]

If there is no essential human being in the way Dewey thinks actual social and cultural conditions, what then is the intuition of Being in which this philosophical position is grounded? Dewey offers one of the most concentrated interpretations of his sense of Being in the opening chapter, "Experience and Philosophic Method," of *Experience and Nature*. Dewey follows James and speaks of (pure or primary) experience as foundational term of all thinking:

> Like its congeners, life and history, it includes *what* men do and suffer, *what* they strive for, love, believe and endure, and also *how* men act and are acted upon, the ways in which they do and suffer, desire and enjoy, see, believe, imagine—in short, processes of *experiencing*.[61]

Experiencing is Dewey's word for Being. As in Heidegger's use of the term Being, it is important to note that it implies a verb-al, a temporal aspect—it is not a noun substantive. Experiencing opens a world in which humans and things exist in ongoing relations; it opens a world of *what* and *how*, of *essentia* and *existentia*, the classical determinants of Being. Subjects and objects are secondary formations arising out of the constant processual differentiations of Being. Human nature arises out of experiencing as a temporal mode of relating to a world always already part of that specific experiencing or, as Dewey says in *Freedom and Culture*, of ways of interaction.

Dewey's way of thinking Being as experiencing stresses the primordial relatedness of what we (*a posteriori*) call humans and their environment;

---

[59]Ibid., 77–8.
[60]Ibid., 142.
[61]*LW* I, 18.

Emerson's way focuses on the emergence of all singular beings from Being. Dewey thinks "outward" from Being as processual relatedness toward human beings and their ever-changing environing social and cultural realities; Emerson may be said to think "inward" from any single being as unique event toward its ongoing emergence from Being. These are basic and complementary ways of dealing with the ontological difference of Being and beings rather than ontic and ideological discrepancies between individualism and communitarianism. The difference in Emerson's and Dewey's response to Being and to the ontological difference under the American dispensation of Being is both contingent and necessary. The radical evasiveness of Being—as thought by these two American thinkers—necessitates unforeseeable and therefore contingent differences because they so deeply respond to the basic feature of their vision: the absence of persistent identity in Being.

Even so, the call of Being mandates an essentially identical response that we have named democratic in the sense of describing a possible order of things. Dewey articulates a pluralist ethics of letting beings be that is directly related to Emerson:

> Respect for experience [alias Being] is respect for its possibilities in thought and knowledge as well as an enforced attention to its joys and sorrows. Intellectual piety toward experience is a precondition of the direction of life and of tolerant and generous cooperation among men. Respect for the things of experience alone brings with it such a respect for others, the centres of experience, as is free from patronage, domination and the will to impose.[62]

Piety toward Being[63] in thinking is a motif that Dewey inherited from Emerson. Emerson said in *Nature*: "In the uttermost meaning of the words, thought is devout, and devotion is thought."[64] This piety is an attitude of reception, of letting the way in which Being occurs, letting manifold experiencing, truly and respectfully be. It is this sense of Emersonian *Gelassenheit* in Dewey that results in the demand for an ethics that also looks back to James's "On a Certain Blindness in Human Beings." Emerson's "sympathetic withholding" of ultimate judgment, James's call for imaginative participation in the radically other, and Dewey's piety toward the potentially endless multiplicity of experiencing are versions of an ethics that might make democracy as a non-essentialist process possible:

---

[62]Ibid., 286.
[63]The late Heidegger's conception of "die Frömmigkeit des Denkens" is a similar motif in responding to the question of Being.
[64]W I, 77.

An American democracy can serve the world only as it demonstrates in the conduct of its own life the efficacy of plural, partial, and experimental methods in securing and maintaining an ever-increasing release of the powers of human nature, in service of a freedom which is cooperative and a cooperation which is voluntary.[65]

This wonderfully intricate statement makes all essentialist generalizations and entities disappear in the service of a true process of democratic experimentation or "releasement" or letting be: America goes beyond its own borders and limitations, it empowers others to be themselves, and in thus going away from itself it becomes itself; the freedom of the individual transgresses the limitations of individualism toward the social compact and Dewey's idea of society abolishes its potentially forced collective character in letting individuality truly be. The democratic ethics that arises out of Dewey's thinking Being as America *continues* Emerson's project in its very difference.[66]

Even more frequently than Emerson, Dewey moves from ontological considerations to critical analyses of ontic manifestations of the American dispensation of thinking Being. In 1917 Dewey published "The Principle of Nationality" in the *Menorah Journal*. This cautious and somewhat noncommittal meditation on the necessity, possibility, and desirability of a Jewish national state begins with a distinction of cultural *nationality* and political *nationalism*. The United States, Dewey maintains, find themselves in a special and exceptional condition:

In the United States we have a distinct situation, for we are perhaps the only national state wherein the principle of nationality has no political standing—except as political parties find it expedient to place upon their tickets representatives of various nationalities in order to secure votes. But excepting in an informal way, the principle of nationality receives no recognition in the constitution of a state like ours, where citizenship and nationality are independent.[67]

---

[65] *Freedom and Culture LW* XIII, 187.

[66] These conclusions necessarily invert Quentin Anderson's evaluation of the relationship between Emerson and Dewey and of the way in which they define the ethical possibilities and the supposed essence of a democratic America. Anderson's skeptical and critical essay "John Dewey's American Democrat," *Daedalus* 108, no. 3 (1979): 145–59, quite surprisingly attributes the character of a closed philosophical system to Dewey's interpretation of American democracy. The liberating potential of both Emerson's and Dewey's thought is thus severely curtailed.

[67] *MW* 10, 287.

Dewey denies an antecedent and constitutive cultural and ethnic identity as a necessary ingredient of American political reality. His ontological presuppositions, which he so extensively analyzed in their relevance for the political realm in *Freedom and Culture*, exclude the recognition of a fixed collective cultural essence. Dewey goes on to say that he finds the "concept of uniformity and unanimity in culture ... rather repellent"[68] and that he thinks the theory of the melting pot in which "all the constituent elements ... in the United States should be put in the same pot and turned into a uniform and unchanging product ... distasteful."[69] Dewey summarizes his view in this seemingly innocent way: "Variety *is* the spice of life, and the richness and attractiveness of social institutions depend upon cultural diversity among separate units. In so far as people are all alike, there is no give and take among them. And it is better to give and take."[70]

Passages like these tend to make us forget that we read not only Dewey's political opinions here but the text of a thinker. The term "life" is one of Dewey's synonyms for experiencing and thus for Being; by italicizing *is* he also emphasizes that variety is indeed an ontological trait; and, last but not least, interactive exchange between single beings and environments, the coexistence of activity and reception, the "give and take," is a prime feature of Being itself throughout major texts like *Experience and Nature*. The very differences that tend to invalidate and maybe even endanger the existence and the solid essence of America make it truly vital if perceived from the vantage point of the American dispensation of Being. It seems a little ironic, therefore, when, in an issue of *Daedalus* on *Human Diversity*, Charles Lindholm and John A. Hall try to answer the question "Is the United States falling apart?" by assuring their readers that the very proliferation of difference, which is perceived as so threatening worldwide, is counteracted by a "powerful homogenizing force" in the United States.[71] Even so, they cannot but participate in the basic experience of Being in America when they remind us that civility in society "depends upon a particular social agreement to ... live together with difference."[72] What seems such a commonplace now is, after all, nothing but the almost global acceptance of a response to Being first articulated and thought in and as America. Philosophically speaking, this now common insight into the ontological necessity to let real difference be, this insight was won in the many, in the various radical acts of intellectual declarations of independence that constitute the history of thinking in America.

---

[68] Ibid., 288.
[69] Ibid., 289.
[70] Ibid., 288.
[71] Charles Lindholm and John A. Hall, "Is the United States Falling Apart?" *Daedalus* 126, no. 2 (1997): 202.
[72] Ibid., 201.

Dewey described his own way as a thinker in terms of a struggle against inclinations and education, against his tendency toward and fascination with systems, and against the charisma of Hegel. Overcoming both his personal and philosophical antecedents, he found that he could now think "the concrete diversity of experienced things" as he explains in his autobiographical sketch "From Absolutism to Experimentalism."[73] This thinking is—like that of Emerson—a literal letting go (the antecedent) and letting be (the unforeseen and the unexpected). It is the core of their, Emerson's and Dewey's, common experimentalism. When Emerson said in "Circles": "I simply experiment, an endless seeker, with no Past at my back,"[74] he did not negate the importance of historical studies, persons, or events. Emerson's predilection for roll-calls of past authorities and the whole drift of his argument in "Quotation and Originality" (1868) do indicate his respect for significant traditions. Experimentalism, however, issues from a sense of Being that will always keep the future open as a way of letting the unprecedented freely be. Dewey's scientifically informed experimentalism is ontologically the same mode of thinking. Both Emerson and Dewey think democracy as an experiment always erasing precedent, they think America as always new and yet unapproachable, they think the American anti-essentialist dispensation of Being.

Ultimately, this way of thinking Being does not only affect the possibilities of the future, it also lifts the constraints of a past subjected to the rigidity of an ultimately inhumane philosophy of history that ascribes meanings to events before they even had a chance to occur. Emerson's and Dewey's anti-Hegelianism cannot but think the dispensations of Being, the coming forth of historical eras as contingent. Thus Dewey saw the American Revolution not as a part of a logic of history but, as he said in *Freedom and Culture*, as a "very fortunate conjunction of events";[75] and Emerson stated in his late essay "The Fortune of the Republic" (1878): "The revolution is the work of no man, but the eternal effervescence of nature."[76] Thinking America as a way of thinking Being shows in both Emerson and Dewey as a constant turning away from all conceptual and institutional petrifications and ossifications past and present—including the persistent attempts to believe that America possesses a core, an identity, an unmistakable essence. By evading[77] such a tempting alternative, Emerson's protean thought and Dewey's tireless experimentalism succeed in heeding the call of Being.

---

[73] *LW* V, 147–60.

[74] *W* II, 297.

[75] *LW* XIII, 185.

[76] *W* XI, 412.

[77] I use the term in the sense introduced by Cornel West's *The American Evasion of Philosophy* (Madison, WI: University of Wisconsin Press, 1989).

PART TWO

# American Pragmatism: Thinking Modernism

# 10

## American Thinking
## Out of Bounds

It is one of the characteristic gestures of authentic modern thinking to try and return to the very beginnings of thought, to attempt and recapture the moment of speechless wonder, of *thaumazein*, which Aristotle thought indispensable as the point of departure for genuine philosophical effort.[1] This significant moment, reiterated and re-enacted again and again by modernist thinkers in a variety of ways, is characterized by the absence of any philosophical position-taking; it is a moment that is essentially, fundamentally, ontologically modern because, in Emerson's words from his essay "Circles," it has no past, that is, no *philosophical* past, at its back;[2] it is not beholden to precedents. Both the very beginnings of thinking and their return in the thought of the great modernists may thus be understood as defined by a comprehensive *epoché*, a primary absence or withholding or bracketing of any pre-established judgment and defined interest. In this way earliest thinkers and their modern counterparts practice a foundational phenomenology in which nature, the world, Being is allowed to come forth and show itself *of* and *for* itself. We see this in Emerson's subtle and manifold re-engagements of the Presocratics and in Nietzsche's evocation of Heraclitus, inspired by Emerson; we see it in a variety of ways in the classical American pragmatist thinkers' attempts to envision and experience a pure given-ness that precedes all language and culture; we see it in

This essay was previously published as "Out of Bounds: American Visions of the Thinker and of Thinking" in *Intellectual Authority and Literary Culture in the US, 1790–1900*, ed. Günter Leypoldt (Heidelberg: Winter, 2013), 205–17. Reprinted by permission of Universitätsverlag Winter GmbH.

[1] Aristotle, *Metaphysics*, ed and trans. Hugh Tredennick. Loeb Classical Library 271 (1933; Cambridge, MA: Harvard University Press, 1996), vol. XVII, 982b 10–17, 12–13.
[2] W II, 297.

Heidegger's attempts to allow the first beginnings of thinking in Heraclitus and in Parmenides to speak for themselves. It is in this very moment before any *doxa*—that is, human opinions, philosophical or otherwise—are articulated, before positions are taken; it is in this moment that Parmenides's momentous insight into the identity of Being and thinking[3] manifests itself as self-evidently and plausibly true: one may call this the supreme initial and initiating, the forever and essentially modern, philosophical epiphany, an epiphany that is not replaced or overcome by the consequent acts of philosophizing but rather, as Heidegger argued in his commentary on Aristotle's basic intuition, permeates all genuine philosophical effort and endeavor.[4]

The very possibility and the reality of both a historically primary and a radically modern mode of thinking seriously challenge one of the most sophisticated among sociocultural attempts to delineate the structural dynamics of human creativity in the arts and in philosophy, namely, Pierre Bourdieu's vision and analysis of the field(s) of cultural production. I will offer a condensed and admittedly somewhat pointed critique of Bourdieu's central metaphor of the field and its implications as the basis and backdrop of my interpretations of the foundational ontological intuitions and practices of Ralph Waldo Emerson as the earliest of exemplary modernist thinkers. This will be followed by brief and condensed readings of the core ideas of Emerson's great American successors, the classical pragmatists William James and Charles Sanders Peirce. The single and simple thesis underlying my readings of Emerson, James, and Peirce is that both the historical *and* the modernist versions of primary thinking occur, logically *have to* occur, *outside* the fields of cultural and philosophical production as defined and described by Bourdieu. Such thinking is essentially "out of bounds," that is, *beyond* or *before* any socially or culturally defined fields of collectively determined human creative activities.

Let me briefly focus on two of the most widely discussed or best-known of Bourdieu's texts in this specific context, the essay "The Field of Cultural Production, or: The Economic World Reversed"[5] and the famous critique of Derrida's deconstructive reading of Kant's *Critique of Judgement* under the title "Parerga and Paralipomena" in the "Postscript" to Bourdieu's book *Distinction*.[6] In both texts the fields of aesthetic, artistic production

---

[3]Parmenides, *Die Fragmente: Griechisch-Deutsch*, ed. and trans. Ernst Heitsch (Zurich: Artemis & Winkler, 1995), B3, 16–17.

[4]Heidegger, "Was ist das – die Philosophie?" (1955), in *Identität und Differenz*, ed. Friedrich-Wilhelm von Herrmann, vol. 11.1 of *Gesamtausgabe* (Frankfurt: Klostermann, 2006), 22.

[5]Pierre Bourdieu, *The Field of Cultural Production: Essays on Art and Literature*, ed. Randal Johnson (New York: Columbia University Press, 1993), 29–73.

[6]Pierre Bourdieu, *Distinction: A Social Critique of the Judgment of* Taste, trans. Richard Nice (1979; Cambridge, MA: Harvard University Press, 1984), 494–8.

and of philosophical thought and critique are looked at from within. The boundaries, the defining limits of the respective fields, are only lightly and sketchily touched upon in an afterthought and a footnote to the Derrida critique. The outside does not really, significantly, exist, not as a productive factor impacting the fields, nor as a horizon meaningfully encompassing them. Bourdieu says:

> The literary or artistic field is a *field of forces*, but it is also a *field of struggles* tending to transform or conserve this field of forces ... Every position-taking is defined in relation to the *space of possibles* which is objectively realized as a *problematic* in the form of actual or potential position-takings corresponding to the different positions; and it receives its distinctive *value* from its negative relationship with the coexistent position-takings to which it is objectively related and which determine it by delimiting it.[7]

Here, as in other writings by Bourdieu, the field of historically established and communally realized cultural activities is always already there. Each single and individual creative disposition and action is, in its possibilities and its value and meaning, defined by the contrastive, or negative, relation to other, say, works or aesthetic or philosophical agendas which "determine it by delimiting it." This sociocentric, anthropocentric, and thus radically humanist or subjectivist stance excludes or ignores the vast reaches of the trans-human and the pre-social as possibly major agents in "cultural production," especially in its version as philosophical thought. This also means that for Bourdieu there is no true and independent beginning (historical or systematic), no "original relation to the universe" in Emerson's programmatic words from *Nature*[8]—simply because every position (or mode of thinking) is, according to Bourdieu, always already constrained by the given, by already existing works and thoughts that structure the interior of the moving field of constantly changing, but always related and power-determined positions. At the same time, there is no space for the truly, ontologically, relevant *new*, the new as the quintessential ontological feature of modern thinking. The new has no real place in Bourdieu's ultimately, in spite of all disclaimers, determinist scheme: new relations and new actualizations *within* the determined space of defined possibles are not really, again ontologically speaking, new: they are not unprecedented, with no past at their backs; they are simply and merely innovative, that is, inventions directed and constrained by the already given. Thinking the modern without a genuine possibility of both an authentic beginning and

---

[7]Bourdieu, *The Field of Cultural Production*, 30.
[8]W I, 9.

an ontologically valid conception of the new, however, appears impossible or a contradiction in terms: the work of art or philosophy that arises out of a field can thus never be itself. Bourdieu argues: "In short, it is a question of understanding works of art as a *manifestation* of the field as a whole, in which all the powers of the field, and all the determinisms inherent in its structure and functioning, are concentrated."[9]

Bourdieu's variety of totalizing determinism defines the philosophical field in a similar fashion: "The radical questionings announced by philosophy are in fact circumscribed by the interests linked to membership in the philosophical field, that is, to the very existence of this field and the corresponding censorships."[10] The coercive character of this field and its philosophical positions does allow contradiction and alternatives, radical challenges and provocative innovation, deconstruction and reconstruction; these moves, however, are always already related, constrained in their very nay-saying by the realm of pre-established possibles. One must not overlook the fact that even what Bourdieu calls the "autonomous principle" within the cultural field— for example, *l'art pour l'art*—cannot escape already given economic determinants: "There are," he declares, "economic conditions for the indifference to economy" among the intellectual avant-gardes.[11] How, then, could a truly primary philosophy and its modernist re-enactment or return be thought at all? A historically primary philosophy would naturally find itself before the formation of any field whatsoever, facing Being in wonder. A modernist re-enactment *of* or return *to* this moment would have to position itself, then, by way of mere negation of the established positions in philosophy—and this would merely serve as an implied rehabilitation of the power of the field. A primary philosophical stance, however, comes about only by way of that existentially significant move which Emerson called "abandonment,"[12] which means simply leaving the field alone and behind and move toward the as-yet-undefined open without looking back; it means to go out of bounds. In Bourdieu's threatening words, this would mean "falling into the exterior, into outer darkness, that is, into the vulgarity of the non-philosophical, the coarseness of 'empirical', 'ontic', 'positivist' discourse."[13] But this is not the way one can or should or has to read American Transcendentalist or pragmatist experiments in regaining a primary vision beyond or outside the field.

Let me begin in the 1840s. Emerson had maintained in his essay "History" (1841)—and Nietzsche, a generation later, had succinctly echoed

---

[9]Bourdieu, *The Field of Cultural Production*, 37.
[10]Bourdieu, *Distinction*, 496.
[11]Bourdieu, *The Field of Cultural Production*, 40.
[12]W II, 300.
[13]Bourdieu, *Distinction*, 497.

his position—that the true moment of culture is not within culture, but, individually and collectively, *in* and *as* the transition from the "not yet" of the so-called barbaric, the natural, the unformed, the featureless, the open, the un-appropriated spread that precedes any field.[14] True moments of culture and of thinking, that is, occur in the processes of cultivation and awareness of what we variously and freely name the world, wilderness, nature, Being itself; primary or modern thinking and culture occur in those acts of Emersonian abandonment and Nietzschean productive forgetfulness that Gertrude Stein called "beginning again and again."[15] Beginning again and again in Emerson's case first of all implies the abandonment of any and all positions taken by previous thinkers and their writings: "Books are for the scholar's idle times"—he states succinctly.[16] Previous thought in the field of philosophy is like all writings "for nothing but to inspire," and Emerson continues in "The American Scholar": "I had better never see a book than to be warped by its attraction clean out of my orbit."[17] The constraints of established position-takings are simply ignored here. In the ruthless language of Emerson's address "Literary Ethics," this reads: "Leave me alone; do not teach me out of Leibniz or Schelling; and I shall find it all out myself."[18]

The outside of the field of cultural production, the realm out of bounds: how does it show, what does it look like, how does it make itself felt and heard in Emerson's vision and thinking? The opening statement of the lecture "The Transcendentalist" reminds us that modern thinking in 1842, called "*new views*" by Emerson, is "not new, but the very oldest of thoughts."[19] The identity of primary thinking in its historical mode, most prominently in the Presocratics, and in its present-day re-enactment owes itself to a defining motion which informs both Being as nature and thinking itself and which Emerson speaks of in "The American Scholar" as "circular power returning into itself."[20] That which truly exists *in* and *as* thought and as reality emerges from an unceasing return of Being and thinking into their own inexhaustible and unstructured—that is, emphatically *not* field-like—creative potentiality before any distinction and appropriation. Emerson's thinking finds many names for the ever-present destination of this eternal return into the featurelessly productive; one of the prominent terms is "intellect." In his eponymous essay, Emerson's "new thought" revives, renews, re-enacts the primary, Presocratic thesis of Parmenides that mind

---

[14] W II, 16, 23–4, 27–8.
[15] Gertrude Stein, "Composition as Explanation," in *Look at Me Now and Here I Am: Writings and Lectures 1909–1945*, ed. Patricia Meyerowitz (1926; London: Penguin, 1971), 23.
[16] W I, 92.
[17] Ibid., 91.
[18] Ibid., 156.
[19] Ibid., 311.
[20] Ibid., 87.

or thinking (in the sense of Gr. *nous*) and Being are the same: "Intellect is the simple power anterior to all action or construction ... Itself alone is."[21] Thus, primary unstructured awareness is Being itself, and it knows by way of a vision that "is not like the vision of the eye, but is union with the things known."[22] Intellect allows things simply *to be* (themselves) without reference to a conceiving, grasping, to a positioned self in a socially and culturally structured field. Intellect "discerns [any given fact] as if it existed for its own sake ... and not as *I* or *mine*."[23] This implies that intellect, the Emersonian version of the Presocratic *nous*, does not relate conceptually, possessively to entities in a structured field. "The scholar of the first age [i.e., the Presocratic thinker] received into him the world around; brooded thereon; gave it the new arrangement of his own mind, and uttered it again."[24] What Emerson indicates with the term "intellect" manifests itself in this "first age" as the primary, open space of thinking that precedes all conceptualizations in fields of philosophy as epistemology: "Long prior to the age of reflection is the thinking of the mind."[25]

In "The American Scholar," that which exists outside and before any field is described as "so entire, so boundless."[26] Here Emerson almost literally regains a primary intuition even older than that of Parmenides, namely, Anaximander's *apeiron*, the aboriginal totality without delimitation and defining distinctions. He goes on to speak of that realm of thinking and Being as "without centre, without circumference" (a phrase which in the essay "Circles" he mistakenly attributed to St. Augustine).[27] The beginning, any beginning like the vision of the *apeiron*, ontologically opens a space *void of* but *ready for* any distinction and position-taking, a space of the forever fundamentally new, a space ready to allow for—again and again— manifold centers and multiple circumferences of historically transient fields. These fields or, as Emerson has it, the ages of reflection, the periods of cultural and philosophical production, are always later, *a posteriori*. They always follow, both historically *and* systematically, what he calls "the thinking of the mind." This is also the reason why Emerson thought the Greek language—and that, for him, means especially the Greek of the Presocratic—a language superior to any later cultural successor operating in the field established by primary, by earliest Greek thought; in an interview with students at Williams College he said: "For the Greek is the fountain of language. The Latin has a definite shore-line, but the Greek is without

---

[21] W II, 303.
[22] Ibid., 304.
[23] Ibid.
[24] W I, 89.
[25] W II, 305.
[26] W I, 87.
[27] W II, 281.

bounds."[28] In order to allow for a modern, that is, a renewed primary philosophy, later languages like his own American English would then have to constantly work against the established forms of meaning and expression by a strategy that Emerson criticism has learned to call a specific form of troping, a ceaseless and relentless turning and abandoning of traditional meanings.[29]

In a further move, Emerson's regained Parmenidian insight into the identity of Being and thinking through ontological awareness becomes the background of his refutation and inversion and thus of his abandonment of the Cartesian axiom of possible certainty—and this in turn positions Emerson as the American fountainhead of radical modernism in thinking. Descartes's "cogito ergo sum" becomes, in the essay "Circles" and elsewhere, "*so to be* [sum] is the sole inlet of *so to know* [cogitare]"[30]—or in a variant "*We are* wiser than we *know*"[31]—that is to say, Emerson posits exact reversals of the traditional ground of early modern philosophy. Anticipating Sartre, modernist Emerson allows *existentia* (the undefined *there*, the outside) to precede *essentia* (the culturally defined what-ness of any being in the field). Existentially speaking, the human being is grounded outside and prior to the fields of his or her very own personalized conceptual orientations *of* and *within* cultural *knowing* including philosophy; the *wisdom* of primary thinking is thus not only a singular historical antecedent, for example, in the Presocratics, it is rather the boundless, undifferentiated potential of cultural, of philosophical, and above all of individual renewal that again and again opens in moments of circular return. As individual renewal that wisdom is named "self-reliance"; it signifies the possibility of being outside one's very own individual and personal field of socially determined cultural competence (or knowing), of being what Thoreau once called "beside oneself in a sane sense."[32] It is important to add at this point that from the Emersonian perspective not even the Presocratics and their (sparsely transmitted) writings establish a position, a possible relation, let alone a field. The modern thinker as primary thinker does not so much relate to any predecessors in engaging Being or intellect; just as they are, he is rather defined simply by his relation to the *Sache selbst*, the matter of thinking. The modern thinker is in the role of the aboriginal phenomenologist who allows

---

[28]Charles J. Woodbury, *Talks with Ralph Waldo Emerson* (New York: Baker & Taylor, 1890), 890.

[29]Richard Poirier *The Renewal of Literature: Emersonian Reflections* (New York: Random House, 1987), 131–2.

[30]W II, 299.

[31]Ibid., 263 (my emphasis).

[32]Henry David Thoreau, *Walden, or Life in the Woods*, vol. II of *The Writings of Henry David Thoreau* (Boston: Houghton, Mifflin, 1893–94), 211.

the *unmediated* address of Being or nature or the world to make itself felt as the defining challenge of all proper and authentic thought.

One of the most intriguing aspects of the Emersonian vision of the thinker outside the field of cultural production is the very method of thinking and writing that it entails and necessitates. For many readers the often surprising and unannounced shifts of position, the tropings alluded to just a moment ago, the unabashed contradictions in judgment, valuation, and opinion in Emerson's essays are simply irritating and annoying, the more so since they hardly ever issue in a viable synthesis. The alternations between the universalist and the pluralist points of view in the essay "Nominalist and Realist" are as good an example as the seemingly more concrete unresolved hesitations between socialist and radically individualist stances in the lectures "New England Reformers" or "The Young American." Emerson's strategy is not dialectic—"Life [and this implies authentic thinking] is not dialectics," he insists[33]—his strategy here again is the return of one of the oldest modes of thinking outside the field, for example when he writes: "All things are in contact; every atom has a sphere of repulsion;—Things are, and are not, at the same time." These aphorisms from "Nominalist and Realist"[34] echo sayings of Heraclitus. In *Journals and Miscellaneous Notebooks* Emerson enters a sequence of eighteen Heraclitus fragments, among them: "On the same stream we embark & embark not; we are & we are not."[35] Hans-Georg Gadamer in his "Heraklit-Studien" (in a volume called *Der Anfang des Wissens* = primary philosophy) has offered a subtle reading of these Heraclitean turns:

> The mysterious problem manifesting itself behind all of these oppositions is obviously the fact that the identical shows as the other without any transition. All of these examples manifest what the Greeks called *metabole*, unmediated reversal. It is characterized by extreme suddenness. The experience of thinking underlying this method is that of an essential unreliability of all that which now shows as this and now as that.[36]

This implies that the thinking and writing of Heraclitus and its Emersonian re-enactment take place in a realm where all dogmatic positions and all judgments are suspended, that is, in the realm of a comprehensive *epoché*. Outside any field with its definable relations and positions, thinking is not the assertion of a stand-point, of *doxa*, it is no longer a position-taking as in

---

[33] W III, 61.
[34] Ibid., 233.
[35] *JMN* VI, 379.
[36] Hans-Georg Gadamer, *Der Anfang des Wissens* (Stuttgart: Reclam, 1999), 42–3 (my translation).

Bourdieu's fields. Thinking becomes, as Emerson has it in "Intellect," "a pious reception."[37] The thinker allows Being and beings to show for what they are and he reacts, as Emerson said of Xenophanes, Heraclitus, and Parmenides, by way of "prompt improvisations,"[38] varieties of statements prompted by the self-manifestation of Being that the thinker as writer improvises in *always tentative* language. Challenged by the open, unstructured expanse of Being, he, literally, responds improvidently, without fore- or hindsight, as "an endless experimenter with no Past at [his] back."[39] In this way the thinker as modernist—just like the Presocratic primary philosopher—takes care to "unsettle all things."[40] In order for thinking to be modern, to be able to return again and again into the primary *apeiron* outside any field, each single statement, each position taken, has to be revoked and reversed immediately. This means that thinking cannot reach, let alone establish or position a ground: thinking has to abandon metaphysics. In "Nominalist and Realist," Emerson does this by asserting "Nature is *one thing and the other thing*, in the same moment."[41] This radical *metabole* deletes (i.e., abandons) the validity of one of Aristotle's mainstays of metaphysical conceptualization, the principle of the excluded middle and, by extension, the principle of identity in logic. Without this, fields of positions taken, of strategies employed, of philosophical trajectories reliably established, are impossible. The most radically modern thinker will then have to admit with Emerson: "I am always insincere."[42] This statement from "Nominalist and Realist" undercuts any position-taking, denies the reliable validity of any standpoint, of the very idea of a standpoint, and, at the same time and once again, calls up the time of Presocratics primary intuitions: "I am *always* insincere" poses the same problem of logical undecidability as Epimenides's famous conundrum of the Cretan who maintains that all Cretans are liars.

I would like to summarize at this point: Emerson's persistent returns from established philosophical positions into the as-yet-undecided beginnings of primary intuition provide an inexhaustible reservoir of ever new—that is, radically new but always tentative and therefore essentially contingent—interpretations of reality that are destined for constant and relentless revisions, tropings, and ultimate abandonment in order to ensure the openness of the world for the free unfolding of an inexhaustible wealth of possible but transient meanings.

A brief look at William James's foundational ontological category, at what he calls "pure experience," is most suitable to show *his* version of regaining

---

[37] W II, 306.
[38] W I, 156.
[39] W II, 297.
[40] Ibid.
[41] W III, 225.
[42] Ibid., 235.

a site or space out of bounds, beyond the circumscription of traditional, established readings of reality. For James's pragmatist intuition, it is not only the thinker, or Man Thinking, as in Emerson, but each individual being who emerges and continues to emerge in existentially significant fashion from an unprecedented and culturally un-appropriated realm beyond the boundary lines of socially defined fields. In one of his *Essays in Radical Empiricism* written in 1904, James states:

> "Pure experience" is the name which I gave to the immediate flux of life which furnishes the material to our later reflection with its conceptual categories ... [this means] to have an experience pure in the literal sense of a *that* which is not yet any definite *what*, tho ready to be all sorts of whats; full both of oneness and of manyness, but in respects that don't appear; changing throughout, yet so confusedly that its phases interpenetrate and no points, either of distinction or of identity, can be caught. Pure experience in this state is but another name for feeling or sensation. But the flux of it no sooner comes than it tends to fill itself with emphases, and these salient parts become identified and fixed and abstracted; so that experience now flows as if shot through with adjectives and nouns and prepositions and conjunctions. Its purity is only a relative term, meaning the proportional amount of unverbalized sensation which it still embodies.[43]

James's pure awareness, the unverbalized sensation, the fullness of unnamed reality is the ground out of which—as in Emerson and later in Wittgenstein, who greatly admired James[44]—an unforeseeable number of language games may arise. Existentially foundational experience, however, is itself prior to the *fields* staked out by languages in their historically and socially seemingly inescapable patterns. Like Emerson, James reserves a realm out of bounds, out of which the freedom of individual and collective renewal, an authentic existentially defined modernist condition may arise again and again.

It may sound a little simplistic and reductive, but for the sake of easy comparison one could say that Emerson envisions a realm out of bounds as the always available starting point of authentic philosophical meditation, whereas James considers the beyond of cultural and social fields as the background of every single existence about to realize itself. With Charles Sanders Peirce, finally, the realm out of bounds assumes what may be cautiously generalized as a cosmic dimension of any and all beings, conscious

---

[43]William James "The Thing and Its Relations," in *Essays in Radical Empiricism*, vol. 3 of *The Works of William James* (1912; Cambridge, MA: Harvard University Press, 1976), 46.
[44]Cf. Russell B. Goodman, *Wittgenstein and William James* (Cambridge: Cambridge University Press, 2002), *passim*.

or not. Peirce began to develop this vision as the basis of his philosophy in the late 1880s and early 1890s. His name for this realm out of bounds is "Firstness":

> The idea of the absolutely First must be entirely separated from all conception of or reference to anything else [I would like to add: it is not an *a priori* of a philosophical system or the like] ... The First must therefore be present and immediate, so as not to be Second to a representation It must be fresh and new, for if old it is second to its former state. It must be initiative, original, spontaneous and free; otherwise it is Second to a determining cause [and thus outside any field]. ... it has no unity and no parts. It cannot be articulately thought: assert it and it has already lost its characteristic innocence; for assertion always involves a denial of something else. Stop to think of it, and it has already flown. What the world was to Adam on the day he opened his eyes to it, before he had drawn any distinctions or had become conscious of his own existence—that is First, present, immediate, fresh, new, initiative, original, spontaneous, free, vivid, conscious, and evanescent. Only remember that every description of it must be false to it.[45]

Logically, this immense, ever-present and nameless "presence" can neither be said to be nor not to be. It is the "before" of everything and all, including all philosophical positioning. Out of its unavailable bounty worlds, thinking, and interpretations, signs and languages and fields may possibly emerge; they arise from the un-conditioned, the free, and the fundamentally contingent, from the unforeseeable and therefore forever modern in a profound sense.

Let me conclude: in their different ways Emerson, James, and Peirce return us to the challenging, exhilarating, refreshing, and liberating, but also and ultimately inhospitable expanses of the necessary and inescapable outside of all humanly inhabited and ontologically as well as linguistically definable fields, to places out of bounds where no one can settle, sites that are reminiscent of Thoreau's summit of Mount Ktaadn or Nietzsche's metaphorical icy mountain peaks of radical thinking. These American modernists return us again and again to a wintry region that another radical modernist, the poet Wallace Stevens, memorably imagined as showing "Nothing that is not there and the nothing that is."[46]

---

[45]*Principles of Philosophy*, ed. Charles Hartshorne, Paul Weiss, and Arthur W. Burks, vol. I of *The Collected Papers of Charles Sanders Peirce* (Cambridge, MA: Harvard University Press, 1931), par. 357.
[46]Wallace Stevens, "The Snow Man," in *The Collected Poems of Wallace Stevens* (New York: Knopf, 1954), 10.

# 11

# William James:
# Ontology and Imagery

Ontology should not be understood as a subdivision or version of metaphysics in my attempt to characterize the function of images in William James's thinking. The term "ontology" is rather meant to indicate a thinking of and about Being in the post-metaphysical sense implied by Martin Heidegger's *Seinsfrage*. Also I do not propose to deal with images as the subject-matter of visual culture studies that arose with and after the so-called pictorial (or iconic) turn announced by W. J. T. Mitchell in 1992.[1] Images are here understood neither as exclusively mental and visual representations nor as pictures, a distinction that is basic for the relevant research advanced, for instance, by Horst Bredekamp.[2] In a preliminary way I would like to define images for my purpose as verbal indicators of pre-conceptual (not necessarily and not exclusively visual) awareness, of a *sense* of the event of beings coming into experiential presence. I would like to approach the problem at hand in four steps: part one, "*About* Ontology," will deal with the limited range of explicit, almost exclusively conceptual, approaches to the question of Being in William James; part two, "Images and Philosophy," is designed to present heuristic tools that may be useful in dealing with images as modes of experiencing and means of thinking based on observations and suggestions from Aristotle to Hans Blumenberg. William James's specific

---

This essay was previously published as "The Ontology of William James: Images of Thinking and Thinking in Images" in *Revisiting Pragmatism: William James in the New Millenium*, ed. Susanne Rohr and Miriam Strube (Heidelberg: Winter, 2012), 51–69. Reprinted by permission of Universitätsverlag Winter GmbH.

[1]W. J. T. Mitchell, "The Pictorial Turn," *Artforum* 30, no. 7 (1992): 89–94.
[2]Horst Bredekamp, "Drehmomente, Merkmale und Ansprüche des Iconic Turn," in *Iconic Turn: Die neue Macht der Bilder*, ed. Hubert Burda and Christa Maar (Cologne: DuMont, 2004), 15–26.

and original use of images in dealing with the question of Being is discussed in part three, "Images and Ontology in William James." Part four, "A Philosophy, an Ontology of the Future," tries to do justice to the momentous break in the history of thinking that manifests itself in James's intuition of Being—a break that Alfred North Whitehead analyzed and appreciated in 1925 as the true beginning of philosophical modernism in his interpretation of James that focused not so much on Being as on James's innovative, his revolutionary reinterpretation of the idea of consciousness.[3]

# About ontology

For William James, the existential and the intellectual, that is, philosophical, worth and dignity of a human being and his thinking manifest themselves primarily in his vision: "a man's vision is the great fact about him," he claims with aphoristic emphasis in *A Pluralistic Universe*, and later in the same book he elaborates and urges the reader of philosophy:

> Place yourself ... at the centre of a man's philosophic vision and you understand at once all the different things it makes him write or say. But keep outside, use your post-mortem method, try to build the philosophy up out of the single phrases, taking first one and then another and seeking to make them fit "logically," and of course you fail.[4]

The reader of philosophy needs "living sympathy," James says,[5] and in a letter to a doctoral student he insists that in reading philosophy you should first grasp the "centre of vision, by an act of imagination."[6] Doing and reading philosophy, then, are primarily acts of existential engagement and significance; they privilege the imaginative, the visionary, and—by extension and amplification—the visual in the widest sense, the percept and the image, over the word, the concept, the text, the *logos*. Writing and speaking, terminologies and logical sequence as well as consistency merely follow; they depend on the *a priori* of the intuited, on that which reveals itself without mediation in the intensity of significant experiential awareness. The "centre of vision" in James's philosophy, his primary and foundational intuition, this is my simple thesis, is his radically innovative, his modernist ontological

---

[3]Alfred North Whitehead, *Science and the Modern World* (1925; New York: Free Press, 1967), 143–4.
[4]*A Pluralistic Universe*, vol. 4 of *The Works of William James* (1909; Cambridge, MA: Harvard University Press, 1977), 14, 117.
[5]Ibid., 117.
[6]*The Letters of William James*, ed. Henry James (Boston: Atlantic Monthly P, 1920), vol. 2, 355.

insight. If one considers the way in which the *Seinsfrage*, the question of Being, obsessively informs and, in endless permutations, pervades the 102 volumes of Heidegger's collected works, it seems both daring and naïve to insinuate that William James may have anticipated and possibly even rivaled Heidegger's grandiose project in depth and dimension. It is true, the *term*, the *concept* of Being, is marginal in James. The *Sache des Denkens*, Being as the very matter of thought, however, may be shown to be foundational, of primary and ultimate importance, in his work. This importance is manifest, I maintain, above all *in* and *as* the *function* of images—images that are the outstandingly significant rhetorical mode and argumentative method employed throughout by James to reveal and to think Being.

By comparison, important abstract-conceptual discussions of Being may be found in hardly more than two relatively inconspicuous places in James. The, at first sight, disappointingly brief third chapter on "The Problem of Being" in his last, unfinished book *Some Problems of Philosophy* is announced in these not exactly encouraging terms: "I will start with the worst problem possible, the so-called 'ontological' problem, or question of how there comes to be anything at all."[7] The conclusion of James's meditations is seemingly as disappointing:

> So the question recurs: how do our finite experiences come into being from moment to moment? ... Who can tell off-hand? The question of Being is the darkest in all philosophy. All of us are beggars here ... For all of us alike, Fact forms a datum, a gift, or *vorgefundenes*, which we cannot burrow under, explain, or get behind. It makes itself somehow, and our business is far more with its *what* than with its *whence* or *why*.[8]

The implications of these few meager statements are, however, significantly more than a mere shrugging of shoulders or the expression of a wondering awe at the enigma. Firstly, Being is seen as event, "as com[ing] to be." Being is inescapably temporal, it emerges from "moment to moment." Secondly, our thinking finds itself always already indebted to Being as a *Vorgefundenes*, in a way that makes it impossible to ground Being, to find or identify it objectively and thus metaphysically as a *substantia* that is thought to be independent of its being experienced. James's characteristically modest statements imply these intuitions: a proper response to the question of Being would have to be anti-foundationalist and acknowledge Being as temporal event or as ceaseless ungrounded transition into and out of itself. "There are novelties; there are losses," he declares. "The world seems ... really to

---

[7] *Some Problems of Philosophy*, vol. 7 of *The Works of William James* (1911; Cambridge, MA: Harvard University Press, 1979), 25.
[8] Ibid., 29–30.

grow."[9] Making sure that we have not missed these understated points, James adds a footnote: "one may say that fact or being is 'contingent,' or matter of 'chance,' so far as our intellect is concerned. The conditions of its appearance are uncertain, unforeseeable when future, and when past, elusive."[10] To reiterate: from the point of view of conceptual reasoning (i.e., intellect or *logos*), Being is contingent, un-grounded, and radically temporal.

In a later chapter of *Some Problems of Philosophy*, James briefly returns to the question of Being and states that "being gives *it*[!]self to us abruptly."[11] Being, then, may be understood as a given or rather as a gift; humans are existentially and intellectually at its mercy—"all of us are beggars here." If Being thus shows, as I just said, as an ungrounded, contingent, always temporal self-presentation, you may, if you wish, read this as a premonition of Heidegger's "*Es* gibt Sein und *es* gibt Zeit" in the late essay "Zeit und Sein"[12] with its meditation on the event- or *Ereignis*-character of Being as radically temporal emergence that *knows* no agent, only agency. James justifies the scarcity of his conceptual elucidations concerning the question of the coming to be of Being and beings by pointing to the wonder, the puzzlement, the *thaumazein* occasioned by the problem: "Philosophy stares, but brings no reasoned solution, for from nothing to being there is no logical bridge."[13] This does not mean, as is often assumed, that the question, the problem is abandoned or that we deal with a kind of "negative philosophy" that knows its theme only by a series of negations: James merely argues that Being as the event, the *Ereignis* of coming to be is not a matter of reasoning, of a "logical bridge." If *ratio* and *logos* do not provide answers, maybe the mandatory, the ideal imaginative reader of James's central vision should look for different modes of approaching the problem, for different bridges to think the emergence of Being out of nothing. Before I consider these alternative approaches and test other than logical bridges, let me remind you of the second of the two major conceptualist attempts to articulate Being in James.

James's probably most concise and most profound definition or, more appropriately, conceptual interpretation of Being occurs in the entry "Experience" for J. M. Baldwin's *Dictionary of Philosophy and Psychology* of 1902, where he writes that experience signifies

the entire process of phenomena, of present data considered in their raw immediacy, before reflective thought has analysed them into subjective

---

[9]Ibid., 29.
[10]Ibid.
[11]Ibid., 84 (my emphasis).
[12]"Zeit und Sein," in *Zur Sache des Denkens*, ed. Friedrich-Wilhelm von Herrmann, vol. 14 of *Gesamtausgabe* (1969; Frankfurt: Klostermann, 2007), 9.
[13]*Some Problems*, 27.

or objective aspects or ingredients. It is the summum genus of which everything must have been a part before we can speak of it at all. ... If philosophy insists on keeping this term indeterminate, she can refer to her subject-matter without committing herself as to certain questions in dispute. But if experience be used with either an objective or a subjective shade of meaning, then question-begging occurs, and discussion grows impossible.[14]

Experience designates, I repeat, "the summum genus of which everything must have been a part before we can speak of it at all." This means that, for James, experience, or better, as he was to discuss it a few years later, *pure* experience, is a name for Being in general. As such it necessarily precedes all verbal articulation—like Charles Sanders Peirce's Firstness it does not fall under the jurisdiction of the *logos*. Peirce's version of the experience of Being as Firstness both clarifies and deepens our understanding of James's intuition of Being as pure experience:

The idea of the absolutely First must be entirely separated from all *conception* of or reference to anything else ... The First must therefore be present and immediate ... It must be fresh and new, for if old it is second to its former state. It must be initiative, original, spontaneous and free; otherwise it is a Second to a determining cause. It is also something vivid and conscious ... It cannot be *articulately thought*; assert it and it has already lost its characteristic innocence ... Stop to *think* of it, and it has flown.[15]

For both James and Peirce, Being as pure experience or Firstness is an event, an emergence; it occurs before the subject-object split so dear to traditional metaphysical and epistemological modes of thinking and their conceptual apparatus. James's radically modern ontological thinking therefore demands—in a wonderful pun—that the *term* "experience" and thus the word for Being be kept in-de-*term*-inate, that is, that it be both spoken and unspoken, asserted and denied, maintained and abandoned. Experience as Being is the togetherness of an awareness and its "contents," objects that only emerge as such once "reflective thought," as he states in the dictionary entry on "Experience," approaches the simple *this* and *there*, the *thatness* of the really real, namely Being as the experiential event. Strictly speaking, experience or Being as such in their immediacy cannot be talked about;

---

14"Experience," in *Essays in Philosophy*, vol. 5 of *The Works of William James* (Cambridge, MA: Harvard University Press, 1978), 95.
15*Principles of Philosophy*, ed. Charles Hartshorne, Paul Weiss, and Arthur W. Burks, vol I of *The Collected Papers of Charles Sanders Peirce* (Cambridge, MA: Harvard University Press, 1931–35), par. 357 (my emphasis).

they may issue in nameable aspects and elements only once they have been retrospectively focused in the context of a new event of experience called reflection. Experience as Being is, or shows as, what James called "*knowledge by acquaintance*," as distinguished from retrospective, reflexive knowledge or "*knowledge-about*."[16] James's conceptualist approach to Being, his presentation of knowledge *about* it, then, offers these severely limited results: Being as contingent and temporal emergence entails a monistic understanding of an entity, or entities, called experience, which cannot be spoken, that is, conceptually articulated, because it is pre-linguistic. Critics of James legitimately call this either a neutral monism or, as both Ruth Anna Putnam and Felicitas Krämer would prefer, a neutral pluralism; the latter designation implies Being or experience as signifying a multiplicity of experiential events within each of which emerges an intimately unified, *lebensweltliche* totality of—in traditional metaphysical dualist parlance—mind and matter.[17] In spite of all their terminological precision and academic dignity or maybe because of that, terms like "neutral monism" or "neutral pluralism" strike the imaginative reader of James as the dry husks of a vital ontological vision, as the ossified, static placeholders of that intuitional awareness in James which sets out to allow Being to manifest, to reveal itself primarily in a dynamic philosophical discourse replete with ever new productive images. Ultimately, this implies not merely a radically novel, a truly modernist departure in ontology; it also prepares a fundamental re-valuation of what it means to do philosophy.

# Images and philosophy

By way of preparing my interpretation of the ontological function of imagery in James's thinking, I would like to present a sketch of some representative philosophical positions concerning the functions of imagery in philosophy.[18]

---

[16]*The Principles of Psychology*, vol. 8.1–3 of *The Works of William James* (1890; Cambridge, MA: Harvard University Press, 1981), 1, 221.

[17]Cf. Ruth Anna Putnam, "Introduction," in *The Cambridge Companion to William James*, ed. Putnam (Cambridge: Cambridge University Press, 1997), 5; Felicitas Krämer, *Erfahrungsvielfalt und Wirklichkeit: Zu William James' Realitätsverständnis* (Göttingen: Vandenhoeck & Ruprecht, 2006), 167.

[18]Three relatively recent German publications are devoted to interpretations of the theories and the functions of philosophical imagery in predominantly European philosophers: Bernhard H. F. Taureck, *Metaphern und Gleichnisse in der Philosophie: Versuch einer kritischen Ikonologie der Philosophie* (Frankfurt: Suhrkamp, 2004); Ralf Konersmann, ed., *Wörterbuch der philosophischen Metaphern* (Darmstadt: WBG, 2007); Simone Neuber and Roman Veressow, eds., *Das Bild als Denkfigur: Funktionen des Bildbegriffs in der Geschichte der Philosophie* (Munich: Fink, 2010). It is only in Taureck that we find a few remarks on imagery in James (and Peirce). Taureck limits his observations to the Jamesian pragmatist conception of truth

This may help one see how James's imagistic practice draws upon, utilizes, and transforms established classical and also contemporary, that is, late nineteenth-century interpretations of philosophical imagery and, at the same time, foreshadows major twentieth-century work in this field. My highly selective readings of Aristotle, Rudolf Eucken, and Hans Blumenberg will not even pretend to do justice to the inner consistency of each of these three philosophical analyses and interpretations of what images may do in and for thinking. But the three thinkers will provide me with a series of heuristic devices that, hopefully and pragmatically, will prove their hermeneutic value in reading James's use of images for and in ontology.

Aristotle's *Peri Psyches* (or *De Anima*) discusses the soul as the vital principle, as "that whereby we live and perceive and think in the primary sense."[19] The soul in Aristotle is an equivalent of the existentially self-aware dynamic that James in *The Principles of Psychology* described as the "*first fact for us, ... that thinking of some sort goes on.*"[20] The intimate connection between existence, in the *primary* sense and as *first* fact, and perception and conception—between Being and perceiving and thinking—is the theme that appears most intriguing for my present concern. For Aristotle the object *of* or *within* the mere percept is, in Blumenberg's later terminology, "das Unbegriffliche"—the a- or non-conceptual: "The object of sight ... has in fact no name."[21] It is, in James's terminology, a mere *that*.[22] As such, however, Aristotle concludes: "the perception of proper objects is true."[23] It is only when language begins to articulate attributes that error may arise, or in James's view: "language works against our *perception* of the truth."[24] Mind itself, the conceptualizing faculty, is interestingly not seen as an entity by Aristotle, but rather as a function (as in James's essay "Does Consciousness Exist?"). Aristotle says: "That part of the soul, then, which we call mind ... has no actual existence until it thinks."[25] Thinking as a function, however, is intimately tied to and conditioned by both percepts

---

and—predictably in a somewhat prejudiced European critic—the monetary imagery whose antecedents in Franklin (and Plato and Cusanus) are dwelt upon (360–1); the more significant indebtedness of James to the philosophy of Leibniz and his use of monetary imagery is not discussed.

[19] Aristotle, *On the Soul*, ed. and trans. W. S. Hett, Loeb Classical Library 288 (1936; Cambridge, MA: Harvard University Press, 1957), 414a 13–15; 79. All references to Aristotle will identify the Greek text in the traditional manner, followed by the page number for the English text in the Loeb Classical Library edition after the semicolon.

[20] *Principles* 1, 219.

[21] Aristotle, *On the Soul*, 418a 26–8; 103.

[22] "The Thing and Its Relations," in *Essays in Radical Empiricism*, vol. 3 of *The Works of William James* (1912; Cambridge, MA: Harvard University Press, 1976), 46.

[23] Aristotle, *On the Soul*, 428b 19–20; 163.

[24] *Principles* 1, 234 (my emphasis).

[25] Aristotle, *On the Soul*, 429a 22–4; 165.

and images in this way: "Now for the thinking soul images take the place of direct perceptions ... Hence the soul never thinks without a mental image."[26] And Aristotle adds in the summary of the book: "no one could ever learn or understand anything without the exercise of perception, so even when we think speculatively, we must have some mental picture of which to think; for mental images are similar to objects perceived."[27] The image, then, is the vital and indispensable *bridge* between the silent, the speechless, and thus self-evidently true presence (Being) of the object *of* and *in* perception and the conceptual articulation in the speculative play of truth and error. The image is primarily a *function* within thinking as it goes on from awareness through imagination to conceptualization. One might say that it is an event rather than a mental fact.

The modernist ontological implications of the Aristotelian interpretation of thinking the presence of beings through the function of images (in the wide sense of the term that I prefer) can be briefly sketched with the help of two subtle readings of Aristotle's ontological profundity of vision by Heidegger and Agamben. Heidegger discusses Aristotle's mode of thinking the essence of beings (G. *Wesen*) and concludes:

Was dies ist, jenes Beständige, wird gleichwohl im vorhinein und zwar notwendig gesichtet. Sehen heisst griechisch *idein*; das Gesichtete in seiner Gesichtetheit heisst *idea*. Gesichtet ist das, als was sich das Seiende im vorhinein und ständig gibt. Das *Was es ist*, das Wassein, ist die *idea*; und umgekehrt die "Idee" ist das Wassein und dieses das Wesen. *idea* ist genauer und griechisch gedacht: der *Anblick*, den etwas bietet, das Aussehen, das es hat und gleichzeitig vor sich her zur Schau trägt, *eidos*.[28]

The awareness of what and how something, a being, shows itself, its phenomenal aspect (*"Anblick"*), has the unwavering (*"ständig"*) quality of an image in the wider sense. The image is given, is presented by the being in question (*"zur Schau trägt"*); it is the individual being itself which manifests, that is, shows or makes visible (*"Aussehen"*), the ontological dimension of essence. In his *Metaphysics*, Aristotle had strongly emphasized the unquestionable quality of that which presents itself thus for human awareness, of essence or *quidditas*, before it is thought about and then, *a*

---

[26]Ibid., 431a 15–17; 177.

[27]Ibid., 432a 6–11; 181.

[28]*Grundfragen der Philosophie: Ausgewählte "Probleme" der "Logik,"* ed. Friedrich-Wilhelm von Herrmann, vol. 45 of *Gesamtausgabe* (1937–8; Frankfurt: Klostermann, 1984), 62. I refrain from attempting to translate Heidegger into English here and will paraphrase the quotation to the best of my ability in the subsequent paragraph.

*posteriori*, becomes open to questions, to decisions about right and wrong: "With respect then, to all things which are essences and actual, there is no question of being mistaken, but only of thinking or not thinking them."[29]

It is this strong interpretation of the ontological dimension of the function of imagistic awareness and self-presentation of beings in Aristotle that is remarkably seconded and amplified in a short essay by Giorgio Agamben. In *L'amico* Agamben reads a passage from Aristotle's *Nicomachean Ethics*. That passage, he argues, amounts to a statement of a *prima philosophia*; that is, it deals not only with beings and their essence but with the question of Being itself, with *existentia* in the aboriginal and in the recovered modern sense that may, after all, apply to James. Discussing Aristotle's phrase *aisthesis oti estin* in the context of his reflections on friendship, Agamben writes: "There is a pure perception of being, an *aisthesis* of existence."[30] The phrase bears an uncanny similarity to Emerson's evocation in "Self-Reliance" of "the *sense of being*, which in calm hours rises, we know not how, in the soul, [and which] is not diverse from things ... and proceeds ... from the same source whence their life and *being* also proceed."[31]

The Aristotelian interpretation suggests the function of images as indicators of Being itself and of the *whatness* or essence of beings. Images work as bridges that mediate both the silent self-presence of what shows as experience *and* our later conceptualizations of this primary undivided awareness or "sense of being." This interpretation, Aristotle's primary ontology, has the potential of being recovered in a modern re-enactment: the Aristotelian echo in Emerson's just quoted proto-pragmatist intuition points the way. It prepares the *method* that will come to full fruition in James's use of functional imagery in reading Being. Images, the linguistic place-holders of the sense of being, do not re-represent; they work as events, as indispensable occurrences in the ceaseless and continuous temporal and experiential self-manifestation of beings in their Being on the way toward potential conceptual renderings.

---

[29]Aristotle, *Metaphysics*, 1051b, 30–32; 473. My reading, as supported by Heidegger, presents a strong contrast to and contradicts the analysis of Stephan Herzberg, who reduces images (Gr. *phantasmata*) in Aristotle to examples, to instantiations or exemplifications, of the generalizing mind. This, it appears to me, is a way of imposing traditional metaphysical patterns unquestioned onto Aristotle's vision, patterns that tend to obscure the very ontological complications discussed here. See Herzberg's "Aristoteles und der Begriff des Bildes," in *Das Bild als Denkfigur: Funktionen des Bildbegriffs in der Geschichte der Philosophie*, ed. Simone Neuber and Roman Veressow (Munich: Fink, 2010), 63–5.

[30]Giorgio Agamben, "Friendship," trans. Joseph Falsone, *Contretemps: An Online Journal of Philosophy* 5 (2004): 5.

[31]W II, 64 (my emphasis).

Rudolf Eucken (1846–1926), the 1908 Nobel laureate in Literature, whom James sporadically quoted with mild approval of his activist idealism,[32] published a concise treatise called *Über Bilder und Gleichnisse in der Philosophie* (*On Images and Comparisons in Philosophy*) in 1880. Eucken is acutely aware of a shift in philosophical rhetoric and terminology as the indication of an imminent fundamental re-orientation of thinking, that is, the emergence of modernism. On the one hand Eucken still believes in the primacy of the concept, in Descartes's maxim (inherited from Cicero, Augustine, and Thomas Aquinas) that the foremost duty of thinking consists in *abducere mentem a sensibus*, that is, to move toward ever clearer and more distinct concepts and thus away from the senses and from percepts and images. Eucken's great good sense of historical change, however, forces him, if ever so uneasily and reluctantly, to acknowledge a constitutive role of imagery for philosophy. Images, the historian of philosophy argues, proliferate especially in times of paradigm changes in thinking, for example, in the late Middle Ages and the Renaissance, or, for that matter, in Eucken's own late nineteenth century.[33] Images, Eucken insists, are trailblazers[34] for future innovative conceptualizations as well as, and more importantly for my purposes, necessary correctives of the analytic production of discrete ontologies or of a scientific world of factual, empirical singularities. This is because images alone are apt to lead thinking and intuition back to visionary synthesis; they are necessary for a non-mediated experiential awareness of a coherent and continuous totality. In other words, images have the power to redirect conceptual differentiation toward the intuition of synthesis[35] and toward the actual experience of the world realized in terms (i.e., images) of an indiscrete ontology.[36]

This imagistic practice, Eucken reasons, shows especially in the leading and creative, that is historically innovative, thinkers.[37] The philosophically significant image is inexhaustible for subsequent conceptualizations and, at the same time, functions as a means to literally liquify thoughts and concepts: "die Gedanken in lebendigen Fluss zu bringen."[38] The image may thus serve in leading the rigid and static discreteness of a world analyzed conceptually back into the dynamic and vital continuities and the flow of active perceptual and experiential engagement. Arguments like these, from

---

[32]See, e.g., *Pragmatism: A New Name for Some Old Ways of Thinking*, vol. 1 of *The Works of William James* (1907; Cambridge, MA: Harvard University Press, 1975), 123.
[33]Rudolf Eucken, *Über Bilder und Gleichnisse in der Philosophie* (Leipzig: Veit, 1880), 8.
[34]Ibid., 9 ("Pfadfinder und Bahnbrecher").
[35]Ibid., 27 ("Einheit einer Anschauung").
[36]I use the term "indiscrete ontology" as defined in Wolfram Hogrebe, *Metaphysik und Mantik: Die Deutungsnatur des Menschen* (Frankfurt: Suhrkamp, 1992), 122–3.
[37]Eucken, *Bilder und Gleichnisse*, 7.
[38]Ibid., 29.

which, as I stated, Eucken again and again shies back in order to almost ritualistically invoke the ultimate superiority of a Cartesian language of pure ideas, arguments like these do indeed read like some of the anti-intellectualist passages in James's *A Pluralistic Universe* or like parts of the chapters on percepts and concepts in *Some Problems of Philosophy*. In this way, Eucken's vision of the philosophical image as, firstly, trailblazer of a new epoch in thinking, secondly, as the guarantor of the intuitive vision of a world synthesized by way of a dynamic and indiscrete ontology, and, thirdly, as a resource which guides active thought without ever being exhausted by its conceptualizations, these three aspects may help to properly read the possible function of Jamesian imagery in an innovative, a modern ontological context. Images can then be understood as a means of correcting the deficiencies of predominantly rationalistic and conceptual ways of thinking, but also as alternatives to traditionally atomistic and empiricist philosophical stances. Summarily stated, images tend to erode the dogmatic validity of all discrete ontologies.

In spite of the more detailed and concrete recent analyses of philosophical imagery by Bernhard Taureck (2004), by Ralf Konersmann (2007), and in the essay collection by Simone Neuber and Roman Veressow (2010),[39] Hans Blumenberg's work on images, metaphors, and the significance of the non-conceptual ("das Unbegriffliche") in philosophy stands unrivaled in depth and sophistication. The central insight of Blumenberg's work concerns the ultimate and necessary failure of the Cartesian project of a fully conceptual language of clear and distinct ideas, a project that, once realized, would have entailed the end of the history of philosophy, a problem already discerned by Leibniz and, of course, reinterpreted by Peirce.[40] Niggardly reason, Blumenberg says pointedly, is always negatively contrasted with the lavish profusion of creation, that is, of Being in its fullness.[41] One is reminded here of James's opposition between the thin reductionism of conceptual, rationalist thinking and the thick plenitude of perceptual awareness.[42] While the concept will never be able to fulfill all of the demands of reason according to Blumenberg,[43] its successes often consist in the inversion of its function: it may help to lead thinking back to a freely chosen encounter with the riches of the un-mediated self-presentation of empirical, perceptual reality in the widest sense.[44] In a similar fashion James had argued that all

---

[39]See footnote 18 above.

[40]Hans Blumenberg, *Theorie der Unbegrifflichkeit* (Frankfurt: Suhrkamp, 2007), 10–12, 105–6.

[41]Ibid., 20. ("Die sparsame Vernunft steht gegen die verschwenderische Grosszügigkeit der Schöpfung.")

[42]*Pluralistic Universe*, 64–8.

[43]Blumenberg, *Theorie der Unbegrifflichkeit*, 11 ("Der Begriff vermag nicht alles, was die Vernunft verlangt").

[44]Ibid., 27.

(conceptual) talk ultimately may and should serve as a means toward an enriched "return to life," a re-immersion into the plenitude of ongoing reality most intimately realized in direct perceptual awareness and active (inner) participation.[45] Blumenberg's thinking contrasts this subordinate, menial role of the concept with the powerfully irreducible function of some images in the conduct of thinking. He calls these images or metaphors "absolute metaphors." Absolute metaphors arise out of the profusion of images provided by our *lebensweltliche* background, a profusion richer and more comprehensive and inescapable than that of verbal language.[46] Sentences beginning, for example, with the noun phrase "Das Sein," that is, Being, sentences and arguments dealing with the totalities of either the cosmos or the *Lebenswelt*, the life-world, a pre-conceptual realm in which the thinking subject always already finds herself,[47] such statements will necessarily have to issue in metaphors or images that resist a fully satisfactory translation into a conceptual argumentative context;[48] rather, thinking of and about and within total horizons will persistently find itself indebted to such absolute metaphors or even worlds of metaphors. Absolute images, world-metaphors, reveal a pre-philosophical a-conceptual ("unbegriffliche") space of thinking awareness: the given and inescapable sub-structure of later conceptualizations, a catalytic sphere, Blumenberg says, where concepts are ceaselessly being generated without ever fully consuming and annihilating the foundational reservoir of perceptually generated imagery.[49] Here we find the nutrient solution out of which the crystallizations of a rational discourse emerge, a discourse unable to totally consume and transform the background to which it owes itself. Blumenberg's own images are intended, they have the function, to testify to the validity of an insight into experiential totalities and processes that refuse to find rationalistic closure. His images gesture toward the foundational and irreducible "Unbegriffliche," which both necessitates and forever frustrates all conceptual transformations.[50]

In turning to William James's use of images for and in thinking Being, I would like to employ these insights from Aristotle, Eucken, and Blumenberg as heuristic guidelines: namely, images may function as indispensable bridges between the mute and true ("unbegriffliche") presence of reality in or as perceptual awareness on the one hand and later conceptual articulation on the other; images herald open vistas of un-precedented, that is, modern thinking, they have the potential to act as trailblazers of the new, the essentially novel,

---

[45]*Pluralistic Universe*, 131.
[46]Hans Blumenberg, "Paradigmen zu einer Metaphorologie" (1960), in *Theorie der Metapher*, ed. Anselm Haverkamp (Darmstadt: WBG, 1983), 288.
[47]Hans Blumenberg, *Theorie der Lebenswelt* (Frankfurt: Suhrkamp, 2010), 14–15 and *passim*.
[48]Blumenberg, *Theorie der Unbegrifflichkeit*, 65.
[49]Blumenberg, "Paradigmen," 288.
[50]Blumenberg, *Theorie der Unbegrifflichkeit*, 107.

and they may guarantee the intuition of indiscrete ontological continuities easily sacrificed by conceptualist analytical discernment; lastly, and maybe most importantly, images as absolute metaphors are the indispensable instruments that help convey the meaning of total contexts to which any philosophical questioning always already finds itself indebted, be they called *Lebenswelt*, cosmos, or Being.

# Images and ontology in William James

Undoubtedly, a considerable number of images employed by James are primarily, if not merely, rhetorical: they serve as illustrations, as elegant seductions of the reader or listener to follow and assent to abstract propositions and challenging insights; the comparison, in chapter IX of *The Principles of Psychology*, of the rhythms of the stream of consciousness as it unfolds with the "alternation of flights and perchings" of a bird's life[51] may serve as a representative example. Absolute metaphors and images, however, that is, the images that do ontological work with which I am concerned, come in two major ways in James that definitely go beyond rhetorical persuasion and embellishment: they may occur either as an open-ended series of at first sight incompatible alternatives or as a unified world of internally related, proliferating metaphorical images in Blumenberg's sense, that is, as a *leitmotif* with possibly endless variations.

*Essays in Radical Empiricism* provides impressive examples for the first variant of allowing images to function in ontological thinking: here a series of alternative images is employed to convey the meaning of Being as pure experience that is not to be exhausted by one single perspective or experientially grounded visualization emerging from immediate awareness. In "Does Consciousness Exist?" James argues:

> My thesis is that if we start with the supposition that there is only one primal stuff or material in the world, a stuff of which everything is composed, and if we call that stuff "pure experience," then knowing can easily be explained as a particular sort of relation towards one another into which portions of pure experience may enter.[52]

I do not want to enter in detail into the central *epistemological* concern of the essay, the question of the existence of an independent faculty called consciousness. The *ontological* implications of the text, however, become

---

[51]*Principles* 1, 236.
[52]*Essays in Radical Empiricism*, 4.

apparent once you focus on the controlling image in the text just quoted. The image of the stuff, the material (Gr. *hyle*), arises out of the awareness of an a-conceptual *that*, which precedes all relations of cognition; as such pure experience is "perceived" in the Jamesian sense that goes far beyond mere perception in the exclusively sensualist meaning of the word. As in Aristotle, the nameless given calls for, it elicits or helps provide a quasi-visual dimension within the perceptual awareness. The shapeless *that* acquires a certain specificity in generating, in allowing, in insinuating the image of the stuff, which now in turn guides or leads toward possible conceptual differentiations. Again as in Aristotle's *Peri Psyches*, the image serves as the hinge or bridge that mediates the wordless presencing of undifferentiated Being and possible arguments about it.

Somewhat later in "Does Consciousness Exist?" James offers this alternative image:

> The instant field of the present is at all times what I call the "pure" experience. It is only virtually or potentially either object or subject as yet. For the time being, it is plain, unqualified actuality or existence, a simple *that*. In this *naïf* immediacy it is of course *valid* ...[53]

Pure experience, Being, is now a temporal spread: this imagistic vision of the ever-present field of nowness allows or facilitates thinking, even conceptualizing, Being as spatialized time. At the same time, the image supports Aristotle's point about the unquestionable truth of anything that is purely given in direct awareness: the naïf immediacy is valid, James says, and it precedes as well as supports both image and concept.

In "The Thing and Its Relations," James begins his argument in this way:

> "Pure experience" is the name which I gave to the immediate flux of life which furnishes the material to our later reflection with its conceptual categories ... Its purity is only a relative term, meaning the proportional amount of unverbalized sensation which it still embodies.[54]

The stuff, the instant field of the present, pure experience, Being, now shows as the ever-productive source of its own later verbalization: Being presents itself as the image of a ceaseless continuity, a flux, which allows for and always encompasses an internal structuring which we call language, conceptualization, knowledge, *logos*. As such the flux is immediate, a temporal phenomenal self-presence without static substantial grounding. The three images, and one might add the odd vision of the mosaic organically growing

---

[53]Ibid., 13.
[54]Ibid., 46.

by its edges in the essay "A World of Pure Experience,"[55] these images show that the encounter with the mere *there* or *that* of Being, an encounter that James would have qualified as perceptual, as irreducible awareness, that this encounter activates the thinking imagination and helps produce an open-ended series of images, a world of metaphors according to Blumenberg. These images provide for a potentially endless series of conceptualizations without, as Blumenberg argues, exhausting or replacing, consuming or eliminating their validity. As in Aristotle, the images guide the mind in its speculative ontological endeavor; they are, as Eucken had it, trailblazers of all *a posteriori* intellectualist, rationalist, analytic differentiations. In James's essays just quoted, such differentiations always follow; and yet the vision of an indiscreetly cohesive and unremittingly challenging pre-verbal totality is being retained.

The second mode in which images help to think Being in James, the unified world of internally related visualizations, is not at all surprisingly represented by the vision of water, of flow, streams, liquefaction. The majority among a plethora of variations on this imagistic theme, however, are verbs. As Joan Richardson has pointedly observed, James's "shifting attention away from a substantive-based language" toward a "language animated by the predominance of transitives"[56] may have been actually more successfully implemented by *Henry* James, but the transitives representing and enacting and pointing toward flow and its cognates in William James nevertheless, I believe, deserve more attention. The chapter on "The Stream of Thought" in *The Principles of Psychology* and its central imagery are so well known that I think I may forgo illustrations here. A far from exhaustive, rather unsystematic selection of quotations from other writings may serve as the basis for the decisive point, the contribution of the world of water-imagery to an, again, indiscrete modernist ontology. In *The Varieties of Religious Experience*, we read: "Philosophy lives in words, but truth and fact *well up* into our lives in ways that exceed verbal formulation."[57] The agency of truth and fact, "experience," that is, Being as event, which, as James says in *Principles*, remoulds us incessantly;[58] this agency shows itself here as an irrepressible spring or fountain. In *A Pluralistic Universe*, James writes: "Reality, life, experience, concreteness, immediacy, use what word you will, exceeds our logic, *overflows* and surrounds it."[59] The *logos* appears

---

[55]Ibid., 42.

[56]Joan Richardson, *A Natural History of Pragmatism* (Cambridge: Cambridge University Press, 2007), 19.

[57]*The Varieties of Religious Experience: A Study in Human Nature*, vol. 13 of *The Works of William James* (1902; Cambridge, MA: Harvard University Press, 1985), 360 (my emphasis).

[58]*Principles* 1, 228.

[59]*Pluralistic Universe*, 96 (my emphasis).

inundated and ultimately submerged by the abundance of the ceaseless self-presencing of Being. In another chapter of the same book, James argues that you "can no more *dip up* the substance of reality" with concepts "than you can *dip up water with a net*."[60] This, in turn, may remind readers of the wonderful image in *Principles* where James intuits conceptual entities as pots and barrels surrounded by the swirling waters of the really real, the ongoing flow of ontic continuity as experience.[61]

If we understand Being as experience, this statement from *A Pluralistic Universe* will further manifest the irrepressible power of the images of flow to convey ontological truth: "Every smallest state of consciousness, concretely taken, *overflows* its own definition."[62] Images of "confluen[ce]" with "higher consciousnesses"[63] widen the horizon of ontological intuition toward the realm of religious modes of experience or Being. The foundational quality of the vision of insuperable flow becomes manifest most succinctly, however, in the opening statements of chapter IV of *Some Problems of Philosophy* concerning percept and concept: "concepts *flow out of* percepts and *into them* again, they are so interlaced ... that it is often difficult to impart ... a clear notion of the difference meant."[64] The difficulty to present a clear notion, a concise and distinct Cartesian idea of a difference between percept and concept, argues for a vision of flowing continuity that submerges the very tools of a discrete ontology in the irrepressible dynamic of Being as relentless inundation that admits of no final or static conceptual articulation. The percept, once again not to be limited to mere visual appropriation of experience, the percept as experiential awareness, as individual enactment of Being as ongoing event or *Ereignis*, can be had only as the mute presence, the wordless *this* or *there* of which Aristotle spoke, or as the image which provides—as it functions like a bridge—the basis for, again in Aristotle's view, speculative thinking, for the arsenal of rationalizations according to Blumenberg, an arsenal that cannot ever be replaced by any single concept or system of concepts emerging from it.

The profusion of ontological images in James evokes a total vision that may be understood as initiating a major change in ontology, a paradigm change in thinking, of which, as Eucken surmised in general terms, the very prominence of images in James's text is a significant testimony. The water images reveal an irrepressible tendency in Being that we may qualify, using a Heideggerian term, as *Abbau* (destruction). Being as self-generating emergence and flux consistently and relentlessly erases, destructs, removes,

---

[60]Ibid., 113 (my emphasis).
[61]*Principles* 1, 246.
[62]*Pluralistic Universe*, 129 (my emphasis).
[63]Ibid., 131.
[64]*Some Problems*, 31 (my emphasis).

and submerges the very demarcation lines, the very boundaries or definitions through which we make things into things and concepts into concepts that allow us to conceive identifiable single entities. Every single moment of experience, of Being as experiential moment of consciousness, James had argued in *A Pluralistic Universe,* "overflows its own definition"—or, as Bruce Wilshire has it, creatively expanding the reach of James's imagery of liquifaction: "Essential to the supremacy of the *that,* the world, things finally overflow our pigeonholes and categories, and 'bleed' through their boundaries into the evolving surround."[65] This radical temporality of Being thus does away with the law of (definable) identity, with the law of the excluded middle, among other mainstays of traditional metaphysics. In a world of flowing transitionality self-identical entities and their conceptual definitions are necessarily and constantly eroded. The emergence of images out of the undifferentiated, "begriffslose" *that* of pure experience (according to Aristotle or Blumenberg) may lead toward varieties of conceptualization, which, in turn, however, lead us back into the indiscrete fullness of Being as irrepressible temporal presencing and ultimate validity.

# A philosophy, an ontology of the future

My readings of William James's ontology have so far characterized it not so much as a series of insights or teachings, let alone as a system of metaphysical statements, but rather as a sequence of motions on a way, as a *methodos,* a leading of our imaging and thinking toward conceptualization and back again into primary awareness, toward that silent *thaumazein,* which, according to Aristotle, sets all true thinking into motion, that staring of philosophy at the question of Being of which William James spoke in *Some Problems of Philosophy.* James had insisted in *A Pluralistic Universe* that, ultimately, the thinker should "deafen" his readers or listeners to talk and "make [them] return to life,"[66] that is, into the immediacy of perceptive awareness; in *Pragmatism* he spoke of the function of all knowing as a "leading" "into the particulars of experience,"[67] that is, a move back into the fullness of Being as experiential event. In *Some Problems of Philosophy,* James completed this image of thinking and knowing as a "leading" by reminding us that all our conceptualized worlds, from the everyday to the mathematical, have "flowered out" of the immediacy of awareness only to ultimately "return

---

[65]Bruce Wilshire, "The Breathtaking Intimacy of the Material Word: William James's Last Thoughts," in *The Cambridge Companion to William James,* ed. Ruth Anna Putnam (Cambridge: Cambridge University Press, 1996), 118.
[66]*Pluralistic Universe*, 131.
[67]*Pragmatism*, 98–9.

and *merge* themselves again in the particulars of our present and future perception."[68] Thinking Being thus becomes, as I said above, a being on the way, a *methodos*, which, like the structure of emanations in Neoplatonism, embraces a *proodos* and an *anodos* (or *epistrophe*[69]), a departure, a coming-forth and a return in ceaseless circular reiteration or a forever innovative renewal. In this (literal) *way of thinking Being*, images are the bridges—or in Emerson's words, the conveyances[70]—which lead thought from amazed awareness through the momentary stasis of useful conceptualizations back again into the existentially practical engagement of the unmediated *thatness* or the once again silent wonder at the sheer fact of Being as it issues forth in and as pure experiences. James's ontology is a philosophy of the future not so much because, like Nietzsche's idea of it, it simply heralds a new era of thinking, but rather because in its ceaseless issuing forth from the ever-renewed and novel encounter with the mere *that* of emergent Being, it keeps the future open as the necessary condition of the possibility of its very existence as a thinking on the way.

---

[68]*Some Problems*, 34 (my emphasis).
[69]Eric Robert Dodds, "Tradition und persönliche Leistung in der Philosophie Plotins," in *Die Philosophie des Neuplatonismus*, ed. Clemens Zintzen (Darmstadt: WBG, 1977), 62–4.
[70]"The Poet" W III, 37.

# 12

# William James:
# Ontological Skepticism

## I

In *A Pluralistic Universe*, William James urged the reader and the critic of the work of a thinker to use a holistic and intuitional approach in order to do justice to its overall intent and meaning:

> Place yourself ... at the centre of a man's philosophic vision and you understand at once all the different things it makes him write or say. But keep outside, use your post-mortem method, try to build the philosophy up out of the single phrases, taking first one and then another and seeking to make them fit "logically," and of course you fail. You crawl over the thing like a myopic ant over a building, tumbling into every microscopic crack or fissure, finding nothing but inconsistencies, and never suspecting that a centre exists.[1]

The starting point and center of reading a philosophy should be a "living contemplation or sympathetic acquaintance" with its inner core, a "knowledge by acquaintance" as contrasted with "theoretic knowledge, which is knowledge *about* things."[2] Theoretical thought or conceptual thinking resulting in a mere "knowledge *about*" deals

> solely with surfaces. It can name the thickness of reality, but it cannot fathom it. ... The only way in which to apprehend reality's thickness is

---

[1] *A Pluralistic Universe*, vol. 4 of *The Works of William James* (1909; Cambridge, MA: Harvard University Press, 1977), 117
[2] Ibid., 111.

either to experience it directly by being a part of reality one's self, or to evoke it in imagination by sympathetically divining someone else's inner life.[3]

The center of all thinking and of reality, whether explicitly focused as in Parmenides and Heidegger or implicitly and occasionally even tacitly engaged as in James, is (the question of) Being. Being is the name for reality at its "thickest."

In *Some Problems of Philosophy*, his last and unfinished book that he had thought of as a *summa* of his thinking, James devoted a very short chapter to Being. At first sight the positive comments on Being are rather brief; they tend to strike one as hesitant, inconclusive, and vague. Toward the end of the chapter James seems to dismiss the problem:

> The question of Being is the darkest in all philosophy. All of us are beggars here, and no one school can speak disdainfully of another or give itself superior airs. For all of us alike, Fact forms a datum, a gift, or *vorgefundenes*, which we cannot burrow under, explain, or get behind. It makes itself somehow, and our business is far more with its *what* than with its *whence* and *why*.[4]

Being is a question, a persistent challenge as for Heidegger, it is not a problem waiting for or promising a solution. There is no divine origin or *substantia* preceding, underlying, and thus explaining Being, there is no metaphysical background *behind* it. Being is an opaque *factum* that is always already done and made, something always and already there to be encountered (*Vorgefundenes*); it is a "gift." The word "gift" signals an insight that surprisingly, even uncannily, foreshadows the late Heidegger's succinct and enigmatic pronouncement "Es gibt Sein,"[5] a statement that begs the question insofar as we are now left with the unfathomable *Es* (It), which presents us with, which offers the gift of Being. Neither James nor Heidegger is able or willing to identify the giver of this gift.

The only other truly positive statement about Being in chapter III of *Some Problems* is almost shyly hidden away in a footnote: "one may say that fact or being is 'contingent,' or matter of 'chance,' so far as our intellect is concerned. The conditions of its appearance are uncertain, unforeseeable, when future, and when past, elusive."[6] Being necessitates a skeptical evasion,

---

[3]Ibid., 112.

[4]*Some Problems of Philosophy*, vol. 7 of *The Works of William James* (1911; Cambridge, MA: Harvard University Press, 1979), 30.

[5]Heidegger, "Zeit und Sein," in *Zur Sache des Denkens*, ed. Friedrich-Wilhelm von Herrmann, vol. 14 of *Gesamtausgabe* (1969; Frankfurt: Klostermann, 2007), 9.

[6]*Some Problems*, 29.

a suspension of (final) judgment, an *epoché*, because it is not at the disposal of our intellect. It cannot be predicted and once it is manifest or experienced, its origin remains elusive, ungraspable, un-be-greif-lich, that is, not to be conceived. The ontological question remains open, it cannot be avoided, you have to devote a chapter to it, be it ever so short, in any decent philosophical *summa*; it makes one think, it calls for thinking, but it defeats all solutions. Dogmatic assertions and conceptual delimitations, let alone essentialist definitions, are impossible. Ultimately, the attempts to cope with the question of Being end in silence, in *aphasia* as Greek skeptics would have expressed it.

Being as the "centre of a man's philosophic vision" is the *explicit* concern of James's intense meditation on the last pages of his early essay "The Sentiment of Rationality." An unpublished note for this essay is titled "Ontologic knowledge."[7] Like the final parts of the essay, it is a wonderful companion piece to the late chapter III on Being in *Some Problems of Philosophy*; it thus powerfully demonstrates the fundamental consistency of James's thinking throughout his career. The "universal form of being" or

> the Universe considered as Being must always be inexplicable to us, we must simply find it, take it for granted, remain Empiricists. For the Universal being, having nothing to be discriminated from, cannot be consciously realized in any quale. It is an eternal tastelessness or monotony, only discriminated in our logic from Nothing—but that is not another *quale*. Nor is it *explicable* in the usual sense of explication viz. the being referred to another genus already known—for by the hypothesis there is no such.[8]

Being, once again, is not available for conceptual explication, it is found, it is given or granted, and, above all, it is not a *what*, it is not qualified as an essence; in Jamesian parlance, familiar especially from his *Essays in Radical Empiricism*, it is a mere *that*, pure existence. This means that Being does not refer to anything else and, at the same time, that all beings have to be conceived and are conceptually known in terms of their relations to a manifold of other beings, but never in terms of undefinable Being itself: "Therefore the 'Relativity of Knowledge' is no imbecility of our understanding, but results from the essence of being."[9] The "essence of Being" is not a definite *whatness* or *quidditas* in the traditional sense; rather, and paradoxically, it is an absence of "quality," of *whatness*, which to James shows as "tastelessness or monotony," lack of all distinction or difference. Existence pure and simple cannot be known like beings, that is, conceptually or in their manifold

---

[7]"Notes for 'The Sentiment of Rationality,'" in *Essays in Philosophy*, vol. 5 of *The Works of William James* (Cambridge, MA: Harvard University Press, 1978), 344.
[8]Ibid.
[9]Ibid.

relatedness: "But it don't follow at all that because we don't know being in this old sense, that we are any worse off, or excluded from anything, that it is opaque to us. If it is *upon* us all the while, if we are of it, why seek to pour it in to the form of the known and understood."[10] Being is "known by acquaintance" ("we are of it"), even if we never know *about* it ("the form of the [conceptually] known and understood"). In this way we return to the injunction to approach the "centre of a man's philosophic vision," namely, Being itself, by way of "placing" ourselves, existentially, within that vision, sharing and not merely conceiving it. In this way we reach the

> blind substance of the living man, ... his third dimension extending from the painted surface of the intelligible world into the deep of ontology, and in which he rests, at home, & feels him*self* (though when he looks *at* it it vanishes) why is not this absolute being? Only not understood because above the understanding, and not needing to be understood?[11]

In its groping and tentative way, James's sketchy note for "The Sentiment of Rationality" arrives at the persistent "centre of his philosophic vision," the awareness or *feeling* (as he also says in the note) of the namelessness of Being "above the understanding." Being is wordlessly manifest and felt both and at the same time *in* and *as* the "Universal being" and in the individual's own "absolute" existence, as subjective *and* objective.

In 1902 James found an elegant way of describing the un-definable Being at the "centre of philosophic vision." In one of my favorite passages, he profoundly meditates on *experience* as:

> the entire process of phenomena, of present data considered in their raw immediacy, before reflective thought has analyzed them into subjective and objective aspects or ingredients. It is the summum genus of which everything must have been a part before we can speak of it at all. ... If philosophy insists on keeping this term indeterminate, she can refer to her subject-matter without committing herself as to certain questions in dispute. But if experience be used with either an objective or a subjective shade of meaning, then question-begging occurs, and discussion grows impossible.[12]

The totality of that which shows (itself) is experience. It is—as it occurs—both subject and object, observer and world, human being and nature, not in the sense of two entities somehow intimately combined but rather, faintly

---

[10]Ibid.
[11]Ibid.
[12]"Experience," in *Essays in Philosophy*, 95.

reminiscent of Schelling's aboriginal unity or *Ureinheit*,[13] as one present event out of which subject and object may emerge by separating that which primarily *is*. This is the *summum genus*, the highest that can be thought. It means that James knows, that he intuits *experience as Being* itself, of which everything must have been a part before, as he says—and this is the point we have to emphasize—before we can *speak* of it. Experience as Being is silent, it cannot be said. From a conceptual, purely linguistic, argumentative, traditionally metaphysical standpoint, it is, like Emerson's "To Be," an unsolvable wonder[14] and therefore, according to Aristotle's well-known argument, the beginning of all thinking. It *is*, it *shows*. Wittgenstein speaks of its inarticulate presencing in *Tractatus logico-philosophicus* 6.522: "Es gibt allerdings Unaussprechliches. Dies *zeigt* sich, es ist das Mystische."[15] The *term* experience/Being has to be kept in-de-*term*-inate, James says. It is a term that negates itself, a non-term term: facing, identifying with, thinking Being necessitates a fundamentally, an ontologically skeptical disposition that results in both *epoché* and *aphasia*.

In *Essays in Radical Empiricism*, James refined his thinking about experience as Being itself. Here he speaks of Being as *pure* experience and his meditations expand and deepen what he had adumbrated in his dictionary definition of experience in 1902:

> "Pure experience" is the name which I gave to the immediate flux of life which furnishes the material to our later reflection with its conceptual categories. … [It is] an experience pure in the literal sense of a *that* which is not yet any definite *what*, tho ready to be all sorts of whats; full both of oneness and manyness, but in respects that don't appear; changing throughout, yet so confusedly that its phases interpenetrate and no points, either of distinction or of identity, can be caught. Pure experience in this state is but another name for feeling or sensation. But the flux of it no sooner comes than it tends to fill itself with emphases, and these salient parts become identified and fixed and abstracted; so that experience now flows as if shot through with adjectives and nouns and prepositions and conjunctions. Its purity is … the proportional amount of unverbalized sensation which it still embodies.[16]

---

[13]Rüdiger Bubner, "Schelling," in *Deutscher Idealismus*, ed. Bubner (Stuttgart: Reclam, 1978), 222.

[14]Emerson, "Natural History of Intellect" W XII, 15.

[15]Ludwig Wittgenstein, *Tractatus logico-philosophicus: Logisch-philosophsiche Abhandlung* (Frankfurt: Suhrkamp, 1963), 115: "After all, there is the unspeakable. It *shows*, it is the mystical" (my translation). The mystical here, I would argue, is that which makes itself silently felt in the contemplation of Being, as in Parmenides's poem.

[16]"The Thing and Its Relations," in *Essays in Radical Empiricism*, vol. 3 of *The Works of William James* (1912; Cambridge, MA: Harvard University Press, 1976), 46.

As in the dictionary definition, pure experience is that which is above all itself—it is *immediate*, that is, non-mediated, it does not know or accept an in-between that separates it and a knower, it just is. As immediate event it has the Heraclitean quality of dynamic ever-changing flow; it is a flux. Conceptual knowledge *about* pure experience as the result of reflection, as opposed to knowledge by existential acquaintance, comes later, *a posteriori*. Pure experience is a mere *that*; there is a sense, a feeling awareness of it, but one cannot say what it is, or how many *whats*, entities or things, it implies. One cannot decide as to whether it is one or many, possesses parts or not. In short, all conceptual distinctions are absent from it; in this respect it is similar to, maybe even identical with, Peirce's intuition of Firstness.[17] As a flowing event it is intuited as finally allowing distinctions, differences, nameable entities, and language to emerge. Pure experience itself, however, always remains and thus induces or demands, once again, the suspension of judgment, that postponement of articulation which defines genuine skepticism. Pure experience is the residue that always envelops all specifics that emerge from it and can be conceptualized. Like a halo forever receding from our attempts to grasp it, it is the unverbalized, unverbalizable background of our specific modes of knowing which come forth from the pure *that* which we are aware of, which we feel.

As early as 1890, in the terminologically often still scientistic *Principles of Psychology*, James had already envisioned, experienced, perceived, or intuited reality/Being in its pre-verbal fullness as something that systematically and necessarily eludes any attempts at dogmatic fixation or linguistic expression of its essence. This is why he states succinctly: "language works against our perception of the truth."[18] The perception or awareness of truth, of what basically or primarily or inescapably *is*, the open presence of Being overflows, as James says metaphorically in *A Pluralistic Universe*, all our concepts and attempts at saying anything: "Reality, life, experience, concreteness, immediacy, use what word you will, exceeds our logic, overflows and surrounds it."[19] Being as the unsayable, the term that has to be kept in-de-term-inate, has many names in this statement, but ultimately it possesses no proper name. In this way it induces wonderment as well as the beginning and above all the continuation of thinking, a thinking that will not come to rest in a final goal or on a firm foundation. In *Pragmatism* James found a haunting image for our condition as philosophical subjects and as persons conducting lives within experiencing, within Being as restlessly ongoing flow:

---

[17]*Principles of Philosophy*, ed. Charles Hartshorne, Paul Weiss, and Arthur W. Burks, vol. I of *The Collected Papers of Charles Sanders Peirce* (Cambridge, MA: Harvard University Press, 1931–35), par. 357.
[18]*Principles* 1, 235.
[19]*Pluralistic Universe*, 96.

For pluralistic pragmatism, truth grows up inside of all the finite experiences. They lean on each other, but the whole of them, if such a whole there be, leans on nothing. All "homes" are in finite experience; finite experience as such is homeless. Nothing outside of the flux secures the issue of it.[20]

We can only know concrete individual experiences, single realities, and single truths in relation to and meshed with other experiences as concrete instances of this and that, instances of *whats, thusnesses, eachnesses*—to use some of James's interchangeable terms. If we want to conceptually think the totality that surrounds the single instances of our live realities, however, we find that this totality is embedded—is that the right word?—in an absence. We are at home in an overarching homelessness as soon as we try to think Being as the ultimate. We have to conceptually capitulate and keep on looking for a solution that may forever elude us. This is what James emphasizes so passionately at the end of *A Pluralistic Universe*: "The word 'and' trails along after every sentence. Something always escapes. 'Ever not quite' has to be said of the best attempts made anywhere in the universe at attaining all-inclusiveness."[21]

There is one aspect and shade of meaning that I have avoided so far in discussing the way in which Being as a whole defeats the authority of philosophical concepts and challenges us to be skeptical thinkers on the way, thinkers who consider ever new terms and images to indirectly approach that which ultimately refuses to be named and imaged: I have overlooked the dimension of time. "What really *exists* is not things made, but things in the making."[22] This should not simply be read as a statement about beings, about individual things as emergent entities. It is also a statement about existing, about Being. Being, and this includes the Being of things, is not *there*; it is always about to be, in the making, rushing toward us from the abyss of the future. Things may be in transition, but more important for our consideration is the implication that Being itself is not just a temporal event, an instantiation in time, but rather that Being *is* time. Similarly, Emerson had already maintained in "Nature" (1844) that there is in nature and among humans "always a referred existence, an absence, never a presence and satisfaction."[23] Deferral of presence is one of the temporal hallmarks through which Being makes itself felt. This intuition radicalizes, it deepens, it intensifies the necessity to withhold naming and conceptualizing Being

---

[20]*Pragmatism: A New Name for Some Old Ways of Thinking*, vol. 1 of *The Works of William James* (1907; Cambridge, MA: Harvard University Press, 1975), 125.
[21]*Pluralistic Universe*, 145.
[22]Ibid., 117.
[23]"Nature" W III, 185.

itself. As the reason for the inescapable withholding, *epoché*, of any definite ascription of meaning to Being, time nevertheless encourages a continuous philosophical engagement of Being as it emerges in beings, in individual realities, in things; Being as time motivates a search without closure.

As so often in James, it is a seemingly offhand remark, an extraordinarily felicitous phrase that grants a glimpse of the depth and subtlety of his vision as it implies the indispensable dimension of time in any attempt to tentatively approach Being: "the word 'or' names a genuine reality."[24] Genuine reality, true Being is not this or that, it is not (yet) *settled*, in Emerson's terminology from "Circles." It is "*either–or*"; it waits to be determined. That which *is*, everything that *is*, arrives from the future, the realm of the new, the unprecedented, and challenges us to settle it, to name it, to evaluate it, at least tentatively and thus skeptically. Being is about to be the Being of things, an openness on which we wholly depend without ever being able to say a definitive word about or for it. Being is no more than the *not-yet* hungering[25] and waiting to be satisfied, a forever deferred fulfillment in a final or definite *whatness*. This *whatness* is never fully realized because beings, things, entities, do not rest in a stable and unchanging home of Being but continue to be "in the making," waiting to be either this *or* that *or* something else in the relentless passage of time.

# II

It is not very common to characterize the thinking of William James as skeptical, and even among those critics who do use the term there seems little agreement as to which type or school of skepticism might possibly help elucidate central features of his philosophy. Bertrand Russell's in many respects negative critique argues that the skeptical features of pragmatism may result in relativism and an irresponsible indifferentism in choosing one's beliefs: "The scepticism embodied in pragmatism is that which says 'Since all beliefs are absurd, we may as well believe what is most convenient.'"[26] Charlene Haddock Seigfried defends James against the possible charge of such ontological and moral relativism that arises from the skeptical challenge "to the self-evident truth of the world of appearances," a challenge which James overcomes, according to Seigfried, by arresting skeptical

---

[24]*Pluralistic Universe*, 146.

[25]These are concepts and images used by Ernst Bloch in *Philosophische Grundlagen I: Zur Ontologie des Noch-Nicht-Seins* (Frankfurt: Suhrkamp, 1961). Bloch's ontology bears strong resemblances to both Peirce's and James's foundational intuitions.

[26]Bertrand Russell, *Logical and Philosophical Papers, 1909–1913*, ed. John G. Slater and Bernd Frohmann, vol. 6 of *Collected Papers of Bertrand Russell* (London and New York: Routledge, 1992), 280.

reduction "while acquiescing in the opacity of being and getting on with life." Seigfried's refutation of skepticism in James rests on the assumption that "Skepticism is akin to nihilism, that is, the loss of meaning in life, in its removal of justifiable grounds for action."[27] Jonathan Levin interprets skeptical aspects of a pragmatist belief in "dynamic, transitional processes" positively, since skepticism prevents a dogmatic settling down in fixed "particular beliefs" and thus allows the critical imagination to "balance visionary and skeptical impulses."[28] Ross Posnock emphasizes the central philosophical and cultural importance of a genuine skeptical disposition in James's thinking: "[S]kepticism toward identity and the exclusionary bias of concepts"[29] dissolves existential (e.g., racial) dogmatism and the ideological delimitation of beings. In this way Jamesian pragmatism embodies a (not only political) "liberating skepticism."[30]

When one considers William James's own use of the term "skepticism," the picture does not become more consistent and unified. In *Pragmatism* he presents one of his many contrastive comparisons of the "tender-minded" and the "tough-minded" philosophical temperaments and summarizes: "The rationalist finally will be of dogmatic temper in his affirmations, while the empiricist may be more skeptical and open to discussion."[31] In *A Pluralistic Universe*, James charges the skeptical critics of rationalism—from Protagoras to Hume and James Mill—with insufficient consistency in their questioning of the intellectualist position; only Bergson and, by implication, James himself are sufficiently radical and skeptical.[32] This is a milder form of an earlier attack on "the stupidity of unimaginative opponents" of rationalism who cowardly shy away from "the very extreme and climax of skepticism."[33] We find a more judicial attitude toward skepticism as a feature of (radical) empiricism in *Some Problems of Philosophy*: Empiricists, he says, "may be dogmatic about their method of building their arguments on 'hard facts,' but they are willing to be skeptical about any conclusions reached by the method at a given time."[34]

---

[27]Charlene Haddock Seigfried, *William James's Radical Reconstruction of Philosophy* (Albany: State University of New York Press, 1990), 27–8.

[28]Jonathan Levin, *The Poetics of Transition: Emerson, Pragmatism, and American Literary Modernism* (Durham, NC: Duke University Press, 1999), 14, 196.

[29]Ross Posnock, "The Influence of William James on American Culture," in *The Cambridge Companion to William James*, ed. Ruth Anna Putnam (Cambridge: Cambridge University Press, 1997), 337.

[30]Ross Posnock, "Going Astray, Going Forward: Du Boisian Pragmatism and Its Lineage " in *The Revival of Pragmatism: New Essays on Social Thought, Law, and Culture*, ed. Morris Dickstein (Durham, NC: Duke University Press, 1998), 187.

[31]*Pragmatism*, 13.

[32]*Pluralistic Universe*, 106.

[33]"Notes," 365.

[34]*Some Problems*, 24.

In all of these statements, James does allow skepticism as an ingredient, as one feature among several, in his characterizations of his preferred "tough-minded" empiricism and anti-intellectualism. In chapter XIV of *The Varieties of Religious Experience*, James inserts an important digression on skepticism in matters of religious conviction that strikes me as applicable to philosophical beliefs as well. James defends himself against the imagined charge of "systematic skepticism" and of "embark[ing] upon a sea of wanton doubt" when he allows for, as he sees it, justifiable and necessary historical changes in religious beliefs, or when he takes the different types of "inner needs" of human beings into consideration that are the basis of varieties of legitimate religious convictions. He does not want his rejection of the "dogmatic ideal" understood as "a perverse delight in intellectual instability. I am no lover of disorder and doubt as such. Rather do I fear to lose truth by this pretension to possess it already wholly. That we can gain more and more of it by moving always in the right direction."[35] The refutation and critique of a deliberate and radical skepticism does not imply an assent to dogmatic positions.

It seems to me that James's resulting moderately skeptical disposition calls for more precision when I speak of skepticism as a possibly essential and defining feature of his temperament as a thinker and a crucial trait of "the centre" of his philosophic, of his ontological vision as whole. My brief survey of critical and of James's own comments on skepticism in his thinking indicates that, on the one hand, skepticism may be seen negatively: as irresponsible relativism (Russell), as a dangerous nihilistic disposition (Seigfried), or, in extreme cases, as amoral and "perverse delight" in "wanton doubt"—as James himself is careful to admit. On the other hand, skepticism shows as a critical corrective of dogmatic and authoritarian beliefs (Levin, James), as a necessary concomitant of experimentally empirical and anti-intellectualist thinking (James), and, importantly, as a way, an intellectual *methodos* of liberation from essentialist fixation (Posnock). Finally, as James argues in *Varieties*, skepticism may ideally be enacted as an open-ended movement in the direction of an always desired, but possibly never fully granted, insight. This spectrum of opinions and definitions calls for a little clarification and, at least, for a schematic overview of varieties of skeptical thinking.

Apart from the popular and vague idea of skepticism as a kind of disgruntled aversion to all kinds of established beliefs, genuine and serious philosophical skepticism comes in at least three or four varieties, which should be carefully distinguished. It may be a surprise to many that Plato himself was considered a skeptic during classical antiquity. Cicero argued

---

[35]*The Varieties of Religious Experience: A Study in Human Nature*, vol. 13 of *The Works of William James* (1902; Cambridge, MA: Harvard University Press, 1985), 266–8.

the case because of the often incompatible views in Plato's works. Ever so much later Hegel agreed when he declared the dialogue *Parmenides* to be a prime example of genuine skepticism because of its inconclusive discussion of the world as one or as many.[36] Pyrrhonic skepticism and the variety espoused by Arcesilaus and Carneades at the Athenian Academy after Plato's death tend to demonstrate that nothing can ever be fully and safely known. The possibility to contradict any dogmatic statement by an equally plausible alternative, by an *equipollent* argument,[37] leads to an *aporia*, an intellectual impasse that necessitates the withholding of any judgment, *epoché*, and, finally, results in philosophical silence, *aphasia*.[38] Contemporary historians of ancient thought like Jonathan Barnes have called this variety of skepticism negative metadogmatism.[39] The so-called Neopyrrhonists criticized the older skeptics, the negative metadogmatists of the Academy, as being quite as dogmatic as positive dogmatists like Aristotle or the Stoics, because they dogmatically assert that nothing can be truly and safely known. The most important representative of the Neopyrrhonists is the prolific Sextus Empiricus (late second to early third centuries CE). As in the case of Emerson,[40] I will argue that Sextus Empiricus in his *Outlines of Pyrrhonism* provides a thoroughly convincing heuristic model for what I understand as the Jamesian version of ontological skepticism in practice. I deliberately exclude modern European skepticism from, say, Descartes through Kant to Santayana from my considerations. The skeptical method in the Cartesian tradition is designed to find its fulfillment and justification in the reflective assertion of and insight into a *fundamentum inconcussum*, an unquestionable ontological or epistemological basis—be this Descartes' *cogito*, Hume's nature, Kant's unity of transcendental apperception, or Santayana's essences. I think it is a justifiable simplification to say that modern European skepticism is a method that is designed to bring about

---

[36]*Historisches Wörterbuch der Philosophie*, ed. Joachim Ritter et al. (Darmstadt: WBG, 1995), vol. 9, 942, 962. I will base the following comments on the Greek skeptics on one of the most precise introductions to skepticism in classical antiquity: Jacques Brunschwig, "Skepticism," in *Greek Thought: A Guide to Classical Knowledge*, ed. Brunschwig and Geoffrey E. R. Lloyd, trans. Catherine Porter (Cambridge, MA: Harvard University Press, 2000), 937–56.

[37]The importance of the concept of "equipollent" arguments is described in detail in Markus Lammenranta, "The Pyrrhonian Problematic," in *The Oxford Handbook of Skepticism*, ed. John Greco (Oxford: Oxford University Press, 2008), 9.

[38]For the Greek terms describing reactions to skeptical awareness, see Thomas McEvilley, *The Shape of Ancient Thought: Comparative Studies in Greek and Indian Philosophies* (New York: Allworth Press, 2002), 450–5.

[39]Jonathan Barnes, "Diogenes Laertius on Pyrrhonism" (1992), in *Mantissa: Essays in Ancient Philosophy IV*, ed. Maddalena Bonelli (Oxford: Clarendon Press, 2015), 524 ff.

[40]Cf. Chapter 2 in this book, also for more detailed discussions of Neopyrhhonism and Sextus Empiricus.

and issue in its own ultimate overcoming. Neopyrrhonism, however, delights in being and continuing to be skeptical.

# III

Sextus Empiricus's massive and carefully detailed, encyclopedic *Outlines of Pyrrhonism* provides the terms and ideas that can function as heuristic tools for a relatively precise presentation and analysis of basic assumptions and insights that characterize the classical and, as I would like to propose and make plausible, also the later and the modern versions of Neopyrrhonist skepticism in Montaigne or Emerson or William James. I will limit myself to some of the central tenets.

Sextus Empiricus begins his book *Outlines of Pyrrhonism* by distinguishing three basic philosophical dispositions:

> The natural result of any investigation is that the investigators either discover the object of search or deny that it is discoverable and confess it to be inapprehensible or persist in their search. So, too, with regard to the objects investigated by philosophy, this is probably why some have claimed to have discovered the truth, others have asserted that it cannot be apprehended, while others again go on inquiring. Those who believe they have discovered it are the "Dogmatists," specially so called—Aristotle, for example, and Epicurus and the Stoics and certain others; Cleitomachus and Carneades and other Academics treat it as inapprehensible: the Sceptics keep on searching.[41]

This simple statement has far-reaching implications. The skeptics who ceaselessly search are called the seekers, Gr. *zetetikoi*, by Sextus. Both the Neopyrrhonist *zetetikos* and the Jamesian pragmatist embark on an endless endeavor without closure. In *The Varieties of Religious Experience* James had argued: "I fear to lose truth by this pretension to possess it already wholly ... we can gain more and more of it by moving always in the right direction." This ceaseless movement and energetic search, however, will not, as in the utopian promise of a final agreement of all thinkers in Peirce's "How To Make Our Ideas Clear," come to an end in the epiphany of a total and definitive interpretation of Being. In his address before the Philosophical Union at Berkeley on August 26, 1898, James described the fate of the thinker as *zetetikos* with colorful intensity:

---

[41]Sextus Empiricus, *Outlines of Pyrrhonism*, trans. R. G. Bury, Loeb Classical Library 273 (1933; Cambridge, MA: Harvard University Press, 2000), 3.

So I feel that there is a center in truth's forest where I have never been: to track it out and get there is the secret spring of all my poor life's philosophic efforts; at moments I almost strike into the final valley, there is a gleam of the end, a sense of certainty, but always there comes still another ridge, so my blazes merely circle towards the true direction; and although now, if ever, would be the fit occasion, yet I cannot take you to the wondrous hidden spot to-day. To-morrow it must be, or to-morrow, or to-morrow; and pretty surely death will overtake me ere the promise is fulfilled. Out of such postponed achievements do the lives of philosophers consist. Truth's fulness is elusive; ever not quite, not quite![42]

The title and subtitle of James's last and unfinished book reinforce his skeptical, his Neopyrrhonist evaluation of the grand project of (his) philosophy. He does not offer a Hegelian *Encyclopädie der philosophischen Wissenschaften im Grundrisse*, he is content to deal with *Some Problems*, and instead of tracing the way from mere consciousness to absolute knowledge as in the *Phänomenologie des Geistes*, James offers *A Beginning of an Introduction to Philosophy*, that is, modestly tentative first steps in (once again) beginning an endless search.

To achieve and maintain this openness, the Neopyrrhonists of classical antiquity and their successors use a methodology of argumentation that is supposed to go back to Pyrrho himself. In his *Lives of Eminent Philosophers*, Diogenes Laertius reports that Pyrrho and his followers "showed ... on the basis of that which is contrary to what induces belief, that the probabilities on both sides are equal."[43] Sextus succinctly describes this kind of skeptical method as a mode of experimentation that keeps basic questions of philosophical belief necessarily undecided: "The main basic principle of the Sceptic system is that of opposing to every proposition an equal proposition; for we believe that as a consequence of this we end by ceasing to dogmatize."[44] As in the case of Pyrrho and his negatively metadogmatic followers Arcesilaus and Carneades, the unceasing presentation of equipollent judgments by the Neopyrrhonists helps abandon dogmatism, but it does not terminate philosophical inquiry or searching. When one surveys the richly varied landscape of William James's explorations of alternative models of ontology, metaphysics, and epistemology, one is struck by the consistency with which

---

[42]James, "Philosophical Conceptions and Practical Results," in *Pragmatism*, 258. Siegfried uses this passage as a concluding statement of her remarkable study *William James's Radical Reconstruction of Philosophy*. The first part of her book bears the title "Overcoming Nihilism and Skepticism." Obviously, her understanding of skepticism is far removed from the energetic, open-minded, and liberal version proposed by Neopyrrhonism.

[43]Diogenes Laertius, *Lives of Eminent Philosophers*, trans. R. D. Hicks, Loeb Classical Library 185 (1931; Cambridge, MA: Harvard University Press, 2005), vol. 2, 491.

[44]Sextus Empiricus, *Outlines*, 9.

he—from early publications like "The Sentiment of Rationality" through mature works like *Pragmatism* and *A Pluralistic Universe* to the posthumous *Some Problems*—keeps relentlessly juxtaposing equipollent philosophical visions, discussing again and again their relative merits and deficiencies from ever-changing points of view. The tender-minded vs. the tough-minded disposition, rationalism vs. empiricism, monism vs. pluralism, nominalism vs. realism, simplicity vs. clarity, concepts vs. percepts: these are the varieties of a ceaseless search for an ever-receding solution, for an ultimate decision in favor of one or the other side of ontologically and metaphysically and epistemologically equipollent alternatives. In its unfinished state, *Some Problems* cannot propose a resolution, but it seems unlikely that James is about to propose an unequivocal—and thus dogmatic—justification of the empiricist, the pluralist, the nominalist, or tough-minded disposition and perspective. The ending of *A Pluralistic Universe*, I believe, presents James's final word on the impossibility of final words:[45]

> Whatever I may say, each of you will be sure to take pluralism or leave it, just as your own sense of rationality moves and inclines. The only thing I emphatically insist upon is that it is a fully coordinate hypothesis with monism. This world *may*, in the last resort, be a block-universe; but on the other hand, it *may* be a universe only strung-along, not rounded in and closed. Reality *may* exist distributively just as it sensibly seems to, after all. On that possibility I do insist.[46]

Even though it is more than obvious that James is the champion of pluralist empiricism, he goes on to argue that the final decision depends on a vital pre-logical disposition toward a "will to believe" that gives rise to arguments following each other on a "faith-ladder," arguments that will be binding and convincing exclusively for the individual believer.[47] The systematically skeptical indecision continues to the very end of the book when James urges his readers to "gather philosophic conclusions of any kind, monistic or pluralistic, from the *particulars of life*."[48] A true Neopyrrhonist skeptic, James has it both ways in two ways: he urges—dogmatically—a true equipollence of monist and pluralist visions and then—skeptically—reopens the way of inquiry, of search, for the *zetetikoi* of the future by

---

[45]Seigfried reaches a similar conclusion when she acknowledges that James is consistently engaged, by means of his "radical empiricism," in "developing the strengths and weaknesses of two extreme positions" of the debate, though without finally succeeding; Seigfried, *Radical Reconstruction*, 395.
[46]*Pluralistic Universe*, 148.
[47]Ibid.
[48]Ibid., 149.

insisting on the particulars waiting to be transformed, tentatively, into either a rationalist monism or an empiricist pluralism.

A central concern in Book I of Sextus's *Outlines of Pyrrhonism* is the insistence that sense impressions have to be taken for what they are and as they appear. This simple and unquestioning preference of the truth value of perceptual, of phenomenal reality returns in a sophisticated form in James's *Some Problems*, especially in chapter IV, "Percept and Concept."[49] Sextus argues that "we shall, indeed, be able to state our own impressions of the real object, but as to its essential nature we shall suspend judgment,"[50] and he elaborates: "For while we are, no doubt, able to state what each of the underlying objects [of our perception] appears to be, relatively to each difference [in the physical or mental condition of the perceiver], we are incapable of explaining what it is in reality."[51] The distinction between the certainty of perception and the present incapability to assert real essence necessitates a linguistic correction: "But this point we must notice—that here as elsewhere we use the term 'are' for the term 'appear,' and what we virtually mean is 'all things appear relative.'"[52] With some passion Sextus returns to the problem of real being: "we are compelled to suspend judgment regarding *the real nature* of external objects."[53]

The core of the skeptical vision is an ontological problem. It is the abiding uncertainty of "the real nature," of the *Wesen*, of the Being of beings that keeps the skeptic as *zetetikos* searching and experimenting. If we simplify just a little, Sextus engages the problem of the *Ding an sich*, but he refuses Kant's negative metadogmatic position that legislates that it is forever, always, and necessarily inaccessible. Like the speaker in Robert Frost's wonderfully skeptical, almost Neopyrrhonist poem "For Once, Then, Something," the *zetetikos* keeps searching and hoping because he is "not simply someone who seeks or who has sought: he is someone who up to this point has done nothing but seek without finding, and who has the intention of continuing to seek, without giving up hope of finding."[54] When James discusses the problem of the *Ding an sich* in Kant and his idealist followers, he adds this caveat: "the reality *an sich* from which in ultimate resort the sense-appearances have to come remains forever unintelligible to our intellect."[55] The limitations of the intellect are strictly the same in Sextus and in James: "The one thing it [intellect] cannot do is to reveal the inner nature of things."[56] James, however, is careful to add: "if you wish to *know*

[49]*Some Problems*, 31–60.
[50]Sextus Empiricus, *Outlines*, 37.
[51]Ibid., 53
[52]Ibid., 79–81.
[53]Ibid., 93 (my emphasis).
[54]Brunschwig, "Skepticism," 939.
[55]*Pluralistic Universe*, 107.
[56]Ibid., 112.

reality ... turn your face towards sensation."[57] Sensation, the immersion in the perceptual flux, provides "knowledge by acquaintance" with reality as changing, but it does not unequivocally reveal Being as the—according to Leibniz—indispensable ground. Awareness of reality *as it appears*, for Sextus as well as for James, necessitates a continuous search, while the nature, the essence of things grounding the phenomenal world keeps receding. Sextus summarizes: "we conclude that, since all things are relative [to changing conditions of perception], we shall suspend judgment as to what things are absolutely and really existent."[58] The ontological quest is suspended; it is not abandoned in Sextus, it is not fully discarded in James, it keeps hovering in the background and calls for recurrent reflective attention—from the early comments in "The Sentiment of Rationality" to the chapter on Being in *Some Problems*.

As ontological skeptics Sextus Empiricus and William James share a sense of what it means to achieve a (at least temporary) balanced insight into a phenomenal world whose *possibly* inaccessible or *maybe* even absent grounding could be read as—in James's words in *Pragmatism*—metaphysical "homelessness." The sometimes only temporary solution of a philosophical problem, James avers in "The Sentiment of Rationality," is recognized by certain marks: "A strong feeling of ease, peace, rest, is one of them. The transition from a state of puzzle and perplexity to rational comprehension is full of lively relief and pleasure."[59] This sensation of "mental ease and freedom,"[60] whatever the solution may be, is a perfect equivalent of the unperturbedness, *ataraxia*, which the Neopyrrhonist Sextus describes as the hallmark of a momentary philosophical resting-place in the ongoing quest in a world of manifold perspectives and changing interests and fleeting sensations:

> For the Sceptic, having set out to philosophize with the object of passing judgement on the sense-impressions and ascertaining which of them are true and which false, so as to attain quietude thereby, found himself involved in contradictions of equal weight, and being unable to decide between them suspended judgement; and as he was thus in suspense there followed, as it happened, the state of quietude in respect of matters of opinion.[61]

The possibility to achieve momentary mental ease and rest in James or, for Sextus, moments of quietude within a phenomenal world without ultimate

---

[57]Ibid., 113.
[58]Sextus Empiricus, *Outlines*, 79.
[59]"The Sentiment of Rationality," in *Essays in Philosophy*, 32.
[60]Ibid., 33.
[61]Sextus Empiricus, *Outlines*, 19.

ontological certainty, these are the preconditions for a successful practical life.[62] James liked to urge his audiences to always return from philosophical speculation and conceptual thinking to life, to practice, to the realm of the ordinary with its contingent cultural realities. Sextus similarly insisted that one trust in the sensually given phenomena in order to make what he thinks of as a "normal" life possible.

> The criterion, then, of the Sceptic School is, we say, the appearance, giving this name to what is virtually the sense-presentation. For since this lies in feeling and involuntary affection, it is not open to question ... Adhering, then, to appearances we live in accordance with the normal rules of life, undogmatically, seeing that we cannot remain wholly inactive.[63]

When one looks at William James's philosophical oeuvre as a whole in the light of the basic intuitions, strategies, and arguments of Neopyrrhonist skepticism, one does find a strong family resemblance. Its prominent features are the continuing, even though continuously frustrated, interest in and engagement of the question of Being, of the "real nature" of things, a pervasive phenomenalism and privileging of the perceptual over the conceptual approach to reality, a persistent and ultimately not conclusive debate between antithetic but equipollent metaphysical interpretations, and the achievement of momentary resting-places of satisfactory, of rational insight that are experienced as (transitory) ease and rest, as unperturbed quietude, in a world that needs and calls for normal and common activities amidst the undogmatically accepted realities of given cultural circumstances.

---

[62]*Pluralistic Universe*, 131.
[63]Sextus Empiricus, *Outlines*. 17.

# 13

# Kitaro Nishida and William James

A survey of the modern philosophical landscape from a cosmopolitan point of view reveals William James as a truly pivotal figure in the international context of a radical reconstruction of thinking at the turn from the nineteenth to the twentieth centuries. The impact of James's thought on F. C. S. Schiller in England, Papini in Italy, Husserl in Germany, Bergson in France, and Nishida in Japan is well documented in each single instance.[1] Especially the early studies of James's oeuvre as a whole have made us aware of the nowadays-often-overlooked fundamental challenges to traditional modes of thinking that have issued from James's original primary philosophical intuitions that go far beyond pragmatism in a narrow sense of the term.[2] These challenges account for the worldwide reverberations and repercussions of his thinking especially between 1890 and 1930. Europeans, however, have not continued to give James appropriate credit for his achievements. The prevalent parochial European perception of, for example, Bergson as the representative philosopher of early modernism is a good example of the way local interests, cultural prejudices, and customary perspectives prevented and continue to prevent a thorough, comprehensive, and well-founded international appreciation of James's far-reaching and

---

This essay was previously published as "Global Aspects of American Pragmatist Thinking: William James and Kitaro Nishida on the Purity of Pure Experience" in *Amerikastudien/ American Studies* 46, no. 2 (2001): 177–205. Reprinted by permission of Damien B. Schlarb, managing editor of *Amerikastudien/American Studies*.

[1]Consider as a representative example these seminal studies on James and Husserl: Bruce Wilshire, *William James and Phenomenology: A Study of "The Principles of Psychology"* (Bloomington: University of Indiana Press, 1968); James M. Edie, *William James and Phenomenology* (Bloomington: University of Indiana Press, 1987).

[2]The most important early critical analyses are: Théodore Flournoy, *La Philosophie de William James* (Saint-Blaise: Foyer Solidariste, 1911); Émile Boutroux, *William James* (Paris: Colin, 1911); Horace Meyer Kallen, *William James and Henri Bergson: A Study of Contrasting Theories of Life* (Chicago: University of Chicago Press, 1914).

preeminently innovative thought through today.[3] Like James, Henri Bergson waged war against rationalist claims as to the predominant and exclusive authority of conceptually ascertained truth. At the same time, however, Bergson, even though he was seventeen years younger than James, proposed merely another metaphysical system to replace the stately mansions of Neo-Kantianism and of the late Hegelian schools. In his writings and in his letters to and about Bergson, James politely and very cautiously objected to the anti-modernist implications evinced in a renewed system-building on the basis of the *élan vital*.[4] Even so, James's trans-metaphysical stance and his anti-foundationalist pluralism have to this very day not been sufficiently appreciated for their daring advance toward new ways of reading human existence and the world, especially if one compares these positions to modernist European philosophy with its obstinate traces of traditional thinking, like Bergson's vitalistic foundationalism or Husserl's transcendental ego, to name some rather obvious instances.

It is interesting and highly instructive that in his time James played a similarly exemplary role in Japan as in Europe. Kitarô Nishida[5] (1870–1945), the founder of the famous Kyôto School of philosophy,[6] avowedly based his first and highly influential work *Zen no kenkyû, An Inquiry into the Good* (1911),[7] on central Jamesian insights, concepts, and terms. As in the case of Bergson, however, the appreciation of the relationship between James and his successor in a different cultural context was not untroubled. Nishida himself and, above all, many of his followers and critics, both in Japan and in America, have tried to diminish the significance of James's insight and impact. More often than not this could only be achieved by means of a more or less disingenuous and possibly culturally or ideologically biased misreading of James's works or because of a lack of the necessary

---

[3]For a critical refutation of this predominantly European view, see Herwig Friedl, "The World as Fact, the World as Event: Varieties of Modernist Thinking in William James, Henri Bergson, and John Dewey," in *Transatlantic Modernism*, ed. Martin Klepper and Joseph C. Schöpp (Heidelberg: Winter, 2001), 51–91.

[4]See the chapter on Bergson in *A Pluralistic Universe*, vol. 4 of *The Works of William James* (1909; Cambridge, MA: Harvard University Press, 1977), 101 ff., and *The Letters of William James*, ed. Henry James (Boston: Atlantic Monthly Press, 1920), vol. 2, 179, 184, 291–3, 308–9, 314.

[5]Names of Japanese philosophers, scholars, and critics will be given in the customary Western order, with the given name followed by the family name.

[6]One of the best introductions to the thinking of the Kyôto School is the collection of texts with critical introductions by Ryôsuke Ohashi, *Die Philosophie der Kyoto-Schule: Texte und Einführung* (Freiburg: Alber, 1990); see also Peter Pörtner and Jens Heise, *Die Philosophie Japans: Von den Anfängen bis zur Gegenwart* (Stuttgart: Kröner, 1995), *passim*; Lydia Brüll, *Die japanische Philosophie: Eine Einführung*, 2nd ed. (Darmstadt: WBG, 1993), *passim*.

[7]Kitarô Nishida, *An Inquiry into the Good*, trans. Masao Abe and Christopher Ives (New Haven, CT: Yale University Press, 1990).

devotion, to say the least, to the subtle implications of James's elegant and profound textual articulations. Few thinkers of such importance as James have written so deceptively engaging, lucid, and seemingly easy and accessible works. James's stylistic excellence, however, has more often than not been an obstacle to the patient reading a thinker of such magnitude both demands and deserves. This is why a thorough appreciation of James's role in helping to provide a firm basis for the great achievement of an innovative and modernist Japanese philosophy at the beginning of the twentieth century calls for a careful appreciation of the subtleties of the literary renditions of his ideas.

Today it seems both ironic and plausible that James assumed a global role as a thinker at the very time the United States of America entered the imperialist phase of its historical career with the annexation and subjection of the Philippines, the building of the Panama Canal, and the role of arbiter in the Russo-Japanese war of 1904/05. It is ironic because James was a vehement critic and fervent public opponent of such policies early on: his active membership in the Anti-Imperialist League begins in 1899. On the other hand, James's international reputation as a philosopher may plausibly have profited from the global visibility and the political and military impact of the United States, even though his thinking subverts any hegemonic interpretation of human and other relations, let alone a justification of American imperialism. James's pluralistic ontology and his later panpsychist vision do not allow for the legitimacy of hierarchic and exclusive locally or regionally centered structures of order and authority. His thinking is uniquely qualified to offer the ontological basis for a decentered egalitarian world; it is expressly designed to let individual units be. In order to appreciate James's global impact, it is therefore just as necessary to overcome simplistic politically correct pieties—whether in Europe, Japan, or America—as it is mandatory to pay respectful attention to the intricacies of his elegantly articulated and still profoundly provocative vision.

The central problem in any evaluation of the seminal importance of James's thinking for Kitarô Nishida's work and for an appropriate appreciation of the difficulties that their philosophical relationship poses, is the concept of *pure experience*, if concept is the right designation for this elusive entity. James began to develop his own highly original interpretation of pure experience around 1895, having borrowed the term from Richard Avenarius's *Kritik der reinen Erfahrung* (1888–90),[8] a work whose biologistic explication of the central idea did not continue to intrigue William James.

---

[8]On James and Avenarius see David C. Lamberth, *William James and the Metaphysics of Experience* (Cambridge: Cambridge University Press, 1999), 83–7. Lamberth summarizes on p. 87: "it is more than just likely that his engagement with Avenarius' work contributed meaningfully to the development of his thought in the 1890s. There is, however, no doubt that James's rendering of pure experience is substantively his own."

In James's oeuvre, the term assumes the function of a tentative designation for Being, Being before it is appropriated, transformed, and maybe obscured as such in either consciously perceptual or conceptual modes of awareness. Pure experience—this may serve as a hesitant preliminary descriptive identification—is a liminal term signifying presence at or rather just beyond the very margins of possible articulation; pure experience is a word pointing at that out of which all possibly definable entities may be thought to arise or, more precisely, it designates a realm from which all definable and nameable entities may be *sensed* as emerging. Pure experience, then, is not a proper object or matter of thinking in a conceptual sense; it constantly and necessarily eludes appropriation. It is obvious that pure experience understood in this way shows some similarities with Mahayana- and especially Zen Buddhist ideas like *sunyata*,[9] the Sanskrit term for that basic, both universal and individualized, nothingness or present absence that is called *ku* in Japanese. Kitarô Nishida had gone through extensive Zen training before he began his career as a philosopher.[10] It seems almost natural therefore that in his attempt to articulate a Japanese understanding of Being in terms of modern, that is, Western philosophy he should have been attracted to James's idea or vision or awareness of pure experience that promised to offer a possible common ground for a meeting of East and West. It seemed as if pure experience might allow space for the continued validity of the primarily religious but non-metaphysical Eastern awareness of nothingness or emptiness while at the same time opening access to a post-metaphysical Western mode of ontological thinking. Nishida himself and many of his renowned followers and critics, however, have subsequently spent considerable intellectual energy in pointing out that James's idea and term of pure experience did not really sufficiently and profoundly enough address the basic philosophical intuition at the core of Nishida's early philosophy in *An Inquiry into the Good*. It is deeply disturbing that the implicit dialogue and many of the misunderstandings between two extraordinary thinkers and their critics should have been occasioned and dominated by the attempt of Nishida and some of his followers to almost exclusively claim and appropriate a term, a word, a mere pointer for a necessary intuition which by definition had to evade and avoid and elude all appropriations, whether in a terminological, philosophical, religious, or cultural sense.

---

[9]See David A. Dilworth, "Nishida Kitaro: Nothingness as the Negative Space of Experiential Immediacy," *International Philosophical Quarterly* 13, no. 4 (1973), 467: "In religious language, Nishida's logic of 'concrete emptiness' is the language of *sunyata*."

[10]A subtle biographical evaluation of the importance of Nishida's training in Zen and his work on the *koan* and the concept of *ku* may be found in the comprehensive study of the philosopher's life and work by his disciple and successor Keiji Nishitani, *Nishida Kitaro*, trans. Seisaku Yamamoto and James W. Heisig (Berkeley: University of California Press, 1991), 22 ff.

# I

A critical reconstruction of the varieties of misreading William James in his intercultural encounter with the definitive modernist Japanese philosophy of Kitarô Nishida and its followers and readers will have to begin with a brief attempt at clarifying at least some of the rich implications of what James means when he addresses experience as pure experience. This will be the basis for retelling and evaluating the story of a series of mostly Eastern failures to recognize, acknowledge, and appreciate a "native" core intuition as soon as it appears in the guise of the Western, that is, American, other.

Long before James systematically employed the term "pure experience" to indicate an as-yet-unappropriated awareness that—from an ontological point of view—is his vision of Being,[11] long before the 1904 and 1905 *Essays in Radical Empiricism*, he sometimes described and attempted to define *experiencing* as it goes on in a fashion that foreshadows his later position, whether he named it the stream of thought, or the stream of consciousness, or simply experience without further qualification. The opening paragraphs of the famous "Stream of Thought" chapter in *The Principles of Psychology* (1890) establish the ontological and epistemological primacy of a conscious awareness that is not subjectively had:

> *The first fact for us, then, as psychologists, is that thinking of some sort goes on.* I use the word thinking in accordance with what was said [earlier], for every form of consciousness indiscriminately. If we could say in English "it thinks," as we say "it rains" or "it blows," we should be stating the fact most simply and with the minimum of assumption. As we cannot, we must simply say that *thought goes on.*[12]

Thinking, in the sense of conscious awareness, of experiencing, is without subject and that is why it cannot be properly *articulated* in English or, for that matter, in any other Indo-European language.[13] As James goes on to

---

[11]Various critics have asserted the identity of experiencing and Being in James's thought. Thus Ralph Barton Perry writes that "reality is immediately given in experience—*is* experience, when that term is properly construed"; *The Thought and Character of William James* (London: Milford/Oxford University Press, 1936), vol. 2, 603; and James M. Edie states: "Being, the *really real*, is *this experienced world itself* ..."; *William James and Phenomenology*, 73. More recently Hilary Putnam has put the same insight in this way in defining James's "neutral monist" ontology: "the properties and relations we experience *are* the stuff of the universe"; "Pragmatism and Realism," in *The Revival of Pragmatism: New Essays on Social Thought, Law, and Culture*, ed. Morris Dickstein (Durham, NC: Duke University Press, 1998), 47.

[12]*The Principles of Psychology*, vol. 8.1–3 of *The Works of William James* (1890; Cambridge, MA: Harvard University Press, 1981), 1, 219–20.

[13]In this context it is interesting and important to note that the lack of the Western grammatical conception of a subject in Japanese would facilitate the articulation of James's insight. On "thinking without subject" in Japanese, see Toratarô Shimomura, "Mentalität und Logik der

explain, experiencing as the stream of awareness has the *tendency* toward personality formation and toward the establishing of an objective world seemingly independent of it. Also, the stream is characterized by continuity or identity and, at the same time, by persistent differentiation.[14] In this early work, which is still predominantly characterized by an apparently dualist position or at least a dualist terminology, James nevertheless leaves no doubt that experience precedes both subjectivity itself and the split between subject and object, person and world. Thinking, awareness, experiencing is also beyond or antecedent to unity or difference, oneness and plurality; in being both continuous or identical *with* and yet at the same time always different *from* itself, experience precedes or transcends conceptualization.

James wrote a remarkable entry on experience for J. M. Baldwin's *Dictionary of Philosophy and Psychology*, which came out in 1902. Like his foundational statements on experience as the event of thinking or as the ongoing temporal awareness before appropriation by and through a subject in "The Stream of Thought," this short text documents the concentrated and disciplined elegance that is the hallmark of James's most intense moments of philosophical vision. For James experience is best defined as:

> the entire process of phenomena, of present data considered in their raw immediacy, before reflective thought has analysed them into subjective and objective aspects or ingredients. It is the summum genus of which everything must have been a part before we can speak of it at all ... If philosophy insists on keeping this term indeterminate, she can refer to her subject-matter without committing herself as to certain questions in dispute. But if experience be used with either an objective or a subjective shade of meaning, then question-begging occurs, and discussion grows impossible.[15]

Experience, and this foreshadows the interpretation of pure experience as does the analysis of the stream of thought, is that which arises out of itself and into the light of phenomenal awareness—without, and that again is the point, without the differentiation of this emergence into subject and object. James's anti-Cartesianism, which Alfred North Whitehead emphasized as

---

Japaner," in *Die Philosophie der Kyôto-Schule*, ed. Ryôsuke Ohashi (Freiburg: Alber, 1990), 382–4. On the linguistic problems of writing a radical empiricist vision of pure experience, see my essay "Thinking in Search of a Language: Pragmatism and the Muted Middle Voice," *Amerikastudien/American Studies* 47, no. 4 (2002): 469–90; see also Chapter 14, "The Necessity of the Lost Middle Voice," in this book.

[14]*Principles* 1, 220.

[15]"Experience," in *Essays in Philosophy*, vol. 5 of *The Works of William James* (Cambridge, MA: Harvard University Press, 1978), 95.

one of his greatest achievements and innovations,[16] implies that there is a non-substantialist pre-logical mode ("before we can speak of it at all' ) in which Being ("the summum genus") manifests itself. This *term* "experience," James goes on to say in a deliberately paradoxical fashion, has to be kept inde*term*inate. The defining delineation, the delimiting circumference (Lat. *terminus*), which allows for a definition, has to be avoided unless one wants to again raise the problems and perplexities that accompany any epistemology based on an aboriginal dualism. If one does indeed *think* about what James has to say and does not merely presuppose the customary and the ordinary, one will have to refrain from any statement whatsoever about experience (in its antecedent purity). It is, for instance, impossible to say whether experience is one or many, whether it is individual or universal, temporal or eternal. Experience is the pre-logical *there* out of which anything may arise, it is Being but not *a* being; it is a *no*-thing. But since it makes *it*self felt, it is not to be understood as a metaphysical entity either; it is not a substantially stable background and backdrop of the phenomenal world.

Experience in this sense, experience as Being, James says, is the genuine subject-matter of philosophy; it is, in Heidegger's words, "die Sache des Denkens." In his late and unfinished masterpiece *Some Problems of Philosophy: A Beginning of an Introduction to Philosophy*, James says about this "matter of thinking":

> What I am contending for is that the non-reproducible part of reality is an essential part of the content of philosophy, whilst ... the logicists seem to believe that conception, if only adequately attained to, might be all-sufficient.[17]

This statement is more than a mere reiteration of James's so-called anti-intellectualist critique of the traditionally dominant role of the concept in philosophical discourse. James attacks an exclusively logocentric mode of thinking because, as we have seen, it cannot do justice to experience, to Being itself as it shows for itself. This position is an exact equivalent of a central concern of Nishida's philosophy, as Toratarô Shimomura has so eloquently argued—while denying that European or Western thinking has ever encountered and successfully dealt with such a problematic.[18]

The attempts to approach Being as the stream of consciousness and simply as experience, without further qualification, show that, from the very start of his philosophical career, James always intuited that which basically

---

[16]Alfred North Whitehead, *Science and the Modern World* (New York: Free Press, 1967), 143.
[17]*Some Problems of Philosophy*, vol. 7 of *The Works of William James* (1911; Cambridge, MA: Harvard University Press, 1979), 47.
[18]Shimomura, "Mentalität und Logik der Japaner," 384–5.

exists as a realm which predates all possibility of articulation, of linguistic determination, and of differentiation into subject and object. Experience is also both identical with itself and the ground of radical difference; it is not yet either one or many. It is the *awareness of Being*, with Being functioning as both subject and object in this phrase.

Pure experience proper is one of the major concerns of the essays written in 1904 and 1905, later collected by Ralph Barton Perry under the title of *Essays in Radical Empiricism*. Here James uses at least three major metaphors in order to convey a sense of this most basic of his philosophical entities: he speaks of pure experience as stuff, as field, and as the flux of life. The very incompatibility of the metaphors helps one understand that James is leading his readers toward a visionary awareness of what pure experience means and is, an awareness that is always endangered by any definitive visualization in a perceptual sense or by a conceptual identification. The seemingly contradictory approaches help to remind one that we are witnessing necessarily oblique approximations rather than clear and distinct ideas or *Vorstellungen* of an objective realm. The first metaphorical approach reads:

> My thesis is that if we start with the supposition that there is only one primal stuff or material in the world, a stuff of which everything is composed, and if we call that stuff "pure experience," then knowing can easily be explained as a particular sort of relation towards one another into which portions of pure experience may enter. The relation itself is a part of pure experience; one of its "terms" becomes the subject or the bearer of the knowledge, the knower, the other becomes the object known.[19]

In the brief supplementary essay "The Place of Affectional Facts in a World of Pure Experience," James offered this variation of the metaphor of a primal "stuff":

> There is no thought-stuff different from thing-stuff, I said; but the same identical piece of "pure experience" (which was the name I gave to the *materia prima* of everything) can stand alternately for a "fact of consciousness" or for a physical reality, according as it is taken in one context or in another.[20]

---

[19]"Does Consciousness Exist?" in *Essays in Radical Empiricism*, vol. 3 of *The Works of William James* (1912; Cambridge, MA: Harvard University Press, 1976), 4–5.
[20]"The Place of Affectional Facts in a World of Pure Experience," in *Essays in Radical Empiricism*, 69.

The idea and the term stuff are clearly hypothetical ("we start with the supposition"). Stuff does not signify matter, not even in the sense of aboriginal substance, even though the term *materia prima* might insinuate this. The term "stuff" is a mere placeholder for an epistemologically as yet unspecified *that* which might be taken, had, thought about in a variety of—always metaphorical—ways. Pure experience accounts for the fact that things not only *are*, but *are known*. The very relationship of things being and being known at the same time is part of pure experience: this is one of the core tenets of radical empiricism. Pure experience allows for the emergence of a world that appears divided into subject and object; it also guarantees their aboriginal relatedness, coordination, identity. With the metaphor of the field, James elucidates aspects of pure experience that go beyond the vision of Being as both primary relatedness and, thus, as the unitary potential of differentiation into knower and known:

> The instant field of the present is at all times what I call "pure" experience. It is only virtually or potentially either object or subject as yet. For the time being, it is plain, unqualified actuality or existence, a simple *that*. In this *naïf* immediacy it is of course *valid*; it is *there*, we *act* upon it; and the doubling of it in retrospection into a state of mind and a reality intended thereby, is just one of the acts.[21]

Pure experience as the field of the present is "at all times" a valid *that* and *there*. This implies, in a wonderfully condensed and disciplined mode of presentation, that pure experience is a *Da*,[22] in Heidegger's sense implied in the term *Dasein*. It is the condition of the possibility of the unfolding of *here* and of *now*, of the time and the place we tend to attribute to ourselves as subjects and to things, to our world of objects, once we turn back on ("doubling … in retrospection") prior instances of pure experience, while pure experience continues to envelop us and our worlds in the very process of unfolding newly emerging contexts. Pure experience, then, allows for space and time without being determined by them; if it were, pure experience would only qualify as another conceptualized objective entity. The metaphor of the flux makes it possible for James to expand these implications of pure experience and account for what we could call the relationship of Being and *logos*:

> "Pure experience" is the name which I gave to the immediate flux of life which furnishes the material to our later reflection with its conceptual

---

[21]"Does Consciousness Exist?," 13.
[22]It is tempting to think about the possibility of James's thought as foreshadowing here both the conceptions of *Dasein* in Heidegger and the philosophy of place (Jap. *basho*) in later Nishida and in the work of Hajime Tanabe.

categories. Only new-born babes, or men in semi-coma from sleep, drugs, illnesses, or blows, may be assumed to have an experience pure in the literal sense of a *that* which is not yet any definite *what*, tho' ready to be all sorts of whats; full both of oneness and of manyness, but in respects that don't appear; changing throughout, yet so confusedly that its phases interpenetrate and no points, either of distinction or of identity, can be caught. Pure experience in this state is but another name for feeling or sensation. But the flux of it no sooner comes than it tends to fill itself with emphases, and these salient parts become identified and fixed and abstracted; so that experience now flows as if shot through with adjectives and nouns and prepositions and conjunctions. Its purity is only a relative term, meaning the proportional amount of unverbalized sensation which it still embodies.[23]

This is a clear and impressively concrete metaphorical visualization of the Jamesian intuition that Being as pure experience is an ongoing event that is both unified and endlessly differentiated, a mere unspecified, always antecedent and anterior[24] *that* or *there*, both present and in transition, a true *presence-ing* without specificity, a paradoxical plenitude without nameable content, a veritable no-thing-ness in action. Pure experience as an event[25] contingently issues in a verbalized and nameable world, in a *logos* to which humans may respond in speech. The purity of pure experience, James adds, hints at or designates that inexhaustible residue of the as yet unverbalized which—we may add—accounts for the central fact of the world as persistently emergent and therefore coherent dynamism and as realm of potential newness.

The three metaphors of the stuff, the field, and the flux supply experimental modes of indirect access to that which, by definition, avoids the definitive, whether in the perceptual or the conceptual mode. The three metaphors for pure experience help account for the way the knower and the known are aboriginally related; they convey a vision of a *there*, a place that provides both for temporal and spatial differentiation and for continuity; and they allow for the innovative emergent productivity of a realm within which we may name and rename, define and revise what we call a world or worlds.

---

[23] "The Thing and Its Relations," in *Essays in Radical Empiricism*, 46.

[24] It is important that James's ontic illustrations in which he uses the examples of newborn babes or men in semi-coma be always understood as implying the ontological dimension of pure experience. A wonderful example of a similar Japanese intuition relating childhood and pure experience (Buddha-mind) before differentiation is this poem by Shinkei (1406–75): "Such a mind is, indeed, / that of a Buddha! / The infant-child / is still free from drawing / distinctions"; *Zen Poems*, ed. Peter Harris (New York: Knopf, 1999), 187.

[25] One may, if one is inclined to be generously imaginative, detect a certain similarity between James's vision of pure experience as flux, as the ongoing event of non-determined Being, and the foundational conception of Chinese and Japanese (religious) ontology, the *dao*.

Before analyzing the specific difficulties of Nishida and other Asian thinkers in doing justice to James's innovative concept of pure experience, it may be useful to remind oneself that even thoroughly sympathetic contemporary American critics find it difficult to adequately render the elusive subtleties of James's vision. John E. Smith has rightly stressed the fact that James was "above all a thinker of participles";[26] that is to say, he was a thinker of ongoing events and of tendencies rather than of solidified facts and stable entities. In studying pure experience, James—according to Smith—not only overcomes the aporias of traditional atomistic empirical theories in the Humean tradition, he manages "to recover what we actually live through ... without the encumbrances of such habitual constructions as 'mind,' 'body,' 'subject,' etc."[27] This appreciation of James's attention to the actual existential event always preceding conceptualized entities does not, however, prevent Smith from criticizing the idea of pure experience thus:

> But the position is inadequate because the stream of experience does not contain all of the concepts and relations in terms of which it is to be understood and interpreted. ... The stream of experience is neither self-organizing nor self-interpreting. A world of pure experience consistently adhered to as a philosophical doctrine would lead, if not to a world of pure nonsense, at least to one of unreason.[28]

Smith obviously and quite wrongly identifies pure experience with experience as *had* by a subject, with what he calls direct experience. Pure experience, though, is not what we or anyone or anything *has*, it is what and how we *are*, a word for Being. Pure experience is also not a "world," not a matter of thinking in the sense of a "doctrine," not an object "to be understood and interpreted." In this respect David C. Lamberth's study *William James and the Metaphysics of Experience* does mark a decisive step forward in the direction of a more subtle understanding of pure experience as "a limit conception" indicating "both a state of being and a state of knowing."[29] Other than Smith, Lamberth realizes that for James "both concepts and percepts, as well as relations, must be understood to be functions of experience, rather than experience a function of concepts and percepts."[30] Lamberth clearly stresses the importance of James's vision of "the continuity of thought without a substantive soul (or transcendental ego)."[31] In a thorough appreciation of

---

[26]John E. Smith, "The Reconception of Experience in Peirce, James and Dewey," in Smith, *America's Philosophical Vision* (Chicago: University of Chicago Press, 1992), 26.
[27]Ibid., 27.
[28]Smith, "Radical Empiricism," in *America's Philosophical Vision*, 83.
[29]Lamberth, *William James*, 43, 35.
[30]Ibid., 40–1.
[31]Ibid., 88.

the necessity of metaphorical indirection he tries to approximate James's ultimately inexpressible sense of Being by naming it "a continuous stream of fields."[32] But in spite of all this care Lamberth nevertheless occasionally lapses into a way of speaking which recalls the old dualist preconceptions concerning experience which are so woefully inadequate when we deal with James. One example is Lamberth's notion that pure experience is "the meeting point of the objective and the subjective,"[33] just as if these seemingly indestructible entities preceded experience in the purity of its foundational *there-* and *that-ness*. These observations on more recent American criticism of James may induce an appropriate leniency when we now turn toward a reconstruction of the story of Japanese ways of at the same time engaging and distancing James's thought.

# II

*An Inquiry into the Good*, Kitarô Nishida's first book, was published just one year after the death of William James. The basic term, concept, idea, or vision is that of pure experience, on which Nishida bases his projects of an ontology, an ethics, and a philosophy of religion.[34] The book as a whole is characterized "by intensity and eloquence ... coupled with [a] comprehensive assimilation of central ideas in Western philosophy," especially ideas of the British philosophical psychologists Bain and Stout and, most importantly, of James and Josiah Royce.[35] At the same time, Nishida achieved a novel perspective "in terms of an Eastern way of seeing renewed by Western thought or of a Western way of thinking renewed by an Eastern way of seeing."[36] It was above all the function of the idea and concept *and* vision of pure experience to provide the ground where Eastern, predominantly Zen Buddhist, and Western, especially Jamesian, intuitions of Being could meet. This is why the focus of the following reconstruction of the scope and limitations of Nishida's interpretation of pure experience will be its ontological dimension. Only in this way is it possible to adequately evaluate the modes of Nishida's appropriation of the Jamesian vision as it has been introduced and characterized above.

---

[32]Ibid., 93.
[33]Ibid., 30.
[34]Rolf Elberfeld, "Einleitung," in Kitaro Nishida, *Logik des Ortes: Der Anfang der modernen Philosophie in Japan*, trans. Rolf Elberfeld (Darmstadt: WBG, 1999), 4–5.
[35]D. S. Clarke, Jr., "Introduction," in Nishitani, *Nishida Kitarô*, ix.
[36]Nishitani, *Nishida Kitarô*, 40–1. Nishitani's dichotomies are problematic, though: he stereotypes both philosophical cultures by identifying "thought" with the West and "vision" with the East. His appreciation of William James on this basis will almost necessarily prove not quite satisfactory.

One of the most condensed statements on pure experience as the basis of his philosophical project in his early works is this passage from Nishida's preface to the first edition of *An Inquiry into the Good* in 1911:

> Over time I came to realize that it is not that experience exists because there is an individual, but that an individual exists because there is experience. I thus arrived at the idea that experience is more fundamental than individual differences, and in this way I was able to avoid solipsism.[37]

This is a rather precise equivalent of James's idea in *The Principles of Psychology* that experience as the stream of thought *tends toward* personality formation, and of his argument in "Does Consciousness Exist?" concerning the *a posteriori* position of the subject (and the object in relation to pure experience. It is, however, worth noting that Nishida calls (pure) experience "more fundamental" than individualized existence. It is possible to read this as a tendency to attribute a universally substantialist character to (pure) experience whereas James, as we saw, is inclined to refrain from characterizing pure experience as either individual or universal, fundamental or phenomenal. James's reticence prevents him from falling back on metaphysical and foundationalist positions. Instead, he implicitly approaches that Eastern vision so well known from Zen texts that avoids the ascription of any characteristic whatsoever to the "nothing that is"—in Wallace Stevens's words from his poem "The Snow Man."[38]

In his preface to the 1936 printing of *An Inquiry into the Good*, Nishida says: "The world of action-intuition—the world of poiesis—is none other than the world of pure experience."[39] With the concept of action-intuition, Nishida had moved back into the speculative metaphysical foundationalism of the German idealists, in this case of Fichte.[40] The two passages from the Prefaces of 1911 and 1936, respectively, indicate a tendency which is already implicitly present in *An Inquiry into the Good* itself, a tendency to occasionally jeopardize the radical modernism of Jamesian thought, which can be seen as ideally suited for the integration of traditional Asian ontological and religious intuitions concerning absolute nothingness as the proper word for Being. There are early, even if faint, indications of an

---

[37]Nishida, *Inquiry*, xxx.
[38]For a Zen interpretation of this poem, see Robert Aitken, "Wallace Stevens and Zen," in *Original Dwelling Place: Zen Buddhist Essays* (Washington: Counterpoint, 1997), 188–93. Such readings help us to understand the extraordinary contiguity of some American modernist modes of thought or forms of sensibility and of Asian ways of interpreting existence.
[39]Nishida, *Inquiry*, xxxiii.
[40]See Kogaku Arifuku, "Fichte und Nishida: Intellektuelle Anschauung versus handelnde Anschauung," in *Komparative Philosophie: Begegnungen zwischen östlichen und westlichen Denkwegen*, ed. Rolf Elberfeld et al. (Munich: Fink, 1998), 25–38.

inclination to abandon or correct the Jamesian point of view in favor of a traditionalist, metaphysical, predominantly European conceptualization. Detailed analyses of Nishida's meditations on pure experience in the opening chapters of *An Inquiry into the Good* may substantiate this suspicion.

The first part of Nishida's book and the first chapter of that first part are both entitled "Pure Experience," and the philosopher most frequently referred to in the text and the footnotes throughout the first fourteen of a total of thirty-two chapters in the book is William James. These first fourteen chapters could be called the ontology of Nishida's early philosophy. In order to denote or hint at or talk about Being, Nishida, like James, does not only use the term "pure experience": the terms "consciousness," "reality," "sole reality," and "principle" are used, as it seems, interchangeably. The first and probably most significant "trait" of pure experience is its unmediated presence:

> To experience means to know facts just as they are, to know in accordance with facts by completely relinquishing one's own fabrications. What we usually refer to as experience is adulterated with some sort of thought, so by *pure* I am referring to the state of experience just as it is without the least addition of deliberative discrimination. ... When one directly experiences one's own state of consciousness, there is not yet a subject or an object, and knowing and its object are completely unified. This is the most refined type of experience.[41]

Like James, Nishida cannot quite avoid occasional problems in properly articulating his awareness of what the presence of pure experience means. If pure experience is anterior to both subject and object, it does not make much sense to speak of "one" directly experiencing "one's own state of consciousness" because this kind of rhetoric presupposes the very subject-object dichotomy to be overcome. James began with a similar mode of speaking about pure experience in *The Principles of Psychology* before his deepened understanding allowed him more refined ways of addressing the problem in *Essays in Radical Empiricism*.

In a second step Nishida tries to emphasize the temporal and semantic implications of pure experiencing. He argues that "pure experience has no meaning whatsoever, it is simply a present consciousness of facts just as they are."[42] It is questionable in the context of both James's and Nishida's writings whether pure experience is properly addressed as "consciousness *of* facts" and not rather as presence of Being. The important point here, however, is the emphasis on the pure givenness of pure experience, its present, wordless

---

[41]Nishida, *Inquiry*, 3–4.
[42]Ibid., 4.

authority as a mere *that* which is not yet a *what*, as James had more subtly explained. The presence of pure experience, Nishida adds, is not a *subject-matter* of awareness: "The present of pure experience is not the present in thought, for once one thinks about the present, it is no longer present."[43] Having stressed the un-mediated and radically present character of pure experience, Nishida turns toward what he calls its unity: "The directness and purity of pure experience derive not from the experience's being simple, unanalyzable, or instantaneous, but from the strict unity of consciousness."[44]

The "unity of consciousness" is here used as a kind of synonym of pure experience. Like James, Nishida allows for both simplicity and complexity in pure experience. Nishida, however, begins to think about pure experience in a troublingly metaphysical way as something that is not simply there, mere Being in its pure suchness, but as *derived* from, maybe grounded in something both intimately related (consciousness) and different at the same time. This, as it seems, innocent and "merely" rhetorical slippage indicates a problem Nishida has in accepting the radically innovative vision of James. Such deviations from the Jamesian intuition will lead toward a resumption of more traditionalist (European) perspectives. In certain basic respects, on the other hand, Nishida continues to follow James. This becomes apparent when he insists on the fact that there "is no fundamental distinction between internal and external in experience, and what makes an experience pure is its unity, not its kind."[45] Nishida's sense of the unity of pure experience, however, seems to differ from the Jamesian understanding. James believes in the un-circumscribed oneness of an open field, in a homogeneous, continuous expanse. Nishida moves in the direction of a more traditional view that posits a unified and therefore delimited entity. He begins by adapting a Jamesian terminology to convey his own sense of how pure experience occurs as a unifying event: "When a consciousness starts to emerge, a unifying activity—in the form of a feeling of inclination—accompanies it. This activity directs our attention, and it is unconscious when the unity is strict or undisturbed from without."[46]

Nishida quite obviously utilizes James's ideas about the function of feelings of tendency in organizing the stream of consciousness, when he speaks of "a feeling of inclination" and its contribution to the unification of pure experience.[47] In the next paragraph, however, Nishida moves forward into

---

[43]Ibid., 5.
[44]Ibid., 6.
[45]Ibid., 7.
[46]Ibid., 8.
[47]It is obvious that the translators did not pay detailed attention to Nishida's reworking of Jamesian terminology in Japanese. For someone who has no command of the language, it is impossible to ascertain whether Nishida's use of "inclination" for "tendency" is a matter of philosophical choice or a problem of translation. Similarly, the unfortunate term "unconscious"

the past. Introducing the concept of the will in a way reminiscent of Fichte and/or Schopenhauer, he argues concerning the unity of pure experience:

> the mode of the development of consciousness is, in a broad sense, the mode of the development of the will, and the aforementioned unifying inclination is the goal of the will. ... The essence of the will lies not in desire concerning the future but in present activity. ... In fact, the zenith of this unifying activity is the will.[48]

The active or dynamic aspect of pure experience in its emergence into unity is determined by the metaphysical entity of the will, a faculty possessed of an unchanging and obviously definable essence. This idealistic argument is saved from being a total anachronism in the context of Nishida's analysis of pure experience by the insight that the will is not *teleological* but, rather, that the will is itself by willing itself. Nishida speaks of pure experience in its dynamic aspect, in its becoming, as the will to will—which is exactly the way Heidegger later described the last metaphysical stance of Western ontology in Nietzsche.

There are other instances of an uncertain wavering between traditional foundationalist metaphysics and modernism in Nishida's utilization of Western thinking. On the one hand, he believes that thinking, *other than* willing, guarantees an apperceptive unity within experience that is merely subjective; on the other hand, he approves of James's argument in "The World of Pure Experience" that thinking *like* willing "constitutes" [sic] pure experience.[49] The chapter on "Thinking" ends on this undecided note. A preliminary summary of the relationship of thinking and pure experience reads like a variation on motifs by Hegel mediated by Josiah Royce:

> Because pure experience is a systematic development, the unifying force that functions at its foundation is the universality of concepts; the development of experience corresponds to the advance of thinking; and the facts of pure experience are the self-actualization of the universal. Even in the case of sensations and associations of ideas, a concealed unifying activity operates in the background.[50]

---

in the preceding quotation may be the result of a language problem. It might be argued that—like James in a related context—Nishida here speaks of a non-reflexive awareness. See also Joel W. Krueger, "The Varieties of Pure Experience: William James and Kitaro Nishida on Consciousness and Embodiment," *William James Studies* 1 (2006). Available online at williamjamesstudies.org.

[48]Nishida, *Inquiry*, 8.
[49]Ibid., 8, 13.
[50]Ibid., 17.

The tentative character of Nishida's early work as a whole shows in the fact that the introduction of the "universality of concepts" is sudden and unprepared. The idea of the universal implies a transcendental point of view whereas the emphasis on "sensations and associations of ideas" shifts back into the empirical. Lastly, the (unidentified) "concealed unifying activity ... in the background" endows the whole paragraph with the air of a (late) idealist speculation on the realizations of the absolute and the substantialist underpinnings of all awareness.

The real and concluding summary of chapter 2 "Thinking"—by way of contrast—reads like a Jamesian critique of the preliminary summary. One is immediately reminded of James's radical empiricist demolition of idealist rationalism in *A Pluralist Universe*:

> In summary, thinking and experience are identical. Although we can see a relative difference, there is no absolute distinction between them. I am not saying that thinking is merely individual and subjective. Pure experience can, as discussed earlier, transcend the individual person. Although it may sound strange, experience knows time, space, and the individual person and so it is beyond them. It is not that there is experience because there is an individual, but that there is an individual because there is experience. The individual's experience is simply a small, distinctive sphere of limited experience within true experience.[51]

In this paragraph Nishida understands thinking in James's sense of an active awareness that obviously includes categories, percepts, and concepts. Fields of experience are wider than individual selves, as James had argued in *A Pluralistic Universe*, where he had appropriated and transformed the speculations of Gustav Theodor Fechner.[52] This analysis of experience is an ontic, an empirical, and not a transcendental argument as was the preceding comment on thinking as the self-actualization of the universal through concepts. The two approaches are not mediated or reconciled; Nishida's thought remains undecided between traditionalist, idealist European approaches and a modern, post-metaphysical reconstruction of thinking in the American grain.

The most important aspect of the summary of "Thinking," however, is Nishida's Jamesian intuition that experience precedes, permits, issues in, shows as individuals and as time and as space. Pure experience is neither one nor many; it is neither temporal nor atemporal, neither localized nor cosmic and universal. Nishida allows pure experience to assume the

---

[51]Ibid., 19.

[52]Nishida occasionally refers to Fechner and one does get the impression that his references and quotations were inspired by or taken over from James.

full Jamesian, radical empiricist meaning of Being as expressed in "Does Consciousness Exist?" and "The Thing and Its Relations." As such it is emptied of distinctions and entities and yet it allows all kinds of *whats* to emerge and to be.[53] It is in statements like the conclusion of the chapter on "Thinking" that the intimate relationship, the true convergence of Nishida's background in Zen and James's post-metaphysical vision become apparent. Thomas Merton has clearly identified this congruence of the two modes of thinking:

> But the chief characteristic of Zen is that it rejects all these systematic elaborations [of discursive philosophical thinking] in order to get back, as far as possible, to the pure unarticulated and unexplained ground of direct experience ... "In this sense Buddhism is radical empiricism or experientialism."[54]

This insight into the congruence of Eastern and Jamesian thinking is so important for Nishida that he keeps returning to it whenever he attempts to incorporate another traditional European category in his endeavor to articulate his and the Japanese sense of Being in terms of Western thought, namely, when he speaks of the fact that all categories including time, space, and individuality emerge from Being as pure experience in its undivided state. Schelling's *intellektuale Anschauung* is made to stand for pure experience in this way: "from the standpoint of pure experience in the strict sense, experience is not bound to such forms as time, space, and individual persons; rather, these discriminations derive from an intuition that transcends them."[55]

Intellectual intuition is appropriated by Nishida, in order to function in his various approaches toward a clarification of the meaning of pure experience, in the same fashion in which he had already used the idea of the will or the concept of the self-actualization of the universal. The problem, however, seems to be that Nishida cannot enact the same radical turn away from metaphysics which we find in James because he allows the terminology of European rationalism and of idealism to function as an aid toward a definition of pure experience, and not merely as indirect or metaphorical indicators of an entity or event beyond the reach of ordinary language and philosophical discourse. In short, he does not sufficiently heed James's injunction to keep the "term indeterminate."

---

[53]See Lamberth, *William James*, 39: "In contrast to Kant, James's notion of experience is both ontologically fundamental and potentially indeterminate ..."
[54]Thomas Merton, "A Christian Looks at Zen," in *Zen and the Birds of Appetite* (New York: New Directions, 1968), 36–7. Merton is quoting D. T. Suzuki.
[55]Nishida, *Inquiry*, 31.

In spite of these limitations, Nishida works his argumentative way toward an expression of his vision that repeatedly at least approximates the Jamesian intensity and profundity. With chapters 7 "The True Features of Reality" and 8 "True Reality Constantly Has the Same Formative Mode,' the ontological project begins to reach its completion. Nishida keeps returning to this statement:

> In pure experience, our thinking, feeling, and willing are still undivided; there is a single activity, with no opposition between subject and object. Such opposition arises from the demands of thinking, so it is not a fact of direct experience. In direct experience there is only an independent, self-sufficient event, with neither a subject that sees nor an object that is seen.[56]

The single activity, the Jamesian event of thinking going on—or, in other words, the flux of life or the stream of consciousness—incorporates and predates thinking, feeling, and willing. This means that Nishida tries to find a common ground for the faculties and activities of the mental apparatus as it was interpreted by traditional philosophy. For Nishida this common ground, then, is pure experience. In addition, the quotation does offer an interesting new insight into the unresolved tensions that have emerged so far in Nishida's experiment of mediating a Jamesian, a Japanese or Zen Buddhist, and a conventional European idealist position. Obviously without becoming aware of it, Nishida uses the term *thinking* in two senses. Firstly, it is an aspect of pure experience and may mean thinking as James understood it, the awareness of Being. Secondly, thinking is used to designate the activity of apprehending givens, or facts, or beings in a world that is characterized by dualism, by the "opposition between subject and object." This ambiguity is another indicator of the fact that Nishida's great project hovers—without satisfactory resolution—between the alternatives offered by idealist traditionalism and Jamesian modernism.

One last aspect of the basic, even if neither consistent nor persistent, agreement between James and Nishida in conveying a view of Being as pure experience is dealt with in chapter 9, "The Fundamental Mode of True Reality." In *The Principles of Psychology*, James had indicated his sense of the compatibility of identity and difference within the stream of consciousness as one of the ways in which pure experience may be approached indirectly and metaphorically. Nishida says:

> On a fundamental level, contradiction and unity are simply two views of one and the same thing. Because there is unity there is contradiction, and

---

[56]Ibid., 48. Variations of this statement may be found on pages 49 and 51.

because there is contradiction there is unity ... The fundamental mode of reality is such that reality is one while it is many and many while it is one; in the midst of equality it maintains distinctions, and in the midst of distinctions it maintains equality.[57]

In his comments, Masao Abe, the editor and translator of Nishida's book, has pointed out that these ideas were to be developed in Nishida's later work under the heading of "absolute contradictory self-identity" and that they were indebted to the Mahayana Buddhist view of the identity of distinctions and equality.[58] At the same time, it is obvious that Nishida also echoes James's analyses of pure experience in "The Thing and Its Relations," where James had emphasized pure experience as the coexistence, the identity of a manifold and a unified entity. Once again, we encounter the correspondences and agreements between the Japanese (Buddhist), the Jamesian, and Nishida's ontological intuition.

Chapter 10 of *An Inquiry into the Good*, with the title "The Sole Reality," promises a concentrated exposition of the insights gathered during the preceding ontological meditations. Given Nishida's terminological and philosophical vacillations in chapters 1 through 9, it does not come as a total surprise that he should, once again, jeopardize the Jamesian point of view and its innovative potential by reverting to outmoded and almost tritely conventional European strategies of explication and summary statement. Like James, Nishida believes that it is pure experience that allows time, space, and beings to emerge; like James, he does not posit a world disposed spatially and temporally in an *a priori* fashion. But Nishida's relapse into nineteenth-century patterns of European thought occurs when he tries to essentialize pure experience in a foundationalist way. We read:

The unifying activity of consciousness [i.e., pure experience] is not controlled by time; on the contrary, time is established by the unifying activity. At the base of consciousness there is a *transcendent, unchanging reality apart* from time ... There is *always a certain unchanging reality at the base of mind* ... All people believe that there is *a fixed, unchanging principle* in the universe and that all things are established according to it ... Just as a principle is the same no matter who thinks about it, at the base of our consciousness there is *something universal*. By means of it we are able to communicate with and understand one another. *Universal reason* runs throughout the base of our minds.[59]

---

[57]Ibid., 56–7.
[58]Ibid., 56–7 n.1-2.
[59]Ibid., 60–2 (my emphasis).

James had kept the term "pure experience" truly indeterminate. In this way he could account for Being as ongoing awareness without establishing it as a separate and substantialist entity. Pure experience as a no-thing, as "the nothing that is," makes plural worlds possible; it lets identity and difference, time, space, and individuals be. There is no need to account for such ultimately incomprehensible events as creation or determination by means of which everything that *is* owes its very Being to something else, something ultimately alien. Nishida's "transcendent, unchanging reality," the forever fixed "principle," or "universal reason" revive the by then outmoded and discredited metaphysical *Hinterwelten* from Plato and Aristotle through Hegel. At the same time, the very terminology Nishida uses in such cases can be understood as a betrayal of the non-metaphysical Buddhist ontology with its ultimately wordless insight into *sunyata*, the plenitude of emptiness, which is a truly indeterminate term. If compared to the Buddhist view, James's interpretation of pure experience does offer, if not an identical, then at least a corresponding and responsive view. Nishida had sensed this. His attempt to articulate Being as pure experience is both refined in terms of its modernist reconstruction of the native Zen Buddhist tradition and in its tentative approximation of the analogous Jamesian belief. If one understands Nishida's project in *An Inquiry into the Good* in this way, one is tempted to treat his intermittent metaphysical evasions and his corresponding terminological lapses with the gruff amiability James showed in his reactions to Royce's idealism: "Damn the Absolute!"[60]

It is therefore fitting and a sign of respect if one ends these critical remarks on Nishida's impressive, but often fitful and inconsistent, appropriation of James's radical empiricist analysis of pure experience with a quotation from Nishida and a comment that allow a glimpse of further productive possibilities for a comparative study of these two major thinkers:

> The state of consciousness in which subject and object have dissolved into the union of thinking, feeling, and willing is true reality. Independent, self-sufficient true reality manifests itself in the form of this union. We must realize the true state of this reality with our entire being rather than reflect on it, analyze it, or express it in words.[61]

This is an early indication in *An Inquiry into the Good* that the ontological analysis of true reality as pure experience is the preparation of an (religiously grounded) ethics: "We must realize the true state of this reality with our entire being rather than reflect on it, analyze it, or express it in words." James's work as a whole may also be read as an attempt to provide the

---

[60]*Letters* 2, 134–5.
[61]Nishida, *Inquiry*, 51.

ontological foundations for a proper kind of conduct and for a religious awareness. *The Will to Believe* and *The Varieties of Religious Experience* are different realizations of this ethically and existentially motivated study of religious attitudes and experiences.[62] In the chapter "The Continuity of Experience" in *A Pluralistic Universe*, James also pointed to the absolute necessity of an *existential* realization of the wordless presence of what we call pure experience or Being, a realization "with our entire being," which a Zen Buddhist might call *practice*. James says:

> As long as one continues *talking*, intellectualism remains in undisturbed possession of the field. The return to life can't come about by talking. It is an *act*; to make you return to life, I must set an example for your imitation, I must deafen you to talk, or to the importance of talk, by showing you ... that the concepts we talk with are made for purposes of *practice* and not for purposes of insight. Or I must *point*, point to the mere *that* of life, and you by inner sympathy must fill out the *what* for yourselves.[63]

A serious meditation on James's words reveals that in 1909 he prepares the paradox at the core of Nishida's verbal injunction to go beyond language in the existential realization of pure experience, a paradox that is also constitutive of the Zen Buddhist tradition of talking and writing about direct transmission of religious awareness without or outside of texts. James privileges practice over intellectualized talk. We appreciate what he says only if we understand practice as (moral and existential and religious) conduct. James, the teacher, can achieve this goal only by paradoxically telling his students to ignore (his) language, or by pointing. One may be pardoned if one is, maybe legitimately, tempted here to be blasphemous and compare James's urgent injunction to wordlessly become aware of the "mere *that* of life" with the Buddha's flower sermon, so often invoked as the initial moment of the Zen Buddhist tradition. It is thus not only James's ontological intuition, it is the total endeavor of his thinking which offered Nishida a so-called Western rendition and model of that awareness of Being and its ethical and religious consequences which constitute the center of his own both different and identical philosophical quest.[64]

---

[62]See Lamberth, *William James*, 6 and *passim*. It is one of the central theses of Lamberth's book that the idea of pure experience, the philosophy of radical empiricism, and James's meditations on religion are intimately related.

[63]*Pluralistic Universe*, 131.

[64]See Clarke, "Introduction," in Nishitani, *Nishida Kitarô*, viii: "[In Nishida's *An Inquiry into the Good*] the term 'pure experience' used by the nineteenth century psychologists was introduced and given a novel interpretation in terms of a special kind of religious experience." It is the argument of this essay that a similar statement might be made about James as Nishida's source of inspiration.

# III

Keiji Nishitani's study of Kitarô Nishida's development as a thinker, with special emphasis on the seminal importance of *An Inquiry into the Good*, is one of the most significant Japanese responses to Nishida's philosophy and one of the most interesting attempts to assess his place in a global philosophical context. It is also a good starting point for a study and an evaluation of ideologically or culturally determined misreadings of this very context, and especially of William James's crucial role in the emergence of the thinking of the Kyôto School. Together with Nishida himself and Hajime Tanabe, Nishitani belongs to the founding fathers of this prestigious philosophical movement.

Nishitani begins the extensive chapter "Nishida's Place in Philosophy" by quoting Nishida to the effect that it is mandatory, for any appropriate evaluation of a thinker, to find "a kind of intellectual intuition at work behind all thinking," a "unifying intuition."[65] In the light of Nishitani's misapprehension of James's importance for Nishida and of his not quite adequate analysis of James's philosophy, it is ironically revealing that Nishida's and Nishitani's concern with the "unifying intuition" should so obviously echo this passage from James's *A Pluralistic Universe*:

> Place yourself ... at the centre of a man's philosophic vision and you understand at once all the different things it makes him write or say. But keep outside, use your post-mortem method, try to build the philosophy up out of the single phrases, taking first one and then another and seeking to make them fit "logically," and of course you fail. You crawl over the thing like a myopic ant over a building, tumbling into every microscopic crack or fissure, finding nothing but inconsistencies, and never suspecting that a centre exists.[66]

Nishitani sets out to find this center, this unifying intuition in Nishida. He fails to do so in the case of James. Basically, Nishitani interprets Nishida's philosophy as a critical response to the challenges of science and materialism and to their threat to religious awareness and the importance of the inner life. The split, as Nishitani sees it, between experience and metaphysics in Western thought could not be overcome by Western thought itself: "Based on [a] two-world theory, traditional Western philosophy has proved virtually incapable of establishing a standpoint of transcendence while maintaining a foothold in experience and fact."[67]

---

[65]Nishitani, *Nishida Kitarô*, 66.
[66]*Pluralistic Universe*, 117.
[67]Nishitani, *Nishida Kitarô*, 71.

This view is the somewhat dubious premise for Nishitani's evaluation of Nishida's supposedly unique achievement and for his inadequate appreciation of James's significance as *the* central philosophical figure on the threshold of modern globalized thinking. Firstly, it is obvious and generally accepted that James overcame and discarded traditional Cartesian dualism. Secondly, it is as obvious that James, in his vehement attacks on the scientific positivism of, for example, Clifford, strove to provide a basis for belief in experience. James's thought offers the very foothold in experience for any kind of religious (transcendent—in Nishitani's words) orientation that Nishitani demands. Nishitani acknowledges the importance of the idea of pure experience in turn-of-the-century Western psychology but then goes on to say, without explanation, "that philosophies based on this approach" are not "particularly important."[68] In describing the historical moment in which Nishida's thinking emerged, Nishitani states:

> The problem called for a philosophy that would keep its feet firmly planted in immediate and pure experience ... and yet be able to offer new answers to the same fundamental questions that the old metaphysics had addressed. ...
>
> In other words, we must ask again whether or not the pure experience we are talking about is truly immediate experience prior to any device. The question carries with it the call for a new metaphysics different from a philosophy grounded only in psychology.[69]

It is clear that Nishitani does not believe that Jamesian thought is philosophical. He thinks of James as a psychologist, a scientist, a metaphysical dualist, whose idea of pure experience is "not truly immediate" because it is only "subjectively immediate."[70] This is a seriously deficient interpretation of James's view. Nishitani's critical reconstruction of pure experience in Nishida is elegant and philosophically impressive. At the same time, however, he continues to address the "psychologists"—and above all James—as incapable of thinking such thoughts because "they are viewing experience from the outside, not as the occasion of a true unity of subject and object."[71] Nishitani rightly asserts that what "we usually call mind and matter, or spirit and body, do[es] not belong to pure experience but [is] only the result of artificial constructs added to it."[72] This, however,—and there is no need to belabor the point—is exactly the unifying intuition of James's

---

[68]Ibid., 75.
[69]Ibid., 77, 79.
[70]Ibid., 79.
[71]Ibid., 82.
[72]Ibid., 84.

thinking in *Essays in Radical Empiricism*, the kind of intuition that Nishitani believes to be central for the appreciation of any thinker. Nishitani credits James with having acknowledged relations as indispensable ingredients of experience, but he does not allow or admit that James could think a truly monistic concept of pure experience like Nishida—as a Western thinker, James, this is the necessary implication and presupposition, was *essentially, constitutionally*, and *culturally* unable to do this. The prejudices inherent in and germane to Nishitani's cultural politics and his insufficient attention to James's "unifying intuition" are the foundation for his cavalier dismissal of James's overpowering presence as a thinker and for the assertion of Nishida's philosophically singular achievement in dealing with the ontological, existential, and religious significance of the purity of pure experience. One is tempted to call Nishitani's position a philosophical variant of *nihonjin-on*, the ideology of Japanese exceptionalism. His refusal to accept James's crucial role in the formation of modern Japanese thinking possesses a curious complement in the fact that he does not identify Nishida's intermittent terminological and thematic borrowings from German idealism, especially from Fichte, Hegel, and Schelling, as violations or at least temporary eclipses of that consistent radical empiricist position of Nishida's that he has identified as the "unifying intuition."

Few scholars—with the possible exception of D. T. Suzuki in the field of the philosophy of religion—have done so much to promote intercultural understanding between Eastern and Western philosophical positions as Masao Abe.[73] His work as a cultural mediator, especially between Japan and the United States, was duly and deservedly celebrated with an impressive *Festschrift* on the occasion of his eightieth birthday in 1998.[74] His introduction to his own and Christopher Ives's translation of *An Inquiry into the Good*, however, is another example of the difficulties Japanese scholars and thinkers have in adequately understanding and evaluating the globally relevant role of William James in the formation Nishida's philosophy. The misreadings of Nishitani and Abe show interesting similarities and significant differences. In distinguishing two kinds of philosophy, a desire for "a purely rational and theoretical system based on logical thinking" and "an existential, religiously oriented discipline,"[75] Abe believes that traditional Eastern thought is closer to thinkers like Augustine, Schopenhauer, and Kierkegaard than to Descartes, Kant, and Hegel. This leads to the rather curious generalization that whereas in the East "philosophy and religion are originally undifferentiated and inseparable," in the West "philosophy and religion occupy two different

[73]See the essays in Masao Abe, *Zen and Western Thought*, ed. William R. LaFleur (Honolulu: University of Hawaii Press, 1985).

[74]*Masao Abe: A Zen Life of Dialogue*, ed. Donald W. Mitchell (Boston: Tuttle, 1998).

[75]Abe, "Introduction," in Nishida, *Inquiry*, viii.

arenas."[76] It is Abe's strategy to create relatively clear oppositions between the two philosophical cultures, his own examples to the contrary, like Augustine, notwithstanding. The task of a modernized Eastern thinking, then, is to "go beyond the demonstrative thinking that is characteristic of the West."[77] Abe's abstract theses serve an interesting implicit purpose: they erase the possibility of modes of thinking in the West that might be identical with or similar to traditional or modernist Eastern thought in important respects. Abe insists that the lack of logic and purely theoretical doctrines in the East implies a preference for "the unity of practice and knowledge."[78] He also says that the "Eastern way of thinking is qualitatively different from the Western with its emphasis on verbal and conceptual expression."[79] In this way, two central and indispensable elements of Jamesian thinking—the pragmatist credo with its emphasis on precisely "the unity of practice and knowledge" and the attack on conceptualist intellectualism—are claimed as essentially Eastern. This makes it possible for Abe to ignore important facets in James as sources of inspiration for Nishida.

Other than Nishitani, Abe accepts the anti-dualist and anti-metaphysical tendencies in James's philosophy whose concept of pure experience, however, he blithely equates with that of Mach and Wundt, without regard for fundamental and insuperable differences between the philosophical traditionalism of Mach and Wundt and James's radical innovation. In this way, the philosophical achievement of James is severely diminished:

> [James, Mach, and Wundt] generated a philosophical standpoint by reducing experience to its pure and direct form. Behind the emergence of this kind of philosophy loomed the historical situation of mistrust of both traditional metaphysics and two-world theories and dissatisfaction with positivism and materialistic philosophy.[80]

It is rather difficult to understand why James's insistence on pure experience as *materia prima* should be a reduction whereas Nishida's version is lauded as the basis of a future philosophy.[81] Abe also evaluates Nishida's references to Fichte as a positive trait, even though he had just praised the overcoming of traditional metaphysics as intellectual progress. The strategy in Abe's attempt to deny a productive dialogue between James and Nishida becomes painfully obvious, however, as soon as he paraphrases several of Nishida's objections to Western concepts of pure experience, uttered in an

---

[76]Ibid.
[77]Ibid., x.
[78]Ibid., viii.
[79]Ibid., ix.
[80]Ibid., xiii–xiv.
[81]Ibid., xiv.

(untranslated) essay written in 1911, the same year *An Inquiry into the Good* was published. These are Abe's summary renditions of Nishida's criticism of Western ideas of pure experience:

> First, they explain pure experience on the basis of many uncritical assumptions, such as the claim that experience is individual and conforms to the categories of time, space, and causality. ...
>
> Second, they grasp pure experience not from within but from without, thus missing the true reality of pure experience. To see it from without means to analyze the concrete, dynamic whole of pure experience into abstract psychological elements like perception, feeling, and representation, and then to reconstruct them. In this explanation, living individual experience is generalized.
>
> Third, true pure experience is direct experience, that is, experience direct to the subject. But in the above psychological philosophies, the observed consciousness and the observing consciousness stand dualistically opposed. Consequently, pure experience observed in this way is not direct experience.[82]

It is more than obvious that these strictures do apply to some of Mach's and Wundt's relatively simplistic analyses. It is equally obvious that James does *not* conceive of experience as merely individual or as dependent on time and space. It is obvious that James does *not* look at pure experience from without; his intuitional approach is clear and unequivocal. It is obvious that James radically *negates* any dualistic implications of his interpretations. Rather, we did observe that Nishida tends to universalize and generalize "living individual experience" when he relapses into conceptions like "transcendent, unchanging reality," or a "fixed, unchanging principle," or "universal reason."[83] In addition to this, it is fairly curious that, according to Abe, Nishida should, firstly, criticize James's (and the others') vision of pure experience as individual and then, in the second critical point, complain of his generalizing "living individual experience."

Abe goes on to contrast his sense of Nishida's achievement with the Jamesian position by interpreting two elaborate diagrams.[84] They are supposed to show that Nishida is the proponent of the idea that there is an individual because there is experience, whereas James et al. insist on experience as dependent on the antecedent existence of an individual. No sincere reading of *Essays in Radical Experience* would allow such a

---

[82]Ibid., xv.
[83]Nishida, *Inquiry*, 61–2.
[84]Abe, "Introduction," xvi–xvii.

conclusion. Abe finally praises Nishida's "unique" philosophical achievement as summarized in three points:

1. Pure experience is realized prior to the distinction between subject and object. ...

2. Pure experience is active and constructive ...

3. In pure experience, knowledge, feeling, and volition are undifferentiated.[85]

This is certainly an astute and appropriate interpretation of Nishida's position. At the same time, Abe in spite of himself wonderfully summarizes James's central vision since 1890.

Abe differs from Nishitani in accepting a tentative movement in Western thought in the direction of Nishida's central post-metaphysical and monistic intuition. Like Nishitani, however, he nevertheless essentializes both perspectives. This leads to the elimination of differences between European and American, between relatively traditionalist and radically innovative positions. The result of Abe's endeavor is that he credits Nishida with the sole authorship of his remarkable insights instead of revealing the far more interesting active and productive dialogue between two major philosophical personalities and between Japanese and American original thought.

Nobuo Kazashi represents a Japanese *and* a cosmopolitan point of view in the ongoing critical re-evaluation of the dialogue between James and European as well as Asian philosophy. In a 1998 paper, read at the Twentieth World Congress of Philosophy in Boston, Kazashi is interested in the, to him, obvious and "clear convergence of the most fundamental concern ... to bring to light the ontologically primordial layer of experience" in James's radical empiricism, in Nishida's *An Inquiry into the Good*, and in the phenomenology of Maurice Merleau-Ponty.[86] Kazashi appreciates James's world historical position in transforming and overcoming Cartesian dualism. Here he joins Whitehead's well-known view and admiration of James. In abandoning a dualist metaphysics, Kazashi argues, "James also transformed the very design of modern Western philosophy in such a way as to, without knowing it, open its stage to the Eastern philosophical tradition."[87] In the light of the earlier Japanese attempts to obscure James's seminal role in transforming Japanese philosophy, it is truly fascinating to come across this 1910 statement by Nishida as translated by Kazashi: "These days I have

---

[85]Ibid., xvii–xviii.
[86]Nobuo Kazashi, "The World Becomes the Self's Body: James, Merleau-Ponty, and Nishida," in *PAIDEIA: Comparative Philosophy* (Papers of the Twentieth World Congress of Philosophy, Boston, August, 12–15, 1998), http://www.bu.edu/wcp/Papers/Comp/CompKaza.htm.
[87]Ibid.

been reading the recently published articles of James. I find them interesting. They seem to bear clear resemblance to Zen."[88]

Both Nishitani and Abe had thoroughly discussed and appreciated the importance of a Zen Buddhist perspective in Nishida's elaboration of the meaning of pure experience. They were not ready and willing, however, to allow such an intuition in a Western, let alone an American, thinker. Kazashi's brief, but extremely valuable, observations provide the foundation for future explorations of the non-Christian religious implications of Jamesian thought. When one considers the fact that Zen Buddhism made its first appearance in the United States in 1893, during and after the Parliament of World Religions at the Chicago World's Fair,[89] one is invited to ponder the significance of the cultural moment that also witnessed an "Eastern turn" in the so-called Western philosophy of William James. Kazashi's article provides the critical openness, the intercultural generosity, and the freedom of appreciation that are needed in order to discover the immensely productive, the globally significant potential of James's intuition and interpretation of that "ontologically primordial layer" called pure experience.

The following, highly selective survey of American attempts to assess the global importance of the original intercultural dialogue between James and Nishida will have to begin with David A. Dilworth's influential essays.[90] Dilworth is generally fair and precise in his analysis of James, but he does not exhaust the deeper ontological and religious implications of the Jamesian view of pure experience. In respect to Nishida, he maintains that "the main thrust of his elaboration was to identify the structure of concrete experience with an intuitive religious horizon of experience."[91] It is this dimension, however, which also characterizes James's oeuvre as a whole. Dilworth finds a religious dimension in Nishida's early thinking that he might just as legitimately have detected as a necessary implication in James's idea of pure experience. This is why this interpretation of Nishida's early ontological position could easily have been seen as a rewriting of a true Jamesian insight: "What is primal, or primordial, is rather the world's irrational, and pre-rational, concrete immediacy. This is Nishida's principle of the self-determination of the dynamically concrete world of the 'absolute present.'"[92] Like Nishitani and Abe, Dilworth tends to overlook such problematic

[88]Ibid.

[89]See Rick Fields, *How the Swans Came to the Lake: A Narrative History of Buddhism in America* (Boston: Shambala, 1992), 119–29.

[90]David A. Dilworth, "The Initial Formations of 'Pure Experience' in Nishida Kitaro and William James," *Monumenta Nipponica* 24 (1969): 93–111; see also Dilworth, "Nishida Kitaro."

[91]Dilworth, "Nishida Kitaro," 468.

[92]Dilworth, "Introduction: Nishida's Critique of the Religious Consciousness," in Nishida, *Last Writings: Nothingness and the Religious Worldview*, trans. Dilworth (Honolulu: University of Hawaii Press, 1987), 19.

aspects of Nishida's early masterpiece as the inconsistent characterization of the "pre-rational, concrete immediacy" of pure experience as "universal reason." It is here that a more generous appreciation of James's ontological and religious refinement might have sharpened the critical analysis of Nishida's sometimes erratic appropriation and transformation of James's argument.

David Putney is the only scholar who has offered a sustained critique of these fundamental inconsistencies in Nishida's way of dealing with his Western sources, inconsistencies that, in Putney's view, tend to subvert the very goal of Nishida's attempt to create a logic of the East with the help of Western conceptualizations:

> It is my thesis that Nishida ... has embraced the very "object logic" abandoned by the Buddhists as well as by Western philosophers such as Nietzsche, James and Derrida. Nishida insists that he is attempting to create a concrete logic. To be truly concrete, however, Nishida cannot describe experience in the abstract, or in terms of abstract logical categories. Nishida's approach, nevertheless, moves away from the phenomenological towards logical abstraction, and, in so doing, this methodology moves him away from his own stated objectives. The irony is that Western figures such as Nietzsche, Heidegger, James and Derrida have tried to develop a methodology to attain what, in effect, Nishida calls a "logic of the East" by abandoning the very categories that Nishida resurrects from more traditional Western philosophy.[93]

This is a rather brusque, but ultimately well-founded summary of the problematic that emerged in our diagnosis of Nishida's relapses into, mostly, European metaphysical, that is, German idealist positions in *An Inquiry into the Good*, relapses that endanger the integrity of the consistently modern, post-metaphysical, Jamesian ontology at the center of Nishida's reconstructive efforts.

The most refined and consistently sophisticated interpretations of the importance of James's concept of pure experience in Nishida's early work are to be found in three essays by Andrew Feenberg. Feenberg credits James with a subtle and importantly innovative experiential ontology that provided the single most important starting point for Nishida's career as a thinker. In this respect he goes beyond Dilworth and provides a welcome counter-argument to the either nationalistic or philosophically narrow points of view of older Japanese critics like Nishitani and Abe. At the same time he articulates positions that contemporary Japanese scholars like Kazashi

---

[93]David Putney, "Identity and the Unity of Experience: A Critique of Nishida's Theory of Self," *Asian Philosophy* 1, no. 2 (1991): 141.

could easily agree with. In Feenberg's and Kazashi's interpretations, then, international scholarship on American-Japanese philosophical relations is reaching a dignified and highly cultivated, interculturally respectable level of liberal mutual appreciation.

In "Experiential Ontology," Feenberg and Yoko Arisaka analyze the importance of the new concept of (pure) experience as "an important international crossroads" of modernist thinking.[94] They discuss the relationship between James and Nishida in general terms and strongly emphasize their common vision of experience preceding subjectivity. In this endeavor, both are seen as preparing the way for Husserl and Heidegger. The detailed comparison of James's and Nishida's concepts of pure experience includes critical comments on various misunderstandings of James's position in, for example, Nishitani, which in turn are interpreted as being derived from Nishida's misreadings of James. Feenberg and Arisaka also comment on Nishida's failure to realize all of the major implications of James's radical empiricism and those aspects of his thinking that move in the direction of a radical phenomenological position. With the exception of a few, maybe culturally determined, clichés about James's "crudeness" [sic], about his supposed "rugged individualism," and the unwarranted inclusion of his thought under the heading of European philosophy, this essay manages to solidly establish James as the initiator of both a Western and a Japanese reconstruction of thinking, the consequences of which are still with us.[95]

In "The Problem of Modernity in the Philosophy of Nishida," Feenberg elaborates on Nishida's own view of a global culture and stresses the fact that, as Whitehead had said, James laid the groundwork for the very critique of Western metaphysics that Nishida was about to undertake. This is why Feenberg appropriately concludes: "In the early 20th century, James was not a bad place to look for access to [an] emerging world culture."[96] Feenberg's last essay on Nishida and pure experience begins with a detailed analysis of the possible meanings of experience as it was adopted as a philosophical term in Japanese philosophy (J. *keiken*). Feenberg distinguishes a. the traditional empiricist concept, b. experience signifying life as felt, c. experience as *Bildung* or the process of self-constitution, and, finally and most importantly, d. experience as "ontological foundation: the phenomenological-existentialist idea of experience as unsurpassable horizon of being ... This fourth definition of experience is the most important for the interpretation

---

[94]Andrew Feenberg and Yoko Arisaka, "Experiential Ontology: The Origins of the Nishida Philosophy in the Doctrine of Pure Experience," *International Philosophical Quarterly* 30, no. 2 (1990), 174.

[95]Ibid., 175–82 and *passim*.

[96]Andrew Feenberg, "The Problem of Modernity in the Philosophy of Nishida," in *Rude Awakenings*, ed. James W. Heisig and John C. Maraldo (Honolulu: University of Hawaii Press, 1994), 162 and *passim*.

of Nishida ... This notion promises a radical transcendence of the subject-
object split."⁹⁷ Feenberg devotes some excellently appreciative paragraphs to
the importance of James's rejection of "Cartesian substantialism"⁹⁸ and to
his achievement in ontologizing experience as the precondition for Nishida's
gradual approximation of a phenomenological position. In this way James is
properly credited with the crucial initiation of a fundamental Western and—
by extension and, for example, through Nishida—a globally reconstructive
critique of experience, as well as with the decisive preparatory move toward
phenomenology and existential ontology.

John E. Smith has written the most thorough and dignified rejoinder to
the Japanese claims that Nishida had to correct inadequately subjectivist
Western ideas and that he had to rewrite an insufficient Jamesian concept
of pure experience. In his kindly refutation of Masao Abe's position, Smith
comes close to the critique of Abe's and Nishitani's views implicitly and
explicitly offered by Kazashi, Putney, and Feenberg. My own evaluation
of Abe's position finds itself in almost total agreement with the arguments
offered by Smith, even though he does not dwell on the traditionalist
inconsistencies and idealist anachronisms in *An Inquiry into the Good*.
Smith politely brings out the strengths of Abe's and Nishida's new views of
the ontological meaning of pure experience. He then turns to their arguments
against James and concludes:

> for James any distinction between subject and object is always consequent
> and not primordial ... James did not think of an individual consciousness
> or self coming "first" to be succeeded by a world of objects, and the point
> is reenforced by his speaking of a "world" of pure experience and by his
> description of the radical empiricism that follows from the idea of a pure
> experience as a *Weltanschauung*.
>
>     In light of the foregoing, it is reasonable to conclude that Nishida and
> Abe are mistaken in the claim that James *assumes* pure experience to be
> individual at the outset. In fact, we might turn the tables ... and point out
> that Nishida, in his charge that Western thinkers see pure experience only
> from without and "generalize" it through abstractions, is the one who
> assumes that such experience is *individual* from the outset; otherwise,
> what would there be to generalize?⁹⁹

The Japanese and the American critics of the dialogue between James and Nishida
agree that either one or both these philosophers deserve an extraordinarily

---

⁹⁷Andrew Feenberg, "Experience and Culture: Nishida's Path 'To the Things Themselves,'"
*Philosophy East and West* 49, no. 1 (1999): 34.
⁹⁸Ibid., 35.
⁹⁹John E. Smith, "Kitarô Nishida, William James, and Masao Abe: Some Comments on
Philosophy East and West," in *Masao Abe*, ed. Mitchell, 266–7.

prominent place in the history of modern thinking because of the ways in which they reopened the *Seinsfrage*, the question of Being, as the question of pure experience. The older generation of Japanese scholars and philosophers show a tendency toward an essentialist view of Eastern and an exceptionalist view of Japanese philosophy. In this way the momentous event of the productive global encounter of two major intellects is redefined as the correction of an insufficient Western approach from the perspective of a superior and anterior Eastern wisdom. Whether these evaluations in the case of Nishitani and Abe are reflections of national and personal histories is less important than the fact that an almost exclusively Eastern, that is, Japanese claim to a proper understanding of pure experience does indeed violate the very vision implied in the concept, the awareness of a primordial layer, of a mere unspecified *that*, which by its very nature has to escape all claims to appropriation. Younger Japanese philosophers like Kazashi and the majority of American scholars prefer a relatively even-handed approach that acknowledges at least James's precedence if not his superior sophistication as a thinker. Most critics, however—with the prominent exception of Putney and some hints in Feenberg's latest essay—do not pay sufficient attention to the intellectual inconsistencies that arise out of Nishida's inability or unwillingness to strictly distinguish between the traditionalist European philosophers and psychologists and the radical departure evinced in the daring innovations of a basically different, an American mode of thinking. From a Japanese perspective, the unfortunate label "Western" obliterates the important and productive tension between the ultimately disparate philosophical traditions in Europe and in America.

# IV

Both William James's and Kitarô Nishida's philosophical projects begin in a crisis and end in a religious vision of human existence and Being as a whole. James's personal intellectual despair and existential anxiety of the early 1870s in the context of a seemingly inescapable scientistic determinism finds a complement in the fundamental uncertainties that arose from the confrontation of traditional (Zen) beliefs and modernist challenges during the later Meiji era when Nishida tried to find his way toward a renewed and unified interpretation of life.

It is sometimes overlooked that James does not only intermittently address questions of belief.[100] An essay like "Human Immortality: Two

---

[100]Important contributions to the subject are Ellen Kappy Suckiel, *Heaven's Champion: William James's Philosophy of Religion* (Notre Dame, IN: University of Notre Dame Press, 1996), Robert J. O'Connell, *William James on the Courage to Believe* (New York: Fordham University Press, 1997), and, most comprehensively, David C. Lamberth, *William James*.

Supposed Objections to the Doctrine" (1897) is not an isolated instance; *The Varieties of Religious Experience* is not a singular masterpiece in the field of psychology (as Nishitani saw it[101]); both must be seen as integral parts of the endeavor to express an awareness of Being that precedes and transcends any individual appropriation in language or thought. The concluding chapters of *A Pluralistic Universe* are sufficient evidence that, from "The Sentiment of Rationality" through the essays collected in *The Will to Believe* and the *Essays in Radical Empiricism*, James consistently dealt with the functions and importance of belief and faith in "a universe of spiritual relations surrounding the earthly practical ones."[102] In Nishida there is no occasion for the slightest doubt from the very beginning of his philosophical career that the religious motivation and dimension of his thought is foundational. In *An Inquiry into the Good*, he states unequivocally:

> The pinnacle of learning and morality can in fact be reached only by entering the realm of religion.
>     People often ask why religion is necessary. This is identical to asking why we need to live. Religion does not exist apart from the life of the self, and the religious demand is the demand of life itself.[103]

The common ground of James and Nishida, then, is their total vision, their intuition, their religious and philosophical awareness of "life itself," of Being. This does not mean that James and Nishida accept a universally accessible, underlying substantiality. Rather, they truly reopen the question of Being by refusing to understand this most difficult of terms, once again, as the highest and most fundamental of beings. Like Heidegger, James and Nishida try to let Being be. The complicated attempts of both thinkers to cope with their visions of pure experience, which is their name for Being, are testimonies to the difficulty of their innovative projects. James showed the way. Nishida could follow James because his Zen training had conditioned him to deal with the truly and forever *indeterminate term* of Being as nothingness, as *sunyata*, as *ku*. His 1910 comment on James's *Essays in Radical Empiricism* as expressions of the spirit of Zen[104] supports this assumption. In a concentrated comparison of Buddhism and pragmatism, Sandra Rosenthal and Rogene A. Buchholz have provided a wonderfully convincing basis for this proposition, which is intended to stand as the summary justification of

---

[101]Nishitani, *Nishida Kitarô*, 77–8.
[102]"Answers to a Questionnaire," in *William James: Writings 1902–1910*, ed. Bruce Kuklick (New York: Library of America, 1988), 1183.
[103]Nishida, *Inquiry*, 152.
[104]Kazashi, "The World," 2.

our in-depth inquiry into the problems of articulating pure experience in different cultural contexts:

> it can be seen that classical American pragmatism, like Buddhism, finds an important role for the pure immediacy of experience which defies articulation, and for a religious experience as the immediate, preconceptual attunement to the totality of interrelated conditions which constitute our embeddedness in nature. ... Both positions view nature not as a collection of substances but as an indefinitely rich, dynamic process which overflows any attempts to grasp and articulate its features. Because of this, they both reject the false reifications of past philosophy which have absolutized conceptual distinctions, thus bringing about the self defeating dilemmas and alternatives which still haunt much of philosophy today.[105]

Thomas Merton's short essay "Nishida: A Zen Philosopher" provides further support for the thesis that James's and Nishida's fundamental ontologies are in basic agreement because they are ultimately religiously motivated. Merton writes:

> For Nishida ... what comes first is the *unifying* intuition of the *basic unity of subject and object in being* or a deep "grasp of life" in its existential concreteness "at the base of consciousness." This basic unity is not an abstract concept but being itself. [106]

This characterization of Nishida's "unifying intuition" is directly applicable to James's earlier vision. Merton adds in another context that the central problem of such philosophical and religious awareness has to do with the inherent and ineradicable insufficiency of language, with the very problem of keeping the "term indeterminate":

> We quickly forget how to simply *see* things and substitute our words and our formulas for the things themselves, manipulating facts so that we see only what conveniently fits our prejudices. Zen uses language against itself to blast out these preconceptions and to destroy the specious "reality" in our minds so that we can *see directly*. Zen is saying, as Wittgenstein said, "Don't think: Look!"[107]

---

[105]Sandra B. Rosenthal, and Rogene A. Buchholz, "Experimental Inquiry and Experiencing Nature Religiously: The Converging Paths of Pragmatism and Buddhism," in *Komparative Philosophie*, ed. Elberfeld et al., 229–30.
[106]Merton, "Nishida: A Zen Philosopher," in *Zen and the Birds of Appetite*, 68–9.
[107]Merton, "A Christian Looks at Zen," 49.

The analyses of Nishida's appropriation of James and the interpretations of the critical responses to their relationship in dealing with the enigma of pure experience, with the central emptiness of Being, have shown how difficult it is "to blast out ... preconceptions," even in a culture like the Japanese whose rich religious past has consistently tried to evade verbal transmission of religious insight into Being as no-thing-ness.

Shigetsu Sasaki (1882–1945)—his Buddhist name is Sokei-an—established the first Zen center in New York City in the 1930s. He knew that he brought his religious vision of Being to a culture that—through thinkers like Emerson and James—was prepared to become aware of the paradoxical fullness of the undefinable emptiness at the core of all beings. He also knew that even so the verbal and conceptual bent of all humans had to be consistently criticized and overcome, because "[e]mptiness means pure existence that has no notion in it—like pure water."[108]

---

[108]*The Zen Eye: A Collection of Zen Talks by Sokei-an*, ed. Mary Farkas (New York, Tokyo: Weatherhill, 1993), 72.

# 14

# The Necessity of the
# Lost Middle Voice

*I am only teaching you to leave the provisional and return
to the real.
After you return to the real, the real has no name either.*

HUI-NENG (638–713 CE)

Pragmatism does not trust language. However, one ought to remember that
John Dewey valuated certain functions of language highly and therefore
called it "the tool of tools,"[1] the essential and indispensable instrument of
thinking in the mode of a socially oriented and responsible instrumentalism.
One could also point to the terminology of Martin Heidegger's "pragmatist"
phase in *Sein und Zeit*[2] and define language as "das eigentliche Zeug der
Eröffnung von Welt." And one must not forget that Richard Poirier has
extensively demonstrated the pragmatist view of the flexibility of words—
the "vehicular and transitive" character of signs, in Emerson's phrase from
"The Poet"[3]—a flexibility and "superfluity" as Poirier calls it, which allows
for the constant turning and troping of meaning in the endlessly revisionist

This essay was previously published as "Thinking in Search of a Language: Pragmatism and
the Muted Middle Voice" in *Amerikastudien/American Studies* 47, no. 4 (2002): 469–90.
Reprinted by permission of Damien B Schlarb, managing editor of *Amerikastudien/American
Studies*.

[1] *Experience and Nature* LW 1, 134.
[2] On pragmatist aspects in Heidegger, cf. Mark Okrent, *Heidegger's Pragmatism: Understanding,
Being, and the Critique of Metaphysics* (Ithaca, NY: Cornell University Press, 1988).
[3] W III, 37.

enterprise of making and remaking our respective worlds.[4] But even so, even if language *works* in pragmatism, language is also considered to be fundamentally and severely deficient in its possibilities to articulate the Being of beings, to capture, to determine, and to recreate reality as experienced.

We find two aspects of this deficiency in William James's and in John Dewey's thinking. The first aspect indicates an intrinsic inadequacy of human speech and of writing. If reality or Being is the stream of experiencing or awareness or thought or consciousness as it goes on, as it is for James, then language is challenged to articulate and represent or refer to a continuous, transitional, and temporal event that is subject to constant change without essential breaks and radical divisions. In the attempt to interpret Being, language is faced with the task of rendering a manifold that is also a unified flow, a flow that is at the same time one and yet always different from itself since thought or awareness or feeling are both "sensibly continuous" and "always changing"[5]: "whatever was true of the river of life, of the river of elementary feeling, it would certainly be true to say, like Heraclitus, that we never descend twice into the same stream."[6]

This stream of identity and difference is filled with the awareness of things in temporal transition, of bodily presence, of relations, of feelings of tendencies, of overtones, halos, and fringes of sensation that color, impede, or direct the ongoing event of individualized Being. If Being in James is thus showing introspectively as "it thinks," as "*thought goes on*,"[7] this radically temporalized mode of existing will not prove hospitable to permanently existing ideas or representations that may be named singly and unambiguously. The "whole organization of speech,"[8] James argues, in supporting the stability of conceptualized entities for reasons of practical orientation, the nature of language itself works against an adequate articulation of *what* and *how* humans are. For James, the forgetting of Being is due to *logos* itself. A "*permanently existing 'idea' or 'Vorstellung'*"[9] may be useful, but it lies about what really *is* in and as experience. James, like Nietzsche before him in "Über Wahrheit und Lüge im aussermoralischen Sinne," implies a radically nominalist vision of reality. James's view, however, presents an even greater challenge to language as a mediator of beings in their Being. He thinks not only a manifold that transcends any lexicon, as does Nietzsche; James, as we will presently see, proposes a fundamental incompatibility of

[4]Cf. Richard Poirier, *The Renewal of Literature: Emersonian Reflections* (New York: Random House, 1987) and *Poetry and Pragmatism* (Cambridge, MA: Harvard University Press, 1992).
[5]William James, *The Principles of Psychology*, vol. 8.1–3 of *The Works of William James* (1890; Cambridge, MA: Harvard University Press, 1981), 1, 220.
[6]Ibid., 227.
[7]Ibid., 220.
[8]Ibid., 230.
[9]Ibid.

linguistic structures and Being as event. In the famous analysis of the psychic realization of a thunder-clap, James shows that sudden emergences in the stream of awareness (like thunder) do not separate the stream in its essential and inescapable togetherness of continuity and change:

> Here, again, language works against our perception of the truth. We name our thoughts simply, each after its thing, as if each knew its own thing and nothing else. What each really knows is clearly the thing it is named for, with dimly perhaps a thousand other things. It ought to be named after all of them, but it never is. Some of them are always things known a moment ago more clearly; others are things to be known more clearly a moment hence.[10]

Language and especially naming violate the character of what temporally *is*, and it does so in two ways. Names do not respect the inescapably complex contexts of seemingly separate single entities in and as experience. Each so-called thing as it is experienced is one with and merges into a variety of receding contexts of variable distinctness. Secondly, a moment of experience is not a clearly circumscribed temporal entity either. A single name again ignores the character of continuity within ongoing experience.

The different rates of change in the velocity of the ongoing stream of experience disclose a further difficulty in the relationship of language and Being, if we define the latter as the event of the stream of individualized consciousness:

> When the rate is slow we are aware of the object of our thought in a comparatively restful and stable way. When rapid, we are aware of a passage, a relation, a transition *from* it, or *between* it and something else. As we take, in fact, a general view of the wonderful stream of our consciousness, what strikes us first is this different pace of its parts. Like a bird's life, it seems to be made of an alternation of flights and perchings. The rhythm of language expresses this, where every thought is expressed in a sentence, and every sentence closed by a period. The resting-places are usually occupied by sensorial imaginations of some sort, whose peculiarity is that they can be held before the mind for an indefinite time, and contemplated without changing; the places of flight are filled with thoughts of relations, static or dynamic, that for the most part obtain between the matters contemplated in the periods of comparative rest.
> *Let us call the resting-places the "substantive parts," and the places of flight the "transitive parts," of the stream of thought.* It then appears

---

[10]Ibid., 234.

that the main end of our thinking is at all times the attainment of some other substantive part than the one from which we have just been dislodged ...

Now it is very difficult, introspectively, to see the transitive parts for what they really are. If they are but flights to a conclusion, stopping them to look at them before the conclusion is reached is really annihilating them ...

As a snowflake caught in the warm hand is no longer a flake but a drop, so, instead of catching the feeling of relation moving to its term, we find we have caught some substantive thing, usually the last word we were pronouncing, statically taken, and with its function, tendency, and particular meaning in the sentence quite evaporated ...

The results of this introspective difficulty are baleful. If to hold fast and observe the transitive parts of thought's stream be so hard, then the great blunder to which all schools are liable must be the failure to register them, and the undue emphasizing of the more substantive parts of the stream.[11]

The difficulty lies in the tendency of the introspective awareness of what is going on to focus on substantive aspects of experiencing that, at least temporarily, insinuate closure. In doing so, the parallel privileging of the substantive aspects of named reality makes it impossible to know or to appropriately speak of what flights or transitive parts of the stream *really are*, as James says. Their Being is ignored. Language tends to be ontologically blind to the relational and event-character of Being itself, because the verbs, the adverbs, and the prepositions seem subservient to the noun substantives as they reveal what is really real in the sense of an identifiable stability and a stable identity. James's analysis, at least implicitly, explains the relationship between traditional metaphysics and its emphasis on solid underlying identities or substances on the one hand and the importance of substantive concepts in philosophical language on the other. It will be James's and especially Dewey's revolutionary achievement to again and again argue against the predominance of the noun[12] and to stress the importance of the verb as the linguistic indicator of real events. Grammatical categories—as Nietzsche has insinuated time and again—are expressions of the will to power and to interpretation and thus represent a kind of metaphysical fate that helps determine the kind of Being we are able to know and to articulate.

---

[11]Ibid., 236–7.

[12]See Dewey, *Experience and Nature LW* 1, 66: "It is a plausible prediction that if there were an interdict placed for a generation upon the use of mind, matter, consciousness as nouns ... we should find many of our problems much simplified."

In addition to the ontologically reductive implications of merely naming parts of the stream of thought and the stabilizing falsifications that are due to the privileged status of nouns, relations pose another difficulty for language, a difficulty that again exposes its essential inadequacy in coping with the fullness of ongoing experience. Relations, in James's thinking, are not imposed on experience by antecedent rational structures as the conditions of the possibility of coherence; relations themselves are experienced; they are of the very stuff of the stream of experiencing itself. This is one of the central tenets of radical empiricism. Relations, however, as one central ingredient of reality, cannot be fully expressed:

There is not a conjunction or a preposition, and hardly an adverbial phrase, syntactic form, or inflection of voice, in human speech, that does not express some shading or other of relation which we at some moment actually feel to exist between the larger objects of our thought. If we speak objectively, it is the real relations that appear revealed; if we speak subjectively, it is the stream of consciousness that matches each of them by an inward coloring of its own. In either case the relations are numberless, and no existing language is capable of doing justice to all their shades.

We ought to say a feeling of *and*, a feeling of *if*, a feeling of *but*, and a feeling of *by*, quite as readily as we say a feeling of *blue* or a feeling of *cold*. Yet we do not: so inveterate has our habit become of recognizing the existence of the substantive parts alone, that language almost refuses to lend itself to any other use.[13]

Reality as it shows itself in and as experience, Being as experiential event is severely impoverished in its essence once it is articulated. In this context James speaks of the egregious error of metaphysics to suppose "that where there is no name no entity can exist":

All *dumb* or anonymous psychic states have, owing to this error, been coolly suppressed; or, if recognized at all, have been named after the substantive perception they led to, as thoughts "about" this object or "about" that, the stolid word *about* engulfing all their delicate idiosyncrasies in its monotonous sound.[14]

It has not yet been sufficiently appreciated that James has thus drawn attention to one specific kind of *Seinsvergessenheit*, which is due to the fact

---

[13] James, *Principles*, 1, 238.
[14] Ibid., 238–9.

that language, the *logos* itself, in revealing always conceals. James's implicit ontology insists that "namelessness is compatible with existence."[15] This is the wider philosophical background of his urgent plea: "It is, in short, the re-instatement of the vague to its proper place in our mental life which I am so anxious to press on the attention."[16] James, as so often, has found a wonderful image to convey his sense of the losses that are due to an atomistic, a merely conceptual, a merely linguistic approach to experience as Being itself. The traditionalists in psychology and philosophy talk "like one who should say a river consists of nothing but pailsful, spoonsful, quartpotsful, barrelsful, and other moulded forms of water. Even were the pails and the pots all actually standing in the stream, still between them the free water would continue to flow."[17]

James is the philosophical champion of the rights of the free water of consciousness, of the as-yet-unnamed aspects of reality as they continuously show in and as experience. In his pragmatist reconstruction of theology, John E. Smith has paid tribute to the continuing importance of this Jamesian revision of the relationship of language and experience: "Experience, then, needs to be rescued ... from the restrictive force of approaching it only through expression, that is, only through language."[18] Smith adds that "experience never fails to transcend expression" and he summarizes: "from the proposition that experience demands expression in language or some symbolic medium—which is true—it does not follow that everything encountered actually does find expression or that all of what does find expression has been adequately expressed."[19]

Experience—in the sense of the event of Being—is thus characterized in relation to language by a kind of excess, an abundance and exuberance, a potential and a promise. This asymmetry of the riches of experience and the poverty of language was forcefully analyzed early on by, among others, Ralph Barton Perry, who drew attention to the fact that in James "reality cannot be analyzed or described, but only conveyed" and that, even though language and especially "concepts somehow *work*," they do, after all, "misrepresent reality."[20] If we read Perry's term *reality* as one of the many possible names for experience and Being, we realize that James's linguistic skepticism was always associated with the problem of an adequate ontology to express the pragmatist vision. The continuing

---

[15]Ibid., 243.

[16]Ibid., 246. Cf. also William Joseph Gavin, *William James and the Reinstatement of the Vague* (Philadelphia: Temple University Press, 1992).

[17]James, *Principles*, 1, 246.

[18]John E. Smith, *Experience and God* (1968; New York: Fordham University Press, 1995), 13.

[19]Ibid., 45, 41.

[20]Ralph Barton Perry, *The Thought and Character of William James* (London: Milford/Oxford University Press, 1936), vol. 2, 601–2.

importance of and fascination with this question is clearly attested by the frequency with which, for instance, Richard Poirier returns to it in his last collection of essays in the pragmatist grain, *Trying It Out in America: Literary and Other Performances*. One of Poirier's *leitmotifs* in this book is the awareness that "any word should be treated *not* as if it necessarily represents an established reality."[21]

James's vigorous battle against transcendental idealism, classical empiricism, and all kinds of intellectualism culminated in his late works. It is here that James articulates his mature sense of the necessary inadequacy of language in thinking Being as experience, an inadequacy that is also a great existential and philosophical boon: it implies the ontological guarantee of the possibility of real innovation, of the truly new, and the vision of the inexhaustible potential of the unprecedented.[22] In his 1910 essay "Bradley or Bergson?" James finds a succinct way of stating the difficulty for conceptual language to do justice to reality as "the continuity and wholeness of a transparent much-at-once." He asserts that "all concepts are discrete; and though you can get the discrete out of the continuous, out of the discrete you can never get the continuous again. Concepts, moreover, are static, and can never be adequate substitutes for a perceptual flux of which activity and change are inalienable features."[23]

James thinks Being in its perceptual givenness in and as the stream of consciousness and experience in terms of an indiscrete ontology. Discreteness is the result of essentially reductionist mental operations that will never result in a reconstruction of live and indiscrete reality as it goes on. Language essentially supports and is tied to discreteness.[24] James's battle against "the ruling tradition in philosophy" and its belief "that fixity is a nobler and worthier thing than change"[25] had to be a fight against the status of the metaphysical concept in the context of intellectual, rationalistic knowledge: "Instead of being the only adequate knowledge, it is grossly inadequate, and its only superiority is the practical one of enabling us to make short cuts through experience and thereby save time. The one thing

---

[21]Richard Poirier, *Trying It Out in America: Literary and Other Performances* (New York: Farrar, Straus and Giroux, 1999), 213. Cf. also the general comments on James's skepticism: 201, 240, 242.

[22]Cf. "The Problem of Novelty," in *Some Problems of Philosophy*, vol. 7 of *The Works of William James* (1911; Cambridge, MA: Harvard University Press, 1979), 76–9.

[23]*Essays in Philosophy*, vol. 5 of *The Works of William James* (Cambridge, MA: Harvard University Press, 1978), 151–2.

[24]On language and its relationship to discrete and indiscrete ontologies, cf. Wolfram Hogrebe, *Metaphysik und Mantik: Die Deutungsnatur des Menschen* (Frankfurt: Suhrkamp, 1992), 113–34.

[25]*A Pluralistic Universe*, vol. 4 of *The Works of William James* (1909; Cambridge, MA: Harvard University Press, 1977), 106.

it cannot do is to reveal the inner nature of things."[26] The true Being of beings, the "inner nature of things" can only be revealed in the perceptual awareness of the stream of experience. It is radically temporal and therefore, by its very nature, resists all verbalization with its implicit segmentation and partition of the ongoing flow of consciousness. Conceptual knowledge is essentially practice-oriented, as Dewey was going to emphasize, and language, therefore, proves to be fundamentally pragmatic. James combined his critique of traditional metaphysics and his celebration of the sensational stream of experience by claiming that the stream concretely exhibited the very traits that were supposed to be inherent only in his favorite *bête noire* of idealist philosophy, the Absolute:

> The absolute is said to perform its feats by taking up its other into itself. But that is exactly what is done when every individual morsel of the sensational stream takes up the adjacent morsels by coalescing with them. This is just what we mean by the stream's sensible continuity. No element *there* cuts itself off from any other element, as concepts cut themselves from concepts. No part *there* is so small as not to be a place of conflux. No part there is not really *next* its neighbors; which means that there is literally nothing between; which means again that no part goes exactly so far and no farther; that no part absolutely excludes another, but that they compenetrate and are cohesive; that if you tear out one, its roots bring out more with them; that whatever is real is telescoped and diffused into other reals; that, in short, every minutest thing is already its hegelian "own other," in the fullest sense of the term.[27]

The continuity of reality or Being goes on in the form of the stream of experience, sensation, perception, or thought. In this way it makes a world possible. Concepts do not do justice to the continuity and compenetration and cohesiveness of Being as it unfolds. If every real event of or within Being is its "own other," then this also means that no single term, no single statement will ever do justice to the experienced "much-at-once." Like the Absolute of transcendental idealism, the temporal "units" or pulses of the flow of plural and individualized reality are beyond linguistic fixation. Language may and does arise out of such a world, but it will never encompass it in its inner nature or true Being. Bruce Wilshire has summarized James's late position on Being and language in his analysis of the supremacy of the *that*, the pure existence of any given and experienced world, over its *what*, that is, its particular and definable essence:

---

[26]Ibid., 112.
[27]Ibid., 121.

Essential to the supremacy of the *that*, the world, things finally overflow our pigeonholes and categories, and "bleed" through their boundaries into the evolving surround.

If experienced or experienceable things bleed through their boundaries, every pulse of experienc*ing* does this exceedingly. Every pulse is "its own other." It "buds out of" what it is and spreads into what it is not (not, according to intellectualist logic). Every pulse contains a spread or stretch that includes in immediate experience past, present, and future indissolubly fused and evolving.[28]

The character of the world of experience and of all entities experienced within it is that of a plurality of emergent events indiscreetly merging into each other in temporal spreads without closure. No lexical and no syntactical unit can ever do justice to what is thus going on. This is why James concludes one of his chapters on percept and concept in his last, unfinished, book *Some Problems of Philosophy* in this way:

If the aim of philosophy were the taking full possession of all reality by the mind, then nothing short of the whole of immediate perceptual experience could be the subject-matter of philosophy, for only in such experience is reality intimately and concretely found. But the philosopher, although he is unable as a finite being to compass more than a few passing moments of such experience, is yet able to extend his knowledge beyond such moments by the ideal symbol of the other moments. He thus commands vicariously innumerable perceptions that are out of range. But the concepts by which he does this, being thin extracts from perception, are always insufficient representatives thereof; and, although they yield wider information, must never be treated after the rationalistic fashion, as if they gave a deeper quality of truth. The deeper features of reality are found only in perceptual experience. Here alone do we acquaint ourselves with continuity, or the immersion of one thing in another, here alone with self, with substance, with qualities, with activity in its various modes, with time, with cause, with change, with novelty, with tendency, and with freedom.[29]

The wide range of symbols, of linguistic signs in general and of philosophical concepts in particular, must not obscure the fact that they are only pale and

---

[28]Bruce Wilshire, "The Breathtaking Intimacy of the Material World: William James's Last Thoughts," in *The Cambridge Companion to William James*, ed. Ruth Anna Putnam (Cambridge: Cambridge University Press, 1997), 118.
[29]*Some Problems*, 53–4.

thin surrogates of experience as had in perception, with all its thickness, depth, continuity, and the free play of the constant emergence of novelty.

The reasons for the pragmatist skepticism as to the ontological possibilities of language—as William James represents it—may now be summarized in this fashion: 1. language possesses no means to articulate the intimate togetherness of identity and difference in the ongoing stream of Being as experience; 2. language cannot render the spatial and temporal continuity of so-called single things or entities within the stream of awareness; 3. language necessarily suppresses the transitional aspects of the flow of consciousness, it bypasses the flights connecting more stable phases of thinking as it goes on; 4. language is not equipped to represent the multiplicity of experienced relations; and 5. language cannot say the indiscrete ontological events that constitute the perceptual emergents of temporal reality. Language can only do what I have done just now: it may conceptually hint at a fullness whose presence is always bought at the price of silence or namelessness and whose absence allows the thin surrogates of intellectualism to create a deceptive aura of felt solidity.

John Dewey shares James's critique of intellectualism and the role of concepts. Chapter 5 of *Experience and Nature*, entitled "Nature, Communication and Meaning," is an extended analysis of the pragmatist conception of language as a socially constructed and historically emergent tool in the service of progressive changes in the interaction of humans and their environment, leading toward possible amplifications and augmentations of reality as experienced. "Language considered as an experienced event"[30] does not provide access to Being itself independent of the pursuit of constructive changes within it. Language does not correspond to "things and meanings ... prior to discourse and social intercourse."[31] Language in action, that is, communication, creates a world of means and ends that are ultimately inseparable:

> Communication is uniquely instrumental and uniquely final. It is instrumental as liberating us from the otherwise overwhelming pressure of events and enabling us to live in a world of things that have meaning. It is final as a sharing in the objects and arts precious to a community, a sharing whereby meanings are enhanced, deepened and solidified in the sense of communion.[32]

Implicitly, then, language cannot but *work within* reality as ongoing individual and communal experience. It is never over against and truly

---

[30]*Experience and Nature LW* 1, 137.
[31]Ibid., 136.
[32]Ibid., 159.

*about* reality as experience going on. Like philosophy, language for Dewey is primarily a means of constructive criticism *within* the world and not *about it*. The way Being *is*, as a plurality of experiences characterized by the intimately interactive togetherness of person and environment, may perhaps be *conveyed*, but it cannot be conceptually, linguistically *had* or *represented*. Language helps Being to go on; it is *of* it, but not a means of access *to* it.

The first and the most fundamental aspect of the deficiency of language in pragmatist thinking demonstrates that *logos* cannot directly engage Being, whether it is talked about as stream of consciousness, as the flow of awareness, as the reality of individualized experience, or as the interactive event of person and environment. These terms merely convey or hint at the way Being *is*; they do not ontologically reveal its presence-ing, its mode of making itself presently felt (I apply "presence-ing" here in the sense of Heidegger's use of German *wesen* as a verb). The problem of language in pragmatism is therefore, first and foremost and literally, an *onto-logical* problem: how do you say what and how *is* is?

There exists, however, a second kind of imperfection in language of which pragmatist thinking is more or less implicitly aware. This inadequacy concerns the problem of an appropriate verbalization of the basic structures emerging from Being as—ultimately unnameable—temporal event. Prominent among these basic structural relations are the interactive dependencies of human being and world, of agency and undergoing, of observant reception and active interpretation of what is given in and as experience—in short, the modes in which Being reveals itself to and in beings. This second shortcoming has occasioned a moderate amount of verbal experimentation in James and Dewey, an experimentation seemingly rather innocent if compared to the massive array of neologisms that Heidegger thought necessary in his parallel attempt to overcome and destruct the metaphysical tradition. Thomas M. Alexander has contrasted the two kinds of linguistic strategies necessitated by a fundamentally new approach to thinking in Heidegger and Dewey:

> [Dewey's] manner of approach is quite the opposite of someone like Heidegger, who forces the difficulty of his thought upon the reader by a bewildering technical style. Dewey's thought is equally difficult and elusive, I believe, but this fact is often hidden by Dewey's conscious adoption of terms with an established meaning, both in popular as well as philosophical senses. Dewey, in other words, sought to reconstruct an existing language rather than fabricate a new one.[33]

Both James and Dewey, as I will try and show, reconstruct the possibilities of ordinary language and common usage not only terminologically but

---

[33]Thomas M. Alexander, *John Dewey's Theory of Art, Experience, and Nature: The Horizons of Feeling* (Albany: State University of New York Press, 1987), xii–xiii.

also stylistically and grammatically. They obviously felt challenged by the way the available structures of English and the prevalent usage impeded their innovative, their modern and post-metaphysical attempts to at least approximate and talk of the ways Being shows itself in the structures of individual worlds emerging as pluralities of experiencing. By way of explaining the title of my essay let me say right away that it is the middle voice, the medium—as one of the historically earliest *genera verbi*, or in Greek: *diathesis*—whose absence[34] in contemporary language is putting such a strain on pragmatist thinking once pragmatism begins to try and approach the problem of saying and conveying, or at least hinting at, the inner workings of Being as it unfolds. The second aspect of the linguistic difficulty in saying Being, in doing *onto-logy*, has to do with the erosion of historically early possibilities of speech that seemed to voice the emergence, the revealing of experienceable worlds more satisfactorily than the linguistic means now at hand. William James was well aware of the fact that languages other than English and especially the older philosophical idioms of Latin and Greek provided ways of getting closer to what is happening in the stream of consciousness, as the mode in which Being opens and unfolds through beings as well as in and as time:

> if language must thus influence us, the agglutinative languages, and even Greek and Latin with their declensions, would be the better guides. Names did not appear in them inalterable, but changed their shape to suit the context in which they lay. It must have been easier then than now to conceive of the same object as being thought of at different times in non-identical conscious states.[35]

James here addresses a theme of modern thinking that was elaborated extensively in Dewey's critique of the philosophical tradition and in Heidegger's attempt to go back into and even behind the beginnings of Western metaphysics. In both cases the implication is that early thought was closer to successfully articulating a vision of the emergence of beings out of Being. This vision was necessarily sacrificed or at least obscured by the development of metaphysical conceptual strategies, by the language(s) of the history of thinking itself.

---

[34]There are, of course, uses of the middle voice, in the specific variety of the mediopassive, in contemporary English. Examples like "These books sell well" may be easily adduced. However, compared with the systematic significance of the active and passive voices and the specific and limited functions of the mediopassive, the original middle voice of the early historical stages of some Indo-Germanic languages is no longer a viable category in almost all modern European languages, with the exception of contemporary Greek, as my friend and colleague Joan Richardson kindly reminded me.

[35]James, *Principles*, 1, 230.

I will now, and with a certain glee, indulge in a dilettante's extravaganza and poach in the field of historical linguistics in order to prepare my reading of the central *fundamentalontologische* concern and problem of pragmatism, which—I hasten to confess—is one of my favorite topics and, from my point of view, probably the decisive and most radical, even if it is not the most spectacular, innovation in the thinking of William James and John Dewey. The question of Being itself, as we have seen, can never be resolved verbally once and for all, if only for the simple reason that, from a post-metaphysical and pragmatist perspective, Being itself is not a something, not a being. Keeping the question alive may be more important than striving for any, ever so tentative, resolution. The question of Being is either a central and necessarily ongoing and open-ended concern of a thinker, as in the case of Heidegger,[36] or it is a constant, a never-ending, an experimental, an underlying accompaniment of all other thematic interests of a philosophical agenda, a kind of *basso continuo* in the *Gesamtkunstwerk* of a thinker. This seems to be the case with James and Dewey. In addition to their awareness of what I called the first aspect of the insufficiency of language, that is, the literally *onto-logical* inability to say Being, James and Dewey worked toward a solution for the resultant second problem, the lack of appropriate grammatical forms like the middle voice to express relations and structures within Being. Since these structures necessarily address the way human beings relate to the Being of their world of beings, I have decided to, once again, use Heidegger's precise terminology and call this problem *fundamentalontologisch*, since it primarily deals with the relationship of Being and human being as distinguished from the primary and antecedent ontological problem of Being itself and its linguistic representation to which my opening remarks were addressed.

The following sketch of the semantic implications and possible historical origins of the meanings and functions of the middle voice is intended to create a sense of the specific character of *fundamentalontologische* structures that are germane to the pragmatist vision. The demise of the original middle voice and its semantic potential created an identical challenge for James and Dewey to which they, however, responded by creating and using different linguistic means.

Most linguistic dictionaries agree on the simple fact that, systematically speaking, the middle voice is a *genus verbi* placed between the active and the passive voice: "Das M.[edium] nimmt eine Mittelstellung zwischen Aktiv und Passiv ein und ist in semantischer Hinsicht dem dt. Reflexivum ähnlich, insofern es Handlungen bezeichnet, die vom Subjekt ausgehen und sich auf das Subjekt zurückbeziehen."[37] Some definitions dealing

---

[36]Cf. Joan Stambaugh, *The Finitude of Being* (Albany: State University of New York Press, 1992).

[37]Hadumod Bußmann, *Lexikon der Sprachwissenschaft* (Stuttgart: Kröner, 1983), 315.

with modern usage are slightly more differentiated in their analysis of the semantic implications. Pei's explanation, for instance, goes somewhat beyond the merely reflexive implications of what is more accurately called the contemporary mediopassive. He says of the middle voice (including the mediopassive): "A verbal form expressing that the action denoted by the verb is DYNAMIC (performed by the agent for himself, or generally affecting the agent); or REFLEXIVE (with the agent and the object the same)."[38] Such a definition tends to stress not only a usage and a meaning already dominant in Greek. The hint that the middle voice articulates an action or an event that "generally affects" the agent implies an existential situation in which the clear-cut contrast of subjective agency and undergoing becomes questionable. This is why Werner Abraham adds a valuable distinction for our purpose when he says about one of the possible meanings of the middle voice in Greek: "Was das Medium (wenn es in Opposition zum Aktiv steht) bedeutet, ist, daß die 'Handlung' oder der 'Zustand' das Subjekt des Verbums bzw. seine Interessen berührt."[39] The important point here is that the middle voice allows us to envision the action or a state of affairs as preceding and determining the subject involved in it. In his useful distinction of medium and mediopassive in Greek, Rudi Conrad also emphasizes this semantic feature that is related to what I have underscored so far: "daß das Subjekt nun eine Handlung in sich aufnimmt, die ein anderer durchführt."[40] The one tentative and preliminary result of this cursory glance at some definitions almost randomly collected is the insight that the middle voice tends (or tended) to subordinate the noun subject to an event preceding, co-determining, and possibly affecting it without transforming the subject into a mere recipient as, for example, in the case of the passive voice.

It may also have become obvious that in this particular case a mere synchronic analysis will not do. In keeping with the assumption that modern thinking like pragmatism in fact does resuscitate lost possibilities implied in the very beginning of Western thought, one will have to look at the corresponding linguistic situation in order to understand former possibilities of thinking the structures of Being as they issue in beings. In his classic *Lateinische Laut- und Formenlehre*, Manu Leumann explains the historical background of the Latin passive forms and the *deponentia*: "Die idg. Grundform für lat. Passiv und Deponens war das Medium"; and he adds, "Die Passivfunktion der idg. Medialformen in lat. und griech. Praesenssystem ... ist eine Neuerung, deren Anfänge bis in die Grundsprache

---

[38]Mario Pei, *Glossary of Linguistic Terminology* (New York: Columbia University Press, 1966), 163.
[39]Werner Abraham, *Terminologie zur Neueren Linguistik* (Tübingen: Niemeyer, 1974), 265.
[40]Rudi Conrad, *Kleines Wörterbuch sprachwissenschaftlicher Termini* (Leipzig: VEB Bibliographisches Institut, 1975).

zurückreichen müssen."[41] This means that the original *genera verbi* in the Indo-Germanic languages were the active voice and the middle voice.

In his extensive analysis of the emergence of the passive voice, Wackernagel begins by stating that its very existence is cause for wonder and puzzlement; he calls it a "Luxus der Sprache."[42] This luxury, Wackernagel contends, is the result of a specific cultural development: "Im ganzen kann man sagen, dass der Wunsch nach passivischem Ausdruck und dessen Anwendung in den Sprachen zunimmt, je mehr die Abstraktion, je mehr das sogenannte gebildete Sprechen zur Herrschaft kommt."[43] I would like to translate this statement in the context of my considerations as meaning that the replacement of the active-middle voice opposition in the *genera verbi* is a result of the development of conceptualization and metaphysics that includes the constitutive subject-object dichotomy of Western epistemology. This is supported by Wackernagel's observation "dass es Sprachen, die man als primitiv betrachtet, eigen ist, dasjenige, was wir als persönliche Tätigkeit auffassen, vielmehr als unpersönlichen Vorgang zu geben, z. B. der Grönländer bedient sich, wo wir 'ich höre' sagen, des Ausdrucks 'es ertönt mir' ... Er hat damit eigentlich recht."[44] The event as preceding the subject and the realization of an object is thus thought to be the earliest form of envisioning the basic structure within the event of Being issuing in beings in time. Wackernagel's example of the Inuit phrase "it sounds for me" is a perfect equivalent of James's modern and post-metaphysical attempt to redefine the way experience as Being goes on. Instead of the "I think" of metaphysics, James would like to say "it thinks" in order to convey his sense of how the event of experiencing begins to show for it-self while allowing a self and a world and their later active/passive relations to emerge.[45]

Wackernagel's approach to the middle voice is a structural equivalent of the modern philosophical attempts to retrieve forgotten beginnings. Today active and passive voices are felt as normal ways of expressing our ways of relating to objects in our world and to our worlds themselves. Going back, first to Latin and then to Greek and Greek linguistics, Wackernagel realizes that the Greek grammarians felt the same way about passive and active voices as we do. This is why they found a "der Trägheit entsprungenen Terminus"[46] (*mesotes*, i.e., that which lies in the middle) for those verbal forms that did not fit the "natural" opposition of active and passive voices,

---

[41]Manu Leumann, *Lateinische Laut- und Formenlehre*, vol. 1 of *Lateinische Grammatik*, by Leumann, Johann Baptist Hofmann, and Anton Szantyr (1926–28; Munich: Beck, 1977), 505–6.

[42]Jacob Wackernagel, *Vorlesungen über Syntax* (1926; Basel: Birkhäuser, 1981), 135.

[43]Ibid., 144.

[44]Ibid., 118.

[45]James, *Principles,* 1, 220.

[46]Wackernagel, *Vorlesungen über Syntax*, 121.

as they saw it. Going even further back, however, one discovers that the "natural" way of expressing relations within Being utilizes either the active or the middle voice.[47] The terms coined by the Sanskrit grammarians for the active and the middle voices open a world that is different from the world of subject and object, action or undergoing, as constituted by the active and passive voices as we have come to understand and interpret them. Wackernagel summarizes ancient Indian grammar in this respect:

> Die aktiven Formen nennt sie *parasmaipadam*, wörtlich "Wort für einen andern", das Medium *atmanepadam* "Wort für sich selbst", d. h. einen solchen Gebrauch des Verbums lassen sie durch die Formen des Atmanepadam ausgedrückt sein, bei dem die Handlung dem Handelnden selbst zugute kommt. Also wird etwa das Medium gebraucht, wenn die Handlung an einem Besitzstück des handelnden Subjekts vollzogen wird.[48]

This implies that the middle voice may articulate any event that pertains to the world of the subject (insofar as one may characterize the world as a "possession," a *Besitzstück*, of the subject). In his careful listings of possible uses of the middle voice, Wackernagel pays special attention to verbs expressing motion, that is, events. Here the middle voice implies the "Bewirkung einer Tätigkeit ..., die auf den Handelnden zugeht."[49] The vision of an event enabling the subject to enact the very event which conditions her or him, such a vision places a process at the center of the world. Both subjects and objects, humans and their world, are beholden to this event in their very Being. This structure of Being expressed by the original middle voice is abandoned as soon as the active and the passive voices of "gebildetes Sprechen," of metaphysical conceptualization and its subject-object dualism take over.

I pause to summarize: the middle voice tends to designate actions or the letting-be of events that intimately concern the subject; the middle voice thinks the agent integrated in her or his world, as not different from the world of events. Active forms (or "words for an other" in the terminology of Indian grammarians) are less frequent in Sanskrit and presuppose a separation of the agent and his world. The passive voice, in the historical development sketched by Wackernagel, is also possible only when the object may be thought as radically separated from the agent. The historical development of languages and the gradual loss of the original middle voice coincide with the emergence of an epistemologically dualistic world that we think of as characteristic of Western metaphysics. This way of thinking Being

---

[47]Ibid.
[48]Ibid., 125.
[49]Ibid., 127.

and its structure is beginning to be overcome in philosophical modernism and its attempts to retrieve lost beginnings. What it cannot really retrieve are the original forms of utterance like the middle voice.

In an American study of post-metaphysical thought, Charles E. Scott provides an important philosophical elaboration of the linguistic facts that I have briefly recounted. Scott argues that the middle voice implies the absence of what later came to be known as the spectator-subject of metaphysics. In order to more thoroughly clarify the uses which the middle-voice had for a way of thinking that was not (or not yet) metaphysical, I will quote at some length from Scott:

> The middle voice has lost a significant part of its meaning, its semantic significance, in Western languages. It survives in a limited way primarily in the reflexive function. In early Sanskrit ... the middle voice speaks in the sphere of the subject. On the one hand, it may be reflexive, and on the other, it may speak nonreflexively of an action in the action ... The middle voice is used when the subject is in some way specifically implicated in the result of the action but is neither the active subject nor the passive object of the action. ... This middle-voiced intransitivity is ... found in the Greek middle perfect form, *phainesthai*, meaning 'to appear appearing or appearing appears,' and *gegonesthai*, 'to become becoming' or 'to come becoming.' In both instances the activity of the middle-voiced perfect expresses its temporal movement out of itself.
>
> I note particularly the intransitive uses of the middle voice, because that is one form of the middle voice that is difficult to retrieve in our languages now, but one that plays a significant role in contemporary efforts to think outside of the domain of subjectivity ... [In the intransitive form of the middle voice] there is neither an active subject nor a passive object, and the peculiarity of that structure for our grammar is lost by the reflexive form ... the middle voice ... can indicate a whole occurrence's occurring as a whole without self-positing or reflexive movement throughout the event ... Oiomai 'to think' is also a middle form and suggests an activity that speaks in its own sphere and reverts to itself of itself prior to a subject's taking charge of it. Thinking in this case would be an activity that enacts itself out of its own processes ...
>
> The middle voice suggests something that goes beyond subject-object formations. It is able to articulate nonreflexive enactments that are not for themselves or something else ... It is the voice of something's taking place through its own enactment.[50]

---

[50]Charles E. Scott, *The Question of Ethics: Nietzsche, Foucault, Heidegger* (Bloomington: Indiana University Press, 1990), 19–20, 24.

It is obvious: if the non-dualistic character of Being unfolds in events that concern the subject but are neither initiated nor undergone by the subject, then this character of Being cannot be expressed by the *genera verbi* now in use, neither by the active voice nor by the passive and not even by the reflexive mediopassive. Scott adds importantly to my historical argument because he shows that the middle voice may express "a temporal movement out of itself." It would thus be appropriate for a modern form of thinking outside or beyond subjectivity: it could speak of self-enacting processes like thinking before a subject takes charge of it. This means that non-dualistic modes of thinking that question the primacy of the subject as the foundational place, as the *origo* of Being as it shows itself, that such ways of thinking, which privilege temporal processes, would actually demand the middle voice to properly say how Being eventuates.

William James once said: "It is high time to urge the use of a little imagination in philosophy."[51] In a modest way I would like to follow that injunction and simply read a few passages from James and Dewey more imaginatively in order to indicate that both were aware of a central deficiency in the grammatical structures at their disposal once they were bent on thinking and articulating Being in a non-dualist metaphysical way. They used a variety of strategies to indicate the absence of the middle voice in order to think the structures of Being as experience, as pure or primary experience.[52] By making this deficiency felt, James and Dewey, long before Heidegger, found their own original ways of retrieving lost and forgotten beginnings as the precondition for the possibility of a radical new departure in thought. The modernist gesture of going back "behind" the metaphysical tradition in James and Dewey does not show in a seemingly forced re-translation of Greek thought in order to recapture the suppressed other of thinking; rather, in admitting an absence in language itself, in making the absence of the middle voice show for itself, they seem to open the possibility of thinking beyond the structure of the traditional subject-object-relation in their ontology, without allowing the essentialization that tends to go with all naming. The indirect acknowledgment in James and Dewey not only of the general, but also of this specific deficiency in language, in order to indicate the way Being is structured, shows that they are aware of a process of forgetting (aspects of) Being that is inescapably tied to the history of *logos* itself.

---

[51]*Pragmatism: A New Name for Some Old Ways of Thinking*, vol. 1 of *The Works of William James* (1907; Cambridge, MA: Harvard University Press 1975), 38.

[52]Ruth Anna Putnam speaks of radical empiricism as James's ontology and explains that a "key element of James' radical empiricism is his rejection of mind/matter dualism as well as of its reduction to either materialism or idealism. In its place, he offers ... a world of pure experience... . Ultimately there are only pure experiences"; Putnam, "Introduction," in *The Cambridge Companion to William James* (Cambridge: Cambridge University Press, 1997), 5.

As I have already indicated: experience—more precisely: pure or primary experience—is one of the pragmatist words for Being. Even though pure experience is the central term to them, I would like to begin with a few statements by James and Dewey that foreshadow the problem of thinking structural aspects of Being as event in the pragmatist mode of radical empiricism by using other terms of ordinary language that allow the free play of its deficiencies. In *The Principles of Psychology*—read as a foundational text of the philosophy of the human being, of Being showing as being-there, as *Dasein*—we should consider this well-known passage:

> *The first fact for us, then, as psychologists, is that thinking of some sort goes on.* I use the word thinking ... for every form of consciousness indiscriminately. If we could say in English "it thinks," as we say "it rains" or "it blows," we should be stating the fact most simply and with the minimum of assumption.[53]

As John Dewey explained in one of his centennial essays on James in 1942,[54] this is a statement that prefigures the continuous and unbroken monist and radical empiricist position in James's thinking.[55] What really *is*, namely Being issuing in a human being, is, to borrow Scott's words quoted above, a temporal movement out of itself; Being as *Dasein* is something that takes place through its own enactment. James clearly states that he lacks the linguistic possibility to predicate a pure event without a positioning or positing of either subject and object—he cannot find a middle voice. And we would do well to consider that what we call person or individual or self or subject is only a secondary formation in James, arising out of this stream of thinking that "tends"—as he says—toward a personal consciousness. Alfred North Whitehead was one of the first readers of James who clearly saw that James, in a revolutionary move, had overcome Cartesian dualism without replacing it with a naïve subjectivist solipsism.[56]

In his later works *Experience and Nature* (1925/29) and *Art as Experience* (1934), John Dewey repeatedly stated, implicitly and explicitly, that he thought of mind and art not as noun substantives but rather as verbs. If we consider that mind is the word for experience had from the subjective pole,

---

[53]James, *Principles*, 1, 219–20.
[54]Cf. Dewey, "The Vanishing Subject in the Psychology of James," *LW* 14, 154–67.
[55]Hilary Putnam specifies: "James' way involved what others ... have described as a 'neutral monist' ontology. In such an ontology, the properties and relations we experience *are* the real stuff of the universe; there is no non-experiential 'substratum'"; see Putnam, "Pragmatism and Realism," in *The Revival of Pragmatism: New Essays on Social Thought, Law, and Culture*, ed. Morris Dickstein (Durham, NC: Duke University Press, 1998), 46.
[56]Cf. Alfred North Whitehead, *Science and the Modern World* (New York: Free Press, 1967), 143.

so to speak, that mind is the name for—again—the human being as *Dasein*, then we do realize that Dewey tended to think of Being as an *a priori* event that implied the *a posteriori* possibility of personhood. The important aspect for us, however, is the insistence that this ontological factuality cannot be properly named: we do not have a verb form, the middle voice for a processual emergence of "mind," without objective or subjective core. In Charles E. Scott's words, it is difficult, or better: it is well-nigh impossible in modern English to articulate "an activity that speaks in its own sphere and reverts to itself of itself prior to a subject's taking charge of it."[57] Being human remains word-less; are we not indeed witnessing the fact here that *Seinsvergessenheit*, the forgetting of Being, is remembered as such in Dewey or James without being irresponsibly conceptualized in yet another metaphysical move of usurpation by the very act of naming it, of speaking of it? Art in Dewey, as we know, is continuous with Being as process; it is the consummate form of experience, called *an* experience by Dewey.[58] In this way art—thought of as a verb—makes us aware of the fact that Being as the event of experience in its ultimate and highest conformation precedes its maker and its recipient (logically, even if not temporally); it is an occurrence without prior self-positing of subject or object, a true intransitive middle-voice situatedness.

One of the high points in Dewey's *Experience and Nature* is the simple defining clause in his chapter on "Experience as Precarious and as Stable": "Every existence is an event."[59] Maybe we appreciate this sentence properly only if we translate it into German and thus lift it out of the elegance of its ordinary articulation: "Jedes Seiende ist ein Ereignen." I stress the verb-from here: *Ereignen*. In the context of his meditations on radical temporality, Dewey cannot really but think any being or the Being of beings other than as the structural form of a subjectless occurring. The nouns and the noun phrases in Dewey's sentence ("event" or "every existence") obscure, but they do not hide the verb-like character of Being, the middle-voiced event-character of all existing. By showing and yet not naming, by using the inadequate noun substantive (e.g., "event") for the unavailable middle voice, so it seems, James and Dewey manage the major philosophical feat of letting the event-character of Being be without appropriating it again metaphysically in any supposedly adequate grammatical form whatsoever.

Before we turn to major passages from James and Dewey, it may be appropriate to point out the fact that even though there are only very few explicit statements on Being in the works of both thinkers, we do have distinct and precise comments by James that justify the *fundamentalontologische* approach in this essay. In his last and unfinished masterpiece, *Some Problems*

---

[57]Scott, *The Question of Ethics*, 20.
[58]*Art as Experience LW*, 10, 42–4.
[59]*LW* 1, 63.

*of Philosophy*, James has a short chapter on "The Problem of Being." Here—in a footnote betokening the preliminary character of the text—James calls Being both absolutely contingent and radically temporal, an unforeseeable and ungrounded temporal event: "In more technical language, one may say that fact or being is 'contingent,' or matter of 'chance,' so far as our intellect is concerned. The conditions of its appearance are uncertain, unforeseeable when future, and when past, elusive."[60] In his entry on "Experience" for Baldwin's *Dictionary of Philosophy and Psychology* (1902), James makes it clear that for him—as for Dewey—experience is strictly synonymous with Being: "It is the summum genus of which everything must have been a part before we can speak of it at all."[61] James adds that philosophy should keep that term (experience in the sense of Being) indeterminate. The interesting aspect for my argument here is that Being, for James, is thus ultimately pre-verbal—we do not have signs (any more) that signify experience in its pure *there*. An "indeterminate term" is, after all, not only a paradox; it is no term at all. In its radical contingency, Being is merely here and now as an ongoing event. What follows from this definition, of course, is that in James, and in Dewey, we do not *have* experiences, we *are* experience. However, the middle-voice, as a category no longer available to James and Dewey, does remind us that there may have been a time when the experience of experience, the experience of Being, the *Seinserfahrung* could be articulated—but that was, as we have seen on our linguistic excursion, before the subject established itself as the indispensable center of speaking and knowing. Now, it seems, one can only speak of experience and Being "as if" it were something or *a* something or "as if" it belonged to someone—but one can know that "as if."

The most impressive passages on Being as pure experience may be found in James's *Essays in Radical Empiricism* and in Dewey's *Experience and Nature*. In both cases we find strategies that seem designed to attract attention to the lost possibility of an adequate speech about the ways Being comes to pass, strategies that make us aware of the muted middle voice as the verbal means to express "an activity that enacts itself out of its own processes."[62] In James the strategy is a variation of metaphors used to make pure experience "show for what it is" without essentializing it metaphysically; in Dewey we find a pervasive use of both the active and the passive voice in his descriptive analyses of what is going in or as primary experience (this is Dewey's term for what James calls pure experience).

In his summary of "Does Consciousness Exist?" James asserts that *"thoughts in the concrete are made of the same stuff as things are."*[63] The

---

[60]*Some Problems*, 29.

[61]"Experience," in *Essays in Philosophy*, 95.

[62]Scott, *The Question of Ethics*, 20.

[63]"Does Consciousness Exist?," in *Essays in Radical Empiricism*, vol. 3 of *The Works of William James* (1912; Cambridge, MA: Harvard University Press, 1976), 19.

term "stuff" is a mere pointer indicating a continuity; it does not mean substance, let alone matter. "Stuff" only makes us aware of the fact that in being aware, in experiencing, there is always, firstly and lastly, a *one*, the continuity of experiencing, a simple ongoing *that*. Subject and object thus become secondary and relational terms and dualism is overcome, a dualism that James wittily debunks by stating as its maxim: "Let no man join what God has put asunder."[64] Having joined the separate spheres torn apart in the Christian-Platonic and especially in the Cartesian tradition, James may confidently offer his special version of (individualized) monism: "It means that not subject, not object, but object-plus-subject is the minimum that can actually be."[65] Experiencing as Being goes on in eachnesses, in individual instances, but each instance is non-dualistic. These non-dualistic eachnesses, these temporal *thats* which precede the separation of subject and object are difficult to describe in the way they are "structured." It seems impossible to talk about the way they go on because, grammatically speaking, the nouns, indicating subject and object, as well as the verb are collapsed into one event. Since there are no *genera verbi* like the middle voice ready to articulate an activity "that speaks in its own sphere and reverts to itself of itself prior to a subject's taking charge of it," as Scott says, James offers a variety of metaphorical versions in *Essays in Radical Empiricism*, indicating not what Being as experience *is*, but *what it is like*. The metaphors convey a sense, they facilitate an experience of the structural properties of Being as event; at the same time their number and variety reveal the fact that there is no longer any adequate form of representing them in language. Language has become a search for experience as Being, demonstrating that the initial self-revelation of Being has been lost or forgotten. All that can be retrieved by means of metaphorical indirection is the sense of an absence.

James offers this first metaphoric view of how experience shows itself of itself:

My thesis is that if we start with the supposition that there is only one primal stuff or material in the world, a stuff of which everything is composed, and if we call that stuff "pure experience," then knowing can easily be explained as a particular sort of relation towards one another into which portions of pure experience may enter. The relation itself is a part of pure experience; one of its "terms" becomes the subject or bearer of the knowledge, the knower, the other becomes the object known.[66]

This passage, to state the obvious, is about "pure experience." Pure experience we accept as James's word for Being. Being is a relational event imaged here

---

[64]Ibid.
[65]Ibid., 5.
[66]Ibid., 4–5.

by the use of the philosophically familiar, even if misleading, term "stuff." The functioning of this relational stuff is called consciousness, which is—in this essay—denied the status of an entity. The stuff of pure experience is therefore to be understood as a process. This process, however, cannot be named by means of the use of a verb. We have grammatically nothing at our disposal but the active and the passive voices, and these both presuppose subjects and/or objects; the functioning of the stuff, however, presupposes the togetherness, the continuity of subject and object. There is no thing in or as the stuff to take the role of subject or object in a sentence about it. It is an event. For such an event there is no proper, no middle voice in our language indicating its self-enactment.

James offers a second metaphor in "Does Consciousness Exist?" for the structural character of the singular totality of Being called pure experience:

> The instant field of the present is at all times what I call the "pure" experience. It is only virtually or potentially either object or subject as yet. For the time being, it is plain, unqualified actuality or existence, a simple *that*. In this *naïf* immediacy it is of course *valid*; it is *there*, we *act* upon it; and the doubling of it in retrospection into a state of mind and a reality intended thereby, is just one of the acts.[67]

The stuff has been replaced by the instant field, a temporalized space a literally momentary *Da*, a total immediacy in time containing all its possible subjective states and objective referents. This immediate experience in its passing is always true, James adds. However, there is, as will be easily understood, no statement possible to articulate this truth. This truth is subject- and objectless: it happens. Being as pure experience evades articulation—what would be needed were, again, an intransitive form of the middle voice. The truth of the instant field of pure experience—just as the event-character of the stuff of pure experience—remains silent; our speech is always already too late, having to rely on entities that have emerged out of the field of the present. Our experience and our language, however, remember an earlier state of affairs, a simple *that* which once, in the earliest beginnings of thought and language, could be spoken as the utterance of nobody, as—in Wallace Stevens's phrase—"the cry of its occasion."[68]

In "The Thing and Its Relations," we find a third metaphor that is intended to make Being as pure experience show:

> "Pure experience" is the name which I gave to the immediate flux of life which furnishes the material for our later reflections with its conceptual

[67]Ibid., 13.
[68]Wallace Stevens, "An Ordinary Evening in New Haven," in *The Collected Poems of Wallace Stevens* (New York: Knopf, 1973), 473.

categories. Only new-born babes, or men in semi-coma from sleep, drugs, illnesses, or blows, may be assumed to have an experience pure in the literal sense of a *that* which is not yet any definite *what*, tho ready to be all sorts of whats; full both of oneness and of manyness, but in respects that don't appear; changing throughout, yet so confusedly that its phases interpenetrate and no points, either of distinction or of identity, can be caught. Pure experience in this state is but another name for feeling or sensation. But the flux of it no sooner comes than it tends to fill itself with emphases, and these salient parts become identified and fixed and abstracted; so that experience now flows as if shot through with adjectives and nouns and prepositions and conjunctions. Its purity is only a relative term, meaning the proportional amount of unverbalized sensation which it still embodies.[69]

This wonderful image that replaces or, rather, varies the "stuff" and "the instant field of the present" visualizes the emergence of conceptualizations within a flow of experiencing, within the temporal process which we also call Being. The interesting point, for us, is that language arises and works *in* pure experience, it is not *about* it. As in the case of the preceding metaphors, we lack a verbal strategy to say what is happening. Instead we are offered a description, an image, which—as we now see distinctly—is only one in a possible variety of indirect, of slant approaches to what we are talking about when we talk about pure experience. Pure experience allows things to be as experienced; it shows and reveals beings (*entbirgt* in Heidegger's terminology) but—in the very act of showing or letting a world of beings emerge—Being as pure experience also hides (*verbirgt sich*). It hides because, as we have now amply seen, the grammatical category for the event of appropriation (*das Ereignis* in Heidegger) is lacking. James's images and metaphors for pure experience create a world of "as ifs," none of which has authority. The middle voice could have spoken directly and without authorizing authority: it might have been a way of letting Being be. This, however, is ir-re-vocable because, literally, we have lost that voice. James's very varieties, which image what *is*, testify to that event.

Readers of Dewey's works, especially of the later works, will be impressed, or pained, by his consistent and insistent use of the active and passive voice in one and the same sentence. "Doing and undergoing" is the standard variety of the many recurring phrases that seem designed, especially in *Experience and Nature* and *Art as Experience*, to catch the interactive rhythms of environmentally co-determined individual experience. Already in "The Need for a Recovery of Philosophy" (1917), the earliest programmatic statement of his later philosophical vision, Dewey spoke of the person as agent-

---

[69]"The Thing and Its Relations," in *Essays in Radical Empiricism*, 46.

patient,[70] as aspect of a total environmental event transcending what used to be called subject and object or self and world. It is important, however, not to take Dewey's biologistic metaphors literally.[71] In *Experience and Nature*, we find a passage in which the stylistic feature of the passive-active dualism and the environmentalist metaphor coalesce in order to redefine what James called pure experience.

> We begin by noting that "experience" is what James called a double-barrelled word. Like its congeners, life and history, it includes *what* men do and suffer, *what* they strive for, love, believe and endure, and also *how* men act and are acted upon, the ways in which they do and suffer, desire and enjoy, see, believe, imagine—in short processes of *experiencing*. "Experience" denotes the planted field, the sowed seeds, the reaped harvests, the changes of night and day, spring and autumn, wet and dry, heat and cold, that are observed, feared, longed for; it also denotes the one who plants and reaps, works and rejoices, hopes, fears, plans, invokes magic or chemistry to aid him, who is downcast or triumphant. It is "double-barrelled" in that it recognizes in its primary integrity no division between act and material, subject and object, but contains them both in an unanalyzed totality.[72]

Dewey's evocation of Being as *experiencing*—he properly uses the verbal form—speaks from within experience. It is here that subjects and objects, active and passive, *existentia* and *essentia*, the *how* and the *what* of a world as experienced may be talked about. The "unanalyzed totality," however, remains—naturally—silent. Analysis presupposes agent and object, the active and the passive voice. Being, in this passage, shrinks to a mere pointer, a hint. Its fullness or totality cannot be said: a whole occurrence's occurring *as* a whole, without the self-positing of an agent or reflexive movement throughout the event, would demand the presence of the lost middle voice. Instead, Dewey's constant movements back and forth between the active and the passive voice not only indicate the togetherness of person and environment in the "unanalyzed totality"; these movements are oscillations about the silent central event of Being as it goes on, oscillations that remind us of the lost *genus verbi* that once voiced the true middle.

James and Dewey make us realize the deficiency of language in speaking of the ways of pure experience or Being. This is a significant achievement. Language—our Western languages at least—has forgotten how to say *what*

---

[70]"The Need for a Recovery of Philosophy" *MW* 10, 10–11.
[71]Cf. Raymond D. Boisvert, *John Dewey: Rethinking Our Time* (Albany: State University of New York Press, 1998), 1 ff.
[72]*LW* 1, 18.

*is* in its pure event-like happening. The middle voice can only be recalled as an absence. In recalling this absence through their insistence on the verb-like character of Being, through their variations on metaphor, and through their incessant play of the active and passive voices, James and Dewey make it possible to think the structures of Being or pure experience as that which both hides (itself) and gives presence (to worlds of experience) without subjecting it to our appropriative ways of speaking.

It is remarkable and significant that one of the greatest works of modern Japanese philosophy appeared only five or six years after the publication of James's articles later collected as *Essays in Radical Empiricism.* In *Zen no kenkyu (An Inquiry into the Good*[73]), published in 1911, Kitarô Nishida reconstructed traditional Japanese religious and philosophical thought by using William James's concept of pure experience as the center and focus of his critical argument that established an innovative, post-metaphysical monist philosophy. As Nishida's disciple Toratarô Shimomura has explained, in using a language that does not necessarily imply a subject in its syntax, Nishida managed to let pure experience speak in an unprecedented way.[74] The English translation of the Japanese original still retains traces of a semantic potential that closely approximates the possibilities of reading Being associated with the former middle voice of the Indo-Germanic languages. This potential, then, is not wholly lost—even though muted. The modern (American) attempt to regain the non-subjectivist implications of forgotten beginnings must realize that, for example, Japanese thinking, emerging out of a horizon opened by a radically different language, is possibly one of its most powerful allies.[75]

---

[73]Kitarô Nishida, *An Inquiry into the Good*, trans. Masao Abe and Christopher Ives (1911; New Haven, CT: Yale University Press, 1990).

[74]Toratarô Shimomura, "Mentalität und Logik der Japaner," in *Die Philosophie der Kyôto-Schule: Texte und Einführung*, ed. Ryôsuke Ohashi (Freiburg: Alber, 1990), 382–3.

[75]Martin Heidegger was well aware of the importance of Japanese thought and language for his own project of overcoming the metaphysical tradition; cf. Heidegger, "Aus einem Gespräch von der Sprache," in *Unterwegs zur Sprache*, ed. Friedrich-Wilhelm von Herrmann, vol. 12 of *Gesamtausgabe* (1959; Frankfurt: Klostermann, 1985), 79–204. One must not forget, however, that Heidegger was less than candid about the degree to which his own thought had profited from Eastern sources; cf. Reinhard May, *Heidegger's Hidden Sources: East Asian Influences on His Work*, trans. Graham Parkes (1989; London: Routledge, 1996).

# 15

# Polite Disagreements:
# James and Bergson

A proper way of thinking modernism differs fundamentally from working out a theory of modernism. A proper way of thinking modernism differs from any attempt to write the historical genealogy of the modernist period; it differs substantially from any descriptive or prescriptive cultural theory about it, be that theory of modernism based on sociological, on political, or on *ideengeschichtliche* assumptions or on the phenomenological description of changing practices in cultural and artistic expression. As we know from Emerson, Nietzsche, Husserl, Dewey, or Heidegger, thinking modernism tends often to energetically reactivate the very earliest moments of Greek thought, those modes and models of philosophical meditation and reflection that necessarily seem to all later philosophers without precedent and therefore truly innovative. These earliest instances appear as modern in the most basic and radical of senses: the earliest Greek moments of philosophy were and are destined to always remain new and exemplary for all later modernisms because, so we assume, nothing ever came before, because, we assume, there were and could be no antecedents. These very earliest moments of thinking, pre-European, Presocratic, have, among many other momentous injunctions, powerfully and effectively reminded their post-metaphysical heirs of American and European modernism that—in Parmenides's starkly simple and measured words—thinking and Being are one: *to gar auto noein estin te kai einai.*[1] My proposition to discuss proper

---

This essay was previously published as "Proper Ways of Thinking Modernism: The Amiable Disagreements of William James and Henri Bergson" in *Proceedings of the German Association of American Studies Annual Conference 2005*, ed. Christa Buschendorf and Astrid Franke (Heidelberg: Winter, 2007), 85–99. Reprinted by permission of Universitätsverlag Winter GmbH.

[1]Parmenides, *Die Fragmente*, ed. and trans. Ernst Heitsch (Zurich: Artemis und Winkler, 1995), 16.

ways of thinking modernism, then, should properly challenge us to explore the implied or explicit ontologies, the modes of thinking Being, of thinking the way the world is, of thinking the modes and modulations of the real as they inform and ground the representative modern efforts of William James and Henri Bergson on either side of the Atlantic—by which I emphatically do not mean that dubious space of recent academic fantasy called "North Atlantic Culture," but much rather an open field of tensions and, above all, of productive and enriching differences *between* cultures.

# Agreements on philosophical methods

The philosophical *way* toward a modern mode of thinking Being, the *methodos* of both William James and Henri Bergson, is most adequately defined and described as anti-intellectualism. Anti-intellectualism as a philosophical method is easily misunderstood, and this is why I would like to begin with a few very plain preparatory remarks that may help to contextualize as well as define the term and its potential uses in reconstructing ontological concerns within a genuine modernist departure in thinking. Anti-intellectualism is basically and always anti-conceptualist. The central dignity of the concept as the essential means of articulating the stable, underlying, and unchanging aspects of Being, the *substantia* or *hypokeimenon* that is thought to be indispensable in any metaphysical system, this central dignity is fundamentally shaken and questioned on either side of the Atlantic by, firstly, Emerson[2] and then, following and inspired by Emerson's example, in Nietzsche's philosophy. Emerson's systematically unreliable and ultimately evasive terminology, which refuses to capture, to hold or conceive, any real entity in any *Begriff* whatsoever, this terminological strategy with its emphasis on "the accidency and fugacity of the symbol"[3] finds its Nietzschean equivalent in the typically hyperbolic implications of "Über Wahrheit und Lüge im aussermoralischen Sinne" where Nietzsche shows how concepts necessarily lie to us *whenever* and *as* they insinuate the existence of separate, well-defined stable self-identical entities or beings.[4] The anti- or post-metaphysical thrust of these positions needs no elaboration: the world of substances and identities seems endangered or even abandoned.

In his wonderful critical appreciation of Bergson's anti-intellectualist method in the chapter entitled "Bergson and Intellectualism" in *A Pluralistic Universe* (1909), James explains:

---

[2]Cf. Herwig Friedl, "Ralph Waldo Emerson und die Erosion der Metaphysik," in *Subversive Romantik*, ed. Klaus Lubbers (Berlin: Duncker & Humblot, 2004), 53–78.

[3]"The Poet" *W* III, 25.

[4]Friedrich Nietzsche, "Über Wahrheit und Lüge im aussermoralischen Sinne," *KSA* 1, 879.

The essence of life is its continuously changing character; but our concepts are all discontinuous and fixed, and the only mode of making them coincide with life is by arbitrarily supposing positions of arrest therein. With such arrests our concepts may be made congruent. But these concepts are not *parts* of reality, not real positions taken by it, but *suppositions* rather, notes taken by ourselves, and you can no more dip up the substance of reality with them than you can dip up water with a net, however finely meshed.

When we conceptualize, we cut out and fix, and exclude everything but what we have fixed. A concept means a *that-and-no-other*.[5]

In a letter dated March 11, 1909, Bergson responded enthusiastically to the manuscript of *A Pluralistic Universe*, and he commented on the passage quoted by saying: "Sur le rôle purement pratique des concepts vous vous exprimez beaucoup mieux que je n'aurais pu le faire, mais dans le sens même où je l'aurais fait."[6] This may serve as one example of the predominant style of genuine and elegantly intense appreciation in which both Bergson and James expressed their deep mutual respect. Anti-intellectualism, so it seems, meant for both a critique of the essential inadequacy of conceptual thinking, and thus of an important or maybe even *the* central aspect of traditional Western metaphysics, as a way, a *methodos* to articulate, to grasp, to convey, to evaluate that which truly *is*. Anti-intellectualism in James and Bergson indicates that, for them, a modern ontology would have to find new modes of saying Being, a new *logos*.

As I have indicated, the methodological consonance of James and Bergson could not have been more thorough, more fundamental, and more amiable. James's enthusiasm for Bergson's anti-intellectualist position seemed boundless, occasionally even exorbitant. After his first perusal of *L'Évolution créatrice* he wrote to Bergson on June 13, 1907: "To me at present the vital achievement of the book is that it inflicts an irrecoverable death-wound upon Intellectualism. It can never rescussitate!"[7] To his most intimate and trusted pragmatist friend and colleague in England, Ferdinand Canning Scott Schiller, James exulted on July 15 of the same year: "Bergson will be the *great* intellectualism-smasher,"[8] and a few months later, on October 16, he answered Schiller's definitely low-keyed and unenthusiastic response to his own ravings about *L'Évolution créatrice* by insisting somewhat peeved and stubbornly: "but he has *opened new horizons*, and he has surely given

[5]*A Pluralistic Universe*, vol. 4 of *The Works of William James* (1909; Cambridge, MA: Harvard University Press, 1977), 113.
[6]*The Correspondence of William James*, ed. Ignas K. Skrupskelis and Elizabeth M. Berkeley (Charlottesville: University of Virginia Press, 1992–2004), vol. 12, 175.
[7]*Correspondence* 11, 376.
[8]Ibid., 388.

*intellectualism its coup de grace."*[9] In that respect and in spite of Schiller's misgivings, James certainly felt greatly reassured when Bergson on January 27, 1908, kindly stated: "Pour ma part, je n'ai jamais mieux saisi l'affinité qui existe entre nos deux méthodes de penser."[10] Methodologically, I would like to emphasize, there indeed seemed to be no discrepancy between James's own approach to vital reality, to life, to Being in and through thinking and the strategies of his younger colleague-in-arms, the anti-intellectualist dragon-slayer Bergson.

Not everyone, however, saw it that way, and anti-intellectualism, Jamesian fashion, became the target of an acrimonious attack early on, an attack by Walter B. Pitkin, professor at Columbia, who, in a paper published in the *Journal of Philosophy, Psychology and Scientific Methods* in 1910, thought it necessary to point out that James's anti-intellectualism reduced concepts to mere practical tools of conducting inquiries, whereas Bergson still and undoubtedly held sway as the champion of intellect as the central avenue, the *camino real*, to true Being.[11] Professor Pitkin certainly lost his first battle against what he saw as James's reductive anti-intellectualism, even though, in the long run, he could—amazingly—recruit such prominent allies as Bertrand Russell to the cause of what remain to this day basically unsophisticated attacks on the Jamesian position. Horace M. Kallen at Harvard and Henri Bergson himself came to the rescue: they both published subtle and incisive refutations of Pitkin's position in the same journal in 1910. Kallen, quoting profusely from James and Bergson, showed that *both* thinkers saw concepts as essentially pragmatic tools that are by necessity inadequate and ineffectual for the purpose of revealing reality, life, Being. Concepts help us organize our approaches to real thinking, they function as and within preparatory arguments, but they do no ontological work at all. As Kallen says, "Forms and concepts are invariably abstractions that miss the heart of reality."[12] Bergson himself concluded his essay "À propos d'un article de Mr. Walter B. Pitkin intitulé: 'James and Bergson'" with these words: "Sur tout cela [i.e., anti-intellectualism] [James] a dit exactement ce que je pense. Je voudrais seulement l'avoir aussi bien dit";[13] and in the letter dated March 11, 1909, Bergson emphasized, once again, his full agreement with James's pragmatist version of anti-intellectualism and his insistence on "le role purement pratique des concepts."[14]

---

[9]Ibid., 461.

[10]Ibid., 531.

[11]Walter B. Pitkin, "James and Bergson: Or, Who Is against Intellect?," in *Pure Experience: The Response to William James*, ed. Eugene I. Taylor and Robert H. Wozniak (Bristol: Thoemmes Press, 1996), 201–8.

[12]Horace Meyer Kallen, "James, Bergson, and Mr. Pitkin," in *Pure Experience*, ed. Taylor and Wozniak, 209–13.

[13]*Correspondence* 12, 525.

[14]Ibid., 175.

# Mutual appreciations

The identity, or at least the thorough parallelism, in James's and Bergson's interpretations of the function of concepts in a philosophical inquiry does not prepare their readers for a major, a significant, an amazing divergence or disagreement in their philosophical engagement of the question of Being. Their ways of thinking life, the world, the real as innovative at its very core, of thinking Being as ontologically modern, of celebrating, as James once said to Bergson, "a truly growing world,"[15] these seemingly identical goals lead into different directions, toward ultimately incompatible positions. The fundamental transatlantic difference in thinking modernism, however, never shows quite as dramatic as it really is when we look at the way James and Bergson charmingly negotiated, politely appreciated, and amiably obscured their disagreements both in their letters and in their mutual interpretations within their philosophical writings. At the very beginning of their correspondence in 1902, James welcomed the daring innovations in Bergson's *Essai sur les données immédiates de la conscience* (1889) and in *Matière et mémoire* (1896). At the same time he began the strategy of hiding some of his misgivings under the guise of not being quite able to follow the intricacies of the argument. Concerning the spatialization of matter, for instance, James would write to Bergson: "I think I understand the main lines of your system very well at present though of course I can't yet trace its proper relations to the aspects of experience of which you do not treat. It needs much building out."[16] As late as 1908, in a letter to his Swiss supporter Professor Théodore Flournoy of Geneva, and after a visit with Bergson in London, James admitted: "I can't say that I follow the *folds* of his system much more clearly than I did before."[17] The system, the ontological interpretation of the relationship of energetic durational becoming and static spatialized matter in Bergson, remained not the only enigma to James. As he argues in a letter dated February 1903, it seemed to him as if Bergson, in his ontology, was drifting back into traditional substantialist metaphysics and had even found new ways of allowing the old Transcendentalist or even idealist concept of the soul to re-emerge under the guise of his conception of *mémoire*.[18] James found a rare candid characterization for his philosophical unease with Bergson when, in a letter to A. O. Lovejoy, he confessed in 1904: "He is the puzzle for me just now. Such incessant gleams of truth on such an obscure background."[19]

---

[15]*Correspondence* 11, 377.
[16]*Correspondence* 10, 167.
[17]*Correspondence* 12, 101.
[18]*Correspondence* 10, 203.
[19]Ibid., 377.

The single most intensely celebratory and, at the same time, the most ambiguous instance of private appreciations and critical reservations is James's letter welcoming the publication of *L'Évolution créatrice* in 1907. The style of the new book alone, James believes, is worthy of a Flaubert, the imagery impeccable and immensely serviceable for the ontological argument: "Oh indeed you are a magician," James exclaims; and then he starts to hedge and imagine what others—not he himself, at least not openly—might object to: "the *élan vital*, all contentless & vague as you are obliged to leave it, will be an easy substitute [for the metaphysical soul] to make fun of."[20] The critics will not be long in waiting to say, James adds, that "Schopenhauer's blind will, Hartmann's unconscious, Fichte's aboriginal freedom ... will all be claimants for priority."[21] In short, Bergson's central ontological intuition of a relentlessly innovative, creative, modern mode of Being and becoming may, after all, only be a return of the suppressed late idealist substantializations; the old in the guise of the modern. In fact, James's Swiss friend Théodore Flournoy was the first to insist, only one month after James's letter to Bergson, that the "*élan vital* is much like the unconscious thrust of German monists," naming Schopenhauer, Hartmann, and Fichte as possible predecessors, just as James had.[22] Writing again to Lovejoy, James felt he could say it all less indirectly: "Have you read Bergson's *Évolution créatrice*? I find it perfectly glorious, though terribly obscure and unfinished."[23] Unhampered by feelings of personal fascination with and admiration for Bergson, F. C. S. Schiller in Oxford expressed openly and soberly what we find implicit in James's hesitations: "And now I must confess," he wrote to James, "that I was rather disappointed in Bergson. Perhaps you had pitched my expectations too high. But he did not remove any of the difficulties I had with him before. E.g. I can't make out how he comes by his conception of matter, what is his epistemological attitude & his relation to idealist arguments ... he never really explains what he means by his élan vital."[24] Schiller's diagnosis of a return to a late idealist ontology in Bergson, without precisely articulated epistemological underpinnings and a persistent confusion of the ontic and the ontological in the analysis of the *élan vital* as it supports both biological evolution and Being in general, this frank diagnosis goes far toward explaining James's focus, or rather the reasons for his omissions, in his greatest tribute to Bergson, the chapter devoted to him in *A Pluralistic Universe*. As James explained to Bergson

---

[20]*Correspondence* 11, 376.
[21]Ibid., 377–8.
[22]Ibid., 616.
[23]Ibid., 445.
[24]Ibid., 450.

on July 19, 1908: "You see that I suppress almost all of your philosophy [in this chapter] for the sake of emphasizing all the more your critique of intellectualism."[25]

Bergson fully matched James in tasteful or, should we say, timid reticence. He was always terribly apprehensive and nervous that he might be considered James's mere disciple in his interpretation of the world, of Being as Flow, and fearfully angry when this was indeed insinuated.[26] Bergson, with the prominent exception of his cheerful acknowledgment of their common foe of intellectualism, hardly ever responded to James's propositions in his letters that a truly tychistic and synechistic world, a world of chance and continuity and of unprecedented, undetermined becoming, might be pluralistic rather than understood in terms of a massive monist entity like Bergson's élan vital. In Bergson's comments on James, as in James's chapter on Bergson in *A Pluralistic Universe*, there is only the indirect admission of an unbridgeable gap, a true disagreement, an admission of differences—mostly by means of omission. In his introduction to the 1911 French translation of James's *Pragmatism*, Bergson admiringly and approvingly sketches James's thinking as a whole by emphasizing the way his ontology, his foundational concept of reality, respects the plenitude and messiness of the world and its lack of clear boundaries, all of which, of course, defeats any intellectualist approach. Toward the end of his essay, however, Bergson cautiously and almost inaudibly distances himself from any idea of a pluralist world of multiple emerging self-awarenesses as it was advanced in James's centrally important *Essays on Radical Empiricism*.[27]

---

[25]*Correspondence* 12, 55.

[26]There are at least two cases in which Bergson's irritation with any imputation of too close a dependence of his thinking on William James as a possible predecessor becomes manifest (see also Chapter 16 in this book): 1. In his 1905 report on the Fifth International Congress on Psychology in Rome, where James had read a paper, Gaston Rageot stated that central ideas proposed by Bergson in his *Essai sur les données immédiates de la conscience* were obviously inspired by James. Bergson refuted this imputation energetically in the same issue of the *Revue philosophique*, and he reported to James that he had to emphasize "des points de départ différents et des methodes différentes" in their respective thinking; see Bergson, *Mélanges* ed. André Robinet (Paris: Presses Universitaires de France, 1972), 661. 2. When Horace Kallen sent his study *William James and Henri Bergson: A Study in Contrasting Theories of Life* (1914) to Bergson, the latter refuted a fundamental difference in their basic philosophical intuitions while at the same time insisting on the quite incompatible ways of thinking by which James, as a psychologist, and he himself, using mathematical modes of thinking, had arrived at the conception of a durational flow or "stream of consciousness"; ibid., 1194.

[27]Bergson, "Introduction," in James, *Le Pragmatisme*, trans. E. Le Brun (Paris: Flammarion, 1911), *passim*.

# Fundamental differences

The first step of my argument has indicated the basic agreement or parallelism of the philosophical strategies, the methods in James's and Bergson's attempts to think modernism as a consistently innovative departure in the dispensation of Being: their anti-intellectualism denies the possibility to use concepts and thus refuses to follow the metaphysical tradition, ever since Plato and Aristotle, in ascertaining what Being is, what existing means, how the emerging world shows. My second concern was a sketch of the transatlantic dialogue of the two thinkers that appears as devoted to mutual appreciation and gracious acknowledgment as to a careful avoidance of a possibly deep and momentous discrepancy and maybe even an antagonism in their central intuitions of existence, in their ontologies. My third and last focus will be on these central ontological intuitions of James and Bergson in their essential, their defining and characteristic difference, the very difference never fully faced by the two philosophers.

Let me begin by introducing a simple, but helpful, distinction. Ontologies, *Seinslehren*, have a way of coming in basically two forms: as discrete and as indiscrete ontologies. Discrete ontologies prevail under the sway of Western metaphysics; indiscrete ontologies characterize much Asian and most truly modern, post-metaphysical thinking. Wolfram Hogrebe has provided this useful and succinct distinction and definition:

> Der Gegenstandsbereich, der durch die diskrete Ontologie erfaßt wird, ist nämlich nicht nur anderer Art als der der indiskreten, er hat auch, wie man sagen möchte, eine andere Dimension. Die diskrete Ontologie erfaßt alle Gegenstände. Wenn man auf ihrem Boden fragt, was es gibt, dann ist … in der Tat mit Quine zu antworten: alles. Die Dimension der diskreten Ontologie könnte man daher auch "horizontal" nennen.
>
> Die indiskrete Ontologie hingegen erfaßt nicht alle Gegenstände, sondern gewissermaßen die gesamte Gegenständlichkeit. Sie geht nicht "nach außen" auf den Umfang, sondern "nach innen" in die Tiefe der Dinge und beansprucht die "vertikale" Dimension.[28]

In the context of my inquiry and on the basis of what we generally know, it seems obvious, at least at first sight, that both James and Bergson are not primarily devoted to an ontological conception and interpretation of "everything" in its horizontal and cosmic spatial disposition. It is rather the inner and vertical depth of experiential Being, as Hogrebe insinuates, that appears to characterize their projects. It is not the world as potentially

---

[28]Wolfram Hogrebe, *Metaphysik und Mantik: Die Deutungsnatur des Menschen* (Frankfurt: Akademie Verlag, 1992), 122–3.

endless addition of distinct entities—things or concepts or beings in general—they are ostensibly concerned with but rather the transitional, *entgrenzte*, fluxional, dynamic, emergent character of the way in which the world possibly and ceaselessly renews itself, innovates itself, shows as, in James's words, a "truly growing world," a modern world. James and Bergson both show as champions of the "indiscrete" charm of an emergent mode of Being within which clear-cut, conceptually available singularities are mere *a posteriori* constructions for practical purposes. One thing is certain in worlds in which the paradigm of evolution and emergence, of "streams of thought" and "élans vitals" has replaced the paradigm of a mechanical interaction of distinct entities, in worlds in which metamorphic and dynamic transformations replace rigid entities: in such worlds, concepts with their inflexible and delimiting boundary lines are fundamentally inadequate. Indiscrete ontologies must have difficulties with conceptual language, with intellectualist methodologies of thinking.

What, then, do indiscrete ontologists do, what do they say, how do they articulate their most intimate sense of Being? The answer is simple and not at all surprising: indiscrete ontologists use images, they indulge in metaphors, they become poets (in a way)—just as Emerson had prophesied it for a philosophy of the future in his *Natural History of Intellect*.[29] Vico and Goethe had already asserted that "erste nothwendige Ur-Tropen,"[30] necessary and inescapable primal tropes, are always at the beginning and ground of all proper thinking and interpretation of Being. With truly modernist thinking, with Emerson and Nietzsche, however, this reliance on original, foundational tropes is abandoned and a new variety of images for the purpose of proper thinking takes center-stage: the fugacity and fluxional quality of all imagistic symbolizations in Emerson, as he stated it in "The Poet,"[31] and Nietzsche's "bewegliches Heer von Metaphern"[32] insinuate that language, just like the constantly renewed emergent reality that it tries to think at the beginning of modernism, that the true language of thinking does not and cannot possess original, foundational, *ursprüngliche* metaphoric symbolizations. A true modernist indiscrete ontology would prefer, would have to indulge in a persistent metaphorical revisionism or troping[33] when

---

[29]"Natural History of Intellect" W XIII, 12. Emerson says here, projecting a "philosophy of the future," Nietzschean style: "I think that philosophy is still rude and elementary. It will one day be taught by poets."

[30]Johann Wolfgang Goethe, "Orientalischer Poesie Ur-Elemente," in *West-östlicher Divan*, ed. Karl Richter, vol. 11.1.2 of *Sämtliche Werke* (Munich: Hanser, 1998), 185.

[31]"The Poet" W III, 25 and 37: "For all symbols are fluxional; all language is vehicular and transitive."

[32]Nietzsche, "Über Wahrheit und Lüge," 880.

[33]A seminal reading of troping as central linguistic strategy of the American pragmatist tradition is found in Richard Poirier, *The Renewal of Literature: Emersonian Reflections* (New York: Random House, 1987), 13–19; and, more extensively, in Poirier's *Poetry and Pragmatism* (Cambridge, MA: Harvard University Press, 1992), *passim*.

it tries to evoke, and create a sense of what it means by, Being as emergent event. Emerson, as the fountainhead of both the American pragmatist modernism and the Nietzschean variety of European modernist thought, had argued that "[a] happy symbol is a sort of evidence that your thought is just" and that "a good symbol is the best argument" because proper thinking, for Emerson, is persistent "analogizing" in a world of "incessant metamorphosis."[34] Metaphoric symbolizations, then, assume a new role once Being is no longer read as something to be contained in or based on a conceptual or imaginatively *intuited* foundation; a modernist indiscrete ontology calls for a flexible, a revisionist utilization of metaphoric intuition and speech. I want to subject James's and Bergson's metaphors to the test. Who, this is the question, who is the more indiscrete of the two in thinking and saying, in imagining and in imaging that which *is*?

James thought that one of the great achievements of his and Bergson's program of anti-intellectualism was what he called the "liquefaction"[35] of previous and established modes of thinking and speaking. It is one of the hallmarks of James's images and metaphors, which guide and transcendentally inform his elucidations of Being, that they are never allowed to coagulate, to ossify, and thus to assume the character of essentializing signifiers. What we observe in his writings from *The Principles of Psychology* (1890) through the *Essays in Radical Empiricism* (1906) to the final *Some Problems of Philosophy* (posth. 1911) is indeed a constant and deliberate imagistic troping and revisionism. We know that one of James's basic words for Being is experience. In his entry for Baldwin's *Dictionary of Philosophy and Psychology* (1902), he defines it as follows: experience hints at "the entire process of phenomena ... in their raw immediacy, before reflective thought has analysed them into subjective and objective aspects or ingredients. It is the summum genus of which everything must have been a part before we can speak of it at all."[36] The subtle point of this "definition" is that it denies the term "experience" the status of a concept: James, using an obvious pun, insists that one has to "keep the term indeterminate." It is thus merely a liminal signifier indicating the simple *is* or *that* which, as a total awareness, precedes any articulation and thus any concept whatsoever; the *summum genus*, experience, Being, is before objectivity and subjectivity[37] and thus before the possibility of conceptually argumentative language.

---

[34]"Poetry and Imagination" W VIII, 18–20.

[35]*Correspondence* 10, 167.

[36]"Experience," in *Essays in Philosophy*, vol. 5 of *The Works of William James* (Cambridge, MA: Harvard University Press, 1978), 95.

[37]On the non-dualist conception of Being as experience, cf. James M. Edie, *William James and Phenomenology* (Bloomington: University of Indiana Press, 1987), 33; Ruth Anna Putnam, "Introduction," in *The Cambridge Companion to William James*, ed. Putnam (Cambridge: Cambridge University Press, 1997), 5; Hilary Putnam, "Pragmatism and Realism," in *The*

This experience, which beings *are*, which they do not *have*, indicates what Hogrebe calls the "Tiefe der Dinge" in a truly indiscrete ontology. James sometimes named this liminal realm "pure experience." Pure experience is imaged, metaphorized as the stream of consciousness before it allows a subject and her or his or its world of objects to emerge from within. In the *Essays in Radical Empiricism*, pure experience, sheer pre-conceptual awareness as ongoing event is called flux[38] in order to allow provisional conceptual comments on its temporal dimension; it is called stuff[39] when James tries to provisionally comment on its possibly pervasive character; the image of a field[40] is chosen for the spatial aspects that pure experience does not possess but show from the shifting points of view of inquiries within the space opened as awareness for all kinds of philosophical considerations; the metaphor of the mosaic[41] lends itself to a perspective focusing on the way the emergent stream of awareness adds what we tend to call objective content onto itself. The open-ended series of Jamesian metaphors—stream, flux, field, stuff, mosaic—provides a flexible, a liquefied arsenal, if there is such a thing, a growing and revisionist variety of phenomenal guidelines for the always tentative and preliminary comments phrased in conceptual language, that thin language which, in James's terminology, points toward but always misses the thick presence[42] for which changing images provide the inexhaustible background and challenge in order to think Being as process, as relentlessly self-modernizing indiscrete event or, rather, continuity of events. Pure experience does not come as a monist totality; it comes as a pluralist manifold, an endless series of ontologically full eachnesses, as James has it. Both statements are true: 1. Being is always one: it is monistic in its primal togetherness of world and awareness; 2. Being is always many: it persistently emerges as a multiplicity of such singular or individual awarenesses. In order to know all this, according to James, all we need is what we are, what each thing is before it knows itself as a subjective suchness—namely, "thought going on":[43] we have to be indiscrete as thinking beings.

---

*Revival of Pragmatism: New Essays on Social Thought, Law, and Culture*, ed. Morris Dickstein (Durham, NC: Duke University Press, 1998), 47.

[38]"The Thing and Its Relations," in *Essays in Radical Empiricism*, vol. 3 of *The Works of William James* (1912; Cambridge MA: Harvard University Press, 1976), 46.

[39]"Does Consciousness Exist?," in *Essays in Radical Empiricism*, 4, 19.

[40]Ibid., 13.

[41]"A World of Pure Experience," in *Essays in Radical Empiricism*, 42.

[42]One of the more extensive passages on the difference between "thin" conceptual language and "thick" ways of thinking and writing experience is found in *Some Problems of Philosophy*, vol. 7 of *The Works of William James* (1911; Cambridge, MA: Harvard University Press, 1979), 53–4.

[43]*The Principles of Psychology*, vol. 8.1–3 of *The Works of William James* (1890; Cambridge, MA: Harvard University Press, 1981), 1, 219–20.

*L'Évolution créatrice* is Bergson's ontological *summa philosophica*. I will mark the fundamental difference in comparison with James by simply elaborating the implications of his master metaphor in this his greatest work, the image whose function as transcendental background of the tentative conceptual explorations of Being as energetic becoming open a world radically different from that of James. Bergson offers his image, other than James, as a "erste nothwendige Ur-Trope," as his one, his dominant, his necessary and guiding metaphor for the energetic, dynamic, emergent character of Being like this:

> Let us imagine a vessel full of steam at a high pressure, and here and there in its sides a crack through which the steam is escaping in a jet. The steam thrown into the air is nearly all condensed into little drops which *fall back*, and this condensation and this *fall* represent simply the loss of something, an interruption, a deficit. But a small part of the jet of steam subsists, uncondensed, for some seconds; it is making an effort to raise the drops which are *falling*; it succeeds at most in retarding their *fall*. So, from an immense reservoir of life, jets must be gushing out unceasingly, of which each, *falling* back, is a world.[44]

And he adds somewhat later, a variation of the same image:

> If our analysis is correct, it is consciousness, or rather supra-consciousness, that is at the origin of life. Consciousness, or supra-consciousness, is the name for the rocket whose extinguished fragments *fall back* as matter; consciousness, again, is the name for that which subsists of the rocket itself, passing through the fragments and lighting them into organisms.[45]

Yes, Bergson's world is one of ceaseless becoming, of a relentless emergence out of which single entities are distilled only later; so essentially, the *élan*, the productive supra-consciousness provides for an indiscrete ontology, for a world of transformative processes. At least, that is what is revealed at first sight. But this is what a closer look permits us to see: Bergson's indiscrete world of energetic renewal, of evolutionary modernism, ontologically speaking, is a world that rests on a *hypokeimenon*, a transcendental and transcendent entity; a supra-consciousness, as he says, subsists. This productive power, the "need for creation,"[46] allows its own other to come

---

[44]*Creative Evolution*, trans. Arthur Mitchell, ed. Pete A. Y. Gunter (1911; Lanham, MD: University Press of America, 1983), 247 (my emphasis). I use the first English translation because this text, in its initial stages, was supervised by William James himself and may thus stand as another document of the intimate exchange of ideas between him and Bergson.
[45]Ibid., 261 (my emphasis).
[46]Ibid.

forth: *discrete* realms, worlds falling back like drops from a giant steam engine, briefly lighted fragments disappearing into the night as the rocket of creation races onward and upward (mindlessly, like Schopenhauer's will after all). Even Gilles Deleuze, who in his fascinating attempt at rehabilitating Bergson's significance as modernist thinker tries to show that Bergson goes beyond traditional metaphysics, has to concede: "[the *élan*] is a becoming that endures, a change that is substance itself."[47]

What we are facing now is that aspect of the system, the core of Bergson's ontology, which proved such a headache for James and for Schiller and for Flournoy and for Kallen: Bergson's Being is a monist substance divided against itself, rising energy against falling spatialized matter—is this not a traditional metaphysical dualism, a conceptually clear-cut *Zweiweltenlehre*? Becoming, the indiscrete, is now supreme, indeed. Plato stands on his head, so it seems: the transient has replaced the ontological authority of the eternally stable ideas. But is Platonism, are traditional metaphysics and discrete ontology in this way really overcome, as Bergson claims in the later sections of *L'Évolution créatrice*?[48] The changeable sublunar world in Platonism is the (Gr.) *me on*, the bad, the insufficient Being: in Bergson it is stably discrete spatialized matter, solidly available for conceptual and especially scientific thinking based on mathematics, that is the new, the modern *me on*. Plato is inverted and thus reaffirmed in his dualist conception of opposing ontological realms. This is so amazing: Bergson offers only a seeming substantialist monism (the world is all productive energy); in actual fact he folds his one world into a dualistically antagonistic system: if we look closely at the metaphors (and somewhat nonchalantly appropriate Schopenhauer), the world that Bergson intuits in its rise of energy and its richly ambivalent fall into material concreteness is the world as will and trash, as ceaseless becoming and ultimately frozen *me on*. In doing so Bergson reconceptualizes his ontology and, in a way, violates the first commandment of his and James's cherished method of anti-intellectualism: thou shalt not conceptually essentialize anything. It is this very conceptualization of an essentialist dualism, however, that Deleuze cannot but acknowledge as a persisting problem in Bergson: "[The élan vital] is always ... a simplicity in the process of differentiating, a totality in the process of dividing up."[49] Here, in Deleuze's reading, it is obviously the re-emergence of a Plotinian metaphysical conception[50] of a cosmology

---

[47]Gilles Deleuze, *Bergsonism*, trans. Hugh Tomlinson and Barbara Habberjam (New York: Zone Books, 1988), 37.

[48]*Creative Evolution*, 316 ff.

[49]Deleuze, *Bergsonism*, 94.

[50]In a letter to Horace Kallen, Bergson himself emphasized his affinity with Plotinos. cf. Bergson, *Mélanges*, 1192. The Plotinian influence may also help account for the disrespectful, the negative evaluation of material reality as product of a *fall* in *Évolution créatrice*.

defined by emanation that demonstrates Bergson's continuing indebtedness to the metaphysical tradition just as much as his mere inversion of the Platonic dualism.

It is also fitting and appropriate, then, that in order to *know* this world, to deal with it philosophically and practically, Bergson would revive what Nietzsche made fun of in German idealism: a *Fakultätenpsychologie.*[51] *L'Évolution créatice* knows these faculties of knowing: intuition, instinct, and intellect; the three "i's" stand for fixed, conceptually solid entities within our knowing apparatus. James's indiscrete thought or awareness as it goes individually on, his vision of unpredictably manifold eachnesses allows for a world, a multiverse, a pluralistic universe that is truly growing in many places, unforeseeable, tychistic and yet locally coherent, synechistic. Mark Bauerlein has convincingly shown how such thought consistently utilizes conceptuality, if it has to, only in order to demonstrate "the nondiscrete alterity" that encompasses and enfolds and always transcends and thus ultimately dissolves "any discrete thought."[52] Bergson's powerful vision of energetic productivity, the dynamism of indiscretely innovative, truly modern becoming is in a way reined in, tamed, by the substantialist implications of the *élan*, by the re-emergence of a discrete conceptualization both of Being *and* of becoming *and* of epistemological categories. While James allows manifold eachnesses tentatively to progress in the direction of the real newness of an open future,[53] Bergson's thinking, somewhat like his metaphorical rocket of productive energy, relentlessly opens a future whose products fall back on established modes of Being and thinking. The implications of these ontological meditations for the interpretation of modernist cultures in Europe and America may yet reaffirm what I believe are major and important and productive differences, differences not to be criticized but to be appreciated. Dewey, from a Jamesian perspective, articulated the difference very well, even if he did not do it as amiably as James would have stated the case: he thought that it would have been more serviceable for a radically post-metaphysical or reconstructed mode of thinking if Bergson, in dealing with a truly indiscrete world, "had commenced, not with the view that is afterwards corrected, but with the corrected view."[54]

---

[51]Nietzsche, *Jenseits von Gut und Böse,* KSA 5, 24–6.

[52]Mark Bauerlein, *The Pragmatic Mind: Explorations in the Psychology of Belief* (Durham, NC: Duke University Press, 1997), 126.

[53]The best interpretation yet of the transitionality of thought and world in James is Jonathan Levin, *The Poetics of Transition: Emerson, Pragmatism, and American Literary Modernism* (Durham, NC: Duke University Press, 1999), 45–66.

[54]"Perception and Organic Action" *MW* 7, 7.

# 16

# Congruences and Divergences: James, Bergson, Dewey

It has been one of the perennial challenges of philosophy to think the relationship and the mode of interdependence of the permanent and the transient, of Being and becoming, of the factually given and the emergent event, of, in John Dewey's terms, the stable and the precarious.[1] The Platonic solution assumed and posited an immutable and eternal realm of regulative entities providing orientation for a permanently changing, unreliable, and fallen world of merely temporal events. This solution informed the long and varied tradition of Western metaphysics with its virtually ubiquitous assumption of a conceptually ascertainable and solidly substantial underpinning of all mutability.[2] If there is one common trait to be found in the diverse forms of the modernist turn away from metaphysics, it may well be the abandoning of a belief in a single and central and stable domain of well-defined entities supplying unfailing points of reference for all that happens in the sublunar realm of essential instability. Emerson's essay "Circles" (1841) and Nietzsche's *Die fröhliche Wissenschaft* (1882) are among the prime movers of this momentous change in America and Europe, respectively. The conspicuous privileging of contingent becoming

---

This essay was previously published as "The World as Fact, the World as Event: Varieties of Modernist Thinking in William James, Henri Bergson, and John Dewey" in *Transatlantic Modernism*, ed. Martin Klepper and Joseph C. Schöpp (Heidelberg: Winter, 2001), 51–91. Reprinted by permission of Universitätsverlag Winter GmbH.

[1] "Existence as Precarious and as Stable" *LW* 1, 42–68.
[2] The intimate and necessary coexistence of a metaphysical belief in stable and substantial identities and in the power of the concept to totally contain such substances is succinctly analyzed by Michel Haar, "Nietzsche and Metaphysical Language," in *The New Nietzsche*, ed. David B. Allison (Cambridge, MA: MIT Press, 1985), 5–36.

over Being in modernist post-metaphysical thought,[3] however, never really allowed thinkers to completely discard and abandon the traditional problem of the *relationship* of stability and flux. I will try and show the fundamental differences underlying the seemingly related attempts of modernist thinkers on both sides of the Atlantic to cope with this crucial question. The intense, thorough, and charmingly amiable dialogue between William James and John Dewey on the one and Henri Bergson on the other side must not obscure the deep and not always readily discernible difference in their basic assumptions and foundational visions. In focusing on the ways these three thinkers thought and evaluated the world in its circumscribed factual manifestations *and* in its character as essentially unpredictable emergent event, I hope to elucidate the varieties of possible modernist solutions and help appreciate major differences that are often only tacitly granted and yet respectfully upheld in their transatlantic dialogue.

# The problem

When speaking of the problem posed by the reconciliation of reading the world as both a collection of facts or data and as a series of events in the work of thinkers like James, Dewey, and Bergson, one uses relatively new terms for an old question of thinking. The evocation of a few rather randomly chosen names and concepts may illustrate the illustrious background of the philosophical challenge met in a variety of ways by the three prominent modernists in the context of a fundamentally altered existential and intellectual environment. Traditional dualistic metaphysical systems allowed for a basic distinction between ways of the world and modes of thought. Spinoza's influential differentiation of *natura naturans* and *natura naturata* provided one model of reconciling the essentially stable productive character of a temporal world and the appearance of a systematic distribution of factual entities available for rational or scientific categorization.[4] Goethe, Emerson, and Nietzsche continued to profit from

---

[3]After Emerson and Nietzsche pragmatism may be said to be the first consistently post-metaphysical or anti-metaphysical way of thinking even before Husserl's phenomenology in its partial dependence on William James: cf. James M. Edie, *William James and Phenomenology* (Bloomington: University of Indiana Press, 1987), 68, 71.

[4]The pertinence of referring to Spinoza in our context is corroborated by a critical observation made by Horace Kallen who maintains that Bergson in his opposition of *élan vital* and spatialized intellect rewrites the Spinozistic relation of the "free, self-caused, and self-determining substance" (*natura naturans*) to its diversification (*natura naturata*) that allows the conceptualization of the world by the human mind; see Kallen, *William James and Henri Bergson: A Study of Contrasting Theories of Life* (Chicago: University of Chicago Press, 1914), 108.

this reading in their interpretations of the interpenetration of the transient and permanent. The double and duplicitous character of the world as essential, but now ultimately meaningless flow and as a possible system of positive and distinct items assumes a new quality in Schopenhauer's famous vision of the interdependence of will and representation. One cannot but notice the obvious shift here toward a conception of Being in which human faculties (will, representation) and objective qualities become more and more identified till they finally merge, as we will see, in the monistic[5] or pseudo-monistic ontological visions of James, Dewey, and Bergson.[6]

In late Emerson "fate" and "power" emerge as modes both of the way the world *is* and of the approaches through which this world offers itself for and in interpretation. The inflexible factuality and fatality of givenness and the indomitable energy of overcoming join in a new and modern, in a non-substantialist ontology that will become popular in Nietzsche's conceptual trinity of *amor fati*, will to power, and eternal return of the same.[7] A related vision was exhibited by Kierkegaard whom William James quoted approvingly: "We live forward, we understand backward, said a danish writer."[8] The existential push of all beings into the future as counteracted and necessarily accompanied by the retrospective factualization of experience, by its transformation into givenness, is a version of reading the fact-event dichotomy that—like Emerson's and Nietzsche's position—closely approximates the Jamesian and Deweyan solutions. In moving from Schopenhauer to Emerson, Nietzsche, and Kierkegaard, we begin to leave the metaphysical substantializations and enter a realm of thinking in which both the fluxional and the static are modes of difference in the way beings may occur or be understood, rather than essences (as in Spinoza or, still, in Schopenhauer).

Philosophical reflection on reality as interpreted by science remained tied to metaphysical positions much longer than ontological or so-called epistemological thinking. Even so, within the framework of fairly traditional assumptions concerning the status of matter and motion, the nature of cause and effect, a new reading of the fact-event dichotomy was propagated by

---

[5]The term "monistic" is used here to designate a non-dualist constitution of Being as experience, the aboriginal togetherness of "subject" and "object." Such a monism does not preclude a vision of a pluralistic universe of monistically defined eachnesses. A similar explanation of the compatibility of monism and pluralism in James's thinking may be found in Edie, *William James and Phenomenology*, 33.

[6]James saw a possible tradition linking Schopenhauer's concept of the will and Bergson's vision of the *élan vital*; see *The Letters of William James*, ed. Henry James (Boston: Atlantic Monthly Press, 1920), vol. 2, 293.

[7]Cf. Herwig Friedl, "Fate, Power, and History in Emerson and Nietzsche," *ESQ* 43 (1997): 267–93.

[8]*A Pluralistic Universe*, vol. 4 of *The Works of William James* (1909; Cambridge, MA: Harvard University Press, 1977), 109.

George Henry Lewes as early as 1875. His terminology was to become the core of the conceptual framework of emergent evolutionism as variously interpreted by Dewey, Alexander, Morgan, Broad, and—most importantly—by Whitehead in the first half of the twentieth century. In the second volume of the *First Series* of *Problems of Life and Mind*, Lewes discusses "Force and Cause" as Problem V in his sequence of analyses of the principles of rationality and science. In the course of his argument, Lewes distinguishes two kinds of effects and thus of beings in the natural world: stable and predictable resultants and processual and unpredictable emergents. Resultants (or, in our terminology, facts) are foreseeable and well-defined issues of the interaction of known natural factors of the same kind. Lewes's example is the shape of the orbits of planets as the resultant of component forces. An emergent (or event) is the essentially unpredictable outcome of the interaction of known natural factors that are not of the same kind: for instance, the ongoing process of the appearance of a new species. A causal relation among the multiplicity of factors differing in kind that effect the emergence of the new species does exist; the causality, however, is, if at all, describable only after the fact. This is what James means by reminding us of Kierkegaard: processes of living are emergents, their logic and explicability, their conceptual facticity, are accessible only once they are solidified and ready for retrospective analysis.[9] You can explain a new species once it is there, established, and no longer in the making, but you cannot—on the basis of its antecedent conditions—predict its coming into being: it is a true emergent event.[10]

Depending on which kind of vision is privileged, whether the basically spatial world of well-defined and stable and calculable entities is prized higher or whether an essentially temporal universe of emergent events always on the way toward ultimately unavailable closure and precision is given precedence, depending on this primary decision one will either find oneself defending a cosmos dangerously close to what Heidegger calls the *Gestell* or one will appreciate a realm of events ultimately due to an ineluctable dispensation, to the forever clouded workings of the *Ereignis*. The problem we are dealing with arises out of the perennial question of all thinking: what and how is the world and what and how is Being? The historical varieties of addressing the problem just touched upon and the varieties of modernist thought, which will be our main concern, may be synoptically summarized by using the conceptual opposition of discrete and indiscrete ontology. Wolfram Hogrebe has articulated the far-reaching

[9]On the similarity of Lewes's conceptions and some pragmatist assumptions, cf. Herwig Friedl, "Art and Culture as Emerging Events: Gertrude Stein, Pragmatism, and Process Philosophy," in *Emerging Structures in Interdisciplinary Perspective*, ed. Rudi Keller and Karl Menges (Tübingen: Francke, 1997), 43–64.
[10]George Henry Lewes, *Problems of Life and Mind. First Series: The Foundations of a Creed* (Boston: Osgood, 1875), vol. 2, 368–77.

implications of the conflict, contrast, and interdependence of what we call fact and event in the following way:

Der Gegenstandsbereich, der durch die diskrete Ontologie erfaßt wird, ist nämlich nicht nur anderer Art als der der indiskreten, er hat auch, wie man sagen möchte, eine andere Dimension. Die diskrete Ontologie erfaßt alle Gegenstände. Wenn man auf ihrem Boden fragt, was es gibt, dann ist … in der Tat mit Quine zu antworten: alles. Die Dimension der diskreten Ontologie könnte man daher auch "horizontal" nennen.

Die indiskrete Ontologie hingegen erfaßt nicht alle Gegenstände, sondern gewissermaßen die gesamte Gegenständlichkeit. Sie geht nicht "nach außen" auf den Umfang, sondern "nach innen" in die Tiefe der Dinge und beansprucht die "vertikale" Dimension …

So gehört schließlich die Welt aus dem Blickwinkel nicht nur ihrer irreversiblen Veränderlichkeit, sondern vor allem ihrer Unverwechselbarkeiten und ihrer Individualität zur indiskreten Ontologie, d. h. die menschliche Geschichte ebenso wie aufs Ganze gesehen der indiskrete Charme eines anmutenden Universums. (Und wenn man den Gedanken der Evolution wirklich ernst nimmt, dann muß man sagen, das Indiskrete ist das Erste und das Diskrete erst das Zweite.)[11]

The two worlds resulting from or described by a discrete and an indiscrete ontology seem basically different: a discrete ontology offers a plenitude of singular objects out there, whereas an indiscrete ontology reveals the fullness of objecthood seen from the multiplicity of irreducible individual interiorities of temporal beings. Hogrebe obviously privileges the world of indiscrete ontology as the one that is "original," basic, and fundamental. We will see that this vision is shared in different ways by the founding fathers of twentieth-century modernism, by James, Bergson, and Dewey. Their differences in turn also affect and help define the diverse ways in which the world of discreteness and the world of indiscrete transitions, the world of sharply defined facts and that of only vaguely delimited events are *related* in their thinking.

The problem of fact and event and its constituent elements may now be described more succinctly. The world as fact is a world dependent on a discrete ontology. It may be seen as a series of mathematically quantifiable differences and predictable relations following stable laws; even if it is a matter of change and temporal development, it is a world in which resultants prevail, an ultimately static affair, because change itself is thought of as subject to the stability of invariable laws. In the world as fact constancy and

---

[11]Wolfram Hogrebe, *Metaphysik und Mantik: Die Deutungsnatur des Menschen* (Frankfurt: Suhrkamp, 1992), 122–3.

predictability must rule phenomena of temporality themselves. This is the world of traditional (metaphysically oriented) science. It is justified, upheld, and verified by science in an established sense, by that kind of science that was philosophically so thoroughly challenged by Dewey in *The Quest for Certainty* (1929). In this context the term "fact" refers to both the object and to its availability for signification, for language and its conceptualizations: "The concept of 'fact' in the sense of a sharply delineated content describable in terms of universally applicable categories is one that has been constructed for the special purposes of theoretical science [in a traditionalist, non-pragmatist sense]."[12] Gilles Deleuze has characterized such a world as ruled by "differences of degree." It is the world of both metaphysics and science that "invokes a spatialized time, according to which beings no longer present anything but differences of degree, of position, of dimension, of proportion."[13] This is—in Bergson's view as interpreted by Deleuze—the inauthentic world of mere spatialized appearance.

By contrast the world as event or a world of events is a stream (or streams) of qualitative differences, of beings or entities shading into each other, a world appropriate for an indiscrete ontology alone. It necessarily implies the possibility of constant and unpredictable and thus of real innovation, of contingent emergents. This world shows, possesses, has or rather *is* radical ontological modernity or persistent innovation. William James, John Dewey, and Henri Bergson have insisted on the element of real newness as a central aspect of authentic Being. Thinking newness makes for a world that is existentially modern. At the same time thinking the world as emergent event(s) makes thinking itself modern in an ontological sense. Deleuze has spoken of this innovative world of indiscrete ontology and emergent events as ruled by differences in kind instead of differences of degree.

The specific urgency of the problem articulated in the opposition of the world as fact and as event for the modernist thinker who sees himself forced to question, revise, or abandon the transcendent and transcendental guarantees of metaphysics, the urgency of that problem becomes visible in an aphorism by Nietzsche that probably expresses more of a desire or a perplexity than a solution: "Dem Werden den Charakter des Seins *aufzuprägen*—das ist der *höchste Wille zur Macht*."[14] If it is the highest will to power, that is, the highest mode of true existence, to forcefully impress the character traits of Being (in the sense of fact) onto becoming (event), then Nietzsche responds

---

[12]John E. Smith, *Experience and God* (1968; New York: Fordham University Press, 1995), 39.
[13]Gilles Deleuze, *Bergsonism*, trans. Hugh Tomlinson and Barbara Habberjam (New York: Zone Books, 1988), 23.
[14]Nietzsche, *Nachgelassene Fragmente 1885–1887, KSA* 12, 312.

to the modern version of this problematic by salvaging stability in the face of and through the very force that makes for the constant destruction and re-structuring of beings, that is, through the will to power as the ultimate and primary dynamic event. Heidegger has tried to show that this move results in a last stance of the metaphysical substantialization of Being that Nietzsche professedly tried to overcome.[15] We will have to inquire and analyze in how far James, Dewey, and Bergson manage to allow for a non-substantialist revision of the fact-event dichotomy in reading Being, and we will have to find out in what respect they feel forced to retain traces of a metaphysical underpinning in order to cope with said dichotomy. The experience of the world as both a constantly destabilizing and a constantly productive and innovative flow, the literally de-constructive character of the world, the erosion and reconstitution of factuality as persistent event, this is Emerson's foundational vision. All three thinkers of high modernism—James, Dewey, and Bergson[16]—are indebted to Emerson and respond to this basic feature of his innovative post-metaphysical ontology in their unique ways.

The several facets of the problem may now be tentatively listed as follows: how is it possible to accommodate the stability of quantified or quantifiable relations in a world that is essentially productive of unpredictable newness? How can a world characterized by differences of degree be made to coincide with a reality determined by differences in kind? How is it possible to think a discrete and an indiscrete ontology at the same time? What is the role of the stabilizing concept in an experience essentially represented by the "paramount reality" of the "primacy of perception,"[17] which is understood as a flowing event attuned to what James called the ontologically central but conceptually "non-reproducible part of reality"?[18] And, maybe most importantly, how are the two horns of the problem, the two sides of the question, the ontological alternatives within one experience and one world, how are the fact- and the event-character of Being *evaluated* by James, Dewey, and Bergson?

---

[15]Heidegger, *Nietzsche II*, ed. Brigitte Schillbach, vol. 6.2 of *Gesamtausgabe* (1961; Frankfurt: Klostermann, 1997), 256 ff.

[16]James's positive response to Emerson may be seen above all in his essay "Emerson" (1903), in *Essays in Religion and Morality* (Cambridge, MA: Harvard University Press, 1982), 109–15. Dewey expressed his view of Emerson as a new beginning of thinking comparable only to the impact of Plato on the last two millennia in "Emerson – The Philosopher of Democracy" (1903) *MW* 3, 184–92. Bergson was familiar with Emerson through his readings while attending school in England.

[17]Edie, *William James and Phenomenology*, 3–4.

[18]*Some Problems of Philosophy*, vol. 7 of *The Works of William James* (1911; Cambridge, MA: Harvard University Press, 1979), 47.

# The dialogue

The exchange of ideas between William James and Henri Bergson has been thoroughly documented and critically appraised in several, mostly early publications.[19] Mutual quotations, explicit appreciations of, and implicit allusions to each other in their published works as well as the exchange of letters facilitated comprehensive analyses of the character of this intense and intimate intellectual relationship. Dewey and Bergson were much less close and the transfer of ideas, at least from my perspective and on the basis of my knowledge, is essentially limited to a series of important critical responses to Bergson in Dewey's writings. These have not yet received the philosophical attention they doubtlessly deserve. Dewey may be said to have extended and supplemented James's view of Bergson's achievements and especially of what he saw as his weaknesses as a thinker. Dewey obviously did not feel impeded, as did James, by the natural reservations arising out of a close friendship in expressing an acute sense of deficits in Bergson's oeuvre.

The following sketch of the responses of the three thinkers to each other is designed to establish a wider context of philosophical agreements and differences. This context will allow a more precise analysis and appreciation of their specific ways of understanding the core problem of the interpenetration of the fact- and the event-character of Being in their mature thought. A more thorough presentation of these approaches will be attempted in the third part of this chapter under the heading of *Solutions*.

The year 1905 turned out to be of crucial importance in the relationship of William James and Henri Bergson. The two great modernist thinkers met—after years of correspondence—for the first time in Paris on May 28. In the same year, a report by Gaston Rageot on the Fifth International Congress of Psychology in Rome was published in the *Revue philosophique*. James had read a paper at the conference, and Rageot used the occasion to claim that major psychological insights in Bergson's *Essai sur les données immédiates de la conscience* (1889) were inspired by James.[20] Bergson responded vehemently in writing, denying any such influence.[21] He meticulously details which essays by James he had read when

---

[19]The story of the relationship is told and documented by the letters reprinted in Ralph Barton Perry, *The Thought and Character of William James* (London: Milford, 1935), vol. II, 599–636, and—together with other correspondence—in Henri Bergson, *Mélanges*, ed. André Robinet (Paris: Presses Universitaires de France, 1972), 566–1227. The most comprehensive analysis to date is still Kallen's *William James and Henri Bergson*. A succinct and even today pertinent evaluation of the relationship of the two thinkers may be found in Théodore Flournoy, *La Philosophie de William James* (Saint-Blaise: Foyer Solidariste, 1911), 179–86.

[20]Perry, *Thought and Character of William James*, vol. II, 599–600.

[21]For the full text of Bergson's reply cf. *Mélanges*, 656–8. Bergson summarized his comments in a letter to James dated July 20, 1905, and stated as his intention: "J'ai cru devoir couper à la racine ce commencement de légende, parce que, à mon avis, un des arguments les plus

he wrote the *Essai* and he asserts and insists that he did not know "On Some Omissions of Introspective Psychology" (1884), which, with some changes, was to be incorporated into *The Principles of Psychology* as the famous chapter IX, "The Stream of Thought." Bergson freely admits that there is a far-reaching similarity between his own *durée réelle*, as introduced in the *Essai*, and James's stream. However, he also claims that James's idea is of a psychological origin whereas the concept of *durée* arises out of the critique of linear time as conceived in mathematics and physics. It seems to have been immensely important for Bergson to stress this difference. Some ten years later, he repeats his position almost verbatim in a somewhat angry letter to Horace M. Kallen, in which he otherwise tries to refute the assertions of major differences between the portraits of a progressive and "democratic" James and a traditionalist Bergson in Kallen's book:

> Certainement, James était arrivé à son "stream of consciousness" par des voies purement psychologiques. Certainement aussi, c'est par la critique de l'idée mathématique et physique de temps, et par la comparaison de cette idée avec la réalité, que j'ai été conduit à ma "durée réelle."[22]

It is telling, too, that Bergson in his refutation of 1905 tries to widen the time gap between the publication of his *Essai* (1889) and James's *Principles* (1890) in his favor by dating the latter as published in 1891. It seems as if Bergson, who was seventeen years younger than James (Bergson was born two days before Dewey in 1859), attempted to overcome all indications of James's (now obvious) priority in the discovery of the central and basic and foundational intuition of true Being as productive personalized flow or continuous event, an insight that James had first published in 1884. In spite of Ralph Barton Perry's conciliatory and generally appropriate remarks stating that neither James nor Bergson were ever making claims to priority and that they were "almost extravagantly appreciative of the other's merit,"[23] it is apparent that for Bergson James's early central vision of 1884 came too close for comfort. Even so, there is a legitimate aspect of Bergson's claim of difference in the very context of their common basic idea. James does indeed envision Being as stream of thought or experiential awareness[24]

---

frappants qu'on puisse invoquer (du dehors) en faveur du 'pragmatisme' américain et de la 'nouvelle philosophie' française est précisément que ces deux doctrines se sont constituées indépendamment l'une de l'autre, avec des points de départ différents et des méthodes différentes"; 661.

[22]Bergson, *Mélanges*, 1194.

[23]Perry, *Thought and Character of William James*, vol. II, 600.

[24]The ontological equation of Being and the flow of (pure) experience in the philosophy of James has been maintained by critics with quite different intellectual orientations. Perry says: "reality is immediately given in experience—is experience, when that term is properly construed"; *Thought and Character of William James*, vol. II, 590. Edie states: "Being, the

psycho-logically, as Bergson says. The term "psychology," however, does not only mean the branch of scientific inquiry. It should and does indicate James's philosophical approach. James thinks Being in the way it shows as and in and for the psyche—in the sense of human being; he conceives of the stream of consciousness as it reveals itself in and for and as (individual) experience. James's ontological approach is modern because he thinks that which *is* neither in a unified theo-logical nor in a totalizing cosmo-logical but in a pluralist psycho-logical fashion. Bergson, as he himself claims, thinks of *durée réelle* as the essential feature of Being *überhaupt*, of *la realité en soi*. One can easily see the first intimations of a major difference here to which I will return again: James thinks the event, the flow, the stream of Being as constituted by and to be deduced from each-nesses, from single and singular (human) beings; whereas Bergson tends toward a vision of *durée* as a comprehensive, a total event in which human beings may or do participate.

In going through the correspondence of James and Bergson between 1902 and 1910, one discovers one major and a number of minor agreements as well as one important area of serious dispute, even though that is often addressed only indirectly. James always credited Bergson with having helped him to overcome intellectualism, that is, the belief in the capability of stable concepts to actually hold and convey reality as experienced. It is interesting and sheds some light on James's famed generosity toward others that Bergson wrote to him as early as 1903 concerning a *résumé* of one of James's courses:

> Le résumé que vous avez bien voulu m'adresser du cours que vous faites en ce moment m'a profondément intéressé. Il contient tant de vues neuves et originales que je n'arrive pas encore à en embrasser suffisamment l'ensemble, mais une idée maîtresse s'en dégage pour moi dès à présent: c'est celle de la nécessité de transcender les concepts, la logique simple, enfin les procédés d'une philosophie trop systématique qui postule l'unité du tout.[25]

Obviously Bergson felt that James's so-called anti-intellectualist stance did help *him* toward a new departure in thinking the verbal and logical possibilities of a modernized philosophy. Having read James's *Pragmatism*

---

*really real,* is *this experienced world itself"*; *William James and Phenomenology,* 73. And Hilary Putnam, in defining James's "neutral monist" ontology, has put the same insight in this way: "the properties and relations we experience are the stuff of the universe"; "Pragmatism and Realism," in *The Revival of Pragmatism: New Essays on Social Thought, Law, and Culture,* ed. Morris Dickstein (Durham, NC: Duke University Press, 1998), 47.

[25]Bergson, *Mélanges,* 589.

(1907), Bergson reiterated his appreciation of James's advance in the right direction of future anti-intellectualist thinking:

> C'est le programme, admirablement tracé, de la philosophie de l'avenir … la philosophie souple et flexible qui est destinée à prendre la place de l'intellectualisme … Quand vous dites que *"for rationalism reality is readymade and complete from all eternity, while for pragmatism it is still in the making,"* vous donnez la formule même de la métaphysique à laquelle je suis convaincu que nous viendrons, à laquelle nous serions venus depuis longtemps si nous n'étions restés sous le charme de l'idéalisme platonicien.[26]

Bergson envisions James and himself as overcoming the conceptualized, static, and factualized world of traditional rationalist and idealist metaphysics *in toto*. James would continue to praise Bergson lavishly for his anti-intellectualist stance on concepts in his published writings; his letters, however, are relatively subdued whenever he speaks of anything in Bergson's thinking that goes beyond this *single major point* of convergence in their thinking. In 1908 James writes: "There are many points in your philosophy which I don't yet grasp, but I have seemed to myself to understand your anti-intellectualistic campaign very clearly, and that I have really done it so well in your opinion makes me proud."[27] A few days earlier James had paid Bergson this slightly ambivalent compliment in describing the lecture version of the chapter on Bergson's philosophy to be incorporated in the projected *A Pluralistic Universe*: "You see that I suppress almost all of your philosophy for the sake of emphasizing all the more your critique of intellectualism, which was the point my own lectures were chiefly concerned with."[28]

In addition to their agreement concerning the reduced function and importance of factualizing and stabilizing concepts in modernized thinking and their inadequacy to hold and convey the real or Being itself in its flowing event-uality, Bergson and James share common views in the philosophy of religion (as expressed by Bergson's appreciation of *The Varieties of Religious Experience*), and they both hold a belief in the importance of a true pluralism of consciousnesses that transcend human existence, a belief substantiated for both by Gustav Theodor Fechner.[29] More importantly though, Bergson also supports James's radical empiricist idea of pure experience as the ultimate "form" in which Being is given and which is neither subjective nor objective. In a letter dated July 20, 1905, he insists on the necessity for philosophy to

---

[26]Ibid., 727.
[27]*Letters* 2, 308–9.
[28]Perry, *Thought and Character of William James*, vol. II, 625.
[29]Cf. Bergson, *Mélanges*, 579–80, 587–8, 785–6, 791.

adopt James's stance on this question.[30] James had found occasion to praise Bergson for a similar thesis advanced in *Matière et mémoire* (1896). He writes in 1902:

> The *Hauptpunkt* acquired for me is your conclusive demolition of the dualism of object and subject in perception. I believe that the "transcendency" of the object will not recover from your treatment, and as I myself have been working for many years past on the same line, only with other general conceptions than yours, I find myself most agreeably corroborated.[31]

As soon as one moves beyond the problems of the relationship of concept and reality and of the epistemological realism founded on the radical empiricist vision of pure experience, one does encounter major differences in James's and Bergson's thinking. This is especially true of their basic ontological orientations and their respective views of the nature or character of philosophical inquiry.

James's early letter of 1902 in praise of Bergson's *Essai sur les données immédiates de la conscience* and his *Matière et mémoire* exhibits a reservation, a withholding of a final judgment, and some critical implications that were to be the hallmark of almost all of James's responses to ontological aspects of Bergson's work:

> I think I understand the main lines of your system very well at present— though of course I can't yet trace its proper relations to the aspects of experience of which you do not treat. It needs much building out in the direction of Ethics, Cosmology and Cosmogony, Psychogenesis, etc., before one can apprehend it fully.[32]

Even though the same letter speaks of Bergson's work as effecting another "Copernican revolution," James clearly finds Bergson's thinking inadequate in doing justice to the fullness of experience and thus to Being or reality as they reveal themselves. James becomes more precise in 1903 when he objects to Bergson's concept of memory as both a personal and transpersonal, underlying, and thus stable and factual entity that seems to revive the traditional metaphysical substantialist soul in another guise: "your unconscious or subconscious permanence of memories is in its turn a notion that offers difficulties, seeming in fact to be the equivalent of the 'soul' in another shape."[33]

---

[30]Ibid., 660.
[31]*Letters of William James*, vol. 2, 179.
[32]Ibid.
[33]Ibid., 184.

Bergson undoubtedly realized the seriousness of the charge and tried to defend himself by simply denying any intention to retain the idea of fixed transcendental substances constituting the Being of human beings as solidified fact: "Cette existence de quelque réalité en dehors de toute conscience actuelle n'est pas, sans doute, l'existence *en soi* dont parlait l'ancien substantialisme; et cependant ce n'est pas de l'*actuellement présenté* à une conscience, c'est quelque chose d'intermédiaire entre les deux."[34] James obviously felt that Bergson and his idea of memory were endangering the basic intuition of Being as a present and thus radically contingent and unconditioned and therefore free stream or event.

The disagreement between James and Bergson became serious when James wrote his most deceptively enthusiastic letter to Bergson after having read *L'Évolution créatrice* (1907). It seems to me that critics have not sufficiently paid attention to James's fundamental objections, embedded as they appear in congratulatory exuberance. After unstinting and serious praise of the book as a "marvel," of the writer as a "magician," of the book's style as comparable only to Flaubert, James goes on to stress these points:

> And if your next book proves to be as great an advance on this one as this is on its two predecessors, your name will surely go down as one of the great creative names in philosophy ...
>
> To me at present the vital achievement of the book is that it inflicts an irrecoverable death-wound upon Intellectualism. It can never resuscitate! But it will die hard ... The *élan vital*, all contentless and vague as you are obliged to leave it, will be an easy substitute to make fun of ... your reality lurks so in the background, in this book, that I am wondering whether you *could n't* give it any more development *in concreto* here ... I feel very much in the dark still about the relations of the progressive to the regressive movement, and this great precipitate of nature subject to static categories. With a frank pluralism of *beings* endowed with vital impulses you can get oppositions and compromises easily enough, and a stagnant deposit; but after my one reading I don't exactly "catch on" to the way in which the continuum of reality resists itself so as to have to act, etc., etc.[35]

James begins with a valuation that is only superficially complimentary. He actually reduces the importance of the *Essai* and of *Matière et mémoire* considerably without acknowledging the status of *L'Évolution créatrice* as a

---

[34]Bergson, *Mélanges*, 652.
[35]*Letters of William James*, vol. 2, 291–3.

future classic—this honorific might be reserved for a new book representing another major advance over its predecessors. One could almost speak of "damning by faint praise." James is genuinely convinced by Bergson's attack on concepts as a means of conveying true Being. The attack on intellectualism, however, must not obscure these major deficits: 1. the *élan vital* appears as an empty version or place-holder of the traditional substance or the absolute[36]; 2. with its emphasis on the dualism of *élan* and spatialized matter *L'Évolution créatrice* seems to miss the opportunity to really cope with the question of reality or Being as concretely lived and experienced; 3. James is puzzled by the opposition of progressive and dynamic *durée* or *élan* and regressive, static matter. Against Bergson's construction of an opposition of event and fact as constituents of a transcendental binary system, James pleads for the reality of a plurality of individualized instances of real *beings* as they unfold as existential events, which, one may add, may capture and conceptually construct transient worlds of fact as they go on.[37] As much as he loved the man and as much as he admired his anti-rationalist strategies,[38] James would continue to question or simply ignore Bergson's ontology, his metaphysical system. Having met him again in London in 1908, James confessed in a letter to his Swiss colleague and admirer Théodore Flournoy: "I can't say that I follow the folds of his system much more clearly than I did before."[39]

In addition to the differences emerging from a closer look at their respective ontological positions, the letters allow at least a glimpse of another disagreement of major importance. In 1903 Bergson attributes James's problems in appreciating his concept of memory to a problematic and old-fashioned understanding of thinking: "Je crois ... que, parmi ces difficultés, il en est qui tiennent simplement à des habitudes invétérées de notre esprit, habitudes qui ont une origine toute pratique et dont nous devons nous affranchir pour la spéculation."[40] James—and Dewey proved even more insistent on this point—would never be ready to heed Bergson's call for a liberation of thinking for the purpose of "spéculation." The very core of the pragmatist turn was and remained its passionate defense of the (in the widest and most refined sense possible) practical consequences of all

---

[36]James's critique of its vagueness reminds one of Nietzsche's satirical fables on the progressive dilution and ultimate evaporation of the idea of a transcendent reality in the course of the history of thinking; cf. "Wie die 'wahre Welt' endlich zur Fabel wurde," in *Götzen-Dämmerung*, KSA 6, 80–1.

[37]Cf. Kallen, *William James and Henri Bergson*, 47: "Where Bergson desiderates unknowably pure metaphysical substrata, James requires only directly experienced objects."

[38]Kallen sees "an authoritative criticism of intellectualism" and, more precisely, the agreement on the limited value of concepts as the only points of a true affinity between James and Bergson; ibid., 43.

[39]*Letters of William James*, vol. 2, 314.

[40]Bergson, *Mélanges*, 588.

thinking. Philosophy for James would have to *work within* Being, *within* the world, and not *speculate about* it.

James could follow Bergson whenever he subordinated the static constructions of intellectual conceptualizations to the perceptual flow. He had to part company once Bergson moved toward what James saw as the substantialization and thus the transcendental fixation of, firstly, memory and then of the opposition of *élan* and matter. Stable metaphysical entities, relations, or transcendental facts contradicted James's sense of Being as a plurality of individualized flowing events of pure experience, and they contradicted his idea of thinking as an effectively ongoing practical project in an ultimately messy and unfinished emergent world.

In his published work, James refined his own early anti-intellectualist position[41] by rendering tribute to Bergson's achievement. The most important texts are chapter VI, "Bergson and his Critique of Intellectualism," in *A Pluralistic Universe* (1909) and the late essay "Bradley or Bergson?" (1910).[42] "Bradley or Bergson?" is a conveniently condensed version of the nuanced subtleties of the Bergson chapter in *A Pluralistic Universe*. The essay begins with an elegant summary of the problem and of Bergson's position as James understands it:

> The idealist tradition is that feelings, aboriginally discontinuous, are woven into continuity by the various synthetic concepts which the intellect applies. ... [Bergson destroys] the notion that conception is essentially a unifying process. For Bergson all concepts are discrete; and though you can get the discrete out of the continuous, out of the discrete you can never construct the continuous again. Concepts, moreover, are static, and can never be adequate substitutes for a perceptual flux of which activity and change are inalienable features. Concepts, says Bergson, make things less, not more, intelligible, when we use them seriously and radically. They serve us practically more than theoretically.[43]

What we might call the "Humpty Dumpty paradox" does allow the "cutting up" of the stream of perceptual awareness into concepts, while it does not permit a reconstruction of the stream out of the static factualizations of these

---

[41]A germ of this stance may be seen in chapter IX of *The Principles of Psychology*, vol. 8.1–3 of *The Works of William James* (1890; Cambridge, MA: Harvard University Press, 1981), 1, 246: James here contrasts conceptualized sensations and their flow, illustrating this opposition with the image of the pails and barrels in a stream: conceptualized entities, factualizations, will never "hold" the ongoing perceptual reality of experience.

[42]James's last word on the concept-percept problem in the context of the anti-intellectualist debate is to be found in chapter IV, "Percept and Concept," in *Some Problems*, 31–60.

[43]*Essays in Philosophy*, vol. 5 of *The Works of William James* (Cambridge, MA: Harvard University Press, 1978), 151–2.

same concepts. The descriptions of a discrete and an indiscrete ontology, to return to Hogrebe's argument, are related but asymmetrical. Concepts do not hold the fullness, the thick richness of reality; they are useful signposts for a predominantly practical orientation within the ongoing events of fluxional Being. It is interesting that James should avoid Bergson's own terminological triad of instinct, intellect, and intuition even while recreating his position in great detail in the Bergson chapter of *A Pluralistic Universe*. James focuses phenomenologically on the way experience is *had*, either conceptually and factually or as a transitive event; in his analysis of Bergson's arguments, he does not abandon the "view from the inside" that offers a sight of the ontological "foundation" of Being as an individualized ongoing event. Bergson, especially in *L'Évolution créatrice*, looks at the mind from the "outside" and presents a *Fakultätenpsychologie* of the human mind that is strongly reminiscent of idealist strategies of interpretation. James obviously feared the transcendental implications of such categories and concepts as intuition and intellect.[44]

In addition to this rather generalized criticism, James obviously saw a major problem in Bergson's rigid dualistic oppositions such as the *absolute* antagonism of concept and percept, of intellect and intuition, and of theory and practice. One of the keywords and key insights of James's philosophy is *continuity*. Tucked away in a longish footnote we find a challenge to Bergson's world of stark contrasts in the mental and ontological realm. James does not believe that it is legitimate to solely attribute—as does Bergson—a practical function to concepts and to deny them any theoretical value whatsoever.[45] James's seemingly marginal and low-keyed critical comment, however, has the same function as the omission of the terms "intellect," "intuition," and "instinct" in his generally appreciative renderings of Bergson's anti-intellectualism. In both cases James abandons the kinds of concepts whose validity in general Bergson himself keeps refuting in his anti-intellectualist critiques. The rigid separation of essentialized faculties like intuition and intellect and of the theoretical and practical modes of knowing in Bergson's work establish unchanging and clearly circumscribed, well-defined factual entities which resist continuity with and integration into the world as a plurality of individually ongoing events which constitute the only reality that is experientially given and therefore entitled to be called true Being. In

---

[44]James also rather graciously veils his disagreement with what he considers to be the obscurities of Bergson's metaphysics. Thus he writes in *A Pluralistic Universe*, 101–2: "I have to confess that Bergson's originality is so profuse that many of his ideas baffle me entirely. I doubt whether anyone understands him all over, so to speak; and I am sure that he would himself be the first to see that this must be, and to confess that things which he himself has not yet thought out clearly, had yet to be mentioned and have a tentative place assigned them in his philosophy."
[45]Ibid., 122–4.

short, Bergson does not heed his own critical comments on the theoretical inadequacy of (metaphysical) concepts.[46]

Bergson published his own tribute to James in 1911 when he wrote a wonderfully appreciative and refined introduction for the French version of *Pragmatism*.[47] Bergson emphasizes the fact that James introduced a new concept of reality which respects the plenitude and messiness of the world and its lack of clear boundaries in ongoing experience. He naturally praises James's contribution to an anti-intellectualist way of thinking and underlines the importance of James's insistence on the fact that relations are themselves an integral part of experience and not rationalistically imposed on sensations. He does justice to the mystical or intuitional basis of James's pragmatism that allows for the world of felt reality to immediately manifest itself as an event. At the same time Bergson appreciates the possibility of a plurality of trans-human consciousnesses, even though he is no longer ready to take seriously James's interest in Fechner in this context. The ultimate achievement of James's pragmatism, however, for Bergson, is the new understanding of truth as "invention" rather than "discovery," an interpretation that allows one to see truth as that which successfully leads toward ever more rewarding consequent experiences. Toward the end of his generally eulogistic interpretation, Bergson cautiously articulates a critique of the basic concept of reality as advanced in the pluralist stance of radical empiricism.[48]

On the basis of this sketchy review of the actual dialogue between James and Bergson, one may find it hard to agree with Perry's summary evaluation that each of the two thinkers could be "the perfect exponent of the other."[49] To be sure, both James and Bergson distrust concepts as purveyors of a factualized and static, a dead and unproductive reality. At the same time James is wary of the traditional metaphysical implications of some of Bergson's ideas, like memory, matter, *élan vital, durée*, intellect, intuition, and instinct. These conceptions—dynamic as some of them may appear to be—seem apt to transcendentally halt and freeze and essentialize the character of Being, which in James's basic philosophical vision reveals itself as an irreducible multiplicity of events.

---

[46]To be fair, James does realize and he tries to refute this possible charge against Bergson; ibid., 122. However, he can only do this so long as he simply ignores such essentialized metaphysical entities as intellect and intuition, theory and practice in Bergson's oeuvre.

[47]Cf. Bergson, "Introduction," in *Le Pragmatisme*, trans. E. Le Brun (Paris: Flammarion, 1911).

[48]Kallen was the first to observe a curious and interesting parallelism here between James's suspicion of Bergson's traditionalist and substantialist metaphysics and Bergson's aversion to the concept of reality in James's radical empiricism; see Kallen, *William James and Henri Bergson*, 46.

[49]Perry, *Thought and Character of William James*, vol. II, 603.

The first personal encounter between *Dewey* and Bergson in 1913 was accompanied by minor personal irritations for Dewey and a major public excitement in New York City. The year before, Dewey had finished his essay "Perception and Organic Action," which he understood as a fundamental critique of Bergson, and sent it for publication in the *Journal of Philosophy, Psychology and Scientific Methods*. When Bergson had agreed to come to Columbia University as a Visiting Professor in 1913, Dewey wrote to the journal's editor, F. J. E. Woodbridge, offering to at least withhold the piece for some time lest it should prove too unfriendly a welcome for the admired guest.[50] The essay did appear as planned in 1912, but Dewey subsequently honored Bergson on the occasion of his visit by writing a highly appreciative "Introduction to A *Contribution to a Bibliography of Henri Bergson*" (1913).[51] Dewey avoids all friction here and makes Bergson sound almost like a natural empiricist and instrumentalist. Thus he stresses the fact that Bergson's concept of intuition is not extra-empirical and approvingly quotes Bergson's arguments against the mathematical mind-set and the necessity for an intensified biologistic and scientifically grounded social approach to reality out of respect for experience. The introduction ends with an extended summary of Bergson's views on evolution and the productive tension of matter and thought, with Dewey's praise for Bergson's synoptic vision of sympathetically collected scientific insights especially in *L'Évolution créatrice*, with an appreciation of Bergson's modernization of the philosophical problematic as a whole, and with gracious welcoming remarks for the new temporary colleague.

Bergson's lectures at Columbia were a resounding public success: "his presence was celebrated like that of a famous actor or general. Fashionable matrons vied for a space with students at his lectures. Gentlemen fought over seats. So great was the interest that, as one observer put it, parts of the city were choked by 'the first traffic jam of the brand-new automotive age.'"[52] The popular interest was a tribute to both the fame of the visitor and the reputation of the Columbia Department of Philosophy under Dewey where, among others, William James had famously lectured to large audiences in the early 1900s. Neither the gracious gestures of his host nor the public success of Henri Bergson at Columbia, however, can obscure the simple fact that Dewey as the foremost spokesman of philosophical opinion in America was about to distance himself from Bergson while continuing to celebrate his own spiritual alliance with William James.[53] The first of a limited number

---

[50]*MW* 7, 497.

[51]Ibid., 201–4.

[52]Pete A. Y. Gunter, "Introduction to the UPA Edition," in Bergson, *Creative Evolution*, trans. Arthur Mitchell, ed. Gunter (1911; Lanham, MD: University Press of America, 1983), xvii.

[53]In order to appreciate the lifelong admiration for and agreement with James's thinking consult—among others—these texts by Dewey: "Three Contemporary Philosophers: A Series of Six Lectures Delivered in Peking" *MW* 12, 206–50; "The Vanishing Subject in the Psychology

of works in which Dewey critically argued with Bergson was the 1912 essay "Perception and Organic Action," already mentioned.[54] In his introduction to volume 7 of *The Middle Works of John Dewey*, Ralph Ross has offered a useful analysis of the basic provocation and irritation that Bergson's thinking represented for Dewey. Bergson separates ordinary experience and philosophy: ordinary experience is concerned with the (factualized) practical world and with the useful, whereas philosophy is concerned with flowing reality as it reveals itself to intuition:

> This duality in Bergson, one important theme among many others in his philosophy, offended Dewey as all dualisms did, but particularly offended him because some ultimate reality was removed from the world in which the questing, adapting human organism acted, and because mind, memory, and life were separated from that organic action that Dewey conceived as the process of life itself. Life and mind became entities in Bergson, however much he tried to avoid it, and in the end he held a panpsychic belief that the material universe is a kind of consciousness.[55]

For Dewey, however, the essential embeddedness of perception within nature reveals the continuity of processes of organic living within a changing environment *and* of (philosophical) knowing: both show as flowing events in which "subject" and "object" always already interdepend and coalesce. "Perception and Organic Action" tries to demonstrate that Bergson does not sufficiently acknowledge and appreciate the workings of perception as integral aspect of the unified occurrences of natural vitality including its self-awareness in thinking. According to Dewey, Bergson not only dichotomizes our inescapable interactions in and with the world into acting (practice within a material, spatialized realm) and intuitional knowing of truly temporal and flowing reality itself (*durée*), but also "cuts" the integral temporal act of perception into single instantaneous and reductive fixations (factualizations) of reality. However, as Dewey sees it, "[p]erception is not an instantaneous act of carving out a field through suppressing its real influences and permitting its virtual ones to show, but is a process of determining the indeterminate."[56]

For Dewey perception does not partake of the factualizing tendencies, the instantaneous reductive dissection of living reality, which Bergson usually and most prominently attributes to concepts. Instead, perception is a progressive co-creation of future interactive possibilities in the temporal field known as

---

of William James" *LW* 14, 155–67; "William James and the World Today" *LW* 15, 3–17; "The Principles" *LW* 15, 18; "William James' Morals and Julien Benda's" *LW* 15, 19–26.
[54]*MW* 7, 3–30.
[55]Ralph Ross, "Introduction," in *MW* 7, XIII.
[56]"Perception and Organic Action" *MW* 7, 13.

the interdependence of man and environment; it is an active participation in the constantly ongoing mutual modification of human being and world in their essential temporalized togetherness.[57] Bergson's view of perception as a series of instantaneous choices imposed on the world is replaced in Dewey by perception as the ongoing activity of intelligent choosing in which world (stimulus) and human being interact. On this basis of reintegrating the only seemingly instantaneous factualizing acts of perceptual choice into the ongoing event of world-making, Dewey radicalizes and deepens the temporal interpretation of Being:

> the traits that are alleged to demarcate perception and the objective material with which it deals from a reality marked by genuine presence of temporal considerations have disappeared. Perception is a temporal process: not merely in the sense that an act of perception takes time, but in the profounder sense that temporal considerations are implicated in it whether it be taken as an act or as subject-matter. If such be the case, Bergson's whole theory of time, of memory, of mind and of life as things inherently sundered from organic action needs revision.[58]

The seemingly technical problem of the appropriate definition of perception in the context of organic events results in a wholesale refutation of essential Bergsonian positions. For Dewey perceptual fixations (facts) are redissolved and integrated into the unitary flow of interactive eventual existence or Being. At the same time Dewey refutes the opposition of theory and practice, of knowledge and action. This in turn denies Bergson's vision of the separate status of philosophy as the intuitive speculative knowledge of vitally flowing reality itself as distinguished from the merely intelligent pragmatic orientation in a spatialized material world defined by measurable differences of degree accessible through static acts of instantaneous perceptual fixation. Dewey was to repeat this fundamental critique of—as he saw it—Bergson's dualist and traditionalist metaphysics without ever again offering a profoundly reasoned refutation as in "Perception and Organic Action." I will therefore conclude this survey of Dewey's part in the transatlantic dialogue by briefly listing the varieties of his later objections.

"The Need for a Recovery of Philosophy" (1917) is Dewey's first major and comprehensive statement of his mature philosophical position

---

[57]Cf. Thomas M. Alexander, *John Dewey's Theory of Art, Experience and Nature: The Horizons of Feeling* (Albany: SUNY Press, 1987), 134: "For Bergson selection is not only preconscious but primarily negative; i.e., it screens or ignores stimuli, subtracting rather than adding. For Dewey, 'perceived objects present our *eventual* action upon the world ...'... The act of perception, for Dewey, is no more just a censor than it is a mere spectator of appearances. It is an actor-writer; it is involved in transforming and participating in the ongoing events."

[58]"Perception and Organic Action" *MW* 7, 30.

and the immediate predecessor of the extensive critique of metaphysics in *Reconstruction in Philosophy* (1920). In his refutation of the atomistic view of sensations and ideas in traditional empiricism and rationalism, in his denial of their static factual character, he briefly glances at Bergson's position in a footnote:

> There is some gain in substituting a doctrine of flux and interpenetration of psychical states, *à la* Bergson, for that of rigid discontinuity. But the substitution leaves untouched the fundamental mis-statement of experience, the conception of experience as directly and primarily "inner" and psychical.[59]

Dewey's argument against Bergson is essentially ontological. If experience is the pragmatists' word for Being,[60] Bergson's denial of a realist interpretation of experience, of the unmediated givenness of the world as experienced, implies a separation of inner and outer, a split of the world into a genuine reality, the flow of *durée* revealed in the immediacy of intuition, and the world of appearance as static fact, as spatial disposition of matter. In spite of his agreement in thinking the world (in experience) as an event, as flux, Dewey cannot share what he sees as the old-fashioned and problematic dualism of Bergson.[61]

The reconstruction of experience in this essay finally leads Dewey toward a radical new description of the functions and character of philosophy:

> If, then, the conclusion is reached that knowing is a way of employing empirical occurrences with respect to increasing power to direct the consequences which flow from things, the application of the conclusion must be made to philosophy itself. It, too, becomes not a contemplative survey of existence nor an analysis of what is past and done with, but an outlook upon future possibilities with reference to attaining the better and averting the worse …
>
> The point that occurs to mind most readily is that philosophy will have to surrender all pretension to be peculiarly concerned with ultimate reality.[62]

---

[59]"The Need for a Recovery of Philosophy" *MW* 10, 13.

[60]Edie, *William James and Phenomenology*, 73: "Being, the really real, is this experienced world itself."

[61]In *Art as Experience* Dewey refuted the possibilities of thinking the world (as experience) as either pure givenness, a block universe of facts, or as its exact opposite, an unmitigated flow of mere events; see *LW* 10, 22–3.

[62]"The Need for a Recovery of Philosophy," 38–9.

Philosophy, pragmatically redefined, is neither *theoria* nor is it the analysis of a factually given world of stable entities. Rather, it becomes an ongoing, future-oriented event that denies the philosophical and ethical authority of antecedents, of "what is past and done with." It is interesting that Dewey should select Bergson in this context as a modernist who ultimately fails and who, in his very failure to become modern in a re-evaluation of the factuality-event dichotomy, does testify to the heavy burden of the metaphysical past:

> The pervasiveness of the tradition is shown in the fact that so vitally a contemporary thinker as Bergson, who finds a philosophic revolution involved in abandonment of the traditional identification of the truly real with the fixed (an identification inherited from Greek thought), does not find it in his heart to abandon the counterpart identification of philosophy with search for the truly Real; and hence finds it necessary to substitute an ultimate and absolute flux for an absolute and ultimate permanence. Thus his great empirical services in calling attention to the fundamental importance of considerations of time for problems of life and mind get compromised with a mystic, non-empirical "Intuition"; and we find him preoccupied with solving, by means of his new idea of ultimate reality, the traditional problems of realities-in-themselves and phenomena, matter and mind, free-will and determinism, God and the world.[63]

Bergson's less-than-half-hearted modernism, from Dewey's perspective, is due to the fact that he does not abandon superannuated problems of traditional philosophy but tries to solve them on the basis of an alternative view of the absolute as flux. Mere inversion of traditional problems, however, is not innovation. Bergson remains a foundationalist and continues to posit a metaphysical substratum in the very shape of the flux designed to replace the fixed entities of Platonism and rationalism. For Dewey, on the other hand, it is necessary to maintain that "the chief characteristic trait of the pragmatic notion of reality is precisely that no theory of Reality in general, *überhaupt*, is possible or needed."[64] The fixities of necessary conceptualization, the facts reductively constructed as tools of knowing in the sense of a cooperative interaction with flowing reality, these are no essences for Dewey; they are momentary "resting-places" (James's term) needed for re-orientation in the ongoing interactivity of human being and world. Thinking, Dewey says—and this is the fifth and summary point of his redefinition of Being as experience in "The Need for a Recovery of Philosophy"—thinking or "reflection is native and constant."[65] Thinking, philosophy, is not over against an absolute static or flowing reality, it and its momentarily fixated and static concepts

---

[63]Ibid., 38.
[64]Ibid., 39.
[65]Ibid., 6.

*constantly* emerge out of, they are born from the stream of experience, they are *native* to it and help to intelligently redirect and re-immerse our vital living processes again into the persistent flow of what is pluralistically going on. Thinking for Dewey is like poetry for Wallace Stevens; it is "Part of the res itself and not about it."[66]

When Dewey lectured on James, Bergson, and Bertrand Russell in Beijing in 1920, he clearly championed James's philosophical position as that of the single most important innovator of philosophical thinking. At the core of his generally fair and sympathetic treatment of Bergson's system, however, we find a profound disagreement, even an aversion to Bergson's basic vision of the world and of the role of material reality in it. This critique may be seen as complementing Dewey's criticism of the interpretation of perception, of the metaphysical essentialization of the flux of *élan vital*, and of the interpretation of the opposition of practical and philosophical knowledge. Dewey's dislike of Bergson's cosmological views becomes apparent in this passage:

> according to Bergson, there was originally no distinction between the material world and the spiritual world; the separation of this continuous universe into discontinuous and discrete units, fixed and dead, is the work of man's intelligence—something man has done to it to adapt it to his needs. Bergson indicates that this is a matter of distress to him.[67]

The implied disparagement and devaluation of intellect, matter, and practical needs must have struck Dewey as invalidating important parts of the very reality he tried to make philosophically respectable. In spite of his admiration of the poetical renderings of the processes of duration and of the analysis of evolution in *L'Évolution créatrice*, Dewey keeps reminding his listeners of the puzzling way in which Bergson looks down on matter as "remnants or 'leavings'" or as mere "vestiges of the will."[68] Dewey finally confesses that he does not understand Bergson's central ontological and metaphysical argument about the way matter originates in the psychological dynamics of the *élan vital*,[69] and he contrasts Bergson's failure to construct a convincingly coherent system out of one single central idea with James's "more sophisticated" plurality of momentous insights.[70]

Dewey's final word on Bergson came in 1935 when he reviewed the American translation of Bergson's book on religion, *The Two Sources of Morality and Religion*. Dewey gives a fair and evenhanded description of

---

[66]Wallace Stevens, "An Ordinary Evening in New Haven," in *The Collected Poems of Wallace Stevens* (New York: Knopf, 1957), 473.

[67]"Three Contemporary Philosophers: A Series of Six Lectures Delivered in Peking" *MW* 12, 226.

[68]Ibid., 228, 231.

[69]Ibid., 234.

[70]Ibid., 235.

the basic ontological and cosmological views of Bergson, goes on to praise the "esthetic charm" and the learned disquisitions on "myths, magic and spirits" in the book, and concludes: "One who finds nothing sound in the philosophical foundations may nevertheless learn a great deal from Bergson's clear and informed discussion of these matters."[71] It seems as if Dewey had finally dismissed Bergson as a serious opponent in the philosophical debate because he went "the way of the older cosmologists," as Kallen had stated in his comparison of Bergson with James's democratic philosophical pluralism.[72]

Dewey clearly and without hesitation named what he saw as major deficiencies of a philosophical system that, in spite of its celebration of the essentially processual character of reality, did not transcend traditional foundationalist metaphysics. In its own way Bergson's philosophy fulfilled Nietzsche's problematic desire and impressed the character of Being onto becoming; it stabilized the very essence of the world as event in the form of a conceptual transcendental fact, in the shape of *élan* or of *durée* as the condition of the possibility of all that is. In addition to this basic disagreement one can, by way of a summary, identify the following divergences in Bergson's and Dewey's thinking: 1. Bergson does not do justice to the full temporal dimension of perception. 2. He maintains a dualism of an inner world of dynamic reality and an outer world of differences of degree, in which spatialized matter may be understood as a series of stable facts; whereas Dewey insists on the indivisible togetherness of human being and environment in and as experience. 3. The *élan vital* shows all the hallmarks of a metaphysical substance as opposed to Dewey's vision of Being as plural temporal interactive fields of experience[73] encompassing individuals and their environments. 4. For Dewey philosophy works within a world of expanding possibilities of experiencing; for Bergson it retains its ancient and problematic dignity of looking at or speculating about all there is instead of engaging Being actively.

Both James and Dewey were well aware of Bergson's achievement in helping to overcome established metaphysical modes of interpreting and evaluating the interactions of stability and change in experience and/as reality. James saw this achievement above all in Bergson's critique of intellectualism; Dewey saw it in the predominant emphasis on temporality. Both James and Dewey, however, radically turned their backs on the very foundations and practices of a type of thinking that had always tended to privilege that which factually persists or endures, even if it showed in the dynamic form of *natura*

---

[71]"Bergson on Instinct" *LW* 11, 430–1.

[72]Kallen, *William James and Henri Bergson*, 51.

[73]Cf. Raymond D. Boisvert, *John Dewey: Rethinking Our Time* (Albany: State University of New York Press, 1998), 20–4.

*naturans*, of the will, of power, or of the *élan vital*. Instead of abandoning the very ground of thinking that had become untenable, Bergson seemed content revising aspects of the problem while retaining the speculative ethos and the substantialist assumptions of traditional philosophy. Musing on Bergson's habit of starting from established positions in order to locally correct them, Dewey thought that it would have been more serviceable if he "had commenced, not with the view that is afterwards corrected, but with the corrected view."[74]

The preceding attempts to define a central problem of modernist thinking on both sides of the Atlantic and the sketches of the explicit and implicit dialogues between James, Dewey, and Bergson will now serve as the background of a series of close readings of such texts by the three thinkers that offer condensed and summary interpretations of the relations of fact and event, of stable Being and contingent becoming, of discrete and indiscrete ontologies. My readings are intended to provide the basis for a critical comparative evaluation of the varieties of modernist answers to this ancient philosophical question.

# Solutions

Dewey has convincingly shown that the thought of James is characterized by a remarkable consistency. In spite of terminological differences in his writings, the basic identity of the foundational philosophical visions of *The Principles of Psychology*, of the *Essays in Radical Empiricism*, and of late works like *A Pluralistic Universe* and *Some Problems of Philosophy* may be taken for granted.[75] The following texts, which deal with the fact-event problem, support the thesis of the essential homogeneity of James's works. One of the most stimulating passages is this well-known excerpt from *The Principles of Psychology*:

> This difference in the rate of change [of the stream of awareness or thought] lies at the basis of a difference of subjective states of which we ought immediately to speak. When the rate is slow we are aware of the object of our thought in a comparatively restful and stable way. When rapid, we are aware of a passage, a relation, a transition *from* it, or *between* it and something else. As we take, in fact, a general view of the wonderful stream of our consciousness, what strikes us first is this different pace of its parts. Like a bird's life, it seems to be made of an

---

[74]"Perception and Organic Action" *MW* 7, 7.
[75]Cf. Dewey, "The Vanishing Subject in the Psychology of William James" *LW* 14, 166.

alternation of flights and perchings. The rhythm of language expresses this, where every thought is expressed in a sentence, and every sentence closed by a period. The resting-places are usually occupied by sensorial imaginations of some sort, whose peculiarity is that they can be held before the mind for an indefinite time, and contemplated without changing; the places of flight are filled with thoughts of relations, static or dynamic, that for the most part obtain between the matters contemplated in the periods of comparative rest.

*Let us call the resting-places the "substantive parts," and the places of flight the "transitive parts," of the stream of thought.* It then appears that the main end of our thinking is at all times the attainment of some other substantive part than the one from which we have just been dislodged. And we may say that the main use of the transitive parts is to lead us from one substantive conclusion to another.

Now it is very difficult, introspectively, to see the transitive parts for what they really are. If they are but flights to a conclusion, stopping them to look at them before the conclusion is reached is really annihilating them. ...

The results of this introspective difficulty are baleful. If to hold fast and observe the transitive parts of thought's stream be so hard, then the great blunder to which all schools are liable must be the failure to register them, and the undue emphasizing of the substantive parts of the stream.[76]

Subjective states are not identical with the stream; they arise out of it together with the objects of their awareness. The stream and its rhythms is that which temporally *is*. This is experience as it goes on. That stream of consciousness, awareness, or thought, however, that stream of experiencing is structured without losing its fundamentally temporal character. It shows in transitive and transitory relations and in intermittent and relatively, but never absolutely, stable substantive parts. The stream is a total event within which transitions and stable entities interdepend. The factually given, the substantive aspect of reality as experience, is intimately connected with and dependent on relational and transitional events. Both, however, are embedded in the primal event of the stream of consciousness or experience as it goes on.

The obvious and germane impossibility of factualizing the stream, of impressing the character of stable Being on essential becoming, this difficulty has led to the traditional attitude of ignoring the event- and the relational character of Being as experience. This is why stability and the substantive character of Being, in a philosophical and in a linguistic sense,

---

[76]*Principles* 1, 236–7.

were privileged. James uses a variety of images in order to convey his sense of an ontological relation of stability and change that is different from the philosophical tradition. His metaphors are not only a hallmark of his superior style, they are necessary linguistic strategies employed in order to avoid the very substantialization of reality that he criticizes in traditional metaphysics. The flights and the perchings of the bird or the image of the joints in the bamboo, which are not breaks but means of indicating both continuity and difference within ongoing experience,[77] these metaphorical images are indications that—as Hogrebe observed—the indiscrete ontology of continuities and transitions is prior to the discrete ontology of factual, substantive entities. The latter, for James, are integral parts of the overall events variously called streams of consciousness, awareness, or experience. The intellectualist conceptualization can never hold or designate stable facts; concepts are mere signposts that serve as means of orientation or as temporary factual consolidations *within* the essential flux as it shows in or for perceptual awareness.

In his radical empiricist attempts to find linguistic approximations to evoke a sense of the basic ontological character of Being as individual event that encompasses what used to be called subject and object, James again used a variety of images. He visualizes pure experience, the primary *there* in its temporal dimension, as a stuff, as a field, and as a stream or flux. This spectrum of images indicates that pure experience as the fundamental ontological presence-ing is beyond conceptualization. The image of the flux also guarantees the continuity of the interpretations of the stream of consciousness in *The Principles of Psychology* and the meditations on its ontological status as pure experience in *Essays in Radical Empiricism*. In "The Thing and Its Relations," we find this passage:

"Pure experience" is the name which I gave to the immediate flux of life which furnishes the material to our later reflection with its conceptual categories. Only new-born babes, or men in semi-coma from sleep, drugs, illnesses, or blows, may be assumed to have an experience pure in the literal sense of a *that* which is not yet any definite *what*, tho ready to be all sorts of whats; full both of oneness and of manyness, but in respects that don't appear; changing throughout, yet so confusedly that its phases interpenetrate and no points, either of distinction or of identity, can be caught. Pure experience in this state is but another name for feeling or sensation. But the flux of it no sooner comes than it tends to fill itself with emphases, and these salient parts become identified and fixed and abstracted; so that experience now flows as if shot through with adjectives and nouns and prepositions and conjunctions. Its purity is only a relative

---

[77]Ibid., 233–4.

term, meaning the proportional amount of unverbalized sensation which it still embodies.[78]

Being as pure event is a kind of liminal concept, a *Grenzbegriff*, a mere pointer hinting at a "reality" or experience neither known nor had.[79] Pure experience is envisioned by James as a mere presence of unstructured flux out of which substantive, relational, and qualitative fixations or facts emerge. Pure experience is the pre-verbal *there* of mere sensation before a division into person and world, subject and object is possible. Ontologically speaking, pure experience is the realm of the indiscrete as such. It exists before and beyond interiority or exteriority; it is a simple flow of event-uality without factual contours: "a *that* which is not yet any definite *what*." Other than Bergson's *élan* or his *durée*, James's pure experience is not available for the kind of privileged access called intuition in Bergson. Pure experience is the diffuse background, the pluralized white noise[80] out of which the compositions of a temporal and always transient factuality emerge. That which can be talked about, that which is available for language with its nouns, adjectives, prepositions, and conjunctions is a series of mutable facts arising out of and ultimately subsiding again into the indistinct, the indiscrete temporal presence-ing event of pure experience.

In his late works James devoted close attention above all to the relationship of concept and percept as purveyors of discreteness and continuity, respectively. Even though James, time and again, appeals to Bergson as a kindred spirit in the field, it is obvious that his own arguments are based on an ontology of the experiential flow that is fundamentally different from Bergson's dualist vision of *élan* and spatialized matter. Discreteness, factualized experience, substantive entities and things, and their concepts have a function that is different from that of the percepts emerging from the fluxional event of living reality; they do not, as in Bergson, belong to a different ontological realm: "Distinctions may be insulators in logic as much as they like, but in life distinct things can and do commune together every moment."[81] The discrete ontology, the ontology of facts, is based on but subordinate to the indiscrete ontology of events. The distinctness of things in the stream of living experience does not exclude togetherness.

---

[78]*Essays in Radical Empiricism*, vol. 3 of *The Works of William James* (1912; Cambridge, MA: Harvard University Press, 1976), 46.

[79]A succinct descriptive analysis of pure experience is offered by Ruth Anna Putnam, "The Moral Impulse," in *The Revival of Pragmatism: New Essays on Social Thought, Law, and Culture*, ed. Morris Dickstein (Durham, NC: Duke University Press, 1998), 67.

[80]Cf. James's related image of the "primordial chaos of sensations" in *Principles* 1, 277.

[81]*Pluralistic Universe*, 116.

James's vision of the continuous stream of Being as experience enabled him to dispense once and for all with his favorite *bête noire*, the absolute, and with its high priest, Hegel:

> The absolute is said to perform its feats by taking up its other into itself. But that is exactly what is done when every individual morsel of the sensational stream takes up the adjacent morsels by coalescing with them. This is just what we mean by the stream's sensible continuity. No element *there* cuts itself off from any other element, as concepts cut themselves from concepts. No part *there* is so small as not to be a place of conflux. No part there is not really *next* its neigbors; which means that there is literally nothing between; which means again that no part goes exactly so far and no farther; that no part excludes another, but that they compenetrate and are cohesive; that if you tear out one, its roots bring out more with them; that whatever is real is telescoped and diffused into other reals; that, in short, every minutest thing is already its hegelian "own other," in the fullest sense of the term.[82]

The guarantee of cohesiveness and continuity of the world as event does not depend on a foundational entity like the absolute that transcends experience; continuity is an essential ingredient of experience itself. Being as event, as experience, is characterized by identity and difference. Each singularity is always and at the same time its own other because it is both distinct, a possible fact ready to be conceptualized, *and* identical with the perceptual flow that allows for the interpenetration of each and all.

A singularly important aspect of James's discussion of the discrete and indiscrete, of concept and percept, of the disjunctive and conjunctive aspects of ongoing experience, then, is the fact that the disjunctive is embedded in the flow:

> Every examiner of the sensible life *in concreto* must see that relations of every sort, of time, space, difference, likeness, change, rate, cause, or what not, are just as integral members ... of the flux as disjunctive relations are. This is what in some recent writings of mine I have called the "radically empiricist" doctrine (in distinction from the doctrine of mental atoms which the name empiricism so often suggests). Intellectualistic critics of sensation insist that sensations are *dis*joined only. Radical empiricism insists that conjunctions between them are just as immediately given as disjunctions are, and that relations, whether disjunctive or conjunctive, are in their original sensible givenness just as fleeting and momentary ..., and just as "particular," as terms are. Later, both terms and relations get

---

[82]Ibid., 121.

universalized by being conceptualized and named. But all the thickness, concreteness, and individuality of experience exists in the immediate and relatively unnamed stages of it.[83]

This is probably the most precise of James's pronouncements on the type of relation that prevails between fact and event. Disjunctive and conjunctive relations are both aspects of the ultimate ongoing event, of the stream of thought or experience. Disjunctions and conjunctions are both temporal: they are "fleeting and momentary." The indiscrete ontology allows, establishes, and encompasses the discrete ontology of nameable facts.

James summarizes his position concerning the concept-percept and the fact-event dichotomy at the end of chapter IV of *Some Problems of Philosophy*:

If the aim of philosophy were the taking full possession of all reality by the mind, then nothing short of the whole of immediate perceptual experience could be the subject-matter of philosophy, for only in such experience is reality intimately and concretely found. But the philosopher, although he is unable as a finite being to compass more than a few passing moments of such experience, is yet able to extend his knowledge beyond such moments by the ideal symbol of the other moments. He thus commands vicariously innumerable perceptions that are out of range. But the concepts by which he does this, being thin extracts from perception, are always insufficient representatives thereof; and, although they yield wider information, must never be treated after the rationalistic fashion, as if they gave a deeper quality of truth. The deeper features of reality are found only in perceptual experience. Here alone do we acquaint ourselves with continuity, or the immersion of one thing in another, here alone with self, with substance, ... with time, with cause, with change, with novelty, with tendency, and with freedom. Against all such features of reality the method of conceptual translation, when candidly and critically followed out, can only raise its *non possumus*, and brand them as unreal or absurd.[84]

Concepts are signs that vicariously represent the whole extent of the possible experience of things, of entities, of facts: this is what Hogrebe calls the horizontal dimension of discrete ontology. Perception, awareness of the basic event of experience as Being opens the "deeper features of reality"; in this context Hogrebe speaks of "die Tiefe der Dinge," of the vertical

---

[83]Ibid., 126–7.
[84]*Some Problems*, 53–4.

dimension of indiscrete ontology.[85] It is the "thickness" of the event of Being, of the stream of thought, of pure experience, which allows the "thin extracts from perception" to temporarily establish a world of concepts and of facts, a world that is, however, always dependent on and ready to be engulfed by the rich flow of real events.

One of James's words for true and basic Being is pure experience. Dewey, as Ruth Anna Putnam outlines, "begins with events. Like Jamesian pure experiences, Deweyan events are essentially neither mental nor physical. They are taken as one or the other (or both) after the fact. Experiencing is a taking, an interaction of the organism with its environment, an environment that includes others like it."[86] The event character of Being is attributed by Dewey to all beings. In *Experience and Nature*, he states: "Every existence is an event."[87] The dynamic and non-dualist character of Being and of beings is also indicated by the term "primary experience," which is professedly indebted to James:

> We begin by noting that "experience" is what James called a double-barrelled word. Like its congeners, life and history, it includes *what* men do and suffer, *what* they strive for, love, believe and endure, and also *how* men act and are acted upon, the ways in which they do and suffer, desire and enjoy, see, believe, imagine—in short processes of *experiencing*. "Experience" denotes the planted field, the sowed seeds, the reaped harvests, the changes of night and day, spring and autumn, wet and dry, heat and cold, that are observed, feared, longed for; it also denotes the one who plants and reaps, who works and rejoices, hopes, fears, plans, invokes magic or chemistry to aid him, who is downcast or triumphant. It is "double-barrelled" in that it recognizes in its primary integrity no division between act and material, subject and object, but contains them both in an unanalyzed totality. "Thing" and "thought," as James says in the same connection, are single-barrelled; they refer to products discriminated by reflection out of primary experience.[88]

Primary experience or Being is an interactive event for Dewey. Single facts like agent and thing, subject and object are *a posteriori* results of intellectual analysis and separation. The interactive event is dynamic, temporal, both passive and active, an "unanalyzed totality" constantly in motion and ready to bring forth single and seemingly stable facts that may be conceptualized

---

[85]Hogrebe, *Metaphysik und Mantik*, 123.
[86]Putnam, "The Moral Impulse," 68.
[87]*LW* 1, 63.
[88]Ibid., 18–19.

primarily in retrospect. The whole of a primary experience in motion is, however, neither shapeless nor without direction. There is a tendency within the interactive dynamics of experiential events to achieve momentary balances of internal relations: the dynamics of Being as primary experience is potentially on the way toward aesthetic perfection—not as final closure, but as starting point of new experiential events. This is why Dewey says in *Art as Experience*:

> Direct experience comes from nature and man interacting with each other. In this interaction, human energy gathers, is released, dammed up, frustrated and victorious. There are rhythmic beats of want and fulfillment, pulses of doing and being withheld from doing.
>
> All interactions that effect stability and order in the whirling flux of change are rhythms. There is ebb and flow, systole and diastole: ordered change. The latter moves within bounds. To overpass the limits that are set is destruction and death, out of which, however, new rhythms are built up. The proportionate interception of changes establishes an order that is spatially, not merely temporally patterned: like the waves of the sea, the ripples of sand where waves have flowed back and forth, the fleecy and the black-bottomed cloud. Contrast of lack and fullness, of struggle and achievement, of adjustment after consummated irregularity, form the drama in which action, feeling, and meaning are one. The outcome is balance and counterbalance. These are not static nor mechanical. They express power that is intense because measured through overcoming resistance. Environing objects avail and counteravail.[89]

"Ordered change" expresses Dewey's idea of the interdependence of static and dynamic conditions, of facts and events. Whereas James has a tendency to envision Being as event in the form of a backdrop for conceptually available formations of experience, Dewey prefers to stress the constant drama, the persistent conflicting interdependence of factual formation and dynamic erosion punctuated by momentary consummations, which are, however, "not static nor mechanical." One of the results of such a vision of the self-organizing character of primary experience in its singularity is the acknowledgment that the world as a whole cannot be thought from the perspective of one single point of view or on the basis of one single physical or metaphysical (factual and persistent) entity:

> Neither self nor world, neither soul nor nature (in the sense of something isolated and finished in its isolation) is the centre, any more than either earth or sun is the absolute centre of a single universal and necessary

---

[89]*LW* 10, 22.

frame of reference. There is a moving whole of interacting parts; a centre emerges wherever there is effort to change them in a particular direction.[90]

The intimate relationship of single facts and a total event without center characterizes what Dewey also called "an aleatory world."[91] In the second chapter of *Experience and Nature* entitled "Existence as Precarious and as Stable," Dewey offered his most extensive analysis of the fact-event relationship within this kind of world as experienced:

> We live in a world which is an impressive and irresistible mixture of sufficiencies, tight completenesses, order, recurrences which make possible prediction and control, and singularities, ambiguities, uncertain possibilities, processes going on to consequences as yet indeterminate. They are mixed not mechanically but vitally like the wheat and tares of the parable. We may recognize them separately but we cannot divide them, for unlike wheat and tares they grow from the same root. Qualities have defects as necessary conditions of their excellencies; the instrumentalities of truth are the causes of error; change gives meaning to permanence and recurrence makes novelty possible.[92]

The vital connection between the stable and the precarious, between what I call fact and event, gives a hint that they emerge from "the same root." This means that the basic flow of primary experience shows as determinate and indeterminate at the same time. Being as experience is both fact-ual and event-ual, discrete and indiscrete. In this togetherness, however, the primacy of the experiential flow is maintained without elevating it to the status of a metaphysical substratum, without impressing the character of Being onto becoming. Dewey summarizes his position and reaffirms the importance of the problem of fact and event:

> the significant problems and issues of life and philosophy concern the rate and mode of the conjunction of the precarious and the assured, the incomplete and the finished, the repetitious and the varying, the safe and sane and the hazardous. If we trust to the evidence of experienced things, these traits, and the modes and tempos of their interaction with each other, are fundamental features of natural existence. ... Structure and process, substance and accident, matter and energy, permanence and flux, one and many, continuity and discreteness, order and progress, law and liberty, uniformity and growth, tradition and innovation, rational will

---

[90]*The Quest for Certainty LW* 4, 232.
[91]*Experience and Nature LW* 1, 43.
[92]Ibid., 47.

and impelling desires, proof and discovery, the actual and the possible, are names given to various phases of their conjunction, and the issue of living depends upon the art with which these things are adjusted to each other.[93]

The very togetherness of fact and event in the ongoing, fluxional process of living, of experience, necessitates and creates the possibility of a way of thinking and of practice that is both ethical and aesthetic: the conduct of life depends on the art of composing and recomposing the stable and the transient elements of the interactive dynamics of experience as it goes on. Dewey's ethics and aesthetics emerge from his vision of those "fundamental features of natural existence" that are the subject-matter of this essay.

Bergson's metaphysics—and the term must be used in its traditional meaning—is most comprehensively presented in *Creative Evolution*.[94] Bergson uses a variety of terms in order to designate Being: *consciousness, supraconsciousness, élan vital,* and *durée* indicate a number of aspects of that which foundationally *is*. The words may mean Being as well as some of the modes of its being known. Even though the *élan* and *durée* have attracted more attention, consciousness is said to be "coextensive with universal life."[95] Consciousness in Bergson does not come in flowing eachnesses as in James and Dewey, consciousness is a universal and metaphysical substratum or substance. The major way in which consciousness as creative flux makes itself generally and individually felt is as *durée*. As a productive urge it bears the name of *élan vital*. It shows in two kinds of beings: inner and temporally enduring realities available to intuition and spatialized matter known to—at its best—mathematical intelligence. On the basis of a transempirical and truly metaphysical entity called (supra-)consciousness, the world we really experience organizes itself dualistically as soul (sometimes called life) and (dead) matter.

Bergson's solution of the fact-event problem is intimately related to this dualistic antagonism:

---

[93]Ibid., 67.

[94]William James had supported and helped with the translation of Bergson's *L'Évolution créatrice* (1907) into English and, as Arthur Mitchell observes, "[i]t was his intention, had he lived to see the completion of this translation, himself to introduce it to English readers in a prefatory note"; "Translator's Note," in Bergson, *Creative Evolution*, v. Because of James's familiarity with Mitchell's translation and because Dewey preferred to read Bergson in English, the 1911 *Creative Evolution* is the text that played a major role in the transatlantic dialogue. In my attempt to critically evaluate Bergson's solution of the fact-event problem, I will therefore quote from this English language edition.

[95]*Creative Evolution*, 186.

All our analyses show us, in life, an effort to re-mount the incline that matter descends. In that, they reveal to us the possibility, the necessity even of a process the inverse of materiality, creative of matter by its interruption alone. The life that evolves on the surface of our planet is indeed attached to matter. If it were pure consciousness, *a fortiori* if it were supraconsciousness, it would be pure creative activity.[96]

Life and matter are at odds. Event and fact oppose each other. Matter is a falling away from the possibility of pure and constant creativity; matter acts as a drag on the productive and persistently innovative energies of the *élan vital*. Bergson's vision seems to rewrite the imagery of the Christian mythology of the fall and to revive the Platonic suspicion of matter as a lesser realm of Being. The pure event of the *élan* is always compromised by the antagonism of its own factual, static, spatialized production. There is no positive togetherness of fact and event in Bergson as in Dewey, no mutually invigorating dependency of the realms of perception and conception of intuition and intelligence as in James.

Bergson's worlds of fact, of spatialized matter open to fixation and calculation, do not seem *embedded* in a plurality of flowing realities:

Let us imagine a vessel full of steam at a high pressure, and here and there in its sides a crack through which the steam is escaping in a jet. The steam thrown into the air is nearly all condensed into little drops which fall back, and this condensation and this fall represent simply the loss of something, an interruption, a deficit. But a small part of the jet of steam subsists, uncondensed, for some seconds; it is making an effort to raise the drops which are falling; it succeeds at most in retarding their fall. So, from an immense reservoir of life, jets must be gushing out unceasingly, of which each, falling back, is a world.[97]

Worlds, palpable realms of relatively stable reality within which the lives of ordinary beings are conducted, are, so it seems, radically deficient if compared with the fundamental and universal productive event in the shape of the ongoing *élan*.

The creative event and impetus of reality, the intuitionally felt *élan* in its durative mode, however, imparts at least some aspects of freedom, of indeterminacy, to the factual space of materialistic predestination:

The impetus of life, of which we are speaking, consists in a need of creation. It cannot create absolutely, because it is confronted with matter,

---

[96]Ibid., 245.
[97]Ibid., 247.

that is to say with the movement that is the inverse of its own. But it seizes upon this matter, which is necessity itself, and strives to introduce into it the largest possible amount of indetermination and liberty.[98]

Bergson's world in its totality is torn by an almost Manichean dualism, the radical split between the forces of factual and inert darkness and the free and event-ful energies of ceaseless productivity literally and metaphorically turned heavenward:

> If our analysis is correct, it is consciousness, or rather supra-consciousness, that is at the origin of life. Consciousness, or supra-consciousness, is the name for the rocket whose extinguished fragments fall back as matter; consciousness, again, is the name for that which subsists of the rocket itself, passing through the fragments and lighting them up into organisms. But this consciousness, which is a *need of creation*, is made manifest to itself only where creation is possible.[99]

Consciousness *subsists*; it is a true traditional metaphysical *substantia*. Its transcendent energies allow the emergence of live, productive and innovative events, even in matter, if only at its highest, "where creation is possible," and this is the human being. The possibility of overcoming material facticity is given in some forms of organic matter in spite of the impediments represented by the rigidities of discrete physical entities.

The interaction of life force and matter, however, does not allow us to think of humans in terms of truly integrated participants in a multiplicity of productive events called experience as in James or Dewey:

> On flows the current, running through human generations, subdividing itself into individuals. This subdivision was vaguely indicated in it, but could not have been made clear without matter. Thus souls are continually being created, which, nevertheless, in a certain sense pre-existed. They are nothing else than the little rills into which the great river of life divides itself, flowing through the body of humanity. The movement of the stream is distinct from the river bed, although it must adopt its winding course. Consciousness is distinct from the organism it animates, although it must undergo its vicissitudes.[100]

Other than in James and Dewey, the event of Being is one and not initially manifold; it is one current that keeps on dividing itself and yet retains its

---

[98]Ibid., 251.
[99]Ibid., 261.
[100]Ibid., 269–70.

original essence.[101] Humanity in Bergson is not a plurality of beings as the only way Being can truly *be*; humanity is the temporal product of a metaphysical stream. The stream, however, indiscriminately called supra-consciousness or *élan*, the basic event of the stream is other than, is essentially different and distinct from its material realizations. The body is simply a temporary home for pre-existent souls which or who are nothing but parts of one original totality. Bergson's Manichean world of pantheistic soul and factual, spatial, dead *res extensa* envisions the human being as inhabited by a part of the stream or, in a different metaphor, by gnostic sparks of the original and ongoing event of creativity, sparks that (may) know their origin by way of intuition. Bergson has openly acknowledged the traditionalist aspects of his metaphysical system: in a lengthy footnote, he compares his own interpretation of "original Being" and matter to Plotinus, especially since Plotinus also views matter as an "enfeeblement" of the essence of original Being.[102] If one considers this kind of textual evidence and the rhetoric and terminology in *Creative Evolution* as a whole, Deleuze's sophisticated attempt to reinterpret Bergson as post-metaphysical and modernist does strike one as disingenuous.[103]

# Summary

Being in James and Dewey is manifold; it is a pluralism without a privileged center or basis. Being is experience as it goes on in eachnesses. The ongoing events of individualized experience do not rest on an antecedent creative substance; they do not depend on a metaphysical fact. Within each experiential event temporary stabilizations and factual ossifications are possible and necessary: in this way individual worlds emerge or are created that we may conceptually know, talk about, and within which one may reliably act. The indiscrete allows, and needs, temporary orders of ontological discreteness. This is above all James's vision. The individualized primary experience in Dewey shows as a dynamic, agonistic, interactive event structured as if it contained the possibilities of forever new aesthetic

---

[101]Cf. Deleuze, *Bergsonism*, 94: "[The *élan vital*] is always ... a simplicity in the process of differentiating, a totality in the process of dividing up ..."

[102]*Creative Evolution*, 210. In his comparative study of Bergson and James, Kallen has pointed out a number of similarities between Plotinus and Bergson; cf. *William James and Henri Bergson*, 61 ff. and *passim*. The footnote on Plotinus in *Creative Evolution* is very suggestive and precise. It is surprising, therefore, that in 1915 Bergson should write to Kallen: "Vous avez sans doute raison de dire que je me rapproche plus que James de la métaphysique traditionelle; vous avez même deviné ma sympathie pour Plotin—sympathie dont je n'ai jamais eu occasion de parler dans me livres ..."; *Mélanges*, 1192.

[103]Deleuze, *Bergsonism*, *passim*.

consummations. These momentary stabilities or facts function as means toward achieving ever-new and ever-widening possibilities of interactive events (experiences) that encompass person and environment in their primordial togetherness. Bergson presupposes a non-empirical supra-consciousness. Even though this consciousness in its realization as life force is characterized as productive, as a transcendent event, it does have the basic nature of an always self-identical and therefore stable, originating, eternal metaphysical fact; it is *substantia*.[104] The world as it shows for humans in the twin modes of intuition and intellect reveals itself as dualistic. The only genuine event is the workings of the *élan* as it subdivides forever, generating matter. Matter is spatialized fact. As such it antagonizes and degrades the pure innovative creativity of the fundamental event. In Bergson's thinking fact and event depend on each other. At the same time each of the two aspects of Being as totality inhibits or endangers the integrity of the other. The worlds of indiscrete and discrete ontology, of event and fact, face each other in a hostile fashion; they do not truly mingle, let alone coalesce as in James or Dewey: "The movement of the stream is distinct from the river bed."[105] Bergson's world consists of two realities before the backdrop of an eternal creativity at one with itself only in its transcendent Plotinian purity.

The differences between the pragmatist and the Bergsonian attempt to reconstruct philosophy were noted early on. The descriptions and evaluations of their achievements in modernizing thinking, however, differ. In 1911 Émile Boutroux succinctly stated the method and the vision of an innovative philosophy according to James:

> La philosophie ... est plutôt affaire de vision passionée que de logique: car la logique ne fait que trouver, après coup, des raisons pour expliquer les données de la vision. ...
>
> Le pluralisme essentiel des choses est ainsi plus vraisemblable que leur absolue réduction à l'unité. Dieu lui-même doit être conçu comme une personne qui n'exclut pas l'existence d'autres personnes.[106]

James is appreciated as an anti-intellectualist like Bergson and, at the same time, as a skeptical pluralist who radically differs from his French colleague because Bergson attributes a totally different task to anti-intellectualist thinking:

---

[104]Even though Deleuze tries to show that Bergson goes beyond traditional metaphysics, he has to concede: "[duration] is a becoming that endures, a change that is substance itself"; *Bergsonism*, 37.

[105]*Creative Evolution*, 270.

[106]Émile Boutroux, *William James* (Paris: Librairie Armand Colin, 1911), 100–1, 105.

From this ocean of life, in which we are immersed, we are continually drawing something, and we feel that our being, or at least the intellect that guides it, has been formed therein by a kind of local concentration. Philosophy can only be an effort to dissolve again into the Whole. Intelligence, reabsorbed into its principle, may thus live back again into its own genesis.[107]

The ultimate objective of thinking in Bergson is regressive in its hope of achieving a visionary, intuitive awareness of a foundational totality. Nothing could be further from the Jamesian point of view as it opens to the irreducible manifold of what is presently going on. Théodore Flournoy has emphasized the cosmological differences by stressing the fundamentally opposed temporal orientations of the two thinkers. For James:

> [la realité] va d'un chaos pluralistique primordial vers un état croissant d'union et d'harmonie, ce qui est juste l'inverse de l'univers bergsonien, lequel, partant d'une unité harmonique originelle, s'achemine pars de lignes d'évolution divergentes vers une dispersion toujours plus grande, comme celle des gouttelettes d'un jet d'eau, suivant la comparaison favorite du philosophe français. Il serait donc difficile d'imaginer deux visions de cours de choses plus contraires l'une à l'autre que celles de James et de M. Bergson ...[108]

According to Kallen, James's emphasis on the present and the future and Bergson's philosophical privileging of origins and the past (as memory) places the latter firmly in the context of the philosophical tradition, whereas James has to be seen as radically modern and his thinking as a truly new departure. This is why Kallen above all stresses the ontological differences in James and Bergson: "Where Bergson desiderates unknowably pure metaphysical substrata, James requires only directly experienced objects. For Bergson, life transcends experience, for James, experience transcends concepts, and not life but experience is the last word of metaphysics."[109] Kallen calls James's radical empiricist and pluralist ontology "a philosophic prevision of the future," whereas he tries to evaluate Bergson's metaphysics as "a philosophic summation of the past":

> James's theory of life seems to me to face forward, to be an expression of the age's underlying and hence vaguely felt and unformulated tendencies. Bergson's theory of life sums itself up as a consummation of the

---

[107]*Creative Evolution*, 191.
[108]Flournoy, *La Philosophie de William James*, 185–6.
[109]Kallen, *William James and Henri Bergson*, 47–8.

philosophic tradition, restated in the modes of thought and harmonized with the modes of feeling of the age.[110]

Most European and some American artists and intellectuals of the time saw it differently, but Kallen is convincing when he finds a genuine modernism in James and only a kind of cosmetic modernization of traditionalist thinking in Bergson. The world itself as ongoing experience in James is ontologically modern and constantly capable of innovation and modernization, whereas Bergson's world, for all its energetic impetus, is ultimately nothing but the realization of a preexistent, an immemorial potential.

In this context the best known and in a sense the most thoroughly documented study of the relationship of James and Bergson is strangely hesitant and imprecise. Ralph Barton Perry lists four major topics that are designed to show that "James' Bergsonism was of the spirit and not the letter."[111] Perry's argument, however, is not credible as soon as he goes on to say that both thinkers share the same vision of "the plenum of being" as "a temporal, changing continuum."[112] Perry knows that

> the general pattern of the evolutionary process tends to be for Bergson divergent and for James convergent. James's unity is in the making—lies ahead as a goal of achievement; while for Bergson there is always a sense of the *aboriginal* unity, as well as of the qualitative sameness, of the stream of life.[113]

Perry realizes but he refuses to properly evaluate Bergson's metaphysical foundationalism and his attempt to impress the character of Being onto becoming. In this way he helps support the mistaken belief in Bergson's innovative and modern ontological vision, and he obscures the cardinal difference between modern and merely modernized thinking as exemplified by James and Bergson.

On the basis of such differences in the cosmological vision, in the temporal orientation of the world and of thinking, and in the ontological analysis of Being itself, the relationship of the factuality and the event-character of reality becomes a central issue that serves to underline the incompatibility of pragmatist modernism and Bergsonian revisions of the tradition of thinking. I will begin and, by way of a summary, present a few representative appreciations of solutions of the problem of fact and event in pragmatism that are available in the critical literature. In her study of classical American pragmatism and phenomenology, Sandra B. Rosenthal concludes:

---

[110]Ibid., viii.
[111]Perry, *The Thought and Character of William James*, vol. II, 601.
[112]Ibid., 603.
[113]Ibid., 602.

for the pragmatists, the structures of objectivities grasped by the knowing mind do not reach a reality more ultimate than do the processive interactions of primordial experience, but rather the lived-through primordial grasp of felt temporality opening onto a processive universe is the very foundation for the emergence within experience of meaningful structure.[114]

The important point here is that structural fixations, objects and meanings, which can be held and known (G. *begriffen*), that such facts arise *within* the individually ongoing process or event of pure or primary experience. The factual is held and encompassed by the event-ful. John J. McDermott offers this variation of the basic pragmatist insight into the relations of knowable fixities and ongoing live events by focusing on Dewey's empirical naturalism: "Following Dewey, we are in, of, and about nature. We are nature's creature, its consciousness, its conscience, however aberrant and quixotic; its organizer, namer, definer, and defiler; a transient in search of an implacable, probably unrealizable, final consummation."[115]

The human being as an ongoing event, indissolubly at one with her or his respective environment, creates momentarily identifiable patterns of meaning and order without ultimate and consummatory closure simply because the individual worlds as ongoing events both allow and ultimately nullify all factual and nameable solidities. This is the world of pragmatic events that Emerson had foreshadowed in "Circles," the world of "the Unattainable, the flying Perfect, around which the hands of man can never meet, at once the inspirer and the condemner of every success."[116] The intimate relationship of fact and event, the integration of factuality into the streams of Being in pragmatism allows a descriptive definition of their interaction which may strike one as almost paradoxical: "Order for Dewey is a dynamic and precarious process."[117] The discrete arrangements of facts and their concepts are subject to the relentless erosions and reconstructions of Being as individual event. Bruce Wilshire has spoken of the "overflowingness" of the real as experienced, of the world of pure and flowing experience in James, and he has distinguished its rich "voluminousness" from the atomistic world known as discrete by means of concepts.[118] He summarizes:

---

[114]Sandra B. Rosenthal, "Classical American Pragmatism: Key Themes and Phenomenological Dimensions," in *Pragmatism Considers Phenomenology*, ed. Robert S. Corrington, Carl Hausman, and Thomas M. Seebohm (Washington: Center for Advanced Research in Phenomenology & University Press of America, 1987), 49.

[115]John J. McDermott, "Experience Grows by Its Edges: A Phenomenology of Relations in an American Philosophical Vein," in *Pragmatism Considers Phenomenology*, ed. Corrington, Hausman, and Seebohm, 166.

[116]W 2, 281.

[117]Alexander, *John Dewey's Theory of Art, Experience, and Nature*, 126.

[118]Bruce Wilshire, "The Breathtaking Intimacy of the Material World: William James's Last Thoughts," in *The Cambridge Companion to William James*, ed. Ruth Anna Putnam (Cambridge: Cambridge University Press, 1997), 111.

The categorial concepts and oppositions of discursive reason must never presume to exhaust the great That, the world ...

It is presumptuous to think that all reality is determinate, that is, determinable by the categories of our reason. Why not suppose chronically borderline tendencies, systems, systematically overlooked? The world is the supreme *that* that cannot be broken down exhaustively into any set of *whats*, no matter how large. Discursive reason cannot penetrate a domain that, by hypothesis, is beyond it.[119]

The discrete, then, is *in* and *of* the indiscrete, and fact always emerges from and then re-enters and is submerged by the events of Being. The *whats* which we know and the concepts by which we know them are both at home in[120] and subordinate to the really real events of experiencing as they go on.

Dewey was wary of Bergson's concept of change just as he eyed the dualist implications of Bergson's interpretation of perception with distrust, as we have seen. Having criticized the tendency of classical metaphysics "to make the stability of meaning prevail over the instability of events," Dewey adds in *Experience and Nature*:

The argument is not forgetful that there are, from Heracleitus to Bergson, philosophies, metaphysics, of change. One is grateful to them for keeping alive a sense of what classic, orthodox philosophies have whisked out of sight. But the philosophies of flux also indicate the intensity of the craving for the sure and fixed. They have deified change by making it universal, regular, sure.[121]

From Dewey's and the pragmatist point of view, Bergson has abandoned the very event-character of Being that he tried to restitute, by elevating change and flux to the status of a transcendent and self-identical entity, a metaphysical fact. The modern possibility of acknowledging reality as contingent, as not grounded on antecedent substances and not ruled by inflexible *a prioris*, this possibility to think real newness and a radical event-character of Being itself is jeopardized by Bergson. Bergson's attempt to surmount the traditional way of thinking the relationship of event and stable fact ends by reaffirming the classical view.

Raymond D. Boisvert has discussed three major concerns of traditional metaphysics overcome and abandoned by Dewey: he calls them the "Plotinian Temptation," the "Galilean Purification," and the "Asomatic

---

[119]Ibid., 114.
[120]This reminds one of Dewey's description of the close relationship of ongoing experience and reflective conceptualization in "The Need for a Recovery of Philosophy" *MW* 10, 6: "There is, apparently, no conscious experience without inference; reflection is native and constant."
[121]*LW* 1, 49.

Attitude."[122] The Plotinian temptation is the philosophical desire to reduce the manifold to an original and total One, the Galilean purification indicates the tendency of scientific rationalism to control and reduce the complexity and messiness in which things and events come in ordinary experience, and the asomatic attitude implies a contempt for the body and a celebration of thinking as purely rational and mental and ideal. Pragmatism as a whole and Dewey in particular emphasize the plurality of Being as experience, the *durcheinander* and vagueness in which the real shows in experience, and the fact that all thinking is inescapably embodied. The anti-modern implications of Bergson's way of thinking the relationship of stability and flux can best be shown by keeping these three traditionalist positions and their pragmatist critique in mind.

In his fascinating but ultimately problematic attempt to claim a future-oriented dimension for Bergson's thinking, Deleuze addresses the question whether Bergson is a dualist or a monist. The world as we know it in experience and as Bergson describes it is inescapably dualistic.[123] The world as thought in philosophy, however, is different. Deleuze states that in thinking according to Bergson, "[w]e go beyond experience, toward the condition of experience."[124] This specific form of transcendental questioning leads Bergson toward a non-conceptual monism: "Dualism is therefore only a moment, which must lead to the re-formation of a monism."[125] In spite of the major difference between, for example, a Kantian mode of thinking the transcendental conditions of experience and Bergson's intuitional approach, Bergson does move toward a monism of supra-consciousness, or memory, or *élan vital*, which deserves the name of a Plotinian strategy in Boisvert's sense of the term. Secondly, whenever Bergson describes life as felt and experienced, he does agree with the pragmatists. Deleuze states: "Bergson is aware that things are mixed together in reality."[126] This means that Bergson does not accept the adequacy of the method of Galilean purification of experience for purposes of a scientific and conceptual domination of reality. This, obviously, is also the reason why he and James could so cordially agree on the limited function of concepts in dealing with reality or in establishing truths. Lastly, Bergson does not think highly of matter and the body. It is in keeping with his predilection for Plotinos that he should disdain bodily reality. Life as transcendent unity actualizes itself in two directions: "life is a movement, materiality is the inverse movement."[127] Deleuze puts it in this

---

[122]Boisvert, *John Dewey*, 5–12.
[123]Deleuze, *Bergsonism*, 21–2
[124]Ibid., 23.
[125]Ibid., 29.
[126]Ibid., 22.
[127]*Creative Evolution*, 249.

way: "Life as *movement* alienates itself in the material *form* that it creates; by actualizing itself, by differentiating itself, it loses 'contact with the rest of itself.'"[128] Matter is fallen reality and the Christian or even Manichean implications of Bergson's images and terminology are too obvious to be missed. The metaphorical rockets of the *élan vital* produce inert fragments, débris, offal—this is the material world we touch and see and smell. Bergson's "asomatic attitude" establishes the dualism of a world as will and trash.

Bergson's vision is fundamentally at odds here with James's sense that the feeling of bodily presence as an ongoing event, that our very breath is the one indispensable and basic aspect of what we may experience as our self. Bergson's vision is also radically at odds with Dewey's celebration of the vital biologistic togetherness of environment and self as the true potential of ongoing and ever-innovative events of experiencing. James and Dewey not only think the continuity of felt event and intellectualized and verbalized fact, they also think the continuity of what used to be called body and mind. They both abandon the mind-body dichotomy as the essential stronghold of all Christian and metaphysical interpretations of Being. For them the mind is truly embodied and matter is not the other of mind. In stressing these continuities, James and Dewey assert their essential modernism.[129] Thinking and its concepts that constitute (temporary) facts—and thus what we call mind—are *at home* in what we sometimes call matter. Bergson, on the other hand, privileges the unchanging change of the *élan* as transcendent fact and considers all bodily realizations, all incarnations as instances of the unavoidable fall into material concreteness in a world of live and palpable events.

In his extensive critique of the metaphysical tradition in chapter 4 of *Creative Evolution*, Bergson attacks the Platonic valuation of the stability and immutability, of the eternal factuality of ideas and the low regard in which temporal matters, events, are generally held because they represent a lesser, a deficient mode of being.[130] In the final analysis, however, Bergson does not question this binary disposition of modes of Being. He simply inverts the order of valuation. Toward the end of the chapter he celebrates the new mode of thinking inspired by a true evolutionism. Now it is the total event of becoming that is honored as the highest mode of Being, whereas matter in its inert fixity and factuality is something which merely descends and falls. Life and consciousness, the intuitional awareness of the *élan*, ascend. The ultimate and highest vision of the philosopher, therefore, makes

---

[128]Deleuze, *Bergsonism*, 104.

[129]The importance of the concept of continuity for an adequate understanding of modernism is analyzed in detail by Daniel Joseph Singal, "Towards a Definition of American Modernism," *American Quarterly* 39, no. 1 (1987): 7–26.

[130]*Creative Evolution*, 317 ff.

the rich plurality of things and facts and events and experiences disappear: "he will see the material world melt back into simple flux, a continuity of flowing, a becoming."[131] The philosopher is and remains the traditional visionary. He contemplates, he intuits, he is one with that which really *is*: the eternal fact of the flux. Bergson's metaphysical foundationalism and his dualism of matter and *élan* reassert the structure, even if not the content of Platonic metaphysics. The possible integration of fact and event in individual events of reality construction and factualization, which Bergson's critique of intellectualism had promised, has not been achieved. He returns to the purely contemplative and theoretical mode of thinking that finds its fulfillment in the vision of one basic fact, even if this fact is called flux.

Dewey's analysis of the objectives of a reconstructed philosophy in *Experience and Nature* may stand for the kind of thoroughgoing modernism that he and James championed in their politely respectful dialogue with their transatlantic colleague who was really with them only in the refutation of rationalism and intellectualism as a strategy for the renewal of philosophy. While Bergson remained committed to thinking as a vision of one substantial fact, Dewey (and James) redefined philosophy as the "criticism of criticisms."[132] Thinking and its concepts *work* within ongoing events of experiencing, within forever concrete temporal situations. The theoretical vision of generalities, of conceptual facts, is nothing but a tool provided for orientation and action in the persistent effort to change and augment the course of events, the individualized experiences as they go on:

> Qualitative individuality and constant relations, contingency and need, movement and arrest are common traits of all existence ... Any theory that detects and defines these traits is therefore but a ground-map of the province of criticism, establishing base lines to be employed in more intricate triangulations.[133]

The extended discussion of ways of rethinking the relationship of fact and event in the context of transatlantic modernism has shown that the most prominent philosopher of early European modernism, Henri Bergson, limited himself to local corrections of old ways of thinking while James and Dewey abandoned superannuated problems and strategies in the course of their open-ended journey toward a thoroughgoing reconstruction of philosophy. It is possible that this is the reason why there is a significant philosophical movement called neo-pragmatism and no comparable venture by the name of neo-Bergsonism.

---

[131]Ibid., 369.
[132]*Experience and Nature LW* 1, 298.
[133]Ibid., 308–9.

# 17

# William James and Charles Taylor

In presenting my thoughts on the significant debate concerning religion, in which the Canadian philosopher Charles Taylor engages William James's *The Varieties of Religious Experience*, I will proceed in three steps: First, I will briefly introduce Taylor's book *Varieties of Religion Today* and its basic attitude toward James; in a second part, I will try to critically reconstruct and evaluate what Taylor calls his "conversation/confrontation with James."[1] I will read this occasionally belligerent conversation as Taylor's argument in favor of the power and significance of, especially, *social* imaginaries, while the third and last part of my remarks will be primarily devoted to James's conception of the philosophy of religion in *The Varieties of Religious Experience*. This last part is intended as both a defense of the Jamesian vision and as a critical description of the boundaries or limitations of imaginaries as Taylor understands them.

## Charles Taylor's *Varieties of Religion Today: William James Revisited*

William James's 1901 Gifford Lectures at Edinburgh University became his best-known and commercially most successful publication under the title *The Varieties of Religious Experience: A Study in Human Nature* in 1902.

---

This essay was previously published as "William James vs. Charles Taylor: Philosophy of Religion and the Confines of the Social and Cultural Imaginaries" in *The Imaginary and Its Worlds*, ed. Laura Bieger, Ramón Saldivar, and Johannes Voelz (Hanover, NH: Dartmouth College Press, 2013), 67–83. Reprinted by permission of the University Press of New England.

[1]Charles Taylor, *Varieties of Religion Today: William James Revisited* (Cambridge, MA: Harvard University Press, 2002), vi.

The literary appeal and the theological as well as philosophical topicality of the work seem not to have diminished during the first 100 years after its initial appearance. In the year 2000, Charles Taylor presented several lectures devoted to a critical appreciation of James's *Varieties* in the Institute for Human Sciences Vienna lecture series. Appropriately these lectures were published by Harvard University Press in 2002, the centenary of James's *Varieties of Religious Experience*, under the title *Varieties of Religion Today: William James Revisited*. The change from "religious experience" in James's title to "religion" in Taylor's marks, for me, one of the central philosophical problems, concerns, and difficulties posed by Taylor's "conversation/ confrontation with James." The question arises: what happens once the philosophical inquiry shifts its focus from the live events or processes of experiencing to a substantive entity called religion? Are we still dealing with the same matter of thinking, with the identical *Sache*, phenomenologically speaking, or does this shift imply a major ontological difference, if not a fundamental reversal?

Taylor begins and ends his critical discussions of James's *Varieties* with deeply respectful, often conciliatory, occasionally genuinely appreciative, and sometimes even admiring statements. He commences by noting that James's position today seems "entirely understandable, even axiomatic, to lots of people" and "central to Western modernity."[2] One of James's great methodological achievements is the application of "wide sympathy, coupled with unparalleled phenomenological insight."[3] The book ends with this compliment for James:

> he [sees] so deeply into an essential feature of our divided age. In some sense religious "experience," the beginning intimations and intuitions that we feel bound to follow up, is crucial as never before, wherever we end up taking them in our divergent spiritual lives. It is because he saw this with such intensity, and could articulate it with such force, that James's book lives on so strongly in our world.[4]

Taylor's repeated positive evaluations of James's study of religious experience are intimately and almost exclusively tied to the seemingly indisputable fact of the ongoing and still impressive contemporaneity or modernity of James's phenomenological descriptions. However, if one considers Taylor's deeply critical assessment of central features of contemporary society and culture, the praise accorded to James tends to take on a decidedly ambiguous hue and character. In his *Ethics of Authenticity*, Taylor diagnoses the

---

[2]Ibid., 13.
[3]Ibid., 22.
[4]Ibid., 116.

fundamental ills of contemporary existential and social reality: he speaks of the three malaises of untrammeled individualism, the pervasive and almost exclusive presence of instrumental reason, and the "alienation from the public sphere and consequent loss of political control."[5] For Taylor these features indicate inescapable and yet decidedly negative side- and after-effects of the originally positive achievement of individual emancipation in the contexts of the Enlightenment and early modernity. One may therefore wonder whether, in Taylor's overall view, James's *Varieties* are, first and foremost, a profound philosophical assessment of at least one of the only potentially ambivalent traits of modern society and culture in the realm of religion, namely, individualism, or whether the book is not rather part and parcel of the latter-day problematic itself that includes the separation of the individually religious and the public spheres. This is a condition that Taylor calls the "post-Durkheimian dispensation"[6] because, according to him, James obviously no longer considers religious phenomena as functional aspects of or within social realities.[7] In addition to that, religious experience is qualified by Taylor as only the "the beginning intimations and intuitions" of—so one may surmise—a fuller spiritual life that would then have to transcend personal, individual experience. This and the seemingly innocuous fact that the term "experience" is set in quotation marks are politely subdued indicators of a fundamental unease in Taylor's encounter with James's vision.

There are ways, Taylor proposes in his preface, in which James's "take on religion could perhaps be considered too narrow and restrictive."[8] The opening of the first chapter, which presents the case against James most concisely, puts the critical charge "slightly more polemically: one could argue that James has certain blind spots in his view of religion."[9] James's approach to religion as a matter of thinking is thus seen as being not comprehensive enough, as limited in scope and marred by fundamental oversights within the very field of vision ("blind spots")—a serious charge especially against a phenomenological thinker. For Taylor the basic problem with James's thinking is simply and essentially the priority, the preeminence, and the valuation of experience:

James sees religion primarily as something that individuals experience. He makes a distinction between living religious experience, which is that of the individual, and religious life, which is derivative because it is taken

---

[5]Charles Taylor, *The Ethics of Authenticity* (Cambridge, MA: Harvard University Press, 1991), 1–12, 10.
[6]Taylor, *Varieties of Religion Today*, 96.
[7]Cf. ibid., 111–16.
[8]Ibid., vi.
[9]Ibid., 3.

over from a community or church. ... churches play at best a secondary role, in transmitting and communicating the original inspiration.[10]

Taylor questions the legitimacy of distinguishing between religious experience as an existentially privileged and authentic personal event and the—from James's point of view—merely formalized participation in various socially organized, politically institutionalized, collectivized, and more or less public forms of religious practice. Taylor asks: "How are the phenomena of religion distorted or narrowed through being conceived in terms of religious 'experience'?"[11] The charges of distortion and narrowing imply a serious deviation in James from a true and comprehensive, an undistorted and exhaustive, that is, a philosophically fully competent vision. I will now move from Taylor's value judgments concerning James's work to his substantial philosophical criticism.

# Taylor's conversation/confrontation with James and the power of social imaginaries

Taylor understands James's interpretation of the validity of (religious) experience as closely and problematically related to the role and potential of language and ideas:

> So the *real* locus of religion is in individual experience, and not in corporate life. That is one facet of the Jamesian thesis. But the other is that the real locus is in *experience*, that is, in feeling, as against the formulations by which people define, justify, rationalize their feelings (operations that are, of course, frequently undertaken by churches). These two are clearly connected in James's mind. Feelings occur, he holds, in individuals; and in turn "individuality is founded in feeling."[12]

A very basic disagreement emerges here: Taylor doubts whether it is ontologically legitimate to confine the reality, the existence of religion to individual experience and not to extend its true being into what he calls the "corporate" realm. Taylor defines James's notion of experience primarily and exclusively as pre-verbal and pre-conceptual, as a matter of feeling in a generalized fashion. This does not do justice to James's sophisticated understanding of the fundamental existential dispositions that he calls

---

[10]Ibid., 4, 5.
[11]Ibid., 20.
[12]Ibid., 7.

feelings. Feelings as inescapable existential dispositions in James not only do *not* exclude rationalizations: like moods in Emerson, feelings in James importantly and inescapably color and inflect all perceptual and conceptual appropriations of experience, they convey knowledge, they are "noetic." Taylor, however, indirectly advances the idea that an adequate analysis of the ontological status of religion demands that it significantly manifest itself primarily in conceptualizations, in "rationalizations," in communally entertained ideas as the basis of conduct. Conduct—socially viable and recognizable and valuable behavior, based on and mediated by ideas and concepts, embedded in a social imaginary, and articulated in language— becomes an indispensable aspect or ingredient of Taylor's understanding of religion, a view that James supposedly does not adequately provide for.[13]

Taylor deepens his critical objections by exploring James's problematic insistence on felt experience as the only true and authentic site of religious awareness by way of a more detailed meditation on the, as he sees it, necessary interrelations between individuality, experience, and language

> one might make the more radical conceptual or transcendental point, that the very idea of an experience that is in no way formulated is impossible ... experience can have no content at all if you can't say *anything* about it.
>
> A similar set of considerations might be deployed to question the sense in which one can really have an individual experience. All experiences require some vocabulary, and these are inevitably in large part handed to us in the first place by our society ... The ideas, the understanding with which we live our lives, shape directly what we could call religious experience; and these languages, these vocabularies, are never those simply of an individual.[14]

Not only mystics, Buddhist or Christian or Muslim, could and would seriously and legitimately challenge the validity of the dogmatic statement that experiences *must* lend themselves to some kind of rendering in language. As James plausibly maintains in chapters 16 and 17 of *Varieties*, in order to be valid experiences, mystical experiences—as quintessential religious experiences—do not need, they even have to dispense with proper linguistic expression in order to remain true to themselves.[15] Taylor also ignores and does not critically engage James's anti-conceptualist stance, his radical linguistic skepticism that he so succinctly expressed in *The Principles of Psychology* by stating that "language works against our perception of

---

[13]Ibid., 23–9.
[14]Ibid., 26–8.
[15]*The Varieties of Religious Experience: A Study in Human Nature*, vol. 13 of *The Works of William James* (1902; Cambridge, MA: Harvard University Press, 1985); see 302 on "ineffability."

the truth."[16] Any perception, as the foundational mode of experiential awareness, James insisted in his last great, unfinished work *Some Problems of Philosophy*, any perception in the fullness of its present givenness always exceeds the capability of any language to do it justice: "the deeper features of reality are found *only* in perceptual experience."[17]

In refuting or ignoring this stance, Taylor reveals that he believes in some version of the prison-house of language view. Neo-pragmatist critics like Richard Poirier have questioned the validity of the metaphor of a prison-house by insisting on the fact that an existing language may and must always be *individually* inflected, changed, and even radically reconceptualized, that is, troped.[18] For Taylor, however, religious experience reveals itself as conditioned by and thus dependent on the always already pre-established, the vast and total cultural, the inescapably communal network of signs and significations called language. I repeat two of Taylor's defining statements and emphasize: "*All* experiences require some vocabulary, and these are *inevitably* in large part handed to us *in the first place* by our society"; "The ideas, the understanding with which we live our lives, *shape directly* what we could call religious experience." This is a primacy of the word certainly not intended by the famous opening sentence of the Gospel according to St. John. Human society and its cultural meanings are a first for Taylor. What he calls the "wider whole" in *Ethics of Authenticity* is the very foundation of true selfhood and individuality; the self is truly a self only if it is grounded in the encompassing other of collective existence. In Taylor's later writings, the "wider whole" becomes the social imaginary. This is defined or described in his book *Modern Social Imaginaries* as a

> wider grasp [that] has no clear limits ... It is in fact that large unstructured and inarticulate understanding of our whole situation, within which particular features of our world show up for us in the sense they have. It can never be adequately expressed in the form of explicit doctrines because of its unlimited and indefinite nature. That is another reason for speaking here of an imaginary and not a theory.[19]

This somewhat simplified and vague resuscitation of Castoriadis's conception of the social imaginary has nothing to say about its ontological status.[20]

---

[16]*The Principles of Psychology*, vol. 8.1–3 of *The Works of William James* (1890; Cambridge, MA: Harvard University Press, 1981), 1, 234.

[17]*Some Problems of Philosophy*, vol. 7 of *The Works of William James* (1911; Cambridge, MA: Harvard University Press, 1979), 53–4 (my emphasis).

[18]Cf. Richard Poirier, *The Renewal of Literature: Emersonian Reflections* (New York: Random House, 1987), 131–4.

[19]Charles Taylor, *Modern Social Imaginaries* (Durham, NC: Duke University Press, 2004), 25.

[20]Cf. Cornelius Castoriadis, *The Imaginary Institution of Society*, trans. Kathleen Blamey (1975; Cambridge: Polity Press, 2005); see esp. Part I, chapter 3, and Part II, chapter 7.

Taylor presents an existentially dubious all-embracing entity without specific location that is supposed to provide the foundation, the orientation, and the possibility of "particular features" and "the sense they have" for our social worlds and thus for its articulation in a communal language and vocabulary, which is subsequently, as Taylor maintains, handed to individuals. Because the individual has no, or only a severely limited, say in saying what or how her or his religious experience is, this experience can never be either primarily individual *or*, as an alternative, momentous and significant in its silence. Religious experience, the individual awareness of the transcendent, tends to become a culturally and socially conditioned and mediated epiphenomenon. It seems ironic, however, that a philosopher who so vehemently argues against the possibility of an "idea of an experience that is *in no way formulated*" (my emphasis) should nevertheless ground all communal meaning and cultural formations of modernity in a determining, constraining, and socially as well as individually empowering totality called "social imaginary" that is characterized as "that large unstructured and *inarticulate* understanding of our whole situation" (my emphasis).

This obvious inconsistency does make sense, though, within Taylor's overall vision of modernity as a "long march"[21] toward a truly emancipated, secular, liberal, democratic society. The numinous, the core of religious experience, has been shifted away from the individual to find a (is it a secularized?) refuge in the transcendental sphere and horizon of the collective social imaginary and its vaguely defined but apparently unlimited power to ground, frame, direct, and provide possibilities of meaning for any and all individual experiences. Taylor's social imaginary, it appears, offers a new version of the Durkheimian social functionalism in reading religion: "a religion," Durkheim had argued, "is a unified system of beliefs and practices relative to sacred things," that is, "beliefs and practices that unite its adherents in a single moral community called a church."[22] Or, more abstractly and even closer to Taylor's vision and terminology: religion is "above all a system of notions by which individuals imagine the society to which they belong and their obscure yet intimate relations with that society."[23] The power of the social imaginary in Taylor's sense similarly provides the possibility of social cohesion through faith and its communal language. The validity of religious experience as an existential dimension is in turn communally sanctioned and grounded and articulated. This is what *Modern Social Imaginaries* describes as the "space for religion in the modern state, for God can figure strongly in the political identity."[24] Instead "of an

[21]Taylor, *Modern Social Imaginaries*, 17 and *passim*.
[22]Émile Durkheim, *The Elementary Forms of the Religious Life*, trans. Carol Cosman, ed. Mark S. Cladis (1912; Oxford: Oxford University Press, 2001), 46.
[23]Ibid., 170–1.
[24]Taylor, *Modern Social Imaginaries*, 193.

ontic dependence [of human society] on something higher," the sacred, the divine "can still be present to us in the design of things, in cosmos, state, and personal life" and as "the inescapable source for our power to impart order to our lives, both individually and socially."[25]

Taylor's position in *Varieties of Religion Today* and in *Modern Social Imaginaries* raises the question whether he is really dealing with religion or religious experience or whether his ultimately reductionist grounding of religious phenomena in social imaginaries implies jeopardizing the religious as a *Sache*, as a *phenomenon* in the philosophical sense of the term. The social imaginary, which is at the basis of the long march toward "order as mutual benefit"[26] in a secular liberal democratic condition, appears in Taylor problematically as total—one hesitates to call it totalitarian—conditioning. This is ominously foreshadowed in *Varieties of Religion Today* when Taylor uses two somewhat haphazardly chosen examples to demonstrate the emergence of religion as a phenomenon of privacy and interiority, as dictated and enforced by constraints of the social imaginary: amazingly, already in the late Middle Ages he sees the spread of the "inward form of religion" as the result of "pressure ... through the preaching of mendicant friars and others"[27]; similarly, the prevalence of private religious experience in France in the nineteenth century "stood at the end of a long process in which ordinary believers had been preached at, organized, sometimes *bullied*, into patterns of practice that reflected more personal commitment.—They had been pressed, we might be tempted to say, into 'taking their religion seriously.'"[28] The total usurpation of the religious by and through the social imaginary in the present is then unmistakably pronounced as dogma in *Modern Social Imaginaries*: "[O]ur social imaginary ... constitutes a horizon we are virtually incapable of thinking beyond."[29] In this way the all-encompassing social imaginary dissolves religious experiencing into the functional historical processes of social, political, and cultural formation.

# James's philosophy of religion and the boundaries of social imaginaries: An apology

For William James, a study of religious experience was not a historical or social, let alone a political or even a cultural, concern. The subtitle of

---

[25]Ibid.
[26]Ibid., 21.
[27]Taylor, *Varieties of Religion Today*, 9.
[28]Ibid., 11 (my emphasis).
[29]Taylor, *Modern Social Imaginaries*, 185.

*Varieties* reminds us that the book is a study of human nature, that is, a philosophical inquiry, presentation, and meditation concerning an essential and indispensable *existential* and thus an ontological feature of being human. An apology, a defense of James's thinking on religion will therefore have to go beyond the implied assumption of Taylor that *all* entities and *all* meaningful aspects of experience, belief, and conduct are primarily and ultimately embedded in and mediated by significations that arise out of the social imaginary as inescapably antecedent transcendental horizon. I will focus on two major areas of contention in Taylor's "conversation/ confrontation" with James's view of the religious that are apt to show the limits of the social imaginary as soon as fundamental ontological and existential questions are raised. The two areas are the interpretations of experience and of the human self. I will occasionally enlist the help of what appears at a first and very superficial glance a highly unlikely ally in the project of defending William James, namely Martin Heidegger. Heidegger's 1920/21 lecture on the phenomenology of the religious life, however, not only agrees with Ernst Troeltsch's evaluation of James's *Varieties* as the best description of religious phenomena extant,[30] it reads the meanings of *existenziale*, that is, foundational, aspects of Being like experience and selfhood in an unquestionably radical empiricist, that is, Jamesian, mode.[31]

Experience in James, as Charles Taylor interprets it, is essentially characterized by feeling and belongs, in terms of its validity as an aspect of the religious life, only with some "beginning intimations and intuitions," that is, not with the fully unfolded reality of religious existence. More fundamental even, and more important for diagnosing the underlying philosophical reasons for their oppositional stances, is this seemingly innocuous statement by Taylor on experience, also already cited above, which will help me to open the *apologia* proper: "James sees religion primarily as something that individuals experience." In this statement religion is an object, a *Sachverhalt*, encountered and appropriated by a subject in an act or event called experience. This, however, is not at all what James means by experience. We find the probably most concise and most profound definition, or interpretation, in James's entry on "Experience" for Baldwin's *Dictionary of Philosophy and Psychology* that appeared in the same year as James's *Varieties* (1902). Here James states that the term "experience" indicates:

> the entire process of phenomena, of present data considered in their raw immediacy, before reflective thought has analysed them into subjective

---

[30]Heidegger, "Einleitung in die Phänomenologie der Religion" (1920–1), in *Phänomenologie des religiösen Lebens*, ed. Matthias Jung, Thomas Regehly, and Claudius Strube, vol. 60.1 of *Gesamtausgabe* (Frankfurt: Klostermann, 1995), 20.
[31]Ibid., 75–86 and *passim*.

or objective aspects or ingredients. It is the summum genus of which everything must have been a part before we can speak of it at all … If philosophy insists on keeping this term indeterminate, she can refer to her subject-matter without committing herself as to certain questions in dispute. But if experience be used with either an objective or a subjective shade of meaning, then question-begging occurs, and discussion grows impossible.[32]

Experience designates the "summum genus of which everything must have been a part before we can speak of it at all." In other words, for James experience is a name for Being in general. As such it necessarily and logically precedes all verbal articulation and the constraints of, for example, social imaginaries. Being as experience occurs before the subject-object split so dear to traditional metaphysical and epistemological modes of thinking. James's postmetaphysical, radical empiricist thinking therefore demands— in a wonderful pun—that the *term* experience be kept inde-*term*-inate, that is, that it be both spoken and unspoken. Experience is the togetherness of an awareness and its "contents," objects that only emerge as such once "reflective thought" approaches the simple *this* or *there* of the really real, the experiential event. Strictly speaking, experience as such, in its immediacy, cannot be talked about. It issues in nameable aspects and elements only once it has been retrospectively focused in the context of a new event of experience called reflection; in this way a prior experience manifests itself in the form of a testimony.

Experience is or provides or shows as what James called "knowledge by direct acquaintance" as distinguished from retrospective, reflexive knowledge or "knowledge-about."[33] Knowledge by acquaintance is quintessentially religious knowledge for James. In this *religionsphilosophische* position, however, he is neither a modernist nor a mere liberal Protestant, as Taylor keeps arguing throughout his study of James's *Varieties*. The non-social, the individual, the pre-verbal and immediate, the socially and culturally un-mediated character of knowledge by acquaintance has been universally attested as the true mark of religious experience in its fullness. In *Varieties*, James simply and consistently reaffirmed the testimony of the world's heritage of sincere religious awareness from the Buddha to Teresa of Avila, Jonathan Edwards, Emerson, and Whitman. Religious experience is, however, not initial, as Taylor maintains; it has no necessary *telos* beyond itself—even though it may, of course, have all sorts of consequences, primarily non-religious. Like perceptual awareness it is, before any appropriation in the

---

[32]"Experience," in *Essays in Philosophy*, vol. 5 of *The Works of William James* (Cambridge, MA: Harvard University Press, 1978), 95.
[33]*Principles* 1, 221.

context of socially created significations, simply itself. This is what Heidegger calls "faktische Erfahrung," the concretely specific primary *here and now* in its ontological authority: in it the self and that which is experienced are not yet, as Heidegger says, "torn apart."[34]

One would, however, overlook the true significance of the Jamesian vision of religious experience, if one did not sufficiently stress its specific noetic character that has often been discussed in connection with the gnostic or mystical implications and connotations of such intimate moments of awareness. James himself has given us this summary appreciation of the noetic dimension of mystical experiences and states of the intimate presence of divine existence or the numinous:

> They break down the authority of the non-mystical or rationalistic consciousness, based upon the understanding and the senses alone. They show it to be only one kind of consciousness. They open out the possibility of other orders of truth, in which, so far as anything in us vitally responds to them, we may freely continue to have faith
>
> It must always remain an open question whether mystical states may not possibly be ... superior points of view, windows through which the mind looks out upon a more extensive and inclusive world.[35]

The characteristic openness and generosity of James's views, his readiness to accommodate and appreciate other modes of awareness than those generally or socially or culturally or scientifically approved, this genuine fairness not only demands that he allow the possibility and even superiority of the noetic dimensions of religious experience, it also makes him energetically fight and refute the exclusive, the severely reductive, and for him always totalitarian, predominantly modern, claims of rational and conceptual interpretations of experience and the world.

Heidegger argues for a similar refutation of what he calls the theoretical or scientific stance in dealing with religious experience.[36] In focusing exclusively on the whatness or thing-character of a phenomenon—in this case of religious experience transformed to the status of a mere object called religion, as in Taylor—the basic meaning and significance of its factual enactment in and as experience, defined in a radical empiricist mode, is abandoned. In Heidegger's terminology, the *Vollzugssinn* is lost; that is, the manifest meaning of the factual presence and event of religious experiencing, which is not attributed by any subject, is jeopardized.[37] Both

---

[34]Heidegger, "Einleitung," 10–14, 9.

[35]*Varieties*, 335, 338–9.

[36]Heidegger, "Einleitung," 6 and *passim*.

[37]Ibid., 62–5.

James and Heidegger allow the *Vollzugssinn* of religious experience as a unified moment of authentic awareness to show for itself in methodologically identical ways: in the *Varieties*, James presents an abundance of testimonies of religious experiences, allowing the verbal traces of silent noetic experience to manifest themselves without evaluating their truth claims; their existential importance is highlighted simply by gathering the religious heritage within plausible categories testifying to certain family likenesses. Heidegger argues for a similar restraint and aversion to objectification. The phenomenologist of religion will have to be content with a "formale Anzeige"—a formal indication or indexing—of the religious testimony.[38] A philosophy of religion will present textual manifestations of moments of actual, existentially pregnant experiential presence. In Heidegger's lecture course, the testimony is that of the New Testament: the philosopher of religion allows it to speak of and for itself. He forgoes any ascription of truth value and meaning in the sense of its possible social or cultural or philosophical or even theological function.

At this point I would like to move toward the second part of this apology that deals with James's philosophical vision of the self as it emerges from his interpretation of experience. This discussion may help refute the strictures in Taylor's reading of James that focus on his seemingly too subjectivist interpretation of religious experience and practice.

In his book *Experience and God*, the neo-pragmatist philosopher of religion John E. Smith has pointedly asked whether the traditional conceptions of experience as "private" are adequate in general and in cases of religious experience in particular. Smith shows convincingly that "the dogma about experience as private, mental content" has to be "challenged as a nonempirical and erroneous view of experience" that leads to "an impoverishment of experience."[39] This critique is legitimate and plausible because the relational character of experiencing established by James's radical empiricism evinces the primary, the intimate and aboriginal co-presence of the so-called subject and the so-called objective content of experience. There is no subject to begin with, no separate self that then or later appropriates experiential objects. Selves *are* experiential; that is, they belong with their worlds. In Heidegger's phenomenological discussion of religious experience, his vision may be paraphrased thus: in the factual enactment of life, I do not even experience an ego-object as a separate entity; experiencing itself always already possesses the character and features of a world, and my self-world is factually indistinguishable from my environing world.[40] Experience, Smith

---

[38]Ibid., 62–3.
[39]John E. Smith, *Experience and God* (1968; New York: Fordham University Press, 1995), 36–7.
[40]Cf. Heidegger, "Einleitung," 13.

insinuates, is not a matter of subjective inwardness; rather, it is a mode in which all of Being truly is and shows. This would necessarily and prominently include what experiences identify as the most significant, essential, or the highest mode of "encounter": the real-ization, the becoming real, in and as experience, of the numinous.

James called the most fundamental mode of experience "pure experience." Pure experience designates anything that shows, or makes itself felt or might be thought of as real in its sheer *thisness*. In one of his *Essays in Radical Empiricism*, "The Thing and Its Relations," James makes it clear that pure experience as the "immediate flux of life," as the process of Being itself, precedes all "conceptual categories" (including subject and object) and that its purity means "the ... amount of unverbalized sensation which it ... embodies."[41] In "Does Consciousness Exist?," James described this silent, yet dynamic, reservoir of possibilities in this way:

> The instant field of the present is at all times what I call the "pure" experience. It is only virtually or potentially either object or subject as yet. For the time being, it is plain, unqualified actuality or existence, a simple *that*. In this *naif* immediacy it is of course *valid*; it is *there*, we *act* upon i.[42]

The field of experiencing is therefore neither primarily nor necessarily subjective. This means that for James (religious) experience in its pre-verbal intensity, as the field of *thereness*, is exactly *not* a private affair, as Taylor insinuates and charges. Pure experience, pure religious awareness is an open field of realization, and within this open field what we later call the self and the "content" or object of his or her experiencing, the numinous or the holy, are continuous with each other, forming a homogeneous spatial realm that *may* issue in a personal identity and his or her beliefs. First and foremost, however, religious experience as pure experience is a vast *this* or *there* that goes beyond any conceptual or subjectivist delimitations or definitions and thus exceeds what may be thought of as existing within the social imaginary.

In the *Varieties*, James calls this aspect of religious experiencing the *More* out of which humans may feel themselves addressed.[43] This *More* is ontologically radically different from Taylor's "wider whole" or "corporate life" or "social imaginary" that he thinks of as determining the language and existence of individuals. James's *More* is a realm "into which the farther limits of our being plunge";[44] it is a space at the further reaches

---

[41]*Essays in Radical Empiricism*, vol. 3 of *The Works of William James* (1912; Cambridge, MA: Harvard University Press, 1976), 46.
[42]Ibid., 13.
[43]*Varieties*, 401 and *passim*.
[44]Ibid., 406.

of experiencing that we encounter only when we allow for self-surrender, the abandonment of the socially and historically realized and culturally mediated self-hood that is constrained by the mandates of social imaginaries. Experience as existential spread without any privileged subject-position is religious experience proper; it resides before and beyond the confines of social imaginaries, beyond any humanly social or subjectivist concerns whatever. Differing again from Taylor's reading of James, one has to insist: "pure experience" is not without language. James says of the *More* within the primary event of experiencing that it contains "ontological messages" that arrive on the horizons of our experiential sites; he speaks not of communications about reality but of the articulate presence of reality within the event of experiencing itself: "There is a verge of the mind which these things haunt; and whispers therefrom mingle with the operations of our understanding, even as the waters of the infinite ocean send their waves to break among the pebbles that lie upon our shores."[45]

Religious experience in James, then, is prior to all the determinations we may ever think of as belonging to our real or imagined, our concrete or desired collective existence; the social imaginary is always already transcended here. The "ontological messages" or "whispers" are James's way of modestly and un-dogmatically reminding his readers of the primacy of a *logos* which speaks within the vast reaches of experiencing and to which we may respond or not, depending on how far we feel ourselves determined, defined, or possibly even hemmed in by the confines of our imaginaries.

---

[45]Ibid., 334.

# 18

# The New

My brief meditation on the American ontological interpretation of the new will—with some concentration and intensity—focus on *nothing*. Emily Dickinson's poem 1563 reads: "By homely gift and hindered Words / The human heart is told / Of nothing - / 'Nothing' is the force / That renovates the World -"[1] Dickinson's *nothing* exists, it is there, it is a powerful agency, a force, and this force renovates the world, "makes it new." A problem arises: the *nothing* is either before or ultimately beyond language, it cannot be properly articulated or conceptualized, it is spoken by hindered words or possibly, in another of Dickinson's central epistemological terms, "slant," but even so, the *nothing* is experienced, it is not a *nihil*.

An extended genealogy of Dickinson's *nothing*, of that which makes it new, would take us back to Emerson's "eternal silence," out of which we have been born,[2] destined to always begin the world anew with no past at our backs.[3] Its ancestry also includes Thoreau's "impervious and quaking swamps," the "impermeable and unfathomable bog,"[4] an unstructured realm out of which everything may emerge; it includes the featureless and a-conceptual wildness in and by which the "preservation of the world"[5] and the remedy for the ravages of civilization, the always necessary renewal, are guaranteed. Moving forward in intellectual history, Dickinson's *nothing* emerges again powerfully in the often-quoted last line of Wallace Stevens's "The Snow Man" in whose passively unfocused mind the wintry world

---

[1] *The Poems of Emily Dickinson*, ed. Thomas H. Johnson (Cambridge, MA: Harvard University Press, 1979), vol. III, 1077. This is poem 1611 in *The Poems of Emily Dickinson: Variorum Edition*, ed. R. W. Franklin (Cambridge, MA: Harvard University Press, 1998), vol. III, 1413.
[2] "Literary Ethics" W I, 155.
[3] "Circles" W II, 297.
[4] Henry David Thoreau, "Walking," in Thoreau, *Collected Essays and Poems*, ed. Elizabeth Hall Witherell (New York: Library of America, 2001), 241.
[5] Ibid., 239.

shows as "Nothing that is not there and the nothing that is,"[6] while the
world waits for poetic renewal and the efflorescence of recreated meaning.
Similarly the creative agency which Gertrude Stein calls "human mind,"
producing "master-pieces," that is, unprecedented and radically new worlds
of meaning, this productive agency is described as an absence, an empty
slate lacking qualitative traits, a *nothing* without identity: "The thing one
gradually comes to find out is that one has no identity that is when one is in
the act of doing anything."[7] From Emerson and Thoreau through Dickinson
to Stevens and Stein—and, as we will see, reaching a culmination point
and summary vision in John Cage—there exists a foundational ontological
intuition of a featureless absent presence, an undefined active awareness at
the core of not only human, but of all beings, of all existing entities, which
assures the ceaseless renewal of Being itself and thus accounts for Being
not as a solid entity but as a continuously self-overcoming and self-creative
event—as a persistent series of actual occasions in Whitehead's terminology
or as the continuous temporal realization of Heidegger's *Ereignis*, to provide
later and slightly distant but parallel European intuitions.

The relentlessly productive *nothing* or *no-thing* of the American poetic
tradition finds its more strictly philosophical equivalent in two central
ontological categories of classical pragmatism: in Charles Sanders Peirce's
Firstness and William James's pure experience. Both, Firstness and pure
experience, are basically identical liminal concepts, intuitions necessarily
betrayed in their very significance by any verbal or conceptual approximation.
The two terms indicate, they point at real *nothings*. Calling Firstness and pure
experience identical philosophical intuitions is then, logically, a *contradictio
in adiecto*: neither Firstness nor pure experience does possess an identifying
core that would allow a statement of either difference between them or
of identity. All that can be said of them is *that* they *are*, but we do not
know *what* they are. Firstness and pure experience imply existence but not
essence. This is the point where the American ontology of Peirce and James
radically challenges and, indeed, renovates, renews Western thinking about
beings and Being.

I would like to examine the two ontological intuitions of a realm of
unprecedented newness and radical pre-verbal otherness more closely. Peirce
says about Firstness:

The idea of the absolutely First must be entirely separated from all
conception of or reference to anything else ... The First must therefore

---

[6]*The Collected Poems of Wallace Stevens* (New York: Knopf, 1954), 10.
[7]Gertrude Stein, "What Are Master-Pieces and Why Are There So Few of Them," in *Stein:
Writings 1932–1946*, ed. Catherine Stimpson and Harriet Chessman (New York: Library of
America, 1998), 355.

be present and immediate, so as not to be Second to a representation. It must be fresh and new, for if old it is second to its former state. It must be initiative, original, spontaneous and free; otherwise it is Second to a determining cause ... It precedes all synthesis and all differentiation; it has no unity and no parts. It cannot be articulately thought: assert it and it has already lost its characteristic innocence; for assertion always involves a denial of something else. Stop to think of it, and it has already flown. What the world was to Adam on the day he opened his eyes to it, before he had drawn any distinctions or had become conscious of his own existence—that is First, present, immediate, fresh, new, initiative, original, spontaneous, free, vivid, conscious, and evanescent. Only remember that any description of it must be false to it.[8]

Firstness is forever now and non-mediated; it is not relational, not determined; neither unity nor difference prevails within or around it; neither language nor conceptual thinking applies. The "negative theology" of Firstness reveals a fundamental novelty, a mere *there* or sheer *this* always now preceding, underlying, or enveloping all defined beings or things or entities in their relational Second- or Thirdness, preceding, that is, their belonging to a world. Firstness is absolutely contingent and only in this way is it fresh and new. Thus the question arises and troublingly prevails and persists: how do we know it?

For William James experience, above all pure experience, is the term for what he calls the "summum genus of which everything must have been a part before we can speak of it at all,"[9] that is, before a separation into subject and object occurs. Pure experience is a word for a phase of Being. In "The Thing and Its Relations," James says:

"Pure experience" is the name which I gave to the immediate flux of life which furnishes the material to our later reflection with its conceptual categories ... [It is] an experience pure in the literal sense of a *that* which is not yet any definite *what*, tho ready to be all sorts of whats; full both of oneness and of manyness, but in respects that don't appear; changing throughout, yet so confusedly that its phases interpenetrate and no points, either of distinction or of identity, can be caught. Pure experience in this state is but another name for feeling or sensation. But the flux of it no sooner comes than it tends to fill itself with emphases, and these salient parts become identified and fixed and abstracted; so that experience now

---

[8]Charles Sanders Peirce, *Principles of Philosophy*, ed. Charles Hartshorne, Paul Weiss, and Arthur W. Burks, vol. I of *The Collected Papers of Charles Sanders Peirce* (Cambridge, MA: Harvard University Press, 1931), par. 357.

[9]"'Experience': from Baldwin's *Dictionary*," in *Essays in Philosophy* (Cambridge, MA: Harvard University Press, 1978), 95.

flows as if shot through with adjectives and nouns and prepositions and conjunctions. Its purity is only a relative term, meaning the proportional amount of unverbalized sensation which it still embodies.[10]

Pure experience is like Firstness because it is pre-verbal, pre-conceptual, unstructured, a mere *that*. James, however, goes beyond Peirce's vision by pointing to an inner dynamic in pure experience, a vectorial aspect as Whitehead would say. The mere *that* in its unceasing newness shows a tendency toward self-organization that brings forth all kinds of *whats*, all kinds of defined entities or things. In traditional ontological terminology, the fundamentally undefined and therefore always new *that* is *existentia* on the way toward a plenitude of nameable entities, *essentiae*. Being, then, is an event, an *Ereignis*, which ceaselessly, again and forever again, begins in or arises out of the novelty of sheer *thatness* or *existentia*, the undefined no-thing-ness of the unnameable and not yet conceptually appropriated realm of the absolutely new—an ever-present event tending toward transient fulfillment in the *quidditas* or *essentia* of solidified, ossified, recognizable, familiarly named things, that is, *whatnesses*, in an already established and articulated world. In Peirce and James temporality enters the inner constitution of Being; existence and essence are no longer statically conjoined as in traditional metaphysics where all beings are simply defined as necessarily and always at the same time both existent and possessing a defining essence. Modern American ontology thinks emergence within Being itself: the new, the pre-verbal no-thing-ness is the indispensable phase of beings in their continuous emergence, their ontological becoming, or—as Gertrude Stein would say—their beginning again and again.

The unanswered question remains: how then, if it can neither be said nor conceived, how can Firstness, how can pure experience, how can the novelty of ceaseless no-thing-ness at the center of emergent beings, how can sheer *existentia* be "known"? Giorgio Agamben, in a subtle reading of passages from *Nicomachean Ethics*, asserts that there is, for Aristotle, "a pure perception of being."[11] Existence, the mere un-defined no-thing or *that*, is thus accessible in perception, in pre-verbal awareness. The long-forgotten sensual, perceptual Aristotelian access—*aisthesis*—to mere existence re-surfaces in Emerson's memorable phrase of the "*sense* of being, which in calm hours rises, we *know not* how,"[12] and it finds its culmination in James's

---

[10]*Essays in Radical Empiricism*, vol. 3 of *The Works of William James* (1912; Cambridge, MA: Harvard University Press, 1976), 46.

[11]Giorgio Agamben, "Friendship," trans. Joseph Falsone, *Contretemps: An Online Journal of Philosophy* 5 (2004): 5. Agamben explains that Aristotle in this context is "mobilising the technical vocabulary of ontology: *aisthanometha oti esmen, aisthesis oti estin*: the *oti estin* is existence, the *quod est* as opposed to the essence (*quid est*, [*ti*] *estin*)"; ibid.

[12]W II, 64 (my emphasis).

so-called anti-intellectual insistence on the primacy of the perceptual over the conceptual in allowing intimate and in-depth experience of what he calls the thickness, the concrete *there* and *that*, of sheer Being or no-thing-ness.[13]

It does take some philosophical imagination, a point on which James repeatedly insisted, to realize the profound pertinence of this stance. Sometimes an omission to enter such a vision or intuition is helpful in clarifying the proper meaning of the newness of or within Being, in this case of James's interpretation of it. Michael North's rich and detailed book *Novelty: A History of the New* offers such an instructive omission as it bypasses the possibility to fathom what he calls the almost "unthinkable problem" of the "nature of ontological novelty."[14] "Newness," North says,

> is expected to "come into the world," apparently from some point outside it, as if there were some other sector, not the world as we know it, with a reservoir of novelty that periodically "leaks" into our space, to take a memorably odd metaphor from William James. The metaphor implies that novelty doesn't belong in the world at all, and that once here, stray droplets of it must soon dry up and cease to be new.[15]

Yes, novelty according to James "leaks" in from a region that is "not the world as we *know* it," from a region that we access not conceptually but perceptually, by way of the *aisthesis oti estin*. James's wonderful metaphor of the ontological leakage reminds us that the new *within* the ongoing process of Being as becoming has no contours, no *whatness*, no clear circumscription—the liquid character of the new shows its no-thing-ness, its transitional and finite character as it again and again moves toward momentary closure in the *whatness* of a fixed being.

Like Emerson, James is a master of aphoristic philosophical condensation. Thinking about Being as an iterative ongoing process of creative renewal everywhere and in every single instance of time, James says about our understanding and tentative verbalization of this process: "the word 'or' names a genuine reality."[16] Genuine reality, true Being, *ontos on*, is something that is always about to be. Genuine reality is on the way toward a possible well-defined *whatness*, either this *or* that. Genuine reality contains in itself a not-yet, a no-thing-ness, an openness waiting to be closed in the process of its *Ereignen*. This central location of the undecided in the very event of

---

[13]*A Pluralistic Universe*, vol. 4 of *The Works of William James* (1909; Cambridge, MA: Harvard University Press, 1977), 64. 112; *Some Problems of Philosophy*, vol. 7 of *The Works of William James* (1911; Cambridge, MA: Harvard University Press, 1979), 31–60.
[14]Michael North, *Novelty: A History of the New* (Chicago: University of Chicago Press, 2013), 7, 8.
[15]Ibid., 15.
[16]*Pluralistic Universe*, 146.

Being is forever new; it keeps the world both open and going. Emerson had foreshadowed and initiated this specific Jamesian version of an American ontology of the new as the always about-to-be-decided when he memorably said of nature as Being in its totality that it is "*one thing and the other thing, in the same moment.*"[17]

The contours and the true significance of a new mode of thinking, in our case of the new American ontology, is often more easily discerned and appreciated when it is looked at from a point distant in time and space. The 1960s witnessed an amazing coalescence of American and German thinking. Jürgen Habermas's 1968 *Erkenntnis und Interesse* with its productive assimilation of Peirce and James and Dewey is one example. In 1961 Ernst Bloch published his ninety-page treatise *Philosophische Grundlagen: I. Zur Ontologie des Noch-Nicht-Seins*, followed by *Atheismus im Christentum* in 1968. Even though Bloch completely misread pragmatism as scientistic utilitarianism, his ontology in both works shows striking parallels with the thought of his American predecessors. Bloch's departure from traditional Western ontology begins at the exact same point as that of Peirce and James: "Ontologie des Noch-Nicht-Seins ergibt durchgehend eine andere Ontologie überhaupt als die bisherige, demgemäss, dass hier Existentia und Essentia nicht mehr direkt-proportional miteinander aufsteigen."[18] Existence and essence are no longer necessarily and simultaneously conjoined in all beings; they are consecutive phases of Being as process; in Bloch, as in Peirce and James, Being is fundamentally temporalized. The guiding and foundational ontological intuition of Bloch is the idea that the ever-present now as the one and only creative event is pregnant with that which is about to be. This, however, means that the now as "noch-nicht-Sein," as Not-Yet-Being or no-thing, is not only not nothing (*nihil*), but that it has more than merely potential status: it is, in Jamesian parlance, a *that* (in Bloch: ein "Dass") on the way toward its *what*. Bloch's "Noch-Nicht" or *existentia* is, as in Peirce and James, the location of newness: "Das *Noch-Nicht*, dies eigentlich Zeithafte, nämlich Heraufkommende in der Zeit, öffnet sich als immer noch mögliches *Novum*, in echter Zukunft"[19]; and he adds: "Zum Nicht gehört es, dass es hungert und sich füllen will. Es ist nicht Etwas, nicht Erscheinung, aber es zieht dazu hin, setzt sie auf dem Weg zu seinem Was, das es nicht hat,

---

[17]W III, 225.
[18]Ernst Bloch, *Atheismus im Christentum: Zur Religion des Exodus und des Reichs* (1968; Frankfurt: Suhrkamp, 1985), 95: "The ontology of Not-Yet-Being consistently results in an ontology different from the one prevalent up to now, an ontology according to which *existentia* and *essentia* no longer arise directly proportionally with each other" (my translation).
[19]Bloch, *Philosophische Grundlagen: I. Zur Ontologie des Noch-Nicht-Seins* (Frankfurt: Suhrkamp, 1961), 25: "The *not-yet*, this authentically temporal entity, i.e., that which arises as time, opens itself as a *novum* still truly possible in genuine futurity" (my translation).

heraus."[20] In a breathtakingly close appropriation of Peircian and Jamesian diction, Bloch concludes concerning the renovating, the renewing force of the "Noch-Nicht" in the event of Being as becoming: "Dies Erste [Firstness] klopft unvermindert im Jetztsein überall, ein Dass [*thatness*] vor den Türen jenes Etwas, das noch nirgends ganz das lösende Was [*whatness*] ist."[21]

A world in which each single entity, atom or human being or galaxy, *is* because it ceaselessly renews itself in its Being by moving out of sheer undefined presence toward a tentatively and always transient identity or *whatness*, such a world is essentially imperfect. As Bloch says: "die ,Schöpfung' der Welt kommt aus dem Ens imperfectissimum."[22] More than a half-century before Bloch, in the philosophical environment of pragmatism, Wallace Stevens said in "The Poems of Our Climate": "The imperfect is our paradise. / Note that, in this bitterness, delight, / Since the imperfect is so hot in us, / Lies in flawed words and stubborn sounds."[23] The world is imperfect because it is not yet, because it keeps forever newly arising in each singularity out of a no-thing, a *Noch-Nicht*. This world is imperfect because it is everywhere always about to be, a realm where the word "or" may name genuine reality. This world keeps forever waiting to be properly named; this imperfect paradise needs or calls for the human being as Adam naming what is not even properly or never fully there yet. In the paradise of the imperfect, "flawed words and stubborn sounds" will have to do; or, as Emily Dickinson had articulated her insight into the ever-new productive no-thing-ness, "homely gift and hindered words," a language of tentative approximation, must suffice.

The variations on no-thing as the productive principle or *arche* of modernist aesthetics and thinking—from Emerson to Stevens and Stein, to Peirce and James (and Bloch, for that matter)—share one defining feature: they are attempts, experiments, which try to ground or describe or explain the emergence of concrete entities, of individuals, of worlds, of works. John Cage inherits this intuition of the aesthetic centrality of no-thing-ness and goes beyond it. The no-thing, the radically undetermined, not only allows entities to emerge, it is also and necessarily their final destination. "Lecture on Nothing" (1949–50) and "Lecture on Something" (1950–52) articulate the philosophical and the aesthetic center of Cage's vision. In the rhythmic and poetic prose of his two "lectures," Cage profoundly widens the

---

[20]Ibid., 47: "That it hungers and wants to fill itself, this is a property of the *not*. It is not a something, not appearance, but it tends toward it, places it on the way toward its *what* which it does not (yet) possess" (my translation).

[21]Ibid., 17: "This *first* knocks undiminished everywhere in now-ness, a *that* before the doors of that something which is so far nowhere the saving *what* in its fullness" (my translation).

[22]Ibid., 80: "The 'creation' of the world emerges from the Ens imperfectissimum" my translation).

[23]Stevens, *Collected Poems*, 194.

foundational interpretation in American modernism of the way structures of philosophical thinking and of making sense, of *poiesis*, arise from and find their "completion" in a site of negation. This is one of the opening sentences of "Lecture on Nothing": "I have nothing to say / and I am saying it / and that is / poetry / as I need it."[24] The open field of primordial silence issues in poetry, in made meaning, but the issue, the poetic and the spiritual result here is manifest as the return into the very emptiness of the no-thing. In the "Lecture on Something" Cage begins in this way: "This is a talk about / something / and naturally / also a talk about / nothing. / About how something / and nothing are not / opposed to each other / but need each other to keep going ... Every something is an/echo of nothing."[25] The world of established meaning in philosophy or in art is a mere echo; the authentic Being is the nothing from which philosophical ideas or works of art arise in their ephemeral and contingent and fleeting evanescence. The *essentia* toward which mere undefined *existentia* urgently tends in Peirce and James and Bloch, but also in Stevens and in Stein, shows in Cage by way of a circular move back into the silent origin itself. This no-thing, the Alpha and Omega of the trajectory of Being, now assumes moral and religious connotations: "if one maintains / secure possession / of nothing / (what has been called poverty of spirit), then there is no limit / to what one may / freely enjoy. / In this free / en-joyment / there is no / possession of things. / There is only / enjoyment. / What is possessed is nothing."[26] The freedom of the ontological no-thing or not-yet and non-possessiveness are the preconditions for philosophical or aesthetic achievements and practice. In the introductory note to "Lecture on Something," Cage says: "The very practice of music, and Feldman's eminently, is a celebration that we own nothing."[27] This, of course, means both that we do not own anything and that we do own *no-thing*. In addition, the gestures of renunciation[28] and the abandonment of spiritual possessiveness in the empty and un-appropriated space of mere *thisness*, pure non-defined existing, become the origin and the goal of a radical and total existential liberation with Franciscan or with Zen Buddhist overtones.

---

[24]*Silence: Lectures and Writings by John Cage* (1961; Middletown, CT: Wesleyan University Press, 1973), 109.

[25]Ibid., 129–31.

[26]Ibid., 132.

[27]Ibid., 128.

[28]Ross Posnock has elucidated the connection between aspects of a (post-)Kantian aesthetics of disinterestedness, the liberating aspect of an absence of possession, and "the basis of poetry (in the large sense of making)" in Cage's "Lecture on Nothing" in *Renunciation: Acts of Abandonment by Writers, Philosophers, and Artists* (Cambridge, MA: Harvard University Press, 2016), 152.

The nothing and the something in Cage's twin lectures merge in a disquieting dialectic, reminding a sophisticated Cage critic like H.-K. Metzger remotely of the opening of Hegel's *Wissenschaft der Logik* with its juxtapositions and identifications of Being, Nothing, and Becoming.[29] Cage, however, playfully designs this dialectic to induce the serenely ascetic religious awareness, "all das, was es gibt, nicht zu überschätzen," not to overestimate the value of that which (merely) exists in the mode of somethings.[30] The philosophical and the aesthetic move, from Emerson to Stein, toward an abandonment of all definable or dogmatic preconditions of beings—of thinking and of making, that is, of creating—culminates in Cage and in his gentle refusal to grant even the results, the ceaselessly emergent new entities of all becoming and doing, a lasting habitation in a seemingly settled and appropriated world.

---

[29]Heinz-Klaus Metzger, "Europas Oper," in *Die Freigelassene Musik: Schriften zu John Cage* (Vienna: Klever, 2012), 122

[30]Metzger, "Anarchie als ästhetische Kategorie," in *Die Freigelassene Musik*, 130.

# INDEX